THE GOSPEL ACCORDING TO
ST. LUKE,

WITH NOTES CRITICAL AND PRACTICAL.

BY THE REV. M. F. SADLER,

RECTOR OF HONITON; PREBENDARY OF WELLS; AUTHOR OF "CHURCH DOCTRINE
BIBLE TRUTH," "CHURCH TEACHER'S MANUAL," "NOTES CRITICAL AND
PRACTICAL ON ST. MATTHEW, ST. MARK, AND ST. JOHN," ETC.

WIPF & STOCK · Eugene, Oregon

Wipf and Stock Publishers
199 W 8th Ave, Suite 3
Eugene, OR 97401

The Gospel According to St. Luke
With Notes Critical and Practical
By Sadler, M. F.
ISBN 13: 978-1-62564-967-6
Publication date 6/12/2014
Previously published by G. Bell & Sons, 1886

INTRODUCTION.

OF the writer of the third Gospel nothing whatsoever is known, except that he was the faithful friend and companion of the Apostle St. Paul. I shall first consider the Scripture notices of him, then the references to his Gospel in the early Fathers, which prove that it has been accepted from the very first as on the same level as regards authority and inspiration as the other three; and, lastly, I shall inquire whether his Gospel can be said to be that of St. Paul—whether we have equal reason for believing that his Gospel is the reproduction of the teaching of St. Paul respecting our blessed Lord's Birth, Life, Death, and Resurrection, as St. Mark's was from the first believed to be the substance of the teaching of St. Peter.

I.

SCRIPTURE NOTICES.

Luke is mentioned by name three times in the Epistles of St. Paul, and always with affection: first in Col. iv. 14, "Luke, the beloved physician, and Demas greet you;" then in 2 Tim. iv. 11, "Only Luke is with me;" and in Philemon, "There salute thee .... Marcus, Aristarchus, Demas, Lucas, my fellow-labourers." From Col. iv. 11, where the companions of Paul, "who are of the circumcision," are distinguished from those afterwards named, we gather that he must have been before his conversion a Gentile. His name is Gentile—Lucanus, shortened into Lucas. These are the only places in which he is mentioned, but there can be not the smallest doubt that frequently in the narrative of the Acts he includes himself amongst the companions in travel of St. Paul by changing the pronoun to the first person plural. Thus in Acts xvi. up to the ninth verse, the historian uses the third person plural, "they." After *they* were come to Mysia, *they* assayed to go into Bithynia: but the Spirit suffered *them* not. And *they* passing by Mysia came down to Troas: " then, in the next verse but one, the tenth, there is a change to the use of the first person plural: " After he had seen the vision, immediately *we* endeavoured to go into Macedonia . . . Therefore, loosing from Troas, *we* came with a straight course to Samothracia." There is no way of accounting for such a change except on the supposition that St. Luke, the undoubted writer of the Acts, joined the party at Troas. St. Luke appears to have been left at Philippi, and joined Paul's company again at Assos (xx. 14) and accompanied him to Jerusalem (xxi. 15). We gather from the same use of the first person plural that Luke was a fellow-voyager with St. Paul to Rome, and was shipwrecked with him.

There is good reason also to suppose that St. Paul alludes to St. Luke in 2 Cor. viii. 18 : " We have sent with him the brother, whose praise is in the Gospel throughout all the churches." If an account of our blessed Lord's Birth, Life, Death, and Resurrection was then called the Gospel—and I do not see why it should not have been so called—then the allusion is most natural and becoming; otherwise it is difficult to understand what St. Paul means by "praise in the Gospel," for his name is not mentioned in any Gospel, nor is his preaching of the Gospel with eloquence ever alluded to, as that of Apollos' is.

These are all the notices of him, direct or indirect, which are to be found in the New Testament. They tell us nothing to satisfy our curiosity; but we cannot but infer from them that he must have been a man of very great zeal and holiness and Christian love, to have been the tried friend and constant companion of the great Apostle.

An immense number of conjectures, all perfectly groundless, are made by various writers respecting him: that he was originally a slave; that there was a medical school at Tarsus, at which he studied, and so became acquainted with St. Paul; that he might have been known to the poet Lucan, and to the philosopher Seneca; and a very late tradition speaks of him as having been a portrait-painter as well as physician.

INTRODUCTION.

II.

EARLY FATHERS.

I now come to the notices of him in the early writers.

First, Eusebius, book iii. chap. 4. " But Luke, who was born at Antioch, and by profession a physician, being for the most part connected with Paul, and familiarly acquainted with the rest of the Apostles, has left us two inspired books, the institutes of that spiritual healing art which he obtained from them. One of these is his Gospel, in which he testifies that he has recorded 'as those who were from the beginning eye-witnesses and ministers of the Word delivered unto him,' whom also, he says, he has in all things followed . . . It is also said, that Paul usually referred to his Gospel, whenever in his Epistles he spoke of some particular Gospel of his own, saying, 'according to my Gospel.'" With respect to Antioch being his birthplace, Godet writes: " If Luke had really found a home at Antioch, we can understand the marked predilection with which the foundation of the Church in that city is related in the Acts. In the lines devoted to this fact (xi. 20-24) there is a spirit, animation, and freshness which reveal the charm of delightful recollections."

Again, Eusebius, book iii. ch. xxiv: "In his own Gospel he delivered the certain account of those things that he himself had fully received from his intimacy and stay with Paul, and also his intercourse with the other Apostles."

Irenæus refers to him frequently by name, as book iii. ch. i.: " Luke also, the companion of Paul, recorded in a book the Gospel preached by him."

Again, Irenæus, speaking of the sacerdotal aspect of Christ, given by St. Luke, writes, book iii. chap. xi. 8: " But that according to Luke, taking up his priestly character, commenced with Zacharias the priest offering sacrifice to God."

Again, Tertullian, in speaking of St. Luke's Gospel, writes : " The same authority of the Apostolic Churches will afford evidence to the other Gospels also, which we possess equally through their means, and according to their usage—I mean the Gospels of John and Matthew, whilst that which Mark published may be affirmed to be Peter's, whose interpreter Mark was. For even Luke's form (*di-*

viii INTRODUCTION.

gestum) of the Gospel men usually ascribe to Paul.": ("Tertullian against Marcion," book iv. chap. 5.)

And lastly Origen, quoted by Eusebius, writes : "And the third, according to Luke, the Gospel commended by Paul, which was written for the converts from the Gentiles." ("Eccles. Hist." book vi. ch. xxv.)

III.

AUTHENTICITY OF ST. LUKE'S GOSPEL.

Three writers, living in different parts of the world before the end of the second century quote St. Luke with the same faith in his authority as any Christian writer would now do. From an index I have now before me I find that Irenæus quotes St. Luke above 150 times, Clement of Alexandria above 100 times, and Tertullian, in his book against Marcion alone, above 300 times.

Each one of these writers recognizes four Gospels, no more, no less ; each one names them as the Church has ever done, and one of them, Irenæus, the first in point of time, gives several reasons—some of them, it is true, not wise ones—for holding that there can be no more than four. Now it is to be remembered that Irenæus, when a young man, could have conversed with aged Christians, whose memories of the history and events of the Church would extend nearly to the days of St. Luke and St. Paul. All the three could have conversed with old men who lived in the first century. Can it be imagined that such men, taking the greatest interest in everything connected with the Church, and holding the truth of the records of Christ as their lives, should be mistaken in the matter of one of their principal books, whether it was genuine or not? Let the reader remember, too, that those who held the Gospel of St. Luke, as we now have it, to be a part of the Divine oracles, lived within seventy or eighty years after its publication, and could have conversed with men who could have known the author, and that the men who are now impugning its authority live 1,700 years later, and have dogmatic reasons for getting rid of it. I have carried this argument out more fully in my Preface to my Notes on St. John's Gospel, to which I refer the reader.

The covert allusion to St. Luke in Justin Martyr, a writer of about 150 A.D., is very interesting. He is speaking of the Lord's Bloody Sweat, and in doing so he distinguishes between the Apostles and their companions: "For in the memoirs which, I say, were drawn up by His Apostles, *and those who* followed them (it is recorded), that His sweat fell down like drops of blood while He was praying and saying, 'If it be possible let this cup pass from me.'"

IV.

THE GOSPELS OF ST. LUKE AND ST. PAUL.

It is quite clear from the extracts given in Section II. that there was an universal belief in the earliest Churches that the Gospel of St. Luke was the embodiment of the Gospel preached by St. Paul, and it will be necessary now to examine whether we can find good grounds for such an assertion in the Pauline Epistles: but first of all we must consider the question, what would be the form of the Gospel of the Apostle of the Gentiles. Would it be, for instance, in the form of an account of Christ, such as the other Gospels present? Would it, that is, be in an historical form—or would it be in the form of an evangelical treatise or essay setting forth, not facts respecting the Son of God, but abstract doctrines, such as Justification, Election, Sanctification, Assurance, and such things?

Now the Apostle answers this question himself, and tells us very distinctly that his Gospel was an historical one, and consisted of certain facts, and these were no other than the Death for sin, Burial and Resurrection of the Lord. Here are his words: "Moreover, brethren, I declare unto you the gospel which I preached unto you, which also ye have received, and wherein ye stand . . . For I delivered unto you first of all that which I also received, how that Christ died for our sins according to the scriptures; and that he was buried, and that he rose again the third day according to the scriptures: And that he was seen of Cephas, then of the twelve," &c., and then there follow the notices of several appearances of our Lord after His Resurrection, ending with that to St. Paul himself. (1 Corinth. xv. 1-10.)

But it is clear that there must be something previous to this to be believed and accepted, and that is the doctrine of the Person of Him Who could thus die for sins—His Incarnation and coming into the world—and this is set forth in the opening words of the most important of his Epistles, where St. Paul tells us that he was "separated unto the gospel of God, concerning His Son Jesus Christ our Lord, which was made of the seed of David according to the flesh; and declared to be the Son of God, with power, according to the spirit of holiness, by the resurrection from the dead." (Rom. i. 1-4.)

There can be no doubt, then, that St. Paul considered his Gospel to be a record of the Birth, Death, and Resurrection of the Son of God—assuming, of course, His previous existence on the one hand (Phil. ii. 6), and the dominion over all things at the Right Hand of God on the other.

Again, if St. Matthew thought it right to leave among the Palestinian Christians an account of the acts and sayings of the Lord, such as is contained in his Gospel,[1] and St. Mark wrote from the lips of Peter the account of the Life of the Lord which he preached, is it to be supposed for a moment that St. Paul would be behind them in his care for his converts, and not leave them in possession of a full account of the words and works of Christ while on earth? If he had not done so, how, for instance, could he have charged his Colossian converts that 'the word of Christ should dwell in them richly in all wisdom'? Such a charge presupposes a full account of, at least, the teaching of Christ.

Is, then, the fact that he did leave such an historical Gospel among them, and that this Gospel was that of St. Luke, which we have seen to be the widespread opinion of the earliest Churches, borne out by an examination of the Epistles?

1. Now, first of all, it is clear that the account of the Institution of the Eucharist is derived not from the tradition in the first two Synoptics, but from St. Paul, who tells us that he himself derived it from a revelation by the Lord Himself: "I have received of the Lord that which also I delivered unto you, that the Lord Jesus the same night in which he was betrayed, took bread: and when he had given thanks, he brake it, and said (Take eat): this is my body, which is broken for you: this do in remembrance of me. After the same manner also he took the cup, when he had supped, saying, This cup is the new testament (or rather covenant) in my blood: this do ye, as oft as ye drink it, in remembrance of me." (1 Cor. xi. 23-26.)

Now this is virtually reproduced by St. Luke in the words, "And he took bread, and gave thanks, and brake it, and gave unto them, saying, This is my body which is given for you: this do in

---

[1] See Eusebius, iii. ch. xxiv.

remembrance of me. Likewise also the cup after supper, saying, This cup is the new testament in my blood, which is shed for you." (Luke xxii. 19, 20.)

The reader will notice that in the revelation of the Lord to St. Paul there are two very important differences from the traditional account. One, that the Lord said, "Do this for my commemoration" (or anamnesis). The other, that He said respecting the cup, "This cup is the new covenant in my blood." Thereby emphasizing both the sacramental reality of the contents of the cup—for a covenant must be in blood, not in wine—and also the covenant nature and value of the ordinance.

Here then, so far as the Eucharist is a Gospel ordinance, conveying to us the most precious promises of the Lord's discourse in John vi., St. Luke's Gospel is that of St. Paul rather than of the other two Synoptics.

This is a very important matter indeed, and opens out to us a very wide field of (I may say) legitimate speculation, for if St. Luke received this important account from St. Paul, and he from the Lord Himself, we cannot help asking, is this the only direct revelation from the Lord respecting what He did whilst on earth, which St. Paul received direct from His Master, and caused to be written in St. Luke's Gospel? If the account of the institution of the Eucharist came thus direct from the Lord through St. Paul to St. Luke, what other matter in which St. Luke is the sole authority, may not have similarly come from the Lord?

2. We now come to a second coincidence, which, even were it by itself, would go far to identify St. Luke's Gospel with St. Paul's.

St. Paul in 1 Cor. xv. sets forth his Gospel to be mainly the evidences of the Lord's Resurrection, and the first of these mentioned by him is an appearance to Cephas: "He was seen of Cephas, then of the twelve." Now it is remarkable that this appearance to Cephas is of the Evangelists only mentioned by St. Luke, and by him, too, as if it was the first. For when the two, Cleopas and his friend, came to the assembled disciples, they were greeted with the words, "The Lord is risen indeed, and hath appeared unto Simon." (Luke xxiv. 34.) Too much stress can scarcely be laid upon this coincidence, as identifying St. Paul's Gospel with St. Luke's.

3. The third which I shall notice seems to me very suggestive

indeed of the closest connection. St. Luke's Gospel has always been believed to have been written for the especial use of the Gentile converts of St. Paul. Now the great battle of St. Paul's life was to free the Gentiles from the yoke of Jewish ordinances, and yet from St. Luke's Gospel alone do we learn that the Lord's infancy and youth were characterized by strict observance of the Mosaic ordinances. St. Matthew, for instance, writing for Jews, takes it for granted that they would know that the Lord received His Name at the time of His circumcision, and does not allude to it; whereas St. Luke not only particularly notices that at His circumcision on the eighth day He received His Name, but that this was followed by the presentation in the temple, and that the accustomed offering was made, and everything was done strictly in accordance with the Mosaic ritual. His account is, "When the days of her purification according to the law of Moses were accomplished, they brought him to Jerusalem, to present him to the Lord (as it is written in the law of the Lord, Every male that openeth the womb shall be called holy to the Lord); and to offer a sacrifice according to that which is said in the law of the Lord, A pair of turtledoves, or two young pigeons." (Luke ii. 21.)

Now we have the key to this anxiety on the part of the Evangelist to show that Joseph and the Lord's Mother in all things conformed to the Levitical Law in the words of the Apostle in Galatians iv. 4: "God sent forth his Son, made of a woman, made under the law, to redeem them that were under the law, that we might receive the adoption of sons."

According then to the Apostle, the submission of Jesus to the requirements of the law was redemptive. He, by this submission, redeemed them that were under the law, in order that they might in due time be delivered from the bondage of that system of things which, according to the words of St. Peter, " Neither their fathers nor they were able to bear" (Acts xv. 10); and if they were thus to be redeemed from this yoke of bondage, much less could it be imposed upon the Gentiles, for whom it was never designed.

Now doctrine like this necessitates some teaching respecting our Lord's ceremonial subjection during His early years on which it could be based. We have no such teaching in the other Gospels. We have it very fully in the Pauline Gospel of St. Luke.

4. With this, as part of the same subject, we have the allusion to

the doctrinal significance of the Lord's circumcision in Coloss. ii. 11: "In whom also ye are circumcised with the circumcision made without hands, in putting off the body of the sins of the flesh by the circumcision of Christ." This teaching seems to require as its basis some distinct allusion to the Lord's circumcision, which is mentioned only in St. Luke's Gospel.

The rest of the instances of identity or close agreement are only coincidences, but are nevertheless of great value to the argument when taken in connection with the more important ones cited above.

5. St. Paul's description of a "widow indeed" in 1 Tim. v. 5: "She that is a widow indeed, and desolate, trusteth in God, and continueth in supplications and prayers night and day," is a reproduction of the account of Anna in Luke ii. 37: "She departed not from the temple, but served God with fastings and prayers night and day."

6. Luke iv. 19: "To preach the acceptable year of the Lord." This quotation from Isaiah lxi. 1 is only to be found in St. Luke, and it agrees well with the preaching of the Apostle of the Gentiles, who alone dwells on the present time being *the accepted time* (2 Corinth. vi. 2).

7. St. Luke alone (xii. 42) designates the minister of Christ as a "steward" (οἰκονόμος), which term in St. Matthew is represented by ἐπίτροπος. St. Paul speaks of the Apostles as "ministers of Christ and stewards (δικονόμοι) of the mysteries of God" (1 Cor. iv. 1), and says that a "bishop must be blameless, as the steward (δικονόμος) of God" (Tit. i. 7).

8. In St. Luke alone (except in one place in St. Matthew) is alienation from God described as being dead, and the return to obedience as being made alive again. (Luke xv. 24, 32.) The reader needs scarcely to be reminded how habitually the Apostle describes a state of sin as death, and a state of conformity to God as life.

9. St. Luke alone of the Synoptics applies the word "revealed" to the second coming of the Lord (Luke xvii. 30); and so St. Paul (1 Cor. i. 7, 2 Thess. i. 7).

10. It is worthy of remark that the order of the commandments of the second table is the same in Luke xviii. 20, and Rom. xiii. 9, so far as this, that "Thou shalt not commit adultery," precedes "Thou shalt not kill, Thou shalt not steal." In the parallel passage in St. Matthew, xix. 18, "Thou shalt do no murder," comes the first. In St. Mark the reading is doubtful.

11. In the account of the Lord's refutation of the arguments of the Sadducees, St. Luke tells us that He concluded with the words, "for all live to him," which are not in St. Matthew's, or St. Mark's account. Now this is a favourite expression with St. Paul; thus, "alive unto God through Jesus Christ our Lord"—"None of us liveth to himself"—"He died for all, that they who live should live henceforth not unto themselves," &c.

12. In their respective accounts of our Lord's great prophecy of the destruction of Jerusalem, St. Matthew and St. Mark seem to recognize no lengthened period of time between the coming in judgment at the destruction of Jerusalem, and the second coming at the end (Matth. xxiv. 29; Mark xiii. 24). St. Luke, on the contrary, speaks of "Jerusalem being trodden down of the Gentiles until the times of the Gentiles be fulfilled" (xxi. 84). Now in the Epistle to the Romans, in speaking of the casting away of the fleshly Israel for a time, St. Paul alludes to these "times of the Gentiles" in an expression exactly analogous to that in St. Luke, "until the fulness of the Gentiles be come in." (Rom. xi. 25.)

13. Again, St. Paul in a very large number of places associates the Ascension of the Lord with His Resurrection. (Thus Rom. viii. 34; Ephes. i. 20, 21; Phil. ii. 9; Coloss. iii. 1-4, &c.) This seems to demand that in his Gospel special mention should be made of it, and so it is, for in St. Luke's Gospel we read that the Lord was taken up into heaven in the act of blessing His disciples. Of the other Evangelists, Matthew and John give no account of the Ascension, and Mark, or the Apostle who concludes his Gospel (I believe St. Peter), very cursorily mentions it. But if we are allowed to consider the first verses of the Book of the Acts as a part of the Gospel, then the Ascension occupies the prominent place in this Gospel which we should suppose that it would have in any Gospel which St. Paul could designate as his.

Again in the last verses of St. Luke we have the Saviour speaking of repentance and remission of sins being preached in His name among all nations, "beginning at Jerusalem," and St. Paul seems to take up this word when he writes (Rom xv. 19), that "from Jerusalem and round about unto Illyricum he had fully preached the Gospel of Christ."

The following are a few verbal coincidences which have some value in connection with the more prominent ones.

INTRODUCTION. xv

St. Paul calls the Christian under instruction ὁ κατηχούμενος (Gal. vi. 6), a reminiscence of Luke i. 4, περὶ ὧν κατηχήθης λόγων. No other sacred writer uses the word.

St. Luke only of the Evangelists makes the Lord mention "children of light" (xvi. 8), and so St. Paul (1 Thess. v. 4).

The only plausible meaning that can be given to 1 Tim. ii. 15, "she shall be saved through the childbearing," is that it is a covert allusion to that particular childbearing by which the Saviour came into the world, and this "childbearing" occupies a far more prominent place in St. Luke than in any other Gospel.

In St. Luke xxii. 43, we read, ὤφθη δὲ αὐτῷ ἄγγελος, and in St. Paul, 1 Tim. iii. 16, ὤφθη ἀγγέλοις.

In Coloss. iii. 16, the Apostle exhorts his converts to let the word of Christ dwell in them richly in all wisdom, and then exhorts them to "speak and admonish one another in psalms, and hymns, and spiritual songs." Now that the word of Christ (as distinguished from that of God in the Old Testament) should thus dwell in them, demands that there should be in use among them a written Gospel in which this word should be embodied, and if this was that of St. Luke, then it is worthy of notice, that that Gospel contains the only Christian hymns (as distinguished from Psalms) to be found in the New Testament, viz., Luke i. 46 and 68, and ii. 29.

Two other matters bearing upon the connection between St. Luke's written Gospel and the teaching of St. Paul, as contained in his Epistles, require to be shortly examined.

The preaching of St. Paul brings forward very prominently that men are saved by faith, and this in order that they may be saved by Grace. (Rom. iv. 16.)

Now if this be so we should expect to find in St. Luke much that would support this, and so we do. Thus, in the very first chapter, we have Zacharias punished for his want of faith (i. 20), and the Holy Virgin pronounced blessed because she believed (i. 45). Again, the woman who is a sinner, no doubt a gross sinner, is dismissed with the words, "Thy faith hath saved thee, go in peace" (vii. 50). Again, as Godet says, the four parables of the lost sheep, the lost piece of money, the prodigal son, and the Pharisee and the Publican, are the doctrine of Paul exhibited in action. Again, salvation comes to the house of Zaccheus the Publican because he receives Christ into it. Again, the teaching of the parable of the unprofitable servant is against any merit of works. Again, to the one

INTRODUCTION.

Samaritan out of the ten lepers the Lord says, "Thy faith hath made thee whole" (xvii. 19). And, lastly, the first words on the Cross, "Father, forgive them," and the absolution of the penitent malefactor, are exhibitions of the fullest and freest grace conceivable.

Again, the earlier chapters especially contain many expressions of a like character, peculiar to this Gospel, as, for instance, the whole of the Magnificat and the Song of Zacharias and of Simeon, and the Song of the Heavenly Host, and St. Luke alone tells us that the Lord, in the synagogue at Nazareth took as His text the words of the Evangelical prophet, "The Spirit of the Lord is upon me, because he hath anointed me to preach the gospel to the poor," &c. (iv. 17-20).

And, lastly, St. Paul, in writing to the Corinthian Christians, beseeches them "by the meekness and gentleness of Christ" (2 Cor. x. 1). We should gather from this that in his Gospel, which must have been in the hands of the Corinthians, and from which they would derive all their knowledge (for the time) of the Lord's character and teaching, the meekness and gentleness of the Lord would be brought into prominence, and so it is. From the Gospel of St. Luke we derive the touching narrative of the gentleness and compassion of the Lord in the raising up of the widow's son and of His treatment of the woman which was a sinner; and we have the record of His own example of His meekness and forbearance in His prayer for His murderers, and in His reception of the penitent malefactor. Again, His teaching, as exhibited in St. Luke's Gospel, inculcates this disposition very strongly, as, for instance, the parable of the good Samaritan, the instruction respecting taking the lowest room, the gentle and forbearing treatment of the sulky and surly elder son by the father in the parable of the Prodigal Son, also the parable of the Pharisee and the Publican, and in connection with this it is worthy of notice that St. Luke does not mention the great indignation manifested by the Saviour against the disciples when they had rebuked those who had brought the little children (xviii. 16), nor the holy violence He used in expelling the buyers and sellers from the temple. (Compare Luke xix. 45 with Matth. xxi. 12 and Mark xi. 15.)

From all these considerations it appears to me to be an absolute certainty that the early fathers were right in identifying the Gospel of St. Paul ("my Gospel") with that of St. Luke, not, of course, that St. Paul himself wrote it, but that it was written by his

INTRODUCTION. xvii

direction and the materials, some of them at least, derived from the highest source, even the revelation of the Lord Himself to the Apostle.

We know that one part of this Gospel came from the Lord through St. Paul, and we know not what other portions may not have had a similar origin. I think it is not unreasonable to suppose that much besides the Institution of the Eucharist was made known to St. Paul by Christ personally.

With respect to other channels of information, St. Luke, in the preface, seems to assert that he derived his materials from the highest human sources. " It seemed good to me, who, having had perfect understanding of all things from the very first " (" or having traced the course of all things accurately from the first "), and this he did apparently from the reports of " those who, from the beginning, were eyewitnesses and ministers of the word."

Now, in carefully examining this Gospel, there seems to be a large number of incidents, the accounts of which must have been derived from eyewitnesses. Thus the account of the miraculous draught of fishes (v. 3-8) must have come from one present, and in whose memory all was indelibly engraved, so also the disciples rubbing the ears of corn (vi. 1), and the healing of the man with the withered hand (vi. 6). (This account is quite as minute as St. Mark's, but not copied from it.) The same may be said of the healing of the centurion's servant (vii. 1-9). This account is far more circumstantial than St. Matthew's, and is not found in St. Mark. Also the account of the woman that was a sinner, peculiar to St. Luke (vii. 36-50). Again, the miracle of the Gadarene demoniac is as graphic as that in St. Mark, but not derived from it. So also the account of the Transfiguration (ix. 28-37) must have come, we should say, from one of the three present. Again, the same may be said of the Lord's Apprehension in xxii. 47-53. We are there told that Judas *went before*—we are told of the Lord's question, " Judas, betrayest thou the Son of man with a kiss ? ", and the disciples' question, " Lord, shall we smite with the sword ? " and the healing of the ear, and the solemn concluding words, " This is your hour, and the power of darkness."

Again, I have noticed that the account of St. Peter's denials, from verses 56 to 59, bears all the marks of coming direct from one who was present; and, lastly, the account of the meeting of the risen Lord with many disciples in xxiv. 36-42, must have been given by an eyewitness.

xviii INTRODUCTION.

All this bears out very fully the statement of Eusebius, that he had received his information "from his intimacy and stay with Paul, and also his intercourse with the other Apostles."

v.

MEDICAL LANGUAGE OF ST. LUKE.

I trust (if God spare me to write on the Acts of the Apostles), to give in an excursus some instances of the use of medical language by St. Luke. This subject seems exhausted in a treatise by the Rev. W. K. Hobart, of Trinity College, Dublin, on "The Medical Language of St. Luke." He seems to prove very clearly, not only that St. Luke uses medical terms in describing the miracles of healing, which the other Evangelists do not use, but that his vocabulary is that of one who had received a medical education and studied medical treatises ; and when writing respecting non-medical matters he yet uses very many words which Hippocrates, Galen, Dioscorides, and other Greek physicians were in the habit of employing even when not writing on diseases and their remedies. To give Dr. Hobart's own words, "There is a class of words running through the third Gospel, and the Acts of the Apostles, and for the most part peculiar to these books of the New Testament writings, with which a medical man must have been familar, as they formed part of the ordinary phraseology of Greek medical language. In thus using words to which he had become habituated through professional training, St. Luke would not be singular, for the Greek medical writers, also, when dealing with unprofessional subjects, show a leaning to the use of words to which they were accustomed in their professional language." I wish I could now give instances, but the extent to which these Notes on St. Luke have already run quite forbids it, and some of the more remarkable instances are to be found in the Book of the Acts.

So that a searching examination of St. Luke's phraseology yields a striking confirmation to the truth of the words of the Apostle, which describe him as a physician.

Almighty God, Who calledst Luke the Physician, whose praise is in the Gospel, to be an Evangelist and Physician of the soul; May it please Thee that, by the wholesome medicine of the doctrine delivered by him, all the diseases of our souls may be healed ; through the merits of Thy Son Jesus Christ our Lord. Amen.

A COMMENTARY.

ST. LUKE.

INTRODUCTORY REMARKS ON THE PREFACE.

1-4. "Forasmuch as many have taken in hand," &c. This is the only place in the New Testament which throws any direct light on the composition of the Gospel narrative. From it we learn that, in the very earliest times, the Church was instructed in the accounts of the Life, Death, and Resurrection of the Lord Jesus, not from books, but from the oral teaching of the Apostles, for the Apostles only can be alluded to in the words, "They delivered them unto us who *from the beginning* were eye-witnesses, and ministers of the word." The things which these original witnesses delivered were historical facts—not abstract doctrines, no matter how clearly deducible from such facts, but the facts themselves; for the true rendering of the words "most surely believed amongst us" is rather "which have been accomplished amongst us" (Godet), or "have been fulfilled amongst us" (Revisers of 1881).

These facts, it appears, were at the first not committed to writing, certainly not by the Apostles or original witnesses, who for some reason confined themselves to teaching them orally.

As might have been expected, many of the first Christians thus orally instructed were dissatisfied with having the accounts only in memory; and for the benefit of themselves and of their friends, and perhaps of the Church, committed to writing in an historical form, more or less imperfectly, the facts which they had heard from the lips of the Apostles.

In a very modest way St. Luke, on the ground that he had carefully informed himself of all the facts from the very commencement, puts forth a claim to write a consecutive account of them, and this, not apparently that the whole Church might possess an orderly account of Gospel facts, but that a certain Theophilus [from the way in which he is addressed as most excellent [κράτιστε], evidently a person of great consideration in the early Church], might know the certainty of the instructions which he had received.

The lessons, then, which we gather from this short preface are of very great importance: they are these—that the Church as an organized body instructed in the teaching, and continuing in the fellowship of the Apostles, was anterior, in point of time, to any book of the New Testament Scriptures—that the instruction in which the first converts were built up in the faith was historical instruction —and that its subject matter was the Life, Death, and Resurrection of Christ; and whatever doctrines were afterwards superadded or deduced, had all of them this account of the Lord's Life and Death as their foundation; but we learn also that from the necessities of the case it was deemed right that in the later Apostolic times the oral accounts of the Lord's Life should be preserved by being put into writing.

There is one important matter deserving attention suggested by this introduction; and that is, its language or style. Godet says: "Not only is it written in most classical Greek, but it reminds us, by its contents, of the similar preambles of the most illustrious Greek historians, especially those of Herodotus and Thucydides. The more thoroughly we examine it the more we find of that delicacy of sentiment and refinement of mind which constitute the predominant traits of the Hellenic character; we do not find a style like it in all the New Testament, except at the end of the Acts, and in the Epistle to the Hebrews." If these one or two Scripture writers use at times most classical Greek, why should not all the New Testament have been similarly composed? Evidently because its composition, according to classical models, would have deprived it of all its usefulness as a book for all, for the poor and uneducated rather than the refined and educated. The Hebrew and Aramaic are, as regards the composition of their sentences, exceedingly simple compared with the Greek and Latin languages. When God then, at the first, caused the account of His Son's Life and Death to be preached in the words and sentences of the Aramaic He enshrined it in that which was especially the language of the poor, and also in the idiom of the poor; and when it was translated into the great classical languages of the period, the phraseology and

CHAP. I.

FORASMUCH as many have taken in hand to set forth in order a declaration of those things which are most surely believed among us.

---

1. "Declaration;" rather "narration;" *ordinare narrationem*, Vulg.; "to draw up a narration," Revisers. "Of those things which are most surely believed among us," or "which have been fulfilled among us," Revisers; "*quæ in nobis completæ sunt rerum*," Vulg.

idiom of the Aramaic were preserved and employed as far as possible, so that what the common people of Palestine heard gladly, the common people of all nations might hear gladly as well. So that we see that it was not from want of ability that one most important sacred writer narrates the words and deeds of the Lord, not in well-turned periods and carefully chosen phrases, of which we see from this preface that he was the master, but in the simple, artless style of the original tradition, so that not the few, but the many might receive in its simplicity the faith of the Lord.

1. "Forasmuch as many have taken in hand," &c. Are St. Matthew and St. Mark to be included amongst these "many?" Certainly not St. Mark, for he most probably wrote in Rome, but it is not at all improbable that St. Matthew may be included; for it is to be carefully borne in mind, that St. Luke, in this preface, pronounces no opinion, favourable or otherwise, about these previous efforts to compose narratives of the Lord's life, but only claims for himself a place amongst them on special grounds, mentioned in the third verse.

Another question is, Are the authors of the productions known as the Apocryphal Gospels to be any of them included amongst these "many?" Certainly not; because the Apocryphal Gospels, all of them, contain much which is, on the face of it, unworthy of the Lord, and were all the production of much later times.

"A declaration of those things which are most surely believed among us." The Revisers of 1881 more correctly render this "a narrative of those matters which have been fulfilled among us,"

2 ᵃ Even as they delivered them unto us, which ᵇ from the beginning were eyewitnesses, and ministers of the word;

3 ᶜ It seemed good to me also, having had perfect understanding of all things from the very first,

ᵃ Heb. ii. 3. 1 Pet. v. 1. 2 Pet. i. 16. 1 John i. 1.
ᵇ Mark i. 1. John xv. 27.
ᶜ Acts xv. 19, 25, 28. 1 Cor. vii. 40.

---

3. "Having had perfect understanding of all things from the very first." See below for translation of Revisers and Godet.

i.e. in our day and generation amongst our contemporaries, though our elders.

"Most surely believed" is a wrong translation.

2. "They who from the beginning were eyewitnesses and ministers of the word." The eyewitnesses from the beginning must have been the Apostles. Thus when one was chosen to fill the place of the traitor, his qualification was that he was one " of those men who had companied with the Apostles all the time that the Lord Jesus went in and out amongst them, beginning from the Baptism of John," &c. These were naturally the first depositaries and deliverers to others of the original account or tradition [paradosis]. From this we learn that the inspiration of the Evangelists did not consist in the Holy Spirit pouring into their mind the knowledge of otherwise unknown facts respecting the Lord's life, but that He so overruled them, that out of a very world of facts, and incidents, and parables, and miracles, and discourses, they were directed to select and set forth those which it was most to the advantage of the future Church to know; so that the mind of the Church might not be distracted or merely amused by a vast multiplicity of incidents, but be led to dwell upon those which, in the eye of the Spirit, were most profitable for faith and practice.

"Eyewitnesses and ministers of the word." This is more correctly rendered by Godet, "who were eyewitnesses of them (the facts or events) from the beginning, and who (afterward, at the Day of Pentecost) became ministers of the word. This emphasizes the fact that only on and after the Day of Pentecost did the Apostles become the ministers of the full and complete word. Before, they preached simply that men should repent and believe, now they preached the sanction of repentance and faith in the full account of the Life, Sayings, Acts, Death and Resurrection of Christ.

3. " It seemed good to me also, having had perfect under-

CHAP. I.]   THE PREFACE.   5

to write unto thee ^d in order, ^e most excellent Theophilus,   ^d Acts xi. 4.
^e Acts i. 1.

4 ^f That thou mightest know the certainty of those things, wherein thou hast been instructed.   ^f John xx. 31.

---

4. "That thou mightest know the certainty of those things wherein," &c. "That thou mightest know the certainty concerning the things," &c.

standing of all things from the very first." Revisers more correctly translate this, "Having traced the course of all things accurately from the first." Godet, "After carefully informing myself of all these facts from their commencement." There seems to be in the words "from the first" or "commencement," an allusion to the circumstance that St. Luke goes further back in his account than the ministry of John, and gives an account of the very first dawning of the Gospel day in the vision of the Angel to Zacharias announcing to him the birth of the Lord's forerunner. So Godet: "The author compares himself to a traveller who tries to discover the source of a river, in order that he may descend it again, and follow its entire course."

"To write unto thee in order, most excellent Theophilus." "In order" would seem to be in order of time. Very probably the narratives which were composed by "the many" were the greater part of them mere memoranda arranged according to the order in which they were received or remembered, rather than with any regard to chronology, or their true sequence in the Lord's Life.

"Most excellent Theophilus." He writes to Theophilus, a man probably of some distinction, and a governor; for the form *Most excellent* was not used except to rulers and governors. As, for example, St. Paul says to Festus, "most excellent Festus," using precisely the same word. In this latter case it must have been used as a form, for there was nothing noble or great about Festus. About Theophilus personally nothing whatsoever is known. It is just possible that as the word means "beloved of God," it may be taken as a general appellation of believers, or Christians, who could not have been called out of darkness into light, except by an act of love on God's part.

4. "That thou mightest know the certainty of those things, wherein thou hast been instructed." Some translate this "instructed" as if it meant "catechized," but it must not be taken to

ZACHARIAS. [St. Luke.

Before the common account called Anno Domini the sixth year.
g Matt. ii. 1.
h 1 Chr. xxiv. 10, 19. Neh. xii. 4, 17.

5 ¶ THERE was ᵍ in the days of Herod, the king of Judæa, a certain priest named Zacharias, ʰ of the course of Abia: and his wife *was* of the daughters of Aaron, and her name *was* Elisabeth.

---

imply that form of instruction by question and answer to which we apply the word " catechize." Theophilus had been instructed in the history of the Lord, but orally, and perhaps by different teachers, and this treatise or narrative being written with care and in due order, and after much investigation, would confirm, *i.e.* invest with more certainty, the oral instruction which Theophilus had received.

5. " There was in the days of Herod, the king of Judæa, a certain priest," &c. The reign of Herod is here mentioned, not simply to indicate the time in the world's secular history, but the time in which prophecy was fulfilled; for this king Herod was an Idumean or Edomite king, imposed upon the Jews by the Romans in virtue of their conquest of the Holy Land. The sceptre had now departed from Judah, so Shiloh was to come, or rather according to the strict meaning of the Hebrew prophecy, " he was to come to whom the gathering of the people should be."

" A certain priest named Zacharias, of the course of Abia," &c. David divided the families of Eleazar and Ithamar into twenty-four divisions, who were in their turn to minister in the Sanctuary—the turn of each course coming twice a year. It was their duty to perform the higher offices of the holy place, to offer the blood of the sacrifices by sprinkling it at the bottom of the altar, to trim the seven-branched candlestick, to put on the shew-bread, and as here mentioned, to burn incense on the altar of incense. The course of Abia was the eighth of these courses, and calculations have been made to show that the course or Ephemeria of Abia would be on duty in the week from the seventeenth to the twenty-third of April, and in that from the third to the ninth of October, but this rests too much on conjecture.

" And his wife was of the daughters of Aaron, and her name was Elizabeth." In this he had fulfilled the will of God, who desired that the priestly tribe should keep its lineage pure by the priests taking wives of the same tribe. Being of the daughters of Aaron,

CHAP. I.]   RIGHTEOUS BEFORE GOD.   7

6 And they were both ⁱrighteous before God, walking in all the commandments and ordinances of the Lord blameless.

7 And they had no child, because that Elisabeth was barren, and they both were *now* well stricken in years.

8 And it came to pass, that while he executed the priest's office before God ᵏ in the order of his course,

9 According to the custom of the priest's office, his lot was ˡ to burn incense when he went into the temple of the Lord.

ⁱ Gen. vii. 1.
& xvii. 1. 1 Kin.
ix. 4. 2 Kin.
xx. 3. Job i. 1.
Acts xxiii. 1.
& xxiv. 16.
Phil. iii. 6.

ᵏ 1 Chr. xxiv.
19. 2 Chr. viii.
14. & xxxi. 2.

ˡ Ex. xxx. 7, 8.
1 Sam. ii. 28.
1 Chr. xxiii. 13.
2 Chr. xxix. 11.

---

9. " His lot was to burn incense when he went into the temple of the Lord." Revisers translate, " His lot was to enter into the temple of the Lord and burn incense." The meaning is that after he and his brother priests had entered that morning into the temple of the Lord they drew lots to determine which part of the service each one should take, and the lot fell to him to burn incense.

she must have been the daughter of a member of one of the twenty-four courses.

6. "And they were both righteous before God, walking in all the commandments," &c. Righteous before God, *i.e.*, righteous before Him Who searcheth the hearts. They were sincere and hearty in their obedience, and this is perfectly compatible with the undoubted theological truth, that being conceived and born in sin "through the weakness of their nature they could not always stand upright."

"Walking in all the commandments and ordinances." The commandments seem to refer to the precepts of the moral law, the ordinances to the Levitical precepts respecting the worship of God.

7. "And they had no child, because that Elisabeth was barren," &c. Inasmuch as fruitfulness was amongst the blessings pronounced by God on the children of Israel if they obeyed Him, the Jews falsely inferred that individual barrenness implied a curse, whereas the mothers of some of the greatest persons in their history, Isaac, Jacob, Samson, Samuel, had been barren till God answered their prayers by special miracles.

8-9. "And it came to pass . . . . his lot was to burn incense," &c. It appears that, in order that there might be no jealousy or

8 THE TIME OF INCENSE. [St. Luke.

10 ᵐ And the whole multitude of the people were praying without at the time of incense.

ᵐ Lev. xvi. 17.
Rev. viii. 3, 4.

11 And there appeared unto him an angel of the Lord standing on the right side of ⁿ the altar of incense.

ⁿ Ex. xxx. 1.

---

unseemly rivalry, all the functions of each day were apportioned by lot amongst the priests who belonged to the particular course in attendance. According to Dr. Edersheim, a priest could only offer incense once in his lifetime. His words are: " While the (morning) sacrifice was prepared for the altar, the priests, whose lot it was, had made ready all within the Holy Place, where the most solemn part of the day's service was to take place, that of offering the incense, which symbolized Israel's accepted prayers. Again was the lot, the third, cast to indicate him, who was to be honoured with this highest Mediatorial Act. Only once in a lifetime might any one enjoy that privilege. Henceforth he was called 'rich,' and must leave to his brethren the hope of the distinction which had been granted him." (" Life of Christ," vol. i. p. 134. 2nd edit.)

10. "And the whole multitude of the people were praying." This was the one time of special daily prayer in the temple. The time of acceptable prayer apparently was not so much the time of offering any bloody sacrifice, however solemn, but the time of incense—incense typifying by its sweet odour the favour with which God regarded true prayer. Thus David says: "Let my prayer be set forth in Thy sight as the incense," and in the Revelation we read: "Another angel came and stood at the altar, having a golden censer, and there was given unto him much incense, that he should offer it with the prayers of all the saints upon the golden altar which was before the throne. And the smoke of the incense which came with the prayers of the saints ascended up before God out of the angel's hand " (viii. 3, 4). It is to be remarked that the incense is not typical of prayer, but ascends up with it as accompanying it.

11. " And there appeared unto him an angel of the Lord standing on the right side," &c. This is the first gleam of the dawn of the Gospel Day, and where did it shine forth? In the temple of God—in the centre and heart of that remarkable system of blended atonement and worship which God had established amongst His people

CHAP. I.] FEAR FELL UPON HIM. 9

12 And when Zacharias saw *him*, ᵒ he was troubled, and fear fell upon him.

ᵒ Judg. vi. 22. & xiii. 22. Dan. x. 8. ver. 29. ch. ii. 9. Acts x. 4. Rev. i. 17.

---

to prepare them for the true Atonement and the spiritual worship of the Church of Christ. It is exceedingly significant how God passed over the teaching or expository system of the popular religion of the day, which had become thoroughly corrupt in the hands of the Rabbis and Scribes, and gave the first sign which heralded the coming change, not in the Synagogues or Rabbinical schools, but in the Holy Place, where was the altar of incense betokening acceptable prayer, and the table of shew-bread showing forth the true Bread, and the seven-branched candlestick the type of the seven-fold Spirit. "It seems indeed most fitting that the Evangelic story should have taken its beginning within the sanctuary and at the time of sacrifice. Despite its outward veneration for them, the temple, its services, and specially its sacrifices, were by an inward logical necessity, fast becoming a superfluity in the eyes of Rabbinism. But the new development, passing over the intruded elements [of Rabbinism] which were, after all, of rationalistic origin, connected its beginning directly with the Old Testament dispensation—its sacrifices, priesthood, and promises. In the sanctuary, in connection with sacrifice, and through the priesthood —such was significantly the beginning of the era of fulfilment. And so the great religious reformation of Israel under Samuel had also begun in the tabernacle."

12. "And when Zacharias saw him, he was troubled, and fear fell upon him." This fear has been ascribed to his sense of sin, but does it not rather arise from the manifestation of the supernatural or spiritual world? The inhabitants of this world are in a sphere above ours. We feel ourselves utterly powerless before them. For what purpose does God permit them to appear? Daniel, a man far greater and holier than Zacharias, felt this fear. On one occasion, in the sight of this very Gabriel, he was afraid, and fell on his face (Dan. viii. 17), on another there remained no strength in him (x. 8).

Great pains have been taken by some commentators to show that before a messenger from the other world can appear, "a condition of peculiar receptivity is required. This condition," it is said, "existed in Zacharias at this time. It had been created in him by

13 But the angel said unto him, Fear not, Zacharias: for thy prayer is heard; and thy wife Elisabeth shall bear thee a son, and ᵖ thou shalt call his name John.

ᵖ ver. 60, 63.

14 And thou shalt have joy and gladness; and ᑫ many shall rejoice at his birth.

ᑫ ver. 58.

15 For he shall be great in the sight of the

---

the solemnity of the place, by the sacredness of the function he was about to perform, by his lively sympathy with all this people who were imploring heaven for national deliverance, and, last of all, by the experience of his own domestic trial." But why thus limit the power of God? What right have we, who know nothing of the conditions under which the denizens of the unseen world exist, much less appear and disappear—what right have we to say that God can only send them to those who are in what we are pleased to call a state of receptivity? One would also think that the state of receptivity would dispel the fear with which their coming seems always attended, but it does not. One thing, however, is most certain, that in every case they appear unexpectedly and suddenly, and disappear as suddenly, as if their manifestation depended on nothing except the Divine Will.

13. "But the angel said unto him, Fear not, Zacharias: for thy prayer is heard,"—*i.e.*, thy prayer for a son. When God moves the heart to pray for some extraordinary blessing, it is a sign that He is about to grant it.

"Thou shalt call his name John." He was commanded to give the child this name, because of its signifying "the Lord is gracious," or "shows grace."

14. "And thou shalt have joy and gladness." This joy and gladness has become the heritage of the whole Church of Christ, for the outward form and utterance of this joy in the Benedictus has ever been the expression of the Church's joy that God has visited and redeemed His people.

"And many shall rejoice at his birth." This must not be restricted to the joy of the family circle (v. 58), or of the neighbouring country, but to the revival of religious hope through his ministry. According to the Lord's words, "He was a burning and a shining light, and ye were willing for a season to rejoice in his light" (John v. 33).

15. "For he shall be great in the sight of the Lord." The Lord

Lord, and ʳ shall drink neither wine nor strong drink; and he shall be filled with the Holy Ghost, ˢ even from his mother's womb.

ʳ Num. vi. 3.
Judg. xiii. 4.
ch. vii. 33.
ˢ Jer. i. 5.
Gal. i. 15.

16 ᵗ And many of the children of Israel shall he turn to the Lord their God.

ᵗ Mal. iv. 5, 6.

17 ᵘ And he shall go before him in the spirit

ᵘ Mal. iv. 5.
Matt. xi. 14.
Mark ix. 12.

---

witnesses to his greatness when He says that he was "more than a prophet," and that " of those born of women there hath not risen a greater."

"And he shall drink neither wine nor strong drink." That is, he shall all his life be under the vow of the Nazarite. Not only was he not to drink wine nor strong drink, but nothing that is made of the vine-tree, from the kernels even to the husk, no razor was to come upon his head, and he was not to touch the dead body even of his father or his mother when they died, because the consecration of his God was upon his head (Numb. vi. 4, 5, 7).

"He shall be filled with the Holy Ghost, even from his mother's womb." "St. John who, before he was born, when yet in his mother's womb, bore witness to the grace of the Spirit which he had received, when, leaping in the womb of his parent, he hailed the glad tidings of the coming of the Lord. There is one spirit of this life, another of grace. The former has its beginning at birth, its end at death; the latter is not tied down to times and seasons, is not quenched by death, is not shut out of the womb" (Ambrose in Catena Aurea).

16. "And many of the children of Israel shall he turn to the Lord their God." By no prophet who went before him was the religious heart of the people of Israel so stirred. "Then went out unto him Jerusalem and all Judea, and all the region round about Jordan." The Lord speaks of "all the people that heard him, and the publicans justifying God being baptized with the baptism of John" (Luke vii. 29). So that his work in preparing the elect remnant for the reception of Christ was pre-eminently blessed of God.

17. "And he shall go before him in the spirit and power of Elias," &c. Go before whom? No doubt before Christ the Son of God, who is here by very sure implication called "the Lord their God." And what wonder, seeing that this same Christ permitted His

and power of Elias, to turn the hearts of the fathers to
the children, and the disobedient ‖ to the wisdom
of the just; to make ready a people prepared for the Lord.

18 And Zacharias said unto the angel, ˣ Whereby shall I know this? for I am an old man, and my wife well stricken in years.

‖ Or, *by.*

ˣ Gen. xvii. 17.

---

apostles to worship Him, and to call Him "Lord and God." Thus Bede, "Now since John (who bearing witness to Christ, baptized the people in His faith), is said to have turned the children of Israel to the Lord their God, it is plain that Christ is the God of Israel."

"To turn the hearts of the fathers to the children." Many early writers consider that "the children" here mean the apostles and Christian teachers who inherited the promises made to the fathers, so that it is the same as turning them to Christianity, which was in a sense the offspring of the older religion; but this seems very far fetched. Do not the words seem to point to a revival of family religion, and home duties and affections, which must have been in a fearfully low state, if divorce was then so common among the Jews, as we know it was? If Christianity was to be a religion of love, what more likely than that love should be revived in the home circle? Coleridge, quoted in Ford, has an observation worth reproducing: "The paternal and filial duties discipline the heart, and prepare it for the love of all mankind. The intensity of private attachments encourages, not prevents, universal benevolence." It is to be remarked that the prophet Malachi, from whom this quotation is cited, mentions both sides—the hearts of the fathers to the children, and the children to the fathers.

"A people prepared for the Lord." By repentance, and works meet for repentance.

18. "And Zacharias said unto the angel, Whereby shall I know this?" &c. This unbelief on the part of this good man seems strange. Was not the appearance of the angel, and in such a sacred place, sufficient to assure him? though, however, many prophets and holy men, Abraham, Gideon, and Hezekiah, had asked for signs. And, besides, we are to remember, that the angels did not on all occasions present a supernatural appearance. They seem to have manifested themselves on most occasions simply as men. Daniel

19 And the angel answering said unto him, I am ʸ Gabriel, that stand in the presence of God; and am sent to speak unto thee, and to show thee these glad tidings.

ʸ Dan. viii. 16. & ix. 21, 22, 23. Matt. xviii. 10. Heb. i. 14.

20 And, behold, ᶻ thou shalt be dumb, and not able to speak, until the day that these things shall be performed, because thou believest not my words, which shall be fulfilled in their season.

ᶻ Ezek. iii. 26. & xxiv. 27.

---

speaks of the "man" Gabriel. There is no ground whatsoever for supposing that they were as represented in pictures, men furnished with impossible wings. But we are to remember that the manifestation of the supernatural by no means necessitates a true belief in God, and in what God requires. The Lord very emphatically says, "If they hear not Moses and the prophets, neither will they be persuaded, though one rose from the dead." The whole book, Old Testament and New, is a strange record of mingled belief and unbelief; and this good man's case is no exception. The very greatness of the tidings, so unlooked for, and yet earnestly prayed for, might instil doubt, as the disciples, when they heard of the Lord's Resurrection, "believed not for joy, and wondered."

19. "And the angel answering, said unto him, I am Gabriel," &c. Gabriel, apparently the second in rank of God's great angelic ministers. He is the one apparently most constantly employed in messages respecting redemption, whereas Michael, who alone is styled Arch-angel, is always at the front of the contest between good and evil (thus Dan. x. 13; xii. 1; Rev. xii. 7; Jude 9).

"And am sent to speak unto thee." From this we gather that there is place, and distance, and motion in the unseen world. However we conceive of it, and speak of it as above this visible state of things, we are not so to speak of it as to rob it of all its reality, and make it a mere vision or transcendental state.

20. "And behold thou shalt be dumb, and not able to speak." This was at once a sign and a chastisement. A sign that the word of God through the angel would be fulfilled; a chastisement, and yet one which should make his heart overflow with joy, for the instantaneous dumbness inflicted at the mere word of the angel was to him as supernatural as the birth of a son would be.

21 And the people waited for Zacharias, and marvelled that he tarried so long in the temple.

22 And when he came out, he could not speak unto them: and they perceived that he had seen a vision in the temple: for he beckoned unto them, and remained speechless.

^a See 2 Kin. xi. 5. 1 Chr. ix. 25.

23 And it came to pass, that, as soon as ^a the days of his ministration were accomplished, he departed to his own house.

24 And after those days his wife Elisabeth conceived, and hid herself five months, saying,

---

21. "And the people waited for Zacharias, and marvelled that he tarried," &c. They waited to receive the blessing, most probably that contained in Numbers vi., "The Lord bless thee and keep thee," &c., which he would pronounce after the incense was consumed. It is not improbable that the angel spake to the aged priest much more than the few words which are preserved.

22. "And when he came out, he could not speak unto them," *i.e.*, he could not pronounce the words audibly, but made signs by which they might understand that he was invoking the benediction upon them. I can give no other meaning to the words, "He beckoned unto them, and remained speechless."

23-25. "And it came to pass . . . to take away my reproach among men." "Hid herself five months, saying, Thus hath the Lord dealt," &c. Various reasons have been given for this conduct on the part of Elizabeth, all unsatisfactory; as, for instance, the natural modesty of females to conceal their state, but this reason would have operated more strongly at the end of the five months. Again, Godet has given an exactly opposite reason,—that she hid herself till it could be seen that the Lord had taken away her reproach. Again, devotion has been suggested, but such would seem to require that her retirement should be stricter as the time drew nigh.

Is it not certain, however, when we take into consideration what immediately follows, that it must have been something not clearly revealed, connected with the visit of St. Mary? For it was at the close of these very five months that the Incarnation took place, and Mary came at once to visit her kinswoman, apparently according

THUS HATH THE LORD DEALT. 15

25 Thus hath the Lord dealt with me in the days wherein he looked on *me*, to ᵇ take away my reproach among men. ᵇ Gen. xxx. 23. Is. iv. 1. & liv. 1, 4.

to the direction of the angel, "Behold thy cousin Elizabeth, this is the sixth month with her who was called barren." It may have been necessary that the Holy Virgin should be sustained in the prospect of Joseph's suspicion, and, perhaps, other cruel slanders, by the salutation and the acknowledgment of her more exalted kinswoman. Would it not add some assurance to even the Virgin's faith in the greatness of Him to Whom she should give birth, to learn that her kinswoman had miraculously conceived him who was to be the forerunner of Mary's Son, the Elias who was to herald Him? Would it not add even more assurance that her kinswoman, because she was filled with the Holy Ghost, prophetically recognized that she was already the mother of the Lord? Whilst fully recognizing her firm faith in God's promise, may we not be permitted to believe that even she required support and comfort?

WHEN THOU TOOKEST UPON THEE TO DELIVER MAN, THOU DIDST NOT ABHOR THE VIRGIN'S WOMB.

We now approach the first and greatest Mystery of the Gospel.

The first in order because it is the beginning of Redemption. It is the root from which all else springs. The Death of Christ for the world's sin, and the Resurrection of Christ to be the world's new Life are both the issues of what the Evangelist is now about to record. Before the Son of God could die and rise again for us, He must have a true human nature, "of a reasonable soul and human flesh," in which He could die and rise again, and the Evangelist is now about to set before us the circumstances, so far as they are revealed, under which this took place.

It is also the greatest of all mysteries, being the most full of mystery, for it is the Infinite personally and permanently uniting Itself with the finite, it is the High and Lofty One Who inhabiteth eternity appearing in time. It is God, without ceasing to be God, becoming man, and man, without ceasing to be man, taken into God.

To express it in Scripture language, it is One Who was in the form of God, and thought it not a thing to be tenaciously grasped,

26 And in the sixth month the angel Gabriel was sent

to be equal with God, emptying Himself, taking the form of a servant and being made in the likeness of men. It is "The Word Who was in the beginning, Who was with God, Who was God"—it is this Word being made flesh and beginning to dwell amongst us so truly that men should "see with their eyes, should look up, and their hands should handle of the Word of life."

Such is the mystery of God's Birth, the humiliation of the Eternal Son, which is the theme of the next few words of the Evangelist.

One or two general remarks are necessary before we consider them word by word.

First, let the reader notice one very great difference between the two accounts of the coming of the Son of God amongst us, as they are given by St. Matthew and by St. Luke respectively.

In St. Matthew the revelation is made to Joseph, and the Virgin is altogether in the background. In St. Luke, the later Gospel, this is altogether reversed. The angel appears, not in a dream, as to Joseph, but to St. Mary personally, so that whilst awake she receives his salutation and converses with him; and to the end of the account of the Nativity and Infancy, all is about Mary, who visits Elisabeth and receives her salutation, and returns thanks to God in the Magnificat. Then comes the account of her giving birth to her Divine Son, and the visit of the shepherds, who found Mary, and Joseph, and the Babe lying in a manger, and then there is her purification and what she offered, and how Simeon prophesied to her of the falling and rising again of many, and of the piercing as by a sword, of her own soul; and then there is the seeking her Son, when, for a few days, He was lost, and her words to Him, the whole concluding with, "His mother kept all these sayings in her heart."

Then, in the next place, let us consider that if no other than the Eternal Son came amongst us by the power of the Holy Ghost, and in a way so above nature, whether it is not reasonable that there should be very many attendant circumstances, in some degree corresponding in their spiritual as well as in their miraculous nature, to so unparalleled a visitation. Is there nothing but the visit of the Magi led by the star, to mark such an advent? St. Luke's account assures us that there is. The Holy Ghost, Who brought about the Incarnation, appeared amongst these holy persons, who were

from God unto a city of Galilee, named Nazareth,

---

favoured with a knowledge of it in the fulness of the spirit of prophecy. Elisabeth in recognition of Mary as the Mother of her Lord, is filled with the Holy Ghost, and the Forerunner in her womb knew the Lord. Mary under the inspiration of the same Spirit poured forth her Magnificat. Zacharias was filled with the Holy Ghost, and prophesied in the words of the Benedictus Simeon came by the Spirit into the temple, and praised God in another hymn universally adopted by the Church. Anna, the prophetess, at that instant came into the temple, and spake of Him to all them that looked for Redemption in Jerusalem. And besides this there had been the message of the angel of the Lord to the shepherds and the anthem of the heavenly host. Now all these formed no part of the original tradition commonly preached; they were scarcely likely to have done so, for they were, most of them, of a more private nature, seen and known by a very few: by the family gathering at the circumcision of the Baptist; by, perhaps at the most, twenty shepherds; by the few that happened to be within reach of the voice of aged Simeon; and so in the course of a generation they would be well-nigh forgotten; but they were nevertheless worthy to become the heritage of the Church, and by the instrumentality of our Evangelist, who was led to "trace all things accurately from the very first," and under the guidance of the Holy Ghost, they have become a part of the Gospel of Christ.

We now come to the examination of this true Gospel of the Infancy verse by verse.

26. "And in the sixth month," *i.e.*, the sixth month after the birth of the Baptist. This, as I noticed, is the starting-point of the chain of events culminating in Redemption.

"The angel Gabriel." In the account of his former appearance to Zacharias, the angel mentions his own name only on the occasion of the unbelief of Zacharias. Now an event in the highest heavens is revealed, "The angel Gabriel was sent from God."

"Unto a city of Galilee named Nazareth." Unto the most despised of the cities of Israel, a place of which even good men scornfully asked, "Can any good thing come out of Nazareth?" And yet God brought about that the greatest event which has ever happened in the universe, even the union of the Godhood and Manhood in the Person of Jesus, should take place in this despised city.

18 THE VIRGIN'S NAME WAS MARY. [ST. LUKE.

27 To a virgin ^c espoused to a man whose name was Joseph, of the house of David; and the virgin's name *was* Mary.

_{c Matt. i. 18.}
_{ch. ii. 4, 5.}

28 And the angel came in unto her, and said,

---

27. "To a virgin espoused." Because of the prophecy, " Behold a virgin shall conceive and bear a son, and they shall call His name Emmanuel."

"To a virgin." Because it was fitting that the all-holy One should come amongst us in the way of the most perfect purity conceivable.

"To a virgin espoused to a man whose name was Joseph." " Scripture has rightly mentioned that she was espoused as well as a virgin; 'a virgin,' that she might appear free from all connection with man; 'espoused,' that she might not be branded with the disgrace of sullied virginity " (Ambrose).

"Of the house of David." His lineage is given in Matthew i. Inasmuch as our Lord was for many years known only among the Jews as the son of Joseph, it is clear that if He was to be held to be the descendant of David, His lineage must be traceable to David himself. It is as certain, as will soon appear, that Mary was a descendant of the same king.

"And the virgin's name was Mary." Mary or Miriam (in the New Testament always Mariam) being the name of the great sister of Moses, was one of the most common, if not the most common, of Jewish female names. There were two, if not three, Maries at the cross. There was Mary the sister of Martha, and Mary the mother of John Mark. Miriam was the most remarkable woman in Jewish history; she seems to have been both leader and prophetess. As prophetess she gave utterance to the sublime ode in which the women of Israel celebrated their deliverance from Egyptian bondage, and their safe passage through the sea. It was through her that Moses was spared to be the future deliverer of Israel, and in the wilderness she seems to have been honoured as a sort of co-leader with her two brothers.

28. "And the angel came in unto her." That is most probably into her chamber, where she was in prayer. That the angel thus came in, seems to imply that the visit took place, not in the field, or by a well, or in the midst of friends.

CHAP. I.]   HAIL, HIGHLY FAVOURED.   19

^d Hail, *thou that art* ‖ highly favoured, ^e the Lord   ^d Dan. ix. 23. & x. 19.
‖ Or, *graciously accepted*, or, *much graced*: See ver. 30.
^e Judg. vi. 12.

"Thou art highly favoured." The two oldest translations, the Syriac and the Latin, both translate κεχαριτωμένη, as "full of grace;" Latin, *gratia plena* ; Syriac, *malith taibotho*.

"Hail" (translated in Syriac *shalōm*, the usual Eastern salutation), "thou art highly favoured." The reader can scarcely be ignorant of the fact, that in all those Churches which use the Latin Vulgate, these words of what is called the "Ave Maria," are translated "full of grace." "Hail thou who art full of grace," richly endowed with grace. Our translation of the Greek word looks rather to the favour with which God regarded her, and is somewhat external in its meaning. God might, for instance, see fit to grant some great favour to a person not of exalted goodness and holiness. But it may be understood as meaning "endowed with internal sanctifying grace," and this being the deeper meaning, is undoubtedly the one to be preferred ; for though it was a favour transcending all thought that she should be the mother of the Lord, yet there must have been in her mind and heart moral and spiritual fitness for such a gift, which fitness she could only receive by the grace of the Holy Spirit: and we have abundant proof that there was. Elisabeth said of her, "Blessed is she that believed." She herself praised God in a psalm of the most exalted devotion. It is said of her, "Mary kept all these things, and pondered them in her heart." And again it is said of her, "Mary kept all these sayings in her heart." And surely if ever woman required the help of the Spirit, it was she to whom was committed the guardianship and earliest training of the Divine Son. Undoubtedly, then, this word should be translated "full of grace," in the sense of endowed by God with the best graces of His Spirit.

And yet, though holding to this deeper and higher meaning, we must not forget that for God to make use of any holy soul is to confer an infinite favour on that soul. We cannot say for a moment that Mary merited to be the instrument by which God became man, but we must acknowledge for the honour of God, Who always chooses the most fitting instruments, that of all human beings she was the most worthy to be the channel of such grace to man.

"The Lord is with thee." This also must be taken in the highest

is with thee: blessed *art* thou among women.

^f ver. 12.   29 And when she saw *him*, ^f she was troubled at his saying, and cast in her mind what manner of salutation this should be.

30 And the angel said unto her, Fear not, Mary: for thou hast found favour with God.

"Among women." See below. "Blessed art thou among women" omitted by ℵ, B., L., two or three Cursives, and Copt.; retained by A., C., D., later Uncials, almost all Cursives, Vulg., Syriac, &c.

29. "And when she saw him." So A., C., almost all later Uncials, almost all Cursives, Itala (but Vulg. *cum audisset*), Goth., Syriac, Æthiopic, &c.; but ℵ, B., D., L., X., and two or three Cursives omit.

possible sense. If the Lord was with the earthly heroes of the Jews, so that fleshly men like Gideon should deliver Israel, in an infinitely higher sense must He have been with this meek and humble saint, that in her the Word should be made flesh.

"Blessed art thou among women." This form of speaking is the Hebrew superlative. There are multitudes of similar forms. "If thou know not, O thou fairest among women," literally "O thou the fair among women." And in fact, measured by the greatness of Him Whom she conceived, and to Whom she gave birth, and to Whom for years she acted the part of a mother, her blessedness as a mother is beyond thought. In her the original curse was reversed. Through the child-bearing of Eve we partake of sin and death; through the child-bearing of Mary there came into the world that second Adam through Whom we receive deliverance from sin and eternal life.

29. "And when she saw him, she was troubled at his saying," &c. Thus the greatness of the blessings which he saw before him is said to make even Israel fear. "Then thou shalt see, and flow together, and thine heart shall fear, and be enlarged; because the abundance of the sea shall be converted unto thee, the forces of the Gentiles shall come unto thee" (Isaiah lx. 5), and those who heard that the Lord was risen were possessed by fear as well as great joy. Notice also that she was troubled at the saying.

"Cast in her mind what manner of salutation this should be." From the three notices of the way in which she regarded the dispensations of God, it is clear that she must have been one of the most reflective of women. "Casting in her mind," "pondering in her heart," "keeping in her heart," the sayings of her Divine Son.

30. "And the angel said unto her, Fear not, Mary: for thou hast

31 ᵍAnd, behold, thou shalt conceive in thy womb, and bring forth a son, and ʰ shalt call his name JESUS.

g Is. vii. 14.
Matt. i. 21.
h ch. ii. 21.

32 He shall be great, ⁱand shall be called the

i Mark v. 7.

---

found," &c. As if he said, "Fear not that the blessing seems overwhelming. Whatever be in store for thee, thou hast no cause of fear, for thou hast found favour with God, Thou hast pleased God: God thy Maker hath seen in thee that which makes thee the fit instrument of His most gracious purpose."

31. "And, behold, thou shalt conceive in thy womb, and bring forth a son, and shalt call his name JESUS." The honour of giving to the Holy Child the most Holy Name, the Name that is above every name, is in St. Matthew given to Joseph. It is here given to Mary.

The name Jesus, which is a shortened form of Joshua, signifies "The Lord our Saviour." And the reason we find in St. Matthew, "He shall save his people from their sins."

32. "He shall be great, and shall be called the Son of the Highest." The same angel said of John to Zacharias, "He shall be great in the sight of the Lord." But were the two greatnesses the same? So far from this, St. John the Baptist himself confesses the greatness of the Lord as infinitely above his, in the words, "He it is who, coming after me, is preferred before me, whose shoes latchet I am not worthy to unloose."

"Shall be called the Son of the Highest." We who have the Gospel of St. John and the Epistles of St. Paul to guide us to the full doctrine of the Person of the Lord, can give but one meaning to these words. To us they mean, " the only-begotten Son of God." But how did St. Mary understand them? We can hardly think that she understood them in the sense of the creeds of the Catholic Church: any adequate sense of such nearness of the Divine Nature would have simply overwhelmed her; and yet it is impossible to suppose that she understood them as merely meaning that her Son would be a child of God as all other children of Abraham were. God said (Ps. lxxxii. 6, 7), of all the children of Israel, "I have said "Ye are gods; and ye are all the children of the most Highest; but ye shall die like men, and fall like one of the princes." But the words of an angel would not be needed to announce such a well-known

THE SON OF THE HIGHEST. [ST. LUKE.

Son of the Highest: and ᵏ the Lord God shall give unto him the throne of his father David:

33 ¹ And he shall reign over the house of Jacob for ever; and of his kingdom there shall be no end.

ᵏ 2 Sam. vii. 11, 12. Ps. cxxxii. 11. Is. ix. 6, 7. & xvi. 5. Jer. xxiii. 5. Rev. iii. 7.
¹ Dan. ii. 44. & vii. 14, 27. Obad. xxi. Mic. iv. 7. John xii. 34. Heb. i. 8.

---

truth as this. The words must have been understood by her in some high and unique sense, very probably an indefinite sense of their greatness and mystery pervaded her mind; just as it was with St. Peter, when he said, " Thou art the Christ, the Son of the living God." He knew not the full meaning of his own language. It was the utterance of one who was yet spiritually a child, but he desired to express by them the highest relationship to God which men could then know or conceive.

32, 33. " And the Lord God shall give unto him the throne of his father David: And he shall reign," &c. All the expectations of the Jews respecting the Messiah as their deliverer and king spring from the promises which God had made to David. Such are, " The Lord hath made a faithful oath unto David, and he shall not shrink from it; of the fruit of thy body will I set upon thy seat " (Ps. cxxxii.); again, in 2 Sam. vii., " I will set up thy seed after thee, which shall proceed out of thy bowels, and I will establish his kingdom. He shall build an house for my name, and I will stablish the throne of his kingdom for ever. I will be his father, and he shall be my son."

Now this promise had never been fulfilled. There was never an approach to a fulfilment of it worthy of the greatness of the terms in which God had promised it in any of the kings of the house of David. They wrought no permanent deliverance. After a few years, sometimes a very few, as in the case of Josiah, they passed away. The one whose youth gave the fairest promise fell under the dominion of degrading sin, and brought upon his descendants the division of the kingdom. The greatest heroes of Jewish history, the Maccabees, were "not of the house and lineage of David."

But the true people of God, those who looked for redemption in Jerusalem, knew that God's promise would not fail, and that the more unlikely the advent of the true deliverance, the greater it would be. And now at last it had come.

34 Then said Mary unto the angel, How shall this be, seeing I know not a man?

35 And the angel answered and said unto her, ^m The Holy Ghost shall come upon thee, and the power of the

^m Matt. i. 20.

"The Lord God shall give unto Him the throne of His father David, and He shall reign," &c. How would the Virgin understand this? At first, and till the sword had pierced her own soul, and the descent of the Spirit had enlightened her as to the true meaning of the kingdom of God, she would understand it as any maiden of the royal house would have understood it,—as the restoration of the kingdom to Israel. But in the light of the Catholic faith, we interpret it as meaning, "He ascended into heaven, and sitteth on the right hand of the Father; and He shall come again with glory to judge both the quick and the dead, Whose kingdom shall have no end."

And yet some of us believe that the greater and wider will not prevent the smaller and the narrower fulfilment, and that He who is King of kings, and Lord of lords, will always retain, in a peculiar sense, the title which He bore upon the Cross, "King of the Jews;" that men will never cease to invoke Him as the Son of David; that the promises to the national Israel will not be totally lost and absorbed in the promises to the Catholic Church, but that " of the increase of his government and peace there shall be no end upon the throne of David and upon his kingdom."

34. "Then said Mary unto the angel, How shall this be, seeing," &c. This is not the question of unbelief as that of Zacharias, who asked, "Whereby shall I know this?" *i.e.*, the truth of your word, but of faith. Believing that it would come to pass, and knowing that she was a pure maiden, and understanding that the child to be born of her was to be hers and hers only, perhaps remembering the ancient prophecy, "Behold, a virgin shall conceive and bear a son," she naturally asked how it could come to pass.

35. "And the angel answered and said unto her, The Holy Ghost shall come upon thee," &c. This is the most explicit declaration of the mystery of the Incarnation, on its human side, which we have in Scripture, whilst the words of St. John, "The Word was made flesh and dwelt among us," are the most explicit declaration of the same mystery on its Divine side. In St. Luke it is the preparation on the part of the Holy Ghost of an undefiled human nature

THAT HOLY THING. [St. Luke.

Highest shall overshadow thee: therefore also that holy thing which shall be born of thee shall be called [n] the Son of God.

[n] Matt. xiv. 33. & xxvi. 63, 64. Mark i. 1. John i. 34. & xx. 31. Acts viii. 37. Rom. i. 4.

in the womb of the Virgin, so that it should be assumed by the Son of God, and the union of the Son of God with that nature, also by the operation of the Holy Spirit. In St. John it is the Word being made flesh, no notice being taken of the operation of the Spirit in the womb of the Virgin.

"The Holy Ghost shall come upon thee, and the power of the Highest shall overshadow thee," &c. The angel here speaks in a Hebrew parallelism. The Holy Ghost being the power of the Highest. The Holy Ghost, the Spirit of the Father, and of the Son, is that Person of the Godhead by Whom the Father and the Son put forth or exert their power. Thus the Lord says to the Apostles, "Tarry ye in Jerusalem till ye be endued with power from on high." Again, "God anointed Jesus of Nazareth with the Holy Ghost and with power." Again, St. Paul's word was "in demonstration of the Spirit and of power, that your faith should not stand in the wisdom of men, but in the power of God." "Christ's humanity itself is thus formed by the power of the Holy Ghost," and again, "His hand [i.e., His Spirit] had carefully selected the choicest specimen of our nature from the Virgin's substance, and separating it from all defilement, His personal indwelling hallowed it and gave it power." (J. H. Newman).

"Therefore also that holy thing which shall be born of thee shall be called the Son of God." We are not for a moment to understand this as if "the holy thing," i.e., the undefiled human nature, was of itself the Son of God; but we are to understand that when the Holy Ghost formed this Holy Thing in the womb of the Blessed Virgin, the Eternal Son began to dwell in it from the first, and this by the operation of the Holy Ghost, and so that which was born of her was the Son of God. Here then are the two natures, but the One Person. The Human nature being formed in the womb of the Virgin, the Divine nature, as St. John tells us, assumes it; but the one Being Who is born is One Person. "That holy thing which shall be born of thee shall be called the Son of God."

"That holy thing." "To distinguish His holiness from ours

36 And, behold, thy cousin Elisabeth, she hath also conceived a son in her old age: and this is the sixth month with her, who was called barren.

37 For ° with God nothing shall be impossible.

° Gen. xviii. 14. Jer. xxxii. 17. Zech. viii. 6. Matt. xix. 26. Mark x. 27. ch. xviii. 27. Rom. iv. 21.

37. *Quia non erit impossibile apud Deum omne verbum,* Vulg. See below.

Jesus is stated in an especial manner to be born Holy, for we, although indeed made holy, are not born so, for we are constrained by the very condition of our corruptible nature to cry out with the Prophet, 'Behold, I was conceived in iniquity.' But He alone is in truth Holy, Who was not conceived by the cementing of a fleshly union, nor, as the heretics rave, one person in His Human Nature, another in His Divine: not conceived and brought forth a mere man, and afterwards by His merits obtaining that He should be God. But the angel announcing and the Spirit coming, first the Word in the womb, afterwards within the womb the Word made Flesh." (Gregory.)

And yet, though thus above us in holiness, yet not separate from us.

"For we confess that which then was taken up from Mary to be of the nature of man and a most real body, the very same also according to nature with our own body. For Mary is our sister, seeing that we have all descended from Adam." (Athanasius in Catena Aurea.)

36. "And, behold, thy cousin Elizabeth, she hath also conceived a son in her old age," &c. This was undoubtedly the first intimation which Mary had received of the miracle wrought in Elisabeth, who had hid herself to this time, by which must be meant that she had kept her state concealed.

This revelation by the mouth of the angel, not by common report, was for the confirmation of Mary's faith. Mary believed, but every degree of human belief is capable of increase; and joy, and strength, and consolation, and hope accrues from such increase.

"Thy cousin Elizabeth." Not necessarily "cousin," but "kinswoman." There is no word in Hebrew, or Aramaic, or Greek to signify strictly "cousin."

37. "For with God nothing shall be impossible." The words

38 And Mary said, Behold the handmaid of the Lord; be it unto me according to thy word. And the angel departed from her.

---

remind us of the word of the angel, or rather of the Lord in angelic form who asked, when Sarah laughed at the thought that she should conceive miraculously, "Is anything too hard for the Lord?"

Their teaching goes far beyond the conception by a virgin, or any other miracle in the world of time and sense. They mean that it is not impossible for the Creator to become a creature—it is not impossible for the high and lofty One, Who inhabiteth eternity, to be born in time—it is not impossible that the Divine and the human should be so united as that God and man should be one Christ—it is not impossible that man should ascend above all heavens and sit on the right hand of God. It is within the power of God to bring about these things.

The sense is precisely the same if we translate thing [no-thing] by "word," as in the Hebrew. If God's Word contains a prophecy or a promise, that prophecy or promise will surely come to pass in its season.

38. "And Mary said, Behold the handmaid of the Lord; be it unto me," &c. "It only remained for Mary to consent to the consequences of the Divine offer. She gives this consent in a word at once simple and sublime, which involved the most extraordinary act of faith that a woman ever consented to accomplish." Mary accepts the sacrifice of that which is dearer to a young maiden than her very life, "and thereby becomes pre-eminently the heroine, the ideal daughter of Zion, the perfect type of human receptivity in regard to the Divine work." (Godet, a Swiss Ultra-Protestant writer.)

Notice how in this, the greatest of all God's dispensations, He requires the free consent of the instrument He uses. It was the part of Mary to submit herself unreservedly to the will of God, no matter what the consequences to herself or to her reputation. It must have at once occurred to her that she would lose the respect and affection of her betrothed, and what a depth of shame and misery was involved in that. She could not then know that her innocence was to be vindicated to him by an angelic messenger, but she left all to God, relying on the promise, "Commit thy way unto the Lord, and put thy trust in him, and he shall bring it to pass; he

MARY AND ELISABETH.

39 And Mary arose in those days, and went into the hill country with haste, p into a city of Juda:

p Josh. xxi. 9, 10, 11.

40 And entered into the house of Zacharias, and saluted Elisabeth.

41 And it came to pass, that, when Elisabeth heard the

---

shall make thy righteousness as clear as the light, and thy just dealing as the noonday." It is to be remembered that though a great part of Christendom has paid her little short of Divine honours, yet by her own people, the Jews, every contumely and blasphemy has been heaped upon her memory.

Immediately upon this, her act of submission, the Incarnation took place, "The Word was made flesh." "He who was in the form of God, and thought it not robbery to be equal with God, emptied himself, and was made in the likeness of men:" "The only begotten Son of God, begotten of his Father before all worlds ... for us men and for our salvation, came down from heaven, and was incarnate by the Holy Ghost of the Virgin Mary, and was made man."

39. "And Mary arose in those days, and went into the hill country with haste, into a city of Juda." Sympathy with one who, like herself, was the instrument of God's highest providential dealings, would lead to this hurried visit; but no doubt it was brought about that they should sustain one another by their mutual faith, and that Mary should receive the acknowledgment of her faith, and of her exalted place in that greatest dispensation of God of which she was the sole human instrument.

The hill country of Judea was that about Hebron, or rather to the south of it, so she would have to go a distance of nearly one hundred miles to visit Elisabeth. Some suppose that the city was Hebron itself, but if so it would have been mentioned by name, as not only a city of great importance, but the first capital of the kingdom of David.

41. "And it came to pass, that, when Elisabeth heard the salutation of Mary, the babe leaped," &c. Some commentators, even believing ones, have attempted to account, on natural principles, for the leaping of the yet unborn child for joy. Thus Godet: "It is not surprising that the intense feeling produced in Mary by the sight of Elisabeth should have reacted immediately on the latter.

salutation of Mary, the babe leaped in her womb; and Elisabeth was filled with the Holy Ghost:

The unexpected arrival of this young maiden at such a solemn moment for herself, the connection which she instantly divines between the miraculous blessing of which she had just been the object, and this extraordinary visit, the affecting tones of the voice and holy elevation of this person, producing all the impression of some celestial apparition, naturally predisposed her to receive the illumination of the Spirit. The emotion which possesses her is communicated to the child, whose life is as yet one with her own, and at the sudden leaping of this being, who, she knows, is compassed about with special blessing, the veil is rent. The Holy Spirit, the prophetic spirit of the Old Covenant, seizes her, and she salutes Mary as the Mother of the Messiah."

But surely all this is little better than impertinent intrusion. If God be personally and peculiarly present, is not all around holy ground? When He, Who was now in the Virgin's womb, was asked to reprove His disciples because they shouted, "Blessed be the King that cometh in the name of the Lord," did He not answer, "I tell you if these should hold their peace, the stones would immediately cry out!" In the Psalms we read, "The hills melted like wax at the presence of the Lord." If we believe that the Incarnation had then taken place, that the Son of God was then present, that the Virgin had then within her the Lord of Elisabeth, and if the Lord of Elisabeth, then the Lord of all men, that Elisabeth had conceived supernaturally, and that he whom she had conceived was to be the forerunner of the then present Son of God—if we believe all this, surely we shall acknowledge that this joy of the unborn forerunner was but consistent with it all. It was the smallest of the wonders that were then in close association with the persons of the Virgin and her kinswoman. To attempt to rationalize about it seems ridiculous. Deny the presence of the Incarnate God if you will, but if you acknowledge it do not lay down, as if you were omniscient, what from your merely human point of view you think can be, or cannot be the accompaniments of such a Thing.

The Evangelist evidently relates it as a thing beyond all natural explanation.

42. "And Elisabeth was filled with the Holy Ghost. And she

42 And she spake out with a loud voice, and said, ^q Blessed *art* thou among women, and blessed *is* the fruit of thy womb.

^q ver. xxviii. Judg. v. 24.

43 And whence *is* this to me, that the mother of my Lord should come to me?

---

42. "With a loud voice." So ℵ, A., C., D., almost all later Uncials, all Cursives, Italian, Vulg., &c. But B., L., read "cry."

spake with a loud voice," &c. "Fruit of thy womb." This is told us in order that we may look upon the words which she said as not her own merely, but as embodying Divine truth.

"Blessed art thou among women." These are the same words as those of the angel Gabriel. We have commented on them fully when they first appeared in the Sacred Narrative. Suffice it to say here that inasmuch as Elisabeth, when she said them, was filled with the Holy Ghost, they are words from God, and declare God's truth; so that whether the words were actually spoken before by the angel or not, they are equally true.

"Blessed is the fruit of thy womb." Blessed, of course, in a far higher sense, because the blessedness of Mary was the blessedness of the creature, whereas the blessedness of her Son—the fruit of her womb—was the blessedness of the Creator.

43. "And whence is this to me, that the mother of my Lord should come to me?" The child in the womb of Mary was the Lord of Elisabeth? How could this be? Evidently because He was "the Son of the Highest." Some, however, suggest that it was because He was to be the Messiah. But why in the counsels of God was He to be the Messiah? Because He was God's Son in that unique sense which no created being, angelic or human, could possibly share with Him.

In the counsels of God the Messiah was to be the God-Man. David addresses Him as "God, whose throne endureth for ever and ever" and as his Lord, to Whom the Lord said, "Sit thou on my right hand;" Isaiah, as "the Emmanuel," the "mighty God;" Jeremiah as the "Lord our Righteousness;" Micah as the "Governor coming from Bethlehem, whose goings forth have been from old of everlasting;" Malachi as the "Lord whom men sought, suddenly coming to his temple."

It was these Divine prerogatives which constituted the true

44 For, lo, as soon as the voice of thy salutation sounded in mine ears, the babe leaped in my womb for joy.

45 And blessed *is* she || that believed: for there shall be a performance of those things which were told her from the Lord.

|| Or, *which believed that there.*

" That believed: for there shall be." See note below.

Lordship of the Messiah, and Elisabeth spake by inspiration of the omniscient Spirit. If these titles of the Christ were not in her mind, they assuredly were in the mind of the Spirit by Whom she was filled.

44. " For, lo, as soon as the voice of thy salutation sounded," &c., "the babe leaped," &c. The babe did not leap merely as sympathizing with his mother in her joy, but with a joy of his own, which the Spirit of God, with whom he was filled from his mother's womb, shed into him.

45. " Blessed is she that believed: for there shall be a performance," &c. Thus early is the dispensation marked out as peculiarly a dispensation of faith. Zacharias is punished for unbelief. Mary receives the promise through faith. The passage may be translated in one of two ways. Either " Blessed is she that believed, for [*i.e.* because] there shall be a performance of those things," &c.; or, " Blessed is she that believed that there should be a performance," &c. The latter seems preferable, for the performance of the greatest things promised had already taken place. In her the Eternal Son was already incarnate, and if God had begun with so stupendous a wonder, all other things, such as the birth, the greatness of Him Who was born, and His eternal reign would follow in due course. Elisabeth could know of the faith exercised by Mary in the word of the angel only by inspiration of the Spirit.

46. " And Mary said, My soul doth magnify the Lord, and my spirit hath rejoiced," &c. In commenting upon this hymn of praise of the Blessed Virgin, it is impossible to put out of view the hymn of Hannah, the mother of Samuel. At first there seem strong verbal resemblances, but the contrast between the tone of the one and of that of the other is very great indeed. In Hannah's hymn we recognize the existence of human feelings of exaltation, must we not say of some degree of bitterness over her personal adversary, Peninnah, who had " provoked her sore, so as to make her fret "? Thus she

46 And Mary said, ʳMy soul doth magnify the Lord,

47 And my spirit hath rejoiced in God my Saviour.

48 For ˢhe hath regarded the low estate of his handmaiden: for, behold, from henceforth ᵗall generations shall call me blessed.

ʳ 1 Sam. ii. 1.
Ps. xxxiv. 2, 3.
& xxxv. 9.
Hab. iii. 18.
ˢ 1 Sam. i. 11.
Ps. cxxxviii. 6.
ᵗ Mal. iii. 12.
ch. xi. 27.

---

sings: "My mouth is enlarged over mine enemies," "Talk no more so exceeding proudly, let not arrogancy come out of your mouth," "The barren hath borne seven, and she that hath many children is waxed feeble." Whilst the Canticle of the Virgin is a far more spiritual hymn, setting forth free grace and the blessedness of the poor in spirit, as we shall see as we proceed.

46. "My soul doth magnify the Lord" .... "He hath regarded the low estate," &c. These are the words of a maiden of the noblest family in Israel, one of the Royal Line, the line of David, Solomon, Hezekiah, Zerubbabel, who had often in secret wept over the fallen fortunes of her house. And now God had looked on them in mercy, and was doing for them more than they could ask or think. A Son was to be born to them Who was God over all, blessed for ever, His throne the Throne of God, His Kingdom the whole creation, visible and invisible.

48. "For, behold, from henceforth all generations shall call me blessed." This title of "blessed," first given to her by the angel, then confirmed by the Holy Ghost speaking by the mouth of this Saint of God, should always be given to the Virgin, for it is the distinction accorded to her not by men, not by the Church even, but by God Himself. If we withhold it, we do not fall into God's mind, we are not conformed to His will. Bishop Pearson has some good remarks on this (Creed, Article iii.): "In respect of her it was therefore necessary, that we might perpetually preserve an esteem of her person proportionate to so high a dignity. It was her own prediction, 'From henceforth all generations shall call me blessed,' but the obligation is ours, to call her, to esteem her so. If Elisabeth cried out with so loud a voice, 'Blessed art thou among women,' when Christ was but newly conceived in her womb, what expressions of honour and admiration can we think sufficient now that Christ is in heaven, and that mother with Him! Far be it from any Christian to derogate from that special privilege granted

32 HIS MERCY IS ON THEM THAT FEAR. [St. Mark.

49 For he that is mighty ᵘhath done to me great things; and ˣholy *is* his name.

50 And ʸhis mercy *is* on them that fear him from generation to generation.

ᵘ Ps. lxxi. 19. & cxxxvi. 2, 3.
ˣ Ps. cxi. 9.
ʸ Gen. xvii. 7. Ex. xx. 6. Ps. ciii. 17, 18.

---

to her which is incommunicable to any other. We cannot bear too reverent a regard unto the mother of our Lord." So long as we give her not that worship which is due unto the Lord Himself, let us keep the language of the primitive Church, "Let her be honoured and esteemed, let Him be worshipped and adored."

49. "For he that is mighty hath done to me great things; and holy is his name." "He has caused me to be the mother of His only begotten Son. He hath made me the outward channel of all redeeming grace to mankind." Mary may not have thoroughly realized all this, but we are bound to give to her words no lower meaning, for in our worship we adopt her words as the words of the Church and of our souls; and we must measure their meaning not by the ignorance which we, in our ignorance, impute to her, but by what the Spirit of God, Who inspired her, has since revealed to us; and He has revealed to us that the Incarnation which took place in her is the first mystery of Godliness.

"His mercy is on them that fear him from generation to generation." Throughout the Old Testament all men's duty to God is expressed by this fear of God, not as excluding the love of God and zeal for His glory, but as meaning a perpetual sense of His holiness, His truth, His greatness, His demands upon our constant obedience, His perpetual presence as a reader of the heart, and an observer of the life. It was because the Holy Virgin excelled in this fear, that His unspeakable mercy in the Incarnation was upon her, and after her upon all who cultivate a similar fear, will this mercy rest.

How miserably then are they mistaken who, on the strength of a few texts which speak against slavish fear, deprecate that godly fear, without which there can be no reverence, no sense of God's greatness, which is the only guard against that familiarity in our intercourse with God, which so often degenerates into impiety, if not blasphemy.

"He hath shewed strength with his arm: he hath scattered the proud in the imagination," &c. He hath put down the mighty . . .

51 ᶻ He hath shewed strength with his arm; ᵃ he hath scattered the proud in the imagination of their hearts.

52 ᵇ He hath put down the mighty from *their* seats, and exalted them of low degree.

ᶻ Ps. xcviii. 1. & cxviii. 15. Isa. xl. 10. & li. 9. & lii. 10.
ᵃ Ps. xxxiii. 10. 1 Pet. v. 5.
ᵇ 1 Sam. ii. 6, &c.

" and hath exalted the humble and meek." The Incarnation was the greatest putting forth of the power of God conceivable, for it was God humbling Himself, God emptying Himself of His glory. It was God becoming what He was not before. It was also the putting forth of the greatest moral power, for it was the Judge abasing Himself to be on a level with the criminal in order to reach his heart, and draw the criminal to Himself, not with the physical strength of chains and bonds, but with the moral attraction of humiliation and sympathy as exhibited in the Cross.

"He hath scattered the proud in the imagination of their hearts." All that man can pride himself upon, whether in the way of brute force, of worldly honour, of glory, of riches, of intellectual superiority, of human philosophy, all is scattered to the winds by the Incarnation; for it is God subduing men, not by strength, but by weakness, not by the great and honourable of the earth, but by the Son of a poor woman, wife of a carpenter, not by rich men, but by very poor ones, not by philosophy, but by the preaching of the Cross. Even in religion men must not attempt to merit grace, but unfeignedly renounce all merit, and cast themselves as guilty and weak sinners upon mere mercy.

52. "He hath put down the mighty from their seats." It has been supposed that the mighty is Satan, the ruler of the darkness of this world, and there appears to be grounds for such interpretation in the words of the Lord, "I saw Satan, like lightning fall from heaven," and " now is the judgment of this world; now shall the prince of this world be cast out;" but is not its meaning more general, and does it not rather look to that great principle of the kingdom of God, so often enunciated by the Lord, "He that exalteth himself shall be abased, and he that humbleth himself shall be exalted"? The weapons of the saints are humility, self-denial, and charity. These are the weapons which are "mighty through God, to the pulling down of strongholds, casting down imaginations, and every high thing that exalteth itself against the knowledge of

53 ᶜHe hath filled the hungry with good things; and the rich he hath sent empty away.

54 He hath holpen his servant Israel, ᵈ in remembrance of *his* mercy;

55 ᵉAs he spake to our fathers, to Abraham, and to his seed for ever.

ᶜ 1 Sam. ii. 5.
Ps. xxxiv. 10.
ᵈ Ps. xcviii. 3.
Jer. xxxi. 3, 20.
ᵉ Gen. xvii. 19.
Ps. cxxxii. 11.
Rom. xi. 28.
Gal. iii. 16.

God, and bringing into subjection every thought to the obedience of Christ."

53. " He hath filled the hungry with good things ; and the rich he hath sent empty away." Here we have again a clear enunciation of the principle of grace. God blesses with the good things of the Gospel, those who feel their need of them, whilst the self-satisfied and self-complacent receive no benefit. Here we have an anticipation of the Lord's beatitude, " Blessed are they which do hunger and thirst after righteousness, for they shall be filled." And the same principle applies to the Eucharistic food. It is the deep sense of spiritual need, the not presuming to come "trusting in our own righteousness, but in God's manifold and great mercies ; " it is the heartfelt confession that we are "not worthy so much as to gather up the crumbs under his table," which is the true preparation for discerning the Lord's Body—for so eating the flesh of the Son of Man, and drinking His Blood that our sinful bodies are made clean by His Body, and our souls washed through His most precious Blood.

54. "He hath holpen his servant Israel, in remembrance of his mercy ; as he spake," &c. The Lord, might seem, in the eyes of men, to have forgotten the promise to Adam, that the seed of the woman should bruise the serpent's head ; to Abraham, that in his seed all the nations of the earth should be blessed ; to David, that of the fruit of his body He would set upon his seat; but "a thousand years is with the Lord as one day." The mystery of sin must be fully worked out, and clearly seen to be beyond the reach of any human remedy : natural religion, the law, philosophy, must all be seen to fail, and then in the fulness of the times, and in the Person of the Lord, Redemption and Regeneration could be brought in.

56. " And Mary abode with her about three months," &c. This is written to show that the Holy Virgin was not with Elisabeth at

HE SHALL BE CALLED JOHN.

56 And Mary abode with her about three months, and returned to her own house.

57 Now Elisabeth's full time came that she should be delivered; and she brought forth a son.

58 And her neighbours and her cousins heard how the Lord had shewed great mercy upon her; and ᶠ they rejoiced with her. _{ᶠ ver. 14.}

59 And it came to pass, that ᵍ on the eighth day they came to circumcise the child; and they called him Zacharias, after the name of his father. _{ᵍ Gen. xvii. 12. Lev. xii. 3.}

60 And his mother answered and said, ʰ Not so; but he shall be called John. _{ʰ ver. 13.}

61 And they said unto her, There is none of thy kindred that is called by this name.

62 And they made signs to his father, how he would have him called.

---

the time of the birth of St. John the Baptist. On her return, no doubt, Joseph was informed, probably by herself, of her state. At first, as was natural, he disbelieved her account of what had taken place, but was reassured by the angel appearing to him in a vision, as is related in St. Matthew i.

57, 58. "Now Elizabeth's full time came . . . they rejoiced with her." Not only because the reproach of barrenness was taken away from an aged woman, but because God had brought this about in so wondrous a manner that the greatest hopes were entertained of the career of one so born into the world.

59-63. "And it came to pass that on the eighth day . . . his name is John." Owing to his dumbness inflicted by the angel in punishment of his unbelief, Zacharias seems to have been under a cloud, and so not consulted by the other chief persons amongst his kinsfolk, who had come to the circumcision. And the name they chose (perhaps, as has been suggested, out of compliment to his father) would have been a most appropriate name, for it signifies "The Lord hath remembered:" but the true name had been sent by God through the angel, and was more clearly connected, not with God's remembrance, so much as with God's mercy and grace, John or Jehochanan meaning, "The Lord hath been gracious."

63 And he asked for a writing table, and wrote, saying, *His name is John. And they marvelled all.

64 ᵏ And his mouth was opened immediately, and his tongue *loosed*, and he spake, and praised God.

65 And fear came on all that dwelt round about them: and all these || sayings were noised abroad throughout all ¹ the hill country of Judæa.

66 And all they that heard *them* ᵐ laid *them* up in their hearts, saying, What manner of child shall this be! And ⁿ the hand of the Lord was with him.

67 And his father Zacharias ° was filled with the Holy Ghost, and prophesied, saying,

marginal notes:
¹ ver. 13.
ᵏ ver. 20.
|| *Sayings.*
¹ ver. 39.
ᵐ ch. ii. 19, 51.
ⁿ Gen. xxxix. 2. Ps. lxxx. 17. & lxxxix. 21. Acts xi. 21.
° Joel ii. 28.

By his being spoken to by signs it seems that the dumbness was accompanied with deafness.

"A writing-table." A tablet of smooth wood on which was a thin coating of wax, on which the answer was written with a sharp-pointed instrument.

64. "And his mouth was opened immediately, and his tongue loosed." This was according to the word of the angel, "Behold thou shalt be dumb, and not able to speak until the day that these things shall be performed." It is to be remarked that the punishment was not removed immediately on the birth of the child, but when Zacharias had done his part by setting aside the wishes of his kinsfolk, and naming the child according to the word of the angel.

65, 66. It is probable that from these wondrous circumstances of his birth, they expected that the child would be himself the Messiah.

"The hand of the Lord was with him." No doubt meaning that he exhibited a devotion and intelligence far beyond his age, because filled with the Holy Ghost from his mother's womb.

67. "And his father Zacharias was filled with the Holy Ghost . . . redeemed his people." The Incarnation in the womb of the Virgin had taken place but some three or four months, but this holy priest, inspired by the Spirit, speaks of Redemption as already accomplished, though it would be thirty years or more before the

68 ᵖ Blessed *be* the Lord God of Israel; for ᑫ he hath visited and redeemed his people,

69 ʳ And hath raised up an horn of salvation for us in the house of his servant David;

70 ˢ As he spake by the mouth of his holy prophets, which have been since the world began:

71 That we should be saved from our enemies, and from the hand of all that hate us;

72 ᵗ To perform the mercy *promised* to our fathers, and to remember his holy covenant;

p 1 Kings i. 48. Ps. xli. 13. & lxxii. 18. & cvi. 48.
q Exod. iii. 16. & iv. 31. Ps. cxi. 9. ch. vii. 16.
r Ps. cxxxii. 17.
s Jer. xxiii. 5, 6. & xxx. 10. Dan. ix. 24. Acts iii. 21. Rom. i. 2.
t Lev. xxvi. 42. Ps. xcviii. 3. & cv. 8, 9. & cvi. 45. Ezek. xvi. 60. ver. 54.

---

72. "To perform the mercy *promised* to our fathers." "To have mercy upon our fathers," *ad faciendam misericordiam cum patribus nostris.* See below.

Lord offered His all-atoning Sacrifice. But if God had begun by so profound an act of humiliation, He would assuredly bring all to its predetermined conclusion. He would not rest with an unfinished work, and so in the mind of the inspiring Spirit all was already accomplished.

69. "And hath raised up an horn of salvation for us in the house of his servant David." The horn is the symbol of strength, and the idea is taken from the horns of animals, which are their most powerful means of defence. The rendering in the Prayer Book, "a mighty salvation," is most true and expressive. The prophecy most directly alluded to is that of Psalm cxxxii., "There shall I make the horn of David to flourish."

70, 71. "As he spake by the mouth of his holy prophets which have been since the world began." This is literally true if we take into account the prophecy of Enoch who lived before the death of Adam, preserved to us in the Epistle of St. Jude, which speaks of "the Lord coming with ten thousand of his saints to execute judgment upon all." This judgment being upon the enemies of Christ and His Church to deliver the godly out of their power. The prophecy of God Himself that the seed of the woman should bruise the serpent's head was now being fulfilled.

72. "To perform the mercy promised to our forefathers." The word "promised" is not in the original, and the passage should be

73 ᵘThe oath which he sware to our father Abraham,
74 That he would grant unto us, that we being delivered out of the hand of our enemies might ˣ serve him without fear,

ᵘ Gen. xii. 3. & xvii. 4. & xxii. 16, 17. Hebr. vi. 13, 17.
ˣ Rom. vi. 18, 22. Hebr. ix. 14.

translated without it. Thus the Revisers, "To show mercy towards our fathers." Williams gives the truest translation, "To perform mercy [on us] together with our fathers. ["God having provided some better thing for us, that they without us should not be made perfect," Hebr. xi. 40.] Thus Origen, "I think that at the coming of our Lord and Saviour Jesus Christ, both Abraham, Isaac, and Jacob were partakers of His mercy. For it is not to be believed, that they who had before seen His day, and were glad, should afterwards derive no advantage from His coming, since it is written, 'Having made peace through the blood (by him to reconcile all things to himself) whether in earth or in heaven.'" And Theophylact, "The grace of Christ extends even to those who are dead, because through Him we shall rise again, not only we, but they also who have been dead before us. He performed His mercy also to our forefathers in fulfilling all their hopes and desires. . . . The fathers also seeing their children enjoy these blessings, rejoice together with them, just as if they received the mercy in themselves."

73. "The oath which he sware to our forefather Abraham, that he would grant," &c. This oath was made or rather renewed to Abraham just after he had in intention offered his son Isaac. "By myself have I sworn, saith the Lord, for because thou hast done this thing, and hast not withheld thy son, thine only son: That in blessing I will bless thee, and in multiplying I will multiply thy seed as the stars of the heaven, and as the sand which is upon the sea-shore; and thy seed shall possess the gate of his enemies. And in thy seed shall all the nations of the earth be blessed " (Gen. xxii. 16, &c.).

How wonderful the fulfilment! Abraham, in obedience to God, withheld not his son, his only son, and now God in mercy to Abraham and to his seed had not withheld His Son, His only Son; only with this amazing difference, that whereas in the case of Isaac a substitute was found, in the case of God's only Son no substitute was found, but He was Himself our substitute.

74. "That we being delivered out of the hand of our enemies." Probably Zacharias in these words looked for liberty from the

CHAP. I.] THE PROPHET OF THE HIGHEST. 39

75 ʸ In holiness and righteousness before him, all the days of our life.

76 And thou, child, shalt be called the prophet of the Highest: for ᶻ thou shalt go before the face of the Lord to prepare his ways;

ʸ Jer. xxxii. 39, 40. Ephes iv. 24. 2 Thess. ii. 13. 2 Tim. i. 9. Tit. ii. 12. 1 Pet. i. 15. 2 Pet. i. 4.
ᶻ Isai. xl. 3. Mal. iii. 1. & iv. 5. Matt. xi. 10. ver. 17.

---

75. "All the days of our life." "All our days." So ℵ, A., B., C., D., F., K., L., most later Uncials, almost all Cursives, and versions.

Roman yoke, that his countrymen might worship God in the holy and beautiful house without fear that it would be polluted by heathen statues, or that the blood of the worshippers would be mingled with their sacrifices; but all such narrower and more local understandings have long vanished away; and the Catholic Church understands "deliverance from our enemies," to be deliverance from the burden of sin and the temptations of Satan; and by "without fear," she understands "in the spirit of filial freedom," as distinguished from that of servile bondage, and that through the faith of Christ, we have boldness and access with confidence to God.

75. "In holiness and righteousness before him, all the days of our life." The end of all God's dispensations, and especially the end of His crowning one, is, that we should serve in holiness and righteousness before Him.

The word "serve" is liturgical, and has to do with religious worship, especially that by sacrifice, so that the meaning is that our lives and our religious services should correspond to the character of the holy and righteous God Whom we worship. It appears to us rather that purity (ὁσιότης) is a negative quality, the absence of stain; and righteousness (δικαιοσύνη) a positive quality, the presence of all those religious and moral virtues which render worship acceptable to God.

76. "And thou, child, shalt be called the prophet of the Highest: for thou shalt go before," &c. The father's thoughts turn now to the little child who is to play so distinguished a part in the immediate future. He is to be a prophet, the prophet of the Highest; but the Lord accords to him a higher place when He speaks of John as "more than a prophet," for no prophet before him had heralded the personal advent of God.

40 THE DAYSPRING FROM ON HIGH. [ST. LUKE.

^a Mark i. 4. ch. iii. 3.
|| Or, *for.*
|| Or, *bowels of the mercy.*
|| Or, *sun-rising,* or, *branch.*
Numb. xxiv. 17. Is. xi. 1. Zech. iii. 8. & vi. 12. Mal. iv. 2.

77 To give knowledge of salvation unto his people ^a || by the remission of their sins,
78 Through the || tender mercy of our God; whereby the || dayspring from on high hath visited us,

77. "To give knowledge of salvation unto his people." The Greek more fully indicates a purpose. "Thou shalt go before the face of the Lord to prepare his way, *by giving* knowledge of salvation to his people by the," &c. The way of Christ was to be prepared in two ways: first, by touching the national conscience, by showing the people what sin really is, and God's wrath declared against it. This the Baptist did when he preached repentance, and fruits meet for repentance, and turned the hearts of the fathers to the children, and of the children to their fathers, *i.e.* by reviving home and domestic religion; and, secondly, by showing what salvation was—that it was not deliverance from a hateful foreign yoke, but the blotting out of sin and the renewal of the heart. This the holy Baptist did when he pointed to Jesus as the Lamb of God that taketh away the sin of the world, and preached that plenary remission and also the gift of the Holy Spirit should attend the baptism of Christ.

78. "Through the tender mercy of our God; whereby the dayspring from on high hath visited us," &c. Literally "through the bowels of mercy of our God." Because God hath forgiven our sins, not for our works' sake, but through His mercy, it is therefore fitly added

"Through the tender mercy of our God; whereby the dayspring from on high," &c. Literally, the rising of the sun, the orient [Vulg.], the dawn. The coming of the Messiah as the true light of the world is often alluded to in the prophets under this figure of a rising luminary. Thus Isaiah: "Arise, shine, for thy light is come, and the glory of the Lord has risen upon thee." And Malachi: "Unto you that fear my Name shall the sun of righteousness arise with healing in his wings." And the Lord says of Himself in the Revelation: "I am the bright and morning star." It was His arising in the world that made the day break and the shadows flee away. The types and figures of the law were then abolished. It was His light that dispelled the mists of ignorance and idolatry: and He alone delivers

79 ᵇTo give light to them that sit in darkness and *in* the shadow of death, to guide our feet into the way of peace.

80 And ᶜthe child grew, and waxed strong in

ᵇ Is. ix. 2. & xlii. 7. & xlix. 9. Matt. iv. 16. Acts xxvi. 18.
ᶜ ch. ii. 40.

---

the soul from the night of sin and the misery produced by it. "All the stars, and the moon with them, cannot make it day in the world: this is the sun's prerogative; nor can nature's highest light, the most refined science and morality, make it day in the soul, for this is Christ's [work]. The sun can make dark things clear, but it cannot make a blind man see them; but herein is the excellency of this Sun, that He illuminates not only the object, but the faculty; doth not only reveal the mysteries of His kingdom, but opens blind eyes to behold them."—Leighton, Sermon on Isaiah lx. 1.

79. "To give light to them that sit in darkness and in the shadow of death." In darkness, of course moral darkness; the darkness of heathenism, of perverted Judaism; the darkness of a blind heart, of a crooked and corrupt will; the darkness of hatred, according to the words of the Apostle, "he that hateth his brother is in darkness, and walketh in darkness."

"The shadow of death." The shadow of death is not death itself, but is a figure to express the close proximity of death. If anyone had been brought to the very gates of the grave, and had been restored, he would have been said to have passed through the valley of the shadow of death. Here it must mean the grossest moral and spiritual darkness possible.

"To guide our feet into the way of peace." The way of forgiveness, of righteousness, of holiness, above all, the way of love—of love not only to God but to our brethren; for if we have the spirit of wrath and contention we cannot have the Spirit of God, Who is the Spirit of Peace.

80. "And the child grew, and waxed strong in spirit," *i.e.*, grew or increased in the Spirit of God. Herein was fulfilled the words of the angel, that "he should be filled with the Holy Ghost, even from his mother's womb."

"And was in the deserts." Not necessarily in uninhabited, but rather in thinly inhabited regions. I cannot help thinking but that it implies that he did not exercise the office of a priest before the spirit, and ᵈ was in the deserts till the day of his shewing unto Israel.

ᵈ Matt. iii. 1. & xi. 7.

people, as being the son of a priest he might have done; but was in solitude and loneliness, prepared by God for the special work of preparing the way of the Lord.

CHAP. II.

Before the Account called Anno DOMINI the fifth year.

AND it came to pass in those days, that there went out a decree from Cæsar Augustus, that all the world should be ‖ taxed.

‖ Or, *inrolled*.

1. "Taxed," properly "enrolled." Vulg., *describeretur*.

1. "And it came to pass in those days, that there went out a decree from Cæsar Augustus, that all the world should be taxed." "In those days," *i.e.*, just after the birth of the Baptist, "there went out a decree from Cæsar Augustus." A difficulty has been made of the fact that we have no specific mention of this particular decree; but the accounts of the latter part of Augustus's reign are very meagre, and we know that in the closing years of his life he was much occupied with compiling a statistical account of the whole empire.

"That all the world should be taxed." Rather should be enrolled with a view to future taxing.

2. "And this taxing was first made when Cyrenius was governor of Syria." There is a still greater difficulty here in reconciling the account given by the sacred historian with secular history. It appears that Cyrenius was not governor of Syria till the year 4 of our era, and he did not execute the enumeration which bears his name till the year 6 A.D., after the deposition of Archelaus, the son and successor of Herod, so that St. Luke seems to represent the journey of Joseph and the Blessed Virgin to Bethlehem as a consequent upon an imperial order for taxing or enrolment, which did

THE ENROLMENT.

2 (ᵃ *And* this taxing was first made when Cyrenius was governor of Syria.)   ᵃ Acts v. 37.

---

2. "This taxing was first made." The article before taxing (ἀπογραφὴ) is found in A., C., L., later Uncials, almost all Cursives, but omitted by ℵ, B., D., which would mean, "This was the first taxing made."

not take place till six years afterwards. The most likely way of reconciling all difficulties seems to be something like this.

Augustus just before the Lord's birth published his decree of enrolment of the whole empire, but there would be necessarily some delay in carrying it out, and particularly in Palestine, where there was a fanatical population which would bitterly resent such an interference by a hateful and idolatrous Power. In order to smooth the way for this enrolment, which he saw to be inevitable, Herod commenced an enumeration which proceeded on Jewish lines; as, for instance, he registered the people, not according to the locality in which they lived, but according to their families and tribes; so that Joseph, being of the house of David, would go up to Bethlehem to be registered. This preliminary enrolment, which it was supposed would answer the end the emperor had in view, was apparently attended with no opposition, being carried out by the national sovereign, so as not to arouse the prejudices of the people; whereas, when Cyrenius, who appears to have been appointed for this purpose, undertook the matter *de novo*, after the banishment of Archelaus, it was the occasion of the dangerous insurrection alluded to by Gamaliel (Acts v. 17). St. Luke then desires to distinguish this abortive enumeration of Herod's from the far more important one which took place some time after. This latter was the census generally known as Quirinius's first census. And so his words may be paraphrased, "There came forth a decree from Cæsar Augustus, that a census of all the world should be taken. As to the census itself, called the first, *it* took place under the government of Quirinius. St. Luke would break off to remark, that prior to the well-known enumeration which took place under Quirinius, and which history had taken account of under the name of the *first*, there had really been another, generally lost sight of, which was the very one here in question; and thus that it was not unadvisedly that he spoke of a census anterior to the first. [I owe the substance of this to Godet].[1]

---

[1] There seems, however, reasonable grounds for believing that

3 And all went to be taxed, every one into his own city.

4 And Joseph also went up from Galilee, out of the city of Nazareth, into Judæa, unto ᵇ the city of David, which is called Bethlehem; (ᶜ because he was of the house and lineage of David :)

5 To be taxed with Mary ᵈ his espoused wife, being great with child.

ᵇ 1 Sam. xvi. 1, 4. John vii. 42.
ᶜ Matt. i. 16. ch. i. 27.
ᵈ Matt. i. 18. ch. i. 27.

---

4. "Lineage," properly "family."
5. "His espoused wife." "Wife" omitted by ℵ, B., C., D., L., one or two Cursives, some old Latin, Coptic, Syriac; retained by A., later Uncials, almost all Cursives, some old Latin (a, b, c), Vulg., &c.

---

3. "And all went to be taxed [or enrolled], every one into his own city." It is very questionable whether Joseph, like Mary, was a native of Nazareth. He might have been a native of Bethlehem, who for some reason, ordered by God's providence, went up to Nazareth, and perhaps temporarily settled there, and found there a virgin, like himself of the family of David, and espoused her. If this be so, it will account for the fact that Matthew, who puts him more prominently forward, speaks of Joseph as turning aside into the parts of Galilee, and coming and dwelling in a city called Nazareth, as if he had had previously little permanent connection with it.

4, 5. "And Joseph also went up from Galilee, out of the city of Nazareth . . . to be taxed with Mary his espoused wife, being great with child." Why this extreme haste? was the matter of the decree so pressing that in the case of a woman just on the point of her delivery there could be no delay of a month or five weeks? No, I believe that this journey, at this exact time, was not so much a matter of necessity, as of faith on the part of both St. Joseph and the Blessed Virgin. Both of them were conscious that they were of the house and lineage of David. To Joseph the angel had promised the birth of Emmanuel, addressing him as "Joseph, thou Son of David." To Mary the angel had said, "The Lord God shall give unto him the throne of his father David." Where was he to be

---

the government of Cyrenius has been made to commence too late. Justin Martyr in three places makes our Lord born in the governorship of Cyrenius. Apol. i. 34; Apol. i. 46; Trypho, 78.

6 And so it was, that, while they were there, the days were accomplished that she should be delivered.

---

born ? They, of all the people of the Jews, knew the prophecy. No prophecy of the expected Son of David could be a matter of indifference to any lineal descendant of David, much less if they were just men, or devout and chaste virgins.

And here let us adore the wondrous providence of God, that the Only-begotten should be brought into the world in the place which God had decreed in His eternal counsels, and foretold by His Prophet. The coming of the Son of God in the flesh was infinitely the most important thing that had taken place in the history of the world. But He must be born of a particular family, in a particular city, and in order to bring this about, the Sovereign of a far distant city of the West, must rule over an ancient province in the East, and publish a decree for a census of it, just at the time when there was a tributary king reigning over it who would attempt to take the census in such a way that each man would be enrolled, not in his domicile, but in the seat of his family and tribe. If it had been but a little later this would have been neglected, and prophecy falsified by the birth of the Lord in Nazareth. Thus Chrysostom: "It was the Lord Who directed Augustus to give the edict, that he might minister to the coming of the Only-begotten: for it was this edict that brought Christ's mother into his country as the prophets had foretold, namely, to Bethlehem of Judæa, according to the word 'to a city of David, which is called Bethlehem.'"

6. "And so it was, that, while they were there, the days . . . no room for them in the inn." Thus did the Lord of Glory begin His visible Life amongst men. In these few simple words is related the appearance amongst His creatures of the Eternal Word. Nine months before this the Only-begotten Son of God "for us men and for our salvation came down from heaven and was incarnate." And now there was a further act of humiliation in that He was born into the world He came to redeem under circumstances of extreme poverty. There was no room for his parents in the apartments of the inn, so they had to take refuge in the stables, and there the Virgin Mother gave a human birth to Him through Whose Divine Power she had herself received her being.

Jesus Christ is the first-born of the Blessed Virgin, and of every creature. His stooping to the weakness of infancy is so much the

HER FIRSTBORN SON.

7 And ᵉ she brought forth her firstborn son, and wrapped him in swaddling clothes, and laid him in a

ᵉ Matt. i. 25.

more worthy to be adored, as it appears [outwardly] more unworthy of His greatness and wisdom. Let human pride blush, since God became an infant of days, submitted to the confinement of swaddling clothes, to the meanness of a manger, to the mansion of beasts, to have recourse to the assistance of His creatures, and to be refused by them. It is the Christian's glory, that his God would do and suffer all this for his salvation. It is his honour to adore Him, to own Him for his King, and to pay Him homage in all His states and conditions [in the womb, in the manger, on the Cross, on His Throne]. (Quesnel.)

It was the opinion of some of the ancient Fathers of the Church, that there were certain supernatural circumstances attending His birth, which are not recorded in Scripture, as that the Holy Virgin gave birth to Him without the usual pains of parturition. Thus Gregory Nyssen: "Though coming in the form of man, yet not in everything is He subject to the laws of man's nature; for while His being born of a woman tells of human nature, virginity becoming capable of childbirth betokens something above man. Of Him, then, His mother's burden was light, the birth immaculate, the delivery without pain, the Nativity without defilement, neither beginning from wanton desire, nor brought to pass with sorrow. For, as she who by her guilt engrafted death into our nature was condemned to bring forth in trouble, it was meet that she who brought life into the world should accomplish her delivery with joy."

7. "Her firstborn son." This by no means implies that she had other children. Jesus being born of a woman, and made under the law, it is said with reference to the requirements of the law. Thus, Exodus xiii. 15, the Israelite is directed to say, "I sacrifice to the Lord all that openeth the matrix, being males; but all the firstborn of my children I redeem." I have shown in an excursus at the end of my notes on St. Mark's Gospel that the only persons who can be supposed to be the brethren of the Lord are expressly said to be the children of another Mary. (Matth. xiii. 55, and Mark vi. 3, compared with Matth. xxvii. 56, and Mark xv. 40.)

"And wrapped him in swaddling clothes." She evidently did this herself, as from her poverty she appears to have been wholly unattended.

manger; because there was no room for them in the inn.

8 And there were in the same country shepherds abiding in the field, keeping || watch over their flock by night. || Or, *the night watches.*

9 And, lo, the angel of the Lord came upon them, and

---

9. "Lo" omitted by ℵ, B., L., but inserted by A., D., all later Uncials, all Cursives, old Latin, Vulg., Coptic, and Syriac.

"And laid him in a manger, because there was no room for them in the inn." There was a tradition as old as the time of Justin Martyr, that the place where the Lord was born was a cave, used as a stable or place for cattle. And this might have been so, as it is never said that the place where He was born was the actual stable of the inn.

8. "And there were in the same country shepherds abiding in the field," &c. A passage from the Mishnah leads to the conclusion that the flocks which pastured there (between Bethlehem and Jerusalem) were destined for temple sacrifices, and accordingly that the shepherds who watched over them were not ordinary shepherds. The latter were under the ban of Rabbinism, on account of their necessary isolation from religious observances, and their manner of life which rendered strict legal observances unlikely, if not absolutely impossible. (Edersheim.)

It has been inferred, because these shepherds were out in the field all night, that the Saviour could not have been born at that (winter) time, but without the smallest reason. The latitude is considerably south of that of Algiers and Tunis, and from the same passage of the Mishnah just alluded to, Edersheim infers that these flocks lay out all the year round, since they are spoken of as in the fields thirty days before the Passover, that is in the month of February, when in Palestine the average rainfall is nearly greatest. Mr. Blunt also notices that any passer-by may see the flocks and their shepherds upon the bleak Wiltshire downs at Christmas time, as well as at all other seasons, and even though the snow should be upon the ground the bleatings of hundreds of lambs during many an hour of the night early in January.

9. "And, lo, the angel of the Lord came upon them, and the glory of the Lord shone round," &c. This revelation of the birth of the Lord to these shepherds is in keeping with the circumstances

48 GOOD TIDINGS OF GREAT JOY. [St. Luke.

the glory of the Lord shone round about them: ^f and they were sore afraid.

10 And the angel said unto them, Fear not: for, behold, I bring you good tidings of great joy, ^g which shall be to all people.

11 ^h For unto you is born this day in the city

^f ch. i. 12.
^g Gen. xii. 3. Matt. xxviii. 19. Mark i. 15. ver. 31, 32. ch. xxiv. 47. Col. i. 23.
^h Isai. ix. 6.

---

of His Incarnation and Birth. He is born in a cave, and cradled in a manger, and the first notice of His birth is sent to shepherds; not to the Sanhedrim, not to the chief priests, nor to Herod, nor to Cæsar, but to these simple men; and sent, no doubt, simply for their poverty's sake and their obscurity: for God is now "scattering the proud in the imagination of their hearts. He is putting down the mighty from their seat, and is exalting the humble and meek." "A set of poor men engaged in a life of hardship, exposed at that very time to the cold and darkness of the night, watching their flocks, to scare away beasts of prey or robbers." To men so circumstanced the angel appeared: one, perhaps the chief, of those mighty ones who "excel in strength," who always behold the face of God, in comparison with whose power and glory that of the mightiest king upon earth is as nothing, to these poor men this messenger, direct from heaven, appeared. He appeared as if to show them that God had chosen the poor of this world to be heirs of His kingdom, and so to do honour to their lot.

"The glory of the Lord shone round about them." Not the glory of the angel shone, but the glory of the Lord Himself, as if for a moment a ray from the throne of the Highest had illumined the plain.

10. "And the angel said unto them, Fear not: for, behold, I bring you good tidings," &c. Literally, I evangelize you a great joy, and all the things which make the Gospel of Christ a matter of joy are to be found in these words of the angel.

"Which shall be to all people." For Jew and Greek, Barbarian, Scythian, bond and free.

11. "For unto you is born this day in the city of David," &c. "To you." Christ was born, and lived, and died for each person. For one and all who hear the call to receive and believe in Him.

"Is born this day in the city of David." By naming David the

CHAP. II.] THIS SHALL BE A SIGN. 49

of David ¹ a Saviour, ᵏ which is Christ the Lord.

12 And this *shall be* a sign unto you; Ye shall find the babe wrapped in swaddling clothes, lying in a manger.

13 ¹ And suddenly there was with the angel a multitude of the heavenly host praising God, and saying,

i Matt. i. 21.
k Matt. i. 16.
& xvi. 16.
ch. i. 43. Acts ii. 36. & x. 36. Phil. ii. 11.

l Gen. xxviii. 12. & xxxii. 1, 2. Ps. ciii. 20, 21. & cxlviii. 2.
Dan. vii. 10.
Hebr. i. 14.
Rev. v. 11.

---

angel connects with the Child thus born all the promises made to David.

"A Saviour,"—from all spiritual, and in due time from all temporal evil, even from death.

"Which is Christ." And so anointed with the fulness of the Spirit to be Prophet, Priest, and King to His people.

"The Lord." Here is His Divine nature and power.

The shepherds may not have understood the angel's message in this fulness of meaning, but we who have the New Testament, and the Catholic Church, are bound to understand them as implying all this; for this message was said to the shepherds and chronicled in God's Word for the use of the whole Catholic Church to the end of time.

12. "And this shall be a sign unto you; Ye shall find the babe wrapped in," &c. The sign by which they were to know the Christ was a miracle of humiliation, confounding all their ideas of the Messiah as invested with all human greatness. As Bede says: "We may observe that the sign given us of the new-born Saviour was, that He would be found, not clothed in Tyrian purple, but wrapped in swaddling clothes; not lying on a gilded couch, but in a manger."

13. "And suddenly there was with the angel a multitude of the heavenly host." Literally, of the heavenly army. The veil between the seen and the unseen was rent, and the sky above Bethlehem was peopled with hosts of angels, for the King of angels was born there. If when Elisha was in a certain city, it was surrounded with chariots and horses of fire, much more would angels circle round the birthplace of the Only Begotten.

14. "Glory to God in the highest, and on earth peace, good will toward men. "Glory to God in the highest," *i.e.*, in the heaven of heavens. The fruit of the Incarnation and Birth of the Son of God,

E

ON EARTH PEACE.

14 ᵐ Glory to God in the highest, and on earth ⁿ peace, ᵒ good will toward men.

ᵐ ch. xix. 38. Eph. i. 6. & iii. 10, 21. Rev. v. 13.
ⁿ Is. lvii. 19. ch. i. 79. Rom. v. 1. Eph. ii. 17. Col. i. 20.
ᵒ John iii. 16. Eph. ii. 4, 7. 2 Thess. ii. 16. 1 John iv. 9, 10.

14. "On earth peace, good will toward men." So L. and all later Uncials, Cursives, Coptic, Syriac, Æthiopic, Armenian, and several Fathers; but ℵ, A., B., D., Ital., Vulg., Gothic, Cyril of Jerusalem (sect. xii., 32), and Irenæus and Origen read "peace to men of good will."

including its issues of Redemption by His Cross, and the presence of Christ by His Spirit in His Church, and its manifold trials and victories, was designed to give the angelic world a higher view of the wisdom of God than was otherwise possible. According to the words of the Apostle, "Unto the principalities and powers in heavenly places might be known by the church the manifold wisdom of God." (Ephes. iii. 10.)

"On earth peace, good will toward (or amongst) men." If this is to be rendered according to the reading of the Received Text, we must supply a copulative,—on earth peace from God, and from God good will towards men. The peace on earth may look forward to some future reign of profound peace amongst mankind, foretold in Psalm lxxii. and Isaiah ii. 4, in which case the "good will toward" or "amongst men," would be in apposition to it. The good will of God to men, and the good will of men toward one another prevailing in the human race.

But the reader is, of course, aware of the variation in the ancient MSS. and in the Vulgate, "peace to men of good will," peace to those on whom God looks with good will, or peace to those who have a good will—a will to receive Christ and be reconciled to God. The last rendering, "peace to men of good will," has undoubtedly the most ancient MSS. and the Vulgate in its favour; but, after all, if we attentively consider these two meanings, they are both true, for it is the fact that the Gospel proclaims God's good will to men generally—in the most unreserved way, so that every one of the race to whom the message comes has a right to it, and is bound to accept it; and yet the peace which is so universally proclaimed avails only to "men of good will," to those whom God regards with good will, and to those who regard God with good will,[1] to those who desire to be reconciled to Him, and to be re-

---

[1] The word eudokia signifies the affection of good will residing

15 And it came to pass, as the angels were gone away from them into heaven, † the shepherds said one to another, Let us now go even unto Bethlehem, and see this thing which is come to pass, which the Lord hath made known unto us.

† Gr. *the men the shepherds.*

16 And they came with haste, and found Mary, and Joseph, and the babe lying in a manger.

---

15. "The shepherds." "The men the shepherds," in margin, after A., D., later Uncials, almost all Cursives, Gothic, Æthiopic; but ℵ, B., L., old Latin, Vulg., Sah., Coptic, Syriac, Armenian, read "shepherds" only.

newed by Him, and these two sets of men are the same. God only regards those with good will who have in themselves the good will to come to Him through His Son. There need be no dispute about this part of the angelic anthem. However taken, it teaches the same lesson, that the Salvation of Christ belongs to all, but is available only to those who accept it.

I need hardly remind the reader that these words of the Angelic Anthem form the first words of the Church's Eucharistic Hymn, the "Gloria in Excelsis."

15. "And it came to pass, as the angels ... Lord hath made known to us." Though the angel had not commanded them to go, he had told them what they should see if they went; and this was sufficient for godly and simple-minded men. "Even unto Bethlehem" would seem to imply that the city of David was at some great distance; but it is not so, for the words need only be rendered, let us go "as far as to," or simply "to" Bethlehem.

16. "And they came with haste, and found Mary," &c. Unless they had come with haste they would not have found the Holy Child in the manger, as doubtless He was soon removed to some human habitation. The simple accordance of the angels' word with the fact was sufficient for these humble believers. They asked for no more, but immediately began to make known the vision of angels which they had seen, and the Divine Message and the Anthem of the heavenly host. If it be true that these shepherds kept the flocks destined for the Temple services, they may have spoken of the vision to the officers of the Temple itself.

---

in the hearts of men in Rom. x. 1, Phil. i. 15, and (according to rendering of Revisers), 2 Thess. i. 11.

52 MARY KEPT ALL THESE THINGS. [St. Luke.

17 And when they had seen *it*, they made known abroad the saying which was told them concerning this child.

18 And all they that heard *it*, wondered at those things which were told them by the shepherds.

p Gen. xxxvii. 11. ch. i. 66. ver. 51.   19 ᵖ But Mary kept all these things, and pondered *them* in her heart.

20 And the shepherds returned, glorifying and praising God for all the things that they had heard and seen, as it was told unto them.

q Gen. xvii. 12. Lev. xii. 3. ch. i. 59.   21 ᑫ And when eight days were accomplished for the circumcising of the child, his name was

---

19. "Things," or "sayings."
21. "Of the child." So D., E., G., H., M., V., very many Cursives, Syriac, Æthiopic; but ℵ, A., B., F. (Wetstein), K., L., R., S., U., &c., nearly 100 Cursives, old Latin, Vulg. (Cod. Amiat.), Gothic, Coptic, read " of him."

18-19. "And all they that heard it, wondered . . . . pondered them in her heart." It seems as if the sacred writer desired to mark a great contrast here. The multitude of hearers wondered at the time, and soon forgot all about it, but Mary kept all these words, "pondering" them—casting them over and over in her heart. The reader will notice how this whole narrative of St. Luke's puts St. Mary into the foreground as a humble, contemplative, observant Saint of God.

20. "And the shepherds returned, glorifying and praising God for all the things which they had seen and heard." They had only seen a new-born Infant in circumstances of deep poverty; but that sight corresponded with what they had heard from the angel. They had heard probably other things from the Virgin and St. Joseph, as particularly how the angel of the Lord had appeared to both of them; and for these things, as certifying that the long-expected Redeemer of Israel had come, they returned "glorifying and praising God."

21. And when eight days were accomplished for the circumcising of the child," &c. Why was it that the Lord, conceived and born without sin, and having pure and holy flesh in which no carnal or worldly lusts could find a place, submitted to receive a rite which betokened the cutting off of the sinful lusts of the flesh? Evi-

CHAP. II.]   HIS NAME WAS CALLED JESUS.   53

called ʳ JESUS, which was so named of the angel before he was conceived in the womb.   ʳ Matt. i. 21, 25. ch. i. 31.

---

dently that He might be "made under the law;" so that through His perfect obedience we might receive "the adoption of sons" (Gal. iv. 4, 5). For it was on His circumcision that the redeeming Blood was first shed, it was on His circumcision that He was first "numbered with the transgressors," for circumcision was for sinners, as baptism now is; so that when circumcised He was treated as a sinner, as if He Himself needed that circumcision of the Spirit which in His kingdom He imparts to His brethren.

Again, in the case of the Lord, the reception of circumcision was a further humiliation, for circumcision was the entrance into the then family of God, and the Lord, the only begotten of the Father, one with Him in nature, in will, in power, consented to be received into His earthly family, and to be the Son of God as a son of Abraham.

Thus His circumcision was the first stage in that outward life of submission to the will of His Father by which He redeemed us. It teaches us, as nothing else can, that submission to God—submission of body, soul, and spirit to God, is at the root of all religion. If they will but receive it, it reads a severe lesson to those professedly spiritual persons who speak and act as if their spirituality put them into some sphere above the ordinances and sacraments of the Catholic Church. For under pretence of being more enlightened by the Spirit, they profess to regard as secondary matters the sacraments ordained by Him from Whom proceeds the Spirit, and Who willingly submitted Himself to observe every ordinance of God which came in His way.

And at this act of submission He received the Name which is above every name.

"His name was called JESUS, which was so named of the angel," &c. The name Jesus is the same as that borne by the great leader of the people of God, who put the Israelites in possession of the land which God had promised to them. It signifies the Lord the Saviour, or the Lord our Saviour, but it signifies infinitely more in the case of the Lord than it does in the case of Joshua; for with Joshua it simply signified that the Lord through him, but apart from him, saved the people of Israel, and subdued their enemies; whereas in Jesus Christ it signifies that the Lord, *i.e.*, the Divine Essence, is

THE PURIFICATION.

22 And when ᵃthe days of her purification

ᵃ Lev. xii. 2, 3, 4, 6.

22. "Her purification;" rather "their" with ℵ, A., B., L., R., later Uncials, most Cursives, Gothic, Sahidic, Coptic, Syriac, Armenian, Æthiopic. Very little MSS. authority for "her."

personally in Him to save His own people from sin ; for, as we learn from St. Matthew, the name of Jesus is given to Him in fulfilment of the prophecy that He is to be " God with us " (Matth. i. 21-23), so that to fulfil the import of His name, He must be personally the Lord, Who is " God with us " to save us.

"Let the Holy Name be ever my refuge and confidence, my strength and support, my peace and consolation ; and let it be truly to me a name of salvation. Exert upon my heart, O Jesus, the right and sovereign power which this Name gives Thee to save me." (Quesnel.)

22. "And when the days of her purification according to the law of Moses," &c. The most probable reading is "their" purification : but the woman only, under the Jewish law, was supposed to be unclean through child-bearing, and no uncleanness was supposed to adhere either to the husband or to the child; so Edersheim with some apparent reason maintains that "their" refers to the Jews. The whole law on this matter the reader will find in Leviticus xii.

Now since all this matter of uncleanness in child-bearing, and consequent ceremonial purification arises from the fact that each one of the human race is conceived and born in sin, how is it that the Virgin Mother, who had conceived the sinless Son of God in a way separate from all sin, needed purification ? The answer is, "Thus it became her to fulfil all righteousness."

Christ, her Divine Son, needed not Circumcision, and yet He was circumcised ; He needed not Baptism, yet to fulfil all righteousness He was baptized. And so, though there was no sin defiling His Conception and Birth, yet God willed that His mother should act in this respect as all other mothers did. Indeed, it arose from the necessities of the case. His immaculate Conception and stainless Birth could not be made known till long after, and if His mother had neglected the separation for forty days, and the offerings for purification incumbent upon every Jewess, it would have been a grievous scandal in the eyes of all who knew her.

CHAP. II.] THE LAW OF PURIFICATION. 55

according to the law of Moses were accomplished, they brought him to Jerusalem, to present *him* to the Lord;

23 (As it is written in the law of the Lord, ᵗEvery male that openeth the womb shall be called holy to the Lord;)

24 And to offer a sacrifice according to ᵘthat which is said in the law of the Lord, A pair of turtledoves, or two young pigeons.

ᵗ Ex. xiii. 2.
& xxii. 29.
& xxxiv. 19.
Num. iii. 13.
& viii. 17.
& xviii. 15.
ᵘ Lev. xii. 2, 6, 8.

"They brought him to Jerusalem, to present him to the Lord." This, of course, was no part of His mother's purification. Every first-born child, if a male, had to be redeemed. It was first presented to the Lord, by being given into the hands of the priest, and then five shekels were paid for its redemption. The law of this, and the reason for that law, the reader will find in Exodus xiii. and Leviticus xii. God took the tribe of Levi to be His special servants in lieu of the first-born being males. The tribe of Levi was numbered and the first-born of the rest of Israel were also counted, and it was found that the first-born exceeded the number of the Levites by 273. These were redeemed at five shekels the head, and the redemption money, 1,365 shekels, was given to Aaron and his sons.

We learn from Numb. xviii. 15, 16, that this redemption of every first-born Israelite, if a male, was to be perpetual.

And this was a further and extraordinary condescension on our Lord's part. He Who had been from all eternity the only begotten of the Father, was presented to God in His human nature; and He Who redeemed all men, was Himself, as a son of Abraham, redeemed for five shekels of silver.

According to Dr. Edersheim (and indeed it seems only natural) the father or mother of the first-born thus redeemed must not be of Levitical descent, which disposes of the legend that the father of the Virgin was a priest, which opinion seems also to have been adopted by Rationalists who desire to show that He had in reality none of the blood of David in His veins.

24. "And to offer a sacrifice, according to that which is said in the law," &c. We read in Levit. xii. 6, that the mother was to bring for the offering of the purification, a lamb for a burnt offering, and one turtle-dove or young pigeon for a sin offering; but if,

SIMEON.

25 And, behold, there was a man in Jerusalem, whose name *was* Simeon: and the same man *was* just and devout, ˣwaiting for the consolation of Israel: and the Holy Ghost was upon him.

26 And it was revealed unto him by the Holy Ghost, that he should not ʸsee death, before he had seen the Lord's Christ.

x Is. xl. 1. Mark xv. 43. ver. 38.

y Ps. lxxxix. 48. Heb. xi. 5.

---

26. " It was revealed." " It had been revealed," Revisers.

being poor, she was not able to bring a lamb, then she was to bring two turtle-doves or two young pigeons—one for the burnt-offering, the other for the sin-offering.

This seems to prove that this presentation could not have taken place after the Magi had presented their offerings, which must have been of considerable value, and would have enabled the Virgin to offer the lamb. Thus the Lord in His mother suffered a further humiliation, being born in a poor family, and this was for our sakes, as St. Paul teaches us, " Ye know the grace of our Lord Jesus Christ, who though he was rich, yet for our sakes he became poor, that we through his poverty might be rich." (2 Cor. viii. 9.)

25. " And, behold, there was a man in Jerusalem, whose name was Simeon." Some have supposed Simeon to have been the son of the great Hillel, the founder of one of the great Rabbinic schools, but without the smallest reason. Simeon, at this time, must have been a very old man, waiting for his departure hence, whereas the Simeon, son of Hillel, became President of the Sanhedrim thirteen years after this. Simeon was one of the most common of Jewish names.

No description of a Christian character can be higher than this of his. He was just in all his relations to men. He was devout, *i.e.*, pious, God-fearing in his service of God, and he waited for the consolation of Israel. He waited for the First Coming of the Lord, just as the true believer now waits for His Second Coming, as the time when he shall receive his crown. And all this not of himself, but because " the Holy Ghost was upon him."

26. " And it was revealed unto him by the Holy Ghost," &c. By some secret intimation of which he could not mistake the origin. Bede remarks well : " To see death means to undergo it, and happy

27 And he came ^z by the Spirit into the temple: and when the parents brought in the child Jesus, to do for him after the custom of the law,   z Matt. iv. 1.

28 Then took he him up in his arms, and blessed God, and said,

29 Lord, ^a now lettest thou thy servant depart in peace, according to thy word: a Gen. xlvi. 30. Phil. i. 23.

---

will he be to see the death of the flesh, who has first been enabled to see with the eyes of his heart the Lord Jesus; having his conversation in the heavenly Jerusalem, and frequently entering the door of God's temple, that is, following the examples of the saints in whom God dwells, as in His temple." (Catena Aurea.)

27. "And he came by the Spirit into the temple." Rather, perhaps, in the Spirit. The Holy Ghost secretly and irresistibly directing his will, so that, perhaps, at some hour when he was not usually worshipping in the Temple he was constrained to come. Thus Jesus was afterwards led by the Spirit into the wilderness.

"And when the parents brought in the child Jesus, to do for him after," &c. "The parents." Joseph, as well as Mary, is here said to be the parent of the Lord. Now, though we believe and confess, as the chief article of the Catholic faith, that Incarnation which requires that He had no human father, yet by virtue of the sacramental mystery of marriage, Joseph was one flesh with Mary, of whose flesh the Lord partook. So that in this sense it is right to call Joseph and Mary united the parents of the Lord.

28. "Then took he him up in his arms, and blessed God, and said." It is nowhere said that he acted here instead of the priest whose duty it was, when a child was presented, to receive him for God by taking him up in his arms. But why should not a little child be taken in the arms of more than one person? Joseph and Mary are not at all likely, from what we have just read, to have neglected so simple a part of the ritual law as that the officiating priest should present the child.

29. "Lord, now lettest thou thy servant depart in peace, according to thy word." The word "Lord" is not the usual one, but is rather to be rendered Master, in the sense of dominion. It is "despotës," and from it comes our word "despot." From this and from the word to "let depart," signifying sometimes to loose from

30 For mine eyes [b] have seen thy salvation,

31 Which thou hast prepared before the face of all people;

32 [c] A light to lighten the Gentiles, and the glory of thy people Israel.

[b] Is. lii. 10. ch. iii. 6.
[c] Is. ix. 2. & xlii. 6. & xlix. 6. & lx. 1, 2, 3. Matt. iv. 16. Acts xiii. 47. & xxviii. 28.

---

bonds, it has been supposed that the idea is here "to dismiss from servitude;" but does it not rather look to the words which had just been spoken of this holy man, that he should not taste of death till he had seen the Lord Christ? In Acts iv. 24, and in Rev. vi. 10 the word despot is used in very solemn invocations of the Great Ruler of all.

Some of the Fathers unite these meanings. Thus Origen:—"Knowing that no one could release him from the chains of his body with the hope of future life but He Whom he held in his arms." And again, as if he said, "As long as I held not Christ, I was in prison, and could not escape from my bonds. Observe, again, that this just man, confined, as it were, in the prison of his earthly frame, is longing to be loosed, that he may again be with Christ."

30. "For mine eyes have seen thy salvation." This is an utterance of very remarkable faith. He held in his arms a little child six weeks old, weak and helpless, to all appearance, as any other child, and yet he discerned in this child the salvation of God. The Holy Ghost had revealed to him that He was the Christ, and this was enough. If He was the Christ, then in Him must be fulfilled all the promises centred in the Christ.

31-32. "Which thou hast prepared before the face of all people, to be a light to lighten," &c. Why *hast* set forth before, &c.? Only four persons, then, knew and recognized the Lord. But when God had thus sent His Son into the world as its Saviour, everything, in the eye of faith, is already accomplished; already He is preached before all the people; already the rays of the Sun of Righteousness disperse the darkness of heathenism; already the name of Israel is the name of the true people and Church of God.

Bede has a remarkable note: "And well is the enlightening of the Gentiles put before the glory of Israel, because when the fulness of the Gentiles shall have come in, then shall Israel be safe."

CHAP. II.]   THE FALL AND RISING AGAIN.   59

33 And Joseph and his mother marvelled at those things which were spoken of him.

34 And Simeon blessed them, and said unto Mary his mother, Behold, this *child* is set for the ^d fall and

^d Is. viii. 14.
Hos. xiv. 9.
Matt. xxi. 44.
Rom. ix. 32, 33.
1 Cor. i. 23, 24.
2 Cor. ii. 16.
1 Pet. ii. 7, 8.

33. "And Joseph and his mother." So A., E., G., H., K., M., and other later Uncials and Cursives, most old Latin, Gothic, Syriac; but ℵ, B., D., L., some Cursives (1, 131, 157), Vulg. and Sah., Coptic, Æthiopic, Armenian, read "his father and his mother."

33. "And Joseph and his mother marvelled at those things which were spoken," &c. There seems to be some probability that the true reading is "His father and his mother." See note on verse 27, as to the freedom with which St. Joseph was called "His father."

Is it not wonderful that after each of them had received angelic messages, and Mary herself had conceived and borne a Son in a way so far above nature, and after she herself had given utterance to the Magnificat, that they should marvel at anything which was told them? And yet this wonder was no proof of unbelief. It was simply that they passed from successive stages of imperfect knowledge to others more perfect. The full Godhead of the Lord could not be revealed to them, or they could not have gone about their daily household work, if they could have even existed at all under any adequate sense of such Nearness. "The rays of Godhead and of glory, that broke forth, filled them with wonder and adoration; while knowing, they knew not what they knew." "Thus we also, though we know the great things of the Gospel long before, and have embraced them, yet on every fulfilment before our eyes and with us, in the development of these promises, we marvel and wonder as at some new thing, gaining new eyes to see that which we had before seen and confessed, and yet knew not." (Williams.)

34. "And Simeon blessed them, and said unto Mary, his mother, Behold," &c. Hitherto all the revelations of the Spirit which accompanied the coming of the Eternal Son amongst His creatures, have been of unclouded glory, now there comes the first shadow of the Cross.

"This child is set for the fall and rising again of many in Israel." Thus the Lord said, "For judgment I am come into this world,

rising again of many in Israel; and for ᵉa sign which shall be spoken against;

ᵉ Acts xxviii. 22.

35 (Yea, ᶠa sword shall pierce through thy own soul also,) that the thoughts of many hearts may be revealed.

ᶠ Ps. xlii. 10. John xix. 25.

35. "Also" omitted by B., L., and some old Latin, Vulg., and some versions; but retained by ℵ, A., D., &c.

that they which see not might see, and that they which see might be made blind."

Here again is fulfilled the prophecy: "He [the Lord of Hosts] shall be for a sanctuary, but for a stone of stumbling, and for a rock of offence." And that of Malachi, "Who shall abide the day of His coming, and who shall stand when he appeareth? He shall sit as a refiner and purifier of silver." The word of the Saviour being the word of God, tried all that heard it as the word of no prophet before had tried them. They that were of God, heard in His words God's word, and so rose; they that were not of God, heard them not, and fell.

"And for a sign which shall be spoken against." This was fulfilled when they said of Him, "He hath a devil, and is mad. Why hear ye him?" When they said of Him, "By the prince of the devils he casteth out devils;" when they said, "He deceiveth the people." He was the Salvation of God, the Light to lighten the Gentiles, and the Glory of God's people Israel; and yet He was to be despised and rejected of men, a man of sorrow, and acquainted with grief. Such opposites meet in the Christ of God.

35. ("Yea, a sword shall pierce through thy own soul also.") It is surprising how most commentators apply this to the grief in the Virgin's heart at the rejection of her Son, when we read of the whole country ringing with the fame of His miracles, and that the common people heard Him gladly. It seems to me that the only adequate fulfilment, the only one worth naming, is the intense grief which must have pierced her soul when she saw her Son upon the Cross.

"That the thoughts of many hearts may be revealed." Is this to be made to depend upon the "sign which shall be spoken against," or with "a sword shall pierce through thy own soul?" I believe with both. The falling and rising again, the sign spoken against, the sword piercing the Virgin's soul, all met in their fulness at the

ANNA A PROPHETESS.

36 And there was one Anna, a prophetess, the daughter of Phanuel, of the tribe of Aser: she was of a great age, and had lived with an husband seven years from her virginity:

Cross. It was that which occasioned the true and permanent fall. It was that which brought about the moral, and will afterwards bring about the actual Resurrection ("I, if I be lifted up from the earth, will draw all men unto me"). It was then that the sign was spoken against, it was then that the soul of the Virgin was pierced, and so, by the Cross, more than by all else in the Lord's Life, are "the thoughts of many hearts revealed." Christ crucified reveals the thoughts of men. To the Jews it is a stumbling-block, and to the Greeks foolishness. It reveals the hidden hypocrisy of the formalist, the hollowness of the multitude, the shallowness of the pretenders to wisdom. As Godet says:—"The hatred of which Jesus will be the object, and which will pierce the heart of Mary with poignant grief, will bring out those hostile thoughts towards God which in the people lie hid under a veil of pharisaical devotion. Simeon discerned beneath the outward forms of Jewish piety, their love of human glory, their hypocrisy, avarice, and hatred of God; and he perceives that this Child will prove the occasion for all this hidden venom being poured forth from the recesses of all their hearts. God does not will the evil: but He wills that the evil when present should show itself; this is an indispensable condition to its being either healed or condemned."

36. "And there was one Anna, a prophetess, the daughter of Phanuel." The fact that she was a prophetess does not imply that she was a public teacher, but that she had a special grace of the Holy Spirit to comfort and edify those who needed it—above all, that she discerned the signs of the times, and looked for the speedy coming of the Hope of Israel.

"Of the tribe of Aser." It seems probable that though the vast bulk of the inhabitants of the Holy Land belonged to the tribes of Judah, or Levi, or Benjamin, yet during the long period when the ten tribes were given up to idolatry, many of those who bowed not the knee to Baal, would have taken refuge in Jerusalem to be within reach of the ordinances of God. To one of these families, belonging to the tribe of Aser, this Anna belonged.

36-37. "She was of a great age, and had lived . . . fourscore and

37 And she *was* a widow of about fourscore and four years, which departed not from the temple, but served *God* with fastings and prayers ᵍ night and day.

ᵍ Acts xxvi. 7.
1 Tim. v. 5.

---

37. "A widow of about fourscore and four years." So later Uncials, most Cursives, Syriac; but ℵ, A., B., L., some Cursives (33, 120), Vulg., and some versions read "until" instead of "about;" *usque ad annos octoginta*, Vulg.

four years," &c. It is possible that the last clause indicates not the time of her widowhood, but her age. If it means the time during which she had lived as a widow, she must have been above one hundred, perhaps nearly one hundred and ten years old.

"Which departed not from the temple." This has been held to mean that she spread her pallet or mat in the Temple and lived there altogether. But would such a thing have been permitted except to some officials of the holy place? May not the words rather be explained by those of Acts i. 14, and ii. 46, " They continuing daily with one accord in the temple," &c.

" But served God with fastings and prayers night and day." It has been said that her form of piety was Jewish rather than Christian; but must not St. Paul have had her in his eye when he speaks of the true type of the Christian widow as " She that is a widow indeed, and desolate, trusteth in God and continueth in supplications and prayers night and day " ? (1 Tim. v. 5.)

Her piety was certainly not of that stamp which finds most favour amongst us now—active, bustling, energetic, and so assumed to be the most *useful;* but have we not gone much too far in despising the contemplative, ascetic, prayerful life? Who knows what may not have been the *use* of Anna's fastings and prayers, in preparing hearts to receive the Lord? God, we doubt not, answered her many supplications in ways which could not be traced out, but which will assuredly be known at the last. Her life of fasting and devotion was evidently her calling of God, known and approved by Him.

And may not, in this very day, the life of religion amongst ourselves be owing not only to sermons, and visitings, and meetings, but to the prayers of the few scattered handfuls of worshippers who here and there are constant at daily service ? A thoroughly ultra-Protestant writer (Girdlestone) remarks on this verse: " The abuses which have attended often on the practice of a mo-

CHAP. II.] THE CHILD GREW. 63

38 And she coming in that instant gave thanks likewise unto the Lord, and spake of him to all them that ʰ looked for redemption in ‖ Jerusalem.

39 And when they had performed all things according to the law of the Lord, they returned into Galilee, to their own city Nazareth.

40 ⁱ And the child grew, and waxed strong in

ʰ Mark xv. 43. ver. 25. ch. xxiv. 21.
‖ Or, *Israel*.
ⁱ ver. 52. ch. i. 80.

---

38. "Unto the Lord." So A., later Uncials, almost all Cursives, most old Latin, Vulg., Syriac, Æthiopic, Armenian; but ℵ, B., D., L., a few old Latin, Coptic, read "to God."
40. "Strong in spirit." So A., later Uncials, almost all Cursives, Syriac, Æthiopic; but ℵ, B., D., L., most old Latin, Vulg., Sah., Coptic, Armenian, omit "spirit."

nastic life, should not render us insensible to the duty of spending large portions of our time in meditation and prayer and fasting."

38. "And she coming in at that instant"—doubtless led "in the Spirit," as Simeon had been led, to come and acknowledge before all the infant Son of David—"gave thanks likewise unto the Lord."

The word "gave thanks," rather means "confessed to the Lord," *i.e.*, confessed to Him, and before all bystanders, that the child in Simeon's arms was the Salvation of the world, and the Hope of Israel.

39. "And when they had performed all things," &c. How carefully St. Luke notices that in the case of this Holy Child, Who was in due time to break from off the necks of God's people the burdensome yoke of the law, all things were done according to the law! This Gospel was, according to the testimony of the earliest Fathers, the preaching of that Apostle who taught so prominently that Christ was born of a woman, and made under the law to redeem them that were under the law, that we might receive the adoption of sons. (Gal. iv.).

"They returned into Galilee, to their own city, Nazareth." Between the first and second parts of this verse we must place, I think, the visit of the Magi and the reception of their offerings, and certainly the flight into Egypt. St. Luke, who has a more vivid apprehension of the prominent part played in all these matters by the Virgin Mother, rather than by Joseph, speaks of their own city, because it was her native place, and because of this, Joseph (as related in Matthew ii. 23), out of all the cities of Galilee chose Nazareth, and so fulfilled the prophecy, "He shall be called a Nazarene."

40. "And the child grew, and waxed strong [in spirit]." If the words "in spirit" are not authentic, and there are considerable

64   THE GRACE OF GOD UPON HIM.   [St. Luke.

spirit, filled with wisdom: and the grace of God was upon him.

^k Ex. xxiii. 15, 17. & xxxiv. 23. Deut. xvi. 1, 16.   41 Now his parents went to Jerusalem ^k every year at the feast of the passover.

A.D. 8.   42 And when he was twelve years old, they went up to Jerusalem after the custom of the feast.

43 And when they had fulfilled the days, as they returned,

---

42. "They went up to Jerusalem." So A., C., later Uncials, almost all Cursives, old Latin, Vulg., Gothic, Armenian, Æthiopic; but א, B., D., L., three Cursives (125, 219, 243), Syriac, Coptic, Sah., omit "to Jerusalem."

---

grounds for their omission, then the whole of the first part relates to the bodily growth and development of the Body of the Lord. His Body appears to have been wholly free from the seeds of disease, and to have been capable of very great exertion, so that He waxed strong, not only in firmness and determination of spirit, but in all the physical powers which became a sinless human nature, which was so far above death, that He alone of all men could say, "No man taketh my life from me, but I lay it down of myself." (John x. 18).

"Full of wisdom, and the grace of God was upon him" (or in Him), as we shall see by what follows.

41. "Now his parents went to Jerusalem every year at the feast of the passover." Notwithstanding their poverty, they performed this annual pilgrimage of above sixty miles in obedience to the law. At a later period a portion of the family went up to the Feast of Tabernacles as well (John viii). It appears also that St. Mary as well as St. Joseph went up, though it was only incumbent upon males to attend the feasts.

42. "And when he was twelve years old." At thirteen He would become what the Rabbis called a Son of the Law. He would then be of a sufficient age to know its obligations, and very probably came up to Jerusalem, anticipating the usual time by a year, to make public profession that he was under such obligations, as our children do at the time of Confirmation.

"And when they had fulfilled the days." Only on the two first days of the Feast of the Passover was personal attendance in the Temple necessary. With the third day commenced the so-called half-holydays, when it was lawful to return to one's home—a pro-

JESUS TARRIED BEHIND.

the child Jesus tarried behind in Jerusalem ; and Joseph and his mother knew not *of it*.

44 But they, supposing him to have been in the company, went a day's journey; and they sought him among *their* kinsfolk and acquaintance.

---

43. "Joseph and his mother." So A., C., later Uncials, almost all Cursives, most old Latin (b, c, f, ff, &c.), Gothic, Syriac; but ℵ, B., D., L., some Cursives (1, 13, 33, 118, 131, 157, 209), Sah., Coptic, Armenian, read "his parents."

---

vision of which, no doubt, many availed themselves. Indeed, there was really nothing of special interest to detain the pilgrims. For the Passover had been eaten—the festive sacrifice or chagigah offered, and the first ripe barley reaped and brought into the Temple, and waved as the omer of first flour before the Lord." (Edersheim.) So that the words, "when they had fulfilled the days,'' cannot necessarily imply that the Holy Virgin and St. Joseph had remained in Jerusalem during the whole Pascal week.

It is important to remember this, as the day of return not being definitely fixed, may have been one of the circumstances which contributed to the Lord having been left behind.

"The child Jesus tarried behind in Jerusalem : and Joseph and his mother," &c. This was probably what we should call accidental, and may have been occasioned somewhat in this way. As they would travel for the sake of mutual protection in large companies or caravans (those which belonged to some particular neighbourhood joining together), through some oversight due notice may not have been given to the Lord, Who spent all His time in the Temple, and so the caravan from Jerusalem to Nazareth set off without Him. When this had occurred, there was no help for Him except to stop where He was, spending His days in the Temple, and receiving food and lodging at night from some friend or relative of his parents, of whom they on their return to seek for Him neglected or forgot to inquire.

44. "But they, supposing him to have been in the company . . . kinsfolk and acquaintance." The caravan consisting of a great number of people and continually moving, they would not miss Him, nor would they be able to search for Him till they halted for the night.

45 And when they found him not, they turned back again to Jerusalem, seeking him.

46 And it came to pass, that after three days they found him in the temple, sitting in the midst of the doctors, both hearing them, and asking them questions.

47 And [1] all that heard him were astonished at his understanding and answers.

[1] Matt. vii. 28. Mark i. 22.
ch. iv. 22, 32. John vii. 15, 46.

---

46. "Seeking him." So ℵ, A., later Uncials, Cursives, but B., C., D., L., read "seeking him diligently."

45-46. "And when they found him not . . . asking them questions." "After three days." This cannot well mean that they were three days searching for Him in the city. It probably dates from the time they set out. The first day would be the first day's journey, the day of their anxious search the second, and the day of their return the third.

We are not to suppose that there was anything unusual in one who sought instruction from the teachers of the law, not only thus hearing them, but questioning them. On the contrary, there seems to have been the greatest freedom in the Rabbinical schools of putting questions to the teachers. The Talmudical writings are full of wise sayings given in answer to questions put at the moment. But what was unusual is contained in the next verse.

47. "And all that heard him were astonished at his understanding and answers." And when we consider the sort of Scripture interpretation and exposition which then began to prevail, well they might be. The Lord's questions, on whatever subject they were upon, would confound these teachers of tradition by their very simplicity—they would come direct from the heart, and so would reach the heart. Think of some of the questions with which the Lord in after times exposed their ignorance: "Have ye not read what David did, when he was an hungered? If David call Christ Lord, how is He his Son? Is it not written in your law, I have said ye are gods?" &c. See how simple these questions are, and yet what a mine of instruction each one opens up!

We are not for a moment to suppose that our Lord in thus hearing them and asking them questions, undertook to teach them. He simply availed Himself of the liberty which seemingly all Jewish scholars had, of questioning their teachers. And in their turn they

48 And when they saw him, they were amazed: and his mother said unto him, Son, why hast thou thus dealt with us? behold, thy father and I have sought thee sorrowing.

49 And he said unto them, How is it that ye sought me?

---

could question Him. A false view of the whole matter is given by the words. "disputing with the doctors," so often applied to this incident. The time had not come for controversy and dispute. No doubt the Lord avoided all appearance of it, and in all simplicity asked and answered as a child would do. But children ask at times the profoundest questions, and this was what would astonish them, not His precocity, so to speak, but the depth of His simplicity—not His learning as men understand the term, but His insight; not His subtlety, but His straightforwardness; not His weaving of cobwebs, but His brushing aside all such things, and laying bare the very heart of the subject which they were considering.

48. "And when they saw him they were amazed." Till then, apparently, He had been reticent of His Divine knowledge, even to them. But most probably they were amazed, not at His questions or answers, which they could not have heard, but at the rapt attention which was accorded to what He was saying by the doctors of the law who were gathered around Him.

"And his mother said unto him, Son, why hast thou thus dealt with us," &c. There is, of course, a sound of reproof about these words. The Holy Virgin thought more of the past anxiety than of the scene before her. This was most likely said as He retired with them. It was the most natural thing for a mother in such circumstances to say, and yet all depended upon the tone and manner of the saying, for it might merely be the expression of inquiry respecting conduct which was unusual.

49. "And he said unto them, How is it that ye sought me? wist ye not that I must be," &c. These words have been translated, "Wist ye not that I must be in my Father's house?" So the Revisers of 1881, and the Syriac. The words literally rendered are, "in the things of my Father." A very little consideration will serve to show that the rendering of the authorized "about my Father's business," does not convey the meaning of the Lord. For it is impossible to suppose that the Lord in asking the question, "How is it that ye sought me?" meant to shame them for coming to seek

[m John ii. 16.] wist ye not that I must be about [m] my Father's business?

---

49. "About my Father's business," rather "in the things of my Father," or "in my Father's house."

Him when He was not to be found in the caravan. He could not blame them for looking after Him. What He does blame them for is for not at once finding Him at the right place—at the Temple—the place where they might have known that He was most likely to be found. If, then, we are to take the words in the most literal way, "in the things of my Father," those " things " must have been the worship and instruction in His Father's house. The things of His Father must indicate some definite place, whereas "His Father's business " might be anywhere; when He had entered on His public ministry, His "Father's business" took Him from the borders of Tyre and Sidon and the east of Jordan, through Samaria to Jerusalem— that is, over the whole circuit of the Holy Land. Whereas His question, " How is it that ye sought me?" viewed in the light of the circumstances which gave rise to it, must indicate that they need not have sought Him, but should have betaken themselves at once to the Temple, where they were most certain to find Him. There were the "things of His Father " in which He must be employed.

These words are remarkable above all others in this respect, that they are the first words of the Lord. As such, they show : 1, His perfect consciousness of His Divine origin, that God, and not Joseph, was His real Father. There is a clear contrast between the Virgin's words, " Thy father and I have sought thee," and the Lord's words, " in the house [or concerns] of my Father." Very many commentators, even thoroughly believing ones, speculate freely about the Lord's human and Divine consciousness, about the development in the human mind of the Child Jesus of the sense of the Divine indwelling of the Second Person of the Godhead, and of the realizing that He was the Divine Son of the Eternal Father ; but is not all this most presumptuous ? The mystery of mysteries is, that there are two whole and perfect natures in one Person, that of Jesus Christ ; that the Personality—the Ego—is that of the Son of God ; and the deepest thing about this mystery is, that the finite nature should, because finite, increase in wisdom, and yet the Personality should be the infinite. And yet there are persons, otherwise believing and reverent, who say that at this juncture it first began to dawn

CHAP. II.] HE WENT DOWN WITH THEM. 69

50 And ⁿ they understood not the saying which he spake
unto them.
                                                                                                                                                             ⁿ ch. ix. 45.
                                                                                                                                                             & xviii. 34.

51 And he went down with them, and came to

---

upon the Lord's mind that God was His true and proper Father. Surely all this should be left to God, and so left in its original mystery; and it should be remembered that these words of the Lord teach us that He was perfectly conscious of His Divine Sonship. But, 2, these first recorded words teach us, that from the first He recognized that it was His mission to be "in" the things of His Father, and therefore in the one place of accredited intercourse with God, where God had 'set His Name,' the 'place where God's honour dwelt.'

50. "And they understood not the saying." Even the Blessed Virgin did not and could not realize as yet that He was the Eternal Son—the Word made Flesh; neither could they understand the nature and scope of His future mission, for which His sojourn in the Temple was a preparation.

It is clear that the Lord, however conscious He was of His Divine Sonship, had veiled it, and with it His superhuman knowledge, so that familiar intercourse with Him in their home, though it deepened their love and admiration, had not brought home to St. Joseph the significance of His name, "Emmanuel," which he had heard from the angel; nor to the Blessed Virgin the sense in which He was to be called "the Son of the Highest." But, indeed, that they should have had any adequate sense of His unutterable greatness was out of the question, for, as I said, to have possessed it would have simply paralyzed them, and made them incapable of performing the daily duties of home in His presence and company.

51. "And he went down with them, and came to Nazareth, and was subject unto them." "But from His very first years, being obedient to His parents, He endured all bodily labours humbly and reverently. For since His parents were honest and just, yet at the same time poor and ill supplied with the necessaries of life (as the stable which administered to the holy birth bears witness), it is plain that they continually underwent bodily fatigue in providing for their daily wants. But Jesus being obedient to them, as the Scriptures testify, even in sustaining labours, submitted Himself to a complete subjection." (Basil, in Catena Aurea.)

Nazareth, and was subject unto them: but his mother °kept all these sayings in her heart.

° ver. 19.
Dan. vii. 28.

How wonderful it seems, that from His twelfth year, when He was taken to the Temple, to his thirtieth, when He was baptized, there is nothing recorded of the Lord, except that He was subject to His parents! With the exception of this obedience, all is wrapped in the profoundest obscurity : not a record of one word that He said, or of any one act which He performed, of one soul that He rescued from evil, or assisted in acquiring goodness. Surely this seems an amazing humiliation—that He Who had evinced such knowledge of Scripture, and such insight into its meaning as to astonish the doctors of the law, should have been contented at the will of His Father so to veil His Light, and to live in such retirement, that, when He did begin to teach, His fellow-townsmen asked, "Whence hath this man this wisdom?" But in this was He not learning to sympathize with that vast mass of His fellow creatures who have to pass through life unknown and unnoticed, obeying in quietness and patience those over them, though such may be vastly inferior to themselves? In this, too, as well as in the pains of the Cross, He "learned obedience by the things which He suffered."

And by this, what a high value has He set upon the faithful performance of home duties, the essence of which is loving subjection to those who are over us in the family! Submission in the smaller sphere of the family prepares us for submission in the wider sphere of the Church, and that for obedience in the still wider sphere of the kingdom of God in the eternal world.

"But his mother kept all these sayings in her heart." It is remarkable that this should be twice mentioned, for in verse 19 we read, "Mary kept all these things, and pondered them in her heart." What is the significance of this repetition? Is it to vindicate the election of God, in that He chose one to be the mother of the Lord whose mind was thoroughly in accord with the purposes of grace, and who would watch with adoring interest all the indications of His higher origin, and of His future greatness ; or is it to assure us that to her observation and memory we owe the few precious notices contained in these chapters of the infancy of the Son of God? They were not learnt by the Evangelist through tradition, but in personal conference with her who, as Origen says, pre-

CHAP. II.] WISDOM AND STATURE. 71

52 And Jesus ᵖ increased in wisdom and ‖ sta-   ᵖ 1 Sam. ii.
                                                 26. ver. 40.
                                                 ‖ Or, *age*.

served all His words in her heart, not as those of a child of twelve years of age, but of Him Who was conceived of the Holy Ghost.

52. "And Jesus increased in wisdom and stature." "In this state of subjection He advanced in wisdom, not as God the Word, but as man, for to perfect manhood growth and increase is needful: but as the separation and distinction between our Lord's Godhead and human Soul is a mystery infinitely above us, and to look into which too curiously, is to look into the ark of God, so this increase in wisdom is mysterious; but no less mysterious would it have been, if He had not grown in wisdom, and unharmonious with the other parts of Catholic truth. He was Almighty in Godhead, yet His Body and Soul received increase; thus not only in bodily affections, but in affections of the soul also, He was as man: He learned obedience; He marvelled; He felt surprise, as at the breaking in of new knowledge." (Isaac Williams.)

In this He can sympathize with us in our infirmities and distresses through partial knowledge. As the apostolic writer says: "He can have compassion on the ignorant, and on them that are out of the way, for that He Himself also was compassed with infirmity," and so partaker of that infirmity which all scholars in the school of experience must have; for, as far as we can judge from the study of our nature, the wisdom gained by experience can only be gained by experience: it cannot be poured into us once for all, but must be acquired by degrees.

"And in favour with God and man." It seems a mystery that One Who had been in the bosom of God from eternity should increase in "favour," or grace, with God and man; but in this respect the Son of God was the representative of His brethren. According to their use of God's grace and gifts, the saints of God increase in the favour of God. God regards them with increasing love and good will according to their devotedness, and it was not otherwise with the Eternal Son. For our sakes He Who was the equal of God in His higher nature, in His lower created nature served God as His servant, and grew in His love and favour, so that it was not only in submission to suffering, but in that which constitutes the bright side of God's dealings with men that He is as we are. It was prophesied of Him, that because "He loved righteousness and hated

ture, and in favour with God and man.

iniquity, therefore God anointed Him with the oil of gladness above his fellows." He said of Himself in respect of His intercourse with His Father, " If ye keep my commandments, ye shall abide in my love, even as I have kept my Father's commandments, and abide in His love." It is no more difficult to believe that on His human side He increased in the favour of God, than that through keeping God's commandments He abode in the love of God.

But with respect to His increasing in favour with men, it has been well said that "*men* suffer for righteousness' sake when the light of their example becomes a witness against others, or excites their envy; but the virtues and holiness of a child consist so much in meekness and subjection, that they kindle love and excite interest among elders; the witness of goodness which displeases and the envy it excites are to be found more among equals in age."

CHAP. III.

Anno
DOMINI
26.

NOW in the fifteenth year of the reign of Tiberius Cæsar, Pontius Pilate being governor of Judæa, and Herod being tetrarch of Galilee,

1. "Now in the fifteenth year of the reign of Tiberius Cæsar," &c. Augustus, the predecessor and uncle of Tiberius, died A.D. 14, and but two years previously he had associated his nephew with him in the imperial rule, so that the ministry of John would commence A.D. 26.

" Pontius Pilate being governor of Judæa," &c. He was appointed in A.D. 26. He was not supreme governor under the Emperor, but procurator under the pro-consul of Syria. His province, or district, embraced Samaria as well as Judæa proper.

"Herod being tetrarch of Galilee," &c. This was Herod Antipas, son of Herod the Great, and the man who beheaded the Baptist. His tetrarchy embraced Galilee and Perea, that is, the country to the east of Jordan, south of the sea of Galilee.

CHAP. III.] THE WORD OF GOD CAME UNTO JOHN. 73

and his brother Philip tetrarch of Ituræa and of the region of Trachonitis, and Lysanias the tetrarch of Abilene,

2 ᵃAnnasandCaiaphas being the high priests, the word of God came unto John the son of Zacharias in the wilderness.

ᵃ John xi. 49, 51. & xviii. 13. Acts iv. 6.

---

2. " Annas and Caiaphas being the high priests," rather "in the high priesthood o. Annas and Caiaphas," א, A., B., C., D., E., G., H., K., L., &c., and most Cursives.

"And his brother Philip tetrarch of Ituræa and of the region of Trachonitis," &c. This was not the Philip whose wife Antipas married, but the son of Herod by his wife Cleopatra. This is the only place in the Gospel history where his name is mentioned. His territory was to the east of the Upper Jordan, and its capital Cæsarea Philippi. Much of it was beyond the bounds of the Holy Land. Ituræa is supposed to have derived its name from Jetur the son of Ishmael (Gen. xxv. 15). Trachonitis was a rocky territory forming part of the ancient Bashan, and is supposed to be the Greek equivalent for the Aramaic Argob. (Smith's Dictionary.)

"Lysanias the tetrarch of Abilene." Abilene was a territory out of the bounds of the Holy Land to the north of Cæsarea Philippi and the east of Damascus. Abilene, near Lebanon, was granted by Augustus to Herod the Great, on whose death he restored it to the heir of a former Lysanias put to death by Antony.

2. " Annas and Caiaphas being the high priests," &c. The oldest MSS. (see above) read "being the high priest." There could be, lawfully, but one high priest, and the one who had the legal claim was Annas, who had been deprived of his office by Gratus, the predecessor of Pilate. Caiaphas was his son-in-law. It is probable that he was considered by the people the only true high priest, and so we read in St. John that the Lord was first taken to him that he might give a sanction and authority to His condemnation which it would not otherwise have had.

"The word of the Lord came unto John the son of Zacharias," &c. This is the phrase used in the Old Testament to describe that the Divine inspiration or afflatus came to a prophet to compel him to deliver some messages from God to the people. Thus Hosea i. 1, " The word of the Lord that came unto Hosea." Also Jeremiah i. 2. It is not elsewhere used in the New Testament to describe the first action of the Spirit on an Apostle or Prophet.

3 ᵇAnd he came into all the country about Jordan, preaching the baptism of repentance ᶜ for the remission of sins:

4 As it is written in the book of the words of Esaias the prophet, saying, ᵈ The voice of one crying in the wilderness, Prepare ye the way of the Lord, make his paths straight.

ᵇ Matt. iii. 1.
Mark i. 4.
ᶜ ch. i. 77.
ᵈ Is. xl. 3.
Matt. iii. 3.
Mark i. 3.
John i. 23.

---

3. "And he came into all the country about Jordan, preaching the baptism," &c. He was not sent, as we should have expected, to Jerusalem, or to any of the cities of Judæa or Galilee; but he took up his station in the wilderness, and the inhabitants of the cities and towns flocked to the wilderness to hear his preaching and receive his baptism.

"The baptism of repentance for the remission of sins." This is the same account of the Baptism of John as that in St. Mark, and it should be noticed that it is the same as St. Paul's account in Acts xiii. 24, and Acts xix. 4. The Baptism of John appears to have been a new thing, as administered to the then people of God. Proselytes when brought into the Church of the Old Covenant were baptized; but there was no baptism for the children of Israel, to indicate that they all needed repentance, and that this repentance was to be followed by a far deeper and more effectual cleansing than the blood of their sacrifices could convey. So that the Forerunner was sent to prepare the way of the Lord, by preaching the Baptism of repentance to the chosen people as, notwithstanding all their privileges, deeply needing it. And yet we must be careful to remember the wholly preparatory nature of John's Baptism. It was not with the Holy Ghost. It was no Burial and Resurrection with Christ. It conveyed no new birth of water and of the Spirit. It baptized into no mystical body. It had to be repeated, even in the case of those who were believers in the Lord. (Acts xix. 5, 6.)

4, 5. "As it is written in the book of the words of Esaias . . . . Every valley shall be filled . . . . rough ways shall be made smooth." As it is the speciality of St. Luke to give (as we shall soon see) the preaching of the Baptist more in detail, describing the way in which he addressed various classes, so in quoting the passage in Isaiah which predicts that teaching, he alone, of the Evangelists, gives it in full, and we find that it sets forth the preparation for the

5 Every valley shall be filled, and every mountain and hill shall be brought low; and the crooked shall be made straight, and the rough ways *shall be* made smooth:

Lord in striking accord with the words of the Blessed Virgin, in the Magnificat. She had prophesied, "He hath shewed strength with his arm; he hath scattered the proud in the imagination of their hearts. He hath put down the mighty from their seats, and hath exalted the humble and meek." And here, in the citation of Isaiah, we have the same figures, "Every valley shall be filled, and every mountain and hill shall be brought low."

"Every valley shall be filled," &c. The valley being low and depressed, represents here the abject mind, the lowly and contrite heart, the spirit broken and depressed on account of sin. The Son of God comes to raise up the poor miserable fearful spirit, always looking upon God in the light of a severe Judge, and to give it assurance of forgiveness, to take away the abject spirit of bondage and to replace it with the spirit of adoption.

"Every mountain and hill shall be brought low." It is the very first law of Christ's kingdom, that all pride whatsoever is to be brought down. Its first beatitude is, "Blessed are the poor in spirit." Its second is, "Blessed are they that mourn." Its third is, "Blessed are the meek." Repentance, if it be worth anything, humbles every man because it makes him ashamed of himself. A true sense of sin never allows a man to compare himself with another to his own advantage, and so the mountains and hills—the self-complacent and conceited souls—must be levelled by repentance.

"The crooked shall be made straight," &c. Repentance unto life rectifies all within. It produces in the soul sincerity of purpose in all our service both of God and of our fellow-creatures. It takes away the double mind, striving to look at once to God and self, and fixes the attention upon fulfilling the will of God.

"And the rough ways shall be made smooth," &c. The rough ways are those which are full of impediments, and the true penitent clears his path of life of all impediments to his Christian walk, such as bad or irreligious company, immoderate desires, self-indulgent habits, and such things; or, as Gregory explains it, the rough ways are changed to smooth when "fierce and savage dispositions by the influence of Divine grace return to gentleness and meekness." (Cat. Aurea.)

6 And ᵉ all flesh shall see the salvation of God.

7 Then said he to the multitude that came forth to be baptized of him, ᶠ O generation of vipers, who hath warned you to flee from the wrath to come?

8 Bring forth therefore fruits ‖ worthy of re-

ᵉ Ps. xcviii. 2. Is. lii. 10. ch. ii. 10.
ᶠ Matt. iii. 7.
‖ Or, *meet for.*

---

6. "All flesh shall see the salvation of God." This may be a prediction of the universal spread of the Gospel, which even before St. Paul's death was so extensive that he wrote of it as being preached to " every creature which is under heaven ;" and it may look to the time of the end when " every eye shall see him," when each one " in his flesh shall see God."

7. " Then said he to the multitude that came forth to be baptized of him, O generation of vipers," &c. In St. Matthew it seems to be said that he addressed these words not to the multitude, but to " many of the Pharisees and Sadducees," but the Pharisees and Sadducees were the representatives of the whole people, who were, as a body, leavened with the leaven of Pharisaism, which made void the law through tradition, or of Sadduceeism, which robbed the promises of God of all their virtue through unbelief.

" O generation of vipers, who hath warned you to flee," &c. These words have been pronounced harsh, but are they one whit more harsh than the words of the Lord, " Ye are of your father the devil," *i.e.*, the old serpent, " and the works of your father ye will do "? It is one of the most common of Scripture figures of speech to call men the children of those whose character they have inherited : the good are called the children of God, of Abraham, of wisdom, of light; whilst the bad are called the children of Belial, of the devil, of the wicked one, of vipers. Instead of carping at such plain, outspoken words, let us consider their truth. If men can be called the children of those whom they imitate, surely they are the children of vipers, whose words instill the poison of infidelity, of heresy, of uncleanness, of envy and malice, and so eternally ruin souls.

8. " Bring forth therefore fruits worthy of repentance," &c. If repentance be not merely a change of conduct, but a change of heart from sin to God, then repentance worthy of this must, in the first place, be internal, the sorrow of the heart. It must begin with the contrition of the heart, and the cleansing of the conscience. The heart must loathe its old sins, and if it does not, earnest prayer for a

Chap. III.] WE HAVE ABRAHAM TO OUR FATHER. 77

pentance, and begin not to say within yourselves, We have Abraham to *our* father: for I say unto you, That God is able of these stones to raise up children unto Abraham.

---

deeper and more thorough repentance must be offered to God. We sometimes find persons speaking boastfully of their former state of sin as enhancing the grace of God in their present case; but such can have no genuine abhorrence of sin. Men cannot speak lightly or complacently of that of which they are thoroughly ashamed.

But if repentance be a genuine change of heart, it will not stop for a moment in internal emotions. If the tree be made good its fruit will be good, and that good fruit must answer to the corresponding evil fruit; avarice must be changed into generosity, uncleanness into purity, malice into goodwill. And, again, there must be restitution if anyone has been wronged; as Zacchæus said, "If I have done any wrong to any man I restore him fourfold." If any one has seduced another from either faith or virtue, there must be every effort made, and constant prayer offered, to bring the seduced back to faith and virtue.

Again, he brings forth fruit worthy of repentance, who, when converted, serves God with as much zeal and ardour as before he served Satan and the world; according to the words of the Apostle, "As ye have yielded your members servants to iniquity unto iniquity, so now yield your members servants to righteousness unto holiness" (Rom. vi. 19).

"Begin not to say within yourselves, We have Abraham," &c. It was no small matter to be the children of Abraham. God very solemnly promised that if the children of Israel after departing from Him yet returned to Him again, He would remember His covenant with Abraham, and receive them again (Levit. xxvi. 42). Again, the Lord calls Israel by Isaiah, "The children of Abraham His friend." But that which was intended to be, and was, a blessing, if rightly remembered, would be turned into a curse if used as a license for sin.

"God is able of these stones to raise up children unto Abraham." This may be hyperbolical, but on that account it more deeply impresses the truth. Abraham shall not want children though you be cut off; the stony hearts of the Gentiles shall be softened by the piercing influences of His grace. He Who could quicken Sarah's

9 And now also the axe is laid unto the root of the trees:
g every tree therefore which bringeth not forth good fruit is hewn down, and cast into the fire,

g Matt. vii. 19.

9. "And now also." "Even now," already. *Jam enim*, Vulg.

womb and Abraham when old, can supply him with truer sons than you. (Williams.)

9. "And now also the axe is laid unto the root of the trees," &c. This, no doubt, primarily refers to the Jewish people. They were about to have offered to them such mercy and grace as they never had before, but corresponding to this greatness of their salvation was their danger. The figure is remarkable. It is as if a wood-cutter had been to some noble tree of the forest, and had laid the axe at its root ready to fell it, but had gone away for some reason, and it had a short respite; and so the Son of Man had come to the Jewish Church, and His coming must be, in the case of the whole Church, and of every single soul which composed it, for mercy or for judgment—for mercy to every tree which suffered itself to be made good by Him, for judgment if it would not be renewed but would remain as it was.

"Every tree therefore which bringeth not forth good fruit," &c. Vengeance will be executed not only on those whom men account wicked, but on the idle, and the slothful, and the barren, and the unprofitable. Thus in the Vision of Judgment in Matth. xxv. those on the left hand are placed there because they have not done good. "I was an hungred, and ye gave me no meat," &c., and to the man who had laid up his pound in the napkin, the Lord says, "Out of thine own mouth will I judge thee, thou wicked servant" (Luke xix. 22); and to the man who hid his talent in the earth the Lord says, "Thou wicked and slothful servant" (Matth. xxv. 26).

"Cast into the fire." In the case of Jerusalem, which refused to be gathered, it was the condign punishment of its siege and destruction, the account of which, in Josephus, is more terrible than any other passage in history; in the case of the unfruitful soul, it is the outer darkness, where is the wailing and the gnashing of teeth, and something described in yet more terrible words as the aionian punishment, answering to the aionian life.

10. "And the people [lit. the multitude, the crowds] asked him . . . . let him do likewise." The people or crowds mean here,

CHAP. III.]   WHAT SHALL WE DO?   79

10 And the people asked him, saying, ^h What shall we do then?

^h Acts ii. 37.

11 He answereth and saith unto them, ⁱ He that

ⁱ ch. xi. 41.
2 Cor. viii. 14.
James ii. 15, 16.
1 John iii. 17.
& iv. 20.

probably, the masses, consisting mostly of working men or labourers.

"What shall we do?" &c. Do, that is, to avoid the condemnation of being "hewn down and cast into the fire." It means, what particular fruit must we bear?

The answer is exceedingly remarkable if we consider that St. John's mission was to prepare the way for Christ. If this question were put to many amongst ourselves who profess to lead men to Christ, they would answer, "You can do nothing. All works of men in your unreconciled state are displeasing to God. You can in no way, by any works of your own, further your own salvation. It is the worst of errors to think so." But the Baptist, filled with the Holy Ghost from his mother's womb, gives an answer implying the very reverse. It is, "You must do something. You must do what is in your power. You can, at least, give food and raiment to the poor starving creatures around you. Begin with this. If you begin thus with denying your selfishness, God will soon show you a more excellent way—the way of grace in His Son. But till that Son comes and reveals Himself to you, do what your hand finds to do. Do some good to your fellow creatures. The way for you to obtain mercy is to be merciful." Now in saying this did St. John, in the least degree, swerve from his mission of preparing the way for Christ by preaching of repentance? No, not for a moment. When the people asked him what they were to do to avoid the wrath to come, it was a plain sign that God had touched their hearts with some degree of repentance, and this repentance was no repentance at all unless it cut at the root of their selfishness, and every unselfish, self-denying act would deepen it.

Notice, also, that St. John said this to the masses. Instead of saying to them, "You have little to give, and so God will excuse you from contributing," he says to them, "Whatever you have that you do not absolutely need, give it." Looked at in this light, the words are very strong, very searching. If they make such a demand on the crowds, what do they make on the few who have abundance of this world's goods?

hath two coats, let him impart to him that hath none; and he that hath meat, let him do likewise.

^k Matt. xxi. 32. ch. vii. 29.

12 Then ^k came also publicans to be baptized, and said unto him, Master, what shall we do?

Of course such words of the Holy Baptist are to be understood in the light of common sense: men are not to give to enable others to be idle, and so St. Jerome applies the words of St. Paul as the best commentary on this passage: "I mean not that other men be eased, and ye burdened; but by an equality, that now at this time your abundance may be a supply for their want, that their abundance also may be a supply for your want: that there may be equality." (2 Cor. viii. 13, 14.)

Calvin has some very suggestive remarks which it would be well for many preachers who admire him to lay to heart: "A true feeling of repentance produces in the mind of the poor sinner an eager desire to know what is the mind and will of God. John's reply explains in a few words the fruits worthy of repentance, for the world is always desirous to acquit itself of its duty to God by performing outward acts of worship (ceremonies), and there is nothing to which we are more prone than to offer to God pretended worship whenever He calls us to repentance. But what fruits does the Baptist here recommend? The duties of charity and of the second table of the law, not that God disregards the outward profession of godliness, and of His worship; but that this (the duty towards our neighbour) is a surer mark of distinction, and less frequently leads to mistakes. For hypocrites labour strenuously to prove themselves worshippers of God by the performance of ceremonies, paying no regard, however, to true righteousness, for they are either cruel to their neighbours, or addicted to falsehood and dishonesty. It was therefore necessary to subject them to a more homely examination, if they are just in their dealings with men, if they relieve the poor, if they are generous to the wretched, if they give liberally what the Lord has bestowed upon them" (Calvin *in loco*).

12. "Then came also publicans to be baptized, and said unto him," &c. The former words ("he that hath two coats," &c.) were to the multitude, and the precept would reach all; now, two specific classes or professions are named, viz., publicans and soldiers. Why should these be singled out for mention, except for this, that of all

DO VIOLENCE TO NO MAN.

13 And he said unto them, ¹ Exact no more than that which is appointed you.

14 And the soldiers likewise demanded of him, saying, And what shall we do? And he said unto them, ‖ Do violence to no man, ᵐ neither accuse *any* falsely; and be content with your ‖ wages.

¹ ch. xix. 8.
‖ Or, *Put no man in fear.*
ᵐ Ex. xxiii. 1. Lev. xix. 11.
‖ Or, *allowance.*

---

14. "Demanded" is too strong. It should be simply "asked."

then existing means of livelihood, they were the two in which the practice of religion was most difficult. We should have supposed that he would at once have bidden them quit their present calling, and choose some other free from such urgent temptations; but he does not. To the publicans he says:—

"Exact no more than that which is appointed you." The publicans were the farmers of the revenue which was imposed on the country by the Romans. Being Jews, they were held in detestation by all classes of their countrymen, as lending themselves to the conquerors to help them to oppress and plunder their own nation. Being thus held up to opprobrium, in a sort of despair they took no pains to prove the falsehood of the accusations against them, but rather gave themselves to all manner of extortion: so that to call a man a publican was to call him a rogue and a scoundrel. If St. John suffered such men to continue in their calling, and simply bade them resist the temptations incident to it, then there is no profession which is capable of being honestly pursued which men may not raise and sanctify by their personal integrity and religion.

14. "And the soldiers likewise demanded of him, saying, And what shall we do?" The word "soldier" is not the usual one, but rather signifies soldiers going on an expedition, or on the march. These were probably mercenaries in the pay of Herod Antipas, and were not likely to have been Roman soldiers, as such would have understood neither the language nor the teaching of the Baptist. St. Augustine comments on this passage, as showing the lawfulness of bearing arms: "For he knew that soldiers, when they use their arms, are not homicides, but the ministers of the law; not the avengers of their own injuries, but the defenders of the public safety." The mention of the military profession in Scripture is very honourable. There is the centurion whose faith is commended;

82   I BAPTIZE YOU WITH WATER.   [St. Luke.

15 And as the people were || in expectation, and all men || mused in their hearts of John, whether he were the Christ, or not;

|| Or, *in suspense*.
|| Or, *reasoned, or, debated*.

16 John answered, saying unto *them* all, ⁿ I indeed baptize you with water; but one mightier than I cometh, the latchet of whose shoes I am not

ⁿ Matt. iii. 11.

---

16. "One mightier than I," rather " he that is mightier than I," Revisers.

the centurion at the cross; Cornelius; and the centurion who had charge of St. Paul on occasion of his shipwreck.

15. "And as the people were in expectation, and all men mused in their hearts," &c. The reader will remember the words of the Lord respecting John : " He was a burning and a shining light, and ye were willing for a season to rejoice in his light" (John v. 35); and how the Jews sent priests and scribes from Jerusalem to ask him, " Who art thou ? "

16. " John answered, saying unto them all, I indeed baptize you with water," &c. It is to be remarked that in each of the Evangelists it is expressly recorded that the Baptist denies that any spiritual grace attends his baptism (Matt. iii. 11; Mark i. 8; John i. 26, 33). The holy Baptist had to prepare the way of Christ, not only by preaching, but by baptizing; but if his baptism was the same as that of Christ—*i.e.*, if he baptized with the Holy Ghost, so that men should be grafted into Christ (if such a thing be conceivable), then there would be no need for the Lord to come, for the Lord's coming was in order that men should receive the Holy Ghost that they might be united to Him spiritually and sacramentally in the unity of His Body.

"But one mightier than I cometh, the latchet of whose shoes I am not worthy to unloose." St. Matthew tells us that he said, " whose shoes I am not worthy to bear." But St. Mark and St. Luke that he said, " whose shoe latchet I am not worthy to stoop down and unloose." But is it not probable, as St. Augustine suggests, that he used both these expressions at times ? They involve an acknowledgment of the infinite difference between Christ and all other men. St. John was by family great among his countrymen. His birth was foretold by an angel. His calling as the forerunner of Christ was foretold by two prophets, Isaiah and Malachi.

CHAP. III.] WHOSE FAN IS IN HIS HAND. 83

worthy to unloose: he shall baptize you with the Holy Ghost and with fire:

17 Whose fan *is* in his hand, and he will throughly

---

17. "And he will throughly purge." So A., C., D., L., all later Uncials, all Cursives, many old Latin, Vulg.; but ℵ, B., old Latin (a, e), Coptic, Armenian, read "to throughly purge."

He was "the friend of the bridegroom," "a burning and shining light." Of those born of women, none had risen greater than he. His character was one of the noblest in all Scripture. For him, then, to say such a thing of a fellow man certifies the believer that He of Whom such a thing could be said was more than man, and if more than man, Who and What was He?

"He shall baptize you with the Holy Ghost and with fire." Does this refer to Christ alone, considered apart from all visible agents or agency, such as His Church and ministers; or does it refer to Christ as present in His Church, and acting through His ministers? Unquestionably the latter. What are the last words of the Lord? "Go ye and disciple all nations, baptizing them," and "Lo, I am with you alway." I am with you in all your ministrations, that they should be Mine, not yours. Whatsoever ye do in My Name I do it.

Do Christ's ministers, then, when they baptize in His Name, baptize with the Holy Ghost, and with fire? Yes, unquestionably. If Christ, through their hands, imparts any gift of the Spirit, He imparts that which is likened to fire in its power of heating and purifying. How, then, is it that the members of the Church are so cold, so unpurified? Because this fire has to be watched, to be fed, to be shielded, to be at times almost rekindled. And both ministry and people are negligent, and take no heed to retain the gift— perhaps scout the idea that any gift worth speaking of is given. The reader will see, if he refers to my note on Matthew iii. 11, the various meanings and interpretations of this "baptism of fire," and all in a sense true. I find that Origen and Bede, quoted in "Catena Aurea," both understand it of that fire which shall try every man's work, alluded to by the Apostle in 1 Corinthians iii. 13.

17. "Whose fan is in his hand, and he will throughly purge his floor, and gather," &c. The fan here is not a winnowing fan, putting the air in violent motion, but rather a shovel where-

84   THE WHEAT AND THE CHAFF.   [St. Luke.

purge his floor, and °will gather the wheat into his garner;
but the chaff he will burn with fire unquenchable.

° Mic. iv. 12.
Matt. xiii. 30.

"And will gather." So A., C., D., L., later Uncials, Cursives, &c.; but א, B., old Latin (e), Armenian, read "to gather."

---

with the grain is tossed up, and, as it falls, the wind drives away the light chaff. It is ever to be remarked how closely grace and judgment are associated in the Gospel. We have in the last verse the crowning promise of grace: "He shall baptize you with the Holy Ghost." And here we have the certainty of judgment and separation by the same Divine Baptizer.

"Whose fan is in his hand." It is even now in His hand. The judgment of Christ, separating the radically evil from the good, goes on from the first, and is always going on, though it may be secretly, but it will be manifested in its fulness at the last day.

"And he will throughly purge his floor." The word for "throughly purge" seems to signify "He will purge it right through." It represents the husbandman as beginning, so to speak, on one side of the floor—the windward side,—and prosecuting his winnowing or cleansing operation right through, or through to the other side (Morison).

And, of course, it means, "will so thoroughly purge or cleanse it that not one grain of chaff shall remain hidden among the wheat. There shall in no wise enter into it anything that defileth."

"And will gather the wheat into his garner." "By this comparison the Lord shows that on the day of judgment He will discern the solid merits and fruits of virtue from the unfruitful lightness of empty boasting and vain deeds. . . . For that is, indeed, the more perfect fruit which was thought worthy to be like to Him who fell as a grain of wheat, that He might bring forth fruit in abundance " (Ambrose in "Cat. Aurea").

"But the chaff he will burn with fire unquenchable." It is idle to dispute whether this fire is metaphorical or real. Suppose it is a metaphor, yet those metaphors which represent things of another world do not generally exaggerate the reality and intensity of the things designed to be shadowed out by them.

Again, it has been suggested that this fire, whatever it be, annihilates, as material fire is assumed to do; but fire never annihilates. If it seizes upon wood, some parts of that wood it converts into

CHAP. III.] MANY OTHER THINGS PREACHED HE. 85

18 And many other things in his exhortation preached he unto the people.

19 ᵖ But Herod the tetrarch, being reproved by him for Herodias his brother Philip's wife, and for all the evils which Herod had done,

p Matt. xiv. 3.
Mark vi. 17.
A.D. 30.

20 Added yet this above all, that he shut up John in prison.

21 Now when all the people were baptized, ᑫ it

A.D. 27.
q Matt. iii. 13.
John i. 32.

---

18. "With many other exhortations preached he glad tidings" (Revisers). *Multa quidem et alia exhortans, evangelizabat populo.* (Vulg.)

19. "His brother Philip's wife." So A., C., K., some later Uncials and Cursives; but ℵ, B., D., I., most later Uncials, and very many Cursives, old Latin, and Vulg., omit "Philip."

cinder, and some is dispersed as steam or gas; but not a particle is annihilated.

18. "And many other things in his exhortation," &c. This may be more properly translated, "with many other exhortations preached he good tidings [or the Gospel] unto the people."

Among, then, many other things, was the proclamation of the "Lamb of God that taketh away the sin of the world;" and if all the latter verses of John iii. contain the Baptist's teaching, then at times he must have set forth very deep truths respecting the Son of God and His relations to His Father.

19. "But Herod the tetrarch, being reproved by him for Herodias," &c. This very slight mention of Herod's criminal marriage, and his conduct to John, is the only one in this Gospel; but in St. Luke only have we the account of the Lord being sent by Pilate to Herod, and of His being set at nought, and mocked by him. From St. Luke's words, "for all the evils which Herod had done," we learn that Herod's infamous union with Herodias was by no means the only crime for which St. John reproved him.

20. "Added yet this above all," &c. "Above all." The imprisonment of John was his greatest crime, for it came nearest to the sin against the Holy Spirit, Who was emphatically in St. John. It was not a mere yielding to lust; it was a desire, as far as possible, to quench the Light itself.

21. "Now when all the people were baptized," &c. The mention of this circumstance, that the baptism of Jesus took place the last

came to pass, that Jesus also being baptized, and praying, the heaven was opened,

---

of all, is peculiar to St. Luke, and requires notice. It cannot mean that it was at the conclusion of St. John's ministry of Baptism, for such a circumstance as that recorded in John iii. 23 (which took place long after the Lord's baptism), seems to forbid the idea. The only reason for its notice seems to be to show that the Lord was not baptized privately or separately, but after a crowd of others had received the same rite. "Thus do we behold Him, as in a scene brought before our eyes, going down with that promiscuous crowd as a man amongst men, as a sinner amongst sinners, yet Himself the Maker and Judge of all " (Williams).

"It came to pass that Jesus also being baptized, and praying." The mention of this, that our Lord was in the act of prayer when the Holy Ghost descended upon Him, is also peculiar to St. Luke; and it is very remarkable that St. Luke alone mentions that our Lord was praying when He began to be transfigured. This teaches us a lesson. The sacraments of Christ do not depend, as regards their inward part, on our prayers; but unless we pray earnestly, both on and after their reception, they are more likely to be to us a source of death unto death than of life unto life. As the article of the Church says: "Faith is confirmed and grace increased by virtue of prayer to God." If the Eternal Son, full of all grace, prayed so on the occasion of His Baptism, how earnestly ought parents and sponsors to pray on behalf of the young, and those baptized in riper years on behalf of themselves—that the seed may remain in them; that they may hold fast their profession; that the good work begun in them may be continued till the day of the Lord Jesus!

21, 22. "The heaven was opened, and the Holy Spirit descended in a bodily shape," &c. The words of St. Luke seem distinctly to express that the Holy Spirit was seen, at least by St. John the Baptist, to come down and alight on the Lord. Thus we read in John i. 33, that God said to him: "Upon whom thou shalt see the Spirit descending, and remaining on him." Now, if St. John was to see this great thing, the Spirit must take some form or appearance, and each of the four Evangelists assures us that He took the form of a dove; and to put this beyond doubt that the bodily eyes of John saw this outward and visible sign, St. Luke tells us

THE HOLY GHOST DESCENDED.

22 And the Holy Ghost descended in a bodily shape like

that the Holy Ghost descended *in a bodily shape* (or as the Revisers of 1881), "in a bodily form," as a dove. It is surprising how some believing commentators have endeavoured to explain this away. One tells us that we need not believe that the Spirit appeared under any specific form, but that He came upon the Lord with a hovering motion.

But what amazing absurdity! How could He be seen to hover if He had no visible form? A hovering motion cannot be seen. It must be something visible which descends, and hovers, and alights on any one.

Of all the forms which the Blessed Spirit could take, that of the dove seems the most appropriate, seeing that His fruits are love, peace, and gentleness. The Lord Himself, too, bids us be "harmless as doves."

And now a deeper question arises: Why did the Holy Spirit thus descend upon the Lord at this time? Had He not the fulness of the Spirit? Nay, inasmuch as He is the Second Person in the Godhead, does not the Spirit proceed from Him? Yes; but in the economy of His humiliation, He had to partake of our sanctification, He had to be baptized by that Spirit by which we are baptized. This, of course, was only with respect to His human nature, but that human nature was the instrument by which the Divine redeems us and sanctifies us, and unites us to Himself; and so, in some mysterious way, He to Whom in the Trinity the Holy Spirit is subordinate, condescended to lay aside His own power, and to do His mighty works by the Holy Ghost. Thus we read, "God anointed Jesus of Nazareth with the Holy Ghost, and with power, Who went about doing good, and healing all that were oppressed with the devil" (Acts x. 38); and even in the matter of the instruction of the Apostles, we read that the Lord "through the Holy Ghost gave commandment to the Apostles whom he had chosen" (Acts i. 2). Again, in the very next chapter it seems that He preached by the Spirit, for He claims for Himself the prophecy, "The Spirit of the Lord is upon me, because he hath anointed me to preach the Gospel to the poor." His Baptism was the commencement of His ministry: and as His ministers are fitted for their work by the consecration of the Spirit, so was He. In fact, the Spirit of God co-operates in all the Redeeming Work: through

88 THOU ART MY BELOVED SON. [St. Luke.

a dove upon him, and a voice came from heaven, which said, Thou art my beloved Son; in thee I am well pleased.

23 And Jesus himself began to be ʳ about thirty years of age, being (as was supposed) ˢ the son of Joseph, which was *the son* of Heli,

ʳ See Num. iv. 3, 35, 39, 43, 47.
ˢ Matt. xiii. 55. John vi. 42.

---

23. "And Jesus himself began to be about," &c.; or, as Revisers, "And Jesus himself, when he began to *teach*, was about," &c.

Him the Lord was Incarnate; through Him He was baptized; through Him He did His mighty works. Even in the work of the Cross the Spirit was present, for we read, "Through the Eternal Spirit he offered himself without spot to God" (Hebrews ix. 14). "By the Spirit he was raised from the dead" (Rom. i. 4), and by the Spirit he will raise us from the dead (Rom. viii. 11).

"A voice came from heaven, which said, Thou art my beloved Son; in thee I am well pleased." St. Matthew says that the voice of the Father said, "This is my beloved Son." St. Mark and St. Luke agree in representing the words to have been "Thou art my beloved Son, in thee I am well pleased." No doubt we must take the testimony of the two latter as being the more accurate, and St. Matthew by no means contradicts it, but gives the same sense. It is not impossible that the words as addressed to the Lord sounded, "Thou art my beloved Son," whereas in order that St. John, and it may be others, might be certain as to the Person, the Divine Voice sounded to them, "This is my beloved Son."

We now come to St. Luke's account of the genealogy of the Lord.

The following remarks will, I trust, be sufficient (in addition to the excursus on these genealogies at the conclusion of my commentary on St. Matthew) to enable the reader to form some judgment respecting the difficulties of the whole matter, and how little they affect any truth respecting the Lord Himself, or any view which reasonable persons may entertain respecting the inspiration of the Evangelists.

1. The truth that our Blessed Lord was the lineal descendant of David, and the inheritor of the promises made to him, depends (in the case of Gentile Christians, such as ourselves), in no respect upon either of these genealogies, but amongst other Scripture testimonies upon the express words of the Lord Himself, when He says, "I

CHAP. III.] THE GENEALOGY OF CHRIST. 89

24 Which was *the son* of Matthat, which was *the son* of Levi, which was *the son* of Melchi, which was *the son* of Janna, which was *the son* of Joseph,

25 Which was *the son* of Mattathias, which was *the son* of Amos, which was *the son* of Naum, which was *the son* of Esli, which was *the son* of Nagge,

---

am the Root and the Offspring of David " (Rev. xxii. 16), and those of two of His Apostles, one of whom says, "God had sworn with an oath to David, that of the fruit of his loins he would set one upon his throne," and then declares that this is fulfilled in the Lord's Resurrection (Acts ii. 31), and the other with equal clearness writes that the Lord was made of the seed of David according to the flesh (Rom. i. 3).

2. But though we who believe in the truth of the New Testament do not depend upon the testimony of these documents for the truth that the Lord was the Son of David, they were absolutely necessary for the Jews at the time when the New Testament was written; for the Jews had a right to demand that the lineage of Him Whom they supposed to have been the Lord's earthly father, should be traced up to David. This, it appears to me, must have been, in any serious investigation, the first preliminary. Whatever the nature of the Lord's miracles and discourses, if it could have been shown that His reputed father was not of the house of David, His claims would not have been listened to, even by candid and well-disposed Jews.

3. The two genealogies preserved to us must have been copied verbatim from well-known documents, and must represent the difficulties, and if there were such, the omissions or inaccuracies of such documents. If the Evangelists had attempted to correct what they found in the public rolls, it would immediately have been objected against them that they had not faithfully reproduced what they had found written therein. It seems clear that they did not correct these documents by the Old Testament itself, as they might have done in one instance at least, that is, in the case of the parentage and the family of Salathiel, for in the Chronicles (1 Chron. iii. 17), Salathiel is the son of Jeconiah, whereas in St. Luke he is the son of Neri; and in the Chronicles Zorobabel is the son of Pedaiah, whereas in both St. Matthew and St. Luke he is the son of Salathiel.

26 Which was *the son* of Maath, which was *the son* of Mattathias, which was *the son* of Semei, which was *the son* of Joseph, which was *the son* of Juda,

27 Which was *the son* of Joanna, which was *the son* of Rhesa, which was *the son* of Zorobabel, which was *the son* of Salathiel, which was *the son* of Neri,

---

27. "Rhesa, which was the son of Zorobabel." Some suppose this name Rhesa to have been a title, that of " head " or " chief," mistaken for a proper name. Rhesa is not mentioned in the Chronicles as a son of Zorobabel.

4. All the original documents containing the Lord's lineage, together with any notes which may have explained their difficulties and cleared up their obscurities, having perished utterly, it follows that all the ways suggested by all subsequent authors, of reconciling any supposed discrepancies between the two genealogies, are the merest conjectures; the greater part wholly the creatures of imagination. This remark applies to *every* scheme of explaining these difficulties.

5. It applies, for instance, to a popular explanation, which, as far as I can see, is worthless in removing any difficulty, that St. Matthew gives the royal line of succession, and St. Luke the natural pedigree. Of course the line in St. Matthew between David and Jeconiah or Zorobabel is the royal line, but it is equally a natural line, the son succeeding his father without a break from David to Jeconiah, and though in one case three generations are omitted, yet the fourth generation descends lineally from the first of the three, *i.e.*, Uzziah or Ozias from Joram (Matth. i. 8).

But what ground can there be for designating the line from Zorobabel to Joseph as a Royal Line, as distinguished from a natural line ? Is there a shadow of evidence that the Jews recognized the line of Zorobabel's son Abiud as inheriting, rather than any other, the kingly succession ? If so, what authority designated each member of the chain as the heir of David's Royalty ? It is absolutely impossible to say which of the two lines, that of Jacob, the father of Joseph, from Abiud, the son of Zorobabel, or that of Heli, the father of Joseph, from Rhesa (or, if Rhesa be a title), from Joanna, the son of Zorobabel, be the inheriting line. It is impossible to say whether any one member of either of these successions succeeded the one before him by natural generation, by Levirate raising

CHAP. III.] THE GENEALOGY OF CHRIST. 91

28 Which was *the son* of Melchi, which was *the son* of Addi, which was *the son* of Cosam, which was *the son* of Elmodam, which was *the son* of Er,

29 Which was *the son* of Jose, which was *the son* of Eliezer, which was *the son* of Jorim, which was *the son* of Matthat, which was *the son* of Levi,

---

29. "Which was the son of Jose." So A., E., G., H., K., M., S., and some other later Uncials ; but ℵ, B., L., a few Cursives (13, 33, 69, 346), read Jesus ('Ιησοῦς). *Qui fuit Jesu* (Vulg.).

of seed, by adoption from some collateral branch, or by intermarriage; and so, through a female link which would be quite admissible in the point of succession to all rights of property, though the name of the female might not appear on the rolls. We may also add that the words of the prophet Jeremiah in chapter xxii. 30, seem to cut off the seed of Jeconiah (and he is assumed to have seed) from inheriting the throne ; and this curse very probably applies to his descendants, or to any whom he would desire to make the heir of his pretensions.

6. I think that respect for the letter of Scripture would make us regard the succession given in St. Matthew as direct, *i.e.*, from father to son, by natural generation, because St. Matthew uses in the case of each member of the succession the word "begat." "Abraham begat Isaac," and in the case of the last link, where the reputed father did not beget, the mother, who was the real link, is mentioned. "Jacob begat Joseph, the husband of Mary, of whom was born (or begotten) Jesus."

Whereas the term used by St. Luke "son of," or rather simply " of," is more open to succession by adoption or by marriage with a daughter. In both the first and last links of the chain, Jesus, the son of Joseph, and Adam, the son of God, there is no descent by natural generation.

7. It appears that in St. Luke's line from Nathan, the son of David, to Joseph, there are forty-one generations. Now I need hardly remind anyone who has given even the most cursory attention to the subject, that the probabilities are exceedingly great against a genealogy extending over above a thousand years being preserved except through female links. In fact, taking into account the law of probabilities, it would require a miracle to keep it up

30 Which was *the son* of Simeon, which was *the son* of Juda, which was *the son* of Joseph, which was *the son* of Jonan, which was *the son* of Eliakim,

31 Which was *the son* of Melea, which was *the son* of Menan, which was *the son* of Mattatha, which was *the son* of ᵗ Nathan, ᵘ which was *the son* of David,

<small>ᵗ Zech. xii. 12.
ᵘ 2 Sam. v. 14.
1 Chr. iii. 5.</small>

solely in the male line. Several of our own oldest titles of nobility are preserved through female succession. Now the law of Moses makes express provision for the succession of property through female heirs. Though then the names of females may, in accordance with Jewish custom, be omitted from the rolls—the rights of property, and, if of property, no doubt other rights must descend through them, in default of male heirs. So that in the genealogies of St. Matthew from Zorobabel to Joseph, and in that of St. Luke from Nathan to Joseph, involving very probably sixty acts of succession, there must have been, according to the law of probabilities, many cases of succession through females, unless, of course, it was ordered otherwise by some providential interference.

The way is now open to us for considering anew the great *crux* in these genealogies as compared together, and that is the relation of Joseph, the Lord's reputed father, to Jacob, who in St. Matthew's genealogy is said to have begotten him, and to Heli, of whom, in St. Luke's genealogy, he is said to have been the son (" of Heli," however, is the expression), but without specifying the nature of the sonship, which St. Matthew does.

Since St. Matthew specifies that the relation between the two, Joseph and Jacob, was by natural generation (Jacob begat Joseph), it would seem to require overwhelming evidence to set this aside, and consequently we must at first take it for granted, and consider how St. Luke can with propriety call Joseph the son of Heli otherwise than by natural generation.

Three ways of so doing—all of them, of course, in our present state of knowledge, conjectural—have been put forth.

1. By calling in the operation of the Levirate law.
2. By simple adoption.
3. By intermarriage: Joseph marrying a daughter of Heli, who had no sons, and so becoming of his family, and consequently his heir.

CHAP. III.] THE GENEALOGY OF CHRIST.

32 ˣ Which was *the son* of Jesse, which was *the son* of Obed, which was *the son* of Booz, which was *the son* of Salmon, which was *the son* of Naasson,

ˣ Ruth iv. 18, &c. 1 Chr. ii. 10, &c.

---

1. The first of these is a very old opinion in the Christian Church, being adopted by most of the Christian Fathers. It can be traced to Africanus, a writer of the third century, and is to be found at length in the seventh chapter of the first book of Eusebius. This Africanus professes to give the genealogy as handed down amongst the descendants of the Lord's own relatives; but whether he himself investigated the matter carefully, or even received it at first hand from these relatives, is very doubtful. The account he gives is this:—" Matthan, whose descent is traced to Solomon, begat Jacob; Matthan dying, Melchi, whose lineage is from Nathan, by marrying the widow of the former, had Heli. Hence Heli and Jacob were brothers by the same mother, and Heli dying childless, Jacob reared up seed to him, having Joseph, according to nature, belonging to himself, but by the law to Heli. Thus Joseph was the son of both."

This is, as far as I can make out, the *fons et origo* of all the opinions of the later Fathers, and the reader will see in a moment how utterly worthless it is, for Julius Africanus in reproducing it cannot have taken the trouble to refer to the genealogies in the Gospels, for if he had he would have seen that Melchi was the grandfather of Matthat (or Matthan, supposing them to have been the same person), and could not, if any reliance is to be placed in St. Luke's account, have married as his second wife Matthat's widow.

This oldest opinion, then, though supposed to be derived from the descendants of our Lord's relatives, is on the face of it worthless in explaining the discrepancy in our two Evangelical genealogies.

The Levirate hypothesis is, in the case of the Lord's genealogy, a singularly difficult and unlikely one, for from Salathiel to Joseph there are two separate lines of succession, each member of which has a different father and grandfather, and these two lines have to be assumed to coalesce, so that two members of them (contemporaries) should be brothers by the same father. In order to this it has to be assumed, without the smallest atom of evidence, that a member of one line marries a widow of the other, who has had already one child, and he has one child by her; that of these two half-brothers

33 Which was *the son* of Aminadab, which was *the son* of Aram, which was *the son* of Esrom, which was *the son* of Phares, which was *the son* of Juda,

---

33. We have no less than five genealogies, or parts of genealogies, witnessing to the sequence of names in this verse as being Naasson and Aminadab, Aram or Ram and Esrom, viz., Numb. ii. 3; Ruth iv. 18, 19; 1 Chron. ii. 9, 10; Matt. i. 3, 4; and the universally received reading of this place in St. Luke. The Septuagint reproduces these names exactly, so does the Syriac; and yet, in the face of all this, we have such a critic as Tischendorf reading [the son] of Naasson, of Aminadab, of Admin, of Arni, thus introducing another generation, totally unknown before, into this sacred genealogy, simply because א reads [son of] Adam, of Admin, of Arni (three generations, where in the sacred text there is but two; and substituting a word beginning with א, aleph, for a word beginning with ע, ayin). And we have also Professors Westcott and Hort reading [son of] Naasson, of Admin [or Adam], of Arni, thus perpetuating the blunders of the scribes of two MSS., א and B., who, contrary to all other authorities, wrote Adam or Admin and Arni. Surely these two learned men cannot believe, on the strength of two unknown scribes, that Naasson's father was ever called Admin or his grandfather Arni!

one is childless, and the other being his uterine brother, and so not bound by the Levirate law to raise up seed to his half-brother, consents to do so, and a woman hitherto childless bears seed to him. Add to this the opinion of Jewish doctors that the Levirate law had not been enforced from before the Captivity, and the balance of probabilities against the citation of it to solve difficulties seems overwhelming.

2. Adoption, unless it be from a collateral branch, breaks the line of succession, for the original line is supposed to be practically extinct, and an offshoot from some parallel line is chosen by some childless member of the first line. But there are two great difficulties attending it. In the first place, the ancestors of the adopted scion become virtually *the direct* line. If, then, the adopted person be of the lineage of David, his ancestors displace the ancestors of the members of the line which has adopted him. If he is not of the lineage of David, then that lineage becomes extinct, for no adoption can confer the reality of that blood relationship which is implied in the words "He was of the house and lineage of David," or "I am the offspring of David."

3. Then remains the hypothesis of intermarriage. In which case Joseph, by marrying the daughter of Heli, would become his son by marriage as really and truly as he would have been if Heli had died childless, and his brother Jacob had begotten him of Heli's widow, or if Heli had simply adopted him from the collateral branch.

Chap. III.] THE GENEALOGY OF CHRIST. 95

34 Which was *the son* of Jacob, which was *the son* of Isaac, which was *the son* of Abraham, ʸ which was *the son* of Thara, which was *the son* of Nachor,

ʸ Gen. xi. 24, 26.

There is but one objection to this—a very strong one in appearance at first, but which becomes weaker and weaker the more it is examined. It is that the Christian Fathers never adopt this way of reconciling the two genealogies, but prefer bringing in the Levirate law. But the more the Fathers are examined, the more ignorant they will be found to be of all Jewish matters. The greater part of them seem to recognize no meaning in the Old Testament except some typical one. Now it appears from the testimony of Dr. Mill that both St. John Damascene and St. Ambrose virtually adopt the testimony of Julius Africanus without any attempt to correct his manifest blunder respecting Melchi taking as his second wife the widow of one who, according to St. Luke's genealogy, is his grandson. The fact is, that the Fathers took without examination the testimony of one who offered them a tradition, which he said was traceable to the descendants of the Lord's family.

Now against this we have to set a tradition handed down, singularly enough, from the most bitter enemies of the Lord and of His Mother, viz., that Mary was the daughter of Heli,[1] and being without brothers, Joseph, by marrying her, would become the heir, and in all probability the adopted son of Heli. Mill urges against this that we receive this tradition from the enemies of the Lord, but on that very account it is almost certain to be true, for from what source could the Jews have received such a tradition? Evidently not from the Evangelists, for neither of them mention Mary's name in the genealogy, and it is to the last degree improbable that

---

[1] I have given it in my excursus at the end of my notes on St. Matthew. Lightfoot gives a remarkable citation in point, so blasphemous, however, that one hardly likes to write it. It is this:— "One who had been in hell, vidit etiam Mariam filiam Eli suspensam in umbris per glandulas mamillarum." "Hieros: Sanhedrin," fol. 23, 3, et "Babyl. Sanhedrin," fol. 44, 2, quoted also in Schoetgen's "Horæ Hebraicæ et Talmudicæ," tom. ii. lib. ix. cap. ii.

96 THE GENEALOGY OF CHRIST. [ST. LUKE.

35 Which was *the son* of Saruch, which was *the son* of Ragau, which was *the son* of Phalec, which was *the son* of Heber, which was *the son* of Sala,

---

the Jews would assist the Christians to reconcile a serious discrepancy between two of their sacred books. No account whatsoever can be given of the origin of such an opinion amongst the Lord's enemies, except its foundation in the truth. If it be asked, how was it that the Fathers of the Christian Church did not adopt it, we answer that they were most probably in profound ignorance about it. They had no communication with the Jews; very few among them understood the Hebrew of the Old Testament, fewer still the Talmudic Hebrew. The later Jewish literature seems to have been utterly unknown to them. I believe, then, that this Levirate tradition is the solution of the difficulty. Joseph could not have had two natural fathers. Jacob is expressly said to be his father by natural generation (Jacob begat Joseph). Joseph, then, could not be the true son of Heli. He must be his son either by Levirate " raising of seed," in which case we have to invent most unlikely hypotheses to make Jacob and Heli brothers, though they have both different fathers and grandfathers—or by adoption ; but Heli must have had some reasonable ground for adopting Joseph, and what more reasonable than that which supposes the Blessed Virgin to be the daughter of Heli ?

One more difficulty which arises from the comparison of the two genealogies, requires examination. The two lines coalesce in Salathiel and Zorobabel, but in Matthew i., Salathiel is the son of Jeconiah, whereas in Luke iii. 27, Salathiel is said to be the son of Neri. This has been explained on the hypothesis that Jeconiah was absolutely childless, and that whilst in Babylon he adopted Salathiel, whose real father was Neri, as being the head of the collateral family. Jeconiah is assumed to have died childless, because of the curse pronounced upon him in Jeremiah xxii. 30, " Write ye this man childless." But in the verse but one before this, he is assumed to have " seed." " Is this man Coniah a despised broken idol ? is he a vessel wherein is no pleasure? wherefore are they cast out, he and his seed, and are cast into a land which they know not ? " Also in 1 Chron. iii. 17, he has apparently eight sons. There can be no doubt that the word barren (" ariri "), in Jeremiah xxii.,

CHAP. III.] THE GENEALOGY OF CHRIST. 97

36 ᶻ Which was *the son* of Cainan, which was *the son* of Arphaxad, ᵃ which was *the son* of Sem, which was *the son* of Noe, which was *the son* of Lamech,

37 Which was *the son* of Mathusala, which was *the son* of Enoch, which was *the son* of Jared, which was *the son* of Maleleel, which was *the son* of Cainan,

ᶻ See Gen. xi. 12.
ᵃ Gen. v. 6, &c. & xi. 10, &c.

---

really signifies "desolate," and its meaning is to be ascertained from the latter part of verse 30, "A man that shall not prosper in his days, for none of his seed shall prosper, sitting upon the throne of David, and ruling any more in Judah." This evidently means that his desolation should consist in himself and his family being deprived of the kingly crown and succession. Neither Assir nor Salathiel succeeded to the kingly title; and though great honour was done to his faithful grandson, Zorobabel, in that he took part in the building of the Temple, yet he did not this as a king, but simply as the head of a chief Jewish family. All through Ezra and Nehemiah he shares the authority with others, with Joshua, with Nehemiah, and their compatriots. There is then a *primâ facie* case for taking the words of St. Matthew: "Jeconiah begat Salathiel," literally; in which case, probably, he had married the daughter of Neri, and so Salathiel was, as in St. Luke, "of Neri," being his grandson. This, of course, is a conjecture, but it is quite as reasonable as bringing in a Levirate marriage. It is also more reasonable than the supposition of simple adoption on the part of Jeconiah, for both in St. Matthew and in the Chronicles, Jeconiah is said to be the father of Salathiel, and Salathiel was one of several brothers.

There is also a minor difficulty in reconciling both the New Testament genealogies with that in the Book of Chronicles, respecting the children of Zorobabel, but at this distance of time, and with no contemporary information at hand, all such attempts are mere conjectures; and the two Evangelists, by taking no notice of the genealogy in 1 Chron. iii., seem to have set it aside, and to rely on their own sources of information as preferable.

St. Luke then in giving the genealogy of Heli, the father of the Blessed Virgin, follows up the line which he had already taken in bringing her into the foreground, and showing her exalted position as the one real parent of the Lord. Both of the genealogies were

H

38 Which was *the son* of Enos, which was *the son* of Seth,
which was *the son* of Adam, ^bwhich was *the son*
of God.

^b Gen. v. 1, 2.

---

necessary to the Jew. In the first stage of Gospel preaching the rightful claims of Joseph were all important, but afterwards, in the second stage of that preaching, when the Lord's miraculous conception was more fully realized, it was well that there should be the evidence of a double descent. The custom of the Jews would forbid the name of the inheriting female, but every one of common sense, when he came into possession of the two Evangelists, would know that because Joseph could not have two natural fathers, St. Luke's expression "(son) of Heli" must be explained otherwise than of natural generation. That the parentage of Mary should be so soon forgotten, or not known accurately, is, I grant, very strange, but the strangeness almost vanishes when we consider the extraordinary ignorance of the Christian Fathers of all purely Jewish matters, and the tradition amongst the bitter enemies of the faith, that she was the daughter of Heli, is perfectly unaccountable except on the hypothesis of its truth.

In verse 36 there is also a difficulty of a lesser sort, that a second Cainan should be inserted into the line. In this St. Luke follows the Septuagint, which both in Genesis x. 24 and xi. 12, introduces this name.

St. Luke carries back the genealogy to Adam. "Adam, who was the [son] of God." Thus the Lord, though He be the only-begotten Son of God, and the Son of God because His pure human nature was created in the womb of the Virgin by the power of the Holy Ghost, is yet the Son of God in the same sense as all His brethren, for we all are, as St. Paul, quoting a Greek poet, says, "the offspring of God."

CHAP. IV.

AND ^a Jesus being full of the Holy Ghost returned from Jordan, and ^b was led by the Spirit into the wilderness,

2 Being forty days tempted of the devil. And ^c in those days he did eat nothing: and when they were ended, he afterward hungered.

^a Matt. iv. 1. Mark i. 12.
^b ver. 14. ch. ii. 27.
^c Ex. xxxiv. 28. 1 Kin. xix. 18.

---

1. "Into the wilderness." So A., E., G., H., K., M., other later Uncials, almost all Cursives, some old Latin (c, e, f, l), Vulg., Coptic, Syriac; but ℵ, B., D., L., some old Latin (a, b, g¹, q), Sah., read, "In the wilderness."

"And was led," &c. Revisers translate, "And was led by the Spirit in the wilderness forty days, being tempted of the devil."

1. "And Jesus being full of the Holy Ghost returned from Jordan," &c. "Full of the Holy Ghost." This carries us back to iii. 22, where we are told that the Holy Ghost "descended upon him in a bodily shape." The genealogy, then, is to be considered as in a parenthesis, and the temptation by Satan follows immediately upon the Baptism of the Spirit, and the witness of the Father that He is His beloved Son.

"Returned from Jordan." Some think that this expresses the Lord's human intention to return to Galilee, and commence a ministry there, but that in this He was overruled by the Will of His Father, Who foresaw that He must be perfected for His Messianic Ministry by the endurance of temptations especially adapted to try His fitness for that ministry. As I have shown in my notes on St. Matthew, all the recorded temptations are addressed to Him as the Christ, the Second Adam.

2. "Being forty days tempted of the devil." Comparing this with Mark i. 13, there can be little doubt but that the Lord was during the whole forty days exposed to the assaults of the evil one, and that the three temptations actually recorded are the last and crowning ones.

"And in those days he did eat nothing." These words seem intended to teach us that the Lord's fast was a total abstinence

3 And the devil said unto him, If thou be the Son of God, command this stone that it be made bread.

---

from all nourishment. He must, consequently, have been miraculously sustained to endure so prolonged a deprivation of necessary food.

Now, for what purpose did He endure this? It was not merely to teach us that, after His example, we must subdue the flesh to the Spirit, but to give the tempter every advantage, and so to bring out more fully the strength of His devout and obedient will. After such abstention, the demand of the exhausted body for nourishment would be overpowering. The Lord would feel Himself fainting, sinking unto death, and so the tempter would seize the opportunity to urge Him to sustain His life by a miracle, which, if He were the Son of God, would be a very small, and apparently harmless, exertion of His power.

2. "And the devil said unto him, If thou be the Son of God [as thou wast proclaimed to be] command this stone that it be made bread." What would have been the sin of working a miracle to sustain an almost ebbing life? Evidently this. By assuming our nature, and becoming the Son of man for our sakes, He had voluntarily submitted to all the conditions under which we, as creatures of God, have to exist. One of these, in fact, the very first, is that we are to depend upon God for all the things needful for the support of our life. And as *we* have to depend upon God's providence for our daily bread, so must the Son of God. For the Lord to have used His miraculous power to sustain His own life, would have been to lift up Himself above His own sphere as a Son of man. He had taken our flesh and blood, in order that He might experience to the uttermost the privations to which that flesh and blood is exposed, and set us an example that we are not to deliver ourselves from such privations in our own way, and at our own time, but to await God's providence, to be exercised in His own time. The Father had given to the Son a commandment "what he should do," and to deliver Himself from His present straits by a miracle was not in that commandment. The Lord was now about to commence a ministry which He was to commend to the people's notice and acceptance by miracles, and He must show that the power which He exercised was never to be exercised independently of God: in fact, that it was not strictly

CHAP. IV.] NOT BY BREAD ALONE. 101

4 And Jesus answered him, saying, ᵈ It is written, That man shall not live by bread alone, but by every ᵈ Deut. viii. 3. word of God.

5 And the devil, taking him up into an high mountain,

---

4. "But by every word of God." So A., D., all later Uncials, all Cursives, old Latin, Vulg., Syriac, Gothic, Armenian; omitted by ℵ, B., L., Sah., and Coptic.

5. "Into an high mountain." So A., later Uncials, all Cursives, some old Latin (c, b), Gothic, Syriac; but omitted by ℵ, B., L., some old Latin (b, g 1 2), Vulg. (Cod. Amiat.), Sah., Coptic.

His own power as the Second Person of the Trinity, but the power of the Spirit Who proceeds from God, and so was never to be exercised, except at the express will of God.

4. "And Jesus answered him, saying, It is written, that man shall not live by," &c. The answer is taken from the Book of Deuteronomy (viii. 3), where God, through Moses, tells the children of Israel that He fed them in the wilderness by the miraculously produced food of manna, to teach them that God could sustain His creatures by any means which He chose. By food which seemed to come down from heaven, or, if it seemed to Him good, by no external food at all, but by His mere Word infusing internal strength of body. So He sustained Moses and Elijah in their long fasts, and so He had for the last forty days sustained the human nature of His Son.

"But by every word." Or, perhaps, by every "thing spoken by" God, because the words of God are always with power, making that to be which was not before in existence. Making bread where there was no bread, or bringing water out of the rock of flint.

This temptation, and our Lord's answer to it, teaches us a most needful moral. "It may be taken as a type of a class of temptations to which the greater part of men are especially liable. In our Lord's hunger we may see a type of the straits and necessities into which we sometimes fall in our worldly condition; and in the temptation of Satan an example of the unlawful and indirect ways in which men are tempted to escape from them." . . . "Our Lord's conduct is an example of trust in the providential care of God, and of the duty of abstaining from all unsanctioned ways of providing for ourselves" (Manning's Sermons, vol. ii. ch. vi.).

5. "And the devil, taking him up into a high mountain, shewed unto him," &c. We shall consider fully in a note at the end of the

shewed unto him all the kingdoms of the world in a moment of time.

6 And the devil said unto him, All this power will I give thee, and the glory of them: for ᵉthat is delivered unto me; and to whomsoever I will I give it.

ᵉ John xii. 31.
& xiv. 30. Rev.
xiii. 2, 7.

---

account of the temptation whether it is more reasonable to consider this transportation of the Lord to the top of the mountain to have been objective or subjective, *i.e.*, whether Satan led the Lord's Body to the top of an actual mountain, or whether it was all in vision, and took place entirely in the brain of the Son of God, and had no outward reality. Anyhow, we must treat it as if the Lord saw, or had pictured before Him, all the kingdoms of the world, so that the sight of them should stir up any feelings of ambition, or desire of rule over men, or of outward pomp and glory which Satan might assume to be in One Who, being the Son of God, was of necessity the heir of unbounded power and greatness.

Assuming the occurrence to have been objective, *i.e.*, taking place in the outer world of time and sense, there was a mountain not far off, which seems adapted to be the scene of such a display. "Directly west," writes Dr. Thompson, "is the high and precipitous mountain, called Quarantania, from a tradition that our Lord here fasted forty days and forty nights, and also that this is the high mountain from whose top the tempter exhibited 'all the kingdoms of the world, and the glory of them.' The side facing the plain is as perpendicular and apparently as high as the rock of Gibraltar." Of course, the highest mountain in the world would not afford a prospect of above one or two hundred miles; but any mountain of great elevation, and with an unimpeded view, would afford a far more suitable scene for such a display than the plains beneath it.

6. "And the devil said unto him, All this power will I give thee . . . for that is delivered unto me." These words of Satan are peculiar to St. Luke. Were they a mere impudent falsehood, or is there a truth in them? Unquestionably the Lord admits a certain degree of truth in then, when He speaks of Satan being "the prince of this world." The Holy Ghost, by the mouth of St. Paul, bears witness to it when he calls Satan the "god of this world." And St. John, also, when he speaks of the whole world "lying in the evil one" (1 John v. 19, Revisers).

CHAP. IV.] GET THEE BEHIND ME, SATAN. 103

7 If thou therefore wilt || worship me, all shall be thine.

8 And Jesus answered and said unto him, Get thee behind me, Satan: for ᶠ it is written, Thou

|| Or, *fall down before me.*

ᶠ Deut. vi. 13. & x. 20.

---

7. All shall be thine ;" or, rather, "It shall be all thine." So ℵ, A., B., D., L., later Uncials, almost all Cursives.
8. "Get thee behind me, Satan," omitted by ℵ, B., D., L., several Cursives (1, 8, 22, 33, 118, 131, 251), some old Latin, Vulg., Gothic, Sah., Coptic, Syriac, Armenian ; retained by A., later Uncials, most Cursives.

Taking Satan to be the ruler of this world by means of its idolatry and wickedness, what he means is, that if the Lord will do him but one single act of homage—for the word need mean no more than the obeisance which an inferior pays to his lord—he will leave the world to Christ, so that from that moment the war between good and evil would end; so that the Lord, without any further humiliation or suffering, may at once set up His Church, and gather all nations into it, without conflict, without martyrdom, without persecution, without apostasy, without the loss of a single soul. This was the intended sting of the temptation. It is impossible to suppose that such a being as Satan, intent upon frustrating the will of God, should have allowed himself to be ignorant of the contents of those Scriptures which set forth God's designs. He must then have known that He Whom he was tempting was—if He was the Christ—the Heir of the world; but that it could only be after a long and bitter conflict that He would enter upon His inheritance. By what, then, did he attempt to seduce the Lord? Not merely by dazzling His eyes with the glory of the world, but by holding out to Him the prospect of a speedy and easy acquirement of it. This was the very essence and spirit of the temptation. So the Lord would take it; and it is very remarkable that when the same allurement of an easy and painless conquest was suggested by his chief follower, it was repelled by the same words, "Get thee behind me, Satan" (Matt. xvi. 23).

8. "And Jesus answered and said unto him, Get thee behind me, Satan," &c. Worship such as Satan demanded would have been an acknowledgment that Satan was a lawful power in God's universe. When men bow before God they acknowledge that He is the rightful Ruler of all, and that He rules all things rightly, and is the source of all power and blessing. And the very least homage to Satan from our Lord would mean that Satan's dominion was

104 HE BROUGHT HIM TO JERUSALEM. [ST. LUKE.

shalt worship the Lord thy God, and him only shalt thou serve.

g Matt. iv. 5. 9 ᵍ And he brought him to Jerusalem, and set

---

not usurped, but of right; that it was not only by God's sufferance, but by His will. Godet expresses this well where he writes on this passage: "The act of prostration in the East is practised to every lawful superior, not in virtue of his personal character, but out of regard to the portion of Divine power of which he is the depositary. Satan had a certain tolerated, and yet usurped and wrongful, power over the world and its kingdoms; but this was only to last till a kingdom should be established which was 'not of this world.' The Lord, now tempted by Satan, was to establish this kingdom; and the smallest inclination of His head to Satan would have been an acknowledgment of the rightful power of the god of this world, in that no kingdom could be in it except by his allowance and sanction."

The reader will see at once the moral lesson. He who would seek to establish the truth by the smallest concession to falsehood (known to be such), bows to Satan. He who would use superstition or pious fraud for the upholding of the Church, bows to Satan. He who would make deliberate use of fanaticism for the advance or maintenance of religion, bows to Satan. And, in the broadest and most universal sense, he who would do evil that good may come, bows to Satan.

"For it is written, Thou shalt worship the Lord thy God, and him only shalt thou serve." Our Lord repels the temptation; not by quoting the mere words, but the full meaning and spirit of two or three passages out of Deuteronomy—one (vi. 13), "Thou shalt fear the Lord thy God, and serve him, and shalt swear by his name. Ye shall not go after other gods, of the gods of the people which are round about you." The others, Deut. x. 12, and xiii. 4. All these imply that God was the sole object of such obeisance or reverence as Satan asked for.

9. "And he brought him to Jerusalem, and set him," &c. This temptation, which is put last in St. Luke, is, according to St. Matthew's account, the second in order. The last words of the Lord, "Get thee behind me, Satan," seem a final dismissal of the evil one; and so St. Matthew adds, "Then the devil leaveth him,

him on a pinnacle of the temple, and said unto him, If thou be the Son of God, cast thyself down from hence:

10 For ^h it is written, He shall give his angels charge over thee, to keep thee: ^h Ps. xci. 11.

---

9. "If thou be the Son of God." Article omitted before "Son" in ℵ, A., B., D., L., later Uncials, and most Cursives.

and behold angels came and ministered unto him." And yet there is a deep reason why St. Luke should put this the last, for it is, in a sense, the culminating one. It directly addresses itself to our Lord's sense of His highest spiritual relationship to His Father—in fact, to His faith in God,—that the Lord should exaggerate that faith, that sense of the constant nearness of God's gracious help, and turn it into presumption. The first temptation was that He should act independently of God, and turn the stones into bread, apart from His Father's will; the second, that He should receive aid to establish His kingdom from another than God; but this third is that He should rely upon God's help, where and when that help was not promised.

"A pinnacle of the temple"—probably the roof of a porch built by Herod, called the Royal Porch, from which, as Josephus says, the eye looked down into an abyss.

The evil one now, in his turn, cites Scripture. He quotes Ps. xci.: "He shall give his angels charge over thee to keep thee in all thy ways. They shall bear thee up in their hands, lest thou dash thy foot against a stone." This Psalm is not specially Messianic, and is full of promises of comfort to every godly man; but, of course, it must *à fortiori* apply to One Who could be, in any true sense, called God's Son.

This temptation, as I have said, suggested "a presumptuous dependence upon God in circumstances to which He had not promised to extend it, and a consequent presumption in running into dangers." Such a temptation can only be addressed to religious persons, but in various shapes and ways it is constantly held before them, so that it behoves every child of God to be assured before he takes any unwonted line of action that in doing so he is strictly in the path of duty.—that there can be no doubt respecting what is the will of God in the matter, or else he cannot claim the Divine Protection or the Divine Blessing. Suppose, for instance, a reli-

THOU SHALT NOT TEMPT THE LORD.

11 And in *their* hands they shall bear thee up, lest at any time thou dash thy foot against a stone.

i Deut. vi. 16.   12 And Jesus answering said unto him, ¹ It is said, Thou shalt not tempt the Lord thy God.

---

gious person thinks himself called to preach the Gospel in some way which experience shows to be sure to end in multiplying or intensifying the divisions in the Church,—ought he not to pause, and consider how earnestly Christ prays for the unity of His Church, and how solemnly and frequently the Apostles commend that unity to the Churches under them ? Can he ask God's blessing on undertakings and schemes which tend more and more to break up the unity of the mystical body, and should this not make him, at the cost of trouble, and renouncing the indulgence of his self-will, look for means whereby the truth may be proclaimed, and yet that which is so dear to Christ's heart, the unity of His Church, be preserved ?

Again, both the Scriptures and the experience of Christian life teach us that no Christian, no matter how advanced in the Divine life, can afford to forego watchfulness and self-denial—that at no time can habits of prayer and self-discipline be safely relaxed. The calls to watchfulness on the part of Christ and of His Apostles are simply incessant. Now it is this watchfulness and constant care which constitutes the Christian's firm standing, and to relax is to " cast himself down " in the hope that he may be preserved when he neglects the means by which God has bidden him preserve himself. And of course by this temptation, and our Lord's conduct under it, we are warned against all needless exposure of ourselves to temptation. The Christian who best knows himself knows that he is always on narrow ground—that there are always precipices near his path, if not all around him; and that the prayer, " hold up my goings in Thy path, that my footsteps slip not," is never out of place.

12. " And Jesus answering said unto him, Thou shalt not tempt," &c. The Lord again repels the tempter by the use of Scripture, and his citation is remarkable. It is from Deut. vi. 16, " Ye shall not tempt the Lord your God, as ye tempted him in Massah." Its gist may be familiarly expressed by such words as, " Ye shall not try the patience of God." God was sustaining the people by daily

13 And when the devil had ended all the temptation, he departed from him ᵏ for a season.   ᵏ John xiv. 30. Heb. iv. 15.

miracles, and they tried His patience—they trifled with His forbearance by murmuring, and chiding, and unbelief. Our Lord, then, raises a particular precept into a most general one. Thou shalt in no way act presumptuously with God; thou shalt keep strictly in the path which He has set before thee; thou shalt not court danger which is not in thy Divinely appointed course, but if it be in thy path thou shall not try God's patience by doubting His presence with thee, as did the Israelites when they tempted God in Massah.

13. "And when the devil had ended all the temptation, he departed," &c. "All the temptation," rather "every temptation," implying, I think, that there were many more than the three recorded.

"For a season." Till the time of which the Lord said, "The prince of this world cometh, and hath nothing in me;" and when He said, "This is your hour and the power of darkness."

WAS THE TEMPTATION OBJECTIVE OR SUBJECTIVE?

Two considerations connected with our Lord's temptation now demand attention.

1. In what sphere did the temptation take place? Did it take place in this outward visible state of things? Was it an objective reality? Did the Lord feel actual hunger? Were there stones lying about which seemed to suggest the miracle that they should be made bread? Was there a mountain at hand, which from its position and extensive view, seemed fitted for the scene of some panoramic display? and was such display created before the eyes of the Lord by a powerful spirit? Did the Lord accompany Satan, or was He in some outward way conveyed by Satan to the top of some pinnacle of the actual Temple, where, if His human nature was the same as ours, He would actually feel a sense of extreme danger, such as those necessarily experience who look from some dizzy height into an abyss, and are tempted to throw themselves over?

Or did all take place within the Lord's brain, or mind, or spirit, *i.e.*, was it all subjective? Was His hunger mere spiritual, or mental, or imaginary hunger? Were the stones to which the tempter alluded, when he said, "Command that this stone" (or "these stones," Matth.), phantoms of stones injected into the Lord's imagination? It is necessary to draw attention to this, because commentators of note explain the first temptation on one principle—the objective, and the second and third on another—the subjective. Was the Lord transported only in very vivid imagination to the top of the pinnacle, so that whilst He was in perfect safety on the sward of the wilderness He was deceived, and thought Himself in a position of extreme danger; and was the Lord's mind or brain so acted upon that He thought that He was on the top of a mountain, with a scene of earthly grandeur and power spread before Him, while all the while He never stirred from His place?

Now it is remarkable that this latter view of the temptation is taken, not merely by rationalists or semi-rationalists, but by believing commentators, such as Godet, who writes:—"We believe that had He been observed by any spectator whilst the temptation was going on, He would have appeared all through it motionless upon the soil of the desert."

But the whole narrative *seems* to be the account of as outward and visible a transaction as any other in the life of the Lord. The tempter "came to Him" (Matth. iv. 3), "spoke to Him," "took Him up into a high mountain," "brought him to Jerusalem," "leaveth him," "departed from Him." Why are all these plain intimations to be set aside? 1. Because (it is alleged) nowhere else in the New Testament is the devil said to take a visible form. 2. Because (it is also alleged) it is not to be supposed that Satan should have power to transport our Lord through the air. To the first of these we answer, The good spirits evidently take a form, a human form, or are seen under a human form, so that they can be discerned by mortal eyes. Why, then, cannot the evil spirits similarly appear, if permitted by God? 2. But the second is to my mind beyond measure weak and inconsistent, for it makes a difficulty of giving to the evil one such power over our Lord as that he should be able to lead Him or bring Him to certain heights (the words used by St. Matthew and St. Luke by no means implying that the devil actually carried Him), whilst it assumes that he had such power over the Lord's brain, which in human beings is the seat of consciousness, as to make Him suppose that He looked down into a particular abyss which had no existence. For how are mental delusions, such as imagining ourselves on the brink of a precipice, or seeing a vision of distant scenes as if close at hand, produced—I mean, naturally produced? Evidently by an abnormal state of the brain or nerves. To deny, then, to Satan, temporary power over our Lord's person to bring about that He should change His place, and yet to give him power over that in the Son of Man, whatever it be which connects His mind and body, so as to set aside His proper consciousness, and make Him the subject of delusions, seems to me a straining at a gnat and a swallowing of a camel, to which nothing in the whole range of Scripture misinterpretation can approach.

It was evidently intended by the Saviour, or by His Father, to give Satan every possible advantage, so that he should never be able to assert that if he had had the ordering of the circumstances he would have been successful. The hunger after so long a fast must have been overpowering, and necessitated a corresponding strength of holy will in the Lord to overcome it. And so the circumstances of the second temptation (in St. Luke) were so ordered that the visions of worldly grandeur and worldly power were placed before the Lord in the best setting, so to speak, not in the bottom of a ravine, but on a commanding eminence. The Lord, of course, was not shown the actual capitals in which the kings of the earth were displaying their greatness, but He saw it all reflected, as in a faithful mirror, and recognized the truth of the representation, and if there had been anything of the world in Him it would have overcome Him. But does not this imply that Satan must be a being of immense power and knowledge, to conjure up before the Lord such representations? Certainly, I answer; and that is what the Spirit of God, speaking by the Apostles, implies that he is, when He speaks of him as the "god of this world," the prince of the power of the air, the head "of principalities, of powers, of the rulers of the darkness of this world."

I believe, then, that it is most natural, most in accordance with the fitness of things, and if the word must be spoken, that it makes the less demand upon our credulity, to consider the whole transaction as outward, visible, and objective. I have the strongest repugnance to believe that Satan was allowed such power over the Lord's inner person, His brain or mind, as to make Him the victim of delusions or illusions. I think it far more reverent to give any power to Satan to conjure up, or form, or paint, or mirror images from without, than to ascribe to him power over the Son of Man within.

110 THERE WENT OUT A FAME OF HIM. [St. Luke.

Anno Domini 30.
1 Matt. iv. 12.
John iv. 43.
m ver. 1.
n Acts x. 37.

14 ¶ ¹ And Jesus returned ᵐ in the power of the Spirit into ⁿ Galilee: and there went out a fame of him through all the region round about.

If it be replied that, after all, the visions of the kingdoms of this world and their glory were delusions, I answer most emphatically—no, they were not delusions, they were representations. A faithful picture is neither a delusion or illusion, though it may be used as such: it is a representation. But if the man before whom it is displayed is aware that it is a perfectly faithful picture, he is not deluded by it, but his mind can be excited by it to desire what is represented, with the certainty that if he ever does possess it, he will find it exactly as has been represented in the picture.

2. Another and a practical remark. The example of the Lord in beating back His tempter by the use of Holy Scripture teaches us how we are similarly to use Scripture in our spiritual warfare. If we are tempted habitually to any form of sin, we must have constantly in our minds those precepts or examples of Scripture which are directed against that sin. Are we tempted to unclean thoughts, we must be ready with the Lord's beatitude, " Blessed are the pure in heart, for they shall see God." Is our temptation to sudden and causeless anger, we must call up in memory and say the words, "Be ye angry and sin not." " Let all bitterness, and wrath, and anger, and clamour, and evil speaking be put away from you." Are we tempted to covetousness we must be ready with, " How hardly shall they that have riches enter into the kingdom of God." Whatever our besetting sin be, we shall find in Holy Writ not one, not two, not three, but a multitude of words of warning against it, with which we must be ready, as the saying is, at a moment's notice, or the enemy may effect an entrance, and "lay our honour in the dust."

14. "And Jesus returned in the power of the Spirit into Galilee." This did not take place immediately after the temptation; on the contrary, the order of events probably was—

1. Jesus returning to where John was baptizing.

2. Attaching to Himself James, John, Andrew, Philip, and Bartholomew, or Nathaniel (John i. 29-51).

3. The marriage in Cana; the first cleansing of the Temple; the

CHAP. IV.] HE CAME TO NAZARETH. 111

15 And he taught in their synagogues, being glorified of all.

16 ¶ And he came to °Nazareth, where he had been brought up: and, as his custom was, ᴾ he went into the synagogue on the sabbath day, and stood up for to read.

17 And there was delivered unto him the book of the prophet Esaias. And when he had opened the book, he found the place where it was written,

_{Anno
DOMINI
31.
° Matt. ii. 23.
& xiii. 54.
Mark vi. 1.
ᴾ Acts xiii. 14.
& xvii. 2.}

---

interview with Nicodemus: and, on His way to Galilee, the meeting with the woman at the well; and the healing of the nobleman's son. In fact, a ministry of some length and importance in Jerusalem and Judæa, the account of which is contained in John ii. 13 to iv. 43.

"In the power of the Spirit," shown in the mighty works which He had wrought, especially in Judæa and Jerusalem, the fame of which preceded Him to Galilee.

14, 15. "There went a fame of him through all the region round about. And he taught," &c. St. John describes this in the words, "Then when he was come into Galilee, the Galileans received him, having seen all the things that he did at Jerusalem at the feast; for they also went unto the feast" (John iv. 45).

16. "And he came to Nazareth, where he had been brought up . . . . to read." There were, in all probability, two visits of the Lord to Nazareth, of which this was the first, as I have shown in my note on Mark vi. 1.

"As his custom was, he went into the synagogue." Some think that "as his custom was" refers to His custom in early years in this very synagogue; but I think it was much more probable that in most synagogues He stood up to read and teach, if permitted by the rulers. The Jews seem to have allowed great liberty, even for strangers, to teach and exhort in their synagogues. Thus, at Antioch, in Pisidia, the rulers of the synagogue invited Paul and Barnabas, who were absolute strangers, to address the congregation (Acts xiii. 15).

17. "And there was delivered unto him the book of the prophet Esaias," &c. It is uncertain whether he asked for the roll containing Esaias, or whether the reading or, as we call it, "lesson," was

112 HE HATH ANOINTED ME. [St. Luke.

18 ^q The Spirit of the Lord *is* upon me, because he hath
q Is. lxi. 1.   anointed me to preach the gospel to the poor;

---

on that Sabbath a portion of that prophet. I should think the former, for the wording seems to imply that he sought out and found an appropriate passage.

18. "The Spirit of the Lord is upon me, because he hath anointed me . . . . . acceptable year of the Lord." This passage from Isaiah lxi. is taken to be a prophecy of the deliverance of the people of God from the Babylonish captivity; but, like many others, the reference to anything occurring in the times of the Jewish dispensation seems very remote and obscure; so that we, living in the light shed upon it by the Gospel, cannot rest in—indeed, can scarcely tolerate—the low, narrow, temporal sense in which it may have been once understood, and we take it as very plainly setting forth the grace and power which accompanies the present preaching of the Gospel.

There seems to have been a twofold thought in the mind of the prophet—the proclamation of the return from the captivity in the terms of the proclamation of the year of Jubilee. As in the year of Jubilee, the poor had their alienated lands restored to them, the slaves were manumitted, the captives set free; so at the return from Babylon, when the decree came from Cyrus, "Who is there among you of all his people? The Lord his God be with him, and let him go up," the tidings would be especially the "Gospel," *i.e.*, good news, to the poor of the people, who had for years been subject to the grinding oppression which was the common lot of the poor in the great heathen cities, and which would be still more bitter in the case of the poor Jews, whose captors would look upon them as aliens as well as slaves. And when the prophet speaks of deliverance to the captives, and setting at liberty them that were bruised, the captive Jews would understand it as the promise of liberty in their own land, reaching to the prisoners who, through the cruelty of heathen masters, had been "fast bound in misery and iron."

There is great difficulty, however, in applying the promise of restoration of sight to the blind to the times of Cyrus; and it has been understood as meaning that those in dark dungeons should be restored to the use of their eyes in the light of day. Such is the temporal local Jewish application.

But the Lord now transforms and regenerates the passage—gives

CHAP. IV.]   HE HATH SENT ME TO HEAL.   113

he hath sent me to heal the brokenhearted, to preach deliverance to the captives, and recovering of sight to the blind, to set at liberty them that are bruised,

---

18. "To heal the brokenhearted." So A., all later Uncials, almost all Cursives, Goth., Syriac, and some versions; but omitted by ℵ, B., D., L., a few Cursives (13, 33, 69), old Latin, Vulg. (Cod. Amiat.), and some versions.

it a new, world-wide, and eternal meaning, which every true Christian has been made by the Spirit to apprehend.

The anointing of Jesus by the Spirit, and in and through Him of His ministers, is especially that they should preach the Gospel to the poor. This means, first, that they should preach a message from God respecting redemption and sanctification and eternal life, which the very poor and the uneducated can not only understand, but are in a better position to receive than the rich and educated, because they are better able to apprehend it in its simplicity; secondly, it means that the poor, who have little of this world's comforts, and very much of its privations, should have the offer of a complete reversal of their state in the eternal world, so that they who have received here evil things, if they be true to God and to Christ, should be eternally comforted.

But we are also to remember that the word in the Hebrew for "poor" also signifies meek and lowly in heart. And the meek only, the poor in heart only, can effectually receive a Gospel which humbles whilst it exalts—humbles on earth, and with respect to all earthly things, whilst it exalts to heaven.

"He hath sent me to heal the brokenhearted." Not only to apply to those broken hearted through the sense of sin the consolation of the Gospel, but to comfort every heart broken through loss of property, loss of reputation, loss of friends and dear relatives, with the glorious hopes of that future when God shall wipe away all tears from all eyes.

"To preach deliverance to the captives." So that being made free from sin, which is the worst of bondage, they should be the children of Him Whose service is "perfect freedom."

"And recovering of sight to the blind." So that they who were blind to the light of God's truth should even see God, should "endure as seeing Him Who is invisible."

"To set at liberty them that are bruised." This, in its spiritual

I

ALL BARE HIM WITNESS. [St. Luke.

19 To preach the acceptable year of the Lord.

20 And he closed the book, and he gave *it* again to the minister, and sat down. And the eyes of all them that were in the synagogue were fastened on him.

21 And he began to say unto them, This day is this scripture fulfilled in your ears.

22 And all bare him witness, and ʳ wondered at

r Ps. xlv. 2.
Matt. xiii. 54.
Mark vi. 2.
ch. ii. 47.

significance, seems something different to the emancipation of the captives just mentioned. Bede and, after him, Didacus Stella, interpret it as deliverance from the galling chain of the Jewish ceremonial law—a yoke which, according to St. Peter, "neither he nor his fathers were able to bear." All false opinions of God and His ways, however, at first men may freely accept them, and take to them, and glory in them, become in time galling, bruising, unbearable fetters. What a yoke, for instance, has that view of God's dealings, popularly called Calvinism, become to thousands upon thousands of Christians once nurtured in it!

"To preach the acceptable year of the Lord." The acceptable year, *i.e.*, the time in which God will accept men. This is, of course, the whole Christian time or dispensation. Now—now till Christ comes to judge,—now is the time when every sinner is invited to receive the Gospel, and be saved.

Some have thought from this that the Lord's ministry was only for one year; but such literalness is alien to the whole Gospel narrative.

Something of the former sort we may reverently assume was the evangelical meaning of this prophecy which the Lord set forth when

21. "He began to say unto them, This day is this scripture fulfilled in your ears." Mark how He passed over unnoticed every former fulfilment, and called attention to that only which He Himself brought about.

22. "And all bare him witness, and wondered at the gracious words," &c. The reader will remember the words of the Psalmist: "Full of grace are thy lips, because God hath blessed thee for ever."

Note the description of the Lord's speaking "gracious words," not merely words of wisdom or of power, but words of grace. And

the gracious words which proceeded out of his mouth. And they said, ⁸Is not this Joseph's son?   ˢ John vi. 42.

23 And he said unto them, Ye will surely say unto me this proverb, Physician, heal thyself: whatsoever we have heard done in ᵗCapernaum, do also here in ᵘthy country.

ᵗ Matt. iv. 13. & xi. 23.
ᵘ Matt. xiii. 54. Mark vi. 1.

24 And he said, Verily I say unto you, No ˣprophet is accepted in his own country.

ˣ Matt. xiii. 57. Mark vi. 4. John iv. 44.

---

23. "In Capernaum." So A., E., F., G., H., K., M., other later Uncials, almost all Cursives. "For" or "to Capernaum" in ℵ, B., D., L., four Cursives (13, 69, 124, 346).

well may they have been such if they were an application of the words of the Evangelical prophet which He had just read. And note, also, that He stops short of the last words, "the day of vengeance of our God," as if on this first offer of salvation to His countrymen, He spake words of invitation only—words of mercy, not of judgment.

"And they said, Is not this Joseph's son?" Their admiration passes away at once, and turns into criticism. "Is not this the youth brought up amongst us? Why does He take upon Himself to teach us, and apply to Himself one of the chiefest prophecies of our greatest prophet?"

23. "And he said unto them, Ye will surely say unto me this proverb, Physician," &c. There seems to be no room for doubt respecting the sense in which the Lord cites this proverb: "You have healed strangers, heal your own citizens, heal your own flesh and blood." And yet some have taken it to mean, "Deliver yourself from your poverty," or, "Assert your Messiahship" by some mighty work.

24. "And he said, Verily I say unto you, No prophet is accepted," &c. It is very hard for those amongst whom a man has been brought up, to consider him as in any way above themselves. And in this case especially, for during the time of His sojourn in Nazareth—which was before His entrance on His public ministry—He had done no miracles. In all probability His private life had been very unobtrusive. It is impossible to suppose that He even preached, or, on the first recorded occasion of His preaching, they would not have expressed such astonishment at His words of grace.

116 MANY WIDOWS, MANY LEPERS. [St. Luke.

25 But I tell you of a truth, ʸ many widows were in Israel in the days of Elias, when the heaven was shut up three years and six months, when great famine was throughout all the land;

26 But unto none of them was Elias sent, save unto Sarepta, *a city* of Sidon, unto a woman *that was* a widow.

27 ᶻ And many lepers were in Israel in the time of Eliseus the prophet; and none of them was cleansed, saving Naaman the Syrian.

28 And all they in the synagogue, when they heard these things, were filled with wrath,

29 And rose up, and thrust him out of the city, and led him unto the ‖ brow of the hill whereon their city was built, that they might cast him down headlong.

ʸ 1 Kin. xvii. 9. & xviii. 1. James v. 17.
ᶻ 2 Kin. v. 14.
‖ Or, *edge.*

25, 26, 27. "But I tell you of a truth, many widows were in Israel . . . Naaman the Syrian." Elijah and Elisha were both Israelites, and yet Elijah, in the time of famine, supported by his miraculous power but one widow, and she not of the chosen people, but a Gentile: and Elisha healed but one leper, and he a Syrian. Elijah could have supported all the widows who would have asked his help, Elisha could have healed every leper; but because of unbelief none came to claim the exercise of the power which God had given to them.

And so it was with the Nazarenes: "He could do no mighty works there, because of their unbelief."

But there can be little or no doubt that the Lord in these words looks far beyond Nazareth and Capernaum. We cannot but see in them the casting away of the Jews through unbelief, and the call of the Gentiles. The Jews put away from themselves the message of salvation: in the words of the Apostle, they "held themselves unworthy of eternal life," and God, through His Church, "turned to the Gentiles."

28, 29. "And all they in the synagogue, when they heard these things, were filled with wrath." What an inconceivably rapid change from "bearing Him witness," and "wondering at His words of grace," to anger and persecuting hate, which made them thirst for His Blood. We must remember that what intensified their

CHAP. IV.]   HIS WORD WAS WITH POWER.   117

30 But he ^a passing through the midst of them went his way,

31 And ^b came down to Capernaum, a city of Galilee, and taught them on the sabbath days.

32 And they were astonished at his doctrine: ^c for his word was with power.

a John viii. 59. & x. 39.
b Matt. iv. 13. Mark i. 21.
c Matt. vii. 28, 29. Titus ii. 15.

---

persecuting rage, was their familiarity with Him in times past. That one whom they had known familiarly as a child, and as a workman in a carpenter's shop, should take to Himself a leading prophecy of Isaiah, should not only call Himself a prophet, but cite the examples of Elijah and Elisha, to show that if they rejected Him, it was to their own inconceivable loss and peril, was more than they could bear, and so they

29. "Rose up, and thrust him out of the city . . . might cast him down headlong." The place of this attempted murder seems clearly capable of identification. "Nazareth spreads itself out upon the eastern face of a mountain, where there is a perpendicular wall of rock from forty to fifty feet high."

30. "But he passing through the midst of them, went his way." Some believing commentators deny that there was anything miraculous about this. One of them (Godet) writes: "The deliverance of Jesus was neither a miracle nor an escape; He passed through the group of these infuriated people, with a majesty which overawed them." But if it was His majestic appearance or bearing that overawed them, why did not this same majestic appearance prevent their thrusting Him out of the city, and ignominiously hustling Him till they came to the brow of the hill? The power of suddenly changing a meek and defenceless demeanour into one so overpoweringly majestic that it overawed a brutal and bloodthirsty mob, either belongs to the sphere of the miraculous, or is a piece of stage acting, which we scarcely dare to name in connection with the Lord, but must do so if it is imputed to Him.

31. "And came down to Capernaum, a city of Galilee . . . with power." Notice how St. Luke, writing his Gospel for distant Gentile churches, explains that Capernaum, which from its size and importance must have been well known to dwellers in the Holy Land, was "a city of Galilee."

"His word was with power." Not merely with power in the

118   A SPIRIT OF AN UNCLEAN DEVIL.   [St. Luke.

33 ¶ [d] And in the synagogue there was a man, which had
a spirit of an unclean devil, and cried out with
a loud voice,

[d] Mark i. 23.

---

sense of incisiveness and directness of appeal to the conscience, but commended to their acceptance by such works of power, as those which follow.

33. "And in the synagogue there was a man which had a spirit of an unclean devil." The account of this miracle is to be found in St. Mark, but not in St. Matthew. It was probably not contained in the body of tradition usually preached, but was peculiar to the preaching of St. Peter; the miracle having taken place before St. Matthew and the greater part of the apostles were called to follow Jesus. Certain small differences seem to forbid us to believe that St. Luke copied it from St. Mark. He probably took it down from the lips of St. Peter himself.

"Which had a spirit of an unclean devil." St. Mark speaks of the man as "having an unclean spirit." St. Luke as "a man which had a spirit of an unclean devil," thereby emphasizing the fact that the devil was the source of uncleanness, having probably in the first instance tempted the man through the lust of uncleanness.

With respect to demoniacal possession, I have given a short excursus on it in the end of my commentary on St. Mark, and must refer the reader to that.

I would here remark that every account of our Lord's casting evil spirits out of men, implies that he looked upon possession by them as a real thing, very different from the usual forms of madness or insanity. He gives the apostles and disciples power to cast out devils (Luke ix. 1.) In Mark ix. 29, he distinguishes a certain kind as not yielding to ordinary forms of exorcism, but as going out only by prayer and fasting. In Luke xi. 21, he refers the subjection of the devils to His disciples (the seventy), to the fact that He had seen "Satan as lightning fall from heaven."

With respect to the fact that instances of demoniacal possession were much more common in the time of our Lord, than either before or after, Godet asks: "Are there not times when God permits a superior evil power to invade humanity? Just as God sent Jesus at a period in history when moral and social evil had reached its

34 Saying, ‖ Let *us* alone; what have we to do with thee, *thou* Jesus of Nazareth? art thou come to destroy us? ᵉ I know thee who thou art; ᶠ the Holy One of God.

‖ Or, *Away.*
ᵉ ver. 41.
ᶠ Ps. xvi. 10.
Dan. ix. 24.
ch. i. 35.

34. "Saying." So A., C., D., later Uncials, all Cursives, Ital., Vulg., Goth., Syriac, &c.; but omitted by א, B., L., and Coptic.

culminating point, did not He also permit an extraordinary manifestation of diabolical power at the same time? By this means Jesus could be proclaimed externally and visibly as the conqueror of the enemy of men, as He Who came to destroy the works of the devil, in the moral sense of the word." (1 John iii. 8.)

Upon possession by *unclean* spirits, Quesnel remarks: " He who has his soul possessed by uncleanness is far more miserable than he whose body only was heretofore possessed by a devil. An unchaste person appears to the eyes of the mind much more demoniac than any other sinner. Our having so little abhorrence of such is a sign that we are not yet in a capacity to judge well of the opposition there is betwixt the Spirit of God and the unclean spirit, betwixt grace and sin."

34. "Saying, Let us alone; what have we to do with thee, thou Jesus of Nazareth? " Notice how the presence of the All-Holy disturbed and distracted the unholy being. And is not this a parable? Those who live in criminal pleasure cannot endure that anyone should disturb their miserable peace. At times I have noticed the impure studiously avoid the company of the good, though there was no chance of their receiving rebuke from them.

"I know thee who thou art." Some commentators (amongst them Williams) have thought that these words imply on the part of the evil spirits, some late reception of the knowledge that Jesus was the Messiah, and they suppose that at the temptation the Lord was manifested to the unseen spiritual world as its Judge and King; but is it not most likely that all purely spiritual existences have a knowledge of one another by a sort of intuition which those in the flesh cannot have?

"The Holy One of God." He spoke of Him not as a holy one of God, as if He were like to the other saints, but as being in a remarkable manner *the* Holy One (with the addition of the article). For He is by nature holy, by partaking of Whom all others are called holy.]

HOLD THY PEACE. [St. Luke.

35 And Jesus rebuked him, saying, Hold thy peace, and come out of him. And when the devil had thrown him in the midst, he came out of him, and hurt him not.

36 And they were all amazed, and spake among themselves, saying, What a word *is* this! for with authority and power he commandeth the unclean spirits, and they come out.

37 And the fame of him went out into every place of the country round about.

g Matt. viii. 14. Mark i. 29.
38 ¶ g And he arose out of the synagogue, and entered into Simon's house. And Simon's wife's mother was taken with a great fever; and they besought him for her.

---

35. "And Jesus rebuked him, saying, Hold thy peace, and come out of him." By this He both refused to receive testimony to His Godhead from these evil spirits, and yet evinced His Divine power over them by expelling them, not by some laboured process, or doubtful form of exorcism, but by a single word. "And when the devil had thrown him in the midst, he came out of him," &c. Here was exhibited the power of Christ, that this last and fiercest effort of the despairing spirit to destroy his victim was harmless. The words "and hurt him not" reproduce in a striking manner the impression of eye-witnesses: they ran towards the unhappy man expecting to find him dead, and to their surprise on lifting him up they found him not the least injured by the violent paroxysm.

36. "And they were all amazed, and spake among themselves, saying, What a word is this!" They probably compared the short, decisive, and irresistible command of the Lord with the feeble, and in most cases, abortive exorcisings of those amongst them who attempted to cast out evil spirits.

38-39. "And he arose out of the synagogue . . . ministered unto them." The healing of Peter's wife's mother is given to us by the three Synoptics. The speciality of St. Luke's account is that the Lord stood over her and *rebuked* the fever, using the same expression, "rebuked," as when he gives the account of the Lord casting out the evil spirit. It is to be noticed how often this word is used when it cannot be understood of moral rebuke of intelligent creatures. Thus He rebukes not only the evil spirits, but "the winds and waves," as if in all evil things he discerned an evil intelligence

39 And he stood over her, and rebuked the fever; and it left her: and immediately she arose and ministered unto them.

40 ¶ ʰ Now when the sun was setting, all they that had any sick with divers diseases brought them unto him; and he laid his hands on every one of them, and healed them.

ʰ Matt. viii. 16. Mark i. 32.

---

behind the physical evil, as if he knew or recognized not dead laws, but evil spirits who worked in or under them. Thus he speaks of a woman who had an infirmity, that "Satan had bound her these thirty years."

St. Luke speaks of the fever as a *great* fever, and it is thought by some that this expression is technical, and used by St. Luke the physician as denoting that the fever belonged to a particular class; but it is best to understand it as describing a strong or malignant disease.

St. Luke also emphazises the fact that the cure was not only instantaneous, but so was the restoration to perfect strength. "Immediately she arose and ministered unto them"—teaching us that those whom the Lord raises from the fever and weakness of indulged passions may be instantly able to serve Him. In fact, their beginning in some way to serve Christ and his Church is the true sign of their restoration to spiritual health.

St. Cyril gives the spiritual significance of the miracle when he writes, "Let us therefore receive Jesus. For when He has visited us we carry Him in our heart and mind. He will then extinguish the flame of our unlicensed pleasures, and will make us whole, so that we minister unto Him, that is, do things well-pleasing to Him." [Cyril in Catena Aurea.]

40. "Now when the sun was setting," &c. That is, when the Sabbath was over, when it would be lawful for them to carry the burdens of the sick bodies.

"He laid his hands on every one of them." So that virtue might be clearly seen to go from His most sacred Person [must we not say his Body?] into them. St. Luke alone mentions that on this occasion He healed them by the laying on of hands. This, considering the great multitudes, must have much enhanced His labour and consequent bodily fatigue. Godet has an admirable passage on this: "Whenever Jesus avails Himself of any material means to

41 ¹And devils also came out of many, crying out, and saying, Thou art Christ the Son of God. And ᵏ he rebuking *them* suffered them not ‖ to speak: for they knew that he was Christ.

42 ¹And when it was day, he departed and went into a desert place: and the people sought him, and came unto him, and stayed him, that he should not depart from them.

43 And he said unto them, I must preach the kingdom of God to other cities also: for therefore am I sent.

44 ᵐ And he preached in the synagogues of Galilee.

ⁱ Mark i. 34. & iii. 11.
ᵏ Mark i. 25, 34. ver. 34, 35.
‖ Or, *to say that they knew him to be Christ.*
¹ Mark i. 35.
ᵐ Mark i. 39.

41. "Thou art Christ." So A., later Uncials, most Cursives, some old Latin, Goth., Syriac, Æth. "Christ" omitted by ℵ, B., C., D., F., L., three Cursives (33, 130, 220), old Latin, Vulg., Copt., Arm., &c.
43. "Other;" "the other," Revisers.
44. "Synagogues of Galilee." So A., D., later Uncials, old Latin, Vulg., Goth., Syriac, &c.; but ℵ, B., C., L., a few Cursives, Copt., Syriac, read, "Judæa."

work a cure, whether it be the sound of His voice, or clay made of His spittle, His aim is to establish, in the form best adapted to the particular case, a personal tie between the sick person and Himself; for He desires not only to heal, but to effect a restoration to God, by creating in the consciousness of the sick, a sense of union with Himself, the organ of Divine grace in the midst of mankind."

42. "And when it was day he departed," &c. . . . . "preached in the synagogue of Galilee." St. Mark is much more circumstantial in his relation of what took place: according to him the Lord rose up early and departed into a desert place to pray, and He was followed by Peter, and "they that were with him," who told Him of the eagerness of the multitude to hear him, and of their desire that He should not leave them.

"Therefore am I sent." His first work in order of time was preaching, not that it was greater than His Atoning work on the Cross, but because preaching presses upon men the acceptance of the things of the Kingdom of God, introduces it, explains what it is, and prepares men to receive it.

CHAP. V.

AND ^a it came to pass, that, as the people pressed upon him to hear the word of God, he stood by the lake of Gennesaret,

^a Matt. iv. 18.
Mark i. 16.

2 And saw two ships standing by the lake: but the fishermen were gone out of them, and were washing *their* nets.

---

2. "Two ships." So ℵ, B., D., most later Uncials, most Cursives, old Latin, Vulg.; but A., E., L., five or six Cursives (1, 33, 40, 53, 237, 259), read "little ships."

1-4. "And it came to pass, that, as the people pressed upon him to hear the word of God . . . taught the people out of the ship." It is very difficult indeed to come to any decision respecting the question, Is this the same call of Apostles which is mentioned in Matthew iv. 18, and Mark i. 16-20?

First we will note the differences. St. Matthew and St. Mark say nothing about the multitudes who were pressing upon Him to hear the word of God. On the contrary, we should gather from this account that the Lord was alone. In St. Luke the fishermen were gone out of the boat. In St. Matthew they were casting their net into the sea. According to St. Luke, He entered into one of the ships and taught the people out of it. Of this nothing is said in St. Matthew. In St. Luke's account, having finished teaching, the Lord ordered them to launch out into the deep; of this we have nothing in the other two Synoptics. St. Luke alone gives the words of St. Peter: "We have toiled all night and have taken nothing," whereas St. Matthew and St. Mark, as we have seen, represent that they were then casting their net into the sea. St. Luke alone mentions what follows, the immense draught of fishes, the breaking of the net, the calling for help to their partners, the sinking of the boat, the words of St. Peter, "Depart from me," &c. The words of Christ are quite different in each case, and correspond to the different circumstances. In St. Matthew the brethren were simply fishing, nothing being said of their success, and the Lord calls them to be fishers of men; but in St. Luke's account they had actually caught an overwhelming number, and the Lord says to

3 And he entered into one of the ships, which was Simon's, and prayed him that he would thrust out a little from the land. And he sat down, and taught the people out of the ship.

4 Now when he had left speaking, he said unto Simon, ᵇ Launch out into the deep, and let down your nets for a draught.

ᵇ John xxi. 6.

Peter alone, the caster in of the net, " From henceforth thou shalt catch (or take alive) men."

The accounts then are almost totally different, and we should all, I think, pronounce them to refer to two different callings: but the difficulty of this is that the conclusion of each is the same, which is the final renunciation of " all " on the part of the four to follow the Lord. It is asked, How can this have occurred twice ? I grant the difficulty, but nevertheless, I assert that such a first and then a second and final forsaking is not at all unlikely.

First, then, they all four knew the Lord previously, having been directed to Him by the Baptist. He then very probably spoke to them about following Him, and to some extent they did, for they were with Him at the Marriage Feast in Cana, and during part of His ministry in Jerusalem. After this came the call whilst they were fishing, recorded in St. Matthew and St. Mark; they then began to follow Him more closely, but, perhaps, with fears about their livelihood. He set before them no means of employment whereby they might be sustained ; so taking into account that even after the Resurrection they went back to their boats and fishing, it may be that after some slight separation they returned again to their occupation. But now at last the miracle of the overwhelming draught beyond measure humbled and overawed them. There must be no further hesitation, no further looking back : and so they forsook not their nets only, as is mentioned by St. Matthew and St. Mark, but all besides, as we have in our Evangelist.

4-6. "Now when he had left speaking ... net brake." Many of the older commentators notice how this shows that the Lord would be no man's debtor. Simon had let Him have the use of his ship as a pulpit, from which to preach the Word of God, and now He rewards him with the immense haul; but had we not rather concentrate our view on the miracle which follows as addressed to the

WE HAVE TOILED ALL NIGHT.

5 And Simon answering said unto him, Master, we have toiled all the night, and have taken nothing: nevertheless at thy word I will let down the net.

6 And when they had this done, they inclosed a great multitude of fishes: and their net brake.

---

faculty of faith in Simon and his companions? As the star was to the Magi, so was this to the Apostles. It met them in the work of their daily calling, and convinced them that He Who had such power to fill their net after they had toiled all night in vain, must be One in Whom they could put entire trust for their future, whether in this world or in the next.

5. "Master, we have toiled all the night, and have taken nothing: nevertheless at thy word I will," &c. This is not the answer of despondency, but of faith. It is to be remembered that St. Peter had been a witness of the turning of the water into wine, and perhaps of many other miracles in the Lord's ministry in Judea, and his own wife's mother had been healed in his house. In faith, then, that something great would happen, he said, "At thy word I will let down the net."

6. "And when they had this done, they inclosed a great multitude of fishes," &c. Was this a miracle of creative power, or of knowledge, or of the two combined? If the Lord had created new fish it would have been the first; but there is no reason to suppose this, as the lake swarmed with fish. Was it then a miracle of knowledge, He being aware that there was in that part of the lake into which they cast their nets at that moment a vast shoal of fish? This, though not impossible, is unlikely, for they had apparently been fishing in that part without success, and the usual time for taking fish was then past. It was most probably a work of power and knowledge combined. He brought within the reach of their nets a shoal which was not there before, or quick-sighted fishermen would have seen the indication of it.

The following is from Tristram's "Natural History of the Bible." "The thickness of the shoals of fish in the lake of Gennesareth is almost incredible to anyone who has not witnessed them. They often cover an area of more than an acre, and when the fish move slowly forward in a mass, and are rising out of the water, they are packed so close together that it appears as if a heavy rain was beating

7 And they beckoned unto *their* partners, which were in the other ship, that they should come and help them. And they came, and filled both the ships, so that they began to sink.

---

down on the surface of the water." It is plain, then, that the Lord by His power brought such a shoal from the depths within reach of St. Peter's net: for if it had come naturally he or his comrades would have discerned it afar off, and there would have been no miracle in their eyes.

" And their net brake," (7) " And they beckoned . . . began to sink." The breaking of the nets and the beginning of the ships to sink are parables. The first betokens the destruction of discipline, owing to the numbers of men of all sorts, good and bad, that are taken in the net of the Church. The second symbolizes a worse evil by far. It is the depressing and destructive effect of the world which has been received into the Church, which threatens to overwhelm it, and if Christ were not in the boat, would do so.

The first, the want of discipline, leads to the second. The discipline of the Church is its way of asserting publicly that those who belong to a holy company should be holy, and if the Church is unable to do this, she is wanting in her principal witness against sin, and so the world within her asserts itself in its lawlessness and impurity, and self-will, and irreligion, and unless God interfere by His own sharp discipline she sinks. But, to take our own case, is it possible to exclude from the Church of England the world which has for centuries been within its pale, and well nigh ruled it? It seems impossible. No disestablishment, no disendowment, no possible political or ecclesiastical movement would effect it. Must then the Church sink? No, the remedy is in its true members—all those who realize it as the mystical body of Christ, exercising discipline over themselves, exercising self-denial, labouring incessantly, "reproving, rebuking, exhorting with all long-suffering." It is a token for good that there has been such a revival of effective discipline among the clergy, so that those who disgrace their holy calling are so much more easily removed or punished. And we must remember that the word in the original is not to be sunk, as if the action was completed, but " begin to sink." The Church is always in danger, both from without and from within, and its safety is in those who are aware of its constant state of peril, crying

8 When Simon Peter saw *it*, he fell down at Jesus' knees, saying, ᶜ Depart from me; for I am a sinful man, O Lord.   ᶜ 2 Sam. vi. 9. 1 Kings xvii. 18.

9 For he was astonished, and all that were with him, at the draught of the fishes which they had taken:

10 And so *was* also James, and John, the sons of Zebedee, which were partners with Simon. And Jesus said unto Simon, Fear not; ᵈ from henceforth thou shalt catch men.   ᵈ Matt. iv. 19. Mark i. 17.

---

incessantly to the Lord that He would raise up His power and come and help us, and in His great might succour us.

8. "When Simon Peter saw it, . . . I am a sinful man, O Lord." In these words we have the first feelings of sinful man, when he realizes the presence of God. It is the sum and confession of his own uncleanness, and the unutterable holiness of Him Who has revealed it. We may compare it with the words of Job: "I have heard of thee with the hearing of the ear, but now mine eye seeth thee; therefore, I abhor myself" (Job xlii. 5, 6), or with those of Isaiah, "Woe is me, for I am undone, because I am a man of unclean lips . . . mine eyes have seen the King, the Lord of Hosts." Such is the natural and appropriate feeling for those who know and realize God's holiness, and yet know not the way of reconciliation and the fulness of Divine grace in Him who has opened it for us. Thus, when Peter knew something of this, his "Depart from me" is changed into "To whom shall we go? thou hast the words of eternal life."

9. "For he was astonished, and all that were with him . . . taken." Unless it was clearly a miracle, he would not have been thus overwhelmed with awe. And being a fisherman, he was the best judge. It is clear from his unbounded astonishment, and that of his partners, that nothing like it had occurred in their experiences on the lake.

10. "And so was also . . . from henceforth thou shalt catch men." Thou shalt not only be a fisher of men, but shalt catch them, and not only catch them, but catch or take them alive. It means, "Thou shalt catch them not for death, but for life." Those whom the Gospel net catches are slain, it is true, to the world, but at the same time they are raised to a far higher, because a spiritual life.

128 A MAN FULL OF LEPROSY. [ST. LUKE.

11 And when they had brought their ships to land, ^e they forsook all, and followed him.

12 ¶ ^f And it came to pass, when he was in a certain city, behold a man full of leprosy: who

^e Matt. iv. 20, & xix. 27. Mark i. 18, ch. xviii. 28.
^f Matt. viii. 2. Mark i. 40.

---

11. "And when they had brought their ships to land, . . . followed him." In St. Matthew's and St. Mark's account, the ships are already brought to land, and in the one case the nets only, in the other "their father Zebedee, with the ship and hired servants," were left: now it is "all"—they forsook all. Are not then the accounts in the two first Synoptics those of a different event to this, and this in St. Luke the final call, after which they never resumed their first occupation?

12. "And it came to pass, when he was in a certain city," &c. It is worthy of remark that though all the three Synoptics give the account of the instantaneous cleansing of the leper, yet in not one is the place where it occurred named. The name of the place had evidently dropped out of the memory of the Apostles. St. Luke's remark that it took place in a certain city, is also worthy of notice. The leper, whose proper place was without the walls, seems to have penetrated, perhaps surreptitiously, into the city, to come near the Lord. It may be, however, that the Lord was passing the quarter assigned to these miserable men. Dr. Thomson, in his work "The Land and the Book," has a most terribly graphic account of his straying by accident into the quarter assigned to the lepers in the city of Jerusalem: "Sauntering down the Jaffa road, I was startled out of my reverie by the sudden apparition of a crowd of beggars. They held up towards me their handless arms, unearthly sounds gurgled through throats without palates." And in describing the beginning and progress of the disorder, he writes: "New-born children of leprous parents are often as pretty and as healthy in appearance as any, but by-and-by its presence and working become visible in some of the signs described in the 13th chapter of Leviticus. The 'scab' comes on by degrees in different parts of the body; the hair falls from the head and eyebrows; the nails loosen, decay and drop off; joint after joint of the fingers and toes shrink up and slowly fall away. The gums are absorbed and the teeth disappear. The nose, the eyes, the tongue, and the palate are slowly consumed, and finally the wretched victim sinks into the

seeing Jesus fell on *his* face, and besought him, saying, Lord, if thou wilt, thou canst make me clean.

---

earth and disappears, while medicine has no power to stay the ravages of this fell disease, or even to mitigate sensibly its tortures " (p. 634).

To the sentence of exclusion pronounced on the leper in Levit. xiii. 45, Rabbinism, ever exaggerating every seemingly harsh precept, ever merciless in binding heavy unendurable burdens, added still more to make the leper's lot intolerable. No one was even to salute him. If he even put his head into a place it became unclean. No less a distance than four cubits (six feet) must be kept from a leper : or if the wind came from that direction a hundred were scarcely sufficient. One would eat nothing purchased in a street where there was a leper. Another boasted that he threw stones at them to keep them afar off—Edersheim (chap. xv.)—who also well remarks, " We can judge by the healing of this leper of the impression which the Saviour had made upon the people. He would have fled from a rabbi: he came in lowliest attitude of entreaty to Jesus."

" Fell on his face, and besought him, saying, Lord, if thou wilt, thou canst," &c. In my St. Mark I noticed how this suppliant could not have addressed the Lord differently, if he had believed in His Godhead. Let us add one or two remarks which we have there left unsaid.

1. The leprosy was held to be, as indeed it was, incurable, except by Divine power. " Am I God," exclaims a king of Israel, " to kill and to make alive, that this man doth send unto me to recover a man of his leprosy ? " (2 Kings v. 7.) For this man to kneel to Jesus, and say to Him, " If Thou wilt, Thou art able," was to ascribe to Him the power of God. Whether he believed that that power resided in Him as the Son of God, or as the Messiah, the especial Messenger sent by God, we need not now inquire. Anyhow, he believed that the Lord's power of healing extended to a disease which all his nation believed incurable, except by the finger of God.

2. This prayer of this unknown outcast of an unknown city, is the very type of the prayer of faith. It is the outcome of intense faith, recognizing more fully than any other prayer addressed to Jesus, the Lord's power ; and yet it bows before the Lord's will, as

13 And he put forth *his* hand, and touched him, saying, I will: be thou clean. And immediately the leprosy departed from him.

g Matt. viii. 4. 14 ᵍ And he charged him to tell no man: but go, and shew thyself to the priest, and offer for

---

13. "Be thou clean." "Be thou made clean," Revisers.

being the will of a wise as well as of a good Being, Who in this present state of things, sets bounds to the benevolent exercise of His omnipotence, and permits fearful evils to afflict those created in God's image. His prayer is humble, plain, and full of confidence in God, Who can do all things, and of dependence upon His will, which orders all things well. It is peculiar to God alone, that He need only will what He intends to perform. His power is His will. It is because He wills it, that thereby He effects all, both in nature and grace.

13. "And he put forth his hand, and touched him, saying, I will: be thou clean." The Lord, as we have noticed all through this commentary, if possible, brings His Body into contact with the bodies of those whom He heals, thereby to certify to them and to us that His very Body overflows with healing life and power, and He makes no exception even in the case of lepers whom it was pollution to touch. But His Sacred Body receives no pollution from the uncleanness even of the leprous body. On the contrary, the pollution flees before it. As soon as it touches it finds the flesh pure, for it was the outward and visible sign of the Divine Will which accompanied it. (See passage from Chrysostom in my Notes on St. Mark.)

"I will: be thou clean." If thou wilt. I will. The answer was instantaneous. All Christ's miracles are revelations also. Sometimes, when the circumstances of the case required it, He delayed His answer to a sufferer's prayer. But we are never told that there was a moment's pause when a *leper* cried to Him. Leprosy was an acknowledged type of sin, and Christ would teach us that the heartfelt prayer of the sinner to be purged and cleansed is always met by instantaneous acceptance.

14. "And he charged him to tell no man." Either that He might not be hindered in His spiritual ministry by men crowding about Him to be healed of bodily diseases, or rather, perhaps, to prevent the priests at Jerusalem from refusing to certify that the man was

thy cleansing, ʰ according as Moses commanded, for a testimony unto them.

ʰ Lev. xiv. 4, 10, 21, 22.

15 But so much the more went there a fame abroad of him: ⁱ and great multitudes came together to hear, and to be healed by him of their infirmities.

ⁱ Matt. iv. 25. Mark iii. 7. John vi. 2.

16 ¶ ᵏ And he withdrew himself into the wilderness, and prayed.

ᵏ Matt. xiv. 23. Mark vi. 46.

17 And it came to pass on a certain day, as he was teaching, that there were Pharisees and doctors of the law sitting

---

cleansed when they heard that the word of Jesus was the occasion of his cleansing. They are to see him and pronounce him clean before they hear of the means which brought it about.

"For a testimony unto them." May mean either for a testimony of My power even over leprosy, or for a testimony that in all things I desire that the law of Moses should be obeyed.

16. "And he withdrew himself into the wilderness, and prayed." How was it that when the Lord was doing so much good (for it is said "great multitudes came together both to hear and to be healed") He withdrew Himself? We may answer in the words of Quesnel: "It is for the advantage of souls, as well as of ministers, that these [ministers] should be absent from those for a time. To speak to God on behalf of souls is not to forsake them. It is the most effectual way of serving them for a man to purify himself by retirement, that he may serve them the better, and replenish himself with God and His truths; that so he may dispense them in greater abundance, and after a more holy manner."

This place shows us the need, if possible, of retirement for prayer. The Son of God was always in communion with His Father: yet it may be that even His perfectly holy human Soul was, like ours, distracted by the presence and the importunity of the multitudes, and so not on this occasion only, but continually He sought retirement.

17. "And it came to pass on a certain day . . . . present to heal them." We gather from this that the growing fame of the Lord's miracles and teaching had thoroughly excited the fear of these teachers of false tradition, who now realized that if the Lord's

by, which were come out of every town of Galilee, and Judæa, and Jerusalem: and the power of the Lord was *present* to heal them.

^{1 Matt. ix. 2.}
^{Mark ii. 3.} 18 ¶ ¹ And, behold, men brought in a bed a man which was taken with a palsy: and they sought *means* to bring him in, and to lay *him* before him.

---

spiritual doctrine became known it would supersede and destroy theirs. So even in these comparatively remote parts they were present in force amongst His hearers for the purpose of cavilling and opposing.

"Present to heal them." Not, of course, the Pharisees and doctors, for they would be the last to come in faith to be healed, but the multitude.

18. "And, behold, men brought in a bed a man which was taken with a palsy," &c. I have commented very fully in my Notes on St. Mark on this miracle, since that Evangelist gives the circumstances more fully. In these notes I shall have principally in view its evangelical and practical import.

First of all let us notice the genuineness of the faith of those who brought the man in—that it overcame all difficulties. The house, which was probably a good-sized square building erected round a court, was so crowded, both in the room where the Lord was teaching, the court-yard, and all about the doors, that there was no possibility of entrance, especially for four persons bearing the sick man on his pallet. Then there would be a natural fear that the crowds who were eagerly listening would resent the interruption, and perhaps some apprehension also that the great Teacher Himself would not approve of so apparently untimely an approach; but they knew that the Lord could heal, they knew that He never sent any away unblessed from His presence, and their faith made them determined to come at Him. If Jewish houses were then like what they are now this must have been a matter of much trouble, for we are told that the houses of the Holy Land have flat roofs. Dr. Robinson thus describes their construction:—" First, large beams, at intervals of several feet, then rude joists, on which again are arranged small poles close together, or brushwood, or, as in this case, slabs of tile or dried clay underneath, and over this a thick

19 And when they could not find by what *way* they might bring him in because of the multitude, they went upon the housetop, and let him down through the tiling with *his* couch into the midst before Jesus.

20 And when he saw their faith, he said unto him, Man, thy sins are forgiven thee.

---

compost of earth or gravel, on the top of which grass sometimes grows, on which goats browse." One sees how to remove such a covering would be a work of labour, so as not to interfere with the structure of the house. Of course this forced entrance through the roof must have taken place by the permission or connivance of the owner.

So that their faith was one which overcame outward difficulties, and not unreasonable apprehension, and so the Lord " saw " it and commended it by rewarding it. This faith, too, was exerted not for their own benefit, but on behalf of another. And should not we have something of this faith in bringing not only our own spiritual wants, but those of others to the feet of the Lord ? Is there anything like the spirit of intercessory prayer amongst us that there ought to be ? May we not find out at the last that vastly more good might have been done both in the world and in the Church if we had prayed and worked more diligently and faithfully ? Quesnel remarks : " True friendship consists in taking a friend out of the way of sin and perdition, in carrying him to Christ, in bringing him into His house, and in laying him, as it were, before Him, by admonitions, instructions, reading, and prayers."

20. "And when he saw their faith, he said unto him, Man, thy sins are forgiven thee." No doubt, however, the true words of the Lord are to be found by comparing St. Matthew and St. Mark's accounts. " Be of good cheer," or " Take courage." " Son, thy sins be forgiven thee." It is noticeable that these words were said on seeing the faith of the bearers, but not *to* them, only to the sick man. The paralytic then, very probably, had some deep feeling respecting past sin, which made him afraid even in the presence of the Great Healer. What was the nature of his fear? Very probably it arose from the doctrine inculcated by the Rabbinical teachers that all such bodily infirmities were the punishment of sin in himself or in his parents (John ix. 2), or connected with this

21 ᵐ And the scribes and the Pharisees began to reason, saying, Who is this which speaketh blasphemies? ⁿ Who can forgive sins, but God alone?

ᵐ Matt. ix. 3. Mark ii. 6, 7.
ⁿ Ps. xxxii. 5. Is. xliii. 25.

---

that his bodily affliction could not be removed unless his sins had been remitted; and who could do this? To this fear the Lord addressed himself in the absolving words: "Thy sins be forgiven thee." A question has been raised whether the Lord by the words He uses signifies: "Thy sins are forgiven thee," *i.e.*, then, at that time, through the power of the Lord's absolving words, or "Thy sins have been forgiven thee," *i.e.*, at some time of his past life which the Lord knew, because He knew the history of every man's soul. In this last case the Lord's word would be in no way absolving, being totally unconnected with the man's forgiveness, which had taken place long before.

Now it is as clear as possible that the Lord meant His words to be absolving, because when the Pharisees objected: "Who can forgive sins, but God only?" instead of disabusing them by saying, "I merely meant that by My knowledge of men's past spiritual history, I know that this man's sins have been forgiven," He says, "That ye may know that the Son of man hath power on earth to forgive." A plainer claim to exercise by His mere Word the power of Absolution cannot be imagined.

21. "And the scribes and the Pharisees began to reason . . . Who can forgive sins, but God alone?" In my Notes on St. Matthew I dwelt somewhat on the fact that here we have the most unspiritual men, opposers of Christ to the uppermost, professing to uphold against Him the sole honour of God, in that God and God only forgives sin. In asserting this they asserted one side of a truth, another side of which is that God, Who is invisible, is wont to dispense the benefits of His kingdom of grace through the lips or the hands of others. This great principle was asserted partially under the old dispensation under which these Pharisees and Doctors lived, in that certain degrees of cleansing and reconciliation were dispensed by the priests through the blood of sacrifices; but it was to be much more fully carried out in that kingdom of grace which Christ was to inaugurate. In it His Apostles were in His absence far more fully to represent Him than Aaron and his brethren represented God. Its beginning was, "As my Father sent me so send I you."

22 But when Jesus perceived their thoughts, he answering said unto them, What reason ye in your hearts?

23 Whether is easier, to say, Thy sins be forgiven thee; or to say, Rise up and walk?

24 But that ye may know that the Son of man hath power upon earth to forgive sins, (he said unto the sick of the palsy,) I say unto thee, Arise, and take up thy couch, and go into thine house.

It contained such promises as, "He that heareth you heareth me." "He that despiseth you despiseth me." "I am with you alway." By their hands the Lord was to baptize. By their hands He was to dispense the Spirit in Confirmation and Ordination. By their hands He was to feed the faithful with His Body and Blood, and by their lips He was to absolve. And one of the ways in which He prepared men to receive this was by claiming to absolve, not as the Son of God, but as the Son of Man, "That ye may know that the Son of man hath power on earth to forgive sins."

Let no one then be surprised or moved by hearing even religious persons speak against the Absolutions of the Church. It is not a sign of piety or spirituality. It is rather a sign that such persons know not the Scriptures nor the power of God, they have no notion of what the Kingdom of God or the Church of Christ really is; for the Lord has set forth in His Word, in the plainest terms, that He will exercise that Headship through a ministry set apart to His service, which will exist and exercise its functions till He comes again.

22, 23, 24. "But when Jesus perceived ... go into thine house." The Lord shows them that all He did was in the Name and Power of God by two signs. First He showed them that He read the thoughts of their hearts by exposing their secret reasonings that He was claiming a power in the invisible world to which He had no right. "I do not claim this power unreasonably, with no sign to show that what I do is ratified at God's secret tribunal. On the contrary, I will work a work on this man's body, which only God can bring about, and which, if I were a blasphemer, He would not permit me to do. I will say to this man 'Arise and walk;'" and the Lord said this, and His word was with power, for

25 And immediately he rose up before them, and took up that whereon he lay, and departed to his own house, glorifying God.

26 And they were all amazed, and they glorified God, and were filled with fear, saying, We have seen strange things to day.

25. "Immediately he rose up before them .... glorifying God." If it be rejoined to what I have said above respecting the power of Absolution that the ministers of Christ have no right to claim it except they can prove their right by miracles similar to this, I answer, No, for such miracles of Christ as this, followed by His Resurrection, the crowning sign of all, prove not only that He had Himself power on earth to forgive, but that He had also authority to inaugurate a system, viz., His Church, and a ministry which should represent Him and dispense His forgiving and strengthening grace, not only to sinners during one age when miracles were common, but to the many generations in which there would be few or none. To assume to give the Holy Ghost in such a rite as Ordination or Confirmation, or to feed men with What can with any propriety be called His Body and His Blood, are each of them surely as great, if not greater things, than to pronounce a guarded Absolution in His Name in which all ultimate power of forgiveness is reserved to God alone.[1] [For further discussion of this matter see my Notes on John xx. 21-23.]

25, 26. "And immediately he rose up before them .... strange things to-day." It was indeed worth while that the Lord should be interrupted in His preaching if the interruption should be the occasion of a miracle such as this, for it would show the hearers that if His word was thus with power it must be true, and would all be fulfilled in its season.

---

[1] Nothing can be more guarded against the idea that the Priest absolves by his own power than the Absolution in our Service for the Visitation of the Sick. First, Christ has left this power for the benefit of those only "who truly repent and believe;" then He Himself is invoked to forgive, "of his great mercy forgive thee thine offences;" and then the Priest absolves not in his own name, but "in the Name of the Father, and of the Son, and of the Holy Ghost."

27 ¶ ᵒ And after these things he went forth, and saw a publican, named Levi, sitting at the receipt of custom: and he said unto him, Follow me.   ᵒ Matt. ix. 9. Mark ii, 13, 14.

28 And he left all, rose up, and followed him.

29 ᵖ And Levi made him a great feast in his   ᵖ Matt. ix. 10. Mark ii. 15.

---

27. "And after these things he went forth, and saw a publican, ... follow me . . . . followed him." It is impossible to suppose that this was the first time that St. Matthew saw the Lord, or, indeed, that this was his first interview with Him. If we had only the Synoptics we should have, perhaps, imagined that the Lord first made acquaintance with Peter and his brother and his partners James and John when He went into his house, as we are told in the last chapter. Whereas from St. John's narrative we know that long before this He had conversed with them and attached them to Himself as, in some sort, His disciples. And so, no doubt, Matthew had seen many of the Lord's miracles and heard many of His discourses, and was deeply moved by what he saw and heard, so that these words, "Follow me," merely decided what had long been in the mind of Matthew, that he should give up a calling hateful to his co-religionists and full of temptations, and from henceforth attach himself to the Lord.

But there can be no doubt that the narrative seems to set forth a sort of miracle in the mind of the Evangelist, in that he was in a moment, as it were, set free from all covetous desires, and at once enabled to surrender himself to the Lord, to follow Him in poverty and persecution and contempt of a very different kind from that which he had hitherto endured from the unpopularity of his occupation. In my Notes on St. Mark's Gospel I gave several proofs of the great probability that there was then a religious movement among the publicans as a class, which had influenced this Matthew, or Levi. The change in his name, very probably by the will of Jesus Himself, was what had taken place in the case of the greater part of the Apostles. It seemed right in His sight that they who were to live such totally new lives should bear new names. In their case was fulfilled the words of the prophet, "Thou shalt be called by a new name, which the mouth of the Lord shall name."

29. "And Levi made him a great feast . . . . sat down with them." From St. Matthew and St. Mark we should simply gather

own house: and ꟴ there was a great company of publicans
ꟴ ch. xv. 1.   and of others that sat down with them.

30 But their scribes and Pharisees murmured against his disciples, saying, Why do ye eat and drink with publicans and sinners?

31 And Jesus answering said unto them, They that are whole need not a physician; but they that are sick.

ʳ Matt. ix. 13.
1 Tim. i. 15.   32 ʳ I came not to call the righteous, but sinners to repentance.

---

30. "But their scribes and Pharisees." So A., E., F., K., M., other later Uncials, almost all Cursives, Goth., Syriac, Æth.; but (א), B., C., D., L., a few Cursives (1, 33, 131, 157), old Latin, Vulg., Copt., Arm., read, "The Pharisees and their scribes."

that Jesus took refreshment in the house; but St. Luke tells that Levi, or Matthew, made Him a great feast, and that he did this with the view not only of taking leave of his former associates, but of bringing them and others into the company of the Lord, that they might hear from His own lips the words of salvation which had separated him from his former evil life.

30. "But their scribes and Pharisees murmured against his disciples," &c. In St. Matthew and St. Mark (by implication) the Pharisees complain to the disciples against the Lord. "Why eateth your Master with publicans and sinners?" Here they murmur against the Apostles themselves: "Why do ye eat and drink?" But this is a sign of the truth of the narrative. They would at one moment complain against the Lord, at another against the Lord and His Apostles together.

31, 32. "And Jesus answering said .... sinners to repentance." This is a truth of the widest application possible. It was because the race of mankind was not righteous like the angels, but sinful and corrupt by nature, that the Lord came amongst us. If any of the race of men were absolutely righteous they would have no need of the Saviour as a cleanser and healer. If any of the race think themselves righteous, they, of necessity, must think themselves less in need of the Saviour as a cleanser and healer. Well, then, has God ceased to love righteousness? Does He desire that men should commit unrighteousness in order that they may realize the healing power of Christ? God forbid. If God be truly "righteousness," He must approve of righteousness in everyone, believer

33 ¶ And they said unto him, *Why do the disciples of John fast often, and make prayers, and likewise *the disciples* of the Pharisees; but thine eat and drink?

*Matt. ix. 14.
Mark ii. 18.

33. "Why do." So ℵ*, A., C., D., R., later Uncials, almost all Cursives, old Latin, Vulg., Syriac, other versions; but "why" omitted by B., L., (33, 157), Copt.

or unbeliever, heathen or Christian, converted or unconverted. Suppose then, that a man has lived a comparatively righteous life, has the Saviour come to call him? Yes, and the call of the Saviour will, no matter how innocently the man has lived, convince him of sin and of his need of the cleansing and strengthening power of the Lord. We have a remarkable example of this in Scripture. God himself witnessed respecting holy Job, "that there was none like him in the earth, a perfect and an upright man, one that feareth God and escheweth evil" (Job i. 8), and, yet, when God came near to Job, so that Job could say, "I have heard of thee with the hearing of the ear, but now mine eye seeth thee," then Job "abhorred himself, and repented in dust and ashes" (xlii. 5, 6). Now the call of Christ will do this to the most righteous man. It will reveal to him God, and it will reveal to him himself; and the man will soon see his need of the Physician, and in all probability his after life will be humbler, and his walk more careful than the man whom Christ calls out of the slough of wilful sin.

Mark too, that the call of Christ is to repentance—that is, to shame for past sin and a loathing of it, and a desire to be rid of it, and to serve God with a perfect heart and cleansed conscience.

33-35. "And they said unto him, Why do the disciples of John fast often . . . . fast in those days." The Lord had instituted no fasts, whilst the strict Jews kept two days of the week as days of abstinence, and it may be that John had also instituted some weekly fasts which the disciples of the Lord kept not. The Lord excuses them on the ground that the time when He was with them was a time of joy; times of distress and hardship and bitter persecution were to overtake them after He had left them, but these days were not as yet. When He left them He prophesied that they would "fast in those days." It is to be observed that the Lord in no respect blamed the Pharisees and the disciples of John for fasting, as He did the former for making void God's law by their traditions. He does not class their fasts among the burdens grievous and heavy to be borne. He had, in

THE BRIDEGROOM WITH THEM. [St. Luke.

34 And he said unto them, Can ye make the children of the bridechamber fast, while the bridegroom is with them?

35 But the days will come, when the bridegroom shall be taken away from them, and then shall they fast in those days.

t Matt. ix. 16, 17. Mark ii. 21, 22.
36 ¶ ᵗ And he spake also a parable unto them; No man putteth a piece of a new garment upon an old; if otherwise, then both the new maketh a rent, and the piece that was *taken* out of the new agreeth not with the old.

---

36. "No man putteth a piece," &c. So A., C., later Uncials, almost all Cursives, Ital., Vulg., and some versions; but ℵ, B., D., a few Cursives (1, 22, 33, 131, 157, 251), Copt., Syriac, read, "No man putteth a piece that he hath torn from a new garment."

His Sermon on the Mount, actually joined fasting with prayer and almsgiving as a means of grace which, if rightly and humbly and unostentatiously used, would call down the blessing of God.

35. "Then shall they fast in those days." Christians, in and from the New Testament times, have always thus fasted, as I have shown in my Notes on St. Mark. [See Acts xiii. 2, xiv. 23; 2 Corinth. vi. 5, xi. 27.] I cannot help noticing how English Protestant commentators try to get rid of this prophecy, one saying that the true fasting is fasting from sin, forgetting that the question might be put to him, When are we allowed to feast in sin? Surely the English-speaking races have, as yet, shown no disposition to err on the side of self-denial, that they should be cautioned against fasting, as if they were in the smallest danger from such a quarter. Taking the very lowest ground, fasting is useful as a discipline. How can we, according to the precept of the Apostle, present our *bodies* a living sacrifice truly acceptable to God (Rom. xii. 1)—how can we, after the example of the same Apostle, keep under our bodies and bring them into subjection (1 Cor. ix. 27), if we of set purpose neglect the precept and the example of the Lord Himself (Matth. iv. 2; vi. 18), in this matter?

36. "And he spake also a parable unto them; . . . shall perish." If the new cloth is put in to patch up the old, then the new, when washed or exposed to the rain, will shrink, and the borders of the new will soon start from the old, and there will be unsightly rents or openings: and if new wine is put into old wine-skins, the new

NEW WINE, OLD BOTTLES.

37 And no man putteth new wine into old bottles; else the new wine will burst the bottles, and be spilled, and the bottles shall perish.

38 But new wine must be put into new bottles; and both are preserved.

38. "And both are preserved." So A., C., D., later Uncials, almost all Cursives, old Latin, Vulg., and various versions; omitted by א, B., L., five or six Cursives (1, 33, 131, 157, 209, 301), Copt.

wine will be sure to burst the old skins, because in the new the fermentation is not altogether finished, and the old skins being weak and unelastic will give way. The explanation, notwithstanding the difficulties which have been made of the passage, seems very easy. The old cloth and the old wine is the old or Jewish dispensation, the new cloth or new wine is the Christian, and the Lord here teaches a lesson which even the Apostles were very slow in learning, viz., that the Christian Church cannot be put as a patch on to Judaism, but the old garment must be altogether laid aside and the new one put on. Again, the new dispensation has a spirit, as it were, which cannot be tied down to the old forms, but must have forms of its own, adapted to its own catholic diffusive character. Take, for instance, that which was most of all characteristic of Judaism, its strictly local and national character. It is clear that a religion which required yearly pilgrimages to Jerusalem, and held all sacrifices unlawful, except those offered at one altar by one tribe of national priests, could never be transformed into a Catholic Church. It must "vanish away," and the new state of things which is so able to subdue all nations to the obedience of faith, cannot be made to patch up or supplement the old, but must take its place.

39. "No man also having drunk old wine straightway desireth new . . . old is better." Most modern commentators seem agreed that the Lord uttered this short additional parable in a spirit of large-heartedness, or charity, as making an excuse for the slowness, or even inability, of His countrymen to embrace the Gospel. And this seems more probable if we take one fact into full account, viz., that for many years the Lord did not require those Jews who accepted Him, to give up the profession and rites of Judaism. On the contrary, we read that many years after the Ascension, and the outpouring of the Spirit, there were in Jerusalem myriads of Jews

39 No man also having drunk old *wine* straightway desireth new: for he saith, The old is better.

---

39. "Straightway" omitted by ℵ, B., C., L., and a few Cursives; retained by A., later Uncials, most Cursives, Vulg., Syriac.

who were all zealous for the law: and that there was the greatest difference made (no doubt with God's approval) between them and the believing Gentiles; for whereas in the Gentiles it was something akin to apostasy to put on a national ceremonial yoke never intended for them, the Jews were allowed to observe the law in its fulness to the last, *i.e.* to the time when to observe it became impossible, because the temple, which was its only lawful home and centre, was destroyed.

The Jews then were those who had drunk the old wine, and were permitted to continue as far as possible so to do: the Gentiles, on the contrary, having never drunk the old wine, having never been brought up in these exclusive doctrines and ordinances, were forbidden so to do.

CHAP. VI.

AND ᵃ it came to pass on the second sabbath after the first, that he went through the corn fields; and his disciples plucked the ears of corn, and did eat, rubbing *them* in *their* hands.

ᵃ Matt. xii. 1.
Mark ii. 23.

---

1. "On the second sabbath after the first," or, "second first sabbath." So A., C., D., E., H., K., M., other later Uncials, almost all Cursives, a few old Latin (a, f*), Vulg., Goth., Syriac, &c.; but "on a sabbath" in ℵ, B., L, a few Cursives (1, 22, 33, 69, 118, 157, 209), some old Latin (b, c, e, f**, l, q), Copt., Syriac, Æth.

1. "And it came to pass on the second sabbath after the first, that he went through, &c. . . . rubbing them in their hands." The second sabbath after the first, literally the second-first sabbath. This is a very difficult phrase, and all explanations of it must be conjectural, as there is apparently no sabbath designated by this name in any Rabbinical writing. One of the two following explanations seems most likely: (1) either that it was the sabbath

CHAP. VI.] NOT LAWFUL ON THE SABBATH. 143

2 And certain of the Pharisees said unto them, Why do ye that ᵇ which is not lawful to do on the sabbath days?   ᵇ Ex. xx. 10.

A.D. 31.   3 And Jesus answering them said, Have ye

2. "To do." So ℵ, A., C., L., later Uncials, Copt., Syriac; omitted by B., old Latin, Vulg.

which occurred during the Octave of Pentecost—the greatest sabbath of the year being the Passover sabbath (that sabbath day was an high-day), and the one occurring at the next greatest feast, that of Pentecost, would be the next greatest, or next-first, or second-first, the Passover sabbath being the first-first, or by far the greatest. The feast of Tabernacles would be the third. But very many take it to be a sabbath at the Passover, either the first sabbath after the second day of that festival, from which the sabbaths to Pentecost are numbered, or the last day of the feast, which was to be observed as a sabbath.

Whichever of these is the true meaning, it appears to me that St. Luke does not designate this day as the second-first, to mark the date when the transaction occurred, but to mark the peculiar holiness of the day. The disciples were in their estimation breaking no ordinary sabbath, but one of the most sacred of all. The breaking of the sabbath on the part of the disciples did not consist in their plucking the ears of corn, but in rubbing them with their hands.[1]

3-4. "And Jesus answering them said, . . . priests alone?" If so very sacred a law as the eating of the hallowed bread, or shewbread, by the priests alone, was to give way to the necessities of

[1] The reader will find an immense number of ridiculous ways of breaking the sabbath in Edersheim's "Life of Christ," Appendix xvii. The following bear on this sin of " rubbing with their hands : " " If a woman were to roll wheat to take away the husks, she would be guilty of sifting with a sieve. If she were rubbing the ends of the stalks she would be guilty of threshing. If she were cleaning what adheres to the side of a stalk she would be guilty of sifting. If she were bruising the stalk she would be guilty of grinding. If she were throwing it up in her hands she would be guilty of winnowing it " (vol. ii. p. 783).

not read so much as this, ^c what David did, when himself was
^c 1 Sam. xxi. 6. an hungred, and they which were with him;

4 How he went into the house of God, and did take and eat the shewbread, and gave also to them that were with him; ^d Lev. xxiv. 9. ^d which it is not lawful to eat but for the priests alone?

5 And he said unto them, That the Son of man is Lord also of the sabbath.

---

4. After verse 4 Codex D. alone of MSS. inserts the following: "On the same day having beheld a certain man working on the sabbath, He said to him, Man, if thou knowest what thou doest thou art blessed, but if thou knowest not thou art cursed, and a transgressor of the law." It is exceedingly improbable that the Lord said anything of the sort, for He never gave man a licence to work on the sabbath, though He reprobated the Pharisaical enactments which made it a burden.

David and his companions in arms, much more should such a ridiculous straining of the law as forbade the removal of husks from wheat, give way before the necessities of the disciples of Him Who was "Lord of the sabbath."

I have enlarged so fully in my Notes on St. Matthew and St. Mark, on the Son of Man being Lord of the sabbath, that I need only here mention the two particulars in which He has shown His lordship: first, by changing the day of the weekly festival, so that our day of rest is kept, not on the seventh day, on which God rested, but on the first day of the week, in which Christ rose from the dead; and, secondly, by relaxing the strictness of the Jewish law, so that the sabbath instead of being a burden always fretting the conscience, may be a day of spiritual refreshment to those who, by the Spirit working in them, and sanctifying them, can keep it as such. If we are to keep the Christian sabbath aright, we must be risen in Spirit with Him Who on it brake the bands of death.

And yet all are bound to abstain from exacting work from others on Sunday, if it is "made for man" as the Lord so emphatically says that it is. It is made especially for those who have on the six days to labour for their daily bread, that they may have one day for rest, and for attendance at Christian Instruction, Prayer, and Eucharist.

6. "And it came to pass also on another sabbath," &c. From St. Luke's account alone we learn that this was on another sabbath.

CHAP. VI.] HE KNEW THEIR THOUGHTS. 145

6 ᵉAnd it came to pass also on another sabbath, that he entered into the synagogue and taught: and there was a man whose right hand was withered.

ᵉ Matt. xii. 9. Mark iii. 1. See chap. xiii. 14, & xiv. 3. John ix. 16.

7 And the scribes and Pharisees watched him, whether he would heal on the sabbath day; that they might find an accusation against him.

8 But he knew their thoughts, and said to the man which had the withered hand, Rise up, and stand forth in the midst. And he arose and stood forth.

---

7. "An accusation against him." So A., E., F., H., K., L., M., and other later Uncials, most Cursives, Goth., Copt., Arm.; but אֵ, B., three or four Cursives (1, 22, 28, 124, 131), Vulg. (Amiat.), &c., "Find how to accuse him."

This emphasizes the fact that the Lord by preference chose the sabbath for the performance of His miracles of healing. His miracles were as much acts of instruction as His discourses. They taught that He was Himself the source of all good to the bodies and souls of men. They directed the attention of the multitudes who frequented the synagogues to Himself, as exhibiting the Divine Mercy and Compassion as well as the Divine Wisdom and Power.

"Whose right hand was withered." Not only was the diseased nerve incapable of conveying sensation and the power of motion, but its impotence deprived the arm and hand of that necessary function of all living healthy flesh of renewing itself, so that it was shrivelled and to all intents and purposes a dead thing. This is a parable teaching us that spiritual life and activity are ever united. Life is seen in action and sensation, and seems unable to exist if it is not in constant use of some sort.

7. "And the scribes and Pharisees watched him, whether he would heal on the sabbath day," &c. What extraordinary malignity, to watch in order that they might accuse a man for benefiting his fellow-man, and the Benefactor doing it by a power which, being always exercised on the side of goodness and virtue, must be from the Author of all good! How near in all this did they come to committing the sin against the Holy Ghost!

8. "But he knew their thoughts, and said to the man which had the withered hand," &c. According to St. Matthew the Scribes first asked the question, "Is it lawful to heal on the sabbath day?" According to St. Mark and our Evangelist they watched whether

L

9 Then said Jesus unto them, I will ask you one thing; Is it lawful on the sabbath days to do good, or to do evil? to save life, or to destroy *it?*

10 And looking round about upon them all, he said unto the man, Stretch forth thy hand. And he did so: and his hand was restored whole as the other.

11 And they were filled with madness; and communed one with another what they might do to Jesus.

---

9. "I will ask." So A., D., later Uncials, most Cursives, many old Latin (a, b, c, &c.), Syriac, Arm., Æth.; but ℵ, B., L., some old Latin, Vulg., Copt., " I ask."

"Whether it is lawful" in A., E., K., M., S., &c., very many Cursives; but ℵ, B., D., L., some old Latin (a, c, e, f, n), Vulg.. Copt., Syriac, &c., read, " If it is lawful," &c.

10. "Whole as the other." "Whole" omitted by ℵ, A., B., D., K., L., many Cursives, old Latin, Vulg., and so is doubtful. "As the other " omitted by ℵ, B., L., some Cursives (33, 34, 63), some old Latin (a, e), Vulg.

He would heal. Perhaps we must reconcile these statements by supposing that as soon as they saw the man with the withered hand they anticipated the Lord's action, because He had constantly chosen the sabbath as the fittest day for such exhibitions of Divine power. They then asked, " Is it lawful to heal on the sabbath?" thus endeavouring to cast a doubt on the lawfulness of what they supposed He was about to do. But having made the man rise up and stand in the midst in order that all in the synagogue might see his deplorable state, He gave an unexpected turn to the question by putting it in the form, "Is it lawful to do good on the sabbath day?" "Surely it is right to do good to a fellow-creature on any day!" must be the answer. And especially when they considered that the sabbath day was instituted for the most benevolent of purposes, " That thy man servant and thy maid servant may rest as well as thou."

But, as St. Mark tells us, they gave no answer, " They held their peace." Having then looked round about upon them all, with mingled grief and anger, He healed the man by restoring the withered hand whole as the other.

11. " And they were filled with madness; . . . do to Jesus." St. Luke alone describes the effect upon them in these terms.

Now all this teaches us Christians this lesson—that men who are in their whole habit of mind utterly apart from God, and alienated

12 ᶠ And it came to pass in those days, that he went out into a mountain to pray, and continued all night   ᶠ Matt. xiv. 23. in prayer to God.

13 ¶ And when it was day, he called *unto him* his dis-

---

from Him by envy, rancour, malice, and hypocrisy, may seemingly assert the honour of an outward law like that of the sabbath, and accuse the holiest men of breaking it; and this because the latter understand the highest of all laws, the law of liberty—not the law of licence, which prompts to the breaking the commandment, but the very spirit and intent of the law, which often refuses to be enclosed in the bare letter.

12. "And it came to pass in those days, that he went out into a mountain to pray," &c. The Lord, having the same nature as ours, would desire retirement for closer intercourse with His Father. The company which always seem to have flocked around Him, the importunity of those who desired healing for themselves and for their friends, the questioning of friends and foes, the consciousness that some were always watching Him—all these things must have tended to hinder His human soul in the matter of unburdening itself to God, especially at such a juncture as this, when He must now choose those who were to represent Him, to found His Church, and ultimately in the future world to share His glory.

Now this teaches us that the Lord can feel for those who are distracted in prayer. He can sympathize with those whose circumstances seldom or never allow them to be in retirement; but it also teaches us that, if possible, we must seek retirement for devotion. Thus Cyril: "Let us examine then in the actions which Jesus did how He teaches us to be instant in prayer to God, going apart by ourselves, and in secret, no one seeing us; putting aside also our worldly cares, that the mind may be raised up to the height of Divine contemplation; and this we have marked in the fact that Jesus went up into a mountain apart to pray."

13. "And when it was day, he called unto him his disciples: and of them," &c. I have enlarged in my Notes on St. Matthew and St. Mark on the significance of the Lord Himself, and not the body of the disciples, choosing the Apostles, choosing a definite and almost sacred number, so that not all were Apostles, separating them from the rest of His followers, always to be with Him, giving them special instruction which He withheld from the rest, and in every

ciples: ᵍand of them he chose twelve, whom also he named apostles;

ᵍ Matt. x. 1.

---

way seeming to designate them as as an order of men in His Church who were especially to lead, to command, to bind, to loose; so that, from the very first, the Christian ministry, as contained in the Apostles, should be the commencement of the organization of the Church: an organization in His absence connecting Himself in heaven with His Church on earth; an organization by, and in, and through which, He would ordinarily work in the Church; though, of course, reserving to Himself the right of raising up faithful men to act as Apostles in reforming the Church, in extending it, in deepening its piety, in bringing before it long-forgotten truths.

"And when it was day, he called unto him his disciples: and of them," &c. Quesnel has a remark which I cannot help reproducing:—"Jesus prays as man, but chooses as God, and as the Sovereign Pastor in the Name of God, He consults neither those He chooses, nor those from among whom He chooses them; but without any human respect whatever executes His Father's will. Mission is so essentially necessary to a man's having authority in the Church, that Christ would have His first ministers bear the name of Apostles, or envoys, to the end that their mission might be as well known as their very name; and that all the world might be convinced that there is no true mission in the Church but His."

The word "Apostle" means, of course, one sent, and the extent of the "sending," or "mission," we gather from the Lord's own words, "As my Father sent me, so send I you." His Apostles were sent by Him to represent Himself, and in His place to do all things which He did which are capable of being done by mere men. Did He govern as Bishop? So are they to do the same. Did He preach and teach? So are they. Did He expiate sin? They cannot do this, but they can apply His own all-sufficient expiation, and this they must do. And so, did He absolve? So are they to absolve. Did He celebrate the Eucharist? So are they. Did He offer to men His Body and Blood for their spiritual food and sustenance? So must they offer it to their brethren. So that the ministry which was in its fulness in Him is to be in them, and as He transmitted it to them so are they to transmit it to others, and this is to last till He comes again.

SIMON AND ANDREW.

14 Simon, (ʰ whom he also named Peter,) and Andrew his brother, James and John, Philip and Bartholomew, ʰ John i. 42.

14. "James and John, Philip." ℵ, B., D., K., L., many Cursives, old Latin (a, b, c), some Codices of Vulgate, Syriac, and Arm., read "and" before "James" and also before "Philip;" but A., E., M., other later Uncials, most Cursives, some old Latin and Vulg. (Amiat.) as in Rec. Text.

14. Simon, (whom he also named Peter,) and Andrew his brother." As I promised in my commentary on St. Mark, I shall here notice very shortly what is said in Scripture and ecclesiastical history respecting the remainder of the Apostles after the three first, Simon, James, and John.

"Andrew his brother." Andrew is not a Jewish, but a Gentile name, and signifies "manly." He was, at first, a disciple of the Baptist, and began to follow the Lord, when the Baptist pointed to Him as the Lamb of God. Through him his brother Simon was brought into the presence of the Lord. Once only he is found in company with the more favoured three, when Peter, James, John, and Andrew asked the Lord privately, "When shall these things be?" Again we find him associated with Philip in bringing before the Lord the request of certain Greeks. The only other separate notice is where he mentions the lad having the five loaves. According to Eusebius he preached in Scythia.

For James and John see my Notes on St. Mark, and for John my Introduction to his Gospel.

"Philip." The first mention of this Apostle is by St. John, who tells us that the Lord found him (John i. 43) either on His way to, or in, Galilee. He then brought Nathanael to Christ. It was to Philip that the Lord put the question, "Whence shall we buy bread that these may eat?" He joined with Andrew in telling Jesus of the Greeks who wished to see Him, and in the last discourse he put in the word, "Lord, shew us the Father, and it sufficeth us," and received the memorable answer, "He that hath seen me, hath seen the Father." After this there is no mention whatsoever of him in the New Testament.[1] The place where he preached and ended his days is unknown. One tradition places it in Parthia, another in Scythia.

---

[1] The article on him in Smith's "Dictionary of the Bible" gives a number of wild legends from apocryphal books not worth attention.

15 Matthew and Thomas, James the *son* of Alphæus, and Simon called Zelotes,

---

15. "Matthew." "And" inserted by much the same authorities (א, B., D., L., &c.) as those mentioned in last critical note as inserting it before "Philip;" omitted by A. and some who omitted it there.
"James." "And" here inserted by א, B., D., L., &c.; omitted by A., E., M., &c., as in previous verses.

"Bartholomew," or son of Tolmai. Very probably the same as Nathanael. Nathanael seems to have been of the number of the twelve from his being mentioned as an Apostle in John xxi. 2. He is always associated with Philip in the lists of the Apostles. Nothing more is known of him than that the Lord witnessed respecting him that he was "an Israelite indeed, in whom there is no guile." Nothing further is mentioned of him under either the name of Bartholomew or Nathanael. He is said by Eusebius to have preached the Gospel in India.

15. "Matthew." Respecting Matthew, called also Levi, and said to be the son of Alphæus, I must refer to my Introduction to St. Matthew's Gospel. After his call to the feast that he made for the Lord, he is never mentioned in the New Testament as speaking any one word, or doing any particular act apart from the others. He is said by Eusebius to have preached the substance of his Gospel to his countrymen in Palestine in an unwritten form and afterwards on his leaving them to preach in more distant parts, he committed it to writing that they might the better remember what he had preached.

"Thomas." We have no notice whatsoever taken of St. Thomas in the three Synoptics except the mention of his name in their lists of the twelve. St. John, however, records three sayings of his, in each case calling him Didymus. First, when he heard that the Lord, Whose life had been threatened by the Jews, intended to go to Bethany again, Thomas said to his fellow disciples "Let us go also, that we may die with him." On a second occasion he asks, "Lord, we know not whither thou goest, and how can we know the way?" and elicited from the Lord the memorable answer, "I am the way, the truth, and the life; no man cometh unto the Father but by me." The third, the scene which occurred on the eighth day after the Resurrection, is too well known to require further mention. After this he appears as one of the five who were with the Lord at His showing himself on the lake of Galilee: and then he is mentioned no more in Scripture, except as one of the Apostles who were in the

16 And Judas [1]*the brother* of James, and Judas Iscariot, which also was the traitor. [1] Jude i.

---

upper room after the Ascension. He is said to have preached in Parthia, or Persia, and to have died at Edessa, where his tomb is mentioned by St. Chrysostom as actually existing in his time.

"James the son of Alphæus." Respecting this James, if he be not the Bishop of Jerusalem, and the writer of the Epistle bearing the name of James (and I do not see how he well can be) nothing whatsoever is said in Scripture. In an appendix on "the brethren of the Lord," in my Commentary on St. Mark, I have given many reasons for believing that the Bishop of Jerusalem, the Lord's brother, and James the son of Alphæus, were three different persons. Alphæus, the name of his father, or Cleophas, or Clopas, seems to have been a common name among the Jews, so that it is impossible to say whether Alphæus the father of Levi or Matthew, and Alphæus the father of this James, and Alphæus the husband of the Mary who stood by the cross, were the same, or two, or even three different persons.

"Simon called Zelotes." The same as Simon the Kananite (not Canaanite as in the Authorized), in the lists in St. Matthew and St. Mark. No word said or act done by him has come down to us. He is said, on very doubtful authority, to have preached in Egypt and Cyrene, and on equally doubtful authority to have been crucified in Judæa in the reign of Domitian.

16. "And Judas the brother of James." In St. Matthew he is designated as Lebbæus, whose surname is Thaddeus; but the true reading may be simply Thaddeus, as he is described in Mark. It is not at all improbable that he should have two names, as indeed almost all the Apostles had. One saying of his is recorded by St. John: "Lord, how is it that thou wilt manifest thyself to us and not unto the world?" He is there carefully distinguished from his namesake the traitor, "Judas (not Iscariot) saith unto him." (John xiv. 22.) Respecting his sphere of work nothing certain is told us in tradition and ecclesiastical history, but he seems to have for some time preached the Gospel at Edessa, and beyond it in Assyria.

The three names, James, Judas, and Simon, are the same as those of three out of the four persons who are named as the Lord's brethren, in Matth. xiii. 55, and the parallel place, Mark vi. 3. Whether they were all the sons of Alphæus, and how they were

17 ¶ And he came down with them, and stood in the plain, and the company of his disciples, [k] and a great multitude of people out of all Judæa and Jerusalem, and from the sea coast of Tyre and Sidon, which came to hear him, and to be healed of their diseases;

18 And they that were vexed with unclean spirits: and they were healed.

19 And the whole multitude [l] sought to touch

[k] Matt. iv. 25. Mark iii. 7.

[l] Matt. xiv. 36.

---

17. "The company." So A., D., later Uncials, almost all Cursives, old Latin, Vulg.; but ℵ, B., L., two Cursives (1, 118), and Syriac, insert, "A great" (πολὺς).

---

related to the Lord is exceedingly difficult to decide. If the reader desires he will see the matter very acutely argued in favour of their being the sons of Alphæus, in Smith's "Dictionary of the Bible" (Article "James," page 920 to 923 of vol. i.).

"Judas Iscariot." Several interpretations have been given to the surname Iscariot—the most probable by far being that which connects it with Keriot in the tribe of Judah. Respecting the mystery of the fall of this man, see my notes on John xiii. 18 and 28. Respecting any special act of his in his character of Apostle, not a word has come down to us. We cannot suppose that he was an hypocrite and dishonest man when the Lord chose him, but by yielding constantly to the temptation to do little acts of fraud, he got hardened in sin, and at last ended with betraying the Lord.

17. "And he came down with them, and stood in the plain." This seems to tell us that the discourse which immediately follows is a different one from that called the Sermon on the Mount; the former was delivered before the call of the Apostles, and this evidently after. I believe that St. Luke, if he knew anything whatsoever of the original body of tradition, knew well the Sermon on the Mount, and that it was according to such tradition delivered on a mount; and in what follows he intends to give the draft of another discourse similar in some points, but, as we shall see, very different in others.

"And a great multitude, &c. . . . healed them all." This occurs so frequently in the Lord's ministry, that we cannot with any certainty use it as marking a particular time.

19. "And the whole multitude sought to touch him . . . healed them all." What gave rise to this peculiar action on the part of

him: for ᵐ there went virtue out of him, and healed *them* all.

20 ¶ And he lifted up his eyes on his disciples, and said, ⁿ Blessed *be ye* poor: for your's is the kingdom of God.

ᵐ Mark v. 30. ch. viii. 46.

ⁿ Matt. v. 3, & xi. 5. James ii. 5.

---

the multitude? Some one must have set them an example, and have been the first to receive a cure in this way. It is mentioned in Matthew xiv. 36, and Mark vi. 56, that the multitude did this, and in each case some time after the miracle of the healing of the woman who had the issue of blood. It seems most probable, then, that she was the first, and that the fame of her faith spread far and wide, and many openly availed themselves of this way of receiving healing from the Lord's person.

20. " And he lifted up his eyes on his disciples, and said, Blessed be ye poor," &c. The reader will at once perceive by these opening words that the discourse which follows is especially delivered to the disciples. If it is intended, as no doubt it is, for the whole Church, it is addressed to the Church through the disciples. We hear it with their ears, they receive it as our representatives. The Lord lifts up His eyes on the *disciples*, and the first beatitude is not expressed in general terms, "Blessed are the poor in spirit," but "Blessed be ye poor." Now it seems to me scarcely possible that, if the discourses are the same, St. Luke should have omitted the qualifying words "in spirit," for a poor man may be anything but poor in spirit. In numberless instances he is proud, overbearing, and conceited. It is also difficult to imagine why St. Luke, if he were reproducing parts of St. Matthew's sermon, should have narrowed the general into the particular — should have changed "the poor in spirit" into "ye poor." Indeed, the difference between the Sermon on the Mount and this sermon on the plain are such that each must be treated independently, as if they were distinct discourses, if we would endeavour to explain faithfully the words of the Lord.

"Blessed be ye poor." The Lord, as reported in St. Matthew, pronounces a blessing on a certain disposition of mind wherever and in whomsoever it may be found; here, on the contrary, He blesses certain persons, who, by an act of extreme self-renunciation, had attained to it. The disciples or apostles around Him had suro Is. lv. 1, & lxv. 13. Matt. v. 6.   21 °Blessed *are ye* that hunger now: for ye

rendered their all for His sake. They had surrendered those good things of this world which above all others have a tendency to raise men above their fellows, and make them look down upon them. The poverty or humility of spirit which, doubtless, they must have possessed, through the preaching of the Baptist, and that of the Lord, was increased or perfected when they left their all to follow the Lord, and so He addressed them as those in whom their voluntary poverty had produced the Divinely intended effect. " Ye poor, both actually and spiritually, Blessed be ye."

" For yours is the kingdom of heaven." To the Apostles especially belonged the good things of the kingdom of God in its present manifestation as the Church, the Body of Christ, for they were its founders, they laid down its laws, they shaped its first course. Taking the first marks or features of the Church as we have them in the account of the first Pentecostal Church, doctrine, fellowship, Eucharists, prayers (Acts ii. 42)—how intensely must the Apostles have realized these as theirs—theirs not for themselves, but for all their fellow members! See how St. Peter writes about the doctrine of the Resurrection of the Lord, that it had begotten all men who accepted it "to a lively hope of an inheritance incorruptible and undefiled"; how must they have realized the "fellowship" who so constantly speak of the Church as all one in Christ; how must they have realized the Eucharist when one of them could say, "We being many are one bread and one body, for we are all partakers of that one Bread"! how must they have realized the prayers, when the twelve as one man put from them into semi-lay hands, the serving of tables, and the importance which belongs to it, with the words, "We will give ourselves continually to prayer, and to the ministry of the word"! Theirs was the kingdom of heaven, theirs was the understanding, the realizing, the dispensing of the treasures of Divine grace, long before each was called to sit on his throne in heaven itself.

21. "Blessed are ye that hunger now: for ye shall be filled." This means more than the corresponding blessing in St. Matthew, "Blessed are they which do hunger and thirst after righteousness." It seems to say, Not only blessed are ye that spiritually hunger after every Divine grace, for all shall be poured into you, but "blessed are ye that hunger, having no certain means of livelihood, for ye

shall be filled. ᵖ Blessed *are ye* that weep now : for ye shall laugh.

ᵖ Is. lxi. 3.
Matt. v. 4.

shall be filled, for ye shall lack nothing, the Divine power shall give you all pertaining to life and godliness." Quesnel has a remark of great depth and value upon this beatitude: "How glorious is it to God to make Himself beloved by men at the expense of all things, without the allurement of any sensible good whatsoever, and purely for His own sake ! This is a proof of His existence, a mark of His greatness, of the truth of His religion, and of the power of His grace."

"Blessed are ye that weep now, for ye shall laugh." This looks to far more than the comfort of the Gospel, which follows after the sense of the guilt of sin. It rather looks to the whole present state of things, as revealed in the Gospel, as a serious state, which will not allow those who realize it to live in pleasures and worldly amusements. The men of the present world are in danger, just as the men on the eve of the Deluge, and the sinners of Sodom were in danger, and those who have their eyes opened to understand the danger, will, to the extent to which they realize it, be concerned about it—for the members of their own families, their nearest neighbours, their best friends, may perish by it. Even under the Law the Psalmist could say, "Mine eyes gush out with water because men keep not thy law."

Such were the Apostles. They were men who had a purpose in life, and that the most overwhelmingly serious one that men could possibly have before them, to save men from that untoward generation, from "the wrath to come," from the anger of God revealed against all ungodliness and unrighteousness of men. Such men might not have always solemn looks, much less mournful ones, they might relax at times, but they could not laugh with the world. Such things as frivolity, light-hearted unthinking carelessness, unrestricted enjoyment of even sinless things, must have been in their eyes sin.

"Ye shall laugh." This is more than the "they shall be comforted" of the Sermon on the Mount. It points to exultation in the triumphs of the Gospel, and the extension of the Church. We can well imagine an Apostle laughing when some stronghold of Satan was overthrown, laughing for joy when he heard of some new Church planted in some city steeped heretofore in wickedness.

22 ⁹ Blessed are ye, when men shall hate you, and when they ʳ shall separate you *from their company*, and shall reproach *you*, and cast out your name as evil, for the Son of man's sake.

q Matt. v. 11.
1 Pet. ii. 19, &
iii. 14, & iv. 14.
r John xvi. 2.

Would not holy exultation have lighted up every feature of the Apostle's face, when he wrote, "Thanks be to God, which always causeth us to triumph in Christ, and maketh manifest the savour of his knowledge by us in every place"? (2 Cor. ii. 14.)

22, 23. "Blessed are ye, when men shall hate you .... fathers unto the prophets." In St. Matthew we have, first a blessing pronounced on those who are persecuted for righteousness' sake, then on those who are persecuted for Christ's sake (v. 10, 11). In this case only does St. Matthew make the Lord address the disciples personally as St. Luke does, "Blessed are ye, when men shall revile you." Now it seems plain from this that the Evangelists are reporting two separate discourses, and that this last beatitude was the only one in which the personal form of blessing, "blessed are *ye*," was the same. In fact, the only beatitude which is exactly the same in both. For it is clear that St. Matthew gives the full number of the beatitudes. The Lord must have pronounced each one which St. Matthew records, and yet it is equally plain that He could hardly have pronounced them according to St. Luke's form. He would not have said, "Blessed are ye meek ones," "Blessed are ye merciful ones," "Blessed are ye peacemakers." The four given by St. Luke are the only ones which could well have been pronounced personally on the disciples; so that the beatitudes as given by St. Matthew and St. Luke respectively, could not have been altered forms of the same discourse: and those in St. Luke, as we learn from what goes before, were especially addressed to the disciples, and are especially applicable to them.

"Hate you," because ye persistently press upon them My Redemption, which must, if received, separate them from the sins they love, and My judgment, which shall separate them for ever from the children of God, unless they repent. "Separate you," most probably, in a religious sense; cast you out of the synagogues, cast out your name as evil, *i.e.* erase your name from the synagogue rolls. [So Godet.]

"For the Son of man's sake." St. Matthew has "For my sake." "The latter expression (St. Matthew's) denotes attachment to the

23 ˢ Rejoice ye in that day, and leap for joy: for, behold, your reward *is* great in heaven: for ᵗ in the like manner did their fathers unto the prophets.

24 ᵘ But woe unto you ˣ that are rich! for ʸ ye have received your consolation.

25 ᶻ Woe unto you that are full! for ye shall

ˢ Matt. v. 12. Acts v. 41. Col. i. 24. James i. 2.
ᵗ Acts vii. 51.
ᵘ Amos vi. 1. James v. 1.
ˣ ch. xii. 21.
ʸ Matt. vi. 2, 5, 16. ch. 16, 25.
ᶻ Is. lxv. 13.

Person of Jesus; the former, faith in His Messianic Character, as the perfect representative of humanity." But is not this too refined? Evil men persecuted Jesus, not surely as the perfect representative of humanity, but as the perfect embodiment of that holiness and purity of God which they hated.

"Rejoice ye in that day," &c. They would rejoice because their persecution would be a sign to them that they were one with Christ in His sufferings, and so would be one with Him in His glory. [So Coloss. i. 23, 24; 1 Pet. iv. 12, 13, 14.]

24. "But woe unto you that are rich! for ye have received your consolation." These four woes are the exact counterpart of the four beatitudes. St. Matthew has, in the Sermon on the Mount, nothing corresponding to them, which, I think, he must have had if he and St. Luke reproduce with variations the same discourse: for if the Lord's words are to be faithfully reported, such severe sayings as these must receive some notice.

The Lord here does not enunciate a doctrine so much as declare a fact: for just as when He said, "Blessed are ye poor," He declares a fact which was true of those around Him who had given up all for His sake, so now He sets forth a fact that the rich and learned and covetous Scribes and Pharisees, and Sadducean High Priests, were accursed because their worldly possessions and worldly position hindered them from coming to Him that they might receive His Life. The reader cannot but remember the words of the Blessed Virgin: "He hath put down the mighty from their seat, The rich he hath sent empty away." And those of Abraham to the rich man: "Son, remember that thou in thy life-time receivedst thy good things." This is but one of a hundred places which declare that riches are a curse unless they are parted with, that the only way of neutralizing their ill effect is to give alms very bountifully of them.

25. "Woe unto you that are full." The reader will remember how the Lord said, "Take heed lest your hearts be overcharged

158 LOVE YOUR ENEMIES. [St. Luke.

hunger. ^a Woe unto you that laugh now! for ye shall mourn and weep.

26 ^b Woe unto you, when all men shall speak well of you! for so did their fathers to the false prophets.

27 ¶ ^c But I say unto you which hear, Love your enemies, do good to them which hate you,

^a Prov. xiv. 13.
^b John xv. 19. 1 John iv. 5.
^c Ex. xxiii. 4. Prov. xxv. 21. Matt. v. 44. ver. 35. Rom. xii. 20.

---

25. " Woe unto you that laugh now!" Some read, "Woe ye that laugh now."

26. " Woe unto you." " Unto you" omitted by ℵ, A., B., E., F., H., K., L., M., old Latin, Vulg., and most authorities; but retained only by D., Copt., Syriac, and a few versions.

---

with surfeiting, and drunkenness, and cares of this life, and so that day come upon you unawares " (Luke xxi. 34).

" Woe unto you that laugh now! " &c. See note on latter part of verse 21.

26. " Woe unto you, when all men shall speak well of you!" " When all men speak well of you, it is a sure sign that you have not been faithful witnesses to the humbling and purifying truths of the Gospel. If you are faithful you will raise up against you the hatred and opposition of the world, though you will have the respect and love of the people of God." This is true, in a measure, of all times; but more, of course, of those times in which the world and the Church were in deadly feud, than of times in which the world has been largely influenced and permeated with the truths of the Gospel. It would be well if all successors of the Apostles had the question of the Apostle ever in their minds : " Do I seek to please men? for if I yet pleased men, I should not be the servant of Christ " (Gal. i. 10). Rather, perhaps, we may say, the words of the Lord: " If ye were of the world, the world would love its own ; but because ye are not of the world, but I have chosen you out of the world, therefore the world hateth you " (John xv. 19).

27. " But I say unto you which hear, Love your enemies," &c. " Unto you which hear." Does this signify much the same as " He that hath ears to hear, let him hear " ? Does it not rather mark a change in the purport or in the subjects of the discourses ? In the four beatitudes Christ speaks to the disciples or apostles. In the four woes to those who are in their character, and in the side which

28 Bless them that curse you, and ^d pray for them which despitefully use you.   ^d ch. xxiii. 34. Acts vii. 60.

they take in the great struggle between the world and Christ, the opposite of the Apostles. Now His address becomes perfectly general; it is spoken to *all who hear*.

"Love your enemies." We are bound to look always to the context before we give any interpretation of a passage, and what has gone before, in verses 22 and 26, obliges us to interpret here, in the first place, these "enemies" and "those who hate us," as our enemies for the Gospel's sake. Now, Christian compassion would lead us to do this; for which is most to be pitied, the persecutor or the persecuted, the hater or the hated? Looked at in the light of the Cross and Judgment of Christ, undoubtedly the persecutor: for he hates the Christian because of his real Christianity, because he sees in him the power of the Cross to separate from sin and an evil world. Now what can be more terrible, and so more worthy of Christian compassion, than the case of the man whose love of sin and the world is such that he hates the Cross of Jesus because of its sin-destroying power? And such must be that of the enemies of the religion of the Cross: and what will be their fate when Christ comes to judge? Surely, then, such a precept, though so hard, so above human nature, is reasonable. And ten times more so when we take into account that Christianity is not merely a teaching system, but a system for the conveyance of the Grace, nay, even the Nature of Christ, to enable us to do the works of Christ, and amongst them to love our enemies as Christ loved His.

And the same applies in its measure to all enmity of all enemies. Is a man our enemy because he fancies that we stand in the way of his interests? He is fostering within himself a passion which will, in the end, do infinitely more harm to him than he can possibly do to us. We must set this before us, and we shall soon see that common Christian compassion would make us—at whatever cost to pride and self-love—meet his hatred with good-will.

"Love your enemies." Love is a feeling or affection of the heart, and we cannot command our affections. How is it to be got within us? Let us take some means of attaining to it, and God seeing our earnestness will bless them. Thus amongst those whom we pray for daily, if we know of anyone who regards us with dislike, let us pray for him, and if we find that in our hearts we are continually

29 ᵉ And unto him that smiteth thee on the *one* cheek offer also the other; ᶠ and him that taketh away thy cloke forbid not *to take thy* coat also.

30 ᵍ Give to every man that asketh of thee; and of him that taketh away thy goods ask *them* not again.

ᵉ Matt. v. 39.
ᶠ 1 Cor. vi. 7.
ᵍ Deut. xv. 7, 8, 10. Prov. xxi. 26. Matt. v. 42.

---

dwelling upon the thought of his enmity, and are tempted to wish him evil, let us pray very earnestly to God for a better mind. And if we have opportunity, let us do him some good, and let us pray for him that he also may be brought by God's grace to lay aside all ill-feeling, and be reconciled both to God and his brethren. Even against our inclinations we can force ourselves to do this, and God assuredly will look favourably upon the effort.

29. "And unto him that smiteth thee on the one cheek offer," &c. This is a proverbial saying, and, like many such, would, if obeyed literally, lose the desired effect of conciliating the adversary; and, besides, the Lord Himself did not do this literally, for when smitten He asked, "Why smitest thou me?" Quesnel expresses the spiritual meaning of this precept well, when he writes: "The proof of our love to our enemies is being disposed to suffer from them affronts, contempt, and ill-treatment; to relinquish our rights rather than to lose our meekness and charity towards them. Ever since our Blessed Saviour suffered His enemies to take away His life, it is by His patience that we must regulate our own."

"Give to every man that asketh of thee . . . ask them not again." I have treated this precept at very full length in my notes on St. Matthew v. 42, to which I must refer the reader. Of course such precepts must be taken with certain exceptions and limitations, such as, "We must not give so as to encourage idleness or mendicancy; we must not give where we know that what we give will be spent in sin." Our Lord knew perfectly well how necessary these limitations and exceptions are; but He was desirous of creating the Christian character, and this must be formed by the reception of great and universal principles, not by the contemplation of the exceptions and limitations. May I be permitted to reproduce here what I have written in my Commentary on St. Matthew? "Our Lord lays down one thing at a time in all its breadth and fulness; so that we may be struck by it, and have our minds occupied by it,

31 ʰAnd as ye would that men should do to you, do ye also to them likewise. ʰ Matt. vii. 12.

32 ˡFor if ye love them which love you, what ˡ Matt. v. 46. thank have ye? for sinners also love those that love them.

33 And if ye do good to them which do good to you, what thank have ye? for sinners also do even the same.

34 ᵏAnd if ye lend *to them* of whom ye hope to ᵏ Matt. v. 42. receive, what thank have ye? for sinners also lend to sinners, to receive as much again.

---

34. For sinners also." So A., later Uncials, all Cursives, old Latin, Vulg., &c.; but א, B., L., Coptic, read, "Even sinners," so Revisers.

and then, when we have firmly grasped the principle, there will be time to consider the limitations. It is infinitely more important that we should have within us the patience, the endurance, the charity, by which we resist not evil, and give to him that asketh, than the self-love and prudence, innocent though they are, which will preserve us from injuring ourselves by too literally following the leading of such patience and such charity."

31. "And as ye would that men should do to you," &c. This passage serves a very different purpose in this discourse to what it does in St. Matthew's Sermon on the Mount. In that sermon it follows upon some promises that God will hear prayer. And, as I have shown in my note, it signifies to us that if we would obtain our petitions fron God, we must be ready to grant the reasonable petitions of our brethren. Here, however, it must be taken with what follows.

32, 33, 34. " If ye love them . . . if ye do good to them . . . if ye lend . . . to receive as much again." We must do good to those who have no claim upon our kindness, just as we should wish to be benefited by those upon whom we have no claim since we have conferred upon them no kindness.

It is no virtue to love those who love us. It is no virtue to do good to those who do good to us. It is no virtue to lend to those from whom after a specified time we look to receive what we have lent them, perhaps with interest; and who may assist us because we have assisted them.

If we were penniless and friendless, we should desire that others

35 But ¹love ye your enemies, and do good, and ᵐ lend, hoping for nothing again; and your reward shall be great, and ⁿ ye shall be the children of the Highest: for he is kind unto the unthankful and *to* the evil.

ˡ ver. 27.
ᵐ Ps. xxxvii. 26. ver. 30.
ⁿ Matt. v. 45.

---

35. "Hoping for nothing again." So A., B., L., later Uncials, most Cursives. Old Latin reads, *Nihil desperantes*, Vulg., *Nihil inde sperantes*. Our Authorized is the only translation agreeing with the words before.
"Children;" rather, sons (υἱοί).

would help us out of pure bounty; and even if we had been their enemies, we should still cherish a secret hope that they would forget their enmity when they saw our distress: and so the Lord, building on this secret desire in all of us, that enemies may relent, and niggards be bountiful, and that we all may be treated unselfishly, says:—

35. "But love ye your enemies, and do good, and lend, hoping for nothing again." Upon this Chrysostom well remarks, "Whereby thou wilt confer more upon thyself than upon him. For he is beloved by a fellow-servant, but thou art made like unto God."

"And your reward shall be great." Though no Christian in doing good sets before himself any definite reward, but does good for the sake of God and for the love of the thing, yet God assures us over and over again, that not one good deed shall be forgotten, but that even the giver of a cup of cold water shall " in no wise lose his reward." But though the true Christian seldom, if ever, looks for a reward for himself, so little does he think of his services and self-denials, yet he looks for this reward in the case of others. When he hears of others doing good, spending themselves for the cause of Christ and the good of His poor, then he is free to rejoice, and he does rejoice, because he knows that they shall be welcomed to the joy of their Lord. As regards himself he recognizes no merit in himself, but casts himself wholly on the mercy of God; but in his brethren he recognizes merit, he thanks God for their subjection to the Gospel, and he is sure that as they have sown bountifully they shall reap also bountifully.

"Children of the Highest." Men are children of God by imitating Him. Thus God is the author of all peace, He is the God of peace, and the Lord blesses the peace-makers by the promise that " they shall be called the children of God." What mistakes and mis-

CHAP. VI.] JUDGE NOT. 163

36 °Be ye therefore merciful, as your Father also is merciful, ° Matt. v. 48.

37 ᵖ Judge not, and ye shall not be judged: ᵖ Matt. vii. 1.

---

conceptions there are about this term "children of God"! What numbers of Christian teachers professing to be regenerate, to be converted, to be saved—if they were asked how are we to become children of God, would never think of giving such an answer as the Lord gives here, "Love your enemies, do good, and lend, hoping for nothing again"! And yet it will be found at the last that this is the surest mark of God's true children, that they should be like to Him in forgiving and forbearing love.

"Be ye therefore merciful, as your Father also is merciful." This is the summing up of all that precedes. It is remarkable that in St. Matthew, in the corresponding passage, we have "Be ye perfect;" here we have "Be ye merciful." So that the perfection of God is His mercy; and it must be, if it caused Him to give His Son for us, the just for the unjust, that He might bring us to God.

37. "Judge not and ye shall not be judged, condemn not and ye shall not be condemned." "What Jesus desires to banish from the society of His disciples is the judging *spirit*, the tendency to place our faculty of moral appreciation at the service of natural malignity, or more simply still, judging for the pleasure of judging." (Godet).

The judging in the first clause is, of course, judging so as to censure and condemn; the condemning of the second clause signifies, from the preposition incorporated into the original word, a more downright condemning, a condemning without mercy, and without making any allowance for the circumstances adverse to virtue, or particular temptations in the way of our neighbour. Here the Lord inculcates that charity which is so well described by His servant (or rather by Himself through the pen of His servant) as "rejoicing not in iniquity," but "believing all things," and "hoping all things." The censorious spirit rejoices in the iniquity of its neighbour. It is the food upon which it preys. It looks out for it, and is determined to find it whether it be there or not. The loving spirit, on the contrary, "believeth all things," *i.e.*, believes that the heart is not so bad as the action seems to show; "hopeth all things," *i.e.*, hopes that an acquittal, a palliation, or an excuse will soon be

condemn not, and ye shall not be condemned: forgive, and
ye shall be forgiven:

q Prov. xix. 17.   38 q Give, and it shall be given unto you ; good

---

37. "Forgive, and ye shall be forgiven." The Revisers translate this, "Release, and ye shall be released;" but as the burden from which we are to be released is sin, it is better to retain the old rendering.

found. I have noticed, in my comment on the parallel passage in St. Matthew, that the judgment which the Lord condemns is the judging of the heart, *i.e.*, of the secret motives, on which we who cannot read the heart must pronounce no opinion, as we cannot do so with certainty. Sin, wherever it appears, is sin, and we must pronounce it to be such, if we would be sincere in our allegiance to Christ ; but we must not intrude into the office of the Searcher of hearts. The sin which we see may be the effect of some sudden unknown temptation, and not have its roots so deep as we might suppose.

"Forgive, and ye shall be forgiven." "Forgive" here is "release," and though it most probably primarily refers to forgiveness of all injuries, yet must be extended to releasing from all burdens, as from servitude, and from obligations which those who have contracted them are now no longer able to fulfil. Thus the Lord's prayer in St. Matthew's Gospel is, "Forgive us our debts, as we forgive our debtors."

But are we to take literally, "ye shall not be judged," "ye shall not be condemned," "ye shall be forgiven"? Does not forgiveness depend upon the Sacrifice of the Lord, not upon our forgiving one another? Of course it depends primarily on the Lord's Sacrifice which has opened the way for forgiveness; but we may depend upon it that at the last the Lord Who offered Himself for us will make good His own words, "Forgive, and ye shall be forgiven." We may not be able to reconcile with one another the various words in which the Lord has set forth the mysteries of grace. The Lord has not, as many vainly think, laid it upon us to do so ; but He has asked us to look upon Himself as our sacrifice and our reconciliation to God, and He has also bidden us, on the pain of forfeiting our part in this sacrifice, to be reconciled with one another.

38. "Give, and it shall be given unto you ; good measure, pressed down, and shaken together," &c. Does this refer to generous treat-

CHAP. VI.] MEASURED TO YOU AGAIN. 165

measure, pressed down, and shaken together, and running over, shall men give into your ʳ bosom. For ˢ with the same measure that ye mete withal it shall be measured to you again.

ʳ Ps. lxxix. 12.
ˢ Matt. vii. 2.
Mark iv. 24.
James ii. 13.

---

38. "With the same measure that ye mete." So A., C., later Uncials, most Cursives, most old Latin, Vulg., Syriac; but ℵ, B., D., L., some Cursives (1, 33, 131, 209), old Latin (e), Copt., Æth. read, "With what measure ye mete."

ment by our neighbours in this world, or by God in the eternal world? No doubt the latter, for the word "men" is not in the original. "It shall be given," without specifying the giver; and yet no doubt it will be found true in a sense of God's dealings with generous, open-hearted men in this world, that God will move the hearts of others to deal bountifully with them.

"Good measure, pressed down, shaken together, and running over." "He that soweth bountifully shall reap also bountifully." "It will be 'measure,' because the eternal reward will be dispensed by proportion, and according to deservings; 'good,' because it will be the true good, embracing in itself everything that is really good; 'pressed down,' because it will be to all fulness, having no part empty, nothing to desire (they shall be satisfied with the fulness of God); and 'shaken together,' because it will be firmly established and secure; and 'running over,' or abundant as surpassing all their deserts." (From an old medieval writer quoted in Williams'.)

"Give unto your bosom." Here is an allusion to the form of the Eastern garment, which like a large pocket can contain many things in the fold above the girdle.

"For with the same measure that ye mete withal it shall be measured to you again." "He that soweth sparingly shall reap also sparingly, and he that soweth bountifully shall reap also bountifully." The last final award will not only be judgment or acquittal, or condemnation, or recompense, but it will very much take the form of that sort of judgment which we associate with the word *requital*. This is very clearly brought out in the Parable of the Pounds in this gospel (xix. 12, &c.).

39. "And he spake a parable unto them, Can the blind lead the blind? shall they not both fall?" &c. Commentators have found it difficult to explain how such a parable as this, respecting spiritual blindness, can have a place in this part of the discussion, which is wholly

39 And he spake a parable unto them, ᵗ Can the blind lead the blind? shall they not both fall into the ditch?

40 ᵘ The disciple is not above his master: but every one ‖ that is perfect shall be as his master.

ᵗ Matt. xv. 14.
ᵘ Matt. x. 24. John xiii. 16. & xv. 20.
‖ Or, *shall be perfected as his master.*

39. "And he spake a parable," &c. ℵ, B., C., D., L., R., X., some Cursives (13, 33, 69, 124, 157), most old Latin, Vulg. read, "And he spake *also ;* " but "also" omitted by A., most later Uncials, most Cursives, Copt., Goth., Syriac.

40. But every one that is perfect," &c. "But every one when he is perfected shall be as his master " (Revisers); *perfectus autem omnis erit, si sit sicut magister ejus.* (Vulg.)

occupied with works of forgiveness and charity; but may not this be owing to mistaken views upon the nature of Christian light and its corresponding eyesight? Is not the key to it to be found in the words of the beloved disciple, "He that loveth his brother abideth in the light, and there is none occasion of stumbling in him. But he that hateth his brother is in darkness, and walketh in darkness, and knoweth not whither he goeth, because that darkness hath blinded his eyes"? (1 John ii. 11, 12). Ever since the time of Zwingle and Calvin Protestants look upon light as the possession of clear views upon certain of the doctrines of grace, and being able to express ourselves well and lucidly upon the truths of redemption; but however necessary this may be, the Lord and His Apostle allow no light to be true unless it is united with charity and the love of our neighbour. An essential lens, so to speak, of the spiritual eye is this love or charity; and if we have not this the Lord holds us to be blind, no matter what our intellectual grasp of His truth.

"Shall they not both fall into the ditch?" If men have not love—the light of pure Christian holy love—they cannot lead the Church or its members aright. At the last day we shall know how many errors of the Church have had their root in want of love.

40. "The disciple is not above his master: but everyone that is perfect shall be," &c. This is a very difficult passage, both as to its meaning and its connection with the context. Godet connects the "blind leader" of verse 39 with the man with "the beam in thine own eye " in verse 41, and tries to make this verse (40) a sort of connecting link, but I think very unsuccessfully. Oosterzee makes it to mean, "It is only when the disciple surpasses his master that he

41 ˣAnd why beholdest thou the mote that is in thy brother's eye, but perceivest not the beam that is in thine own eye?   ˣ Matt. vii. 3.

42 Either how canst thou say to thy brother, Brother, let me pull out the mote that is in thine eye, when thou thyself beholdest not the beam that is in thine own eye? Thou

---

42. "Either how canst thou say," &c. So A., C., D., E., H., K., L., M., other later Uncials, almost all Cursives, old Latin, Syriac, Goth., Copt., &c.; but "either" omitted by ℵ, B., Vulg. (Cod. Amiat.).

---

can hope to be preserved from falling into the ditch, into which his blind leader falls. Since, however, the disciple does not usually surpass his master, he has the same danger to fear." The best interpretation, however, seems to be that which makes the Master here to be the Lord Himself, Who came not to judge, but to save. So Cyril: "Since Christ, therefore (thy Master), judged not, why dost thou judge? for He came not to judge the world, but to show mercy." And so Stier: "The Lord intends to say, 'Take care that ye do not, in your rash and unmeasured condemnation of your brethren, exercise a severer judgment than I, in My love and forbearance, have exercised upon you. For does not the censorous judge place himself, as it were, above His forgiving, graciously correcting, long-suffering Master? In this case 'everyone that is perfect,' *i.e.*, perfectly instructed and disciplined, shall be as His Master, *i.e.*, conformed to His image of long-suffering love."

41, 42. "And why beholdest thou the mote that is in thy brother's eye?" &c. It seems strange that amongst reasonable creatures such an illustration as this should be at all needed, yet what is more common than to see persons who have some grave fault, or faults, known to all around them, severe upon others for some error incomparably less offensive or dangerous? But just as the eye cannot see itself, so the moral vision can with difficulty be turned inward, so that we should scrutinize ourselves with the severity with which we scrutinize others. So that one of the most dangerous things for ministers, whose duty it is to teach, reprove, and exhort, is to forego self-examination and strict judgment of themselves. Such become hypocrites; for a man who is constantly censuring others without dealing strictly and severely with himself is a hypocrite, for he is no real hater of evil, for if it was hatred of evil that

A GOOD TREE. [St. Luke.

hypocrite, ʸ cast out first the beam out of thine own eye, and then shalt thou see clearly to pull out the mote that is in thy brother's eye.

ʸ See Prov. xviii. 17.

43 ᶻ For a good tree bringeth not forth corrupt fruit; neither doth a corrupt tree bring forth good fruit.

ᶻ Matt. vii. 16, 17.

---

inspired his judgment, would he not begin by showing this feeling in an unsparing judgment of himself?

" First cast out the beam . . . and then shalt thou see clearly." This teaches us that the most successful combatants against sin in others are those who most thoroughly cleanse themselves.

43. " For a good tree bringeth not forth corrupt fruit; neither doth a corrupt tree," &c. Much difficulty has also been made of the connection of this with what precedes, but it seems very plain. The Lord had said, " Cast out the beam out of thine own eye, and then shalt thou see clearly," &c. What does the illustration " cast out the beam " signify but " cleanse thyself from sin, from all heart sin, as well as from all outward sin," and then thou wilt bear fruit unto God, then thou wilt make thyself a good tree, bearing thyself the fruits of righteousness, and helping and influencing thy brethren to bear the same fruit? The "for" at the beginning of verse 43 evidently implies a close connection with the last clause of verse 42, and what I have said seems to make a very close one, and I think the only one possible.

" A good tree . . . a corrupt tree," &c. The Lord, " who came to destroy the works of the devil, and make us the children of God," could not possibly have said this if every tree was fated to remain always the same. On the contrary, those to whom He said it could only be compared to trees in the sense that each tree bears its own particular fruit. Men are not in all respects like trees: they have wills, hearts, consciences. And these the Lord came to direct, to change, to awaken. So that the good tree might bring forth better fruit, and the bad be converted and bear good.

But does not a good tree, *i.e.*, a good man, sometimes, through the weakness of his nature, commit sin; and does not an evil man, because he yet retains some remnants of his original righteousness, sometimes do good? Yes; and so the Lord's words are only strictly and absolutely true of the *man* in each; the old man, and

44 For ^a every tree is known by his own fruit. For of thorns men do not gather figs, nor of a bramble bush gather they †grapes. _{a Matt. xii. 33.} _{† Gr. *a grape*.}

45 ^b A good man out of the good treasure of his heart bringeth forth that which is good; and an evil man _{b Matt. xii. 35.}

---

the new; the old man, when not hindered by the new, always doing evil ("corrupt according to the deceitful lusts," Ephes. iv.), and the new man, when not hindered by the old, always doing good: So at least we, as Christians, must understand Him, and make it the business of our lives to mortify the old and to cherish the new.

But the Lord speaks in a general way; internal characters produce corresponding external fruits, and so He proceeds to say,—

44. "For every tree is known by his own fruit," &c. The proud man by his pride, the selfish man by his want of care for his brethren, the dishonest man by his fraud; as also the humble man by his humility, the charitable man by his benevolence, the honest man by his truthfulness and fair dealing.

But would it not be better to put all together, and say the converted man (or saved man) by the fruits of conversion? No, it would not, for the change which is generally known as conversion very frequently leaves some bad feature of the original character little altered. The converted man, as the term "conversion" is very commonly understood, is frequently by no means an humble man, and often he is a censorious man who deeply needs the application to himself of the Lord's words, "Judge not, and ye shall not be judged." The Apostles had, if ever men had, accepted the Lord—for they had given up all to follow Him; and yet even they needed a conversion from a spirit of self-aggrandizement; for when they disputed " which should be the greatest?" He answered, "Except ye be converted, and become as little children, ye shall not enter into the kingdom of heaven."

45. "A good man out of the good treasure of his heart bringeth forth," &c. The good treasure in the heart of the good man is not only good knowledge of Scripture and of the doctrines of grace, for there are numberless instances of a very extensive knowledge of the best things in the hearts of bad men. No, the good treasure is first of all a good intention—the bent of the will being turned to God; the good treasure is the new heart and the right spirit. It is new

out of the evil treasure of his heart bringeth forth that which is evil: for ᶜ of the abundance of the heart his mouth speaketh.

ᶜ Matt. xii. 34.

46 ¶ ᵈ And why call ye me, Lord, Lord, and do not the things which I say?

ᵈ Mal. i. 6. Matt. vii. 21. & xxv. 11. ch. xiii. 25.

---

45. "Out of the evil treasure of his heart bringeth," &c. So A., C., X., Γ, Δ, later Uncials, almost all Cursives, some old Latin (c, e, f, g², q), Copt., Syriac, Goth., Æth.; but ℵ, B., D., L., a few Cursives (1, 69, 131), a few old Latin, Vulg. (Cod. Amiat.), Arm., omit "treasure of his heart."

---

affections set on God, new desires longing after righteousness, new hopes of God's eternal good things. These, and these alone, give their value to such things as correct and extensive knowledge, or powers of illustration, or richness of imagination, or a copious flow of language.

And the converse is true: the radically evil state of the heart taints the outpourings of its stores of knowledge and wit in brilliant conversation, or at least renders them nugatory for good.

"Of the abundance of the heart his mouth speaketh." From the abundance, because there is ever more within than is poured forth. The heart is as a deep fountain, these but the streams.

But cannot a wicked man dissemble and speak good words and refrain from evil ones? Not always. No man can at all times, on all occasions, and in all companies, do such violence to himself as never to unburthen his own soul—never to give relief to his very self —always to stifle what his heart prompts him to utter.

46. "And why call ye me, Lord, Lord, and do not the things which I say?" The Person of Christ, God and Man, and all that flows from this union of the Godhead and Manhood, is given to us that through His grace and love working in us we should obey Him. What a mockery to confess Him as "God," if we do not surrender ourselves to Him as God! What a mockery to call Him "Lord" if we do not attempt to obey Him as Lord! What a mockery to call Him "Saviour" and continue in wilful bondage to that from which He died to save us!

Notice how here Christ claims to be what they called Him, and demands that they should obey Him as the Lord. As Cyril says: "Lordship, both in name and reality, belongs only to the highest nature."

CHAP. VI.] IT WAS FOUNDED UPON A ROCK. 171

47 ᵉ Whosoever cometh to me, and heareth my sayings, and doeth them, I will shew you to whom he is   ᵉ Matt. vii. 24. like:

48 He is like a man which built an house, and digged deep, and laid the foundation on a rock: and when the flood arose, the stream beat vehemently upon that house, and could not shake it: for it was founded upon a rock.

---

48. "Upon a rock." "Upon the rock."

"For it was founded upon a rock." So A., C., D., X., Δ, later Uncials, almost all Cursives, old Latin, Vulg., Goth., Syriac, and Arm.; but ℵ, B., L., two Cursives (33, 157), Copt. read, "Because it was well built."

47. "Whosoever cometh to me, and heareth my sayings, and doeth them, I will," &c. This parable differs from that in Matth. vii. in this particular, that "coming to Christ" is spoken of before "hearing His sayings" and "doing" them. It is plain that stress should be laid upon this *coming*. It is not picking out some particular sayings of Christ which an unconverted Hindoo might learn, and attempting to imbibe their spirit and obey them. This is useless unless it leads to something better. But Christ is not only a teacher, He is a Master. He is a bestower of grace and strength to obey His precepts. We must come to Him, by an act of our spirit, to throw ourselves at His feet and commit the care of our souls personally into His hands, all the while endeavouring to follow all His leading. This, and this only, is to dig deep (to dig and deepen, as the Revisers have it). It is getting to the rock, but still be it remembered, when the foundation is reached the house is not built—the act of building is the hearing Christ's sayings and *doing* them, and is, I need not say, the work of a lifetime; but the Lord, it appears to me, speaks here not so much of the process of building as of the coming to, the reaching Himself, the true Rock, in the matter of the laying of the foundation.

48. "When the flood arose, the stream beat vehemently," &c. A house built only on the earth, on the slopes of the hills with which our Lord was surrounded, may not always be washed away by a deluge of rain. It may escape, and doubtless many ill-built houses do, which are not so much in the way of the stream as others: but the Christian building, the house of each man's soul, must always

49 But he that heareth, and doeth not, is like a man that without a foundation built an house upon the earth: against which the stream did beat vehemently, and immediately it fell; and the ruin of that house was great.

---

be tried by the flood. It is a spiritual necessity. It is part of our probation that, at some time or other, or constantly, we should be tempted. And we must be prepared for the stream "beating vehemently." We must be prepared for temptations which nothing but holding on very firmly to Christ, and using all the means of grace, and following in the steps of our Lord in prayer and self-denial and the use of Scripture, will enable us to overcome.

Such is the positive side of building on the rock; but when we come to the negative, "But he that heareth, and doeth not, is like a man that without a foundation," &c., we see a remarkable difference; no mention is made of the "coming," but only of the hearing and the not doing, "doeth not." So that the unsuccessful builder is the one who, even if he has come to Christ, neglects to follow Him and obey His word. It is as if the ceasing to obey of itself removed the man from the foundation.

49. "It fell; and the ruin of that house was great." This is a place of terrible significance. The soul thus ruined and fallen need not have been that of some king or noble or philosopher, but of some obscure man whose fall from truth or goodness none but a few godly neighbours would notice even, much less lament; and yet to the man himself the ruin was unspeakably great, for it was the loss of his spiritual and then of his eternal life—of his all; and yet it is possible that whilst he was in this life he might by repentance begin to build again.

CHAP. VII.

NOW when he had ended all his sayings in the audience of the people, ᵃ he entered into Capernaum.

2 And a certain centurion's servant, who was ᵃ Matt. viii. 5. dear unto him, was sick, and ready to die.

3 And when he heard of Jesus, he sent unto him the elders of the Jews, beseeching him that he would come and heal his servant.

4 And when they came to Jesus, they besought him instantly, saying, That he was worthy for whom he should do this:

5 For he loveth our nation, and he hath built us a synagogue.

---

4. "Instantly." Revisers, "Urgently."
"That he was worthy for whom he should do this." Rather, "He is worthy for whom thou shouldest do this." So א, A., B., C., D., E., H., L., &c., twenty-one Cursives; but as Authorized in G., K., M., S., and most Cursives.

1-5. "Now when he had ended all his sayings .... built us a synagogue." "A certain centurion's servant," &c. This miracle is common to St. Matthew and St. Luke, but all notice of it is omitted by St. Mark. St. Matthew's narrative is much shorter, and if we possessed it alone we should have supposed that the centurion came once in person to the Lord, and that there was but one stage, as it were, in the narrative; whereas St. Luke's account very greatly enhances our opinion, not only of the faith, but of the exceeding humility of the centurion. For no doubt feeling that he was of an alien race whom God as yet had kept at a distance from Himself, instead of coming personally, he sent the elders of the chosen people of his place to the Lord, with the request that "He would come and heal his servant." They seconded his appeal by recounting his good deeds, that he loved the Jews as the people of God, and had built them a synagogue.

6. "Then Jesus went with them .... under my roof." From the accounts of His miracles and teaching this man must have been

6 Then Jesus went with them. And when he was now not far from the house, the centurion sent friends to him, saying unto him, Lord, trouble not thyself: for I am not worthy that thou shouldest enter under my roof:

7 Wherefore neither thought I myself worthy to come unto thee: but say in a word, and my servant shall be healed.

8 For I also am a man set under authority, having under me soldiers, and I say unto † one, Go, and he goeth: and to another, Come, and he cometh; and to my servant, Do this, and he doeth *it*.

+ Gr. *this man.*

9 When Jesus heard these things, he marvelled at him,

---

7. "My servant shall be healed." So ℵ, A., C., D., all other Uncials and Cursives, &c.; but B. and L. read, "Let my servant be healed." Westcott and Hort, Tischendorf, and other editors follow these two MSS., and reject the verdict of the rest of Christendom.

very deeply impressed with the Lord's greatness and goodness and with His nearness to God. This came upon him with such force, when he saw that the Lord was approaching his house, that he sent the remarkable message that the Lord would no further trouble Himself, but heal his servant by His mere word, "Say in a word, and my servant shall be healed."

And the reason which he urged was still more remarkable for its grasp of recognition of the Lord's power and greatness. "Say in a word, and my servant shall be healed. For I also am a man," &c. He looks upon the Lord as having all power over that vast hierarchy with which the unseen and spiritual world is peopled, so that as God is set before us throughout the Old Testament as sending His angels to destroy or to avert destruction, so Jesus had such power with God that He could do the same. For such must be the true meaning of the comparison which he draws between himself as issuing his commands to his under officers or soldiers to do his will at a distance, and the Lord issuing His commands. The Lord was a poor man, having no servants, and the words of the centurion imply that if He healed his servant it would be because invisible messengers of health and strength waited His beck and call.

9. "When Jesus heard these things he marvelled . . . . faith, no, not in Israel." The belief of this Gentile centurion stands in strong contrast with that of the Jewish nobleman whose utmost

CHAP. VII.] NO, NOT IN ISRAEL. 175

and turned him about, and said unto the people that followed him, I say unto you, I have not found so great faith, no, not in Israel.

10 And they that were sent, returning to the house, found the servant whole that had been sick.

11 ¶ And it came to pass the day after, that he went into

---

10. "That had been sick" omitted by אc, B., L., Cursives 1, 157, 209, old Latin (a, b, c, e, &c.), Copt.; retained by A., C., D., E., F., G., H., K., M., other Uncials, almost all Cursives, Vulg., Syriac, &c.

11. "On the day after." אc, A., B., E., F., G., H., L., other later Uncials, seventy Cursives, some old Latin (a, b), &c. read only "afterwards;" but א, C., D., K., M., very many Cursives and versions read as in Authorized.

---

faith was only strong enough to make him say, "Sir, come down, ere my child die." St. Chrysostom also shows how it rises far above that of the sisters whom Jesus loved; for they thought of nothing more than sending for the Lord, and when He came they could only say somewhat reproachfully, "Lord, if thou hadst been here, my brother had not died."

"He marvelled." How is it that the Son of God, Who foresees and knows all things, marvelled, because all wonder arises from want of foresight, from seeing, or hearing, or learning something unlooked for? The answer is, that our Lord fully partook of human nature; and just as according to His human nature He increased in wisdom, so in His human nature He was astonished. It is the greatest of mysteries that God and Man—God with all the powers and perfections of the Godhead, and man with all the limitations and sinless weaknesses of the perfect manhood—should be one Christ; but this mystery pervades the whole Revelation of the Son of God contained in the Gospels. He knows all things, and yet He increases in wisdom. He is the source of all happiness, and yet He suffers pain. He ceaselessly and unweariedly upholds all things, and yet He is weary. He is almighty, and yet He is crucified through weakness. All the mystery of His compound Being is contained in the words, "He was in the form of God" and yet "He emptied Himself." How all this came to pass is a secret of the Trinity. We have but to fall down and worship.

11. And it came to pass the day after, that he went into a city called Nain; and many," &c. This consoling and instructive miracle is only to be found in St. Luke, and the question naturally arises,

a city called Nain; and many of his disciples went with him, and much people.

"Many of" omitted by ℵ, B., D., F., L., some old Latin (a, e, f, l), Vulg., and versions, but read in A., C., E., G., H., K., M., &c., most Cursives, Goth.

why so remarkable an act of Christ's power in raising the dead should not form part of the body of tradition which we have in the first two Evangelists. Perhaps we have been much too ready to ascribe some human or secondary motive to the Evangelists, in that they inserted one account and rejected another—perhaps we have not sufficiently ascribed their choice to the guidance of that Spirit Who "divideth to every man severally as He wills," and Who thought good to order that whilst the four have much in common, each should have the honour of recording special incidents, or as is the case with St. Mark, narrate them with a circumstantiality which takes note of the manner, look, and gesture of the Lord in doing them. Godet suggests that the life of the Lord was so crowded with miracles that little more could be given with any fulness of detail than one or two of each class. As he rightly re marks, "For edification, which was the sole aim of the popula preaching, this was sufficient. Ten cures of lepers would say no more to faith than one. And that as St. Matthew and St. Mark give fully the restoration to life of Jairus' daughter, and St. John that of Lazarus, so to St. Luke is assigned this of the widow's son.' Dean Plumptre suggests that St. Luke received this account from the devout women who followed the Lord, as the miracle was or which, from its circumstances, had specially fixed itself in the. memories.

Attempts also have been made to get rid of the miracle by asserting that it was a case of suspended animation, the young man not being really dead, but only in a death-like swoon; but, if so, the miracle of Resurrection is changed into a miracle of Divine intuition, for the Lord must have in this case foreseen the very moment at which the young man would come again to life, and God must have so ordered the two processions—that of the disciples and followers of Jesus, and that of the funeral in which was "much people of the city," that they should meet at the exact moment; for a few minutes earlier, and the sad concourse would not have left the house of mourning; a few minutes later, and the body would have been quietly deposited in the grave.

THE ONLY SON OF HIS MOTHER.

12 Now when he came nigh to the gate of the city, behold, there was a dead man carried out, the only son of his mother, and she was a widow: and much people of the city was with her.

13 And when the Lord saw her, he had compassion on her, and said unto her, Weep not.

"Called Nain." A spot yet exists called Neen or Nein in the locality where the city must have existed. Dean Stanley writes:—
"On the northern slope of the rugged and barren ridge of little Hermon, immediately west of Endor, which lies in a further recess of the same range, is the ruined village of Nain. No convent, no tradition marks the spot. But under the circumstances the name is sufficient to guarantee its authenticity. One entrance alone it could have had—that which opens on the rough hill side on its downward slope to the plain. It must have been in this steep descent, as according to Eastern custom they 'carried out the dead man,' that nigh to the gate of the village the bier was stopped, and the long procession of mourners staid, and the young man delivered back to his mother." (P. 357.)

12. "Now when he came nigh to the gate of the city . . . . was with her." What a very simple, yet what a surpassingly touching picture of the bereavement! "He has told us the sum of misery in a few words. The mother was a widow, and had no further hope of having children; she had no one upon whom she might look in the place of him that was dead. To him alone she had given suck, he alone made her home cheerful. All that is sweet and precious to a mother was he alone to her." (Greg. Nyss., Cat. Aurea.)

13. "And when the Lord saw her, he had compassion on her," &c. What an honour had this unknown widow, that the Lord saw her grief and had pity on her! But has not the Lord, Who is unchangeable, and Who, from His most eminent place in heaven, sees all grief, has He not compassion now on those who weep? We firmly believe that He has. But what form does His sympathy take? That we know not now, but we shall know hereafter. We shall know then that the grief of every mourner has been specially discerned by Him, and that a particular exercise of compassion has come forth from Him; but whether His act of compassion has met with its due recognition and response from the mourner is another matter altogether.

14 And he came and touched the ‖ bier: and they that bare *him* stood still. And he said, Young man, I say unto thee, ᵇ Arise.

‖ Or, *coffin.*
ᵇ ch. viii. 54.
John xi. 43.
Acts ix. 40.
Rom. iv. 17.

"Weep not." And what He says to the disconsolate one he says to every mourner, "Weep not." For it is He Who takes away all cause for bitter tears. Do we weep for the dead? He is the Resurrection, and He hath abolished death, so that "they who sleep in Jesus will God bring with Him." Do we weep for sorrow of heart for any worldly loss, as of means, of health, of friends? It is He Who has said without any reserve, "Blessed are they that mourn, for they shall be comforted." Let us but strive to receive a message from Him in every visitation whatever it be, and our sorrow will, sooner than we think, be turned into joy. Do we mourn for sin? This is His most precious gift, for He has Himself made us sorry that we may receive from Him remission, reconciliation, restoration.

14. "And he came and touched the bier," &c. There was no coffin fast closed and nailed. The body lay stretched upon a board or plank with raised edges, covered with the white linen graveclothes, and a napkin to hide the face.

"Touched the bier." On almost every occasion when it is possible, He brings His blessed Person into contact with the body of him whom He desired to heal or to raise. Here the act has a peculiar significance which is wonderfully brought out by St. Cyril: "He performs the miracle not only in word, but also touches the bier, to the end that you might know that the Sacred Body of Christ is powerful to the saving of man; for it is the Body of Life, and the Flesh of the Omnipotent Word, Whose power It (the Body) possesses. For as iron applied to fire does the work of fire, so the Flesh, when it is united to the Word which quickens all things, becomes itself also quickening, and the banisher of death." (Cat. Aurea.) And so to each one we give the Communion of the Body of Christ in the words, "The Body of our Lord Jesus Christ, which was given for thee, preserve thy body and soul unto everlasting life."

"And they that bare him stood still." Why was this? It may be through awe at meeting one the fame of whose miracles had filled the Holy Land. Perhaps, also, they vaguely expected some act of power on His part.

15 And he that was dead sat up, and began to speak. And he delivered him to his mother.

"And he said, Young man, I say unto thee, Arise." Here we have the majesty as well as the power of God exhibited in the Lord. Massillon, one of the most eloquent of French orators, thus characterizes it: "Elijah, it is true, raises up the dead, but he is obliged to stretch himself out upon the body of the child whom he recalls to life; and it is easily seen that he invokes a foreign power, that he withdraws from the empire of death a soul which is not subjugated to him, and that he is not himself the master of life and death. Jesus raises up the dead as easily as He performs the most common actions; He speaks as master of those who repose in an eternal sleep; and it is thoroughly felt that He is the God of the dead as of the living, never more tranquil and calm than when He is operating the grandest things."

15. "And he that was dead sat up . . . And he delivered him to his mother." Notice the two deliverances. He delivered him from death to life, and He delivered him to his mother. This is a type or forecast of what will take place at the great day of Resurrection. Then all who rise in Christ will be "delivered" to those from whom they have been separated; delivered to those whom they have loved, so that they shall be theirs in a far higher and better way than they could have thought it possible.

The Fathers consider the deliverance of this young man to his mother by the power of Christ's word as a type of the restoration of all those who are raised by Christ's power from the death of sin to their true and sorrowing mother the Church. The Church weeps for those who are alienated from her through evil lusts and passions. They are dead to her. They cannot support her or strengthen her by prayer and a holy life; but when by Christ's power they are awakened from their sleep, then they become hers again. She has again restored to her their love, their works, their intercessions. Augustine also compares the three forms of death from which our Lord restored Jairus' daughter, the widow's son and Lazarus, and deduces from the comparison how the Lord raises from spiritual death three classes of sinners—one, that of the little maid, is scarcely death, and it typifies the restoration of the sinner who, by consenting to secret sin, is only just dead; a second, like the widow's son, is completely dead, and is no longer of service to religion or the

16 ^c And there came a fear on all: and they glorified God, saying, ^d That a great prophet is risen up among us; and, ^e That God hath visited his people.

17 And this rumour of him went forth throughout all Judæa, and throughout all the region round about.

18 ^f And the disciples of John shewed him of all these things.

c ch. i. 65.
d ch. xxiv. 19. John iv. 19. & vi. 14. & ix. 17.
e ch. i. 68.

f Matt. xi. 2.

Church, but is put away, if not formally at least really; whilst a third, like Lazarus, is not only dead but loathsome and polluting all around by the savour of his ill-deeds. He is as one buried four days, and by an inveterate continuance in sin has become corrupt and noisome, while evil custom lies as a stone upon the grave, and its old sinful habits, like grave-clothes, wrap around the body. So that no form of spiritual death is such that it can resist the quickening power of the word of the Lord.

16. "And there came a fear on all: and they glorified God." This fear was rather what we now call awe: because though it retained much of the nature of fear, as there always must be in the nearness of the supernatural, yet it rather attracted them to God, for they said, "A great prophet is risen up among us," and "God hath visited His people." The words "God visiting" is applied to any deliverance which God wrought. Thus, when Naomi returned to the land of Israel, it was because "she had heard that the Lord had visited his people in giving them bread." The hearty confession of the hand of God on the part of His ancient people in every dispensation of judgment or deliverance, puts the cold, grudging, half-believing recognition of God's interference by some modern Christian nations to shame.

17-18. "And this rumour of him went forth . . . . shewed him of all these things." By the words "throughout all the region round about," St. Luke very probably alludes to the part beyond the Dead Sea where John was imprisoned: so that the rumour reached those disciples which were near him, and had access to him. It is probable that they were somewhat prompted by envy. They could not bear to think that their master should decrease, and that the new Teacher should increase. Of course, in such disciples the teaching of the Baptist had as yet failed to produce the one effect for which John was sent to preach, viz., to prepare men to

LOOK WE FOR ANOTHER?

19 ¶ And John calling *unto him* two of his disciples sent *them* to Jesus, saying, Art thou he that should come? or look we for another?

20 When the men were come unto him, they said, John Baptist hath sent us unto thee, saying, Art thou he that should come? or look we for another?

21 And in that same hour he cured many of *their* infirmities and plagues, and of evil spirits: and unto many *that were* blind he gave sight.

22 g Then Jesus answering said unto them, Go your way, and tell John what things ye have seen and heard;

g Matt. xi. 4.

---

19. "Sent them to Jesus." So אּ, A., Δ, later Uncials, almost all Cursives, old Latin (b, c, f, l, q, &c.), Copt., Syriac, &c.; but B., L., R., Cursives 13, 33, 69, 157, some old Latin (a, g), Vulg. (Cod. Amiat.), Arm., Æth. read, "to the Lord."

receive Christ. Those who had most effectually received the words of the Baptist,—Peter, James, John, Andrew, Philip, Nathaniel,— had long ago attached themselves to Christ.

19, 20. "And John calling unto him two of his disciples . . . . look we for another?" "Art thou he that should come?" &c. The Messiah was emphatically the Coming One. Of His own coming into the world He says, "Lo I come, to do Thy will." It was He that beyond all other messengers of God should "come in the name of the Lord." He was "the Desire of all nations" that should "come," of whom Haggai prophesied, and of whom Habakkuk spake of as "He that shall come will come, and shall not tarry."

21. "And in that same hour he cured many of their infirmities . . . . he gave sight." He did not answer them in words, but bid them stand aside and judge of Him by His works of mercy and power.

22. "Then Jesus answering said unto them, Go your way and tell John," &c. The Lord here asserts that in His personal acts of love and power He fulfils one of the most remarkable prophecies of the Old Testament respecting the Coming One, and the good time which He brings with Him; but when we look to the words of the prophecy, we found that He Who comes is God: "Say to them that are of a fearful heart, Be strong, fear not: behold your God will come with vengeance, even God with a recompense; He will come and save you. Then the eyes of the blind shall be opened, and the ears of the deaf shall be unstopped. Then shall the lame

ʰ how that the blind see, the lame walk, the lepers are
cleansed, the deaf hear, the dead are raised, ⁱ to
the poor the gospel is preached.

h Is. xxxv. 5.
i ch. iv. 18.

23 And blessed is *he*, whosoever shall not be offended in me.

---

man leap as an hart, and the tongue of the dumb sing." Notice, the question of the Baptist was, ",Art Thou He that should *come;*" and the Lord after doing the mighty works foretold by the prophet, sends to John to tell him that the prophecy which speaks of no other than God's coming and saving was fulfilled in Him. To this the Lords adds: "To the poor the Gospel is preached." This seems to belong to another prophecy, that of Isaiah lxi., but must it not be included under the promise of the prophecy of chap. xxxv., which the Lord is now referring to, for the prophet goes on to predict, "In the wilderness shall waters break out, and streams in the desert"? What is this but the Lord by His Gospel giving to thirsty souls the living water?

23. " Blessed is he whosoever shall not be offended in me." St. Ambrose supposes that in these words the Lord anticipates the offence of the cross—the last and most dangerous offence of all. " For the cross," he writes, " may cause offence even to the elect. But there is no greater testimony than this of a Divine Person. For there is nothing which seems to be more surpassing the nature of man than that One should offer Himself for the whole world."

Respecting the motive of St. John in sending the two disciples to the Lord, whether whilst languishing in prison he felt deserted, and so was somewhat shaken in faith, or whether it was only for the sake of his disciples, that, seeing the Lord's work, they might attach themselves to Him—these two matters I have discussed in my note on St. Matthew xi. 2. Upon the whole, the evidence seems in favour of the latter view. Godet supposes that John was moved with the fact that Jesus had not begun to fulfil the programme, if one may use the expression, which John, speaking by the Spirit, had marked out for Him. In particular, He had made no approach to fulfilling that work of judgment which St. John had assigned to Him when he spake of Him as One " whose fan is in His hand, and He will throughly purge His floor," &c.; but this seems unsatisfactory, because John had equally prophesied of the Lord as the Lamb of God.

CHAP. VII.]   MORE THAN A PROPHET.   183

24 ¶ ᵏ And when the messengers of John were departed, he began to speak unto the people concerning ᵏ Matt. xi. 7.
John, What went ye out into the wilderness for to see? A reed shaken with the wind?

25 But what went ye out for to see? A man clothed in soft raiment? Behold, they which are gorgeously apparelled, and live delicately, are in kings' courts.

26 But what went ye out for to see? A prophet? Yea, I say unto you, and much more than a prophet.

27 This is *he*, of whom it is written, ¹ Behold, I ¹ Mal. iii. 1.
send my messenger before thy face, which shall prepare thy way before thee.

---

24. "And when the messengers of John were departed, he began," &c. Particular notice is taken of the fact that the Lord gave this testimony to John, not in the presence of his disciples, but when they had gone to their master. In their then state of unbelief respecting Himself it would probably have been injurious for them to have heard so high a testimony to John as being "more than a prophet." They might have said to themselves, "If he be more than a prophet why should we leave him to follow another?"

24. "What went ye out . . . . live delicately, are in kings' courts." "What went ye out into the wilderness for to see? A reed," &c. They took a long journey into the wilderness: did they go out to see one like one of the reeds growing there in the marshy places?

Again He asks, "What went ye out for to see?" (not naming the wilderness.)

Did they go out to see one clothed according to his exalted rank among them: being a son of one of the chief priests; or wearing long robes as one of the scribes? In other words, did they go to see a fickle, time-serving preacher, who trimmed his doctrine so as to win the applause of the multitude? or did they go to hear one like a court preacher, softening down the denunciations of God against luxury, rapacity, and adultery? No, they left their homes and went into the wilderness to see a prophet, one far greater than any prophet.

27. "This is he of whom it is written, Behold, I send my mes-

184   THE PUBLICANS JUSTIFIED GOD.   [St. Luke.

28 For I say unto you, Among those that are born of women there is not a greater prophet than John the Baptist: but he that is least in the kingdom of God is greater than he.

29 And all the people that heard *him*, and the publicans, ^m^ justified God, ^m^ being baptized with the baptism of John.

^m^ Matt. iii. 5.
ch. iii. 12.

---

28. "There is not a greater prophet." So A., E., G., H., later Uncials, almost all Cursives, some old Latin, Vulg., Goth., Syriac; but "prophet" omitted by ℵ, B., K., L., M., twenty-five Cursives, most old Latin (a, b, c, e, h, &c.).

"The Baptist" omitted by ℵ, B., L., Cursives 1, 131, 157, and a few others; retained by A., E., G., H., K., M., S., other Uncials, most Cursives, old Latin, Vulg., Syriac.

senger before thy face." Greater was John than any prophet before him, in that he heralded the approach of the Lord—in that he prepared His way—in that he pointed Him out as the Lamb of God—in that he even baptized Him.

28. "For I say unto you, Among those that are born of women," &c. It is singular that so many of the Fathers have missed the meaning of this saying. Bede gives from those who preceded him two interpretations, one that the kingdom of heaven means the angelic kingdom, and so the least angel is greater in power at least than such a saint as John; and the other that the Lord refers to Himself, Who at the time of His birth came after John but was far greater in Divine authority.

But the true meaning undoubtedly is that John, having suffered martyrdom before the Lord's Crucifixion and Resurrection, was "under the law," and could not receive that new nature and those sacramental means for its conveyance which were the results of the Resurrection of the Saviour. The least member of Christ's Mystical Body has a nearness to Christ and an union with Him which none of the patriarchs or prophets could have before He finished His Redeeming Work. "As a type or prophecy of grace is less than a pledge and means, as a Jewish Sacrifice is less than a Christian Sacrament, so are Moses and Elias less by office than the representatives of Christ." (J. H. Newman.)

29. "And all the people that heard him, and the publicans, justified," &c. This particular mention of the publicans is remarkable. It seems to me to point to some religious movement amongst them

CHAP. VII.] WHEREUNTO SHALL I LIKEN? 185

30 But the Pharisees and lawyers ‖ rejected ⁿ the counsel of God ‖ against themselves, being not baptized of him.

‖ Or, *frustrated.*
ⁿ Acts xx. 27.

31 ¶ And the Lord said, ᵒ Whereunto then shall I liken the men of this generation? and to what are they like?

‖ Or, *within themselves.*
ᵒ Matt. xi. 16.

---

31. "And the Lord said." This clause omitted by nearly all MSS., ℵ, A., B., D., E., F., G., H., K., L., M., other later Uncials, 150 Cursives, most old Latin, Vulg. (Cod. Amiat.), and versions, though without it the following clause comes in with most unusual abruptness.

as a class. And it may be that God, seeing that they were utterly condemned by the rest of the Jews because they submitted to farm the taxes under the Roman Government (which existed by the decree and providence of God), showed openly, by some strong spiritual influences which He shed upon them, that He was no respecter of persons. (See particularly my note on Mark ii. 14.)

"Justified God," *i.e.*, acknowledged the goodness and righteousness of God in the mission of John, and submitted to it by being baptized by him.

30. "But the Pharisees and lawyers rejected the counsel of God against themselves," rather rejected against themselves (to their own infinite loss) the counsel of God, which was designed to prepare the whole nation for the reception of Christ.

"Being not baptized of him." So that the counsel of God can be rejected by refusing to receive an outward ordinance. And rightly so, because the outward reception of the ordinance was a sign of submission to the counsel of God. The Pharisees might have said, and probably did say, "What good can the reception of such a thing do to us?" It can do no good of itself, but it is a sign of obedience and submission to God the Author of all good. Much more, of course, does such reasoning apply to the devout reception or profane rejection of a Christian Sacrament, which is not only the outward sign, but the means of the conveyance to us of very great "good" from God. They who devoutly and intelligently accept the Christian Sacraments justify God in offering to us such high grace under such lowly forms.

31, 32. "And the Lord said, Whereunto shall I liken the men of this generation?" &c. "Ye have not wept." A considerable difficulty has been made of this parabolic illustration, as I have

32 They are like unto children sitting in the market-place, and calling one to another, and saying, We have piped unto you, and ye have not danced; we have mourned to you, and ye have not wept.

---

noticed in my commentary on St. Matthew, by pressing the correspondence between all the parts of it too far. It has been urged (particularly by Archbishop Trench in his " Studies in the Gospels") that the Lord cannot compare Himself and the Baptist to " the men of this generation," who called unto their fellows and found them untoward and ill-humoured; so that we must explain it as if "the men of this generation " were the unbelieving Jews, who desired that St. John should be laxer; "they would fain have him give up his strict, ascetic ways, his rigid separation from sinners, his stern summonses to repentance, and complained that he would not do so, that he would not 'dance' to their 'piping.' Christ Himself was equally, as they thought, at fault. They mourned to Him, and He would not lament. The Bridegroom and the Bringer of Joy, He would not change for any sadder note that note of joy to which the Gospel that He preached was set." (Luke v. 30-35.) But surely our Lord at times was as stern and uncompromising as the Baptist; and certainly the demands which He made upon some for the forsaking of all worldly goods, and upon all for the cleansing of the heart rather than the reformation of the outward life, went far beyond the demands of the Baptist. The whole difficulty vanishes if we consider that the Lord includes Himself and the Baptist in " this generation." They, equally with their fellow-countrymen, were " men of this generation." The exalted Personality of the Lord, and the greatness of the forerunner, are entirely sunk, or lost sight of; and the one point is that, as two parties of children playing a common game found their playmates untoward and unwilling to play with them, no matter how they endeavoured to engage them, so the men of that generation rejected the messengers of God, no matter how or under what guise they came.

As our Lord was then probably preaching in some public place, it is not improbable that the very scene was going on under His eyes.

The lesson is that worldly and impenitent men will, under all circumstances, reject a true messenger from God; and so the Lord proceeds to show the truth of the illustration.

33 For ᵖ John the Baptist came neither eating bread nor drinking wine; and ye say, He hath a devil.   p Matt. iii. 4. Mark i. 6.

34 The Son of man is come eating and drink- ch. i. 15.
ing; and ye say, Behold a gluttonous man, and a winebibber, a friend of publicans and sinners!

35 ᑫ But wisdom is justified of all her chil- q Matt. xi. 19.
dren.

33, 34. "For John the Baptist came neither eating bread . . . . friend of publicans and sinners." The men of the generation cast about for an excuse for rejecting the messages of both Jesus and John; and, regardless of all consistency, they professed to find this in the manner of life of each respectively: the Baptist led the ascetic life in the desert; the Lord the life of holiness in common life in cities and towns. But the men of the generation would have none of either, because, under different guises, the message of each was the same—"repent," "believe," and, in believing, change your false worldly hopes into spiritual ones, renounce all sin, keep all God's commandments, give alms. The Baptist preached nothing sterner than the words of Christ, respecting the cutting off of the right hand, the plucking out of the right eye, and the fear of Him Who is able to destroy both body and soul in hell; and the Lord preached no more joyful tidings respecting Himself than the Baptist did, when he proclaimed the coming of the Bridegroom.

35. "But wisdom is justified of all her children." The children of wisdom are the true children of God, who are drawn to Him by what is attractive and amiable in His truth, or are driven to Him by what is severe in the same truth.

It is the wisdom of God to use opposite means and instruments, by one or other of which all His children come to Him, and so justify Him.

The use of the word "wisdom," instead of "God," as in the 29th verse, is remarkable. Archbishop Trench (no doubt with absolute truth) refers to the impersonation of Wisdom in the book of Proverbs: "Wisdom here is no abstract quality, no attribute of God, any more than at Luke xi. 49; but a Person, even the same of whom such glorious things are spoken in the book of Proverbs; who appears there as crying in the streets (i. 21, viii. 1-3), as building her mystical house, sending forth her maidens, gathering to herself all those who are willing to hear her voice (ix. 1-6): being, indeed,

36 ¶ ʳ And one of the Pharisees desired him that he would eat with him. And he went into the Pharisee's house, and sat down to meat.

ʳ Matt. xxvi. 6. Mark xiv. 3. John xi. 2.

37 And, behold, a woman in the city, which was a sinner,

37. "A woman in the city which was a sinner." So A., later Uncials, almost all Cursives, old Latin (a, b, e, q); but ℵ, B., L., Z., some old Latin (c, f, l), Vulg., &c., read, " A woman which was a sinner in the city."

no other than the Word as yet (*i.e.*, when the book of Proverbs was written) not made flesh, or rather the Divine Word in ALL His dealings, both before the Incarnation and after, with the children of men; Who, being this absolute Wisdom, must have chosen wisest ways in which to deal with them, and Who, therefore, should not have been lightly charged with waywardness and folly " (Archbp. Trench, " Studies in the Gospels ").

36. "And one of the Pharisees desired him that he would eat with him . . . sat down to meat." It is important that we should consider the state of mind of this Pharisee towards our Lord. He was evidently friendly towards Him, but nothing more. A great teacher and worker of miracles was in his city. He may have been much struck with the wisdom of His discourses, and the evident power from God displayed in His miracles; and he desired a closer intimacy, in order that he might learn more about Him. But I cannot think, with Godet and others, that his spiritual state was that of the debtor who had been forgiven the smaller sum of the ensuing parable. There seems to be no sign whatsoever that the Lord's teaching had so reached his heart that he could in any sense have been said to have had any forgiveness from any act or word of Christ. Everything in the narrative seems to show the uncertainty of his state. He may not have been, or he may have been, far from the kingdom of God.

37. "And, behold, a woman in the city, which was a sinner, when she knew," &c. Who was this woman? There can be no doubt whatsoever that the words " a woman in the city, which was a sinner," mean that she was a harlot. But as to her name, that is forgotten, unless she be Mary Magdalene, which is, I think, unlikely.[1]

---

[1] In my notes on Mark xv. 40, I said, "The Magdalene is most probably the woman mentioned in Luke vii. 37; but this is not absolutely certain." Further consideration makes me think that it is improbable.

when she knew that *Jesus* sat at meat in the Pharisee's house, brought an alabaster box of ointment,

---

That she was Mary, the sister of Lazarus, the woman who sat at Jesus' feet, and had chosen the good part, is impossible. It is true that many of the fathers consider her to have been such, and hold that the two anointings—one at Bethany, another here in Galilee—were the same, but that one or other of the Evangelists made a mistake about the place. But it seems to us marvellous that such an opinion should have been entertained for a moment; for the things which the Lord said of each of these women respectively could not have been said of the same person. Of the one He said, "She hath done what she could; she is come aforehand to anoint my body to the burying;" of the other, "Her sins, which are many, are forgiven, for she loved much." The complaint in the one case was that of the Pharisee, who said within himself, "This man, if he were a prophet, would have known who or what manner of woman this is." In the other case, it was that of Judas: "This ointment might have been sold for five hundred pence, and given to the poor." The only things in common are the two anointings, and the two hosts having the same name of Simon; but the practice of anointing was most frequent, and Simon was the most common of Jewish names.

It has been asked how it was that a woman of such character was permitted to enter after the Lord into the guest chamber; and it is answered that the feasts of the Jews were much more public than ours; that many entered, and even took part in the conversation, who had not been invited to the feast. That the entrance of strangers was not unusual is manifest from the unspoken thought of the Pharisee. He expressed no wonder or indignation at the presence of the woman in the hall; but he did express wonder that the Lord, professing to be a prophet, knew not her manner of life.

"Brought an alabaster box of ointment." Nothing is here said of the value of the ointment; whereas, in the corresponding anointing by Mary at Bethany, its very great preciousness (being equal in value to five hundred pence) was the cause of the envy of Judas, and ultimately, through his disappointment, of the Lord's betrayal. It was a small phial, rather than a box. The alabaster was sup-

38 And stood at his feet behind *him* weeping, and began to wash his feet with tears, and did wipe *them* with the hairs of her head, and kissed his feet, and anointed *them* with the ointment.

---

38. "And kissed his feet." The word in the original (κατεφίλει) betokens kissing with much affection or earnestness. The Revisers in the margin read, "kissed much."

posed to preserve the ointment better than any other material, and being fragile, was easily broken.

38. "And stood at his feet behind him weeping, and began," &c. "Weeping" for sorrow at her past life, of the sin of which some words of the Lord had convinced her, and worked in her godly sorrow unto repentance.

"To wash his feet with tears." This was, no doubt, the first opportunity she had of confessing in His presence the shame of her past life, and that He was the means by which she had been delivered from it. No doubt the Lord, like other guests, had put off His sandals before reclining, and His feet being on the outer side of the couch, the woman would be able to come close behind them, and hang over them, and let her tears fall upon them.

"And did wipe them with the hairs of her head." It is said that, "In order to duly appreciate this act we must remember that among the Jews it was one of the greatest humiliations for a woman to be seen in public with her hair down."

This very remarkable action of anointing His feet and wiping them with her hair is mentioned by St. John in connection with that subsequent anointing by Mary, the sister of Martha, which gives it the appearance of being by the same person,—so that she should be designated by that marked description of "the Mary that wiped His feet with her hair." But the other affecting circumstance of washing His feet with her tears, and kissing His feet, is not mentioned in the latter case, whereas it has a peculiar propriety on this occasion, rather than on the other. It has been well observed that, though many come to Christ under the pressure of bodily maladies, yet this is the only instance of one coming to be released from sins, and to express love for deliverance from an evil life.

I hope I am not wronging Mary of Bethany in suggesting that she may have heard of this wiping of the Lord's feet with hair, and

SHE IS A SINNER.

39 Now when the Pharisee which had bidden him saw *it*, he spake within himself, saying, ⁸ This man, if he were a prophet, would have known who and what manner of woman *this is* that toucheth him : for she is a sinner.

⁸ ch. xv. 2.

---

she may have desired to express as deep and lowly gratitude for the deliverance of her brother from death as did this first woman for her own rescue from a life of sin.

39. "Now when the Pharisee which had bidden him saw it, he spake within himself," &c. It is impossible that this Pharisee should have hitherto received any spiritual benefit from Christ if he could harbour such a thought as this. No doubt, as I said, he invited Christ as a teacher, perhaps from God, and with a view of knowing more about His teaching and mission ; and here the Lord's silent acquiescence in the homage of this penitent decides him that He cannot be even a prophet, or He would have shrunk from the pollution of her touch.

But all the circumstances forbid us to judge very harshly of him, though, as I said, they altogether prevent us from supposing that he was represented by the debtor who owed fifty pence, and had had that debt forgiven him. It is very improbable, indeed almost impossible, that he could have known that this woman had been convinced of the sin of her life by the preaching of the Lord. He looked upon her as yet a sinner, and this was his most grievous fault, that he did not discern and welcome the manifest signs of repentance which he saw her exhibit. If he had been a true penitent himself he would have welcomed the smallest sign of repentance. If he had known the grace of God he would have also known that that grace could reach and raise up the most degraded sinner.

But in common with almost all his countrymen he was not, as yet, delivered from the bondage of the formal and the external. No doubt he judged that the touch of such an one was defilement, for her whole life had been, and perhaps he thought was yet, a life of bodily as well as of spiritual pollution. Such an one as she, in his estimation, had lived apart from ordinances, apart from even ceremonial washing, apart from all temple or even synagogue worship ; so she was as a heathen, and must not so much as be touched by a devout Israelite ; and so he judged not her, but the Lord. Jesus, if a

40 And Jesus answering said unto him, Simon, I have somewhat to say unto thee. And he saith, Master, say on.

41 There was a certain creditor which had two debtors: the one owed five hundred || pence, and the other fifty.

|| See Matt. xviii. 28.

---

prophet, must be zealous for the law, "Had He been a Rabbi He would *certainly*, and had He been a prophet He would *probably*, have repelled such approach. The former, if not from self-righteousness, yet from ignorance of sin and forgiveness; the latter because such homage was more than man's due." (Edersheim, vol. i. p. 567.)

But the Lord read his thoughts, and this alone should have convinced him that He came in the Name and with the Power of the Searcher of hearts, for—

40-43. "Jesus answering said unto him, Simon, I have somewhat to say unto thee . . . Thou hast rightly judged." The larger of the debts would amount to about £16, the smaller to about 32s. This parable must be interpreted on principles of common-sense. There must be, for instance, some likeness or equality of disposition between the two debtors. They must, of necessity, have had the same honesty of purpose which would make them equally desire, if they could do so, to pay their respective debts. Because, of course, if one was indifferent about his obligations, and the other very sensitive about them, the parable would not hold good. This, I need not say, is true quite independently of the spiritual application of the parable. It equally requires some common-sense limitation of this sort whether it be understood of debts owed by men to one another, or of debts owed by all men to God.

But if these considerations be taken into account—if, that is, there be such an equality—then it stands to reason that the greater debt would bring the greater anxiety of mind and the greater relief in its forgiveness, and the livelier feeling of gratitude towards him who had generously removed it.

And now as to the application of all this to spiritual things. Taking what we have said into account it seems easy, for it is not the mere money value of any debt, but its pressure upon the mind which depends upon the state of the heart, whether honest or otherwise.

Chap. VII.] HE FRANKLY FORGAVE THEM BOTH.

42 And when they had nothing to pay, he frankly forgave them both. Tell me therefore, which of them will love him most?

43 Simon answered and said, I suppose that *he*, to whom he forgave most. And he said unto him, Thou hast rightly judged.

And so the relief felt by any sinner at the forgiveness of his sin does not depend upon the actual amount of sin, but upon its burden, the sense of its guilt and loathsomeness; in fact, upon the state of his heart.

And this, of course, depends upon the grace of God; for repentance, contrition, the sense of sin as well as the sense of forgiveness, depend upon the grace of God.

Now, God is a just God, righteous in all His ways, and holy in all His thoughts. Is it right, then, that He should give such a deep sense of sin, and such a lively sense of love at its removal, to a gross sinner as this woman, and withhold the same from a comparatively virtuous person, as we may presume this Pharisee to have been?

The answer to this is, that in a world constituted as ours, God would not be just if He did not; for we must take into account the difference of outward circumstances, over which any particular sinner has no control, which may have contributed to his sinful or vicious life. Take the case of this woman. From what we know of the utter degradation in the matter of purity and chastity of those times and of that country, it is not at all improbable but that in early youth she was sold by others, perhaps by her very parents, to a life of impurity; whilst it is very probable that the Pharisee had, through no merits of his own, been shielded from all the evil influences which had ruined the life of the woman. When, then, this woman was, by the word of Jesus, awakened to a sense of sin, and, with this, to a sense of goodness and virtue, it was the beginning of a new life, rather, perhaps, the reawakening of her true life. It was the first springing up of hope and of holy love. She owed it to the Lord Himself, and so it would seem to her a very small tribute of gratitude to wash His feet with her tears and wipe them with her hair; whereas the guilt of the Pharisee was, that having been brought up under comparatively better influences, and without all doubt having been carefully instructed in the letter of the Word of

o

44 And he turned to the woman, and said unto Simon, Seest thou this woman? I entered into thine house, thou gavest me no water for my feet: but she hath washed my feet with tears, and wiped *them* with the hairs of her head.

---

44. "With the hairs of her head." So E., F., G., H., M., some later Uncials, most Cursives, Cureton Syriac; but א, A., B., D., I., K., L., other later Uncials, twenty-five Cursives, old Latin, Vulg., Copt., Syriac omit "of her head."

God, he was really indifferent to the goodness of God, for he viewed with no thankfulness the signs of penitence and a return to virtue in a fellow-sinner, and he could debate in his mind whether one who taught and performed the mightiest acts of mercy, as did the Lord— whether such as He were even so much as a prophet, because He suffered returning penitents to touch His feet.

Such, it seems, is the relation of the teaching to the penitent woman and to Simon. The great lesson of the whole transaction, taking together the signs of contrition in the woman and the Lord's approval of them, is this, that the publicans and harlots enter into the kingdom of God before the self-righteous; that God may make even gross sinners monuments of His mercy (as He did St. Augustine), whilst men who live decent and respectable lives may be far from God through pride, through selfishness, through coldness arising from indifference, and that indifference having its roots in self-satisfaction and a desire to remain as they are rather than to come nearer to God.

And now we come to the comparison of the conduct of the woman with that of Simon.

44-46. "And he turned to the woman, and said unto Simon, Seest thou this woman? I entered . . . hath anointed my feet with ointment." I think those are wrong who suppose that Simon had intentionally slighted our Lord in not offering Him these acts of courtesy. One who has written a life of our Lord with the special view of illustrating it from Jewish customs and observances (Edersheim) says, "To wash the feet of a guest, to give him the kiss of welcome, and especially to anoint him, were not, indeed, necessary attentions at a feast. All the more did they indicate special care, attention, and respect." Simon, if this be true, had not been intentionally rude and discourteous to the Lord. He had merely contented himself with offering Him the customary common-

Chap. VII.] SHE LOVED MUCH. 195

45 Thou gavest me no kiss: but this woman since the time I came in hath not ceased to kiss my feet.

46 ᵗMy head with oil thou didst not anoint: ᵗ Ps. xxiii. 5. but this woman hath anointed my feet with ointment.

47 ᵘWherefore I say unto thee, Her sins, which ᵘ 1 Tim. i. 14. are many, are forgiven; for she loved much: but to whom little is forgiven, *the same* loveth little.

---

place civility due to an ordinary guest, not the affectionate welcome due to an honoured one. It is important to remember this, Simon received the Lord simply with doubt, as one who might be a prophet, but it was uncertain: the woman treated the Lord as the Prophet whose word had delivered her from the misery of a sinful life; and so Simon took no account of the signs of contrition in the conduct of the woman, and all but pronounced the Lord to be no prophet because He graciously received them. The mighty works of mercy which Simon must have known, or he would not have invited a poor man like the Lord at all, did not make him welcome the Lord as any messenger from God ought to have been welcomed; whereas the words of Christ, which had rescued the woman from the bondage of sin, bowed her whole soul before Him in utter humiliation.

Such is the innermost teaching of the incident, the difference which the true sense of sin makes in the attitude of the whole soul to Christ.

Christ cannot be treated familiarly and on terms of equality by one who has a spark of true and genuine penitence. He cannot be debated about, whether He be this or that. No. The penitent soul will fall down before Him, will kiss His feet, will lavish upon Him all that is costly, all that expresses shame, humility, devotion, self-denial, as well as love.

47. "Wherefore I say unto thee, Her sins, which are many . . . . loved much." She loved much because she *felt* she had much forgiven. If she had felt no deep sense of sin, no fear of its consequences, no shame at its pollution, she would not have behaved thus at her sense of deliverance and at the new hope within her; but her burden was very great, and her love of Him Who had removed it was great in proportion.

48. "And he said unto her, Thy sins are forgiven." That this was said in the sense of absolving her, or, at least, asserting before

48 And he said unto her, ˣThy sins are forgiven.

ˣ Matt. ix. 2.
Mark ii. 5.

49 And they that sat at meat with him began

---

all present that which God only can really know, is certain from what follows.

49. "And they that sat at meat with him began to say within themselves," &c. They could not have said this unless they had understood the Lord's words as pronouncing forgiveness in a way in which it was unlawful for any mere man to do, unless he had a special commission from God "to declare and pronounce to penitents the absolution and remission of their sins." This the Lord had, and the proof thereof was His miracles, which, being all on the side of God and goodness, showed that He was sent by God.

"Her sins, which are many, are forgiven; for she loved much."

48-50. "And he said unto her, Thy sins are forgiven . . . Thy faith hath saved thee; go in peace." It is surprising to think that the conclusion of this affecting incident should have been made the battle-field on which controversialists should have contended, whether this woman was saved by faith alone, "Thy faith hath saved thee;" or by love, "Her sins, which are many, are forgiven; for she loved much;" and as love is assumed to be a work, some on one side would deny that love had anything to do with saving her, whilst others, on the other side, would assert that her faith, unless it was mixed with love or issued in love, would be simply the faith of devils.

Now, let us try and reconstruct, as it were, the spiritual history of this woman. In its leading features I think we cannot be far wrong. Our knowledge of human society, would teach us that she could scarcely have been the only sinner of her class. Very likely great numbers who sinned either openly or secretly after the same sort of sin had heard, along with her, the Lord's call to repentance.

But there was that within her which attracted her to Him, and made her listen to Him, whilst other similar sinners did not. What was that? It was an alteration in her will, a sense of sin as foul and polluting, which made her not only be willing, but "will" (*i.e.*, strongly desire) to be rid of it. This was the root of all. What was it? Being a change of heart, or mind, a turning from sin and turning to God, we may call it repentance; but it was not repen-

WHO IS THIS THAT FORGIVETH SINS? 197

to say within themselves, *Who is this that forgiveth sins also?

y Matt. ix. 3.
Mark ii. 7.

tance alone, if so it would have turned to despair—it was inextricably mixed with faith, faith in God and goodness, a belief in the present excellence and future triumph of purity, as distinguished from the present degradation and future condemnation of impurity. So it was faith as the evidence of things not seen. This gave her the ear to listen to the words of Christ, because in them she heard the words of One Who was Himself divinely pure, and yet showed Himself able and willing to relieve the hearts of all who came to Him under the burden of impurity.

This was a further act of faith on her part. She not only believed in a God of purity, but in Christ as the representative of that God of purity. She consequently came to Him in spirit as she listened to His words, because His words first opened before her the door of hope. So then we have here a confirmation of the truth of the remarkable words of the Apostle, "We are saved by hope."

If the words of Christ had not been full of hope for a person in her sad condition she would not have listened to Him so as to be attracted to Him. But we have used the word "attract:" what is the attraction of soul to soul? Most people would unquestionably call it love, and they would be right; for how could there be the attraction of a penitent soul to a pure, yet loving Saviour, for such benefits as forgiveness and cleansing, without love? What was it, then, which "saved" her. It was her will, the opposite of the will of those to whom the Lord said, "Ye will not come unto me that ye may have life." Being the change of her will it was repentance (metanoia), "repentance unto life;" but repentance which differed from despair or worldly sorrow, because it was inspired by hope ("we are saved by hope").

It was a change of mind Godward, and so was faith in God; and Christward, because it recognized in the Lord the Saviour from sin ("Ye believe in God, believe also in me"); and yet from first to last it was faith, whose very life was holy love. She was attracted to the former guilty partners of her sin by unholy love; she was attracted to Christ by penitent, believing, hopeful, holy love.

It seems to me the height of folly and presumption to try to separate the will, the repentance, the faith, the hope, the love, and assign to each their respective parts in the matter of salvation. God hath

50 And he said to the woman, ^z Thy faith hath

<small>z Matt. ix. 22. Mark v. 34. & x. 52. ch. viii. 48. & xviii. 42.</small>

joined all together; let us not try, even in thought, to put them asunder.

But what is the significance of the Lord's words, "Her sins, which are many, are forgiven; for she loved much"? The real drift of it seems to me to have been extensively misunderstood. The key to it seems to be in the *many* sins (αἱ πόλλαι) and the loving *much* (πολύ), the same Greek adjective. A sinful life such as hers, in which she had laid herself out to seduce others to sin, required a deep sense of guilt, a deep repentance: a superficial, light-hearted sorrow in her case would have been, humanly speaking, of no avail, no repentance at all; but God, in His mercy, gave her true and godly sorrow. This appeared in her whole action, particularly in her washing the Lord's feet with her tears, and wiping them with the hairs of her head. Now, Mary of Bethany similarly poured precious ointment on the Lord's feet, and similarly wiped them with her hair; but in all the three accounts there is not a word said of her shedding a single tear: and if she had, her tears would not have been those of penitence, but of gratitude for the restoration of her brother.

What, then, was the washing of the Lord's feet with her tears? of what, I mean, was it the sign?—of repentance? of faith? of love? Of all three, I answer, all inseparable, all permeating one another, all sustaining and nourishing one another. The whole action, if a sincere one, could not have existed without all three.

The Lord's words, then, cannot have the slightest bearing on any post Reformation disputes respecting faith and works, faith and love, love as preceding forgiveness, or love as following it. They are emphatically natural words, describing the natural effect of the grace of God in the soul; for though grace be above nature, it yet works not unnaturally, but naturally, according to its own nature, and according to the nature of the human being who receives it. Sins such as this woman had lived by, make terrible havoc of the best sensibilities of the soul, no roots of bitterness strike so deep, and to be done away, they require adequate self-abhorrence, adequate prostration before the Author and Giver of grace, or they may resume dominion. The Lord here announces that the work of grace in the soul was sufficient, and so He bids her " go in peace."

saved thee; go in peace.

Be it remembered that after this woman left the Pharisee's house, a very different sign of love to her Saviour would be required of her: the Lord would no longer look for washing of His feet with tears, but for the mortification of sin, and the cultivation of purity and holiness; and unless He had known well that in her case the work already begun in tears and faith and love was deep and would be permanent, He Who knew all things would not have said to her "go in peace."

CHAP. VIII.

AND it came to pass afterward, that he went throughout every city and village, preaching and shewing the glad tidings of the kingdom of God: and the twelve *were* with him.

2 And ^a certain women, which had been healed   ^a Matt. xxvii. 55, 56.

---

1. "And it came to pass afterward . . . twelve were with him." This is the first notice in St. Luke of the Lord commencing, what we call an itinerating ministry; not confining Himself to one spot or its immediate neighbourhood, but taking extensive circuits through districts. Diocesan Episcopacy is in its nature itinerating, if the Bishop is to be the pastor of the laity of his diocese as well as of the clergy.

2, 3. "And certain women which had been healed of evil spirits and infirmities . . . . which ministered unto him of their substance." It appears that all these, as well as Mary Magdalene, the first mentioned, had received some healing benefit from Him, and followed Him, "and ministered unto Him of their substance." It is not implied, of course, that they followed Him as closely as the Apostles did. It would have been inconvenient, to say the least, that a mixed troop of perhaps more than twenty persons ("many others" in addition to the Apostles and the three women expressly named)

200 MARY MAGDALENE. [St. Luke.

of evil spirits and infirmities, Mary called Magdalene, [b] out of
[b] Mark xvi. 9. whom went seven devils.

3 And Joanna the wife of Chuza Herod's steward, and Susanna, and many others, which ministered unto him of their substance.

[c] Matt. xiii. 2.
Mark iv. 1.
4 ¶ [c] And when much people were gathered together, and were come to him out of every city, he spake by a parable:

5 A sower went out to sow his seed: and as he sowed,

---

3. "Unto him." So ℵ, A., L., M., Π, Cursives 1, 33, and many other Cursives, old Latin (a, b, l), Copt., Syriac, Arm., Æth.; but B., D., E., F., G., H., K., other later Uncials, ninety Cursives, some old Latin (c, e, f, g, &c.), Vulg. (Cod. Amiat.), Syriac (Cureton and Schaaf) read, "Unto them."

should always be in attendance. It is probable that they took it by turns to attend to the bodily wants of Himself and the Apostles.

We learn from this that the Son of God Who in His heavenly Being made and sustained all things, in His earthly existence lived on the willing liberality of others. He acted in all this in the way in which He commanded His Apostles to act, to have no settled means of subsistence, but to live on the alms which the faithful, unsolicited by Him but moved by the Spirit of God, tendered to Him.

"Mary called Magdalene," *i.e.*, of the city of Magdala. From being associated with Joanna, the wife of Herod's steward, as ministering to the Lord, she must have been a person of some substance, and could not have been the nameless penitent mentioned in the last chapter. Godet suggests that Chuza might have been the Basilikos (court lord) whose son Jesus had healed (John iv. 46), and who had believed with all his house; but this is the merest conjecture.

4. "And when much people were gathered together . . . spake by a parable." St. Luke omits to mention that this parable was delivered by the Lord from a ship, the people thickly lining the beach. If he had simply constructed his narrative out of the existing body of tradition, he would not have omitted such a circumstance.

5. "A sower went out to sow his seed . . . . it was trodden down . . . . the fowls of the air devoured it." St. Luke alone mentions

some fell by the way side; and it was trodden down, and the fowls of the air devoured it.

6 And some fell upon a rock; and as soon as it was sprung up, it withered away, because it lacked moisture.

7 And some fell among thorns; and the thorns sprang up with it, and choked it.

---

that the seed sown by the way side was "trodden down;" and it is remarkable that in the explanation given by the Lord in verse 12, no notice is taken of this "treading down." But it is one of those touches which makes the similitude true to nature, for seed sown on the road or trodden path, would not germinate, not only because it would be snatched away, but because some of it would be certainly trodden down by the next passer-by. The treading down may be the crushing or destruction of the seed by the allowance of gross sin, as distinguished from the light and trifling thoughts which, like the fowls coming and going, snatch it away.

6. "And some fell upon a rock; and as soon as it was sprung up . . . . lacked moisture." St. Luke speaks here of the seed having been sown upon the rock, whereas St. Matthew and St. Mark speak of its being on rocky ground, *i.e.*, a rock covered with only a thin coating of earth. St. Luke, then, takes for granted that there must be some soil, and only mentions the cause of the mischief, the nearness of the rock to the surface equivalent to the "no depth of earth." St. Matthew and St. Mark speak of its having no root, *i.e.*, none worth speaking of. St. Luke that it withered because it lacked moisture. If it had had any length of root it would have penetrated into the deeper soil, which was always moist; but because of the nature of the ground it had no length of root, so it perished because "it lacked moisture."

7. "Some fell among thorns; and the thorns," &c. St. Luke here has a slight but important difference. St. Matthew and St. Mark have simply the thorns grew up, or ascended; but St. Luke has, the thorns grew up together with it, as if the thorns when the seed were sown were under the earth, and they grew up as the wheat grew, alongside of it.

8. "And other fell on good ground, and sprang up, and bare fruit," &c. St. Luke here has "and sprang up, and bare fruit," whereas St. Matthew and St. Mark have "and gave [*i.e.*, yielded]

8 And other fell on good ground, and sprang up, and bare fruit an hundredfold. And when he had said these things, he cried, He that hath ears to hear, let him hear.

^d Matt. xiii. 10. Mark iv. 10.

9 ^d And his disciples asked him, saying, What might this parable be?

10 And he said, Unto you it is given to know the mysteries of the kingdom of God: but to others in parables; ^e that

^e Is. vi. 9. Mark iv. 12.

seeing they might not see, and hearing they might not understand.

---

fruit." St. Matthew and St. Mark notice the difference in the yield, thirty, sixty, an hundredfold; whereas St. Luke mentions the largest yield only, an hundredfold.

I have noticed the differences, sometimes comparatively trifling, between St. Luke's version of this parable and that of the two other Synoptics, because it seems to me to bear very directly upon the relation of St. Luke's narrative to the original tradition. St. Matthew and St. Mark give almost word for word the same account. Theirs is the same version, with comparatively slight difference, whereas St. Luke is, so far as words are concerned, a totally different version, though with precisely the same meaning all through. On comparing all three it is clear that none of them copied from an original written document, or we should not have the slight discrepancies between St. Matthew's and St. Mark's version; and assuming that there was no original written document, but an original oral tradition, carefully committed to memory for some years, then St. Matthew and St. Mark drew upon, and endeavoured to produce as far as possible, that original body of tradition almost verbatim, and St. Luke did not do this, but received his account from one who knew the original tradition well, and entered fully into its meaning and spirit, but reproduced it more loosely, and with considerable variations, all the while preserving the meaning and spirit of it.

9, 10. " And his disciples asked him, saying, What might . . . they might not understand." I have dwelt upon this and the additional matter which accompanies it so fully in my comments on St. Matthew and St. Mark, that I must content myself with giving the following founded upon a very good exposition of these parables by Thiersch. A time of sifting had commenced among the hearers,

CHAP. VIII.] THE SEED IS THE WORD OF GOD. 203

11 *Now the parable is this: The seed is the word of God.
12 Those by the way side are they that hear;   *Matt. xiii. 18.
                                                Mark iv. 14.

and now the Lord spoke after a different manner—that is to say, by parables. These parables are of the nature of warnings to disciples, and contain also great promises and mysteries of the kingdom of God. The Lord declared these warnings and prophecies purposely in obscure language, in order to hide their meaning from blasphemers and sceptics, whose anger He was unwilling to excite, and yet so as to confirm the faith of the disciples to whom He explained all things. The honest-minded were to be led further into the truth, but only they. All who had treated the earlier discourses of the Lord with levity and unfaithfulness were to receive no further light.

11. "Now the parable is this: The seed is the word of God." That is the message of salvation by Christ, usually called the Gospel; but we must not absolutely confine it to this. An example, a warning, a moral precept even, may be the first means of arousing the attention; but if the word of God, sown by the sower, is to produce its perfect fruit, its full effect, it must be the full word. No part of the Catholic truth respecting the Person, or work, or character, or requirements of Christ must be withheld. When Philip preached Christ to the eunuch it at once elicited from him the question, "See, here is water: what doth hinder me to be baptized?" So that the true proclamation of Christ cannot be without some sacramental teaching.

It is to be remarked that there is no explanation of the field, what it is, as in the parable of the tares in St. Matthew xiii.; but it is needless. It is usually the congregation, all who are assembled to hear the word, but it is all into whose ears the word falls, whether receiving it in a body or singly.

12. "Those by the way side are they that hear," &c. These wayside hearers are the only one of the four classes which absolutely reject the word, so that it never sinks into their hearts so as to germinate and appear above ground. By this hard-beaten ground are described insensible, frivolous, and worldly dispositions, upon whom the Word of God makes no impression. They reject His sovereignty; they are unmoved by His goodness. Like the wicked before the flood, they desire that God should depart from them, and know not what the Almighty can do for them. "Many of these souls, hardened by the continual wear and pressure of the world's

then cometh the devil, and taketh away the word out of their hearts, lest they should believe and be saved.

13 They on the rock *are they*, which, when they hear, re-

---

footsteps, are frequenters of churches and places where prayer is made and sermons are preached. They do so from custom, because others do: but they accustom themselves to hear without attention, and understand nothing. The Word ministered passes by them, neither affecting the heart nor enlightening the conscience. So they remain unprofited, unchanged." (Thiersch.)

It is necessary here to call attention to a particular kind of this wayside hearing, by which many in these days deceive themselves and others as to their real state. The only springing up of the seed recognized by the Lord is that which produces, or is in the way of producing, fruit. Now, there are many who have an intellectual apprehension of the doctrines of grace. They can discourse well upon some of the highest truths of Christianity—they can defend them against heretics or unbelievers—they can take sides in theological controversy, and yet the seed lies crushed and lifeless on the surface of their souls because they have never attempted to put it into practice. The only germinating or springing up of the seed is its action first in the heart, by repentance and prayer, then in the life by good works, and this they have never once seriously attempted.

Let the reader note this also, that the word, being living, its natural result is to spring up in life; and where it does not, it is destroyed by being crushed by deadly sin, or is snatched away by frivolous, worldly, unbelieving thoughts, which are the emissaries of the evil one, instilled by him into the heart for the purpose of counteracting the Divine sowing.

13. "They on the rock are they, which, when they hear, receive . . . . fall away." Stier has a good exposition, which is virtually the same as that which I have given in my Commentaries on both St. Matthew and St. Mark. "He who quickly with joy receives the earnest word of truth, which judges the principle of the heart and conscience, perceives not at all its serious meaning and difficulty; he expends his strength before the time in shallow feeling, and in hasty words, instead of receiving it, as he ought, with the calm earnestness which marks a thorough work slowly effected.

ceive the word with joy; and these have no root, which for a while believe, and in time of temptation fall away.

14 And that which fell among thorns are they, which,

Then the sun arises (in its midday or summer heat), and this the weak seed which has shot up in a way not natural cannot bear. The sunshine and its heat mean no harm to the seed, but come rather as an ordinance from God to promote the growth, and are even necessary to it. . . . Nothing ripens without heat, and in the case of a good root it must promote, and not hinder, the growth."

I noticed in my Commentary on St. Mark how we have several instances of men, apparently with joy, receiving the word and falling away in time of temptation, as Herod, who heard John gladly; as the Pharisees, who were willing for a season to rejoice in the light of the forerunner; as the Galatians, who received St. Paul's message with joy and warmth of affection. (Gal. iv., 14, 15.)

But there is another case of falling away which we have in John vi. in which the temptation, and consequent offence, arose from the very nature of the seed which the Eternal Son Himself sowed. He sowed the seed of a word which required subjection of the reason and understanding to the deepest revealed mysteries of God, and those who had received His Word up to a certain point were startled, and exclaimed, "This is a hard saying, who can hear it?" and "walked no more with Him." And is not this a very powerful temptation in our own day? Men stumbling at what is mysterious and supernatural in the Gospel, asking how can these things be? and refusing the remedy for the deepest evils of our nature because they cannot understand all about it. And all the while taking scientific grounds, whilst they are forced to confess that every single department of science rests on a mystery as unthinkable, and as incomprehensible as any mystery which underlies the Gospel.

Are those that fall away irrevocably lost? They are, unless, God, Who raises the dead, has means of reviving that which is withered. He may have. We trust in many cases, He may see fit to bring about in this life a spiritual restoration, or even resurrection, but His Son has said nothing about it here.

14. "And that which fell among thorns are they, ... no fruit to perfection." Taking the heart to be the earth or ground, the first sort have hard hearts, the second shallow hearts, and the

when they have heard, go forth, and are choked with cares and riches and pleasures of *this* life, and bring no fruit to perfection.

third divided hearts. God, and the things of God have not the foremost place in the heart. The things of this world, worldly anxieties, worldly satisfactions, worldly lusts and desires, have their principal thoughts. When alone their thoughts do not naturally revert to God, and the things of God, as perhaps they once did. Now, God must have the throne of the heart, and such a share in the service of the life, that all duties, even secular duties, are done as to Him, and with a view to His approval. (See particularly Ephes. vi. 5-8.)

Thiersch writes well on this class. "Here is a progress made, though unless the danger that threatens it be removed in time, it must end disastrously. The seed remains, takes root, but in the midst of thorns. The thorns are at first weak and small, and, therefore, made no account of, but little by little they grow up— they strike their roots more and more firmly—they spread abroad above the earth, until they exhaust the strength of the soil. . . . The danger to which such souls as are here described are exposed is this, that they scarcely perceive the quenching of the Spirit of life— the gradual withdrawal of grace, which is the effect of the growth of the thorns, *i.e.*, of the increasing power of the cares of this world, of the esteem and love of riches, and of other lusts. They deceive themselves as to their real state. They suffer from a spiritual consumption, and the evil of this disease consists in this: that the sick person does not know his true condition, and how near he is to spiritual death. The thorns are at first small; that is, this evil does not begin with gross sins, but with things that a man considers lawful and innocent,—such as anxiety about his livelihood, the love of money, attachment to earthly possessions, in efforts to obtain a high position, gratification in the honour that comes from men, seeking after refined enjoyments and pleasures, the pride of science, political excitement." The occupation of the heart by these things brings on spiritual decay, and though we cannot say death, yet the plant is too often as good as dead, being unfruitful.

The Lord, as reported in St. Luke, says not that these are absolutely unfruitful, but " bring no fruit to perfection."

Now, is there no hope for those in this state? Certainly, if they will arouse themselves and do their best to weed the garden of their

15 But that on the good ground are they, which in an

souls, and determinedly pray to God to help them in thus cleansing away all noxious growths from within them. How does the Holy Ghost, by the Apostle, teach us that we are to avoid being barren and unfruitful? "Giving," he says, "all diligence, add to your faith, virtue; and to virtue, knowledge; and to knowledge, temperance; and to temperance, patience; and to patience, godliness; and to godliness, brotherly kindness; and to brotherly kindness, charity; for if these things be in you and abound, they make you that ye shall be neither barren nor unfruitful in the knowledge of our Lord Jesus Christ." (2 Pet. i., 5, &c.)

15. "But that on the good ground are they which in an honest and good heart," &c.

It is to be remarked what trouble (so called) Evangelical commentators have with these words of the Lord, " an honest and good heart." It cuts at the roots of their favourite dogma, that the grace of God is given after such a sort, that the previous state of the heart, and by consequence of the life, is of no avail, *i.e.*, it is never really taken into account by God. But the teaching of this parable from beginning to end is, that the state of the heart or conscience before hearing the word makes all the difference. It does so in the three cases where the sowing fails or seems to fail, and the Lord asserts equally clearly that it does so in the one case out of the four where the sowing is successful. Now, in all this there is the deepest of all mysteries, *i.e.*, the difference between one heart and another— what makes the heart in one case good, and in another evil, before the man himself has had any power over himself to attempt even to cleanse or rectify himself, or to call upon God to help him so to do. All that we know is that " every good gift and every perfect gift is from above," and that God opens hearts to receive the word (Acts xvi. 14). Let us, then, at least in deference to the express words of the Lord, avoid all such teaching as that the disposition of the heart or works done before a certain definite crisis, such as conversion or regeneration, are useless. We know not where, when, and how the Spirit works in the human heart, and if we are not careful, we may be speaking against that secret working of the Holy Ghost whereby He prepares men to receive the Word of God. Whilst acknowledging the deficiency of all natural good dispositions and their fruits, let us equally acknowledge that all goodness is of God,

honest and good heart, having heard the word, keep *it*, and bring forth fruit with patience.

g Matt. v. 15.
Mark iv. 21.
ch. xi. 33.

16 ¶ g No man, when he hath lighted a candle, covereth it with a vessel, or putteth *it* under a bed; but setteth *it* on a candlestick, that they which enter in may see the light.

---

16. "Candle"—"candlestick." Rather, "lamp"—"lampstand."

and pleasing to Him, though He may desire to raise it, and purify it, and enlarge it—in fact, regenerate or renew it.

"Keep it"—that is, hold it fast by the action of their own wills inspired by Divine grace.

"And bring forth fruit," the fruit of works of mercy, corporal and spiritual, for these are the fruit which the Lord mentions in His own account of His procedure at the judgment.

"With patience." "There are three kinds of patience which are necessary in order to bring forth fruit pleasing to God. That of continuance in prayer to keep and preserve the seed, in expectation of the blessing of God upon it to make it fruitful; that of Christian perseverance, in bringing forth fruit to the end without being tired; and that of resistance and suffering in trials and persecutions, either internal from evil habits, or external from the hands of men. What, then, must we always pray and never cease fighting, under the banner of Christ, against His and our spiritual enemies? Yes. This is the lot of the children of God in their present state, the fruit of the Divine word in their hearts, and the continual exercise of their patience." (Quesnel.)

16. "No man, when he hath lighted a candle, covereth it with a vessel," &c. The man who lights the candle or lamp represents the Lord. The lamp or candle which he lighted was the Apostolic company, to whom He had just said, "To you it is given to know the mysteries of the kingdom of God." By the lighting of this lamp, the Lord here alludes to the instruction He had given to them respecting the sowing of the seed of the word. The lampstand or candelabrum (called here wrongly "candlestick") was a piece of furniture which, from its height and the position in which it was placed, could give light as far as possible to the whole house. This candelabrum represented the exalted place which the Lord

17 ʰ For nothing is secret, that shall not be made manifest; neither *any thing* hid, that shall not be known and come abroad. ʰ Matt. x. 26. ch. xii. 2.

18 Take heed therefore how ye hear: ⁱ for whosoever hath, to him shall be given; and whosoever hath not, from him shall be taken even that which he ‖ seemeth to have. ⁱ Matt. xiii. 12. & xxv. 29. ch. xix. 26.

‖ Or, *thinketh that he hath.*

---

had assigned in His Church to the Apostles, that all that enter into the Church may be within the reach of the Light of Life.

17. "For nothing is secret, that shall not be made manifest;" &c. God revealed to them secret things—hidden mysteries, in order that all the world might, through the teaching of the Church, derived at first from the Apostles, be enlightened in the knowledge of the deepest mysteries of God. Consider the secret things of God which were unknown, or known but very dimly by the patriarchs and prophets, and which are now the common heritage of the children of the kingdom, at least so far as finite minds can apprehend them. The Trinity, the Incarnation, the Atonement, the gift of a New Life through the human nature, the Flesh and Blood of Christ, the Church the Body and the Bride of Christ, we, His members, the call of the Gentiles, the equality of all men in Christ, the clear meaning of once obscure prophecies, the significance of types,—all these were revealed, perhaps not at this time, but as men were able to receive them.

18. "Take heed therefore how ye hear," &c. Some have said that we should rather have expected, "Take heed how ye preach, how ye teach," but if they are to preach and to teach aright, they must hear aright.

But how does this agree with the latter clauses of this verse?

"Whosoever hath, to him shall be given; and whosoever hath not," &c. Evidently in this way. Only they who take heed how they hear, who hear reverently, attentively, believingly, "have." *They* only retain, and realize, and make their own of what falls into their ears; and such only are in a condition to receive more. "He alone who assimilates the Lord's teaching by an act of living comprehension, who really 'hath' (the opposite of seeing without seeing, verse 10), can continually receive more. Acquisitions are made only by means of, and in proportion to, what is already pos-

19 ¶ ᵏ Then came to him *his* mother and his brethren, and could not come at him for the press.

ᵏ Matt. xii. 46.
Mark iii. 31.

20 And it was told him *by certain* which said, Thy mother and thy brethren stand without, desiring to see thee.

21 And he answered and said unto them, My mother and my brethren are these which hear the word of God, and do it.

---

sessed . . . . If, therefore, anyone amongst them contents himself with hearing truth without appropriating it, by and by he will obtain nothing, and at last even lose everything." (Godet.)

19. "Then came to him his mother and his brethren . . . . for the press." St. Luke, apparently by using the word "then," places this incident, in point of time, just after the parable of the sower, omitting the other parables, which in the narratives of St. Matthew and St. Mark follow this first parable. St. Matthew places it immediately after the Lord had delivered the parable of the evil spirit returning to the empty house (xii. 43-45,); St. Mark, after He had been speaking of the sin against the Holy Ghost, which itself was called forth by their asserting that He cast out devils through Beelzebub, and that He had an unclean spirit. Gresley, in his "Harmony," places it immediately after the parable of the unclean spirit re-occupying his old abode, though that parable comes in this Gospel much after this (xi. 24, &c.). The discrepancies, both in the Evangelists and in the harmonists respecting the true sequence of this incident, show how impossible it is to arrange the incidents of our Lord's life in any sure chronological order. It seems to me quite clear that for some wise purpose we are forbidden to attempt to harmonise them, *i.e.*, to weave them into one consecutive narrative. God has given to us four Gospels, and we are not to attempt to make them virtually one.

I have commented so fully on this incident as it is related in the other Synoptics that I can only say now that the Lord's words do not imply that He resented the interference, which was no doubt kindly meant on the part of his kinsfolk, but they teach us that He desired to lay the greatest stress possible on the fact that of all relationships spiritual relationship is the closest; and that this spiritual relationship is, in its essence, obedience to God. For in this Gospel He is reported to have said, "My mother and my brethren are those

22 ¶ ¹ Now it came to pass on a certain day, that he went into a ship with his disciples: and he said unto them, Let us go over unto the other side of the lake. And they launched forth.

¹ Matt. viii. 23.
Mark iv. 35.

23 But as they sailed he fell asleep: and there came down

---

who hear the word of God and do it," whilst in St. Matthew's narrative He says, " Whosoever shall do the will of my Father which is in heaven, the same is my brother." In the one case the "doing" alone is mentioned; in the other the hearing, in order to do. Even in earthly relationships communion in will, *i.e.*, in spirit, is far closer than communion in flesh. There may be, and too often is, estrangement in those who have only flesh in common; but in communion of will there is love, and united purpose, and a mingling of thought and intercourse, of soul with soul, tending to make all one. Now this was pre-eminently the case with the Blessed Virgin. She who had said, "Behold the handmaid of the Lord, be it unto me according to Thy word," she also had kept and pondered all the sayings of her Son in her heart: but now she was accidentally, it may be said, associated with those who were taking too much upon themselves, and this drew from the Lord one of His deepest and most searching sayings.

22. "Now it came to pass on a certain day .... and they launched forth." This passage over the sea, of which St. Luke leaves the date uncertain, according to St. Mark took place on the evening of the day on which the Lord had been teaching the multitude by parable out of the ship.

St. Luke, for some reason, does not notice the fact that the Lord went into a ship and taught the people from the ship as they were crowding the shore (Luke viii. 4); St. Mark seems to imply that the ship did not touch the western shore of the lake that evening (iv. 35); whilst St. Matthew places this and the three following miracles much earlier in the narrative and in the midst of totally different incidents—another, as I believe, divinely appointed caution against all our attempts at "harmonizing."

23-25. "But as they sailed he feel asleep .... he commandeth even the winds and water," &c. With respect to this miracle, I have commented so fully upon it in my notes on the other two Synoptics that I can but very briefly advert to it here. The sea of

a storm of wind on the lake; and they were filled *with water*, and were in jeopardy.

24 And they came to him, and awoke him, saying, Master, master, we perish. Then he arose, and rebuked the wind and the raging of the water: and they ceased, and there was a calm.

24. "Then he arose." "And he awoke," Revisers, after ℵ, B., L.; but A., later Uncials, Cursives, &c., as in Authorized.

Galilee was always subject to sudden storms, and the leading Apostles, in plying their trade on it, must have been long accustomed to expect them. From, however, their fear on this occasion, it seems that this storm must have been one of unaccustomed violence, and probably of longer continuance than usual. Cyril notices this: "It seems to have been especially and wonderfully ordained that they should not seek His assistance when first the storm began to affect the boat, but after the danger had increased, in order that the power of the Divine Majesty might be made more manifest. Hence it is said, 'And they were filled with water, and were in jeopardy.' This, indeed, our Lord allowed for the sake of trial, that having confessed their danger, they should acknowledge the greatness of the miracle."

The words with which the disciples awoke the Lord are somewhat differently reported in the three Evangelists. St. Mark has "Carest thou not that we perish?" St. Luke, "Master, master, we perish;" St. Matthew, "Lord, save us, we perish."

But as Augustine says this may have been the case that by the many that awoke Him all these things were said, one by one, and another by another. Indeed, it is extremely improbable that in such an urgent crisis only one should have uttered a word.

All are agreed upon the typical significance of this miracle—that the ship is the Church; the storm, the persecution and opposition of the world; and the Lord, asleep on the pillow, the presence of Christ in the Church, but, though present, at times seemingly regardless of the dangers which threaten to overwhelm it. But those who are in the ship rouse Him, as it were, by their prayers, and He delivers them from their distress.

But Quesnel and others consider that the ship also represents the soul; the passage over the sea, its passage through time into eter-

WHERE IS YOUR FAITH?

25 And he said unto them, Where is your faith? And they being afraid wondered, saying one to another, What manner of man is this! for he commandeth even the winds and water, and they obey him.

26 ¶ ᵐ And they arrived at the country of the Gadarenes, which is over against Galilee. ᵐ Matt. viii. 28. Mark v. 1.

---

26. "Gadarenes." So A., later Uncials, almost all Cursives and Syriacs (Cureton and Pesh.); but ℵ, L., some Cursives (1, 33, 118, &c.), Copt., Arm., Æth. read, "Gergesenes," and B., D., old Latin, and Vulg. read, "Gerasenes."

nity; the lake, the world over which we must pass; the storm of wind, the temptations of our spiritual enemy, which may spring up from any quarter suddenly; and the water with which the ship was filled, and well-nigh ready to sink, the sins and declensions from God, which are the effect of temptations yielded to. But can the Saviour be said to be in the ship of the soul? Assuredly, for He says, "He that abideth in me, and I in him." And, again, His Apostle says, " Know ye not that Jesus Christ is in you, except ye be reprobates." The Church is made up of souls, and Christ is in the Church by His dwelling in the souls of its members.

But can the Saviour be said to be in the soul like one asleep? Yes; for one of the principal exercises which He lays upon the soul is that it should stir up the grace already given to it. He makes as though He were slumbering, in order that we may call upon Him the more earnestly. And "the Lord will wake as one out of sleep," and rebuke the tempest of passion and the waves of temptation, and there shall be a great calm.

25. "And he said unto them, Where is your faith?" Where is your faith in My Divine Mission, if ye are are afraid that any commotion of wind and waves could cut it short, and frustrate the purpose of God in sending Me into the world?

"What manner of man is this! for he commandeth even the winds," &c. The miracle had done its work in them; for this is a question, not of unbelief, but of faith, for the only answer to it is that He is infinitely more than man. There are questions of unbelief which are such as "How can these things be?" But there are questions to which faith only can reply, and this is one, for the answer is, "He is God's only Son, our Lord and our God."

26. "And they arrived at the country of the Gadarenes," &c. I

27 And when he went forth to land, there met him out of the city a certain man, which had devils long time, and ware no clothes, neither abode in *any* house, but in the tombs.

---

27. "Which had devils long time." So A., later Uncials, almost all Cursives, Vulg.; but א, B., L., Cursives 1, 33, 131, 157, and some versions take "long time" with "ware no clothes,"—"and for a long time he ware no clothes" (Revisers).

have shown in notes on St. Mark that the locality of this miracle has been pretty surely identified with a place yet retaining the name of Gersa or Chersa. The name as pronounced by the Bedouin Arabs is Gersa or Kersa; and the natural features of steep declivity and narrow shore of the lake in all respects correspond with the narrative.

27. "And when he went forth to land, there met him out of the city," &c. St. Mark says "there met him out of the tombs." Both may be perfectly accurate. The man belonged to the city, but refused to dwell in human habitations, but had his dwelling-place in the tombs, the remains of which yet exist in the mountain close by.

St. Matthew mentions two possessed persons, St. Mark and St. Luke one only: the general explanation being that the one mentioned by the second and third Synoptics was by far the best known, and the most violent.

"Which had devils long time, and ware no clothes, neither abode in any house," &c. Macarius (quoted in Ford) has an eloquent passage upon this case of possession, in that he was driven to dwell in the tombs. "Whenever you hear mention made of tombs, don't let your thoughts run only upon such as are outward: for thine own heart is the tomb or sepulchre. For when the prince of wickedness and his angels are lurking there, and make paths and thoroughfares, where the powers of Satan walk up and down in thy very mind and thoughts, art not thou a hell, a sepulchre, and tomb, and art thou not dead to God? There it is that Satan hath stamped the reprobate silver (Jer. vi. 30); in thy very soul has he sown the seeds of bitterness, and leavened it with the old leaven. The Lord, therefore, descends to those souls that seek after Him, into the very depths of the heart; and there doth He give forth His commands to death, saying, 'Let out all the souls under your confinement that seek after me, and which you keep by main force.' He breaks, therefore, through the heavy stones that lie upon the soul, opens the sepulchres, raises up

CHAP. VIII.] LEGION. 215

28 When he saw Jesus, he cried out, and fell down before him, and with a loud voice said, What have I to do with thee, Jesus, *thou* Son of God most high? I beseech thee, torment me not.

29 (For he had commanded the unclean spirit to come out of the man. For oftentimes it had caught him: and he was kept bound with chains and in fetters; and he brake the bands, and was driven of the devil into the wilderness.)

30 And Jesus asked him, saying, What is thy name? And he said, Legion: because many devils were entered into him.

---

the true dead, and bringeth the imprisoned soul out of the custody of darkness."

28. "When he saw Jesus, he cried out . . . . torment me not." Throughout the narrative, the human subject, the man, is wholly in the background; he neither addresses the Lord, nor the Lord him. He had been for long tormenting his victim, and yet not the oppressed, but the oppressor, cries to the Lord, "I beseech thee, torment me not." Here he witnesses to the Lord, Whom he calls the Son of God most high, as being the Judge of the whole universe of fallen spirits, as well as of sinful men.

29. "For he had commanded the unclean spirit to come out of the man." How is it that the unclean spirit who held possession of the man allowed him to come into the presence of the Lord? No doubt because the Lord compelled him. The same power which cast him out forced him to present himself before the King and Judge of Angels that he might receive sentence at His hand.

30. "And Jesus asked him, saying, What is thy name? And he said, Legion," &c. Both Trench and Godet, and doubtless many others, suppose that this question was put by the Lord with the view of facilitating the man's cure; for we are told that asking the name of a lunatic or madman throws the man back on his own consciousness, which they assume is a step to the restoration of his reason; but if so, in this case it was unsuccessful, for the man does not give his name, but the Spirit, through the man's lips, gives a name which must have been dictated by Him, and which it is absurd to suppose that the man would have given of himself. We do not know the conditions under which the unseen spiritual world exists;

31 And they besought him that he would not command them to go out ⁿ into the deep.

ⁿ Rev. xx. 3.

32 And there was there an herd of many swine feeding on

---

31. "The deep." Rather, "the abyss."

but if this band of evil spirits was always associated with their leader, and obeyed him as one man, through some necessity unknown to us, then, if the Lord's question forced the evil one to say the truth respecting himself, it is probable that he must give an answer which betokened that he was never alone, and could not be regarded as a simple unit, but wherever he was there was his evil company; and so his strange answer as given in St. Mark is the more exact, "*My* name is Legion, for *we* are many."

31. "And they besought him that he would not command them to go out into the deep." "The deep" is a most inadequate—indeed, according to the circumstances, an absolutely wrong—translation. The word is, the "abyss," rendered several times in the Revelations as the bottomless pit, and always in a bad sense, as the place from which issued the smoke and the tormenting locusts (Rev. ix. 1, 2, 11), and into which Satan was cast bound during the thousand years (Rev. xx. 2, 3). Seeing, then, that this "abyss," whatever it was, was destined to be their prison, and they knew that the time of their final doom was not yet come, they most naturally ask the Lord for a longer respite. In St. Matthew one of them is represented as saying, "Art thou come hither to torment us before the time?"

But, then, the question arises, how are we to make their request, as given in St. Luke, agree with that which is given in St. Mark? "He besought Him much that He would not send them away out of the country." Taking the two places as they stand, and assuming that both requests were made, they can be perfectly reconciled in this way. The country of the Gadarenes, perhaps this small neighbourhood, was the only one in which they were allowed to be at large. It was for them either this city and hill-side, or the abyss. To deprecate, then, being driven out of the country, was to deprecate their imprisonment in the abyss.

32. "And there was there an herd of many swine feeding . . . . he suffered them." Only one likely reason has been given for this request, that the evil spirits foresaw that if they could enter into

HE SUFFERED THEM.

the mountain: and they besought him that he would suffer them to enter into them. And he suffered them.

33 Then went the devils out of the man, and entered into the swine: and the herd ran violently down a steep place into the lake, and were choked.

---

and destroy the swine it would so act upon the fears or the cupidity of the people of the place that they would reject the Lord's mission. Or the real reason for their asking for such a thing may be totally unknown to us. It may have been inexpressible torment for these evil spirits to be left to wander about unclothed with some human, or in default of that, some animal frame which they could torment or worry, and so they asked to be clothed with the bodies of these swine. It may be that they did not desire the destruction of the swine, and that a panic got among these creatures which they were unable to control, and so the Lord punished them by granting their request. But the whole matter is in a sphere above and beyond us, and we can only put forward conjectures which appear less unlikely than others. It has sometimes seemed to me that the Saviour, in performing this miracle, desired not merely to set forth His power over all worlds, visible and invisible, but to give us a slight glimpse of the fearful conditions under which the evil side of the world of spirits exists; how it torments, and is tormented; how it destroys, and is destroyed; how it is a world of unrest, of unsatisfied lusts and longings; how it has affinities with all that is unclean and ignoble, and sensual, and base, in this mixed state of things; how we are encompassed by a hell of evil spirits as well as by a heaven of good angels. Of all such things we have just a glimpse, as it were, in this narrative.

33. "Then went the devils out of the man, and entered, &c. . . . were choked." I observed, in my notes on St. Mark, that this does not at all imply that there was an evil spirit to each separate swine, but that a herd of swine, as of other animals, would follow if a panic seized the leaders. I also showed, by a quotation from Dr. Thompson's "The Land and the Book," that there was close at hand a part of the beach exactly suited to the destruction of an herd of creatures such as these, for there is just at this spot a mountain, or hill, the side of which inclines rapidly to a very narrow strip of beach, so that the swine would, if they rushed violently down, not

218 SITTING AT THE FEET OF JESUS. [St. Luke.

34 When they that fed *them* saw what was done, they fled, and went and told *it* in the city and in the country.

35 Then they went out to see what was done; and came to Jesus, and found the man, out of whom the devils were departed, sitting at the feet of Jesus, clothed, and in his right mind: and they were afraid.

36 They also which saw *it* told them by what means he that was possessed of the devils was healed.

o Matt. viii. 34.   37 ¶ °Then the whole multitude of the country
p Acts xvi. 39.   of the Gadarenes round about P besought him to depart from them; for they were taken with great fear: and he went up into the ship, and returned back again.

---

be able to stop themselves, but would be carried by the impetus into a deep part of the lake.

34-37. "When they that fed them . . . . taken with great fear." This conduct of the Gadarenes must not be ascribed wholly to avarice at the loss of their swine, but to ignorance and fear. We are to remember that the country was more than half heathen, that this was the Lord's first visit, that He had never preached among them or healed any of their sick. In all probability they only half understood what had been done. The swineherds could have heard little or nothing of what had passed between the Lord and the man possessed with the Legion. They only saw three things, the presence of some very powerful stranger, the marked change in one who had probably long been their terror, and the sudden, and to them unaccountable destruction of their swine; unaccountable, I say, for they could not have seen invisible spirits quit their human victim and take possession of the animals; so that much of their seeming sin must be imputed to blind ignorance, and fear at the presence of the supernatural in the Lord.

And yet their conduct is an apt illustration of what is very common, the rejection, by worldly or carnal, or ignorant souls, of the near approach of Jesus, in a true conversion and change of heart and character, because they have an instinctive feeling that His presence will destroy carnal lusts and swinish indulgencies. This is but another form of the very old rejection of God in the

CHAP. VIII.]   RETURN TO THINE HOUSE.   219

38 Now ᑫ the man out of whom the devils were departed besought him that he might be with him: but ᑫ Mark v. 18. Jesus sent him away, saying,

39 Return to thine own house, and shew how great things God hath done unto thee. And he went his way, and published throughout the whole city how great things Jesus had done unto him.

40 And it came to pass, that, when Jesus was returned, the people *gladly* received him: for they were all waiting for him.

---

words, "Depart from us, for we desire not the knowledge of thy ways." (Job xxi. 14.)

38, 39. "Now the man out of whom the devils were departed .... Return to thine own house," &c. It seems strange that the Lord should have refused this man's request to be his follower, as the Apostles were, but He no doubt saw that one so long the terror of the neighbourhood, but now in his right mind, would be a more effectual witness to His love and power amongst his fellow-countrymen, who knew so well what he had once been, than to strangers who knew not his history. That He should command one to spread abroad the fame of a stupendous miracle, and enjoin others with the utmost strictness to say nothing about a similar one, no doubt depended upon each man's particular state of mind. To go about disclosing what God has done for us is not enjoined in all cases, for in one sort of soul it may minister to humility, and in another to self-conceit, which would destroy very much of the good effect, even of a miracle of conversion.

By the living witness of the change wrought in this man the inhabitants of the district might be more ready to welcome the tidings of the Gospel, when it was preached to them after the Resurrection and the Day of Pentecost.

40. "And it came to pass, that, when Jesus was returned .... waiting for him." We should gather from this that the Lord had foreseen how very short His sojourn on the other side of the lake would be, and had made it known; otherwise, if His return had been uncertain they would not "all have been waiting for Him."

41, 42. "And, behold, there came a man named Jairus .... thronged him." "Jairus," the same name as Jair, in Numbers

A MAN NAMED JAIRUS.

41 ¶ ʳAnd, behold, there came a man named Jairus, and he was a ruler of the synagogue: and he fell down at Jesus' feet, and besought him that he would come into his house:

ʳ Matt. ix. 18.
Mark v. 22.

42 For he had one only daughter, about twelve years of age, and she lay a dying. But as he went the people thronged him.

ˢ Matt. ix. 20.

43 ¶ ˢAnd a woman having an issue of blood twelve years, which had spent all her living upon physicians, neither could be healed of any.

---

43. "Had spent all her living upon physicians." This sentence has various readings. Omitted by B., retained by ℵ, A., C., D., L., later Uncials, Cursives, &c.

xxxii. 41. It is possible that he was one of those who interested themselves on behalf of the centurion (Luke vii. 3), as the place where this occurred was most probably Capernaum. If so, his kindly feeling towards his Gentile neighbour was indeed abundantly rewarded. His daughter was restored by a miracle, one of the three recorded cases of the Lord's raising the dead, and his name is handed down in the Gospel narrative as one who, on account of his faith, received this special benefit from the Lord.

43, 44. "And a woman having an issue of blood twelve years . . . . her issue of blood stanched." I have commented so fully on this incident and its typical meaning in my notes on both St. Matthew and St. Mark, that little can be said here. The narrative of St. Luke is much more full and circumstantial than that in St. Matthew, but not so much so as that of St. Mark. It seems to me that St. Mark's is that of an eyewitness who had even conversed with the woman (Mark v. 28, 29), and St. Luke that of one who had received his account from an eyewitness, whilst St. Matthew produces the account in its traditional form very abbreviated.

The woman may be taken to represent human nature convinced of its sin and misery in the sight of God. Her deep-seated and incurable malady may be held to signify the dominion of evil habits. The physicians upon whom she had spent her all seem to set forth the impotence of all human means to deliver the sinner from the guilt and power of sin. The coming behind the Lord on the part of the woman indicates the mind of the sinner to whom

CHAP. VIII.]   WHO TOUCHED ME ?   221

44 Came behind *him*, and touched the border of his garment : and immediately her issue of blood stanched.

45 And Jesus said, Who touched me ? When all denied, Peter and they that were with him said, Master, the multitude throng thee and press *thee*, and sayest thou, Who touched me ?

45. "And they that were with him." So ℵ, A., C., D., L., later Uncials, almost all Cursives ; but B., a few Cursives, Sah., and Syriac omit.

"And sayest thou, Who touched me ?" So A., C., D., later Uncials, &c., Cursives, old Latin, Vulg., Syriacs ; omitted by ℵ, B., L., three or four Cursives, Sah., Copt., Arm.

God had granted faith in His Son,—he would come to the Lord as knowing that in Christ is his only hope of deliverance. The touching the hem or tassel of the Lord's garment is the belief (and consequent acting on that belief) that the Lord's whole Person, Body, Soul, and Spirit, being the Person of the God-man, is the channel of all healing from God to man—not merely the doctrine, nor the example, nor even the power, but the very Person, Body, Blood, Soul, and Divinity of the Redeemer as the Second Adam, of whose very nature we must partake if we are to be in Christ by grace as we are in Adam by nature, for we receive sin and death, not from following the example, but by receiving the nature of Adam, and we must receive life and righteousness, not merely by trying to follow the example, but by, if possible, so coming into contact with Christ, the Second Adam, as to receive His nature.

The fringe or tassels of the Lord's garment adumbrate the means of grace in the Church of Christ by touching, *i.e.*, by partaking, of which the sinner comes into contact, as it were, with the Lord's Person, only with this very great difference, that there was no promise attached to touching the borders of the Lord's garment, whereas to the devout reception of His Body and Blood the Lord joins the greatest possible promise, even " He that eateth my Flesh and drinketh my Blood dwelleth in me, and I in him."

The stanching of her issue of blood is the type of the reception of deliverance from past sin, and power against future sin, which we receive through faith in Christ. I believe that at the last it will be found that this grace against sin has ordinarily come through the channels of grace in the Church : and that where it has not apparently accompanied the use of these means it is simply

VIRTUE IS GONE OUT OF ME. [St. Luke.

46 And Jesus said, Somebody hath touched me: for I perceive that ᵗvirtue is gone out of me.

ᵗ Mark v. 30.
ch. vi. 19.

47 And when the woman saw that she was not hid, she came trembling, and falling down before him, she declared unto him before all the people for what cause she had touched him, and how she was healed immediately.

---

because they have been used mechanically or without faith, and without prayer and self-examination, and above all, without a sincere desire to receive in their use the grace which Christ has promised. We must not only have a general faith in Christ, a faith in His Atonement or Intercession, or His love to us, but a faith " whereby we steadfastly believe the promises of God made to us in that Sacrament."

The comparison between the thronging and pressing of the multitude and the perhaps slight and almost imperceptible touch by the woman, sets forth the difference between the practical unbelief of mere nominal and the real faith of true Christians. The multitude, at least that part of it which was nearest to the Lord's Person, touched Him, hustled against Him, pressed Him, and in all probability came really nearer to Him than the woman, but there was no purpose in their coming near or touching, whereas the woman touched with a purpose—a definite purpose—of receiving healing from His Person through His robe. The multitude, then, may prefigure those who throng our churches, and even frequent the Sacraments, but for mere custom's sake. In coming to church they come into His peculiar presence: in coming to Holy Communion they come far closer still, but they have little or no more purpose in coming than the crowd in surrounding Him, of which crowd, be it remembered, it is said that "they gladly received Him," or, as is in the Revised, " They welcomed him, for they all waited for him."

But the woman adumbrates those who come to His presence in church, or much more to His presence in the Blessed Sacrament, with a purpose—with a will—with a strong definite desire to receive from Him eternal life. It is to such that He manifests His Nearness, even the saving efficacy of His Real Presence.

48. "And he said unto her, Daughter, be of good comfort: thy faith hath made thee whole," &c. " Thy faith hath made thee

48 And he said unto her, Daughter, be of good comfort: thy faith hath made thee whole; go in peace.

---

48. "Be of good comfort." So A., C., E., H., other later Uncials, most Cursives, Goth., Syriac, Æth.; omitted by ℵ, B., D., L., six or eight Cursives, most old Latin, Vulg., Sah., Copt., Cureton Syriac.

whole." What was her faith? It was a faith not only in the general power and goodness of the Lord, but that His very Person overflowed with healing virtue. It was the preparation for that loftier and more intelligent faith of the Catholic Church that the Lord's Person, as the Second Adam, is the fountain of healing Grace, and that He diffuses this Grace through means—means of grace utterly inadequate in themselves, but efficacious because of their Divinely appointed connection with Himself.

Godet has made a remark on the Lord's asking the question "Who touched me?" that should not be suffered to pass unnoticed. He writes: "There is no reason for not attributing to Jesus the ignorance implied in the question, 'Who touched me?' But could the Lord have been ignorant of the particular person on whose behalf the virtue had gone out of Him? Surely the same Divine knowledge which revealed to Him that a particular person in a dense crowd had very gently touched His clothes with a purpose, revealed to Him that purpose, revealed to Him the person in whose breast it had been formed, revealed to Him that she was worthy to receive a cure, and so on. It seems to me the height of superstition to suppose that virtue had gone out of Him at random as it were, without an act of His Divine will suffering it and directing it to the proper object." Godet further remarks, "Anything like feigning ignorance ill comports with the candour of His character." But the Lord did not, in asking this question, "feign ignorance." He asked the question for the sole purpose of drawing out from the woman a full and voluntary confession of what she had done and her reason for doing it. Considering the crowd which surrounded them, He could not have accused any one in particular of touching Him. Her own confession was necessary if the bystanders were to believe that her action was voluntary. With respect to feigning, did God feign when He asked Adam "Where art thou?" or when He asked him "Who told thee thou wast naked?" or when He asked Eve, "What is this that thou hast done?" (Gen. iii. 9, 11, 13).

49 ¶ ᵘ While he yet spake, there cometh one from the
ᵘ Mark v. 35. ruler of the synagogue's *house*, saying to him,
Thy daughter is dead; trouble not the Master.

50 But when Jesus heard *it*, he answered him, saying, Fear
not: believe only, and she shall be made whole.

51 And when he came into the house, he suffered no man
to go in, save Peter, and James, and John, and the father
and the mother of the maiden.

52 And all wept, and bewailed her: but he said, Weep
ˣ John xi. 11, not; she is not dead, ˣ but sleepeth.
13.
53 And they laughed him to scorn, knowing
that she was dead.

54 And he put them all out, and took her by the hand,
ʸ ch. vii. 14. and called, saying, Maid, ʸ arise.
John xi. 43.

---

54. "And he put them all out" omitted by א, B., D., L., most old Latin, Vulg., Cur.
Syriac, Æth.; retained by A., most later Uncials, Cursives, &c.

49. "While he yet spake, there cometh one from the ruler of the
synagogue's house," &c. This must have tried exceedingly the
faith of the ruler. He had not had faith to ask the Lord, " Say
the word only," as the centurion had; but like the nobleman
whose son was at the point of death, he could only believe that the
Lord could work miracles where He Himself was present, and
could lay His hands on the sick. But if he was to receive the blessing he sought, he must believe that the Lord's power could reach to
the very confines of the unseen state into which the souls of the
dead pass, rather even into the unseen realm itself, and so the Lord
upheld him with the words—

50. "Fear not: believe only, and she shall be made whole."
"Believe only." Faith is the one thing needed, for it is that within
us which realizes to us the Son of God in all His attributes of grace
and love as well as in the Divine dignity of His Person: but faith
in the Lord as revealed to us must not stop short at anything
which is within the reach of His Almighty Power. It must not
confer with flesh and blood, and think, as the ruler was tempted
to think, that the Lord's power is limited to this world, and to
this present life.

51-56. "And when he came into the house .... no man what

55 And her spirit came again, and she arose straightway: and he commanded to give her meat.

56 And her parents were astonished: but [z] he charged them that they should tell no man what was done.

[z] Matt. viii. 4. ix. 30. Mark v. 43.

was done." I have sufficiently commented on the substance of these verses in my notes on St. Mark. They have nothing more than what is in the other Synoptics.

CHAP. IX.

THEN [a] he called his twelve disciples together, and gave them power and authority over all devils, and to cure diseases.

[a] Matt. x. 1. Mark iii. 13. & vi. 7.

1. "His twelve disciples." So E., F., H., U., many Cursives, a few old Latin (b, ff², g¹, l, q); but ℵ, C., L., some Cursives (16, 33, 67, 69, 124), old Latin (a, c, e, f), Vulg., &c. read, "his twelve apostles," and A., B., D., K., M., R., S., other later Uncials, about 100 Cursives, and Syriacs read, "the twelve."

1. "Then he called his twelve disciples together," &c. He called them "together" as a "body" or "college," and gave them this their first commission in their corporate capacity, as it were, thus distinguishing them from the rest of His disciples.

"And gave them power and authority over all devils, and to cure diseases." He gave them what in the eyes of men was esteemed to be His own highest prerogative, for the people had exclaimed, "What a word is this, for with authority he commandeth even the unclean spirits, and they obey him."

"Over all devils." The effects of possession by evil spirits were diverse, according to the power and malignity of each one; some were easily expelled, others held to their victims more tenaciously; but the Lord gave them power over *all*, so that, if any resisted them, it was through their own deficiency in faith. (Matt. xvii. 20.)

226 HE SENT THEM TO PREACH. [ST. LUKE.

2 And ^bhe sent them to preach the kingdom of God, and to heal the sick.

3 ^cAnd he said unto them, Take nothing for *your* journey, neither staves, nor scrip, neither bread, neither money; neither have two coats apiece.

^b Matt. x. 7, 8. Mark vi. 12. ch. x. 1, 9.
^c Matt. x. 9. Mark vi. 8. ch. x. 4. & xxii. 35.

2. "The sick" omitted by B. and Cureton Syriac only.

3. "Staves." So A., H., K., other later Uncials, very many Cursives; but אּ, B., C., D., E., F., L., M., &c., many Cursives (1, 11, 22, 28, 33, 69, 106, &c.), old Latin, Vulg., and versions, read, "a staff."

2. And he sent them to preach the kingdom of God, and to heal the sick." "To preach the kingdom of God," *i.e.*, its near approach, so that those who heard should accept it in the Person of the Lord.

Did they themselves then understand all that was meant by the term, "Kingdom of God"? Certainly not. This was not necessary, for in preaching the kingdom, they simply heralded it, and proclaimed its near approach, but did not expound it. Men expected that the Messiah when He came, would introduce a new regime, as it were. This they proclaimed as at hand.

"And to heal." The healing those afflicted in mind or body, in mind by evil spirits, in body by diseases, was their credential. It was the same as the Lord's. In this first mission of the twelve there was a partial fulfilment of that which after the Resurrection was embodied in the words, "As my Father sent me, so send I you." Godet has a valuable remark: "There is something greater than preaching—this is to make preachers; there is something greater than performing miracles—this is to impart the power to perform them. It is this new stage which the work of Jesus here reaches. He labours to train His Apostles up to His own level.

3. And he said unto them, Take nothing for your journey." Go just as you are, make no preparation whatsoever. My Father will see that you need nothing.

"Neither staves." Probably, neither a staff. This does not mean that if they had a staff they were to throw it away, but if they had not a staff already, or if they walked well without one, they were not to procure or buy one.

"Nor scrip," *i.e.*, no wallet or small basket to hold provisions; for when they were hungry God would open the hearts of the first person they called upon to supply their wants.

4 ^d And whatsoever house ye enter into, there abide, and thence depart. ^d Matt. x. 11. Mark vi. 10.

5 ^e And whosoever will not receive you, when ye go out of that city, ^f shake off the very dust from your feet for a testimony against them. ^e Matt. x. 14. ^f Acts xiii. 51.

"Neither bread, neither money." This shows that this mission was a very special one, because in their usual following of the Lord, they took with them some provision of bread ("we have no more but five loaves"), and they had also a common purse or bag, out of which Judas pilfered.

"Neither have two coats apiece." This of course does not imply that they are to go insufficiently clad, but that they are to have no change of garments. They were to travel as poor working men were wont to do.

4. "And whatsoever house ye enter into, there abide, and thence depart." We gather from St. Matthew that they were first to inquire who in the city was worthy, so that their ministry might not be injured by any scandal in the house from which they went forth; and having found such a house they were to continue in it, and not go from house to house in search of better quarters.

These short directions as to the conduct of the Apostles, on this their first missionary journey, imply two things. The most complete unselfishness and indifference to creature comforts on the part of the Apostles, and their absolute faith that God would watch over them and supply their needs wherever they were. This, their faith, was amply rewarded, for when the Lord afterwards appealed to them, "When I sent you without purse or scrip, lacked ye any thing?" they said "Nothing." (Luke xxii. 35.)

5, 6. "And whosoever will not receive you, when ye go out of that city, shake off .... healing everywhere." The Jews were accustomed, on their return from heathen countries to the Holy Land, to shake off the dust from their feet at the frontier. This act signified a breaking away from all joint participation in the life of the idolatrous world. The Apostles were to act in the same way with reference to any Jewish cities which might reject in their person the kingdom of God.

The rejection of the Gospel is not the rejection of a mere theory on which men may innocently entertain different opinions. It is

6 ᵍ And they departed, and went through the towns, preaching the gospel and healing every where.

g Mark vi. 12.

7 ¶ ʰ Now Herod the tetrarch heard of all that was done by him: and he was perplexed, because that it was said of some, that John was risen from the dead;

Anno Domini 32.
h Matt. xiv. 1.
Mark vi. 14.

8 And of some, that Elias had appeared; and of others, that one of the old prophets was risen again.

---

7. "That was done by him." "By him" omitted by ℵ, B., C., D., L., Cursives 69, 157, old Latin (a, b, e, ff², &c.), Sah., Copt., Cur. Syriac, Arm., but retained in A., E., G., H., K., M., S., &c., most later Uncials, almost all Cursives, some old Latin (c, f), Vulg., Goth., Pesh Syriac, Æth.

the rejection of a message which, if faithfully received, reveals God, and subdues us to Him, and transforms us into His likeness. It is the refusal of the only remedy for moral evil which God has given to man. And notice that this remedy, being offered to us by men sent by God, may be rejected in rejecting their message or their preaching. The faults or idiosyncrasies of the preacher are taken no account of by the Lord. It is one with what He says elsewhere, "He that heareth you, heareth me, and he that despiseth you, despiseth me, and he that despiseth me, despiseth him that sent me."

7-9. "Now Herod the tetrarch..... And he desired to see him." There is a remarkable difference between the narratives of the other Synoptics and that of St. Luke, respecting the conduct of Herod on his hearing of the fame of Jesus. According to St. Matthew, Herod himself suggests that it is St. John the Baptist risen from the dead. According to St. Mark, Herod suggests that it is John, and those about him that it is Elias, or some other prophet. But according to St. Luke, the name of the Baptist and other prophets is first suggested by others, and Herod exclaims, "John have I beheaded, but who is this?" The accounts in the two first Evangelists seem to set forth more decidedly the workings of Herod's guilty conscience. It seems not improbable that Herod's fears first suggested to him the reappearance of John from the dead; then those about him, to calm them, would name other prophets, as Elias; and lastly, Herod, having somewhat reassured himself that John could not have risen, exclaimed, "Who is this, of whom I hear such things?"

9 And Herod said, John have I beheaded: but who is this, of whom I hear such things? ¹And he desired to see him. ⁱ ch. xxiii. 8.

10 ¶ ᵏAnd the apostles, when they were returned, told him all that they had done. ¹And he took them, and went aside privately into a desert place belonging to the city called Bethsaida. ᵏ Mark vi. 30. ˡ Matt. xiv. 13.

11 And the people, when they knew *it*, followed him: and

---

10. "Into a desert place belonging to the city called Bethsaida." So A., C., E., G., H., K., M., S., T., Δ, other Uncials, most Cursives, Arm., Goth., Æth. "A city called Bethsaida," B., L., Ξ, X., 33, Sah., Copt. *In locum desertum qui est Bethsaida*, Vulg. (Cod. Amiat), old Latin. There are a number of other different readings. "Into a village (κωμην) called Bethsaida," D., and others.

"And he desired to see him." The reader will remember that St. Luke, who alone records this desire on Herod's part, is the only Evangelist who tells us that the Lord was at the first sent by Pilate to Herod, so that Herod had his profane and godless curiosity gratified, but in a way which only added to his condemnation.

Godet has a suggestive note respecting the source of St. Luke's knowledge of this desire of Herod. "The remarkable detail which Luke alone has preserved—that Herod sought to have a private interview with Jesus—indicates an original source of information closely connected with this king. Perhaps it reached Luke, or the author of the document of which he availed himself, by means of some one of those persons whom Luke describes so exactly in Luke viii. 3, as 'Joanna the wife of Chuza, Herod's steward,' and in Acts xiii. 1, 'Manaen which had been brought up with Herod the Tetrarch,' and who belonged to Herod's household."

10. "And the apostles, when they were returned, told him all ... desert place belonging to the city," &c. According to St. Mark, He thus took them aside, to afford them some needful rest. They were distracted with the constant calls on their powers of healing, so that they had "no leisure so much as to eat."

"Into a desert place belonging to the city called Bethsaida." There are considerable differences of reading; but it is clear that the place into which He led them, being a desert place, could not have been the city of Bethsaida itself.

11. "And the people ... and he received them ... need of healing." Instead of blaming them, and sending them away, be-

230 WE ARE HERE IN A DESERT PLACE. [St. LUKE.

he received them, and spake unto them of the kingdom of God, and healed them that had need of healing.

12 ^m And when the day began to wear away, then came the twelve, and said unto him, Send the multitude away, that they may go into the towns and country round about, and lodge, and get victuals: for we are here in a desert place.

^m Matt. xiv. 15. Mark vi. 35. John vi. 1, 5.

---

cause they broke upon His scanty but well-earned and sorely-needed leisure, He received them. The Son of God is never angry with eagerness and importunity, always with indifference. He seems never to resent interruption, if they who intrude upon Him do so in order to call forth the exercise of His power and goodness.

"And spake unto them of the kingdom of God." In St. Mark this is described as "he began to teach them many things." The kingdom of God has many aspects. It is not a very simple matter, which can be dismissed in a sentence or two. It is full of mystery. "Unto you it is given to know the *mysteries* of the kingdom of God." It is like many things, very different from one another. It is like a field, a hidden treasure, a grain of mustard seed, a net, a man making a supper, and virgins going to meet a bridegroom.

12. "And when the day began to wear away . . . here in a desert place." We now enter upon our fourth exposition of the miracle which seems, in the view of the Spirit of God, the most important of all, for a separate account of it is given in each of the four Gospels; and, if we take into consideration that another miracle, precisely similar in its leading features, *i.e.*, the feeding of the four thousand, is given us in two Evangelists, we have this miraculous multiplication of bread repeated six times in the evangelical narrative. The reader, then, cannot expect more than a "gathering up of fragments;" and yet fragments which must not be lost, *i.e.*, incidental lessons, which ought on no account to pass unnoticed.

In the first place, then, we may notice that there is nothing special in St. Luke's account. He gives no incident or feature which is not to be found in SS. Matthew and Mark; but yet his account is so far independent that it is impossible to suppose that he copied from either of them.

It is also worthy of notice that there were two or three remark-

GIVE YE THEM TO EAT.

13 But he said unto them, Give ye them to eat. And they said, We have no more but five loaves and two fishes; except we should go and buy meat for all this people.

---

able anticipations of this miracle in the Old Testament. There was the unfailing barrel of meal in the history of Elijah (1 Kings xvii. 14). There was the multiplication of the oil in the history of Elisha (2 Kings iv. 1-7); and, in the account of the latter prophet, there was a miracle still more remarkably similar—where Elisha bids his servitor set twenty loaves, and some full ears of corn in the husk, before a hundred men. There is the same objection made by the servitor as by the Apostles. The one asks: " Shall I set this before a hundred men ? " The other: " What are they among so many?" And in each case there was some left. Now these anticipations of this miracle in the Old Testament—a book which must have been familiar to the Apostles—seem very important. The Apostles knew the history of Elisha. In this very Gospel, and in this chapter, we are told they asked respecting the Samaritan village which would not receive them, " Wilt thou that we command fire to come down from heaven, and consume them even as Elias did ? " How is it, then, that having seen our Lord perform miracles greater and more numerous than those of Elijah and Elisha, they did not anticipate that He could multiply food? Was it owing to their want of faith, or to their forgetfulness? Our Lord seems to impute it to their want of understanding; but this want of understanding was providential, for it shows us plainly that they never looked out for miracles. They were never fully alive to the significance of the supernatural in the life and actions of the Lord. In recording these stupendous miracles of creation they record their own extraordinary dulness of apprehension and slowness of belief. We may feel assured that they never imagined a miracle where there was none, and never exaggerated a natural incident into a miracle. On the contrary, their want of apprehension seems at times itself miraculous, as if a supernatural veil was over their hearts. Never once does the Lord reprove them for superstition, or too great readiness to believe; constantly does He blame them for unreadiness to take in the greatness of His claims.

With respect to the teaching of the miracle, in my notes on St. Matthew and St. Mark I have shown how it sets forth the Lord as

14 For they were about five thousand men. And he said to his disciples, Make them sit down by fifties in a company.

---

14. "By fifties in a company." "Make them sit down (or recline) in companies about fifty each."

the Feeder of His people—feeding them both by doctrine and by Eucharist.

With respect to the doctrine, look how the few facts of the Gospel narrative embodied in the creeds have multiplied under His hands, and in the hands of those whom He has sent, into a vast body of truth, practical, consolatory, instructing, correcting, elevating even to heaven, enlightening the soul's eye, so that human beings once blind through sin should see God and His invisible kingdom; and, in the case of the poor and the uneducated, see how at times the smallest modicum of truth is multiplied in the individual mind, so as to furnish it, satisfy it, enable it to overflow and abound. Keble has a remarkable application of this in a sermon of his on this miracle. "He helps our souls as He helps our bodies, through the aid of ordained means; and sometimes He may cause these means to fall short, and then may supply them as suddenly and abundantly as He multiplied these loaves and fishes. A person may have but little learning—he may be quite unable to read, and may seem to himself as if he did not well understand what he hears—and yet, if he have the fear of God in his heart, and try to live accordingly, he shall eat and be filled with spiritual meat and drink. One good lesson, one verse, one prayer may be a treasure to him which he shall never lose. He may be a good way from church, he may have few helps at home; but if he really try to make the most of what little he has, God can and will make a good deal of it—*to him*. Half a prayer remembered as having been learnt in childhood; an old loose Bible or Testament on a shelf; the remembrance of some good Christian formerly known, his sayings, his tone of voice, his manner of coming in and going out, all these and other such things are as the scanty fare of that multitude, which become abundant under His creative hand."

And with respect to the Eucharistic Food, His Body and Blood given to us to make us partakers of Himself, how is His most sacred Body and Blood present at every Eucharist, to be offered to every Christian! We who believe that in that sacred feast He feeds

15 And they did so, and made them all sit down.

16 Then he took the five loaves and the two fishes, and looking up to heaven, he blessed them, and brake, and gave to the disciples to set before the multitude.

---

us, not with representations or figures or emblems, but with realities, must believe that His Almighty grace has so brought it about that every communicant has received His Body and His Blood as surely as each one of these multitudes received what He had taken, and blessed, and broken, and given. Our Blessed Lord seems to have ordered His doings in such a way that the disciples would be sure to remember them when, about a year after, He instituted the Eucharist. The very act of consecration, the taking, blessing, breaking, was anticipated by the Lord when He fed the multitudes. We cannot read the miracle without thinking of the Lord's action on the night of His betrayal.

And the Lord evidently meant us to connect mentally the one with the other, and, as far as I can see, for but one reason,—to enhance our ideas of the greatness of the Sacrament, as a rite or ordinance in which He feeds all with one Bread. Whatever the appearance of the broken element, there is but one nourishing and sustaining Substance. "The bread which we break, is it not the participation of the Body of Christ?" "We being many are one bread and one body, for we are all partakers of that one bread." (1 Cor. x. 16, 17.)

And again, by this miracle our Lord gives believers a lively assurance of the truth of His promise, "Seek ye first the kingdom of God and His righteousness, and all these things (*i.e.*, all things needful for the body) shall be added unto you." These multitudes sought first the kingdom of God. They so hung upon the words proceeding from the Lord's lips; they were so taken with His miracles of healing, that they forgot the things needful for this life; they seem to have even forgotten their hunger, and took no care for their night's lodging, and in this desert place the Lord fed them by this miracle. And I do not think that we can read the account of the life of any poor humble-minded Christian, without finding that when he was in great straits the Lord assisted him unexpectedly by some special providence, which required as distinct an interference on God's part with the course of human

17 And they did eat, and were all filled: and there was taken up of fragments that remained to them twelve baskets.

18 ¶ ⁿ And it came to pass, as he was alone praying, his disciples were with him: and he asked them, saying, Whom say the people that I am?

ⁿ Matt. xvi. 13. Mark viii. 27.

---

events, as did the performance of this miracle demand an exercise of unique power over the elements of human food.

Two subordinate lessons are (1) the necessity of a particular act of giving thanks at each meal to Him that giveth food to all flesh; and (2) the duty of avoiding all waste. Here was an immense quantity of human food produced without labour by a mere word; but by the Lord's blessing it had become fit to sustain life, and so nothing of it was to be lost. There is a sort of sacredness about all human food, for it is God's means of keeping alive one who is created in His image, and so the truly God-fearing man will look upon it with some degree of reverence, and preserve even its fragments for the use of those who are in want, or who have but scanty means of living.

18. "And it came to pass, as he was alone praying," &c. St. Matthew and St. Mark tell us that what follows, *i.e.*, the question of Jesus as to whom the people, and then the disciples, said that He was, took place in the coasts or towns of Cæsarea Philippi. And St. John records that immediately after the feeding of the five thousand, there took place the miracle of the Lord walking on the water, and the discourse of the Lord respecting eating His Flesh and drinking His Blood, which He delivered in the synagogue of Capernaum. St. Luke here, between verses 17 and 18, omits several matters of interest, as the dispute with the Pharisees respecting the eating with unwashen hands—the nature of defilement, the healing of the daughter of the woman of Canaan, the healing of the deaf and stammering man (in Mark vii. 32-37 alone): also the second miracle of the loaves—the Pharisees seeking a sign, the reproof of the disciples for their want of understanding, and, in St. Mark only, the healing of the blind man at Bethsaida. Some of these, as bearing so directly upon the acceptance of the Gentiles, we should have supposed that St. Luke would not have passed over, if it had been his special purpose, in writing his Gospel, to set forth the words and acts of the Lord which foreshadowed it.

CHAP. IX.] WHOM SAY YE THAT I AM? 235

19 They answering said, °John the Baptist; but some *say*, Elias; and others *say*, that one of the old prophets is risen again.

° Matt. xiv. 2. ver. 7, 8.

20 He said unto them, But whom say ye that I am? ᵖ Peter answering said, The Christ of God.

ᵖ Matt. xvi. 16. John vi. 69.

---

18. "And it came to pass, as he was alone praying . . . . Whom say the people that I am?" This is the only instance in which the Lord inquires as to the opinion of others respecting Himself. He does it, no doubt, in the way of catechizing, to draw forth from the Apostles what the multitude thought of Him, and then what they themselves thought; so that they might be more distinctly conscious of the wide difference between the popular opinion and that which they had themselves formed; and this, that they might the better understand, that if they had a truer view of Him than the multitude, it was because they were taught of God. ("Flesh and blood hath not revealed it unto thee, but my Father.")

It is said that He did this when He was "alone praying," and that His disciples were with Him, *i.e.*, only His disciples, not the multitude. Quesnel has a remarkable application of this, "Christ asks His disciples concerning their faith after prayer and in the privacy of retirement, on purpose to teach bishops not to instruct, nor to examine into the faith of inferior pastors in the presence of the people, and to do it with much prudence, after having begged of God the Spirit of Wisdom."

19. "They answering said, John the Baptist; but some say, Elias, and others," &c. This answer is remarkable. The miracles of the Lord had convinced the people that He was come from God, a messenger from the unseen world, and so they thought that He must be some former servant of God, who after his departure had been sent again. It seems strange that they should so far honour Him as to imagine Him to be John or Elias risen again, and yet stop short of the truth. Why should He be a resuscitated prophet, and not the Messiah Himself? The answer is, either that He was a totally different Messiah to what they expected, or (which is more likely to be the truth) that when the true Messiah came, none would recognize Him, except those specially taught of God.

20. "He said unto them, But whom say ye that I am? Peter answering," &c. All the truth of Christ's revelation is wrapped

THE SON OF MAN MUST SUFFER. [St. Luke.

21 ^q And he straitly charged them, and commanded *them*
to tell no man that thing;

22 Saying, ^r The Son of man must suffer many things, and be rejected of the elders and chief priests and scribes, and be slain, and be raised the third day.

23 ¶ ^s And he said to *them* all, If any *man* will

q Matt. xvi. 20.
r Matt. xvi. 21.
& xvii. 22.
s Matt. x. 38.
& xvi. 24.
Mark viii. 34.
ch. xiv. 27.

up in these words, "The Christ of God." For Christ means the Anointed One. If He be the Anointed of God, and is faithful to His anointing, then all that He reveals respecting Himself, respecting the Father, respecting the Holy Ghost, respecting His own Sacrifice, His Intercession, His Mediation, His Judgment, His Flesh being the bread of His people, His perpetual Presence after His departure—all is absolutely true, and will be revealed to the Church, and then to individual souls, as they require it.

Hitherto the Lord had elicited from them the confession of Himself as the Christ. Now He set forth the qualifications which would enable Him to exercise the Messiahship. This was not His Divine dignity, or His Almighty power, but His humiliation and His weakness.

21, 22. "And he straitly charged them that they should tell no man . . . . be raised the third day." But why did He so straitly charge them that they were to tell no man that He was the Christ of God? Because in their then state of ignorance they would be utterly unable to preach the truth respecting His Messiahship. Both they and the people expected a victorious prince; a captain of salvation made "perfect through suffering" would then be unimaginable by either Apostles or multitude.

23. "And he said to them all." Why is it said, "to them all?" This is a very remarkable case of two wholly independent narratives, explaining one another. St. Matthew had said, "Jesus said unto his disciples," and when this conversation was begun the disciples alone could have been present. How is it, then, that St. Luke says, "He said to them all"? The key is given in St. Mark, who tells us that "He called the people unto him with his disciples," and then He proceeded to say words which belong not to Apostles only, but to all who name the Lord's Name. "If any man will [or desire to] come after me, let him deny himself," &c.

There can be no doubt (as I have endeavoured to impress upon

come after me, let him deny himself, and take up his cross daily, and follow me.

---

23. "Daily" omitted by C., D., E., F., G., H., S., &c., nearly 120 Cursives, old Latin (a, b, c, e, ff², l, q); retained by ℵ, A., B., K., L., M., R., &c., Cursives 1, 13, 33, 69, 72, 124, 131, old Latin (f), Vulg., Sah., Copt., and Syriacs (Pesh. and Cureton), Goth., Arm.

the reader), that Christianity has two sides, the attractive, the winning, the merciful, and the severe side. The attractive may be expressed in the words, "Come unto me, all ye that labour and are heavy laden, and I will give you rest." The severe is to be found in, "If any man will come after me, let him deny himself, and take up his cross daily, and follow me." No servant of Christ who looks upon himself as called to teach others can be faithful, unless he does his best to set forth, as occasion requires, these two aspects of the Lord's teaching. No teacher has ever joined these two more effectually than St. Paul, "They that are Christ's have crucified the flesh with its affections and lusts." "Mortify therefore your members which are on the earth." "Fornication," &c. "We beseech you . . . . that ye present your bodies a living sacrifice, holy acceptable to God." "I keep under my body, and bring it into subjection, lest that by any means," &c. One of his faithful sayings is, "If we suffer with him, we shall also reign with him." These are as much His words, and seem to be said with as much earnestness as "By grace are ye saved through faith."

"Deny himself"—that is, at times to abstain from what is pleasurable, though it be perfectly lawful. Without this there is no exercise in godliness, no true discipline.

"Take up his cross daily." The taking-up of the cross is a remarkable figure. For a man to bear on his shoulder two heavy pieces of wood, knowing that at the end of the journey they will be the instrument of a cruel death to him, betokens, *if it be done willingly*, the most determined purpose conceivable to endure all for the cause on which he has set his heart. Now, if the man's heart be set to follow in the blessed steps of his Saviour's holy life, then, to take up the cross daily, implies bearing, enduring, praying, watching, of no ordinary kind; for to take up a cross willingly must have been, even in the times when crucifixion was a punishment, no ordinary thing. It implies willingness to endure no ordinary death; and the figure, as used by the Saviour, must of necessity betoken the determination to go very contrary to flesh

24 For whosoever will save his life shall lose it: but whosoever will lose his life for my sake, the same shall save it.

25 ᵗ For what is a man advantaged, if he gain the whole world, and lose himself, or be cast away?

ᵗ Matt. xvi. 26.
Mark viii. 36.

24. " Will save ; " *i.e.*, wills or desires to save.
" Will lose." The second " will " only the sign of the future tense.

and blood, rather than not follow His example, or not do His will.

" Follow me." Follow Me in the path of purity, holiness, goodness, love, submission to God.

24. " For whosoever will save his life shall lose it: but whosoever will lose," &c. It is to be noticed that the " life " here is one thing : it means the self—that for which a man lives, whether in this world, or in the next.

" Whosoever will save," *i.e.*, whosoever desires, whosoever lays himself out to " save his life," *i.e.*, either to avoid death, which must overtake him if he adheres to the profession of My faith ; or to avoid what comes short of death, *i.e.*, personal discomfort, loss of the world's favour, or whatsoever it be which makes a man feel that this world is not his home, and that he must look for his true home in another world. If a man sets himself to work to avoid these things, and to make the best of this world, then he loses his true life, which is a life " hid with Christ in God."

" But whosoever will lose [not desires to lose, but shall lose] his life," *i.e.*, his temporal life, or all things that in the estimation of the world make the present life worth living ; whosoever shall despise these, if put against the possession of My Favour, then such an one " shall save his life ; " he shall preserve within himself the true life of God, and he shall gain the Resurrection life.

25. " For what is a man advantaged, if he gain the whole world and lose himself," &c. This is one of the plainest of Christ's holy words. It is equally true, whatever we take *life* here to mean. What would it profit a man if he had all the wealth of the world in his possession, and yet, as soon as he possessed it, his soul or life should be required of him ? He could take not one penny of it away with him. He would only find in the other world that which he had parted with in this, for the sake of Christ, or His Church, or

26 "For whosoever shall be ashamed of me and of my words, of him shall the Son of man be ashamed, when he shall come in his own glory, and *in his* Father's and of the holy angels.

u Matt. x. 33.
Mark viii. 38.
2 Tim. ii. 12.

His poor. The gold and silver which he had spent in mere luxury, or vain glory, or sinful pleasure, will then be " a witness against him," and " eat his flesh as it were fire " (James v. 3).

To profit by this saying of the Lord's, we must have real faith in Jesus Christ. Faith in Him, as on His cross losing the whole world, and then, because of His self-renunciation, gaining the empire of the universe. Faith in Him as coming again, and at His coming reversing all human conditions, scattering the proud, putting down the mighty, "raising up the poor out of the dust, and lifting the needy out of the dunghill, that He may set him with princes, even with the princes of His people."

26. " For whosoever shall be ashamed of me and of my words ... holy angels." It seems impossible, now that the Name of Christ is so honoured in the world, that men should be ashamed of Christ; even infidels, or some infidels, speak of him as the wisest and greatest of men. Even those who deny His Godhead confess that no one has made such a mark in the history of the world and in human society as He has. But the Lord connects the being ashamed of His words with being ashamed of Himself. And must we not be delivered from the fear of our fellow-men; must we not hold the opinion of the world and its great ones very cheap, if we are in all companies manfully to confess that we believe in the truth, the absolute truth, of the very words which He has just been uttering, that His true followers must deny themselves, and take their cross daily; that whosoever will save his life, *i.e.*, shall lay himself out to enjoy it to the full, shall lose it, and that the gain of the whole world is worthless when set side by side with the possession of the true Life of God ?

" When he shall come in his own glory," &c. The most abject shame and the highest glory are here contrasted. The ineffable glory of the Son of Man, threefold—His own, that of His Father, that of the holy angels—all enhancing the distress and confusion of the miserable being who has had the opportunity of winning a crown by confessing Him, and has deliberately rejected it for the goodwill of a condemned world.

27 ˣBut I tell you of a truth, there be some standing
here, which shall not taste of death, till they see
the kingdom of God.

ˣ Matt. xvi. 28.
Mark ix. 1.

27. "But I tell you of a truth, there be some standing here, which shall not taste of death," &c. I have spoken twice before of the difficulty of this verse, and that I have never found an altogether satisfactory explanation of it. One thing, however, is certain, that there must be some reference in the Lord's words to the approaching vision of glory, for each of the three Synoptics prefaces his account of the Lord's Transfiguration with it. The difficulty is this. The words, "I tell you of a truth, there be some standing here which shall not taste of death," seem to point to a very prolonged life indeed. They seem to point to far more than a survival of the destruction of Jerusalem, which took place some forty years afterwards, and which is by almost universal consent reckoned as a coming of the Lord, only to be exceeded in the terrors of its vengeance by the consummation at the last day.

It seems at first sight, then, impossible to refer the words with any degree of propriety to the event on the mountain top, which should occur in little less than a week. And so it would be if the Transfiguration had been a public manifestation of the Lord's glory in the sight of all Jerusalem or all Galilee. But the key to the difficulty is, I am persuaded, to be found in the fewness of those to whom the Lord vouchsafed the sight of His glorified Body, and the injunction He laid upon those favoured three, to "tell the vision to no man." The Lord had been speaking of Himself as "the Son of Man coming in his glory," and then "rewarding every man according to his works," and of "coming in his own glory, in that of his Father, and of the holy angels," and of then being ashamed of those who had been ashamed of Him. But this event was in the far distance; ages might intervene, the coming might be long delayed, and the dangers and persecutions alluded to in verses 23, 24, 25 were close at hand. Was there to be any sign, any pledge, any pre-announcement of the final glory? Yes, there was. There were three, and only three, who should be witnesses of a sight of the Lord, arrayed in as much of the Light and Splendour of the Second Coming as mortal eyes would be able to bear. On the steadfastness of the faith of these three God had made the faith of the Church to depend; and the vision on the holy mount was necessary

28 ¶ ʸ And it came to pass about an eight days after these || sayings, he took Peter and John and James, and went up into a mountain to pray.

ʸ Matt. xvii. 1.
Mark ix. 2.
|| Or, *things*.

29 And as he prayed, the fashion of his countenance was altered, and his raiment *was* white *and* glistering.

---

to the steadfastness and perseverance of their faith—necessary, that is, in the counsels of God, for God has made all men's faith to depend in a great measure on the testimony of their fellow-men.

These observations convey in somewhat different language what I have written more fully on Mark ix. 1, to which I earnestly refer the reader.

28. "And it came to pass about an eight days after." St. Matthew and St. Mark write after six days; but there is no discrepancy. These were six whole, unbroken days; and the parts of the day preceding the first of these six, and of the day succeeding the last, would be reckoned by St. Luke as "days."

29. "And as he prayed," &c. St. Luke alone mentions that He retired for prayer, and that the glory began "as he prayed." May we reverently inquire as to the subject of His prayer? We should say the strengthening of the faith of the three, and through them of the whole company of the Apostles. And so the answer to His prayer was the Transfiguration itself, which, more than any miracle that they had seen, upheld them in the overwhelming waterflood through which they had soon to pass.

"The fashion of his countenance was altered." It has been remarked that St. Luke, writing his Gospel for Gentiles, avoids the use of the word which St. Matthew and St. Mark employ to signify the change which came over the appearance of the Lord. They use the word "metamorphosed," a word which would suggest to Gentiles, acquainted with their own mythological system, all manner of abominable stories; whilst St. Luke, writing for Gentiles especially, simply says that His countenance was "other," that is, different, because of its radiance, from what it was before.

"His raiment was white and glistering." This seems to signify that the light of the indwelling Deity streamed, not only from His countenance, but from His whole Person through His garments. What was this radiance—this glory, this all-penetrating brightness? Evidently that of His Divine Nature, which by a miracle of

30 And, behold, there talked with him two men, which were Moses and Elias:

---

restraint He kept from shining forth; but now for a brief space He withheld the restraining power, and He appeared in something of His natural brightness. So that, as I have shown in my notes on St. Matthew, the Transfiguration was not a miracle of superadded glory, but the removal of a veil which hid His state of natural glory from the eyes of His fellows—the real miracle was in the humiliation—the emptying of Himself, the shrouding and restraining of what was ever ready to shine forth.

30. "And behold, there talked with him two men, which were Moses and Elias." "Luke does not name them at first. He says '*two men*.' This mode of describing them reflects the impression which must have been experienced by the eye-witnesses of the scene. They perceived first of all the presence of two persons unknown, it was only afterwards that they knew their names. Behold (ἰδού) seems to express the suddenness of the apparition. The imperfect, 'they were talking,' proves that the conversation had lasted some time when the Apostles first perceived the presence of these strangers." (Godet.)

Two or three questions are suggested by this appearance of these two prophets. The first is, were they mere disembodied spirits? If not, "with what body did they come?" Now it is often remarked, that there was something strange and unique about the departure of these two saints. Elias was taken up to heaven in a chariot of fire and horses of fire, and the death and burial of Moses was still more mysterious, "God," it is said, "buried him, and no man knoweth his sepulchre unto this day." And, besides this, if the Epistle of St. Jude is written under the guidance of God's Spirit, there was a contention between the chief of the good angels and the chief of the wicked ones respecting his body. This seems to teach us that his body did not undergo that which is the common lot of all, but that it was reserved in God's keeping till this appearance of it in the company of the Lord.

Another question seems absurd. It is, "How did the Apostles know them to be Moses and Elias?" Many ways were possible. It might be by intuition from God, or by revelation, it might have been through the words which the Lord addressed to them. It was needful that they should know who these heavenly visitors were,

WHO SPAKE OF HIS DECEASE.

31 Who appeared in glory, and spake of his decease which he should accomplish at Jerusalem.

32 But Peter and they that were with him ˣ were heavy with sleep: and when they were awake, they saw his glory, and the two men that stood with him.

ˣ Dan. viii. 18. & x. 9.

33 And it came to pass, as they departed from him, Peter

---

32. "And when they were awake." Alford translates this, "But having kept awake," Revisers (in margin), "Having remained awake."

because it added to the dignity of the Saviour; and so was intended for the confirmation of their faith, that the law and the prophets should appear in the persons of Moses and Elijah as waiting on the Lord.

31. "Who appeared in glory." That is, radiant with light, as apparently all heavenly visitants are.

"And spake of his decease which he should accomplish at Jerusalem." The word for decease is exodus. His departure, or going out of this evil world, as the children of Israel departed out of the bondage of Egypt. It was evidently for the sake of the three Apostles that the Lord and His two servants conversed upon this. St. Peter had said of that decease or Exodus, "Be it far from Thee, Lord; this shall not be unto Thee." And now they have the two leading prophets of the Old Covenant speaking to the Lord of this only, and as taking place in the Holy City, and no doubt to be accomplished in a very short time.

32. "But Peter and they that were with him were heavy with sleep: and when," &c. This was the effect of the vision, or rather of its beginning. There are several other instances of this sleep, or absence of distinct consciousness in the presence of some supernatural manifestation. Thus, it is said of Abraham when he received the remarkable revelation of God immediately after his justification, that "a deep sleep fell upon Abraham, and lo, a horror of great darkness fell upon him." (Gen. xv. 12.) And of Daniel, "When I heard the voice of his words, then was I in a deep sleep on my face, and my face toward the ground." (Dan. x. 9.)

33. "And it came to pass, as they departed from him, Peter said unto Jesus, Master, it is good," &c. St. Luke alone mentions that they saw the two prophets departing, and that they desired to

said unto Jesus, Master, it is good for us to be here: and let us make three tabernacles; one for thee, and one for Moses, and one for Elias: not knowing what he said.

34 While he thus spake, there came a cloud, and overshadowed them: and they feared as they entered into the cloud.

35 And there came a voice out of the cloud, saying, [a] This is my beloved Son : [b] hear him.

[a] Matt. iii. 17.
[b] Acts iii. 22.

33. "Tabernacles;" rather, "booths."
35. "This is my beloved Son." So A., C., D., all later Uncials and fragments (except L. and Ξ), all Cursives seemingly, most old Latin (b, c, e, f, q), Vulg., Syriac (Cureton and Schaaf); but א, B., L., Ξ, Sah., Copt., and old Latin (a) read, "This is my Son, my chosen." In 2 Peter i. 17, in which we have the same words, all MSS., including א, B., L., read, "My beloved Son." If not St. Peter's, this epistle is of extreme antiquity.

detain them, because of the wonderful things respecting His death upon which they had been conversing.

"Master, it is good for us to be here: and let us make three tabernacles [or booths for dwelling in]; one for thee, one," &c.

"Not knowing what he said." He desired greatly to detain the two heavenly visitants with the Lord, as the revelations respecting Redemption through the Lord's converse with these glorified prophets were far beyond all that he had yet received; but, like men who have an earnest desire after some great blessing, and know not how it is to be brought about, he talked wildly, supposing that Moses and Elias would not remain, unless they had some sort of habitation provided for them. And should we, who despise his words, have said anything more to the point, if we were fainting with fear at the immediate presence of these glorified denizens of the eternal world?

34. "While he thus spake, there came a cloud, and overshadowed them: and they feared," &c. No doubt, from what follows, that this cloud, like the schekinah of old, betokened the immediate presence of the Father. St. Matthew speaks of it as a bright cloud which "overshadowed them." It was first above them, and then seemed to descend over them and envelop them, otherwise it is difficult to explain the words, "They feared as they entered into the cloud."

35. "And there came a voice out of the cloud, saying, This is my beloved Son." Moses and Elias were servants—last of all God sent

CHAP. IX.]   JESUS WAS FOUND ALONE.   245

36 And when the voice was past, Jesus was found alone. ^c And they kept *it* close, and told no man in those   ^c Matt. xvii. 9. days any of those things which they had seen.

His Son. This was He in the company of God's two greatest servants, and in their presence the voice of the Father was heard to say, "Hear him." They had heard Moses and the prophets, now they must hear the Son, Who would teach them the true meaning of both the law and the prophets. Or the significance may be, " This is my beloved Son, hear Him in whatsoever He may say to you. Even though He speak about His departure by a cruel and ignominious death, hear Him."

36. "And when the voice was past, Jesus was found alone." Rather when the voice was—at the time of the voice.

"Jesus was found alone." Godet asks, " Does this contain any allusion to the idea which has been made the very soul of the narrative: the law and the prophets pass away—Jesus [Who is their true fulfilment] and His word alone remain."

"And they kept it close, and told no man in those days." Notice the undesigned coincidence between St. Luke and the other two Synoptics. St. Matthew and St. Mark mention that Jesus charged them that they should tell no man what they had seen. St. Luke says nothing respecting the Lord's charge, but tells us that they kept the matter close. They would certainly not have done so unless Jesus had very strictly bidden them not to make it known.

Such is the Transfiguration. One of the greatest divines of our Church, Dr. Pusey, has treated it as giving an earnest of the Christian's future glory. And certainly it gives a remarkable reality to many intimations of the heavenly state which God sets before us. Among them such as, " He shall change our vile body, that it may be like unto his glorious Body." " Then shall the righteous shine forth as the sun in the kingdom of their Father." " We know that when he shall appear we shall be like him, for we shall see him as he is." " As we have borne the image of the earthy, we shall who bear the image of the heavenly." "When Christ, who is our life, shall appear, then shall we also appear with him in glory." "It is sown in dishonour, it is raised in glory." I believe that in most of these places we have the effects of the teaching of the Transfiguration, even in those which were written by St. Paul. If it be objected against this that both St. Paul and St. John saw the Lord

37 ¶ ᵈAnd it came to pass, that on the next day, when they were come down from the hill, much people met him.

ᵈ Matt. xvii. 14. Mark ix. 14, 17.

38 And, behold, a man of the company cried out, saying, Master, I beseech thee, look upon my son: for he is mine only child.

---

in the glory of His Godhead (Acts xxvi. 13, Rev. i. 13-17), I answer that the glory manifested at the Transfiguration seems to have been milder and more tolerable, and so was more likely to have been the origin and seed of that view of the state of the glorified body of the Christian of which the foregoing passages are intimations.

37. "And it came to pass, that on the next day, when they were come down from the hill." It has been generally supposed from this that the Transfiguration occurred at night, and that Jesus and His three Apostles came down from the Mount early the next day. The expression, "much people met him," corresponds with the statement in St. Mark, "running to him, saluted him."

The miracle which follows is given so much more fully in St. Mark, where I have examined it at great length, that it seems impossible to do more than refer to the account, and the notes upon it, to be found in my comment on that Gospel.

38. "And, behold, a man of the company cried out, saying . . . mine only child." From St. Luke alone we learn that the man pleaded that the sufferer was his only son. Do we not naturally revert to what had just taken place? The Lord had just been recognized by the Father as His Beloved Son; and now one calls upon Him to heal his only son.

"Look upon my son." St. Luke alone represents the parent as asking the Lord to look upon his son. To look upon sinners with a view to extending mercy to them is a divine act. The Psalmist prays for it when he says, "Look thou upon me, and be merciful unto me, as thou usest to do unto those that love thy name." "The Lord turned and looked upon Peter." The father may not have understood it in so deep a sense; but he was led by a higher power to use words which reached far beyond his present thoughts. His words as recorded in St. Mark, "Lord, I believe; help thou mine unbelief," are certainly inspired to express the thought of all sinners

39 And, lo, a spirit taketh him, and he suddenly crieth out; and it teareth him that he foameth again, and bruising him hardly departeth from him.

40 And I besought thy disciples to cast him out; and they could not.

41 And Jesus answering said, O faithless and perverse generation, how long shall I be with you, and suffer you? Bring thy son hither.

---

in the presence of One Who, whilst He gives faith, gives along with it the deep feeling of its imperfection.

Quesnel well remarks: "He who begs one look of mercy begs every thing. God has already looked upon that person who, knowing the absolute necessity of this look, desires and implores it."

39, 40. "And, lo, a spirit taketh him . . . they could not." And yet but a short time before they had been sent on a mission to "cast out devils," and had returned, saying, "Lord, even the devils are subject to us in thy name." There must have been a falling away of their faith—perhaps, owing to the absence of the Lord and the three leading ones; perhaps, in some measure owing to their despondency at the Lord's intimation of His approaching Sufferings and Death.

41. "And Jesus answering said, O faithless and perverse generation, how long?" &c. "Generation" here signifies, not only the Apostles who had declined in faith, but the multitude, the father of the child, who could only say, "If thou canst do anything," the scribes who, from their presumed greater knowledge of the Old Testament Scriptures, ought to have discerned in Jesus the signs of the Messiah. In these almost desponding words there seems to be a tacit reference to the company of the spirits of just men made perfect, which He had just enjoyed. Their holy converse impresses upon Him the more deeply the faithlessness and sinfulness of the generation among whom He must yet labour, and at whose hands He must soon suffer so much.

"After enjoying fellowship with celestial beings, Jesus suddenly finds Himself in the midst of a world where unbelief prevails in all its various degrees. It is, therefore, the contrast, not between one man and another, but between this entire community alienated from God, in the midst of which He finds Himself, and the inhabi-

42 And as he was yet a coming, the devil threw him down, and tare *him*. And Jesus rebuked the unclean spirit, and healed the child, and delivered him again to his father.

43 ¶ And they were all amazed at the mighty power of God. But while they wondered every one at all things which Jesus did, he said unto his disciples,

e Matt. xvii. 22.   44 ^e Let these sayings sink down into your ears: for the Son of man shall be delivered into the hands of men.

f Mark ix. 32. ch. ii. 50. & xviii. 34.   45 ^f But they understood not this saying, and

42. " The devil threw him down, and tare him." " The devil dashed him down " (or "rent him," marg.), " and tare him grievously" (or "convulsed him," marg.), Revisers.

tants of heaven which He has just left, which wrings from Him this mournful exclamation." (Godet.)

42. "And as he was yet a coming, the devil threw him down, and tare him," &c. We learn from this the comforting lesson that the most violent temptations of the evil one may immediately precede his expulsion by the power of God. He "has great wrath because he knows that he has but a short time."

43, 44. "And they were all amazed . . . into the hands of men." Notice the implied contrast here. The people were full of admiration and wonder, and no doubt those warm expressions corresponded to their state of feeling. But the Lord turns from them to the Apostles: " Trust not to this seeming devotion. The Son of Man must be delivered into the hands of men." Men—this very generation—will crucify and kill Him. St. Luke omits what St. Matthew inserts: " The third day he shall rise again," which, no doubt, the Lord really said. But the next verse,

45. "But they understood not this saying, and it was hid from them, that they perceived it not," must be taken as referring to the Lord's approaching Death, which alone St. Luke mentions. It is very marvellous to think how, after the Lord had so distinctly informed them respecting His Death, and that the leaders of the Apostolic band had heard Moses and Elias speaking to Him of His "decease which He should accomplish at Jerusalem," that it should be said with such remarkable iteration, "they understood it not," "it was hid from them," "they perceived it not." Was this because

it was hid from them, that they perceived it not: and they feared to ask him of that saying.

46 ¶ [g] Then there arose a reasoning among them, which of them should be greatest.

[g] Matt. xviii. 1. Mark ix. 34.

47 And Jesus, perceiving the thought of their heart, took a child, and set him by him.

---

all men naturally turn away from, and refuse to contemplate what is distasteful to them, or was it because there was a supernatural veil over their understandings? Very probably from both causes. At first they refused to accept in simple faith those sayings of the Lord which seemed contrary to His honour, and to the end which, not He, but they themselves had assigned to Him, forgetting that it was He, and not they, Who knew best what was most to His glory, so that when they rejected or mentally turned away from His own words respecting His decease, it was through want of real faith; for faith would say, without any reserve, "Thou knowest all things. Thou knowest what is most conducive to the glory of God." And this lack of faith would bring about its own retribution. What they turned away from, God would not allow them to realize; the plainest truth would be hidden from them, so that they should *perceive it not*.

"They feared to ask him of that saying." Does not this mean that they feared lest it should be too true; that they should lose their Master, and be left alone, whereas they knew not that by His departure they would gain a presence and an indwelling above all thought?

46. "Then there arose a reasoning among them, which of them should be the greatest." What can have first given rise to this reasoning? Must it not have been the prospect of the removal of the Lord by death? Hitherto, when as yet they had had no thought of His Death, such a question seems never to have occurred to them. Now, if He was to leave them, who was to supply His place?

How was it, however, that they did not all instinctively turn to Simon Peter? Evidently because the Lord's words respecting his primacy were not intended to reserve for him such pre-eminence as would put him above them as the vicar of Christ.

47. "And Jesus, perceiving the thought of their heart, took a

48 And said unto them, ʰWhosoever shall receive this child in my name receiveth me: and whosoever shall receive me receiveth him that sent me:

ʰ Matt. x. 40.
& xviii. 5.
Mark ix. 37.
John xii. 44.
& xiii. 20.

child, and set him by him." St. Matthew represents the disciples as "coming to the Lord;" St. Mark, that the Lord Himself began the matter by asking, "What was it that ye disputed among yourselves by the way?" St. Luke's account may be called intermediate. There arose amongst them the dispute; and Jesus, as the discerner of the thoughts of the heart, "perceived it." Here we see the relations between the accounts of the three. St. Mark gives the incident verbatim, as the eye-witness, St. Peter, delivered it. St. Luke's narrative is from one who had more accurate information than the account preserved in the common tradition, but more general than St. Mark's history; whilst St. Matthew gives the tradition which, in detail, could hardly be preserved very accurately; but the sense of each is the same, whilst their witness is independent.

"And set him by him." The Lord, of course, would be in the midst of the disciples; so that when, according to St. Mark, the Lord set him in the midst of them, He would set the child beside Himself.

48. "And said unto them, Whosoever shall receive this child in my name, receiveth me." St. Mark has "one of such children." It is clear that the meaning is the same. The child which Jesus took was no different from other children, and so could be taken as the type of any and every child. The principle underlying the words of the Lord, about receiving a child in His name, is this—ambitious disciples or ministers, who are desirous to be great in the world, would strive to minister to the rich, to the educated, to those who are in high places and have influence in the world, and would neglect the poor, the ignorant, the lowly, and the despised. In making such a preference to further their ambitious ends, they would virtually reject Christ; whilst those who would, out of the love of their Master (Who, like His Father, had respect unto the lowly) try to instruct and benefit poor children, or such as are like children, regardless of any consideration except helping forward a poor and despised member of Christ; such receive Christ, and in receiving Him receive God His Father. How have we of the Church of

CHAP. IX.]   THE SAME SHALL BE GREAT.   251

¹ for he that is least among you all, the same shall be great.   ¹ Matt. xxiii. 11, 12.

48. "Shall be great." So A., D., later Uncials, almost all Cursives, old Latin (e, q), Syriac, Arm.; but ℵ, B., C., L., X, Ξ, 1, 33, ten other Cursives, old Latin (a, b, c, f, l, g), Vulg., Copt. read, "is"—"is great."

England been in fault in this matter! How have we built churches in rich streets and squares and fashionable suburbs, and till very lately neglected to bring the means of grace to the doors of the poor in their crowded courts and alleys; and we are reaping the fruit of it now in the alienation of such from the Church of their Fathers.

The spirit of these words of Christ seems exactly expressed in the precept of His servant: "Comfort the feeble-minded, support the weak, be patient towards all men;" and in the same Apostle's other words: "Mind not high things, but condescend to men of low estate." "He who receiveth such an one [by affection to sympathize with him, by converse to console him, by effort to serve him, by patience to suffer with him] he receiveth Me." (Ludolphus, quoted in Williams).¹

"For he that is least among you all, the same shall be [or *is*] great."

"He that is least"—he that abases himself, spares not himself, makes himself, or is ever willing to make himself, the last of all and the servant of all, he shall be great, for true greatness consists in service, in self-sacrifice, self-denial, self-abasement.

---

¹ Alford takes a totally different view of the scope of this incident. "The dispute had been—who among the twelve should be greatest? Our Lord reminds them that no such precedence is to be thought of among those sent (Apostoli) in His Name; for that even a little child if thus sent is clothed with His dignity; and if there be any distinction among such, it is this—that he who is like that child, humblest and least, *i.e.*, nearest the Spirit of the Lord, he is greatest." And then, with reference to what John says respecting his having reproved one who cast out devils, he (Alford) establishes the connection thus: "There arises the thought in the mind of the ardent son of Zebedee of the exclusive and peculiar dignity of those who were thus sent, and he relates what they had done as a proof of his fully appreciating this exclusive dignity." I think, however, the exposition I have given (the usual one) is far better.

HE FOLLOWETH NOT WITH US. [St. Luke.

49 ¶ ᵏ And John answered and said, Master, we saw one casting out devils in thy name; and we forbad him, because he followeth not with us.

50 And Jesus said unto him, Forbid *him* not: for ¹ he that is not against us is for us.

ᵏ Mark ix. 38. See Num. xi. 28.

¹ See Matt. xii. 30. ch. xi. 23.

---

50. "Against us is for us." So E., F., G., H., many later Uncials and Cursives. "Against you is for you" read by B., C., D., K., L., M., twenty-five Cursives, old Latin, Vulg., Goth., Copt., Syriacs, &c. "Against you is for us," read in ℵ, A., Δ.

49, 50. "And John answered and said . . . . we forbad him . . . . against us is for us." Why is it that John *answered* and said ? He apparently *answered* what his conscience struck him as being a reproof in the words of the Lord. He and others had come in contact with one who was little more than an incipient disciple. He could not have been very well instructed in the words of Christ, because the Apostolic company, and those closely connected with them, alone had the Lord's instructions in full; but what he had heard or seen of the Lord had convinced him that He had come from God; and, above all, that the invocation of His Name was with power over evil spirits; and so, in a spirit of faith, he cast out devils in Christ's name. John forbad him; and we gather that he obeyed the rebuke, or John would have mentioned that he refused to obey them; and the Lord's words, "Forbid him not," seem to imply that St. John should remove a prohibition which was yet obeyed. It was the success of his prohibition in this case which seems to have struck the conscience of the Apostle, and made him bring the case before the Lord.

In my notes on St. Mark I entered fully into the present application of this incident—how far it bears upon the forbidding, on the Church's part, of irregular or schismatical ministrations. I desire to notice in addition that, in all probability, the man was animated by no spirit of opposition, much less had he the least idea of setting up some new organization. He had been deeply struck with the Lord's words and works. He tried the invocation of His Name on those possessed, and he found it successful; and so he went on, without a thought that he must be joined to the One Body, for that Body was not yet manifested so that all men should be received into it.

"He that is not against us is for us." This clearly shows that

CHAP. IX.] HE STEDFASTLY SET HIS FACE. 253

51 ¶ And it came to pass, when the time was come that ᵐ he should be received up, he stedfastly set his face to go to Jerusalem.   ᵐ Mark xvi. 19. Acts i. 2.

---

he evidently acted in no antagonistic spirit. If he had done so, the Lord would not have described him as "not against us." Godet speaks of him as the Dissenting disciple, a description utterly opposed to the facts.

51. "And it came to pass when the time was come that he should be received up, he steadfastly," &c. In these words we enter upon a portion of the Lord's ministry, the account of which is peculiar to St. Luke. It extends from this place (ix. 51) to chap. xviii. 15, where St. Luke's narrative rejoins that of the other Synoptics in the account of the Lord blessing the little children. (Matt. xix. 13, and Mark, x. 13.)

Respecting the chronological place of the first incident in this section, that of the conduct of James and John, and the rebuke they received from the Lord, there is considerable difference amongst harmonists. Greswell places it between what is related in Luke xvii. 10, and xvii. 11 (where the Lord heals the ten lepers). In the Speaker's, and most other commentaries, it is put in its order in the Gospel as beginning the section which relates the events of a journey to Jerusalem through South Galilee, Samaria, and Peræa. Alford considers this journey to Jerusalem to be that which ended in his arriving there at the time of the Feast of the Dedication. Godet seems to hold the same view. "Immediately therefore after the Feast of Tabernacles Jesus returned to Galilee, and it was then that he definitely bade adieu to that province, and set out as we read (Luke ix. 51) to approach Jerusalem slowly, and while preaching the Gospel. Not only is such a journey possible, but it is, in a manner, forced on us by the necessity of providing contents for that blank interval in the ministry of Jesus."

"That he should be received up." This, of course, is his Ascension, the termination of His earthly career.

"He steadfastly set his face." The reader will remember how differently the same determination is described in St. Mark, "And they were in the way going up to Jerusalem. And Jesus went before them; and they were amazed." (Mark x. 33.)

52. "And sent messengers before his face: . . . Samaritans, to

254   THEY DID NOT RECEIVE HIM.   [St. Luke.

52 And sent messengers before his face: and they went, and entered into a village of the Samaritans, to make ready for him.

n John iv. 4, 9.   53 And ⁿ they did not receive him, because his face was as though he would go to Jerusalem.

54 And when his disciples James and John saw *this*, they said, Lord, wilt thou that we command fire to come down

---

make ready for him." Travelling with, at least, twelve followers, and those who ministered unto Him, it would be needful to seek out sufficient, though no doubt homely, lodging places beforehand. It might be also to prepare the village for a more spiritual reception of Him.

53. "And they did not receive him, because his face was as though," &c. How different to His former reception by the people of Sychar! Probably to some extent because His face was as though he would go to Jerusalem, to one of the chief feasts ; whereas, on the former occasion, He was coming from Jerusalem. Knowing that He now claimed to be the Messiah, they would be the more exasperated that as the Messiah He should reject their schismatical worship at Gerizim.

This adds the finishing stroke to His rejection by men, His fellow-creatures. He had been rejected by the chief priests, by the Scribes, by the elders, by the Jewish sects, Pharisees, Sadducees, and Herodians, by the people both of Jerusalem and Galilee, and now these aliens, who had before seemed as if they would receive Him and accept His claim, rejected Him.

54. "And when his disciples James and John saw this, they said," &c. How is it that James and John were the ones to show this untempered zeal? Archbishop Trench suggests, "They feel that a greater than Elias is here, for they are fresh from the Mount of Transfiguration, where they had seen how the glory of the foremost prophets of the Old paled and waned before the brighter glory of Him Whom they served, the Lord of the New ; an outrage against Him, and the rejection of Him should not be, therefore, less terribly avenged."

This act of zeal shows our Lord's insight into their characters when He called them "sons of thunder." "Well did they pre-

from heaven, and consume them, even as °Elias did? °2 Kings i. 10, 12.

55 But he turned, and rebuked them, and said, Ye know not what manner of spirit ye are of.

---

54. " Even as Elias did?" So A., C., D., all later Uncials and Cursives, old Latin (a, b, c, f, q), some Copt., Syriac (Schaaf), &c.; omitted by ℵ, B., L., Ξ, 71, 157, Vulg.

55. "Ye know not what manner of spirit ye are of" omitted by ℵ, A., B., C., E., G., H., L., S., &c., about sixty Cursives, including 28, 33, 71, 157, and some versions; retained by D., Fw., K., M., U., &c., most Cursives, old Latin, Vulg. Notwithstanding that the authority of the oldest MSS. are against the retention, it seems to have all the stamp of the Lord's wisdom and goodness. It is easy to see why it has been omitted; it is beyond measure difficult to suppose any one inventing it, and putting it into the Lord's mouth. Its absence seems to me to be so far the condemnation of any MSS. in which it is wanting.

sume," says St. Ambrose, " on bringing down fire from heaven, for they were the Sons of Thunder."

"As Elias did." Whether the words are genuine or not, the Apostles must have had before their eyes the example of Elijah in 2 Kings i., 9, "The king sent unto him a captain of fifty, with his fifty. And he went up to him: and, behold, he sat on the top of an hill, And he spake unto him, Thou man of God, the king hath said, Come down. And Elijah answered, and said to the captain of fifty, If I be a man of God, then let fire come down from heaven and consume thee and thy fifty. And there came down fire from heaven and consumed him and his fifty." There is no other instance of a servant of God invoking fire from heaven upon the enemies of God.

55. " But he turned, and rebuked them, and said, "Ye know not what manner of spirit ye are of." These words of the Lord's rebuke (assuming their genuineness) have been variously understood. The key to the right understanding of them, is that they must be words of rebuke. Now this seems to set aside all such meanings as would make them to be words of blame for their want of mere knowledge. They are paraphrased as meaning, "Ye know not that ye partake of the Spirit of the Old Testament rather than of the New." Thus Hammond (quoted in Trench): " Christ tells them they know not of what spirit they are, that is, they consider not under what dispensation they were. But surely the Old Testament had much of forgiveness and mercy, whilst the New, in its far clearer denunciations of eternal wrath, much exceeds the Old in its real severity. Nothing whatsoever is said about the eternal

56 For ᵖ the Son of man is not come to destroy men's lives, but to save *them*. And they went to another village.

p John iii. 17.
& xii. 47.

57 ¶ ᑫ And it came to pass, that, as they went

q Matt. viii. 19.

---

56. "For the son of man is not come to destroy men's lives, but to save them" omitted by almost all authorities, ℵ, A., B., C., D., E., G., H., L., and others, above sixty Cursives (including 28, 33, 51, 79, 157), and some editions or MSS. of versions. Found only in Fw., K., M., many Cursives, old Latin (a, b, c, e, f, q), Vulg., Cur. Syriac.

---

state of these captains and their fifties that were consumed by fire from heaven, whilst the Lord of all compassion says of those who reject Him, "If ye believe not that I am he, ye shall die in your sins." And these very Apostles had been bidden to shake off from their feet the dust of any city which had not received them, with the assurance that it should be more tolerable for Sodom and Gomorrah in the day of judgment than for that city. It is clear, then, that the Lord, the Searcher of hearts, discerned in them, not so much zeal for His glory, as a vindictive and persecuting spirit because they also were rejected in the refusal to entertain their Master.

Thus Cornelius à Lapide, "Ye think ye are influenced by the Spirit of God, whilst ye are acted on by a human spirit of impatience and revenge."

56. "For the Son of man is not come to destroy men's lives, but to save them." Whatever meaning we give to the word "life," this saying is equally true. If it means the spiritual or eternal life, the life of the soul in the presence of God, then the whole mission of the Lord was to implant and cause to increase the life of God in the soul of man: and if the Lord alludes rather to the temporal life, then by His constant healing of all manner of sickness, and all manner of disease, and by His raising of the dead, He set forth that He came not to cut short, but to prolong the lives of His fellow-men.

57. "And it came to pass as they went on their way a certain man said unto him," &c. There is considerable difference of opinion respecting the chronological plan in the Gospel narrative of the incidents which follow. Godet, for instance, considers that they should most fitly be placed at the commencement of the last journey when the Lord was taking a final leave of Galilee. Archbishop Trench, on the other hand, who has a short chapter on them

in the way, a certain *man* said unto him, Lord, I will follow thee whithersoever thou goest.

58 And Jesus said unto him, Foxes have holes, and birds of the air *have* nests; but the Son of man hath not where to lay *his* head.

---

57. "Lord" omitted by ℵ, B., D., L., Ξ, Cursives 1, 28, 64, 131, 157, old Latin (a, c, e), Vulg.; retained by A, C., Δ, later Uncials, almost all Cursives, &c.

entitled, "The Three Aspirants," in his "Studies on the Gospels," considers that their place in the narrative in St. Matthew is the true one, holding that they must have taken place before the final designation of the Apostles to their office, as he considers each of the three to have been of the number of the twelve, and not ordinary disciples, as such would have needed no special call.

"A certain man said unto him, Lord, I will follow thee," &c. This was a forward disciple, knowing little of his own real motives, and very probably offering to follow the Lord " whithersoever he went," from hopes of worldly advantage in the kingdom of such a Messiah as the ordinary Jew then expected. The Lord cuts him short by setting before the man His own life of absolute poverty and self-denial, having no settled home even, and depending on the alms and offerings of those whose hearts were opened to assist Him. " Foxes have holes, and the birds of the air have shelters [or rather roosting places] but the Son of man hath not where to lay his head." It has been remarked that even on the Cross the Lord had no rest for His Head. When all was over He " bowed His head and gave up the Ghost," and afterwards the resting-place of His Body was not His own.

Archbishop Trench thinks that it is by no means an improbable conjecture that this was Judas Iscariot himself, and that the Lord who read his heart, and knew his double-mindedness, sought here to discourage him, notwithstanding the zeal, and love, and devotion from which so unreserved an offer of service seemed to proceed. There is this to be said for this view, that Judas could not well have been at first chosen by the Lord ; he must have offered himself, and put himself forward before the rest. And there is nothing so likely as that the Lord should so speak to him as to repel him from seeking a nearness to His person which could only end in his greater condemnation.

59 ʳ And he said unto another, Follow me. But he said,
ʳ Matt. viii. 21. Lord, suffer me first to go and bury my father.

---

59. "Lord" omitted by B., D., V., 57; retained by ℵ, A., C., L., later Uncials, almost all Cursives, old Latin, Vulg., Goth., Copt., Syriac, &c.

59. "And he said unto another, Follow me," &c. Here with this man the Lord takes the first step Himself. "He knew that there was more truth in the backwardness of this man than in the forwardness of the other who had·just addressed Him, and so He calls him with that significant 'Follow me' wherewith He had summoned Philip, Matthew, Andrew, Peter (John i. 43; Matth. ix. 9; Mark i. 17)."—Trench. But the man seems to hold back. "Lord, suffer me first to go and bury my father." It is doubtful whether in this case the man's father was lying dead waiting to be buried, or whether it meant that he was very old, and, to use the common expression, "with one foot in the grave." In my notes on St. Matthew I gave an instance of the use of this phrase in this very day in the East, in the case of one who declined to leave home and country till he had performed the last rites to his father, who was then alive and well. But supposing that the father was actually dead, there was ample precedent in the law of Moses, that in certain exempt cases a man must not pollute himself by contact with the dead body of his nearest relative. "The high priest and the Nazarites were not to pollute themselves for the dead, were it even their father or mother (Lev. xxi. 11; Numb. vi. 6, 7); that is to say, they could neither touch the body, to pay it the last duties, nor enter the house where it lay (Numb. xix. 14), nor take part in the funeral meal (Hos. ix. 4). It must be remembered that the pollution contracted by the presence of a dead body lasted seven days (Numb. xix. 11-22). What would have happened to this man during these seven days? His impressions might have been chilled. Already Jesus saw him plunged anew in the tide of his ordinary life, lost to the kingdom of God."—Godet. It is clear also from the words "let the dead bury their dead" (τοὺς νεκροὺς) that there were sufficient numbers of unbelieving relatives to perform the last office. (See my note on the same words in Matth. viii. 19.)

If the man showed his obedience by at once following the Lord, he showed his fitness for the Apostolic office by at once renouncing the secular life. The Lord might see that the wrench to natural feel-

LET THE DEAD BURY THEIR DEAD.

60 Jesus said unto him, Let the dead bury their dead: but go thou and preach the kingdom of God.

61 And another also said, Lord, ^s I will follow thee: but let me first go bid them farewell, which are at home at my house. ^s See 1 Kings xix. 20.

62 And Jesus said unto him, No man, having put his hand to the plough, and looking back, is fit for the kingdom of God.

---

60. "Let the dead," *i.e.*, "Leave the dead to bury," &c.

ings, in leaving others as near as himself to perform the funeral obsequies of his father, might be needful to fit him to hold so unique a ministry as the Apostolic.

St. Luke now mentions a third case unnoticed by St. Matthew.

61. "And another also said, Lord, I will follow thee: but let me first go bid them farewell, which are at home at my house." Does this man offer himself, or has the Lord called him? I think he offers himself, and yet his words are not irreconcilable with the fact that the Lord had first called him. Any how, he makes a condition which the Lord tacitly rejects, and with it the man himself, as not a true-hearted disciple. The Lord, Who searches the hearts of all men, saw in this request a sign of half-heartedness. He compares him to a ploughman who, having put his hand to the plough, instead of keeping his eye looking straight forward at the ridge running right before him, looks back, and so spoils the furrow. Such a man is only half at work, and half work or a marred work will be the only result.

What a view we have in these three instances of the difficulties of the Apostolic life! This is the work which our forefathers in Christ, the founders of the Christian Church, had to undergo. They had to follow closely in the steps of One Who had no settled abode. They had to hold themselves loose to the dearest ties of relationship, and they were required instantly, and without delay, to obey any call of Christ. Their attitude of mind was, "Here am I, send me." They were the slaves, the δοῦλοι, as well as the followers and representatives of Christ. When we look at all this we are forced to exclaim, Is there now on the earth a real ministry of Christ?

CHAP. X.

AFTER these things the Lord appointed other seventy also, and ᵃ sent them two and two before his face into every city and place, whither he himself would come.

ᵃ Matt. x. 1.
Mark vi. 7.

1. "Other seventy." So ℵ, A., C., L., later Uncials, nearly all Cursives, some old Latin (b, f, q), Goth., Copt., Syriac (Schaaf); but B., D., M., R., old Latin (a, c, e, l), Vulg., Cureton Syriac read, "seventy-two."

1. "After these things the Lord appointed other seventy also, and sent them," &c. There is considerable difference amongst harmonists about the chronological place of this mission of the seventy. Greswell (or Williams) in his Harmony assigns it a place after the Lord's departure to the city Ephraim (John xi. 54), but this seems much too near the end to allow time for the work of these thirty-five pairs of disciples in preparing the way for His preaching and teaching in many "cities and places whither He Himself would come." In the harmony in the "Speaker's Commentary" it is placed between xviii. 35 and xix. 1 in St. Matthew, and between John vii. 1-10 and vii. 11. If the reader desires to see the whole subject well discussed, though I cannot but think an unsatisfactory conclusion is arrived at, he should turn to Williams' "Devotional Commentary," third year, part iii., pp. 270-282.

"The Lord appointed other seventy also." The words "other, also," seem used to distinguish this mission from that of the twelve (ix, 1-6), and from that of the mere messengers whom He sent to make ready for Him [ix. 52].

Many interesting questions arise respecting the number as seventy. Some think that this corresponds to the seventy elders chosen by Moses, who all prophesied, and so they conjecture that this was a revival by the Lord of the [so-called] order of prophets. But there never was a fixed order of "prophets," as there was of priests and Levites among the Jews, or of Apostles, Bishops, or Presbyters and Deacons in the Church. The prophets seem to have been raised up as occasion required, and we read of no regular specific duties, not

2 Therefore said he unto them, ᵇ The harvest truly *is* great, but the labourers *are* few : ᶜ pray ye therefore the Lord of the harvest, that he would send forth labourers into his harvest.

ᵇ Matt. ix. 37, 38. John iv. 35.
ᶜ 2 Thess. iii. 1.

---

even of preaching or instruction, discharged by them. Others suppose that the number seventy corresponds to the number of the Sanhedrim, and tell us that the Lord here institutes a spiritual Sanhedrim in opposition to the carnal one. Others fasten upon an old opinion among the Jews, that the nations of the Gentiles were seventy in number, and that this mission of the seventy adumbrates the call of the Gentiles, the Apostles being sent to the lost sheep of the house of Israel only, but no limitation is named in the mission of the seventy.

Some also have supposed that in these seventy the Lord instituted the order of Presbyters, as in the Apostles He did that of Bishops, but all these are the merest conjectures : what, however, strikes the thoughtful mind about this appointment of the seventy is that the Lord's itinerating work was far more extensive than what we gather from the two first Synoptics. Here, at the close of His ministry, we find thirty-five pairs of disciples sent to prepare His way by healing the sick, casting out devils, and preaching the Gospel. Now, supposing that each pair of disciples announced his coming in as few as three cities or villages, here are above one hundred cities and villages which He visited and in which He preached, the name of scarcely one of which has come down to us. How does this force upon us the truth in John xxi. 25, that the works of the Lord were practically numberless!

2. " Therefore said he unto them, The harvest truly is great, but the labourers are few." This is as true of this, the nineteenth century, as it was of the Lord's lifetime. There were then twelve apostles and seventy disciples for the millions of Palestine. Now I suppose that there are not anything like this proportion for the present heathen world. For instance, the inhabitants of China cannot be less than 300,000,000, and the number of missionaries, exclusive of Roman Catholic clergy, is not above one hundred persons.

"Pray ye therefore the Lord of the harvest, that he would send forth labourers," &c. It is often said that this is the foundation of our Ember prayers, but it leads us far beyond either of those which

3 Go your ways: ^dbehold, I send you forth as lambs among wolves.

4 ^eCarry neither purse, nor scrip, nor shoes: and ^fsalute no man by the way.

5 ^gAnd into whatsoever house ye enter, first say, Peace *be* to this house.

6 And if the son of peace be there, your peace shall rest upon it: if not, it shall turn to you again.

^d Matt. x. 16.
^e Matt. x. 9, 10. Mark vi. 8. ch. ix. 3.
^f 2 Kings iv. 29.
^g Matt. x. 12.

---

6. "The son of peace;" rather, "a son of peace." So A., B., C., D., and all other Uncials except א, and nearly all Cursives.

we use at such seasons, for in them we ask for a blessing only on those who have aleady obeyed the call, whereas the Lord here bids us ask that a sufficient number of faithful labourers may be called.

3. "Go your ways: behold, I send you forth as lambs among wolves." *i.e.*, weak and utterly unprovided with means of defence, so that their only safety is His protection, in which they must exercise constant faith.

4. "Carry neither purse," *i.e.*, they are not to provide themselves with money to purchase necessaries. "Nor scrip," *i.e.*, they are to take no supply of food for their next meal, but are to rely upon God opening the hearts of those to whom they preach to provide them with it. "Nor shoes," *i.e.*, they were to have no change of sandals. They were to be shod with sandals, but were not to burthen themselves with carrying any other.

"Salute no man by the way." They were to act like men who feared nothing so much as hindrance in their work. Salutation might lead to conversation, and this to the loss of time. The reader cannot but remember what Elisha says to Gehazi; "Gird up thy loins; if thou meet any man salute him not; and if any salute thee, answer him not again, and lay my staff on the face of the child." (2 Kings iv. 29.)

5. "And into whatsoever house ye enter, first say, Peace be to this house." The reader will remember that in the service for the Visitation of the Sick of our branch of the Church Catholic the minister is directed to say, when he comes into the sick person's house, "Peace be to this house and to all that dwell in it."

6. "And if the son of peace be there, your peace shall rest upon it: if not, it shall turn to you again." This seems to mean that if

7 ʰ And in the same house remain, ⁱ eating and drinking such things as they give: for ᵏ the labourer is worthy of his hire. Go not from house to house.

8 And into whatsoever city ye enter, and they receive you, eat such things as are set before you:

9 ˡ And heal the sick that are therein, and say unto them, ᵐ The kingdom of God is come nigh unto you.

ʰ Matt. x. 11.
ⁱ 1 Cor. x. 27.
ᵏ Matt. x. 10.
1 Cor. ix. 4, &c.
1 Tim. v. 18.
ˡ ch. ix. 2.
ᵐ Matt. iii. 2. & iv. 17. & x. 7. ver. 11.

there be any one in the house favourably disposed to receive the word of God, they should have some sure, but secret intimation from God, that their salutation of peace had not been in vain, but that it had blessed the heart of one inhabitant of the house, and so they might enter and preach the word of God; and they should have a like intimation from God if there were none in the house whose hearts could be moved, and so any labour they bestowed there would be lost. "To every house which they enter is the declaration of peace to be made; for it is not in man to know whether the Son of peace be therein, which the great day only can make known." Williams thus seems to interpret the "Son of peace" of Christ Himself, Who must Himself first be present in any house if they are to labour in it to any profit.

7. "And in the same house remain, eating and drinking such things . . . . as they give," &c. As if the Lord said, "Ye have no call to consider yourselves as under any obligation to those who set meat before you, for you give them that which is of infinitely greater value to them than what they give to you is to you." As St. Paul writes, "If we have sown unto you spiritual things, is it a great thing if we shall reap your carnal things?" (1 Cor. ix. 11.)

"Go not from house to house," &c. Do not choose those houses in which you think you will be best entertained. If you have taken up your abode in one house and the fare is poor, do not leave it for a better.

8. "And into whatsoever city ye enter, and they receive you," &c. This seems to look to the fact that they are sent not to households so much as to cities and communities. "If one household shuts the door upon you, another may receive you and entertain you. Then you are to do the two things which I have done in every place. You are to heal the sick and to proclaim the near

264   THE VERY DUST OF YOUR CITY.   [ST. LUKE.

10 But into whatsoever city ye enter, and they receive you not, go your ways out into the streets of the same, and say,

n Matt. x. 14.
ch. ix. 5. Acts
xiii. 51. &
xviii. 6.

11 ⁿ Even the very dust of your city, which cleaveth on us, we do wipe off against you : notwithstanding be ye sure of this, that the kingdom of God is come nigh unto you.

---

11. Cleaveth on us." So E. and some later Uncials and very many Cursives; but A., C., G., K., L., M., "to our feet"—"cleaveth on us to our feet," and ℵ, B., D., R., most old Latin, and Cur. Syriac read, "to the feet."

"Unto you." So A., C., later Uncials, most Cursives, &c. ; but ℵ, B., D., L., some Cursives (1, 13, 33), most old Latin, and Vulg. omit.

approach of the Kingdom of God in My Person, as I shall shortly follow you and perfect your work."

10, 11. " But into whatsoever city ye enter, and they receive you not. . . . nigh unto you." The message of God's servants cannot be rejected with impunity. It is either the savour of life unto life or of death unto death. Note here, that in the rejection of Christ's message through His servants Christ Himself can be rejected. Indeed, now that His visible presence is withdrawn, He can only be accepted or rejected in and through the ministrations of His ministers.

To "shake off the dust of their feet " as a witness against any city which had wholly rejected their message, signified that they had no more part or lot with the inhabitants—that they would retain nothing of theirs, no, not so much as what accidentally cleaved to their sandals. This was one of the many outward significant symbolical acts of which the special messengers of God made constant use. Thus Jeremiah put on a yoke, and hid a girdle by the side of the Euphrates—thus Agabus bound St. Paul's girdle round his own hands and feet, and Paul himself and Barnabas on one occasion used this very sign of shaking off the dust of their feet against the Jews of Antioch in Pisidia, who had rejected God's word spoken by their mouth. We have given up altogether the use of such signs, and I believe have lost much by our rejection of them.

" Notwithstanding be ye sure of this, that the kingdom of God is come nigh." Mercy here appears to be mingled with judgment. If in time to come ye call to mind our message and repent, the door is yet open. We can do no more, and we have done with you. God

12 But I say unto you, that ⁰ it shall be more tolerable in that day for Sodom, than for that city. o Matt. x. 15. Mark vi. 11.

13 ᵖ Woe unto thee, Chorazin! woe unto thee, Bethsaida! ᑫ for if the mighty works had been done in Tyre and Sidon, which have been done in you, they had a great while ago repented, sitting in sackcloth and ashes. p Matt. xi. 21. q Ezek. iii. 6.

may not have altogether cast you off; and if ye remember our message and repent and turn to Him, He assuredly has not.

12. "But I say unto you, that it shall be more tolerable for Sodom," &c. Sodom was a place of unnameable wickedness, but of little or of no light. There was one righteous man in it, but his witness, from all we can gather of his character, must have been miserably weak; whereas the cities which rejected the testimony of the Lord had messengers direct from Him equipped with His power to enforce the truth of their message, representing Him also not only in words, but in self-denial, in zeal, and in earnestness.

13. "Woe unto thee, Chorazin! woe unto thee, Bethsaida! for if the mighty works," &c. God only knows all possible contingencies, and His co-equal Son here declares that if the people of Tyre and Sidon had had the light of the Lord's preaching and mighty works, as Chorazin and Bethsaida had had, they would have deeply repented. Why was it, then, that Chorazin and Bethsaida were unmoved by the personal witness of Christ? Simply because they and their fathers had gone on for generations resisting light. They had become hardened by continued indifference and the love of sin to the light of Moses and the Prophets; and when the Lord came to them, showing by His holy teaching and mighty works that it was He to Whom Moses and the Prophets bear witness, they hardened their hearts still more and rejected Him. In all probability they of Chorazin and Bethsaida were by no means so immersed in deadly sin as they of Tyre and Sidon, but they were harder in heart. They were self-righteous and self-satisfied, and this made them determinedly resist the entrance of all further truths, which would humble them and bring them nearer to God. And so it may be with multitudes of professing Christians who seem free from open sin. Their case is more hopeless than that of many grosser sinners, because they think that having the outward possession of the Bible, the Church and the Sacraments, they have

14 But it shall be more tolerable for Tyre and Sidon at the judgment, than for you.

15 ʳ And thou, Capernaum, which art ˢ exalted to heaven, ᵗ shalt be thrust down to hell.

16 ᵘ He that heareth you heareth me; and ˣ he that despiseth you despiseth me; ʸ and he that despiseth me despiseth him that sent me.

ʳ Matt. xi. 23.
ˢ See Gen. xi. 4. Deut. i. 28.
Is. xiv. 13. Jer. li. 53.
ᵗ See Ezek. xxvi. 20. & xxxii. 18.
ᵘ Matt. x. 40. Mark ix. 37. John xiii. 20.
ˣ 1 Thess. iv. 8.
ʸ John v. 23.

15. "Which art exalted to heaven, shalt be thrust down to hell." So A., C., all later Uncials except L. and Ξ, almost all Cursives, some old Latin, Vulg., &c.; but ℵ, B., D., L., Ξ, Cur. Syriac, Copt. read, "Shalt thou indeed be exalted . . . thou shalt be thrust down," &c.

need of nothing, and the first step towards really knowing God is a source of need.

15. "And thou, Capernaum, which art exalted to heaven, shalt be thrust down," &c. In what respect could Capernaum be considered as exalted to heaven? Simply and solely by the dwelling of Christ so long within it. This is one of those many sayings which so meek and humble a man as Christ would not have said, unless He had been conscious of the dwelling of the Godhead within Him. The reading of B. and the few MSS. which usually agree with it makes our Lord express Himself in a way very unusual with Him, but does not affect the sense.

16. "He that heareth you heareth me; and he that despiseth you," &c. We should never have dared to say this of any human ministry whatsoever: but as the Saviour has Himself said it, and more than once (Mark ix. 37; John xiii. 20), we must not dare to keep it back, or unsay it, as it were, by diluting it. Quesnel has a very good remark on this. "It is one and the same truth, which is in the Father, by His essence, in the Son, by His Eternal Generation, in the Apostles by His Spirit. So long as the trust is kept inviolable, in hearing these we hear the Father and the Son. The pastoral authority, which, as well as the truth, has God for its fountain, is communicated to the Son by the mission of His Father, *i.e.* by His Incarnation; to the Apostles by the mission of the Son; and to the Church by His Spirit."

17, 18. "And the seventy returned again with joy, saying, Lord,

CHAP. X.] THE SEVENTY RETURNED WITH JOY. 267

17 ¶ And ᶻ the seventy returned again with joy, saying, Lord, even the devils are subject unto us through thy name.   ᶻ ver. 1.

18 And he said unto them, ᵃ I beheld Satan as lightning fall from heaven.   ᵃ John xii. 31. & xvi. 11. Rev. ix. 1. & xii. 8, 9.

19 Behold, ᵇ I give unto you power to tread on   ᵇ Mark xvi. 18. Acts xxviii. 5.

---

17. "And the seventy." "The seventy-two" read by B., D., old Latin, &c. See critical note on verse 1.

19. "I give." So A., D., later Uncials, almost all Cursives, Cur. and other Syriac; but ℵ, B., C., L., a very few Cursives, most old Latin, Vulg., &c. read, "I have given."

even the devils are subject, &c. . . . as lightning fall from heaven." It has been a question amongst expositors whether this exclamation of the seventy, "even the devils are subject unto us through Thy name," was said in holy exultation at the power of Christ manifested in them, or whether there was a degree of self-satisfaction in it which called forth the saying of the Lord, " I beheld Satan as lightning fall from heaven," as if He said, Be not lifted up with pride at your success over the spirits of darkness. Remember that it was pride which hurled from his exalted place in heaven the chief of these spirits. I behold this terrible fall of one once so high in the favour of God, and I bid you take warning from the example." I do not think that the Lord's saying has this significance. It rather seems to mean, "You naturally exult in these triumphs of My power through your hands. I was contemplating (εθεώρουν) a far greater conquest. I was contemplating Satan's power shattered, his strongholds spoiled. The idolatries and false philosophies of the world vanquished by My Cross.". It is to be remembered that the Spiritual Eye of the Lord sees all things, past, present, and to come, and saw in them all their issues. In the first fall of Satan from heaven, and in his subsequent expulsion from every place of eminent power which he has usurped, He clearly discerned the issue of the warfare between good and evil, in the final triumph of good.

It is worthy of notice that Quesnel, a predestinarian, has this remark upon the fall of Satan. "If grace was not in a state of security in an angel of high rank in heaven, what man upon earth, if he have this treasure, ought not to tremble, since he carries it in an earthen vessel ?"

19. "Behold, I give unto you power to tread on serpents and scorpions," &c. In these words the Lord seems to confer an

serpents and scorpions, and over all the power of the enemy: and nothing shall by any means hurt you.

20 Notwithstanding in this rejoice not, that the spirits are subject unto you : but rather rejoice, because ^cyour names are written in heaven.

^c Ex. xxxii. 32.
Ps. lxix. 28.
Is. iv. 3. Dan.
xii. 1. Phil. iv.
3. Heb. xii. 23.
Rev. xiii. 8. &
xx. 12. & xxi. 27.

20. "Rather rejoice." Almost all authorities, א, A., B., C., D., E., F., later Uncials, Cursives, old Latin, Vulg. omit "rather."

additional power over and above that which He had already granted. That they are to be taken literally as well as spiritually is evident from the terms in which the Lord renews the gift just before His Ascension (Mark xvi. 18), where, having mentioned the casting out of devils He separately promises to them the power of taking up serpents, and that if they drink any deadly thing it shall not hurt them.

But what means He by adding the words, " all the power of the enemy " ? The words read as if serpents and scorpions were part of this power, *i.e.*, were the creation of Satan and not of God ; but in the original it is clear that "power" or "authority" not "tread" must be read before "over." "Behold, I give you the power of treading on serpents and scorpions and (power) over all the power of the enemy." Many suppose these malignant and deadly creatures to be here taken as types of evil men, and many suppose that they are to be understood of open and secret sins; but that the Apostles had power given to them over venomous creatures is certain from the incident recorded of St. Paul at Melita (Acts xxviii. 5). I should rather take the treading on serpents and scorpions literally, and "the power of the enemy " to signify the idolatries and false and wicked opinions by which Satan enslaved souls, and which gave way before the preaching of the Gospel.

"And nothing shall by any means hurt you." They were to be "immortal till their work was done," and till God should call them to Himself by a martyr's death. Compare St. Paul's words, " All things work together for good to them that love God." And " thanks be to God, who always causeth us to triumph in Christ."

20. " Notwithstanding in this rejoice not, that the spirits are subject to you : but rather," &c. All outward acts of power, even the casting out of evil spirits, might be done in Christ's name by those

21 ¶ ᵈ In that hour Jesus rejoiced in spirit, and said, I thank thee, O Father, Lord of heaven and earth, ᵈ Matt. xi. 25.

---

21. "Rejoiced in spirit." So A., E., G., H., M., later Uncials, almost all Cursives, &c. "Rejoiced in the Holy Spirit" read in ℵ, B., C., D., K., L., 1, 33, old Latin (b, c, e, i, l), Vulg., Copt., Syriac (Cur. and Pesh.).

who were really not his; thus the Apostle says, "Though I have all faith so that I could remove mountains, and have not charity, it profiteth me nothing." Their names were written in heaven, not by an act of partiality or mere unreasoning will (*sic volo, sic jubeo*), but because they had heard the word of Christ, accepted Him, and were following Him in righteousness and self-denial. "There is no limitation to the truth, that the most magnificent successes, the finest effects of eloquence, temples filled, conversions by thousands, are no real cause of joy to the servant of Jesus, except in so far as he is saved himself."—Godet.

21. "In that hour Jesus rejoiced in spirit, and said, I thank thee, O Father, Lord of heaven," &c. The words of the Lord in this verse are verbatim the same as those of the parallel passage in St. Matthew. In St. Matthew, however, they are prefaced by the words, "At that time Jesus answered and said." A very important question arises: Were these precisely similar words, then, said at one time or at two different times? Trench (in his "Studies in the Gospels"), Alford and others, consider that they were said at two different times, but if so, then that which goes before, the woes on Chorazin and Bethsaida, must also have been repeated twice. I cannot help thinking, however, that as it is freely allowed that St. Matthew at times places parts of discourses together as if they were one discourse, we may take the words, "Then began he to upbraid," of Matth. xi. 20, as not necessarily following upon "Wisdom is justified of her children," but simply as introducing words which St. Luke gives us in their right sequence.

"I thank thee, O Father, Lord of heaven and earth," should be rather, "I confess to thee, O Father," and may be paraphrased, "I confess to thee, O Father, that thou hast done right in hiding these things from the wise and prudent." These "wise and prudent" here, of course, are the Scribes and Elders, the leaders of religion among the Jews. The Lord means the wise and prudent in their own eyes, those who had stifled any life they may have had by their perverse worshipping of "the letter that killeth," and by

that thou hast hid these things from the wise and prudent, and hast revealed them unto babes: even so, Father; for so it seemed good in thy sight.

---

their neglect of, and opposition to "the Spirit which giveth life." The babes signify the twelve, or the seventy, to whom the Lord shortly turns, and says, "Blessed are the eyes which see the things that ye see." In these words we have enumerated the great principle of the kingdom of God, that faith, unquestioning faith, faith which bows itself in adoration before the mysteries of God, is the first requisite in the school of Christ. And rightly so, for if we voluntarily put ourselves under such a teacher as the Eternal, Incomprehensible, and all-wise God, we must feel and acknowledge that what He vouchsafes to teach us respecting Himself and His dealings must be infinitely above us; and so we must receive it in submission, acknowledging that He knows infinitely better than we do all things which require a revelation from Him before we can know them. There are two ways in which men receive knowledge. They receive it so as to be made proud by it ("knowledge puffeth up"), or they receive it so as to be humbled by it, because the more knowledge they receive, the more vast and infinite do they perceive the domain of knowledge to be. The former our Lord means by the wise and prudent, the latter He would class amongst the babes; for it is to be noticed that He does not contrast the "wise and prudent" with the ignorant and foolish, but rather with the docile, the meek, the simple-minded. And the Father reveals these things to babes, not that they should continue babes in knowledge and understanding, but that they should become men in Christ; for the Lord indignantly asks these babes when they did not reflect upon what they had seen, "Are ye yet without understanding?" And His inspired servant says, "In understanding be men."

For these reasons it was good in the sight of the Father to reveal the mysteries unto babes. I have dwelt upon this in my notes on St. Matthew. I have noticed there two other reasons why the mysteries of the kingdom should be revealed to those who were as regards them in the condition of babes: first, that the Revelation would be thus kept the purer, as being in the hands of those who had no temptation to mix it up with human philosophy, and also that it should be commended to the world in the language of the common people rather than of the learned.

22 ᵉ ‖ All things are delivered to me of my Father : and ᶠ no man knoweth who the Son is,

ᵉ Matt. xxviii. 18. John iii. 35. & v. 27. & xvii. 2.
‖ Many ancient copies add these words, *And turning to his disciples, he said,*
ᶠ John i. 18. & vi. 44, 46.

22. "All things are delivered," &c. So ℵ, B., D., L., M., 1, 13, 22, 33, about fifteen others, old Latin (a, b, e, f, g), Vulg.; but A., C., E., G., H., K., S., &c., most Cursives, and Syriac (Schaaf) begin this verse with the words, "And he turned unto his disciples, and said, All things," &c.

22. "All things are delivered to me of my Father; and no man knoweth," &c. The Lord says this contemplating the persons meek and feeble in themselves as mere babes, to whom His Father had vouchsafed the highest revelation of His purposes. How were such persons to bring about the final conquest of sin and Satan, and the victory of the Kingdom of God ? The Lord answers, "All things are delivered unto me of my Father." This is exactly parallel to what He says in giving them their final commission. "All power is given unto me in heaven and in earth. Go ye, therefore, and teach all nations," &c.

This deliverance of all things unto the Son cannot for a moment be taken as implying any inferiority on the part of the Son. It rather implies equality. For if all things are committed by the Father to the Son, the Son must have the same Divine power and knowledge as His Father has, to receive all things at His hands, and henceforth rule over them as His Father had done. These words do not look to our Saviour's dominion over all things by right of creation, but as the Mediator. Athanasius has well expressed this. "The dominion of the Creation is not then, as they [the Arians] think, here meant; but the words signify the dispensation made in the flesh. For after that man sinned all things were confounded; the Word then was made flesh that He might restore all things. All things, therefore, were given Him, not because He was wanting in power, but that as Saviour He should repair all things; that as by the Word all things at the beginning were brought into being, so when the Word was made flesh He should restore all things in Himself.

"No man knoweth who the Son is but the Father." What a wondrous thing for one in flesh and blood to say that no one knows what He is except the omniscient God, and that no one knows who the eternal and infinite God is except Himself. This meek and lowly man, Who was born little more than thirty years

but the Father; and who the Father is, but the Son, and *he* to whom the Son will reveal *him*.

23 ¶ And he turned him unto *his* disciples, and said privately, ^gBlessed *are* the eyes which see the things that ye see:

g Matt. xiii. 16.

---

before this, and within one short year would surrender His life— He alone knows the nature and mode of existence, and mind, and will, and power of the Father, and the Father alone knows His nature and mode of existence, and mind, and will, and power, as the Son. This equality—this sameness of knowledge—implies equality and sameness of nature. It also necessarily implies mutual indwelling, that He is in the Father, and the Father in Him. This saying of the Lord's requires the full Catholic doctrine of the Trinity, at least of the relation of the Father to the Son, as set forth in the creeds of the Catholic Church, to enable us to realize it.

"And he to whom the Son will reveal him." The Son reveals the Father to the soul that will receive His teaching as a little child. He reveals that the supreme Being is essentially a Father, as having from all Eternity One only Son. He reveals the will and heart of the Father towards mankind as reconciled to them, as loving them, as desiring that they should know Him, and partake of His holiness, and be conformed to His image.

Of course the man to whom the Son thus reveals the Father knows Him only in the degree that a finite creature can know the Infinite; but he really does know the supreme Father. All the knowledge that he is capable of receiving is true and right, and to be relied on. He is by this revelation of the Son wholly delivered from all and every form of "Agnosticism" respecting God.

23. "And he turned to his disciples, and said privately, Blessed are the eyes," &c. What are the things which they saw? They saw the holy life, the Divine actions, the miracles, the privations, the sufferings of the Son of God. And in these things they were beginning to discern with the eye of faith One Who was far above any prophet or king, or righteous man. They discerned this no doubt dimly at present; but their faith was a living faith, and so, a growing faith. What it eventually grew to we learn from the words of the last survivor of them all, who looking back on these days of the Son of

24 For I tell you, ʰ that many prophets and kings have desired to see those things which ye see, and have not seen *them;* and to hear those things which ye hear, and have not heard *them.*

ʰ 1 Pet. i. 10.

25 ¶ And, behold, a certain lawyer stood up, and tempted

---

25. "Tempted him;" perhaps, "tried him."

man, wrote, "That which was from the beginning, which we have heard, which we have seen with our eyes, which we have looked upon, and our hands have handled of the Word of Life; for the life was manifested, and we have seen it, and bear witness and show unto you that eternal life which was with the Father, and was manifested unto us." (1 John i.) How manifested? By His Life of consummate holiness, by His words of Divine wisdom, by His acts of almighty power.

These words were said to them privately: just as the parallel words reported by St. Matthew were said to the disciples when they were alone.

24. " For I tell you, that many prophets and kings have desired to see those things," &c. The best explanation of this is in the words of one then present, "of which salvation the prophets have inquired and searched diligently, who prophesied of the grace which should come unto you.... Searching what, or what manner of time the Spirit of Christ which was in them did signify, when it testified beforehand the sufferings of Christ and the glory that should follow." (1 Pet. i. 10.) All the prophets have expressions of devout longing for some great person or some good time coming, which they hoped might even be in their day. Thus David: "Remember me, O Lord, with the favour that thou bearest unto thy people: O, visit me with thy salvation. That I may see the good of thy chosen, and rejoice in the gladness of thy people, and give thanks with thine inheritance."

Is this the same saying, and said at the same time as the parallel one in St. Matthew? I think not. Is it not likely that the Lord frequently repeated sayings which He desired should sink very deep into the hearts of those who heard them?

25. "And behold, a certain lawyer stood up, and tempted him, saying," &c. There is no indication as to the time and place of this narrative. Some suppose that as the scene of the parable is

T

him, saying, ¹ Master, what shall I do to inherit eternal life?

¹ Matt. xix. 16. & xxii. 35.

26 He said unto him, What is written in the law? how readest thou?

ᵏ Deut. vi. 5.

27 And he answering said, ᵏ Thou shalt love

---

laid on the road from Jerusalem to Jericho, that the question was asked of the Lord somewhere near that city; but the road in question was then, as it now is, notorious all over the Holy Land for its insecurity.

"Stood up." This seems as if the Lord was teaching in some house: it might be in a synagogue.

"And tempted him." This may mean with a bad intention to draw from Him something for which he might accuse Him, so Cornelius a Lapide; or it might simply mean, as Edersheim supposes, to try Him, as to which side He would take in a matter much controverted amongst the Rabbis, whether good works or the study of the law was the surest passport to Paradise. Evidently, however, he did not come and ask the question with the same sincerity as the young ruler who came running to the Lord and falling down before Him. (Luke xviii. 18 compared with Mark x. 17.)

"What shall I do to inherit eternal life?" He has been blamed for asking such a question as savouring of legalism; but the Lord does not blame him for so putting the matter, nor does He attempt to set him right in the matter of salvation by faith or by works. The Lord's atoning Death was not at this time understood by any one of the Apostles, how, then, could one not under the Lord's instruction anticipate its significance? The covenant of works was then in force, and the new and better covenant was not yet revealed, at least clearly, and as of universal application; so that if the man really desired to know how he was to get to heaven, he could only ask it in some such terms.

26. "He said unto him, What is written in the law? how readest thou?" The Lord does not answer him, but makes him answer himself, as indeed he afterwards did, when he asked, "who is my neighbour?"

27. "And he answering said, Thou shalt love the Lord thy God," &c. This answer the Lord Himself gave to another inquirer on a very different occasion. The question, then, arises, how came this

the Lord thy God with all thy heart, and with all thy soul,

27. "With all thy soul." ℵ, B., L., 1, 131, 157, 209, and Copt. read, "In all thy soul —in all thy strength—in all thy mind;" but A., C., all later Uncials, almost all Cursives, most old Latin, Vulg., Syriac as in Authorized.

lawyer, evidently a very unspiritual person, to give the same answer—to single out of all the precepts scattered up and down the Pentateuch, these two, out of different books, and put them together? The answer seems to be that these had long before been distinguished from the rest by the Jewish teachers: and, indeed, to any one who has any knowledge of human nature, the law of love must be the strongest of all. All other laws are satisfied with the minimum of obedience, the law of love is never satisfied with the maximum. Take the first two laws of the decalogue. If a Jew acknowledged and worshipped no other God than Jehovah, he had fulfilled the letter of these laws. Take, again, the law of fear; a Jew might say, "I have done, or, I have abstained from doing, quite sufficient to avert punishment"; but no true lover of God could say, "I have done enough to serve and please One Who has done so much for me." So that, as I said, any one who knew well human nature, if he had proposed to himself the question which is the most powerful command, must have singled out those which command or involve love, and we have evidence from Rabbinism that these two commands were thus distinguished.[1]

[1] "As regarded the duty of absolute love to God, indicated by the quotation of Deut. vi. 5, there could, of course, be no hesitation in the mind of a Jew. The primary obligation of this is frequently referred to, and, indeed, taken for granted in Rabbinic teaching. The repetition of this command, which, in the Talmud, receives the most elaborate and strange interpretation, formed part of the daily prayers. When Jesus referred the lawyer to the Scriptures he could scarcely fail to quote this first paramount obligation. Similarly he spoke as a Rabbinic lawyer, when he referred, in the next place, to love to our neighbour, as enjoined in Levit. xix. 18. Rabbinism is never weary of quoting, as one of the characteristic sayings of its greatest teacher, Hillel (who, of course, lived before this time), that he had summed up the law in briefest compass, in these words: "What is hateful to thee, that do not to another. This is the whole law; the rest is only its explanation. Similarly

276 THIS DO AND THOU SHALT LIVE. [St. Luke.

and with all thy strength, and with all thy mind: and ¹ thy neighbour as thyself.

¹ Lev. xix. 18.

28 And he said unto him, Thou hast answered right: this do, and ᵐ thou shalt live.

ᵐ Lev. xviii. 5. Neh. ix. 29. Ezek. xx. 11, 13, 21. Rom. x. 5.

"And thy neighbour as thyself." Godet remarks well on the connection between these two great commands. "The second part of the summary is the corollary of the first, and cannot be realized except in connection with it. Nothing but the reigning love of God can so divest the individual of devotion to his own person that the Ego of his neighbour shall rank in his eyes exactly on the same level as his own. The pattern must be loved above all, if the image in others is to appear to us as worthy of esteem and love as ourselves. Thus to love is, as Jesus says, the path to life, or rather it is life itself. God has no higher life than that of love. The answer of Jesus is, therefore, not a simple accommodation to the legal point of view. The work which saves, or salvation, is really loving. The Gospel does not really differ from the law in its aim; it is distinguished from it only by its indication of means, and the communication of strength."

28. "And he said unto him, Thou hast answered right: this do, and thou shalt live." It has been said that the Lord said this somewhat in irony, or in a sort of benevolent contempt for one so ignorant. On this principle of interpretation it is as if He said, "This do, and thou shalt live; but thou canst not do it, so thou mayest as well let it alone." But one's whole soul revolts from such an interpretation of the Lord's words, which never could have crossed the mind of one who lived before the sixteenth-century controversies respecting justification. Does the Lord, then, mean that he was to be saved by love alone—that he need seek no faith, no reliance on the Lord's merits and strength, and so on? Now the answer to all this is, that at that time, and before " a more excellent way " was revealed to him and pressed upon his acceptance, the very best thing that this inquirer could do was to bend his whole

---

Rabbi Akiba taught, that Levit. xix. 18 was the principal rule—we might almost say—the chief summary of the law." Edersheim's "Life and Times of Jesus Christ," vol. ii., p. 232.

WHO IS MY NEIGHBOUR?

29 But he, willing to [n] justify himself, said unto Jesus, And who is my neighbour?   n ch. xvi. 15.

30 And Jesus answering said, A certain *man* went down

---

soul and spirit to the attainment of this love of God and of his neighbour—to ask God constantly, and with all the earnestness that he could excite within himself, to give him this love of Himself, to write this law of love in his heart, and, at the same time, to ask God for forgiveness for all his breaches of this law of love, and to set before himself all the instances in Scripture and in the history of the chosen race, which were calculated to warm his cold heart with the love of the God of Israel. If he did this—that is, if he took pains to do what the Saviour told him to do—we may be sure, not only that he would not be without Divine Help, but that, in a very short time, he would be led by God's Spirit to see the greatness of Him Who was then conversing with him—to see in Him the exuberant love of God to His fallen creatures, and to be joined to Him, inwardly by faith, outwardly by fellowship in that Church which would be His abiding representative when He was taken away. If the law was a schoolmaster to lead men to Christ, surely the chief precept of the law, the law of Divine love, would lead a sincere soul most directly to Him.

29. "But he, willing to justify himself, said unto Jesus, And who is my neighbour?" This word "justify" cannot be taken in a theological sense. It seems to mean, willing to justify himself for having asked a question which, by so simple a process, he had been himself compelled to answer.

"Who is my neighbour?" Such a question is eminently characteristic of Judaism. The whole spirit of Rabbinism would exclude heathens from all good offices. For instance, in explaining Exod, xxiii. 35, they explain it so as to mean that the burden is only to be unloaded if the ass that lieth under it belongs to an Israelite, not if it belongs to a Gentile; and so the expression, "the ass of him that hateth thee," must be understood of a Jewish and not of a Gentile enemy.

30. "And Jesus answering said, A certain man went down from," &c. It has been made a question whether what follows was a parable composed by the Lord on the occasion, or a narrative of what actually occurred about that time. I should think most probably the former.

278   A CERTAIN PRIEST.   [St. Luke.

from Jerusalem to Jericho, and fell among thieves, which stripped him of his raiment, and wounded *him*, and departed, leaving *him* half dead.

31 And by chance there came down a certain Priest that

"A certain man." No doubt a Jew by nation and religion, or the parable would lose very much of its point.

"Went down from Jerusalem to Jericho, and fell among thieves, which stripped," &c. The road from Jerusalem to Jericho is described so graphically as to its desolateness and solitariness, its dangers and its declivity, in the following passage from Thomson's "Land and Book," that I think the reader will thank me for recalling it to his recollection or introducing him to it. "With noise and pomp such as Arabs only can affect we passed out [of Jerusalem] at St. Stephen's gate, wound our way into the narrow valley of Jehosophat, over the south point of Olivet, by the miserable remains of the city of Mary, Martha, and Lazarus, and then prepared ourselves to descend—for you remember that we must 'go *down* to Jericho.' And sure enough, *down, down* we did go, over slippery rocks, for more than a mile, when the path became less precipitous. Still, however, the road follows the dry channel of a brook for several miles further, as if descending into the very bowels of the earth. How admirably adapted for 'robbers'! After leaving the brook, which turns aside far to the south, we ascended and descended naked hills for several miles, the prospect gradually becoming more and more gloomy. Not a house, not even a tree is to be seen; and the only remains are those of a large khan, *said* to have been the inn to which the good Samaritan brought the wounded Jew. Not far from here, in a narrow defile, an English traveller was attacked, shot, and robbed in 1820. As you approach the plain, the mountains wear a more doleful appearance, the ravines become more frightful, and the narrow passes less and less passable. At length the weary traveller reaches the plain, by a long, steep declivity," &c., p. 613.

31. "And by chance there came down a certain priest that way." This is the only place where chance is mentioned in the New Testament. The Apostolic writers look upon every thing as ordered or controlled by God, and so they seldom use the word. But the expression scarcely signifies absolute chance as we use it of the

way: and when he saw him, °he passed by on the other side.

° Ps. xxxviii. 11.

32 And likewise a Levite, when he was at the

---

chances of dice, or such things. The word really means " concurrence," or " coincidence " of circumstances, all which circumstances are foreseen by God and, in a way unknown to us, ordered by Him; so that though to the priest himself his coming up at that moment seemed fortuitous, it was so ordered that it should display his want of charity, and so bring out into deeper relief the charity of one whom he esteemed his natural foe. This holds good whether the narrative be a real accident or a parable. All through our lives thousands of circumstances which seem like chance to us serve to bring out what is within us.

" A certain priest." He was going up to Jerusalem, in his turn to take part in the sacrificial worship of God, or he was returning from Jerusalem, having assisted in that worship, and that was the worship of One Who had said in words which must have been well known to him. " He . . . loveth the stranger in giving him food and raiment. Love ye, therefore, the stranger, for ye were strangers in the land of Egypt." (Deut. x. 18, 19.)

" When he saw him, he passed by on the other side." He might have made many excuses for doing this. He might have said to himself, " He is well nigh dead already. He cannot recover; besides I shall be too late for the appointed sacrifice if I delay, or I am expected at home, and they will be anxious about me, and the wretches who have murdered this poor man may rush out upon me in so dangerous a part of the road as this." But though we take example from this man, let us not judge him, for distress may have lain in our way, and in countless instances we may have passed by on the other side. All wilful avoiding information respecting any misery or sin which may be in our midst lest, if we know it, our consciences may reproach us with having done nothing to alleviate or remove it, or lest it threaten expense to us, and the loss of valuable time—is not this our way of passing by on the other side?

32. " And likewise a Levite, when he was at the place, came and looked on him," &c. The Levite seems to have been somewhat more humane at the first than the priest; for the priest simply saw him and got out of the way, whereas the Levite came and saw

place, came and looked *on him*, and passed by on the other side.

33 But a certain P Samaritan, as he journeyed, came where he was: and when he saw him, he had compassion *on him*.   P John iv. 9.

34 And went to *him*, and bound up his wounds, pouring in

(looked on) him. It seems as if the Levite examined the case more closely, but declined giving assistance as too difficult, or too dangerous, or too expensive. The Levite seems in one respect to have been more blameable than the priest; for being more of a menial servant of the temple, he was accustomed to rougher work, such as bearing burdens, killing, washing the animals used in sacrifices, and preparing their bodies for the sacrificial fire or feast, so that it would not have been out of the way of his occupation to remove the wounded man to the neighbouring inn.

33. "But a certain Samaritan, as he journeyed, came where he was." Commentators have drawn attention to the fact that the word "Samaritan" is put as the first word of the sentence to emphasize it: "A Samaritan, a certain one." I think that that which emphasizes the mention of the Samaritan most strongly is the fact that just before this the Lord was churlishly denied hospitality by a village of these aliens, because His face was " as though he would go to Jerusalem."

"And when he saw him he had compassion on him." The priest and Levite if they retained in their breasts any human feeling must have felt some degree of compassion; but this is passed over by the Saviour as of no account, because it bore no fruit, whereas the compassion of the Samaritan is mentioned with honour because it made him actively succour and relieve the miserable man.

34. "And went to him, and bound up his wounds, pouring in oil and wine," &c. He poured oil unto the wounds as an emollient, but why wine? As the man was in a fainting state, and no doubt exhausted with weakness through loss of blood, it would seem that the wine must have been given to him as a cordial to revive him; but all expositors seem agreed in the fact that the application of both was external. The wine, which would be more of the nature of vinegar than of wine, was supposed to cleanse the wounds, and the oil to heal.

oil and wine, and set him on his own beast, and brought him to an inn, and took care of him.

35 And on the morrow when he departed, he took out two ‖ pence, and gave *them* to the host, and said unto him, Take care of him; and whatsoever thou spendest more, when I come again, I will repay thee.

‖ See Matt. xx. 2.

---

35. "Two pence." "Two denarii"—double what the householder in the parable in Matth. xx. gave to each of the labourers for their day's work. Supposing that wages were 20s. a week, it would be above 6s. in real value.

34. "And brought him to an inn." Not a mere caravanserai with bare rooms, but a place of rest and refreshment which receives all comers.

"And took care of him," *i.e.*, nursed him till he left him the next day, as we must suppose, out of danger.

35. "And on the morrow when he departed, he took out two pence." He not only stayed till he saw him in the fair way of recovery, but gave the host a sufficiency for the maintenance for two days more, and, if this would not be enough, he gave him permission to spend upon the wounded man whatsoever was necessary, if it was best that he should remain longer at the inn.

Mark the various stages in the goodness of this man, which fully entitle him to the name of "Good" Samaritan. He had compassion on him; he delayed his journey to bind up his wounds, applying to them his own provision for his journey; he set him on his own beast, himself walking by his side; he nursed him himself the first night; he left sufficient for his keep for sometime, and gave the innkeeper a promise to repay him all further expenses. We should particularize all these points, because the Lord does so, in order to bring out the contrast between the trouble—the labour of love which he took—and the mere look of the priest and Levite.

It should be remarked that the word penny (two pence) is a wrong translation, because it conveys a very false impression to the majority of those who hear it, or read it. In the case of nine-tenths of half-educated Englishmen it would convey the idea of extreme stinginess, which would seriously detract from the teaching of the rest of the parable, whereas the sum was amply sufficient for the occasion. The word had better be left untranslated, as the value of money fluctuates and differs in every country.

36 Which now of these three, thinkest thou, was neighbour unto him that fell among the thieves?

37 And he said, He that shewed mercy on him. Then said

36. " Which now of these three, thinkest thou, was neighbour unto him?" &c. Observe how the Saviour here turns the tables, as it were, on His questioner. Instead of asking, " Must not every one be our neighbour, no matter what his religion or race?" He asks, "Who is he who acts as a neighbour, and so sets us an example of true disinterested humanity?" This would come home to the conscience of the lawyer, for he would feel that he ought to have been above asking such a question. The mere fact that he made such an inquiry showed a very imperfect practical knowledge of the law of love. The Lord's question has been admirably put as, " Which now of these three understood best what thou desirest to know?" The Samaritan was the wounded man's neighbour. Neighbour is a correlative term; and the meaning is—which acted as a neighbour, recognized the true love of one's neighbour, and so is to be imitated. Surely it is he who allowed no distinction of religion, or country, or friendship, to straiten his compassions.

37. " And he said, He that shewed mercy on him." Commentator after commentator blames the lawyer, and imputes it to his ineradicable national prejudices that he did not directly name the Samaritan, but " circuitously " replies, " He that shewed mercy on him;" but it seems to me that we must draw an exactly contrary inference, for instead of simply saying " the Samaritan," he designates him by his good deed: " He that shewed mercy on him." It seems as if the good example had struck him, and produced the desired effect. If he wished to disparage him, he would have said, He who assisted the wounded man, or relieved him; but he gives him his full due in naming the word " mercy."

" Then said Jesus unto him, Go, and do thou likewise." And what our Lord says to this man He says to every Christian who hears or reads this most exquisite Divine story (or history, as it may be). " Do thou shut thine eyes to no misery or want which is near thee, or in thy way. Rather do thou visit those afflicted by it. Do thou relieve it, even at the cost of some luxury or even comfort in thine own house. Do thou apply thyself to its removal, even though it give thee trouble, take up thy time, and somewhat hinder

Jesus unto him, Go, and do thou likewise.

---

thy business; for do thou remember well that no business will be found at the last to have been anything like so urgent as the laying up of treasures in heaven, or making to thyself friends of the mammon of unrighteousness." Thiersch has an application very appropriate to these times. "Many in our day consider it a sufficient evidence of their Christian charity, if they pay others to fulfil the works of mercy. And, indeed, the good Samaritan paid the host of the inn for the care of the wounded man. But before all he wrought with his own hand, and spared not the pains of dressing the wounds of the sufferer, walking by his side after placing him on the mule. When, from a pure motive and with prompt resolution, we incur privation, sacrifice pleasure, and undertake a painful personal labour for the benefit of a suffering neighbour, a special blessing rests upon us."

I cannot help saying that I take it as a special token for good in the Church that God, from Whom every good impulse comes, has raised up amongst us such multitudes of nursing Sisterhoods. When one remembers that forty years ago there was not one or only one, and now they are, with their offshoots, about one hundred, it seems as if His Spirit had not forsaken us.

All commentators, Catholic and non-Catholic, seem at one in the spiritual or mystical application of this parable. The Lord has not created for us such an example and model without having Himself, in His own Person, set it before us.

The wounded man is human nature, sick unto death through sin, "from the sole of the foot to the crown of the head, no soundness in it, but wounds and bruises and putrifying sores." The robbers are the powers of evil under their prince: he who was a murderer from the beginning. The priest and the Levite are the law and the prophets, utterly powerless to help or to give life, for "if there had been a law given which could have given life, verily righteousness, [which is the life of all intelligent creatures], should have been by the law" (Gal. iii. 21).

The Lord Himself was the good Samaritan, only infinitely exceeding the type in goodness. He "looked" from heaven upon our miserable condition. He did far more than the Samaritan could do, for the Samaritan and the Jew had but one common nature, whereas the Son of God, retaining all His Divine powers of healing,

38 ¶ Now it came to pass, as they went, that he entered

---

took upon Him our nature, in order that He might bind up our wounds, and pour into us health and consolation and strength. In His human nature He bore our burden—the burden of our sins and sorrows. He brought us to a place of comparative safety, even His Church, ruled by His ministers—the dispensers of His Sacraments. Having first tended us Himself—for the first care-taker of every soul is the Lord Himself,—then He left us in the hostelry which He Himself had built and furnished, and put under ministers —under Apostles, Evangelists, Pastors, and Teachers. In His Commission, in His Word, in His Sacraments, He has given these ministers and stewards all things needful for the restoration of souls; and if there is anything which in reason they, under the guidance of His Spirit, see needful, they are to supply it, and He will allow it at His return. Such is this parable, wondrous alike in its depth and its simplicity, convincing us all of sin—of miserable shortcoming in this matter of Divine and heavenly charity.

" O Lord, who hast taught us that all our doings without charity are nothing worth, send Thy Holy Ghost, and pour into our hearts that most excellent gift of charity, the very bond of peace and of all virtues, without which whosoever liveth is counted dead before Thee. Grant this, for thine only Son Jesus Christ's sake."

38. " Now it came to pass, as they went, that he entered into a certain village." This certain village must have been Bethany, so that if the seventy were sent forth by the Lord when He was journeying in South Galilee and Peræa, this incident must have occurred at one of His visits to Jerusalem.

Edersheim supposes that it took place at the feast of tabernacles, that its proper place is just before John vii. 14. It is there stated that about the midst of the feast Jesus went up into the Temple. Where was He before this? It is suggested that He would not have journeyed during the feast, but that He sent his disciples on to Jerusalem, and He Himself abode at Bethany, at the house of Martha; that they lodged for the most part, not in the house, but, as all law-observing Jews did, in a booth or booths in the court or garden; and that this accounts for the distraction of Martha with the " much serving," as she would have to go to and from the booth to the house—Lazarus, who is not mentioned, being absent, keeping the feast at Jerusalem. This is ingenious, but pure conjecture.

CHAP. X.] MARTHA AND MARY. 285

into a certain village: and a certain woman named ᑫ Martha
received him into her house.

39 And she had a sister called Mary, ʳ which
also ˢ sat at Jesus' feet, and heard his word.

ᑫ John xi. 1.
& xii. 2, 3.
ʳ 1 Cor. vii. 32, &c.
ˢ Luke viii. 35.
Acts xxii. 3.

---

39. "At Jesus' feet." So A., later Uncials, almost all Cursives, &c.; but ℵ, B., C., D., L., old Latin (except b), Vulg., Copt., Syriacs (Cur. and Schaaf) read, "The Lord's feet."

"A certain woman named Martha." Commentators, with one consent, notice the exact similarity of the characters of the two sisters as given in the two Evangelists. Martha, too attentive to household duties, "cumbered with much serving," in St. Luke; and, at the supper mentioned in St. John, "Martha served." Mary, in St. Luke's narrative, sitting at the Lord's feet; and, in St. John, anointing the Lord's feet. Martha forward to speak (Luke x. 40; John xi. 21-27, 39). Mary retiring in silent meditation (Luke x. 39; John xi. 20).

All sorts of conjectures have been made respecting the condition of Martha: that she was a widow; that she was the wife of Simon the leper; that it was even possible that she was the elect lady to whom St. John wrote his second Epistle; but two things must be held with certainty respecting her, first, that she was a true believer, for it was she who answered the Lord's question respecting belief in Himself as the Resurrection and the Life, with the words: "I believe that thou art the Christ, the Son of God, which should come into the world." Secondly, that she must have been a person of some means, probably large means, and so that the whole household would not consist of herself and her sister only. This is most certain from the fact that their family sepulchre was like that of Joseph of Arimathea, a cave hewn out in a rock, with a stone as its door.

39. "And she had a sister called Mary," &c. "A sister called Mary:" such a mode of naming her shows that she could not possibly have been the Mary called Magdalene, of chap. viii. 2, or the woman that was a sinner of vii. 37. This is undoubtedly the first mention of her.

"Which also sat at Jesus' feet, and heard his word." This, of course, means that she was a devout and attentive disciple, like her great namesake, keeping the Lord's sayings, and pondering them in her heart.

40 But Martha was cumbered about much serving, and came to him, and said, Lord, dost thou not care that my sister hath left me to serve alone? bid her therefore that she help me.

"And heard his word" means that she heard them effectually. She had ears to hear, she heard the Lord's words, and believed on Him that sent Him.

40. "But Martha was cumbered about much serving, and came to him, and said," &c., "serve alone." Very much depends upon the meaning of this "serving alone." Were there no other servants to whom such household duties could be committed? From all that we can gather respecting the circumstances of the family, there must have been such. If there were not, and food had to be prepared for the Lord, and perhaps other guests, then it seems selfish in Mary not to have assisted her sister, so that both together might listen to the Lord. But if there were other servants to whom such duties might have been well left, then the case is altered. Martha must have known that the best way of honouring the Lord was not to prepare Him an elaborate entertainment, but to listen to Him, and to receive His words, and through receiving them be made His. The Lord evidently blames Martha. He could not blame her for doing a woman's duty, but he could blame her for overdoing it, for thinking for a moment that anything was so acceptable to him as receiving His Word—and His Word was the Word of God—in the love of it. So that what He undoubtedly blames her for is the display of a worldly spirit—a desire to get credit from the entertainment—and so a woman's vanity.

And now it will be needful to consider an opinion largely held by Christian antiquity, which is this, that both Martha and Mary served the Lord with religious service—the one in her household work, the other in listening to his words; and that the Lord in what He says does not blame Martha, but pronounces the way of Mary to be a more perfect way. Thus Gregory, following Augustine: "One signifies the active life, the other the contemplative; that Martha's care is not blamed, but Mary is praised, for great are the rewards of an active life, but those of the contemplative far better." But I think such an application of the incident is impossible, *i.e.*, an application which treats both Martha's and Mary's conduct on this occasion as religious; but Mary's as the better, for

CHAP. X.] TROUBLED ABOUT MANY THINGS. 287

41 And Jesus answered and said unto her, Martha, Martha, thou art careful and troubled about many things :

---

41. "And Jesus." So A., C., D., all later Uncials, almost all Cursives, old Latin (b, c, f, q), Copt., Syr. (Schaaf), &c.; but ℵ, B., L., old Latin (a, i, l), Vulg., read, "the Lord."

surely the Lord Himself set an example of the active life, and all His Apostles, and all who in other days have extended the borders of His Church, have led active lives—lives never without earnest prayer, never without the reading of Scripture, never without seasons of retirement for devout meditations, but still active ones—lives in which he who led them fed on the words of Jesus, and devoutly accepted His every utterance, and chose the good part, but still such men could not be described as sitting still at the Lord's feet, and doing nothing but listening to His words. For what is such listening as Mary's for ? Surely not merely for private and solitary contemplation, however devout, but for the benefit of others. For as activity, without meditation and constant retirement for devotion, is not according to the Lord's will, and will soon more and more secularize religion, and make it cold and mechanical; so contemplation without activity will make religion unreal and dreamy, and unfruitful, for every doctrine of our religion, without exception, must both be contemplated inwardly and acted out visibly in the conduct.

41, 42. "And Jesus answered and said unto her . . . . not be taken away from her." As if He said, " Thou art distracted with such anxieties respecting the entertainment of thy guests, that thou neglectest the one thing for which I took thy nature. I came not to be ministered unto, but to minister; and I minister the word of salvation. Blame not thy sister; she has discerned the one object of my Mission, the one reception which honours Me, the one entertainment for which I look. If thou hadst been like her, and understood my one purpose in coming to my people, thou wouldst have given less attention to niceties for which I care nothing, and found time for receiving from my lips that word of truth by which thy soul will be made mine for ever."

Did Martha, then, never sit at the feet of Jesus and choose the good part? Did Mary never honour thd Lord's Body with outward service ? The sequel of their history, as given in St. John, tells us ; For Martha in that she confessed, " Yea, Lord, I believe that thou art the Christ, the son of the living God ;" and so, " Thou art the

42 But ᵗone thing is needful: and Mary hath chosen that
good part, which shall not be taken away from
her.

ᵗ Ps. xxvii. 4.

42. "But one thing is needful." So A., C., all later Uncials except L., all Cursives (except 1, 33), some old Latin (f, g¹, q), Vulg., Syriac (Cur. and Schaaf); but א, B., L., 1, 33, Copt., Æth., read, "few things are needful or one." In this case the so-called neutral text substitutes an unintelligible sentence for one of the Lord's most important words. And this against the authority of all Christendom.

Resurrection and Life,"—Martha, I say, in thus confessing Him, manifested with all possible clearness that she had sat at the feet of the Lord, and received His words of life; and Mary, in that she anointed His Body with the box of very precious ointment, paid far more devotion to that adorable Body than Martha did when she was busied about the food of His entertainment. So that they seem to change places, the one received His Word as the Word of God, the other honoured His Body as the Body of God.

CHAP. XI.

AND it came to pass, that, as he was praying in a certain place, when he ceased, one of his disciples said unto him, Lord, teach us to pray, as John also taught his disciples.

1. And it came to pass, as he was praying in a certain place .... John also taught his disciples." It has been supposed that the Lord was praying aloud, that one of the disciples (perhaps one of the seventy who had not heard the sermon on the mount), struck with the fervour and Divine rapture of His prayer, asked to be taught to pray similarly, and added, that His great forerunner had given to his disciples a form of prayer.

2. "And he said unto them, when ye pray, say, Our Father which art in heaven," &c. It is evident by the answer which the Lord gave, that the disciples had asked the Lord to teach them a form of prayer. The Lord's answer is very suggestive. According to the opinion of many bodies of Christians since the time of Calvin,

2. And he said unto them, When ye pray, say, ^a Our Father which art in heaven, Hallowed be thy name. Thy kingdom come. Thy will be done, as in heaven, so in earth.

^a Matt. vi. 9.

2. "Our Father which art in heaven." So A., C., D., all later Uncials, almost all Cursives, most old Latin (a, b, c, f, ff², i, l, q), Copt., Cur. Syriac, &c.; but ℵ, B., L., 1, 22, 57, Vulg., have only "Father," without "our," and without "which art in heaven."
"Thy will be done, as in heaven, so in earth." So ℵ, Λ., C., D., all later Uncials, almost all Cursives, old Latin (b, c, e, f, i, l, q), Copt., Æth., but omitted by B., L., 1, 22, Vulg., Cureton Syriac, Arm.

the Lord should have said, "I cannot teach you any *form* of prayer. Any words that even I could give you would only fetter the freedom of your intercourse with your Father. My Spirit alone can teach you how to pray, and His teaching will raise you up into an atmosphere far above all forms." On the principle of those who discard the use of all forms, such should have been the Lord's answer; but instead of this He at once gave them, a second time apparently, the prayer which He had given in the Sermon on the Mount.

Now, in giving them this well-known form, He gave them words to which, so far from fettering or cramping their freedom, they would never be able to rise up. Do what we will we can never comprehend the depth and fulness—we can never attain to the height of "hallowed be thy name, thy kingdom come, thy will be done."

Consider the first, "Hallowed be thy name." It blends itself with the incessant Trisagion of the Seraphim close to the throne. It unites itself in earth with the praise of "everything that hath breath." It prays against every form of false worship, of superstitious worship, of will-worship, of careless, indevout, cold, formal, hypocritical worship; and it prays for every thing by which God may be better known, better remembered, better loved. It prays for all honour to God, in heaven and in earth, in the heart, in the family, in the senate, in the world, in the Church; above all, in the Eucharistic celebration, because that is the highest act of worship of the Mystical Body.

Consider "Thy kingdom come." The more we know of God's kingdom in the heart, the Church, the world, the more we know of the misery of all adverse rule, and of the blessedness of being ruled by God, and of having every thought brought into subjection to the obedience of Christ, the more we shall realize "Thy kingdom come."

3 Give us ‖ day by day our daily bread.

4 And forgive us our sins; for we also forgive every one that is indebted to us. And lead us not into temptation; but deliver us from evil.

‖ Or, *for the day.*

---

4. "But deliver us from evil." So A., C., D., later Uncials, almost all Cursives, old Latin (b, c, f, i, l, q), (a, e wanting here), Copt., Syriac (Cur. and Schaaf), Æth.; but omitted in ℵ, B., L., 1, 22, 57, 130, 131, &c., Vulg.

And the more we know of the righteousness and goodness of the will of the Supreme Father, with the more fervour and devout submission we shall say, "Thy will be done."

So that no prayer should be so studied as this prayer. Under no other prayer can we gather up and express so many aspirations. No prayer leads us to think so much of God and of His will and designs as this prayer. In the use of no other prayer can the Christian submit himself so unreservedly to God. It follows that no prayer should be said—at times, at least—so slowly, so collectedly, so recollectedly, so humbly, so reverentially. It follows that no prayer requires more teaching of God's Spirit to enter somewhat into its depth and fulness, and so to say it aright.

Like the Eucharist, it can be offered up with a particular intention. If there be any work to be done for God or for the Church, what better way of commending it to God—if there be not time or opportunity for the celebration of the Eucharist—than by this prayer, that in the work on account of which we pray He would glorify His Name, He would advance His kingdom, and carry out His holy will.

I have enlarged upon each petition so very fully in my comment on St. Matthew vi., that I must refer the reader to that, if he desires a fuller exposition of the several parts.

An interesting question arises, however, on this—whether the Lord gave this prayer to His disciples only once or on two occasions: once in His Sermon on the Mount (Matt. vi.), once as related here.

Now it will be necessary to remember that the form in St. Matthew is not only the most perfect form, but that, when we have once known it, we could not possibly be contented with that given in St. Luke; for the form in St. Luke, as given in several ancient MSS., and in the Vulgate, is this—"Father: hallowed be Thy Name. Thy kingdom come. Give us to-day our daily bread. And

5 And he said unto them, Which of you shall have a friend, and shall go unto him at midnight, and say unto him, Friend, lend me three loaves;

---

forgive us our sins, for we also forgive every one that is indebted to us. And lead us not into temptation." Now it is incredible that the Lord should have given the Lord's Prayer in a perfect state, and not taught His people to say, "Thy will be done," and "Deliver us from evil." Supposing, then, that these Manuscripts give the true version of this prayer as it came from the lips of the Lord on this occasion, then St. Matthew, who seems to have been, in most cases, the more perfect reporter of the Lord's discourses, has given us that form from which it is impossible for any Christian to deviate; for it is absurd to suppose that they are alternative forms, so that we should sometimes say the Lord's Prayer with the petitions, "Thy will be done" and "Deliver us from evil," and sometimes, of set purpose, omit them.

If, however, the Lord had previously given to His people the Prayer as it is contained in the Sermon on the Mount, then, when He was asked by one who was ignorant of it to teach them to pray, He might naturally give them what would remind them that He had already taught them the prayer of prayers. He would give them the shortened form, which probably, as He then set it forth, was still shorter, merely to remind them that He had already taught them what they now asked for, and that they must remember His former words. Or it may be that St. Luke, in this account, contented himself with words just sufficient to remind his hearers of the fuller form. Anyhow, there can be no Lord's Prayer without "Thy will be done."

5. "And he said unto them, Which of you shall have a friend, and shall go?" &c. The Lord having taught them the most fitting words of prayer, now adds a short parable respecting frequency and perseverance in prayer. In order to encourage us always to pray and never to faint, and in everything by prayer and supplication to make our requests known unto God, He gives us a short parable, in which the case is put as strongly as it well can be.

Supposing that any one of those who heard Him had a friend who came to him in the dead of night, hungry, and faint with his journey, and he went to a neighbour of his, also his friend, whom he had seldom found wanting in time of need, though he had often

6 For a friend of mine ‖ in his journey is come to me, and
I have nothing to set before him?

‖ Or, *out of his way*.

7 And he from within shall answer and say,
Trouble me not: the door is now shut, and my children are
with me in bed; I cannot rise and give thee.

---

tried his patience, he would not scruple to go to this friend, notwithstanding that it was midnight, and ask for three loaves, for he was bound to show his visitor hospitality, and he had nothing whatsoever in the house. The case was so urgent that he would run the risk of exciting his friend's impatience and ill-temper; and when his friend, perhaps in angry tones, told him to take himself off, for if he got up to supply his want, he would wake up his children, and disturb all the house, the man without, urgently feeling the need, would continue knocking till he within, seeing that there was no help—that, if he would get his night's rest, he must comply with his friend's request, and yield to his shameless importunity,—would rise up, and with ill-humour and, perhaps, some bad words, give him what was needed.

Now see the amazing contrast between the conduct of the angry and churlish friend and that of God. The friend in his house at midnight, in bed with his children, is put in contrast with God, Who never slumbers nor sleeps, Whose ears are always open to prayer, Who is angry and disturbed—to speak after the manner of men—not when His people pray, but when they do not pray; the door bolted and barred is put in contrast with the door of heaven, always open; the trouble that the friend within deprecated is in contrast with the ease with which Almighty God can grant any and every request, without stirring from His place. The impatience of the friend at being disturbed is in contrast with the patience of God, Who, no matter how we have sinned, will hear our prayer. The granting of the request, not for friendship, but for self's sake, is in contrast with the exuberant kindness and mercy of, God, Who gives to us, not as a relief to Himself, but because of His love to us, and His desire for our temporal and eternal good.

The refusal and delay of the man within, in order that the man without might go away, and cease to disturb him, is in contrast with the mind and conduct of our heavenly Father, Who, when He seems to delay His answer, delays not for His ease, but for our sakes,

CHAP. XI.] ASK, AND IT SHALL BE GIVEN. 293

8 I say unto you, [b] Though he will not rise and give him, because he is his friend, yet because of his importunity he will rise and give him as many as he needeth.

[b] ch. xviii. 1, &c.

9 [c] And I say unto you, Ask, and it shall be given you; seek, and ye shall find; knock, and it shall be opened unto you.

[c] Matt. vii. 7. & xxi. 22. Mark xi. 24. John xv. 7. James i. 6. 1 John iii. 22.

---

in order that our faith may be strengthened, our habit of prayer increased, and our appreciation of the value of His gifts deepened because of the trouble and perseverance we have to exercise.

Whether this parable was spoken just after Jesus had taught them the Lord's Prayer seems doubtful; but what immediately succeeds, "Ask, and it shall be given you," was no doubt delivered at the same time by the Lord as the lesson of the parable. There are many spiritual meanings given to various parts of it, as that the three loaves are faith, hope, and charity, or the knowledge of the three Persons of the Trinity; but it seems best to let nothing interfere with *the* lesson, which is, that persevering, importunate prayer will always be answered.

Again, some commentators have taken pains to vindicate the comparison of the conduct of God with that of the churlish man here described; but it seems to be not a comparison, but a contrast, all the way through. The character and conduct of God, as regards prayer, is the opposite of that of the man in question: and so the rather with confidence ask of God, seek His grace, knock at His door.

9. "And I say unto you, Ask, and it shall be given you; seek, and ye shall find; knock," &c. "I say unto you," as the great lesson from the parable I have just uttered, "Ask, seek, knock." These gradations of earnestness are suggested by the parable. The man first, no doubt, simply asked; then he sought the door, or sought to open it, till he found it was fast shut and barred; then he knocked, so as to threaten to awake not only his friend, but the other inmates of the house. Quesnel has a very good exposition: "A man, in order to offer up such a prayer as becometh a sinner, must ask with the humility of a beggar, seek with the carefulness of a faithful servant, and knock with the confidence of a friend."

Or, again, "asking" may be simply putting up words; "seek-

10 For every one that asketh receiveth; and he that seeketh findeth; and to him that knocketh it shall be opened.

---

ing" may be the diligent use of means of grace; "knocking" may signify still further and more decided means of attracting the ear of God, such as, for instance, fasting and almsgiving. Of Cornelius it was said, "Thy prayers and thine alms are come up for a memorial before God;" and as to those who set apart Paul and Barnabas to the Apostolic work, it is said that the command from heaven came "As they ministered unto the Lord, and fasted." The great prayer seasons of the Church, the Ember days, and the Rogation days, are days of fasting as well as of prayer. Again, as to the use of means of grace. Do we ask for strength of soul against sin? We must remember that Christ has left a means of grace for the strengthening and refreshing of our souls, even the Sacrament of His Body and Blood; and we shall show the sincerity of our prayers by diligently using that Sacrament with the earnest desire and definite intention of receiving strength in it. Anyhow, this place teaches us that if we have any sincerity, we must not put up some hasty prayer and have done with it. People who are in earnest about any earthly matter do not so behave. They call to mind all the ways of approaching a friend or patron who has something to give, and neglect none. Particularly if the great man has any friend who can command his ear, they will avail themselves of such an one's intercession. And so the Christian will ask particularly the intercession of the Lord, and also of His people. And if by any memorial act they can remind the patron of some great kindness of his to them in past time, they will most certainly use such memorial; and so the Christian's special times of prayer and intercession will be when the Sacrifice of Christ is represented to God in the Sacrament of His Son's Body and Blood.

10. "For every one that asketh receiveth." He may not receive what He asks for in the exact form in which he expects it; but he shall receive something better, something that God knows that He requires more.

"He that seeketh findeth." He findeth the hidden treasure—the pearl of great price; He finds God.

"To him that knocketh it shall be opened." The door of grace here, the door of heaven hereafter.

11 ᵈ If a son shall ask bread of any of you that is a father, will he give him a stone? or if *he ask* a fish, will he for a fish give him a serpent? ᵈ Matt. vii. 9.

12 Or if he shall ask an egg, will he †offer him a scorpion? † Gr. *give.*

13 If ye then, being evil, know how to give good gifts unto your children: how much more shall *your* heavenly Father give the Holy Spirit to them that ask him?

---

13. "Your heavenly Father," rather "the Father which is from heaven."

11. "If a son shall ask bread of any of you that is a father . . . . scorpion." To what does this similitude look? What being, when he is asked for bread, gives a stone? In all probability the Lord opposes the gifts of the Father to the gifts of the world, or of Satan. It may be observed that each has a slight resemblance to the object put in opposition to it: bread to a stone, fish to a serpent, the egg to a scorpion. Thus it is with the things which Satan bestows; they have always some similarity to the objects which the heart of man seeks, but are useless as is the stone, or in the end fatal as the serpent or the scorpion.

13. "If ye then, being evil, know how to give good gifts unto your children: how," &c. The reader will remember how, in the exactly parallel place in Matth. vii., the heavenly Father, in answer to prayer, is said to give all good things; so that it seems, by comparing the places, that the Holy Spirit is the equivalent of "all good things." But, indeed, is He not much more? What is all knowledge, even of the Scriptures, all eloquence, all skill, not to mention all riches, all earthly happiness, or earthly glory, without the Holy Spirit.

The greatest gift of God, then—the gift of the Renewer, Comforter, Revealer of God, and Giver of Eternal Life—is to be got for the asking.

Notice how the Lord here recognizes the universal presence of sin in the race when He says, "If ye then, being evil."

Notice also, that though thus sinful by nature, we still retain so much of the image of God, that we can infer, from the remains of what is good within us, the perfect goodness of God.

14. "And he was casting out a devil, and it was dumb . . . .

14 ¶ ᵉ And he was casting out a devil, and it was dumb. And it came to pass, when the devil was gone out, the dumb spake; and the people wondered.

15 But some of them said, ᶠ He casteth out devils through † Beelzebub the chief of the devils.

16 And others, tempting *him*, ᵍ sought of him a sign from heaven.

17 ʰ But ⁱ he, knowing their thoughts, said unto them, Every kingdom divided against itself is

ᵉ Matt. ix. 32. & xii. 22.
ᶠ Matt. ix. 34. & xii. 24.
† Gr. *Beelzebul*, and so ver. 18, 19.
ᵍ Matt. xii. 38. & xvi. 1.
ʰ Matt. xii. 25. Mark iii. 24.
ⁱ John ii. 25.

---

people wondered." It is not possible, with any degree of certainty, to fix the time of this miracle. It is almost identical, both in its circumstances and its effects on the people and on the Pharisees with two in St. Matthew, one related in Matt. ix. 31, the other in xii. 22. If much that is in the preceding chapter describes the acts of a ministry in Peræa, then this must be related by St. Luke out of its place. Alford supposes, and with seeming truth, that it was "a portion of the Evangelic history the position of which was not exactly and satisfactorily fixed." In St. Mark's Gospel the blasphemy of the Pharisees, and the Lord's answer to it, come in immediately after the interference of His friends to restrain Him as one "beside himself." (Mark iii. 21, 22, &c.) I would only remark in passing, that the casting out of evil spirits seems to have been viewed with more wonder by the people than any other of the Lord's miracles. They perhaps contrasted His power with the imperfect and abortive efforts of their own exorcists.

15. "But some of them said, He casteth out devils," &c. With incredible folly, as well as wickedness, they ascribed to the power of the evil one miracles of the highest power on the side of good, done with the express purpose of enforcing the highest righteousness and goodness which God has ever revealed to His creatures.

16. "And others, tempting him, sought of him a sign from heaven." With equal folly demanding, as the highest credential of His mission, that He should afford them a sign somewhere in the region of the sky, and not on the surface of the earth.

17. "But he, knowing their thoughts, said unto them, Every kingdom divided," &c. Every kingdom rent by internal divisions, issuing in civil war, is destroyed by such divisions; and every

A HOUSE DIVIDED FALLETH.

brought to desolation; and a house *divided* against a house falleth.

18 If Satan also be divided against himself, how shall his kingdom stand? because ye say that I cast out devils through Beelzebub.

19 And if I by Beelzebub cast out devils, by whom do your sons cast *them* out? therefore shall they be your judges.

20 But if I [k] with the finger of God cast out devils, no doubt the kingdom of God is come upon you.

[k] Exod. viii. 19.

---

17. "A house divided against a house falleth." Some interpret this as meaning "house falleth against house," when there is civil war. The Vulgate translates, *domus supra domum cadet*.

house or family similarly divided cannot maintain its high position. And, if Satan be divided against himself, so that he casts out his own evil angels who maintain his power over the bodies and souls of men, how can his kingdom be maintained?

19. "And if I by Beelzebub cast out devils, by whom do your sons?" &c. As if He said, I, by a power on the side of benevolence and goodness, repeatedly cast out evil spirits, and your sons, invoking the Name of this God of all goodness, at times cast out the same evil spirits, but far less frequently and successfully than I do. If you allow their feeble efforts in this way to be by the power and according to the will of God, why do you impute my far more successful inroads on the kingdom of evil to the author of evil?

"Your sons" cannot well mean the Apostles, as some suppose, for they wrought solely under Christ and His Name. They can be only Jewish exorcists, but not necessarily pretenders or cheats, as the sons of Sceva. (Acts xix. 14.)

20. "But if I with the finger of God cast out devils," &c. Notice how the casting out of evil spirits by the Lord by the power of the Spirit (Matt. xii. 28), or finger of God, as here, is the surest sign of the presence of the kingdom of God. The Lord in saying this must have believed in the reality of the evil world of fallen angels. He could not have said this if His words and His actions respecting possession by devils was only an accommodation to the ignorance of the times. (See my excursus on Demoniacal Possession at the end of my volume on St. Mark's Gospel.)

THE STRONG AND THE STRONGER. [St. Luke.

21 ^l When a strong man armed keepeth his palace, his goods are in peace:

22 But ^m when a stronger than he shall come upon him, and overcome him, he taketh from him all his armour wherein he trusted, and divideth his spoils.

23 ⁿ He that is not with me is against me: and he that gathereth not with me scattereth.

^l Matt. xii. 29. Mark iii. 27.
^m Isai. liii. 12. Col. ii. 15.
ⁿ Matt. xii. 30.

---

21. "When a strong man armed keepeth his palace, his goods are in peace," &c. This, taken with the preceding context, seems to mean that the power of Satan, the strong man, fully equipped with all appliances of evil, is not destroyed by any internal division in his kingdom, but by the Son of God, armed with all the power of God, suddenly coming into his kingdom and taking from him all by which he kept possession of his domain. This is true both of the world and of the soul.

Satan's power was destroyed in the world by the coming of Christ in the flesh, and the setting up of His visible kingdom, the Church. Then the Word of Christ went forth, conquering and to conquer. There was a power given to Christ's servants which if faithfully used would have rooted all idolatry and all falsehood in religion, and philosophy, and morals, out of the world; but because the servants of Christ did not faithfully use this power, their success has been but too partial. And so with the soul. The soul of the impenitent sinner is Satan's stronghold, and its true conversion is not owing to any struggle within it between good and bad principles—the good getting the better by their own strength, but by the coming of Christ to it, regenerating it, renewing it, taking all its faculties and powers, and turning them from the service of self to the service of God.

Notice how the Son of God is the "stronger." He is stronger than any evil lust, or bad temper, or sinful habit, no matter how inveterate. He is stronger than any evil opinion, or heresy, or prejudice, no matter how deeply rooted; He is stronger than the world. "Greater is he that is in you than he that is in the world."

23. "He that is not with me is against me: and he that gathereth not with me scattereth." There can be no neutrality in the war between Christ and evil. Neutrality is treason to Christ. If a man

CHAP. XI.] THE UNCLEAN SPIRIT RETURNING. 299

24 º When the unclean spirit is gone out of a man, he walketh through dry places, seeking rest; and finding none, he saith, I will return unto my house whence I came out.

º Matt. xii. 43.

is not religious, his weight, whether he be conscious of it or not, goes into the scale opposite to that of Christ. A neutral man—a man who says, "I make no profession of religion"—is of the world. He is one unit more to swell the world's power. He is often more dangerous than an avowed unbeliever, or an opponent of what is good. Let us remember that, so far from tolerating neutrality, Christ does not even tolerate lukewarmness: " Because thou art neither hot nor cold, I will spue thee out of my mouth."

"He that gathereth not with me scattereth." Godet supposes that this refers to the Jewish exorcists. Though seemingly on the side of Christ, and against that of Satan, they were not so in reality: for they enabled the adversaries to say that mighty works might be done by those not belonging to Christ, and so that the Lord's power over evil spirits was no infallible sign of the truth of His mission. But the saying is of far wider significance. It means that no one can really uphold the cause of virtue in the world, if he attempts to do it independently of the Christian faith.

24. "When the evil spirit is gone out of a man, he walketh through dry places," &c. This parable or illustration is almost verbatim the same as that in Matthew xii. 43, the most noticeable difference being the conclusion; the words, "Even so shall it be also to this wicked generation," being omitted in St. Luke. I have shown in my remarks on St. Matthew's version of it, to which I refer the reader, that it bears on the face of it a twofold application. It applies, as the Lord distinctly says, to that evil generation. The evil spirit of idolatry and neglect of God's worship had been cast out; but he had then returned with other evil spirits worse than himself. The spirit of idolatry itself had returned; but it returned in the shape of the worship of the letter of Scripture, to the neglect of its spirit, so that the very law of God was made void, and with him came the evil spirits of hypocrisy—the most evil of all evil spirits, of formality, of adultery, and fornication, which appears to have prevailed then as grossly as in the semi-heathen times; of exclusiveness, so that they would deny to the Gentiles the very word of life itself; of disobedience to parents; of false swearing; and, above

25 And when he cometh, he findeth *it* swept and garnished.

26 Then goeth he, and taketh *to him* seven other spirits more wicked than himself; and they enter in, and dwell there: and ᵖ the last *state* of that man is worse than the first.

p John v. 14.
Hebr. vi. 4. &
x. 26.
2 Pet. ii. 20.

---

all, of the deadliest dislike of the holiness of God's character, as set forth in the Life and Example of His Son then dwelling amongst them.

The second application is to the individual soul. The evil spirit may be driven out in Baptism, or even by a conversion sincere at the time; but no pains are taken to invite into his place, or to retain the Holy Spirit of God. Habits of prayer, or reading of Scripture, or careful preparation for the reception of the Lord's Body and Blood are relaxed; and sin by degrees regains its dominion, perhaps not in its first grosser forms, but in the form of covetousness, selfishness, secret impurity, envy, evil-speaking, all of these quite as deadly as gross, open sin. There is the form of godliness, but a complete denial of its power. So that this is a place much to be pondered over by all who have begun well. Quesnel remarks: "A converted sinner is a place which the devil has lost, the weak sides and avenues whereof he perfectly knows, in which he very often keeps a correspondence."

Alford, in his "New Testament for English Readers," has another application to the Christian Church, which, though in many respects fanciful, and tinged by his ultra-Protestantism, nevertheless is worth notice: "Strikingly parallel with this [the application to the Jewish Church] runs the history of the Christian Church. Not long after the Apostolic times, the golden calves of idolatry were set up by the Church of Rome. What the effect of the captivity was to the Jews, that of the Reformation has been to Christendom [?]. The first evil spirit has been cast out [perhaps in England, Scotland, Holland, and parts of Germany]. But by the growth of hypocrisy, secularity, and rationalism, the house has become empty, swept, and garnished—swept and garnished by the decencies of civilization and discoveries of secular knowledge, but empty of living and earnest faith. And he must read prophecy but ill who does not see under all these seeming improvements the preparation for the final

27 ¶ And it came to pass, as he spake these things, a certain woman of the company lifted up her voice, and said unto him, ꝗ Blessed *is* the womb that bare thee, and the paps which thou hast sucked.

28 But he said, Yea ʳ rather, blessed *are* they that hear the word of God, and keep it.

ꝗ ch. i. 28, 48.

ʳ Matt. vii. 21. ch. viii. 21. James i. 25.

---

27. "A certain woman of the company," rather "a certain woman from among the crowd lifted," &c.

development of the man of sin—the great repossession, when idolatry, and the seven worse spirits, shall bring the outward frame of so-called Christendom to a fearful end."

The great lesson, then, of this similitude is that, under a seeming improvement, there may be a far worse alienation from God.

27. "And it came to pass, as he spake these things, a certain woman," &c. This incident is variously placed by harmonists. Greswell supposes that it took place at the same time that His mother and His brethren came, interrupting Him (Matt. xii. 46-50); and it is supposed that when this woman heard His mother named, she broke out into this exclamation; but in common with a vast number of incidents in the Lord's life, it is impossible to fix its place in a harmony. It is peculiar to St. Luke.

So far from derogating from the blessedness of the Holy Virgin, the Lord by implication here declares it to be twofold. He did not deny her blessedness in having brought into the world its Redeemer; but He sets forth a higher than this, that of hearing the Word of God, and keeping it. This was, in one sense, the highest blessedness of the Virgin, in that it sets its crown on the first. If the thing may be so much as imagined, it would not have availed the Virgin to have brought Christ the Son of God into the world, if she had had no part in Him spiritually; but not only blessed was she who gave birth to our Lord and God, but "blessed is she that believed," "blessed is she that kept all the sayings of her Divine Son, and pondered them in her heart." (Luke i. 45; ii. 19, 51.) In this, her second and greatest blessedness, we can share; but it was through her first blessedness that we can now hear the word of God uttered by His Incarnate Son: and it is through the grace of that Incarnation, of which she was the instrument, that we can keep it.

29 ¶ ᵃAnd when the people were gathered thick together, he began to say, This is an evil generation: they seek a sign; and there shall no sign be given it, but the sign of Jonas the prophet.

ᵃ Matt. xii. 38, 39.

30 For as ᵗ Jonas was a sign unto the Ninevites, so shall also the Son of man be to this generation.

ᵗ Jonah i. 17. & ii. 10.

---

29. "Jonas the prophet." So A., C., later Uncials, almost all Cursives, some old Latin (e, f, g), Syriac (Schaaf), some Copt., Æth.; but "the prophet" omitted in ℵ, B., D., L., some old Latin (a, b, c), Vulg. (Cod. Amiat.), some Copt., &c.

29. "And when the people were gathered thick together, he began to say," &c. Why is the crowd of people so expressly mentioned? Seemingly for this reason, that He desired that what He was saying respecting the wickedness of the generation, and the Queen of the South, and the Ninevites rising up in judgment against it, should be diffused far and wide; so that when the time came, as many as possible, taking warning from his words, should "save themselves from that untoward generation."

"They seek a sign." This has evident reference to what is related in verse 16. The sign they asked was evidently a sign from *heaven*. They made light of the miracles of healing; they said that He cast out devils through the prince of the devils; nothing would satisfy them except a "sign from heaven,"—as Moses gave, when he brought down the manna, seemingly from heaven; as Elijah, when at his prayer God sent down the fire on the sacrifice, apparently also from heaven.

"No sign be given them, but the sign of Jonas the prophet. For as Jonas was a sign," &c. The Lord here alludes to His Resurrection, as we learn from St. Matthew's account. The Resurrection of Christ was His Spirit coming out of the unseen and eternal world, and re-animating the Body. It was far more, then, than any bringing down of either manna or fire from the lower region of the sky. It was the Highest Power of the heaven of heavens bringing a soul out of Paradise, and so changing the nature of the resuscitated body, that it became from that time a spiritual body.

30. "For as Jonas was a sign to the Ninevites, so shall also the Son of man be," &c. The resemblances between the two signs are remarkable. Jonas was a sort of piacular victim, his death accepted in the place of the destruction of the crew of the ship; Jonas was

31 "The queen of the south shall rise up in the judgment with the men of this generation, and condemn them: for she came from the utmost parts of the earth to hear the wisdom of Solomon; and, behold, a greater than Solomon *is* here. ^{u 1 Kings x. 1.}

32 The men of Nineve shall rise up in the judgment with this generation, and shall condemn it: for ^x they repented at the preaching of Jonas; and, behold, a greater than Jonas *is* here. ^{x Jonah iii. 5.}

---

31. "A greater than Solomon," literally "more than Solomon."

cast forth from the jaws of death as the Lord was. Jonas was sent to the Gentiles, and the Lord, after His Resurrection, became "a light to lighten the Gentiles." In both cases, as I noticed in my comment on St. Matthew, the persons did not perform a wonder or miracle as a sign, but were themselves the sign. And in both cases they were a sign only to faith, for none of the Ninevites saw the prophet's deliverance from death, they only saw him after his deliverance, and none of the Jews saw the Resurrection of the Lord, only a few chosen ones saw His Body after His Resurrection.

31. "The queen of the south shall rise up in the judgment with the men of this generation," &c. Either the Queen of Abyssinia, or the queen of a district at the south-west corner of Arabia. The Lord, the meekest of men, calls Himself greater, or more than Solomon, the wisest of men; and yet, in the view of the Catholic Church, there is no comparison between the two. The wisdom of the one was that of a created being, given to him, and not his by nature; the wisdom of the other was the Wisdom of God, from Whom that of Solomon himself was derived.

32. "The men of Nineve shall rise up in the judgment with this generation," &c. They repented at the preaching of a servant of God, who, as far as we read, did no miracles, healed no palsied or leprous persons, fed no multitudes, raised no dead, whereas the Son of God did all these things, and rose from the dead, and sent His Spirit. So that His messengers or representatives did greater things, and yet the generation repented not.

Mark the graphic way in which the Lord describes the last judgment, men not only raised up from the dead to be judged, but

33 ⁷ No man, when he hath lighted a candle, putteth *it* in a secret place, neither under a ‖ bushel, but on a candlestick, that they which come in may see the light.

y Matt. v. 15.
Mark iv. 21.
ch. viii. 16.
‖ See Matt. v. 15.

34 ᶻ The light of the body is the eye: therefore when thine eye is single, thy whole body also is full of light; but when *thine eye* is evil, thy body also *is* full of darkness.

z Matt. vi. 22.

---

33. "Under a bushel," or "candlestick," rather "the bushel"—"the lamp stand."

34. "The light of the body." D., most old Latin, Vulg., Copt., Syriac (Schaaf), read, "of thy body."

"Is the eye." So E., G., H., K., L., other later Uncials, most Cursives, Cur. Syriac, Arm.; but ℵ*, A., B., C., D., M., a few Cursives, old Latin, Vulg., Copt., Syriac (Schaaf), read, "is thine eye."

"Therefore when thine eye." "Therefore" omitted by ℵ, B., D., L., Δ, old Latin, Vulg. Copt.; but retained by A., C., later Uncials, almost all Cursives, and Cur. Syriac.

rising up in the judgment to witness against those who had rejected Christ.

33. "No man, when he hath lighted a candle, putteth it in a secret place," &c. This proverb, as it may properly be called, has been twice before used by the Lord, once in the Sermon on the Mount (Matt. v. 15), where it is evidently spoken with reference to the Apostles; once before in this very Gospel (chap. viii. 16), where it seems also to refer to the Apostles. Here, however, it seems to be spoken by our Lord of Himself. He is the Light which God hath lighted; and as God Himself has lighted Him for the purpose of diffusing Divine Light, He will see to it that He shall be put in a position to give light to the world. This was fulfilled at His Resurrection and Ascension, and the consequent descent of the Spirit.

34. "The light of the body is the eye: therefore when thine eye is single, thy whole," &c. Here the Lord seems to pass from Himself the Light to His entrance into the soul to give it light. The light of the luminary, no matter how brightly it shines, is of no avail, unless there be an organ through which it can shine into the body. If the eye, the organ for enlightening man, be clear, and all its parts do their work, the whole body is full of light; but if the eye be dimmed by films stealing over it, or if, in any other way, it does not fulfil its functions, then the body is full of darkness; the eye misrepresents objects so that they appear not in their proper colours, or size, or place.

35 Take heed therefore that the light which is in thee be not darkness.

36 If thy whole body therefore *be* full of light, having no part dark, the whole shall be full of light, as when † the bright shining of a candle doth give thee light.   † Gr. *a candle by its bright shining.*

35, 36. D. and some old Latin (a, b, c, ff, i) omit verses 35 and 36.

Now the soul has a spiritual eye, which is the conscience, or moral sense; if this eye be in a good and healthy state, then it allows the light of the Lord to shine into it, and enlighten the whole soul with the light of God; but if the soul's eye be evil, if the conscience be defiled or unhealthy, it vitiates the very light of Christ as it shines into the soul. Take, for instance, every form of Antinomianism: it apparently gladly welcomes into the soul the light of Christ as an atoning sacrifice, but not as a sin eradicator; so that the very light of Gospel truth is turned into darkness, for no darkness is greater than the belief that Christ saves us *in* our sins, and not from them. Again, what numbers nowadays teach that sin is not sin, *i.e.*, loses its character of sin, in God's children! whereas the Apostle has warned us very solemnly: " Little children, let no man deceive you; he that doeth righteousness is righteous, even as he is righteous : he that committeth sin is of the devil."

35. "Take heed therefore that the light which is in thee be not darkness." Take heed that the light of Christ shining into thee purify thee, fill thee with the love of God and of thy neighbour, make thee peaceable, gentle, honest, and full of mercy and of good fruits.

36. " If thy whole body therefore be full of light . . . . give thee light." This a difficult place. It evidently takes up the argument of the preceding verse, which makes the nature of the light within a man to depend in one sense on himself. It *seems* to mean that if a man's whole body or self be full of light, having no dark places, the illumination will be like that of a very bright light or lamp within, in the very centre of the room, as distinguished from the light entering by a comparatively small aperture in one side. In times before the invention of glass, the apertures to let in the light must have been small, as the weather had to be excluded, so that the most perfect illumination of an apartment would have

x

37 ¶ And as he spake, a certain Pharisee besought him to dine with him: and he went in, and sat down to meat.

ᵃ Mark vii. 3. 38 And ᵃ when the Pharisee saw *it*, he marvelled that he had not first washed before dinner.

ᵇ Matt. xxiii. 25. 39 ᵇ And the Lord said unto him, Now do ye Pharisees make clean the outside of the cup and

---

been from a bright lamp in the centre. "If, then," the Saviour seems to say, "you see to it that the light shines well into you, and is pure light unmixed with darkness, as that which comes from the eye in its perfect state, then your whole interior shall be as perfectly illuminated with the light of truth as when a bright shining candle leaves no dark corners, but illuminates the whole apartment equally." Whether this be the meaning or not, the true interpretation of the passage must depend upon the fact that the illustration requires that a lamp is supposed to give the most perfect illumination to the interior of a room.

This interpretation which I have given is perfectly consistent with the fact that Christ Himself is the lamp within; so that we have to see that Christ is within us. (2 Cor. xiii. 5.)

37. "And as he spake, a certain Pharisee besought him to dine with him," &c. This incident is peculiar to St. Luke, but not the discourse which the Lord delivers in the house. Much of this, if not all, is to be found in Matt. xxiii., which contains a much longer discourse on the same subject, evidently delivered by the Lord in Jerusalem. I do not see why these denunciations should not have been repeated, and in the same words. The Pharisees everywhere seem to have been of the same formal, hypocritical character, and would require them as much in Galilee or Peræa, as in Jerusalem.

"To dine." Rather, to take the morning meal—to breakfast.

38. "And when the Pharisee saw it, he marvelled," &c. On another occasion the Pharisees brought this accusation against the disciples. (Matt. xv. 1, 2; Mark vii. 3.) I think the fact that the Pharisee marvelled shows that he had not invited the Lord with any malignant purpose.

39. "And the Lord said unto him, Now do ye Pharisees make clean the outside," &c. Ye cleanse yourselves externally by constant washings of your hands, but ye take no pains about the puri-

the platter; but ᵉ your inward part is full of ravening and wickedness. ᵉ Titus i. 15.

40 *Ye* fools, did not he that made that which is without make that which is within also?

41 ᵈ But rather give alms ‖ of such things as ye have; and, behold, all things are clean unto you. ᵈ Is. lviii. 7. Dan. iv. 27. ch. xii. 33.
‖ Or, *as you are able.*

---

41. "Of such things as ye have," rather "of the things within," *i.e.*, the food. Vulg., *Veruntamen quod superest, date eleemosynam.*

fication of your hearts from envy, guile, malice, adulterous thoughts, and covetous desires.

40. "Ye fools, did not he that made that which is without make that which is within also?" If He made that which is without, and ordained that it should be kept pure from ceremonial pollution, did not He make that which is within, *i.e.*, the soul or spirit, and ordain that *it* should be kept pure from the contamination of evil, covetous, defiling thoughts, *i.e.*, "ravening and wickedness."

41. "But rather give alms of such things as ye have; and, behold, all things," &c. Instead of "such things as ye have," the words ought rather to be rendered, rather give alms of that which is "within the cup and platter," *i.e.*, of their contents, give food and refreshment to those who need it, and behold all things are clean unto you. This is one of those very many places which assign to almsgiving (of course if practised for the approval of God, and not for vain glory) an almost expiatory value. Thus this Gospel (xvi. 9), "Make to yourselves friends of the mammon of unrighteousness, that when ye fail they may receive you into everlasting habitations." "Thy prayer and thine alms are come up for a memorial before God" (Acts x. 4). "Come, ye blessed of my Father, inherit the kingdom prepared for you. . . . . for I was an hungred, and ye gave me meat" (Matt. xxv. 34, 35). "Charge them that are rich, ... that they do good, that they be rich in good works, ... laying up in store for themselves a good foundation against the time to come, that they may lay hold on eternal life (1 Tim. vi. 17, 18). (Also Psalm xli. 1, 2; Daniel iv. 27; Matt. v. 7; vi. 3, 4; Luke xii. 32, 33.) Godet paraphrases it well: "Do you wish, then, that these meats and these wines should not be defiled, and should not defile you? Do not think that it is enough

42 ᵉBut woe unto you, Pharisees! for ye tithe mint and rue and all manner of herbs, and pass over judgment and the love of God: these ought ye to have done, and not to leave the other undone.

43 ᶠWoe unto you, Pharisees! for ye love the uppermost seats in the synagogues, and greetings in the markets.

44 ᵍWoe unto you, scribes and Pharisees, hypocrites! ʰfor ye are as graves which appear not, and the men that walk over *them* are not aware *of them*.

ᵉ Matt. xxiii. 23.
ᶠ Matt. xxiii. 6. Mark xii. 38, 39.
ᵍ Matt. xxiii. 27.
ʰ Ps. v. 9.

---

43. C., D., Cursives 13, 64, old Latin (b, q), add "the first places (of reclining) at feasts."

44. "Scribes and pharisees, hypocrites!" So A., D., later Uncials, most Cursives, some old Latin (b, f, i, q), Syriac (Schaaf); but these words omitted in ℵ, B., C., L., a few Uncials, old Latin (a, c, e, ff²), Vulg., Copt., Syriac (Cureton), Arm.

---

for you carefully to wash your hands before eating; there is a surer means: let some poor man partake of them."

42. "But woe unto you, Pharisees! for ye tithe mint and rue and all manner," &c. As if the Lord said: Ye are to be scrupulous in paying to God in His temple service, to the minister of God, and to the poor, the utmost of their dues; but, with all this, ye ought by constant prayer and watchfulness to cultivate within you the spirit of righteousness and love. In the parallel passage in Matthew, instead of judgment and the love of God, we have judgment, mercy, and faith; but if men cultivate the love of God, that love will necessarily be accompanied by mercy and faith.

43. "Woe unto you, Pharisees! for ye love the uppermost seats in the synagogues." Some must have the uppermost seats, but what the Lord here denounces is the love of such distinctions. The office of teaching the Word of God ought to humble a man, seeing that he has to set forth such holy truth, seeing that he is bound to live to his teaching, seeing that he has to give account for every word which he teaches.

"Greetings in the markets." As St. Matthew explains it, greetings such as Rabbi, Rabbi, denoting their high place in the theocracy.

44. "Woe unto you, scribes and Pharisees, hypocrites! for ye are as graves which," &c. As the graves which had nothing to dis-

CHAP. XI.]   YE LADE MEN WITH BURDENS.   309

45 ¶ Then answered one of the lawyers, and said unto him, Master, thus saying thou reproachest us also.

46 And he said, Woe unto you also, *ye* lawyers! ¹for ye lade men with burdens grievous to be borne, and ye yourselves touch not the burdens with one of your fingers.

¹ Matt. xxiii. 4.

47 ᵏ Woe unto you! for ye build the sepulchres of the prophets, and your fathers killed them.

ᵏ Matt. xxiii. 29.

48 Truly ye bear witness that ye allow the deeds of your fathers: for they indeed killed them, and ye build their sepulchres.

---

tinguish them polluted those who walked over them, so those who came in contact with these pretenders to righteousness were morally the worse for intercourse with them.

45. "Then answered one of the lawyers, and said unto him, Master, thus saying," &c. The Pharisees were a sect, but the lawyers a profession. They were the authorized teachers and expounders of the law. They, by their teaching, kept up the authority of the traditional interpretations of the law which practically made it void.

46. "And he said, Woe unto you also, ye lawyers, for ye lade men with burdens," &c. The Mosaic law itself was a hard burden, at least so St. Peter said when remonstrating with the Pharisaic party among the Christians; he asks, "Now, therefore, why tempt ye God to put a yoke upon the neck of the disciples which neither we nor our fathers were able to bear?" If, then, the law, pure and simple, could be thus described, with what weight must it have pressed down upon God's people when the load of traditions was added to it!

From this place we gather the hypocrisy of the teachers. They taught what they took no care to observe in their own lives. Theophylact (quoted in Williams) says: "As often as the teacher does what he teaches, he lightens the load, by offering himself for an example."

47, 48. "Woe unto you! for ye build the sepulchres of the prophets, and your fathers killed them. Truly ye bear," &c. This is spoken in deep irony. It would have been an act of virtue to build and adorn the sepulchres of prophets whom their fathers persecuted

310   I WILL SEND THEM PROPHETS.   [ST. LUKE.

49 Therefore also said the wisdom of God, [1] I will send them prophets and apostles, and *some* of them they shall slay and persecute:

[1] Matt. xxiii. 34.

---

and killed, if they were ready to welcome and listen to the prophets whom God was then sending: but if, in like manner as their fathers had done, they persecuted and killed the true prophets of their own time, then they acted with most shameless hypocrisy. Their building of the prophets' sepulchres could not be allowed by God or man to be a repudiation of their fathers' deeds; it must rather be taken as approving such deeds. As Godet well puts it: "By a bold turn, which translates the external act into a thought opposed to its ostensible object, but in accordance with its real spirit, Jesus says to them: 'Your fathers killed, ye bury; therefore ye continue, and finish their work.'" [1]

49. "Therefore also said the wisdom of God, I will send them prophets," &c. This is understood as if it were a quotation from the Old Testament, or from some lost prophetical book. Most probably the latter. If the former, it must be a reminiscence of 2 Chron. xxiv. 18-22. So Alford; but if the reader refers to this place, I think he will not consider it likely. There is a similar passage, but not exactly the same, in Matt. xxiii. 34; but there the Lord assumes to Himself the sending of the "prophets, wise

---

[1] There are enormous rock-hewn tombs yet remaining in the neighbourhood of Jerusalem. Mr. Williams thus describes what are now called "the tombs of the Prophets." "Through a long gallery, first serpentine and then direct, but widening as you advance, one passes into a circular hall, rising into a conical dome, about twenty-four feet in diameter. From this hall run three passages, communicating with two semicircular galleries in connection with the hall, the outer one of which contains in its back wall numerous recesses for the corpses, radiating towards the centre hall. No inscriptions or remains of any kind have been discovered to elucidate the mysteries of these mansions of the dead." Dr. Thompson, to whom I owe this extract, says: "The prodigious extent of these quarries and tombs is one of the most striking indications of a great city, and of a long succession of prosperity which the environs of Jerusalem furnish."

IT SHALL BE REQUIRED. 311

50 That the blood of all the prophets, which was shed from the foundation of the world, may be required of this generation;

51 ᵐ From the blood of Abel unto ⁿ the blood of Zacharias, which perished between the altar and the temple: verily I say unto you, It shall be required of this generation.

ᵐ Gen. iv. 8.
ⁿ 2 Chron. xxiv. 20, 21.

52 ᵒ Woe unto you, lawyers! for ye have taken

ᵒ Matt. xxiii. 13.

---

men, and scribes." If they are the words of no inferior prophet, but of the Lord Himself, then He here speaks of Himself as the "Wisdom of God." Godet supposes that the Lord has in His mind, and gives the sense of Prov. i. 20-31, "Wisdom uttereth her voice," &c.; but there is this difficulty, that throughout that passage Wisdom does not speak of sending any prophets or messengers, but of speaking herself in her own person. So, on the whole, we must consider them either the words of the Lord Jesus Himself, the wisdom of God, or of some one of the numerous prophets whose writings have not come down to us.

50. "That the blood of all the prophets, which was shed from the foundation of the world," &c. Because the truth and love which was very partially set forth in the messages of former prophets, was concentrated, as it were, in the words of Christ and of His Apostles—because the credentials in the shape of miracles wrought by former prophets were far exceeded by the Resurrection of the Lord, and the great Pentecostal sign; so that as that generation sinned against infinitely greater light, so they were visited by a far more tremendous punishment. (See my note on Matt. xxiii. 35.)

"Zacharias." No doubt the son of Jehoiada. Abel and Zacharias seem singled out from the rest because their blood was especially said to cry for vengeance. Thus Gen. iv.: "The voice of thy brother's blood crieth unto me from the ground." And in 2 Chron. xxiv. 29, it is said of Jehoiada that when he was martyred by Joash, under circumstances of the blackest ingratitude, he said, "The Lord look upon it and require it."

52. "Woe unto you, lawyers! for ye have taken away the key of knowledge . . . . ye hindered." The lawyers, who claimed to be the authorized interpreters of the law, by their traditions and false

away the key of knowledge: ye entered not in yourselves,
and them that were entering in ye || hindered.

|| Or, *forbad.*

53 And as he said these things unto them, the scribes and the Pharisees began to urge *him* vehemently, and to provoke him to speak of many things:

54 Laying wait for him, and ᵖ seeking to catch something out of his mouth, that they might accuse him.

ᵖ Mark xii. 13.

---

53. "As he said these things unto them." So. A., D., later Uncials, almost all Cursives, old Latin, Vulg., Syriac (Cur. and Schaaf), Arm., Æth.; but ℵ, B., C., L., 33, Copt., read, "when he had gone out thence."

54. "Seeking." So A., C., D., later Uncials, almost all Cursives, old Latin, Vulg., &c.; but omitted by ℵ, B., L., and a few Cursives, &c.

"That they might accuse him." So A., C., D., later Uncials, Cursives, &c.; omitted by ℵ, B., L., Copt., Æth.

---

expositions obscured its true meaning. The true meaning of the law was either (1) its literal, plain, common-sense meaning, which would have convinced men of sin, and so make them ready to welcome such an one as the Lord, Who engaged to deliver them from the power of sin ; or (2) it meant the spiritual meaning which still more directly set forth Christ as the hope of Israel. By neither of these meanings did the Scribes themselves give the true interpretation of Scripture, and they hindered others from perceiving it, and so being prepared for the coming of the Christ.

53, 54. " And as he said these things . . . . that they might accuse him." On no occasion apparently were they so exasperated at the way in which he exposed their hypocrisy. This scene seems to have taken place after He had left the house of the Pharisee. Their frantic looks and angry gestures and vociferation seem to have collected together the "innumerable multitude" mentioned in the next verse.

CHAP. XII.

IN ᵃthe mean time, when there were gathered together an innumerable multitude of people, insomuch that they trode one upon another, he began to

ᵃ Matt. xvi. 6.
Mark viii. 15.

---

1. In the mean time, when there were gathered together . . . . hypocrisy." The following warnings—for warnings they all are (at least to the 10th or 12th verses)—were all delivered by the Lord on various occasions, and in most cases, with a different object in view, which we shall draw attention to as we proceed. Indeed, this applies to the whole chapter. Dean Burgon has an observation on this well worthy of serious thought: "A strange circumstance it certainly is that of the 59 verses which compose the present chapter, no less than thirty-five should prove to have been delivered *on quite different occasions*, and not in single verses either, but by seven, eight, or even ten verses at a time. He must have a very unworthy notion of the dignity of the Gospel, who can make light of a fact like this. . . . Let us be well persuaded that over and above the advantage to be derived from every passage so repeated, considered in and by itself, there is a further use provided by its repetition ; discoverable, however, only by him who will diligently seek for it by minute comparison, exceeding watchfulness, and patient thought."

"He began to say unto his disciples first of all." He spoke directly to the disciples, but so that the multitude (called "an innumerable multitude ") should hear and profit.

"First of all." By this He emphasized the warning against hypocrisy as the most important of all, because, no doubt, the leaven of hypocrisy was the most subtle and destructive.

"Beware of the leaven of the Pharisees, which is hypocrisy." All sects who, as a body, make a profession, avowed or tacit, of greater or deeper religion than the majority, are in the greatest danger of falling into this soul-destroying vice. The Pharisees, whose very name implied separation, separated themselves and held themselves aloof from the mass of the Jews as being stricter observers of the

say unto his disciples first of all, ᵇBeware ye of the leaven
ᵇ Matt. xvi. 12. of the Pharisees, which is hypocrisy.

---

law, and of that which was held in almost the same estimation as the law, the body of tradition by which it was explained. Every man amongst them who professed to be a sincere member of the sect was bound to join with his fellows in making a stricter profession of obedience than the rest of the people, for such was the one only reason for his existence as a Pharisee. But the strain of making the inward life consistent with such an outward profession could be kept up by a very few. The great majority made no effort to cleanse that which was within, that it might accord with the ceremonial cleanness of that which was without, and so there was an ever-widening difference between the inner state of the heart and the outward apparent sanctity: and this was the hypocrisy which leavened the whole Pharisaic sect, and spread its noxious influence far and wide over the whole nation.

This evil spirit is ever reappearing in the Christian Church, and in all parts of it; particularly where a higher profession of what is called Christian experience or spirituality is required for those who would be members, or admitted to Communion. There is particular danger of fostering this spirit in what are called class meetings, if such meetings are held for the relation of Christian experience—each person being called upon to relate the dealings of God with his or her individual soul. Persons thus called upon would be more than human if they were not under the constant temptation of concealing what is in the least degree discreditable, and of dressing up what is ordinary and common-place; and all this breeds unreality.

The clergy, I need hardly say, have constant daily need to realize this warning of the Lord, for their very calling as ministers of Christ requires a higher standard—a standard which may be observed punctually in the outer life and neglected in the inner one of secret prayer and devout meditation and self-examination.

At the same time, it must be remembered that though we must constantly put Christians on their guard against this vice, this must be done in general terms. To qualify (as Quesnel says) a man to tax others with hypocrisy, he must be able to know the bottom of the heart as Jesus did. We must remember that there may be, and often is, very flagrant inconsistency, with little or no real hypocrisy.

2 ^c For there is nothing covered, that shall not be revealed; neither hid, that shall not be known. ^c Matt. x. 26. Mark iv. 22.

3 Therefore whatsoever ye have spoken in darkness shall be heard in the light; and that which ye have spoken in the ear in closets shall be proclaimed upon the housetops. ch. viii. 17.

---

2. "For there is nothing covered, that shall not be revealed; neither hid, that shall not be known." This saying is often repeated by the Lord, and with different meanings. In Matt. x. 26 it is said in deprecation of the fear of men. In another part of this Gospel (viii. 17) it seems to refer to the spread or divulgence of all and every part of the truth of God; but here it seems to form the natural sequel to the solemn warning against hypocrisy. Secret sins, secret selfishness, secret insincerity, shall all be exposed in the full light of the coming of the Son of Man. So that if men would only believe that the day is fast approaching when the secrets of all hearts shall be disclosed, they would earnestly set to work to put away all guile, all malice, hypocrisy, to be as pure in heart and honest in intention as they desire to seem blameless in outward life.

But though this application, as against hypocrisy, is manifestly both true and necessary, yet the next verse seems to demand that we consider these two verses as parallel to, and so having something of the same significance as those in Luke viii. 16, 17. For we read there:—

3. "Therefore whatsoever ye have spoken in darkness shall be heard in the light," &c. Think not that anything ye say or do can be permanently hidden. On the contrary, it shall spread and be known far and wide. You will be put into such a position in My Church (Luke viii. 16) that your least and most secret words and actions shall be like the rays of a lamp diffusing light through the whole Church. Or the Saviour may mean by the "darkness" and the secresy of the "closets" the comparative obscurity of their present teaching in Galilee; and by "the light" and "the housetops" their proclamation of the truth in the great centres of human concourse and power, Alexandria, Athens, Rome.

The reader will, of course, remember that the houses in Syria were flat-roofed, and the streets very narrow, so that, at a given

4 ᵈAnd I say unto you ᵉmy friends, Be not afraid of them that kill the body, and after that have no more that they can do.

5 But I will forewarn you whom ye shall fear: Fear him, which after he hath killed hath power to cast into hell; yea, I say unto you, Fear him.

ᵈ Is. li. 7, 8, 12, 13. Jer. i. 8. Matt. x. 28.
ᵉ John xv. 14, 15.

---

5. "Hell," not "hades," as in Luke xvi. 23, but "Gehenna."

signal, the roofs would be covered with eager listeners in numbers far greater than could possibly be assembled in the streets below.

4, 5. " And I say unto you, my friends, Be not afraid of them . . . yea, I say unto you, Fear him." The connection seems to be, " What ye have spoken in secret shall be heard far and wide, and it shall draw down upon you the bitter wrath of those in power. They shall persecute you and put you to cruel deaths. But fear them not. They have done their worst when they have slain you. All the indignities which they can inflict on your mangled bodies will not delay for one moment the resurrection of those bodies in the likeness of Mine. Fear them not, but fear Him Who has given you to suffer on My behalf. Fear lest, through fear of men, you fall away and deny Me; for whereas the wrath of your persecutors extends only to your death, His wrath can extend through eternity.

" Fear him who hath power to cast into Gehenna: yea, I say unto you, Fear him." We have ventured to paraphrase this awful place, simply for the purpose of showing how it carries on the sense of verse 3; but, taken as setting forth a general truth, that all, even those whom Christ calls His friends, must have the fear as well as the love of God ruling in their hearts, it is above all exposition, for no words even of the Lord are plainer. We can only direct attention to the plain lessons it teaches, and to the extraordinary seriousness and earnestness of the Lord in saying it.

It teaches us that the highest favour of God does not absolve us from the fear of God; for here Christ warns, not His enemies the Pharisees and Scribes, not the fickle multitude, but his disciples— those whose salvation was so far assured that He could say to them, " Ye have not chosen Me, but I have chosen you and ordained you, that ye should bring forth fruit, and that your fruit should remain." To these He says, " I will forewarn you when ye shall fear."

It teaches us also that in sinful beings, or in beings bearing about

6 Are not five sparrows sold for two ‖ farthings, and not one of them is forgotten before God? ‖ See Matt. x. 29.

---

a remainder of sin as we do, the fear of God cannot altogether be dissociated from the justice of God. We have to do with an exceedingly just Judge, Who though He may not and will not condemn us to condign punishment, has it in His power so to do, and the Lord here tells us very plainly that our fear is to distinctly take into account this tremendous power. Some may dislike this, but I cannot see how else the Lord's words are to be received. The slavish fear which love casts out cannot be the true godly fear which the Lord presses here upon St. John as well as on all else. No faith, as far as I can see, can absolve from this fear, for the Apostle says: "Thou standest by faith; be not high, but fear" (Rom. xi. 20). In fact, it is this fear which makes love to be holy reverential love, and which saves faith from becoming forward and presuming.

And, then, as to the seriousness and earnestness with which the Lord here inculcates this fear. It is scarcely paralleled in any other of His sayings, "I say unto you, my friends, fear not them." "I will forewarn you whom ye shall fear." "Fear him." "Yea, I say unto you, Fear him."

And yet the popular fanaticism of the day, out of the pretence of honouring the finished work of Christ, pushes aside this fear, preaches a Christianity in which it has no place, condemns those who teach it, and brands as unsaved those who feel it. I need hardly say that it is one of the characteristics of the Catholic Church to put it in the foreground of her teaching.

And now the Lord, having taught His friends to fear, as emphatically teaches them to "fear not."

"Are not five sparrows sold for two farthings, and not one of them . . . . more value than many sparrows." The providence of God takes into full account the smallest matters as much as the greatest, for insomuch as the whole course of nature and of human life is made up of an infinite number of small things, and all interdependent, the providence of God would not be all-observing and all-ruling, if it omitted anything, for the smallest omission might put all things else out of gear, as it were.

But is there not a course of nature? Do not all things take place in a natural order, according to (so-called) laws of nature? They may do, but this does not for a moment exclude God's omni-

7 But even the very hairs of your head are all numbered. Fear not therefore: ye are of more value than many sparrows.

8 ᶠAlso I say unto you, Whosoever shall confess me before men, him shall the Son of man also confess before the angels of God:

ᶠ Matt. x. 32.
Mark viii. 38.
2 Tim. ii. 12.
1 John ii. 23.

---

presence, and superintendence, and control, and power of altering such course, though He does not allow us to see how and when He does so. This is the mystery of God's providence. There is a seemingly unbroken chain of cause and effect, and yet not one of the men who deny God's overruling providence would now be in existence if it were not for that providence warding off death and preserving life. If not a single sparrow is now alive except by the express will of God, no more is any human being; and if God takes account of the hairs of our heads, much more does He of our life, both temporal and eternal, and all things that affect either the one or the other. Now, in view of all this, Christ says to the Apostles, and through them to every one of God's children, "Fear not." Nothing can happen to you, no matter how trivial, except as foreseen by Me and controlled by Me; and if you but commit your way to Me and love Me, everything shall work together for your good.

There seems a slight touch of irony in the words, "Ye are of more value than many sparrows." Though all things are equally controlled and ordered by God, all things are not of equal value in His sight. That which He prizes most of all created things in this world is the soul of the Christian, which has surrendered its will to His, and desires to be the instrument of His purposes. It is the price of His Son's Blood. It is the habitation of His Spirit, and nothing can exceed its preciousness in His eyes.

8, 9. "Also I say unto you, Whosoever shall confess . . . denied before the angels of God." The confession of Christ by the Apostles was before the heads of their religion, the chief priests who had crucified Him. It was before rulers and kings, before the philosophers of Athens, the libertines of Corinth. It was the bold, unflinching avowal that the world was *saved* by the cruel and disgraceful death of a Jew, one of a nation regarded with pretty much the same contempt as they are now. They who made this confession always made it at the risk of their lives. This confession

9 But he that denieth me before men shall be denied before the angels of God.

---

of Christ is yet dangerous to life even in this nineteenth century. No man in a Mahometan country, brought up in the national faith, can embrace the Christian religion except at the risk of his life—at least it was so a very few years ago.

In Christian England the confession of Christ has assumed a different form, but it equally requires sincerity and courage to make it: a Christian has now to profess the creating power of God amongst Evolutionists, and the all-ruling providence of God in the company of unbelieving Scientists. In some companies he has to brave the ridicule attaching to the belief in miracles. In the society of filthy-minded men he has to uphold the purity of Christ, and in the society of worldlings he may be called upon to uphold the rooted antagonism between the world and Christ. These may seem very poor and mild ways of confessing Christ compared to what our forefathers in the faith had to endure; but they all try the metal of the Christian. If he is faithful in confessing Christ in these comparatively little matters, he may have a good hope that God would, if called upon, give him grace to make a bolder and more public and dangerous confession if it was laid upon him so to do.

Such is the confession of Christ; and the reward answers to it: "Whosoever shall confess me before men, him shall the Son of man also confess before the angels of God."

"Before the angels of God," *i.e.*, before the court of God—before His special ministers. Notice the extraordinary reality with which the Lord here invests the unseen world of angels. To be honoured before them and receive their applause infinitely outweighs the contempt and persecution of a condemned world. It is to be noticed that in the parallel place of St. Matthew (x. 32) the confession on the part of the Saviour and His corresponding denial is "before the Father." This seems to show that the two sayings of the Lord, though parallel, are different, and come from different traditional sources. Neither of them could possibly have been substituted for the other.

10. "And whosoever shall speak a word against the Son of man, it shall be forgiven him: . . . not be forgiven." Saul of Tarsus spake very many blasphemous words against the Son of man, *i.e.*,

10 And ^g whosoever shall speak a word against the Son of man, it shall be forgiven him: but unto him that blasphemeth against the Holy Ghost it shall not be forgiven.

^g Matt. xii. 31, 32. Mark iii. 28. 1 John v. 16.

11 ^h And when they bring you unto the synagogues, and *unto* magistrates, and powers, take ye no thought how or what thing ye shall answer, or what ye shall say:

^h Matt. x. 19. Mark xiii. 11. ch. xxi. 14.

12 For the Holy Ghost shall teach you in the same hour what ye ought to say.

---

against His claims to be the Christ, and even compelled others to do the same, and yet it was forgiven him; but he had never seen the Lord, he had never conversed with Him. He had never spent so much as one day in His company. If he had had full opportunity of knowing the goodness and holiness of the Lord and the truth and genuineness of His miracles, and yet had pronounced His goodness to be hypocrisy, and His miracles to be due to the power of the evil one, then humanly speaking, there would have been no hope for him. He would have come as perilously near to the blasphemy against the Holy Ghost as we can predicate of any human being. "The sin which is for ever unpardonable, is not the rejection of the truth, in consequence of a misunderstanding, such as that of so many unbelievers who confound the Gospel with this or that false form which is nothing better than a caricature of it. It is hatred of holiness as such,—a hatred which leads men to make the Gospel a work of pride or fraud, and to ascribe it to the spirit of evil. This is not to sin against Jesus personally: it is to insult the Divine principle which actuated Him. It is hatred of goodness itself in its supreme manifestation" (Godet).

11, 12. "And when they bring you unto the synagogues, and unto magistrates, ... what ye ought to say." Thus it is said of St. Peter, when brought before the high priests and their council, that he was "filled with the Holy Ghost" (Acts iv. 8), and of St. Stephen that he was "full of the Holy Ghost" (vii. 55). The Holy Ghost was needed, not so much for their own defence, as that their judges and accusers should have the truth of Christ set before them in a way which would either convince or convict them.

13 ¶ And one of the company said unto him, Master, speak to my brother, that he divide the inheritance with me.

14 And he said unto him, [1] Man, who made me a judge or a divider over you?   [1] John xviii. 36.

---

13. "And one of the company said unto him." Either "one out of the crowd (ὄχλου) said unto him." So ℵ, B., F., L., 33; or "one said unto him out of the crowd," so A., D., later Uncials, most Cursives, Vulg. (Cod Amiat), Sah., Copt., Syriac, &c.

This was a more absolute promise of the guidance of the Holy Spirit than that which was given to them in the matter of their preaching; and naturally so, for in preaching they could choose their time, and place, and audience; whereas, when taken before magistrates, they had to answer for their lives before men of far greater worldly wisdom than themselves. Again, in many cases, such as that of Paul before Felix, they had skilful advocates learned in the law hired against them, to whom they could oppose nothing but what would excite prejudice and ridicule, and it seems meet that both for the sake of themselves and of the truth they should in such cases have a special and very unreserved promise of Divine help.

13, 14. "And one of the company said unto him . . . . or a divider over you?" This was a very natural interruption; one of the crowd, impressed with the wisdom of the Lord's words, and the authority with which he spoke, and having a grievance against his brother, probably the head of the family, that he had kept him out of his share in the inheritance, asks the Lord to arbitrate. His request, and the answer to it, changes the whole subject of the discourse; at least till verse 34. Hitherto it had been on the confession of Christ; now it is upon the danger to the soul of all love of this world's goods—nay, even of all anxiety about them. Commentators notice that the Lord's answer exactly corresponds to that given to Moses by one of the two Israelites he was desirous to reconcile (Exod. ii. 14): "Who made thee a prince and a judge over us?" "Then Moses was by anticipation assuming his office as the ruler of a temporal kingdom, but this Christ refuses, because *His* kingdom was not of this world." I cannot but think that in this case the Lord disclaims, on behalf of His ministers, all temporal rule, such as that of the Bishop of Rome over the States of the Church, the prince Bishops of Germany, and such offices of temporal sovereignty as occupy the time and energies of His ministers with

15 And he said unto them, ᵏ Take heed, and beware of covetousness: for a man's life consisteth not in the abundance of the things which he possesseth.

16 And he spake a parable unto them, saying, The ground of a certain rich man brought forth plentifully:

ᵏ 1 Tim. vi. 7, &c.

---

15. "Covetousness." So E., F., G., H., S., &c., and most Cursives; but ℵ, A., B., D., K., L., M., Q., R., and more than forty Cursives, old Latin, Vulg., Sah., Copt., Syriac, &c., read, "all covetousness."

---

secular business. Still it may often be the duty of the office-bearers of His Church to arbitrate in cases where they clearly see their way to the establishment of peace in families or societies.

15. "And he said unto them, Take heed, and beware of covetousness: . . . which he possesseth." The meaning is somewhat difficult. Read in the light of the succeeding parable it seems to signify that amongst the many things which a rich man may possess he cannot reckon his life, because it may be required by God at any time, and thus he loses every earthly possession along with it. Or it may convey a general truth independent of the parable, which is that a man's life, either his present enjoyment of life, or his true life, his eternal and spiritual life, does not consist in the abundance of the things which he possesses. Let him amass riches ever so much, even whilst he possesses them he may neither enjoy them nor really profit by them; he is not certain of the enjoyment of them for a single day; whereas, if he does not set his heart upon them, so as to tenaciously grasp and hold them, he may make them his own for ever by being rich towards God. If he parts with them now he shall find them hereafter.

16. "And he spake a parable unto them, saying, The ground of a certain rich man," &c. The groundwork of the parable with which our Lord now enforces His warning against covetousness seems to be found in the apocryphal Book of Ecclesiasticus. Indeed, the resemblances, both verbal and material, are so striking that we can hardly resist the conclusion that He either honoured that book by taking His illustration from it; or that the Spirit which was without measure in Him was also given to the Son of Sirach, that he should give us what, if not to be appealed to for *doctrine*, is yet very profitable indeed for "reproof, for correction, for instruction in righteousness." The passage runs: "There is that waxeth rich by

CHAP. XII.]   I WILL PULL DOWN MY BARNS.   323

17 And he thought within himself, saying, What shall I do, because I have no room where to bestow my fruits?

18 And he said, This will I do: I will pull down my barns,

---

18. "My fruits." So ℵ, A., D., most later Uncials, several Cursives; but B., L., X., some ten Cursives, Sah., Copt., Arm., Æth., read, "my corn."

his wariness and pinching, and this is the portion of his reward: whereas he saith, I have found rest, and now will eat continually of my goods: and yet he knoweth not what time shall come upon him, and that he must leave these things to others and die" (Ecclus. xi. 18, 19).

"The ground of a certain rich man brought forth plentifully." It is not said that he amassed his wealth by hard or unfair means. On the contrary, his profits arose from that over which he had apparently no control—the extraordinary fertility of his ground. If, however, that fertility was owing, under God, to himself, by the skill with which he cultivated it, this was to his credit, and would not be blamed by Him Who had laid it upon mankind to replenish the earth and subdue it; and had also said, "Whatsoever thy hand findeth to do, do it with thy might."

17. "And he thought within himself, saying, What shall I do, ... where to bestow my fruits?" This was the beginning of his sin—at least the first indication of his rooted covetousness. He takes counsel with himself, how he is to preserve the profits of his lands for himself and, as the sequel shows, only for himself.

18. "And he said, This will I do: I will pull down my barns, and build greater; .... my goods." It seems never to have crossed his mind—indeed, we may be certain that the idea never for a moment suggested itself to him, "If God has given so much to me, what can I give to others? I have many more goods (ἀγαθά) than what I can enjoy myself, what more good can I do to my poorer neighbours?" His conduct stands in remarkable contrast with an eminent servant of God of the last century, who had an income of some thirty pounds a year, of which he gave away three to the poor; and when his income was doubled, instead of saying to himself, "What greater comfort can I procure for myself by this increase of income?" he said, on the contrary, "I have lived in great comfort, and in reality wanted nothing on my thirty

and build greater; and there will I bestow all my fruits and my goods.

¹ Eccles. xi. 9.
1 Cor. xv. 32.
James v. 5.

19 And I will say to my soul, ¹ Soul, thou hast much goods laid up for many years; take thine ease, eat, drink, *and* be merry.

---

pounds, now I shall be able to give thirty pounds more to those in distress."

"And there will I bestow all my fruits," &c. This man was a landowner or agriculturist; for the Jews, at least those living in Palestine, were not then a commercial nation. If the Lord had laid the scene in England, He would probably have made a slight alteration in the parable. He would probably have said: "The business of a certain rich merchant, or tradesman, was exceedingly profitable;" or, "The practice of a certain professional man, a physician, or lawyer, was very extensive." He would not have made such an one talk of pulling down and rebuilding barns, but he would have made the man speak to himself about investments, securities, percentages of interest, and such like, for these are the things which, though the mention of them may sound vulgar, most assuredly answer to the pulling down and building of barns in the Lord's time; and if any man ever did, the Lord spake to the men of the time and adapted Himself to their mode of life; and if there is to be any reality in what we build upon His words, we must do the same.

19. "And I will say to my soul, Soul, thou hast much goods laid up for many years," &c. The guilt or the innocence of much of this speech depends entirely upon the spirit in which it was said. And the Lord tells us at the conclusion that it was said in a godless, selfish spirit. It would have been perfectly right if he had said, " I have got not only a competency, but an increasing income. I will devote no more of the time which God may give me to moneymaking; I will rest and take my ease from this, and see what good I can do with what I have already accumulated;" but when he says to his soul, "Eat, drink, and be merry," he says what any libertine would say.

Though few Christians would say this even to themselves, is it not what they secretly think and hope? "I will now rest on my oars. I will enjoy life. I can now afford this, that, or the other

CHAP. XII.] THOU FOOL. 325

20 But God said unto him, *Thou* fool, this night ‖ ᵐ thy soul shall be required of thee: ⁿ then whose shall those things be, which thou hast provided?

‖ Or, *do they require thy soul.*
ᵐ Job xx. 22. & xxvii. 8. Ps. lii. 7. James iv. 14.
ⁿ Ps. xxxix. 6. Jer. xvii. 11.

indulgence." Now this rest or indulgence may be perfectly innocent, but to save the thought from guilt, it requires a distinct calling to mind of the will of God with reference to ourselves, a committal of our way to God, a thorough belief and acknowledgment that our times are in His hand, that what He has given us is not for ourselves only, but for our fellow members in Christ's body, that the secular life, even if lived in a godly Christian way is not the highest life, and such things.

20. "But God said unto him, Thou fool, this night thy soul shall be required," &c. "God said unto him." It is asked how God said this. Did He speak directly to this man, did He afford him a presentiment, or a dream? But God may not have spoken to the man at all so that he should hear Him. It may simply represent God's judgment upon the man, *i.e.*, upon his folly, and God's will that he should surrender up his soul to its account at once. Thus God is represented as saying to the King of Assyria what He had determined about him, though it never was intended to reach his ears. (Isaiah xxxvii. 28, 29.)

"Thou fool." He was probably a man of much worldly prudence and foresight, but inasmuch as he was alive only to his temporal interests, and blind to his eternal ones, God Who inhabits Eternity knew his extreme folly.

"This night thy soul shall be required of thee," or rather, "They shall require thy soul of thee." Theophylact (quoted in Trench) has a remarkable passage upon this. "For like pitiless exactors of tribute, terrible angels shall require thy soul from thee unwilling, and through love of life resisting. For from the righteous his soul is not *required*, but he commits it to God and the Father of Spirits, pleased and rejoicing, nor finds it hard to lay it down, for the body lies upon it as a light burden. But the sinner who has enfleshed his soul, and made it earthy, has prepared to render its divulsion from the body more hard: wherefore it is said to be required of him, as a disobedient debtor that is delivered to pitiless exactors."

21 So *is* he that layeth up treasure for himself, °and is not rich toward God.

22 ¶ And he said unto his disciples, Therefore I say unto you, ᵖ Take no thought for your life, what ye shall eat; neither for the body, what ye shall put on.

° Matt. vi. 20. ver. 33. 1 Tim. vi. 18, 19. James ii. 5.
ᵖ Matt. vi. 25.

"Then whose shall these things be which thou hast provided?" By this question God seems to imply that he might have retained them, or rather more than retained them—have received them again in the other world with God's abundant interest added to them; whereas now he has lost them with respect of both worlds. He can now take nothing away with him to the other world; and what St. James calls the canker of his gold and silver unused for God, "and their rust, shall be a witness against him and shall eat his flesh as it were fire" (v. 3).

21. "So is he that layeth up treasure for himself, and is not rich towards God." That is, he is both to be stripped of every thing by death at any moment, and to wake up in the eternal world poor beyond expression, having no deeds of faith or love set against his name in God's books; whereas his poor neighbour, because rich in faith, is "heir of the kingdom which God hath prepared for them that love him" (James ii. 5).

Such is this parable. It is very awful in its reticence. It is not said that he is taken to a place of punishment; nor is it mentioned that his riches pass into the hands of a stranger. He simply lays up treasure for himself, and loses all: whereas if he had been unselfish—if he had, in the words of the Apostle, "done good, and been rich in good works, ready to distribute, willing to communicate"—he might have laid up for himself "a good foundation against the time to come" (1 Tim. vi. 17).

22. "And he said unto his disciples, Therefore I say unto you, Take no thought," &c. These precepts following seem not to be said to the multitude, but to the *disciples*, *i.e.*, to the twelve, or those who followed Him as did the twelve. "They are conceived in a higher tone of unworldliness than the parable which had just been delivered to the people. They are not merely to beware of covetousness, they are to "take no thought [*i.e.*, no anxious thought] for their life." And so the words have a general application.

23 The life is more than meat, and the body *is more* than raiment.

24 Consider the ravens: for they neither sow nor reap; which neither have storehouse nor barn; and ᑫ God feedeth them: how much more are ye better than the fowls?

ᑫ Job xxxviii. 41. Ps. cxlvii. 9.

"Take no thought," rather be not anxious, or as we say, "worried." Archbishop Trench remarks that "take no thought" is a mischievous translation. "It sounds like an exaggeration of the precept of faith, and by the help of assuming that it is so, and the consequent impossibility of carrying out the precept, men justify to themselves the whole extent of their unfaithful anxieties and cares."

Calvin makes a good remark upon the general application to all Christians. "Each of us ought to labour as far as his calling requires and the Lord commands, and each of us ought to be led by his own wants to calling upon God. Christ does not forbid every kind of care, but only what arises from distrust. 'Be not anxious,' says He; that belongs to those who tremble for fear of poverty or hunger, as if they were to be in want of food every moment."

23. "The life is more than meat, and the body than raiment." "He had forbidden them to be excessively anxious about the way in which life might be supported, and now he assigns the reason. The Lord Who has given life itself will not suffer us to want what is necessary for its support; and certainly we do no small dishonour to God, when we fail to trust that He will give us necessary food or clothing; as if He had thrown us on the earth at random."

24. "Consider the ravens: for they neither sow nor reap . . . . better than the fowls?" In the parallel passage in St. Matthew, the fowls of the air are mentioned. Here the ravens are particularized, probably because of the words of the Psalmist, "He feedeth the young ravens which call upon Him." It is said also that the Lord speaks of the young ravens, as they are soon deserted by their parents, and have more difficulty in procuring subsistence, because they feed on flesh or carrion.

"God feedeth them." There is no such thing recognized in Scripture as "laws of nature," by which the various creatures are

25 And which of you with taking thought can add to his stature one cubit?

26 If ye then be not able to do that thing which is least, why take ye thought for the rest?

27 Consider the lilies how they grow: they toil not, they

---

sustained. God is here and elsewhere represented to us as feeding them Himself, "He giveth food to all flesh." He may employ secondary means but He must Himself be present with these secondary means, or they would not continue in action for a single day. And in this respect the Bible is infinitely more philosophical than modern books of science: for these books represent the present state of things as carried on by laws themselves, whereas a law, being an unconscious rule or limitation, can do nothing of itself. It must be kept in action by a will, *i.e.*, an Intelligence, which considering the boundless field it has to occupy, we can hold to be nothing less than the Supreme Will.

25. "And which of you with taking thought can add one cubit?" There is some difficulty in settling whether our Lord here alludes to the increase of the height of the body, or the increase of the term of life. By no carefulness or thought, however intense, can we add the smallest increase to our height; by no thought or care can we add to our term of life when the time decreed by God for our departure hence has arrived. Eusebius (quoted in "Catena Aurea") seems to recognize both. "If no one has by his own skill contrived a bodily stature for himself, but cannot even add the shortest delay to the prefixed limit of his time of life, why should we be vainly anxious about the necessaries of life?"

26. "If ye then be not able to do that thing which is least, why take ye thought for the rest?" Our stature, or the term of our life, trifling things though they seem, are predetermined by God—so fixed that we cannot alter them in the least. If, then, all that we are is so ordered by God, why cannot we resign ourselves to God altogether, with the thought that He who has thus ordered our stature and our allotted time here has ordered all things belonging to us, so that if we but look to Him and do our duty, all will be well both here and hereafter?

27. "Consider the lilies how they grow: they toil not, they spin not." The Lord's argument requires that these should be the wild

spin not; and yet I say unto you, that Solomon in all his glory was not arrayed like one of these.

28 If then God so clothe the grass, which is to day in the field, and to morrow is cast into the oven; how much more *will he clothe* you, O ye of little faith?

29 And seek not ye what ye shall eat, or what ye shall drink, ‖ neither be ye of doubtful mind.   ‖ Or, *live not in careful suspense.*

---

28. "God so clothe the grass, which is to day in the field." So A., most later Uncials and Cursives, but ℵ, B., L., Λ, &c., read, "If God clothe the grass in the field."

lilies, the lilies of the field, as we read in the parallel place in St. Matthew. As they spring up spontaneously, man, by his cultivation, has added nothing to their perfection. They are creations of God on which He has lavished such splendour of form and colour that Solomon's jewelled robes were not to be compared to them, and yet God has thus gorgeously clothed them for no apparent purpose except to exhibit profuseness of beauty; they last but a day, and the next day their withered stalks are gathered for fuel for the oven. Not one in one million delights the eye even of a child; and yet each particular one serves its purpose in creation. Each one is observed and its beauty noted by God—by Him Who numbers the grains of sand and the drops of dew—each particular one, though never to be seen by man, is as perfect of its kind as if it had been destined to adorn the temple of God.

28. "If then God so clothe the grass, which is to-day in the field," &c. Such are the lilies, and their lesson to us is, that we need take no thought for raiment. If God sees to it that the grass which withereth and perisheth is clad so exquisitely, will He not see to it that the bodies of those who commit their way to Him be protected and preserved from shame?

"O ye of little faith"—little faith, not only in the Scriptures, but in the lessons taught by the birds and the flowers.

29. "And seek not ye what ye shall eat, or what ye shall drink," &c. This does not seem to refer, as many take it, to the quality of the food as if it meant seek not to live sumptuously; but rather, "be not anxious how ye shall procure your food." The *ye* is very emphatic.

"Neither be ye of doubtful mind." The meaning of this word,

330   FEAR NOT, LITTLE FLOCK.   [ST. LUKE.

30 For all these things do the nations of the world seek after: and your Father knoweth that ye have need of these things.

^r Matt. vi. 33.   31 ¶ ^r But rather seek ye the kingdom of God; and all these things shall be added unto you.

^s Matt. xi. 25, 26.   32 Fear not, little flock; for ^s it is your Father's good pleasure to give you the kingdom.

30. "All these things." So A., D., K., M., &c., most Cursives, many old Latin (b, c, f, i, l, q), Vulg., Copt., Syriac (Schaaf); but ℵ, B., E., H., L., &c., thirty Cursives, old Latin (a, e), Sah., Cur. Syriac omit "all."

rendered here to "be of doubtful mind," is uncertain. In the Apocrypha (2 Macc. v. 17, &c.), it seems to mean indulging lofty imaginations. In a place in Josephus, however, where the adjective is used (De Bell. Jud. i. 27, 3) it means "agitated with anxious thoughts;" and such signification seems best to suit the context here: "Be not agitated with uneasy, restless thoughts as to how you shall live."

30. "For all these things do the nations . . . . and your Father knoweth," &c. As if He said, "The Gentiles are anxious about these things because God has not clearly revealed to them His personal providence and care of them as a Father, whereas He has revealed to you that He is your Father, and as a Father He knoweth all your needs, and will see that they are supplied."

31. "But rather seek ye the kingdom of God; and all these things shall be added unto you." The kingdom of God in the Person of the Lord had been found by them, and they had preached it as at hand. And yet the kingdom of God has always to be sought—always to be prayed for, as all Christians do when they say, "Thy kingdom come." No one here on earth has fully realized its extent and powers. Each successive revelation of it discloses wonders of grace and love which exceed all former ones.

32. "Fear not, little flock; it is your Father's good pleasure," &c. What means He by this "Fear not"? Evidently that they should put away all fear respecting their daily wants. If it is God's good pleasure to give them the great gift of the kingdom, will He not give them all things pertaining to the life which they must pass through before they can come to the full enjoyment of the kingdom?

"Little flock." The flock of Christ is always, compared to the

CHAP. XII.] SELL—GIVE ALMS. 331

33 ᵗ Sell that ye have, and give alms; ᵘ provide yourselves
bags which wax not old, a treasure in the heavens
that faileth not, where no thief approacheth,
neither moth corrupteth.

ᵗ Matt. xix. 21.
Acts ii. 45. &
iv. 34.
ᵘ Matt. vi. 20.
ch. xvi. 9.
1 Tim. vi. 19.

---

world around it, a little flock. "Many are called but few chosen;"
but when they are all gathered together it will be " an innumerable
multitude " (Rev. vii. 9).

" It is your Father's good pleasure to give you the kingdom." He
had given it to them now; for He had given them to Christ and
Christ to them, and if they continued faithful (some did not) He
would give it to them hereafter.

33. " Sell that ye have, and give alms: provide yourselves bags,"
&c. This, as compared with some modern teaching and expositions, is an astonishing inference. There is a tract upon this
text written by an Evangelical bishop in which this place is
is made to teach absolute confidence that if we have been once
in grace we shall be always in grace. Our ultimate salvation
is secured to us the moment we believe, but assuredly the Lord
draws no such lesson from the good pleasure of God to the little
flock around him. His inference is " Sell that ye have and give
alms. It is your Father's good pleasure to give you the kingdom.
Sell, give alms, provide yourselves bags in which your money will
always be secure, for they cannot have holes in them—a treasure
out of all reach of robbery and decay."

This is one of those many places which teach us that there is a
real virtue in almsgiving, if it be done in sincerity and with a view
solely to God's approval and the benefit of those to whom we give.
It follows up the teaching of the Sermon on the Mount, " Blessed
are the merciful, for they shall obtain mercy." " Let not thy left
hand know what thy right hand doeth; that thine alms may be
in secret, and thy Father, which seeth in secret, shall reward thee
openly." (See also Matth. xix. 21; Luke xvi. 9; Acts ii. 44, 45;
x. 4; 1 Tim. vi. 17-19.)

It is clear from these places that no one can be a faithful minister
of Christ who does not set forth in its integrity the truth contained
in these words of God. Too often are they deprived of all their
force by solemn cautions against self-righteousness and trusting in
almsdeeds, and so forth; whereas we may humbly hope that God

34 For where your treasure is, there will your heart be also.

Who gave us the good-will to part with our possessions, will also see to it that the gift of this liberal mind be not a snare to us.

There can be no doubt but that this and similar precepts moved the Pentecostal Christians to sell all that they had and hold all things in common; but the question arises how far such counsels of perfection are binding in their fulness upon Christians in all ages. Godet has some very sensible remarks on this. "It must not be forgotten that the kingdom of God at this period was identified with the Person of Jesus and the society of disciples who accompanied Him. To follow Jesus (literally) in His itinerant ministry was the only way of possessing this treasure, and of becoming fit to spread it in consequence. Then, as we have seen, it was an army, not merely of believers, but of evangelists, that Jesus was now labouring to form. If they had remained attached to the soil of their earthly property they would have been incapable of following and serving him without looking backwards (ix. 62). The essential character of such a precept alone is permanent. The form in which Jesus presented it arose from the present condition of the kingdom of God. The mode of fulfilling it varies. There are times when to disentangle himself, and practise Christian love, the believer must give up everything; there are other times when, to secure real freedom, and be the better able to give, he must keep and administer. When Paul thus expressed the Christian duty "possesing as though they possessed not" (1 Cor. vii. 30), it is evident that all he had in view was the disengaged and charitable *spirit* commended by Jesus, and that he modified the transient form which this precept had assumed."

34. "For where your treasure is, there will your heart be also." Let a man for but a short time carefully watch the current of his thoughts, and he will see how true this is. If, even in our prayers, we constantly find our heart wandering to our farm, our estate, our office or place of business, our condition, our favourite amusements, it is a sign that we require to be converted from what is earthly to what is heavenly. We have, to use the vulgar expression, no real interest, no stake in the eternal kingdom of God. Bede writes truly, "Now this must not only be felt concerning love of money, but all the passions. Luxurious feasts are treasures, also the sports of the gay, and the desires of the lover."

35 Let your loins be girded about, and *your* lights burning;

36 And ye yourselves like unto men that wait for their lord, when he will return from the wedding; that when he cometh and knocketh, they may open unto him immediately.

37 Blessed *are* those servants, whom the lord when he cometh shall find watching: verily I say

x Eph. vi. 14.
1 Pet. i. 13.
y Matt. xxv. 1, &c.
z Matt. xxiv. 46.

At this point there is a complete change in the scope of the discourse: hitherto it has been on covetousness, and the danger of riches, now it is on preparation for the Lord's second Advent, and the necessity of our looking for the Lord from heaven.

35, 36. "Let your loins be girded about, and your lights burning .... open unto him immediately." Here is an allusion to the long flowing robes then worn, which required to be tucked up, and the ends fastened under the girdle, if there was to be any freedom for either labour or quick walking.

"And your lights burning." There seems an allusion to the burning lamps in the parable of the ten virgins, but with this difference, that there the virgins wait outside to join in the procession; here the watchful servants wait inside, to answer the door the moment the Master knocks. In St. Matthew xxv., the Lord Himself is the Bridegroom; here, on the contrary, He seems to come home from some wedding of one of His friends. Stier ingeniously explains the returning from the wedding as the returning from heaven, where He is already holding the wedding feast; but not in the fulness and perfection of bliss and glory with which it will be held at the time of the end. But this is inconsistent with the general tenor of Scripture, which seems always to place the marriage feast as the consummation itself. Better to take the marriage as symbolizing any entertainment, and the main thought is that He is away at a feast and will return.

37. "Blessed are those servants .... watching .... come forth and serve them." The figure used to express the high blessedness of those found watching, that the Lord will gird Himself and wait upon them, is a very surprising one, and must betoken an honour and blessedness beyond all thought. There is a remarkable foreshadowing of it in John xiii., where the same Lord is said to

unto you, that he shall gird himself, and make them to sit down to meat, and will come forth and serve them.

38 And if he shall come in the second watch, or come in the third watch, and find *them* so, blessed are those servants.

---

have laid aside His garments and taken a towel and girded Himself, and to have begun to wash the Apostles' feet. But there is this difference that in the first, the foreshadowing, the Lord is in a state of humiliation, but then He will be in a state of glory. What the reality will be we cannot so much as attempt to conceive. As Stier says, "Let no one contemplate it but when clothed in the profoundest humility." But be it remembered that all the Lord's acts of humiliation for our sakes are comprehended in the first—the taking upon Him our nature—in doing this He took upon Him the form of a servant, and He would not take upon Him the form without becoming the reality. All His life was a life of service to us. He served us in the pain, the sorrow, the anguish He endured. In submitting to the penalty of our sin He served us as our Sacrifice. In giving His Body to be eaten by us, and His Blood to be drunk by us, He abases Himself to serve the deepest needs of our souls."

Cyril has a good remark on this girding. "'He shall gird himself,' from which we perceive that He will recompense us in like manner, seeing that He will gird Himself with those that are girded."

38. "And if he shall come in the second watch, or come in the third watch, and find," &c. This seems as if the most meritorious watching was that in the first watch. They who watched in the first watch, as the early Church did, understood with most faith His own words respecting the uncertainty of the hour of His return, that it might be at any moment after His first departure; and so, immediately after the disappearance at His Ascension, two angels prophesied His apparently speedy return. But as the ages pass along and the Lord's coming is delayed, men's faith in His speedy and unexpected return grows dim and feeble; but this does not absolve them from the duty of being ready to meet the Lord at any moment, and so He hints the possibility of a long delay; but this delay will in no way affect the blessedness of those who die in a state of preparedness.

39 ᵃ And this know, that if the goodman of the house had known what hour the thief would come, he would have watched, and not have suffered his house to be broken through.

ᵃ Matt. xxiv. 43. 1 Thess. v. 2. 2 Pet. iii. 10. Rev. iii. 3. & xvi. 15.

40 ᵇ Be ye therefore ready also: for the Son of man cometh at an hour when ye think not.

41 ¶ Then Peter said unto him, Lord, speakest thou this parable unto us, or even to all?

ᵇ Matt. xxiv. 44. & xxv. 13. Mark xiii. 33. ch. xxi. 34, 36. 1 Thess. v. 6. 2 Pet. iii. 12.

---

39. "And this know, that if the goodman of the house had known what hour," &c. If the time of the attack by the robber had been known men would have prepared for him, and been safe from his depredation; but as he is known to be meditating a sudden and unexpected attack on the house, there is nothing left but that they should be always on the look-out. Now the Lord compares the secrecy and suddenness of His coming to an attack of this sort, and so He presses upon His disciples the need of being ready at all times.

40. "Be ye therefore ready also: for the Son of man cometh at an hour," &c. From this and many other sayings and discourses of the Lord, we gather that the duty of looking for and expecting the Lord's coming at any time is an attitude of mind towards Him distinct from, and over and above every other. We are not only to believe, but to watch—not only to obey, but to watch—not only to love, but to watch. We are to watch for *Him*, "coming [according to His constantly reiterated promise] in the clouds of heaven." We are not merely to watch, and be prepared for the day of our death—for then we should be draughted out of this world, and go to Him—but we are to be in a constant attitude of expectancy for an unknown day, in which He will come out of the unseen state to this world and to us. We are, therefore, to watch for, and be ready, not for some dispensation of providence, however great, but for a Person Who at His coming will put a stop to the present state of things, and bring in the eternal kingdom of God. [For a full examination of what our watching for Christ's coming is, and what it implies, see my notes on St. Matthew xxiv. 23-27; and on St. Mark xiii. 24.]

41. "Then Peter said unto him, Lord, speakest thou this parable unto us," &c. St. Peter naturally asked this because the discourse

42 And the Lord said, ^c Who then is that faithful and wise steward, whom *his* lord shall make ruler over his household, to give *them their* portion of meat in due season?

^c Matt. xxiv. 45. & xxv. 21. 1 Cor. iv. 2.

43 Blessed *is* that servant, whom his lord when he cometh shall find so doing.

44 ^d Of a truth I say unto you, that he will make him ruler over all that he hath.

^d Matt. xxiv. 47.

---

about covetousness was addressed to the disciples (verse 22). He had spoken to them as "a little flock," and then He bids them be like unto men that wait for their Lord.

42. "And the Lord said, Who then is that faithful and wise steward . . . . meat in due season?" Why does the Lord give the answer in the shape of a question? Apparently because He is struck with the difficulty of finding, amongst fallen sinners, one who combines perfectly faithfulness and wisdom.

"Whom his Lord shall make ruler over his household." This, of course, does not mean the whole household, but each local portion of it. All pastors, as St. Peter, the asker of this question, tells us, have, "To feed the flock of God which is among them." (1 Pet. v. 1, 2.)

Notice how all Church rule proceeds from Christ, not from the people.

"To give them their portion of meat in due season." Here the *wisdom* of the pastor comes in as distinguished from his faithfulness. He has to give to all their portion of meat in due season. He has to see to it that he does not give the strong meat to babes; but he has also to see that through ignorance, or negligence, or prejudice he keeps nothing back, that in its proper place he declares the whole counsel of God. (Acts xx. 27.)

43, 44. "Blessed is that servant . . . . ruler over all that he hath." He will make him ruler over all that he hath. Is this to be considered an hyperbole, because, if taken literally, there would be many rulers over all that the Lord hath? We are to remember that in various shapes this promise is repeated. "How shall he not with him also freely give us all things?" (Rom. viii. 32.) "All are yours" (1 Cor. iii. 22). "To him that overcometh will I give to sit with me on my throne" (Rev. iii. 21). The reward is to

45 ᵉBut and if that servant say in his heart, My lord delayeth his coming; and shall begin to beat the menservants and maidens, and to eat and drink, and to be drunken;

ᵉ Matt. xxiv. 48.

46 The lord of that servant will come in a day when he looketh not for *him,* and at an hour when he is not aware,

---

us, in our present state, inconceivable, and that is just what the Apostle says that it is, when he saith, "Eye hath not seen, nor ear heard, neither have entered into the heart of man the things which God hath prepared for them that love him" (1 Cor. ii. 9).

Bede finds what he considers a suitable meaning by comparing the merits and rewards of watchful servants (verse 37) and watchful pastors. "For what difference there is in the merits of good hearers and good teachers, such also there is in their rewards; for the one whom when He cometh He finds watching He will make to sit down; but the others whom He finds faithful and wise stewards He will place over all that He hath, that is, over all the joys of the kingdom of heaven, not certainly that they alone shall have power over them, but that they shall more abundantly than the other saints enjoy eternal possession of them."

45. "But and if that servant say in his heart, My Lord delayeth his coming," &c. Notice that the beginning of unfaithfulness is the putting away the thought of the nearness of the Lord's Advent. He who is faithful to this idea will keep in mind that he is only a servant, and must be always employed about his Lord's business, for, not at some definite time, but at any moment, he may be called upon to give account; the unfaithful servant, on the contrary, begins to play the master. He begins to oppress the underservants, and to live in self-indulgence.

46. "The lord of that servant will come in a day when he looketh not," &c. Either at the great day, or at death, or it may be by cutting him off from the true vine, so that long before he leaves this world his doom is finally sealed, and he is, as it were, both dead and judged.

"Will cut him in sunder" seems to mean his irreparable destruction. Some commentators, as Alford, see a symbolical reference to that dreadful sundering of the conscience and practice which shall be the reflective torment of the condemned: but this can

and will ‖ cut him in sunder, and will appoint him his portion with the unbelievers.

‖ Or, *cut him off*. Matt. xxiv. 51.
f Numb. xv. 30. Deut. xxv. 2. John ix. 41. & xv. 22. Acts xvii. 30. James iv. 17.
g Lev. v. 17. 1 Tim. i. 13.

47 And ᶠ that servant, which knew his lord's will, and prepared not *himself*, neither did according to his will, shall be beaten with many *stripes*.

48 ᵍ But he that knew not, and did commit things worthy of stripes, shall be beaten with few

---

hardly be the meaning, because this cutting asunder is the man's own doing in this world.

"Will appoint him his portion with the unbelievers." Not with the heathen, but with those who, having the Gospel of light presented to them, refused it, as loving darkness rather than light. This place shows that the man was a believer, or the words would have no point. It is one of those many places which teach us that the term "believer" is not by any means synonymous with true Christian. It is not the unbeliever, but the believer, who has to make his calling and election sure.

47. "And that servant, which knew his lord's will." Knew his Lord's will, *i.e.*, by the ministry of the Church and the possession of the Scriptures.

"And prepared not himself." It is a mistake in the authorized Version to insert "himself." He has not to prepare himself only, but to do an appointed work, upon which he must be employed when the Master returns. (See Mark xiii. 34: "to every man his work.")

48. "But he that knew not, and did commit things worthy of stripes," &c. This appears primarily to refer to the heathen, who, at the second coming of the Lord, will stand before Him for judgment. How is it, however, that those who "know not" are to be punished at all? Evidently because their natural conscience, their moral sense, if they had followed its leading, would have preserved them from doing much evil, and led them to do much good. (Rom. ii. 14, 15, 16 and 26.)

This place is exceedingly important as teaching two truths.

1. That no wrong-doers whatsoever will escape punishment. Ignorance will not shield them, because it will be found that, no matter how ignorant they have been, they have yet judged all around them, and condemned, in others who have injured them, the injuries which they themselves have inflicted upon their fellows.

stripes. For unto whomsoever much is given, of him shall be much required: and to whom men have committed much, of him they will ask the more.

2. But, in the second place, this passage teaches us that the idea is utterly false that God intends to inflict but one punishment in the next world, and that an eternal one, and of a kind so terrible that we can scarcely dare to contemplate it. That God can and will inflict *aionian* punishment on the devil, and those men who have persisted in rebellion against Him, and determinedly continued in impenitence and unbelief, is certain; but this place (Luke xii. 47) most undoubtedly does not contemplate any such punishment.

The "few stripes" is, to my mind, totally incompatible with a never-ending eternity of stripes, for such cannot be called few. The Lord seems to have in His mind a punishment typified and set forth in Deut. xxv., and not at the present time a punishment typified and set forth by the valley of the Son of Hinnom (which latter He unquestionably has set forth in Matt. v. 29, 30; xxv. 41).

Let no sinner, however, reading this, imagine that the "few stripes" will be light, and so it is of comparatively little consequence whether, through grace, we avoid them or not. Look at the years of suffering through disease or imprisonment which God in this world allows His friends—those reconciled to Him—to undergo, and then think what He certainly can and will inflict on wilful sinners; but, notwithstanding this, if we, in the very teeth of many express Scripture assersions, insist upon it that God has, in the world to come, precluded Himself from inflicting any punishment except an eternal one, it seems to me that we go far to destroy the Revelation of future punishment and reward which God has given.

"For unto whomsoever much is given . . . ask the more." All human responsibility is grounded on this principle. We may, then, be quite sure that God, in His apportionment of rewards and punishments, will act according to that principle of justice which He has Himself implanted within us. Only be it remembered that He, and He only, knows the full consequences of sin, either in the outward universe or in the heart. He, and He only, knows the exact history of every man, what each one had at the first, how he has retained it, improved it, or lost it; how each soul has dealt with God and with itself.

49 ¶ ʰI am come to send fire on the earth; and what will I, if it be already kindled?

ʰ ver. 51.

---

49. "I am come to send fire on the earth; and what will I, if it be already kindled?" The connection between the foregoing words respecting wilful and ignorant sinners and their respective punishments, and this verse is very difficult indeed to establish. I confess I have nothing to offer upon it. It seems as if the Saviour was wrapt in intense thought upon the changes which His coming would bring upon mankind, and gave utterance to a soliloquy, of which it seems absurd, as well as most presumptuous, to endeavour to guess the mental cause.

"I am come to send fire on the earth." The ancients mostly explain this of the fire of the Holy Spirit which would enkindle human nature with the fire of Divine love. Thus Cyril: "Now it is the way of Holy Scripture to use sometimes the term 'fire' of holy and divine words. For as they who know how to purify gold and silver destroy the dross by fire, so the Saviour, by the teaching of the Gospel in the power of the Spirit, cleanses the minds of those who believe in Him. This, then, is that wholesome and useful fire by which the inhabitants of earth, in a manner cold and dead through sin, revive to a life of piety." ("Catena Aurea.")

It has been explained by Moderns—Godet, for example, and after him, the authors of the Commentary on St. Luke in the "Speaker's Commentary,"—of the divisions and heartburnings which the promulgation of the Truth occasioned: but surely the two opinions, when carried out, coalesce. What occasioned the divisions but the searching purifying power of the Spirit, making one of a family on fire with the love of God, and leaving the other in the icy coldness of his unrenewed nature, because he refused to be renewed?

"And what will I, if it be already kindled?" The translation of this place has occasioned much difference among critics. It is difficult to understand the meaning of the English translation. Alford renders it, "What will I, would that it was already kindled." This is substantially the same as that given by Cyril, "Our Lord was hastening the kindling of the fire, and hence it follows, 'And what will I, save that it be kindled?'" If thus translated this verse forms a Hebrew parallelism with the text, at least with its latter clause.

CHAP. XII.] NAY, BUT RATHER DIVISION. 341

50 But ¹I have a baptism to be baptized with; and how am I ‖ straitened till it be accomplished!

51 ᵏ Suppose ye that I am come to give peace on earth? I tell you, Nay; ˡ but rather division:

52 ᵐ For from henceforth there shall be five in one house divided, three against two, and two against three.

53 The father shall be divided against the son, and the son against the father; the mother against the daughter,

i Matt. xx. 22. Mark x. 38.
‖ Or, *pained*.
k Matt. x. 34. ver. 49.
l Micah vii. 6. John vii. 43. & ix. 16. & x. 19.
m Matt. x. 35.

---

50. "But I have a baptism to be baptized with; and how am I straitened till," &c. This baptism was His Passion and Crucifixion. Till He had offered that Offering for the sins of the world, He could do comparatively nothing. But when once it was offered the barrier between heaven and earth, occasioned by the sin of man, was broken down, the veil of exclusion was rent, and the Lord was free to operate upon all mankind. Before the Crucifixion and Resurrection the fire was pent up; after the Resurrection and Ascension it could spread on all sides, and enkindle all within its reach. The old translation, then, "What will I, save that the fire be kindled," is parallel to "How am I straitened till it be accomplished!"

51. "Suppose ye that I am come to give peace on earth?" &c. It was natural to expect that the Lord would come to give peace, seeing that He was described in prophecy as the "Prince of Peace," seeing that at His Birth the angels sung "peace on earth," seeing that in His atoning work "righteousness and peace kissed each other:" for He has made peace through the Blood of His Cross. And yet the primary effect of His coming and work must needs be division, for the wisdom which is from above is *first* pure and *then* peaceable. Its purity naturally rouses the opposition of the impure, which opposition lasts as long as they continue in their impurity. So that the first effect of the coming of the Gospel to the kingdom, the society, the family, must be division, and the division will be first and most bitterly felt in the household.

52, 53. "For from henceforth there shall be five in one house divided . . . . daughter in law against her mother in law." This was of frequent occurrence during the centuries of persecution, for then Christians were not unfrequently betrayed to death by their nearest relatives. And now many professedly Christian homes are

and the daughter against the mother; the mother in law against her daughter in law, and the daughter in law against her mother in law.

54 ¶ And he said also to the people, ⁿ When ye see a cloud rise out of the west, straightway ye say, There cometh a shower; and so it is.

ⁿ Matt. xvi. 2.

---

rendered unhappy because the fire of divine love has seized upon one in the household, and his or her godliness and zeal puts to shame the lukewarmness or ungodliness of the rest. Where this is so there must be every effort made to avoid needless offence, and to present true religion under such an aspect that it may win rather than repel. This saying of Christ is a prophecy, and is cited by Chrysostom as witnessing to the Godhead and supernatural knowledge of Christ. "Now hereby He declared a future event, for it so happened in the same house that there have been believers whose fathers wished to bring them to unbelief; but the power of Christ's doctrine has so prevailed that fathers were left by sons, mothers by daughters, and children by parents . . . . But if He were mere man, how could it have occurred to Him to conceive it possible that He should be more loved by fathers than their children were, by children than their fathers, by husbands than their wives, and they too not in one house, or a hundred, but throughout the world. And not only did He predict this but accomplish it in deed."

54. "And he said also to the people, When ye see a cloud rise out of the west," &c. In these verses the Lord uses a similar illustration to that which He had employed in Matthew xvi. 1-4, but though similar as taken from the signs of the weather, it is not the same or addressed to the same persons. On the occasion mentioned in St. Matthew the Pharisees had asked from Him a sign from heaven, and His answer implied that such sign if given, would do them no good. They were accustomed to predict fine or rainy weather from the signs in the sky. The signs of the political sky were quite as distinct in predicting the near approach of the Messianic kingdom, and yet they could not see it. Why this? Because of their insincerity, *i.e.*, their hypocrisy. If we are determined upon any course of action, it is quite in our power to resist the evidence of any sign which makes against it.

The Pharisees, and with them the majority of the Jewish people,

55 And when *ye see* the south wind blow, ye say, There will be heat; and it cometh to pass.

56 *Ye* hypocrites, ye can discern the face of the sky and of the earth; but how is it that ye do not discern this time?

57 Yea, and why even of yourselves judge ye not what is right?

---

56. "Ye do not discern." So A., D., Γ, Δ, Λ, Π, later Uncials, almost all Cursives, most old Latin, Vulg., both Syriacs; but ℵ, B., L., 33, Sah., Copt., Æth., read. "Ye do not know how to discern."

were determined not to see the tokens of the Messiah in Jesus of Nazareth. Their evil instincts led them clearly to see that if they accepted Him they must give up their worldliness, their covetousness, their exclusiveness, their formality, and become new creatures; and so they shut their eyes to the clearest proofs of His Messiahship, and refused to see in such things as the departure of the sceptre from Judah, the fulfilling of the weeks of Daniel, the coming of the Baptist in the spirit and power of Elias, that this was the very hour when the Messiah was to be expected. From the rising of clouds, or the quarter from which the wind blew, they predicted the weather promptly and surely. It was only their double-mindedness, *i.e.*, their hypocrisy, which prevented them from seeing that what was happening to their church and nation, showed the coming of the Christ to be at hand.

And so it may be with us, the time of the second coming may be imminent, and the appointed signs very plain, but only to those who have eyes to discern them. So it is written in the book of Daniel, "None of the wicked shall understand, but the wise shall understand" (xii. 10).

57, 58. "Yea, and why even of yourselves judge ye not what is right? [For] When thou goest with," &c. The Lord had been showing them how they did not read the signs of the times, because of their double-mindedness and hypocrisy. Now He urges upon them the pressing need of repentance towards God, with a view to reconciliation with Him, from their own conduct in their proceedings one with another.

This is a very important saying of the Lord. It may be considered to be the text or motto, or seed of such a book as "Butler's Analogy." Origen remarks upon it, "Had it not been implanted

THE VERY LAST MITE. [ST. LUKE.

58 ¶ ° When thou goest with thine adversary to the magistrate, ᴾ *as thou art* in the way, give diligence that
thou mayest be delivered from him; lest he hale
thee to the judge, and the judge deliver thee to
the officer, and the officer cast thee into prison.

59 I tell thee, thou shalt not depart thence, till thou hast
paid the very last ‖ mite.

° Prov. xxv. 8.
Matt. v. 25.
ᴾ See Ps. xxxii. 6. Is. lv. 6.

ᑫ See Mark xii. 42.

---

in our nature to judge what is right, our Lord would never have said this.

58. "When thou goest with thine adversary to the magistrate, as thou art in the way," &c. Who is the adversary here? It has been variously explained as the Devil, as the Law of Moses, or the law of God, as conscience, or as God Himself. Thus Godet, "God is at once adversary, judge, and officer, the first by His holiness, the second by His justice, the third by His power." A very beautiful application of it is given by Augustus, "If thou sin the Word of God is thine adversary. (John xii. 48.) It is the adversary of thy will, till it become the author of thy salvation. But if thou maintain a good will to thine adversary and agree with him (Matt. v. 25), instead of a judge shalt thou find a Father; instead of a cruel officer an angel taking thee unto Abraham's bosom; instead of a prison, a Paradise. How rapidly hast thou changed all things *in* the way, because thou hast agreed with thine adversary!"

59. "I tell thee, thou shalt not depart thence, till thou hast paid the very last mite." It is assumed that this is impossible, and that the man must continue in prison for ever; but I think that if the Lord had meant this, He would have distinctly said it: for at times He speaks of *aionian* punishment with fearful plainness. (Matt. xxv. 46; Mark ix. 43-49.) If these were the words of a human judge they would certainly imply, that not all who were imprisoned continued there for ever, but that the length of the imprisonment would be according to the amount of the debt.

CHAP. XIII.

THERE were present at that season some that told him of the Galilæans, whose blood Pilate had mingled with their sacrifices.

2 And Jesus answering said unto them, Suppose ye that these Galilæans were sinners above all the Galilæans, because they suffered such things?

---

1. "There were present at that season some that told him of the Galilæans." There is no account in Josephus, the only Jewish contemporary historian, of this massacre of the Galileans. The oldest account of it is in Cyril of Alexandria (about 400 years after it occurred) and runs thus : " For these [Galileans] were followers of the opinions of Judas of Galilee, of whom Luke makes mention in the Acts of the Apostles, who said that we ought to call no man master. Great numbers of them refusing to acknowledge Cæsar as their master were therefore punished by Pilate. They said also that men ought not to offer to God any sacrifices that were not ordained by the law of Moses, and so forbade to offer the sacrifices appointed by the people for the safety of the Emperor and the Roman people. Pilate, thus being enraged against the Galileans, ordered them to be slain in the midst of the very victims which they thought they might offer according to the custom of their law, so that the blood of the offerers was mingled with that of the victims offered." It is also conjectured that this interference of Pilate in slaying these Galileans was the cause of his quarrel with Herod, who resented his interference until a reconciliation took place by his sending Christ to him as one under his own jurisdiction.

2. " And Jesus answering said unto them, Suppose ye that these Galilæans," &c. For the Lord to have answered in such words implies that those who brought the matter under His notice held that such a carnage in so holy a place, and whilst engaged in a religious act, was a direct sign of the anger of God against men who had committed no ordinary sin, and inquired of Him respecting its

346　THOSE EIGHTEEN.　[St. Luke.

3 I tell you, Nay: but, except ye repent, ye shall all likewise perish.

4 Or those eighteen, upon whom the tower in Siloam fell, ‖ Or, *debtors*, and slew them, think ye that they were ‖ sinners above all men that dwelt in Jerusalem?

Matt. xviii. 24.
ch. xi. 4.

5 I tell you, Nay: but, except ye repent, ye shall all likewise perish.

---

3. "Likewise" [ὡσαύτως]. So A., later Uncials, almost all Cursives; but ℵ, B., D., L., Cursives 1, 13, 33, 69, 131, 157, 209, read, "in like manner" [ὁμοίως].

5. "Likewise" [ὡσαύτως]. So ℵ, B., L., M., Cursives 1, 29, 33, 71, 131, 244, 248, 251; but A., D., later Uncials, almost all Cursives, &c., read, "in like manner" [ὁμοίως].

nature and guilt. He at once, as was His wont, brushes aside all mere speculation as to how God looked upon the matter and draws the lesson, "Except ye repent, ye shall all likewise perish."

Did He mean by this word "perish" destruction in this or in the eternal world? It is impossible to shut out an allusion to the future punishment of impenitent sinners at the day of judgment. But it is not at all improbable that the Lord's words here are prophetic of the fearful slaughter of the Jews at the taking of Jerusalem—the city, be it remembered, being crowded with those who had come up to one of the feasts and were not allowed to depart, so adding to the horrors of the siege. And so *in like manner* the impenitent Jews perished.

3. "I tell you, Nay." Mark the authority of these words. He speaks as if He knew the future lot of each one of those men who miserably perished, and their character and deserts at the bar of God, as well as the character and deserts of all those who perished not. And He pronounces, as One who knew the secrets of God's judgment that they were not more guilty, and so their slaughter was. a surer indication of the doom which would overtake, not grievous sinners only, but all the impenitent.

4. "Or those eighteen, upon whom the tower in Siloam fell," &c. They had brought before the Lord the case of men perishing whilst performing religious services in the temple. He now reminds them of another loss of life which apparently had very lately taken place through a mere accident—the fall of a building—and He evidently desires that they should look upon the two as of the same character. Whether the cause of death is the cruelty and profanity

CHAP. XIII.] HE SOUGHT FRUIT THEREON. 347

6 ¶ He spake also this parable; ᵃ A certain *man* had a fig tree planted in his vineyard; and he came and sought fruit thereon, and found none.

ᵃ Is. v. 2.
Matt. xxi. 19.

---

of Pilate, or the fall of a building, it is all the same. We can gather nothing from it respecting the greater or less guilt of those who perished; both died alike by the providence of God, but we can and must gather from each the same lesson of the necessity of repentance to every sinner.

6, 7. "He spake also this parable; A certain man had a fig tree planted in his vineyard," &c. This parable very appropriately follows upon the double warning which the Lord had grounded on what had just then occurred, *i.e.*, the slaughter of the Galileans, and the falling of the tower. "Except ye repent," He had said, "ye shall all likewise perish;" but ye need not perish; ye are as a fig tree planted in the vineyard of God. Hitherto He has looked in vain for fruit. He is minded to cut it down as taking up room which might be more profitably employed. But the judgment, though threatened, is not yet executed. There is an Intercessor Who is pleading for a longer respite in which He will bring to bear upon it more labour and more means of grace. But this respite is not a long one. Let it alone this year also. And if this day of grace be neglected, then even the Intercessor will ask for the removal of the tree. "If not, then after that thou shalt cut it down."

With respect to the interpretation of this short parable I cannot help remarking that commentators who, in explaining other parables, warn us not to insist upon giving a specific meaning to every minute detail, in their exposition of this parable entirely neglect their own advice, and insist upon taking notice of every feature. Some, for instance, say that we cannot explain the fig-tree as the Jewish nation, because according to the analogy of other parables, the vineyard is the nation. But need the planting of the fig-tree in the vineyard betoken anything more than the care taken of the fig-tree that it should be planted in a place eminently calculated to make it produce fruit? It is planted in a cultivated enclosure, not on the road-side. The idea of the parable seems to combine national and individual repentance. The Lord had called all to repentance, not only through fear of the judgment of the last day, but because a terrific destruction threatened the nation. But national repentance cannot be separated from individual. The

7 Then said he unto the dresser of his vineyard, Behold, these three years I come seeking fruit on this fig tree, and find none: cut it down; why cumbereth it the ground?

nation is composed of units, and each unit must repent and be reconciled to God. Each unit stands apart from the rest and must be dealt with by God and man as separately as a fig-tree planted among vines must be treated by itself. Much of the force of the parable would have been lost if the Lord had made the owner look for fruit from one vine amongst many vines, or from one fig-tree in an orchard of figs. When God deals individually with any soul it stands out from among its fellow souls such as a fig-tree in a vineyard stands out amongst the vines.

The fig-tree, then, is any member of the Jewish nation or Church, who, being barren and useless, is taken to represent the whole. The planter of the fig-tree is God. The vineyard in which it is planted is the Jewish Church. The dresser of the vineyard is the Lord Jesus Christ. The three years denote a sufficient time of probation. Various explanations have been given of these *three* years. Some think they mean the three years of our Lord's ministry, and the Lord in other places represents Himself as the Son sent by the Father to receive of the fruit of the vineyard: but in this case how are we to explain the *one* additional year, because at least forty intervened between the Lord's Ascension, followed by the descent of the Spirit and the final execution of vengeance in the destruction of Jerusalem. Ambrose makes the three years cover the whole time of the dispensation. "Behold these three years I came seeking fruit. He came to Abraham, He came to Moses, He came to Mary, that is, He came in the seal of the Covenant, He came in the Law, He came in the Body." Augustine understands by them the times—of the natural law—of the written law—and now of the time of grace. By those who explain it of the individual, the three years are taken to be childhood, manhood, and old age. But the unsatisfactoriness of all these explanations lead us to understand the three years as signifying amply sufficient time, and nothing more.

"Cut it down; why cumbereth it the ground?" It is remarkable how frequently the grace of God is set forth as working on a comparatively small field or area, so that if a church or an individual is unfaithful it takes up room which might be more profitably

CHAP. XIII.] LET IT ALONE THIS YEAR. 349

8 And he answering said unto him, Lord, let it alone this year also, till I shall dig about it, and dung *it*:

9 And if it bear fruit, *well*: and if not, *then* after that thou shalt cut it down.

---

9. "And if not, then after that." "After that" in the last clause in A., D., later Uncials, almost all Cursives, old Latin, Vulg., and Syriacs; but in the former clause, "If it bear fruit after that," in ℵ, B., L., 33, 69, Sah., Copt., &c. Revisers translate "and if it bear fruit thenceforth."

occupied by some other Church or person. (See Matt. xxi. 41, Rom. xi. 19, Rev. ii. 5.)

8. "And he answering said unto him, Lord, let it alone this year also, till," &c. "This year" seems to have nothing to do with some remaining year of our Lord's ministry, because as far as we can see He applied by his preaching to the Jews no further declaration of grace than he had done in the previous years. If it applies to the period between Pentecost and the destruction of their city, then "this year" cannot denote a year of twelve months, but must signify a time in the counsels of God amply sufficient for all purposes of His grace.

The "digging about it" and "dunging it," signifies the setting up of the Christian Church, and its ample means of grace, and the miracles, such as the gift of divers languages, and the extraordinary multitude of conversions greater than those performed by the Son of Man when living amongst men in the flesh.

Theophylact writes, "The dresser is Christ who will not leave the fig-tree cut down as barren, as if saying to the Father, Although through the law and the prophets they gave no fruit of repentance, I will water them with my sufferings and teaching, and perhaps they will yield us fruits of obedience." (Theophylact, in "Catena Aurea.")

The application to the individual soul is very easy and common place, but withal, of overwhelming importance. Each and every impenitent soul living without God, and bearing no fruits of righteousness, is in danger of being cut down and cast into the fire.

There is One Who intercedes for each sinful soul. "If any man sin, we have an advocate with the Father," &c. His intercession is that it may be some time longer under His care. His care for it will be shown in calls to repentance, in the discipline of afflictions and distresses, and in the application of the means of grace.

10 And he was teaching in one of the synagogues on the sabbath.

11 ¶ And, behold, there was a woman which had a spirit of infirmity eighteen years, and was bowed together, and could in no wise lift up *herself*.

But this renewed season of grace is not for ever. It will speedily come to an end. If then there be no return for all this loving care, if there be continued barrenness, then even the Intercessor says, "Thou shalt cut it down."

One more remark. Let the reader notice that the fig-tree is not condemned because it produced evil figs (Jer. xxiv. 3), but for its barrenness: and so God looks for fruit, *i.e.*, good works: He is not for a moment satisfied with a mere respectable abstention from sin. His Son was sent to "purify unto Himself a peculiar people, *zealous of good works.*" (Titus ii. 14.)

10, 11. "And he was teaching in one of the synagogues on the sabbath. And behold there," &c. "A spirit of infirmity." Comparing this with the words of the Lord in verse sixteen, " a daughter of Abraham, whom Satan hath bound," it seems not unlikely that the infliction under which she laboured arose from some sort of possession. We read of deaf and dumb spirits, in which case the influence of the evil spirit must have been on the nerves, by which the soul or spirit acts on the ear in the conveyance of sound to itself, and on the tongue by enabling it to make its thoughts known to the outer world in articulate speech; and this affliction, described as " being bowed down " so that she could not lift up herself, was through the nerves, by which the spirit acts on the muscles of the body; so that this may have been a case of possession, the evil spirit acting on the secret links of connection between spirit or soul, and body.

This evil spirit was in no way permitted to affect her religion, for she came to the synagogue as a devout worshipper, notwithstanding her infirmity.

The Lord, however, in speaking of Satan having bound her, may merely refer to the fall brought on by Satan, through the effects of which she suffered; and so He traces, as it were, all the evils of humanity to their one root.

I may mention, in passing, that the use of the particular terms translated, "lift up herself," "thou art loosed," and "made

CHAP. XIII.] SHE WAS MADE STRAIGHT. 351

12 And when Jesus saw her, he called *her to him*, and said unto her, Woman, thou art loosed from thine infirmity.

13 ᵇ And he laid *his* hands on her : and immediately she was made straight, and glorified God. ᵇ Mark xvi. 18. Acts ix. 17.

14 And the ruler of the synagogue answered with indignation, because that Jesus had healed on the sabbath day, and

---

straight," shews, amongst many similar instances, the medical training of St. Luke. (See Hobart on "The Medical Language of St. Luke.")

12. "And when Jesus saw her, he called her to him, and said unto her," &c. The Lord, it is to be noticed, does not wait to be entreated, but seeing her miserable case, at once, without asking respecting her faith, commences the work of healing. It has been suggested that her attendance at the synagogue might be taken as a sign of faith, but when our Lord did demand faith, it was always in His own power to work a miracle. Probably the woman being bowed down, so that she could not lift up herself, did not see Him till He called her.

13. "And he laid his hands on her, and immediately she was made straight," &c. Another instance to be added to the many others, in which He not only says the word, but brings His most Sacred Person into contact with those whom He desired to heal. Thus Cyril: "We should here answer, that the Divine power had put on the sacred flesh. For it was the flesh of God Himself, and no other, as if the Son of Man existed apart from the Son of God, as some have falsely thought." ("Catena Aurea.")

"And glorified God." Though many more than those distinctly recorded as having done so, may have glorified God for some great and miraculous benefit which they had received of the Lord, yet mention is made of comparatively few who showed any gratitude to God or to Christ. Thus of ten lepers cleansed only one gave thanks, so that it seems that we must sorrowfully conclude that in very few cases the spiritual accompanied the bodily healing.

14. "And the ruler of the synagogue answered with indignation, because that," &c. The malignity and folly of this man seems almost incredible. Instead of falling down and glorifying God that so astonishing an act of Divine power and mercy had taken place in his synagogue, and that he had been privileged to be present and

said unto the people, ^c There are six days in which men ought to work: in them therefore come and be healed, and ^d not on the sabbath day.

15 The Lord then answered him, and said, Thou hypocrite, ^e doth not each one of you on the sabbath loose his ox or *his* ass from the stall, and lead *him* away to watering?

16 And ought not this woman, ^f being a daughter of Abraham, whom Satan hath bound, lo, these eighteen years, be loosed from this bond on the sabbath day?

c Ex. xx. 9.
d Matt. xii. 10.
Mark iii. 2.
ch. vi. 7. &
xiv. 3.
e ch. xiv. 5.
f ch. xix. 9.

---

15. " Thou hypocrite." ℵ, A., B., L., later Uncials, about eighty Cursives, Sah., Copt., read, " Ye hypocrites ; " but D., many Cursives, and Syriacs, read as in Received Text.

---

witness it, he, in his envy and wrath, speaks words which imply that this afflicted woman ought to have absented herself from the synagogue when the Lord was there, lest he should have compassion on her and heal her.

15. "The Lord then answered him, and said, Thou hypocrite, ... on the sabbath day." Well might the Lord call him a hypocrite, for his making zeal for the sanctity of the Sabbath a pretext for his malignant opposition to Jesus. The Lord had simply called to the woman, laid his hand upon her, and spoken a very few words. This did not involve anything like the Sabbath breaking of unloosing an ox, or an ass, and leading him to some place where there was water, perhaps to some considerable distance. In fact, it did not necessitate anything like the labour of opening the synagogue chest, taking out the roll of the Scriptures, unrolling it, finding the place appointed to be read, reading it, and returning it to the officer.

"Be loosed from this bond on the sabbath day?" So far from being forced to continue even a day longer in her wretched state of premature decrepitude lest these hypocrites should be offended, the Lord pronounced that the moment she appeared in His presence her restoration should not be delayed. (See particularly my note on Mark iii. 4.)

Why does the Lord mention her as a daughter of Abraham? The reader will remember that in the case of Zaccheus, He said, " Salvation is come to this house, forasmuch as he also is a son of

17 And when he had said these things, all his adversaries were ashamed: and all the people rejoiced for all the glorious things that were done by him.

18 ¶ ᵍ Then said he, Unto what is the kingdom of God like? and whereunto shall I resemble it?   ᵍ Matt. xiii. 31. Mark iv. 30.

---

18. "Then said he." So A., D., later Uncials, almost all Cursives, Syriac (Schaaf), &c.; but א, B., L., 1, 13, 69, 157, 246, most old Latin, Vulg., Sah., Copt., read, "He said therefore."

Abraham." This may mean that He was sent to the lost sheep of the house of Israel, that the children must first be fed, and so that this woman had a right on the ground of God's covenant with Abraham to receive blessing from Him: or it may mean that, as was seen in her acknowledgment of the mercy, she was a true child of Abraham by faith, and so had a double right to what she had received.

18. "Then said he, Unto what is the kingdom of God like? and whereunto shall I resemble," &c. Whichever reading we adopt, "Then said He," or, "He said therefore," the Evangelist establishes a connection between the enunciation of this parable in this place, and what precedes. Now that which immediately precedes is not the healing of the woman with a spirit of infirmity, but the effect of it, which was the confounding of the Lord's adversaries, and the belief and consequent rejoicing manifested by all the people. This brings before the Lord's prophetic vision the spread of His kingdom from the smallest beginnings. The Lord uses the grain of mustard seed to illustrate this because there was a common proverb among the Jews "as small as a grain of mustard seed." The grain of mustard seed was the seed, not properly of a tree, but of a garden herb, but it grew with the rapidity of the growth of a garden herb into a production of sufficient size to be called a tree, so that not only did birds commonly rest in its branches, but these branches could sustain the weight of a man: and it attained to this size by rapid growth. It would not have served the Lord's purpose to have taken as an example an acorn, or any seed of a forest tree, because such trees are of very slow growth; the mustard seed seems, in fact, the only one which would serve the double purpose of very quick growth, like a garden herb, and the production of such branches that it could rightly be called a tree.

A A

19 It is like a grain of mustard seed, which a man took, and cast into his garden; and it grew, and waxed a great tree; and the fowls of the air lodged in the branches of it.

---

19. "A great tree." So A., later Uncials, almost all Cursives, some old Latin (c, f, q), Syriac, Æth.; but ℵ, B., D., L., old Latin (a, b, e, ff, i, l), Cur. Syriac, Arm., omit "great."

I have shown, in my notes on Matthew xiii. 31, and Mark iv. 31, that the fact that the fowls of the air could take refuge in its branches, is not one of the accessories, so to speak, of this parable, but of its essence. The parable means that the Church shall grow from the smallest of beginnings to be a place of refuge or shelter.

Williams notices in how many ways the Church was, at the first, exceedingly small. It was small in numbers, being all contained in one man, then in twelve, and though it spread rapidly, yet only after more than three centuries, did its children become the majority in the Roman Empire. It was small in point of wealth, very few of the rich or respectable belonged to it, so much so that it was often thrown in the teeth of Christians that they were principally recruited from the slave, or working class: it was small in the scandal of the Cross, Christians gloried in One Who had done no mighty deeds as of a warrior, but endured the most shameful of deaths, and their symbol was the form of the Cross on which He was crucified; it was small in reputation, "ye see your calling, brethren," says one of its greatest teachers, "how that not many wise men after the flesh, not many mighty, not many noble, are called." (1 Cor. i. 26.)

With respect to that which I believe is its leading teaching, that it grows from the smallest beginnings to be a sheltering or protecting institution, this was fulfilled when the nations of the world established it, and adopted its laws and principles as their own, but it has ever been the only true refuge, not only for nations, but for souls.

This was the view, mostly taken by the Fathers, of the birds finding refuge in its branches. Thus Gregory: "In these boughs the birds find rest, because holy souls raise themselves from earthly thoughts in the sayings and consolations of holy preachers, which are the branches, and so find a respite from the weariness of this life." And Jerome: "The branches of the Gospel tree, which have grown of the grain of mustard seed, I suppose to signify the various

IT IS LIKE LEAVEN.

20 And again he said, Whereunto shall I liken the kingdom of God?

21 It is like leaven, which a woman took and hid in three || measures of meal, till the whole was leavened. || See Matt. xiii. 33.

doctrines in which each of the birds (or believing souls) takes his rest."

20, 21. "And again he said, Whereunto shall I liken . . . whole was leavened." This parable is the necessary counterpart of the preceding one, for whereas under the figure of the grain of mustard seed the Church is set forth as a visible and widely ramified institution affording shelter to all who need it, so here it is described as an invisible influence permeating all human society with which it comes in contact.

The leading principle of this parable is, of course, the transforming power of the leaven, but another most essential feature is its working invisibly from within, for the woman hid the leaven in the meal. The grain of mustard seed, as soon as it appears above ground, grows visibly—the leaven works secretly, and has transformed nearly the whole mass before its effects are visible.

With respect to the woman, she is taken to represent the Church, but does not the Lord bring in the woman because making the household bread is a woman's work? Again, I do not think that the three measures of meal have any particular mystical meaning, but must be taken, as Chrysostom says, for an ample quantity —a sufficiency. Archbishop Trench illustrates the influence of the leaven by its secret, one might almost say, stealthy working, in the Roman Empire before the time of Constantine. He cites " the entire ignorance which heathen writers betray of all that was going forward a little below the surface of society, the manner in which they overlooked the mighty change which was preparing, and this not merely at the first, but, with slight exceptions, even up to the very moment when the triumph of Christianity was at hand."

Thiersch, whose valuable work on the parables I have before alluded to, relying on the fact that leaven generally signifies an evil influence, explains it of the rapid corruption of the Church from the first, in doctrine and discipline; but in these parables the Lord is setting forth the necessary principles of the Church, and He would scarcely say that the Kingdom of God was like a corrupting

356 ARE THERE FEW THAT BE SAVED? [St. Luke.

22 ʰ And he went through the cities and villages, teaching,
and journeying toward Jerusalem.

ʰ Matt. ix. 35.
Mark vi. 6.

23 Then said one unto him, Lord, are there few that be saved? And he said unto them.

24 ¶ ⁱ Strive to enter in at the strait gate: for ᵏ many, I say unto you, will seek to enter in, and shall not be able.

ⁱ Matt. vii. 13.
ᵏ See John vii.
34. & viii. 21.
& xiii. 33.
Rom. ix. 31.

24. Gate." So A., later Uncials, Cursives; but ℵ, B., D., L., 1 131, Arm., read, "door."

---

influence, though He might, as in the parable of the tares, show how an enemy had corrupted it. Here the reader will notice that the Kingdom itself is likened to the leaven.

22. "And he went through the cities and villages, teaching, and journeying toward Jerusalem." This seems to indicate a very slow and leisurely progress, taking on His way every place where men were gathered together, and so where a congregation could be made for His teaching. There is not a word said respecting the place from which the journey commenced, nor the route which He took, except its direction; nor have we the name of a single city or village into which He entered. We should think, however, that these cities and villages must have been those in which His way had been prepared by the mission of the seventy (x. 1).

23, 24. "Then said one unto him, Lord, are there few . . . not be able." What gave rise to this question it is impossible to say —indeed after the notice of the extent of the Lord's work in the previous verse it seems absurd to ask. It is to be noticed, however, that two similar questions had but a little before been put to the Lord. One by St. Peter (xii. 41), "Lord, speakest thou this parable unto us, or even unto all?" another, when He was told of the Galileans "whose blood Pilate had mingled with their sacrifices." Our Lord treats each case in a precisely similar way. He does not answer the question but throws it back upon the questioner, that he himself should see to it that he is a faithful and wise steward— that he should repent if he would not perish at last—and here that he should set about the salvation of his own soul in good earnest.

" Strive to enter in at the strait gate: for many, I say unto you, will seek to enter in," &c. The man asks Are there few that be saved? This seems to refer to salvation at the last day; and the

CHAP. XIII.]   LORD, LORD, OPEN TO US.   357

25 ¹ When once the master of the house is risen up, and ᵐ hath shut to the door, and ye begin to stand without, and to knock at the door, saying, ⁿ Lord, Lord, open unto us; and he shall answer and say unto you, ᵒ I know you not whence ye are:

¹ Ps. xxxii. 6.
Is. lv. 6.
ᵐ Matt. xxv. 10.
ⁿ ch. vi. 46.
ᵒ Matt. vii. 23. & xxv. 12.

Lord seems to confine His answer to the final salvation; so that it seems to me to take from the terrible significance of the Lord's words, as Godet seems to do, to interpret them as meaning entrance into the Messianic kingdom. The illustration seems to be formed on the idea of some great house, or castle, into which men enter, not by some grand and lofty portal, but by some narrow postern gate (betokening humility and penitential sorrow) into which if men desire to enter they must throw away all impediments, and the period of entrance is uncertain and may be closed at any moment without warning given. Williams notices that in the Second Book of Esdras there are very similar and striking expressions, as a " city full of all good things, the entrances thereof narrow, and set in a dangerous place to fall, like as if there were a fire on the right hand, and on the left a deep water, and only one path between them both."

25. "When once the master of the house is risen up, and hath shut to the door," &c. There seems to be a difference between the gate, or door, which has to be passed through with difficulty, because of its straitness in this life, and the door of eternal blessedness at last; but if we take the striving to enter in at the strait gate to be self-surrender—the surrender of our corrupt wills to God—then this is only available now on this side of eternity, God will only accept it now. He will not receive our self-surrender at last when it will be in a manner forced upon us, when the time of probation is over, and we begin to realize what we have lost.

"Ye begin to stand without, and to knock at the door, saying, Lord, Lord, open to us." The reader will remember that all this happened to the foolish virgins. They went to buy the oil, but it was too late; they came to the door, and said these very words, "Lord, Lord, open to us; " and they received the same answer.

"I know you not whence ye are." In the parable of the virgins the answer is simply, "I know you not." In the Sermon on the Mount it runs " I never knew you; " but, very probably, the difference is

26 Then shall ye begin to say, We have eaten and drunk in thy presence, and thou hast taught in our streets.

27 ᵖ But he shall say, I tell you, I know you not whence ye are; ᑫ depart from me, all *ye* workers of iniquity.

28 ʳ There shall be weeping and gnashing of teeth, ˢ when ye shall see Abraham, and Isaac,

p Matt. vii. 23. & xxv. 41.
ver. 25.
q Ps. vi. 8. Matt. xxv. 41.
r Matt. viii. 12. & xiii. 42. & xxiv. 51.
s Matt. viii. 11.

---

to be found in a covert allusion to what comes after. "I know you not of what parentage ye are. Ye are not of God—ye are not the children of Abraham by faith."

26. "Then shall ye begin to say, We have eaten and drunk in thy presence, and thou hast taught," &c. We can well imagine many who knew our Lord after the flesh—many who sat down with Him at such a meal as that of the Pharisee in Luke xi. 37, saying these very words.

But it is impossible to read them without our minds reverting to another eating and drinking, and that in the still more immediate presence of Christ, even in the Eucharistic Communion. To plead even this will be of no avail, because for what purpose is Christ present in the Eucharist there and then to feed us with His Flesh and Blood, but to separate and purify us from all sin, and to bring about that He should dwell in us and we in Him. His presence amongst us is for a purpose, and if we have not answered or accomplished that purpose, even His Sacramental Presence will be our condemnation.

Again, with respect to His teaching it is vain to plead that we have heard His teaching either from Himself personally or from His ministers, if it has not brought us to Him by a living faith, and so He reiterates with terrible emphasis His former words.

27. "But he shall say, I tell you, I know you not whence ye are, depart from me, all ye workers of inquity." The last sentence of the Judge has always respect to "doing." They that have done good to the resurrection of life and they that have done evil to the resurrection of condemnation. So to those, who, "by patient continuance in well-doing, seek for glory, honour, and immortality, God will render eternal life," &c. (Rom. ii. 7.)

28. "There shall be weeping and gnashing of teeth . . . . yourselves thrust out." The Lord here speaks to Jews, whose greatest

and Jacob, and all the prophets, in the kingdom of God, and you *yourselves* thrust out.

29 And they shall come from the east, and *from* the west, and from the north, and *from* the south, and shall sit down in the kingdom of God.

30 ᵗAnd, behold, there are last which shall be first, and there are first which shall be last.

ᵗ Matt. xix. 30. & xx. 16. Mark x. 31.

---

names were those of Abraham, Isaac, Jacob, and the prophets. If He had spoken to nominal Christians would He not have said: "When ye shall see the apostles, the martyrs, the true servants of God, the intrepid soldiers of the cross, the lights of the Church in all ages, the true benefactors of mankind—when ye shall see them welcomed to the joy of their Lord, and His face turned away from you."

29. "And they shall come from the east and from the west," &c. This prophecy was very rapidly fulfilled. The Ethiopian eunuch came from the south; men living in the first century were converted to Christ in Spain, in Gaul, in Britain.

About thirty years, or less, after this, a great servant of Christ wrote, "From Jerusalem and round about, unto Illyricum, I have fully preached the Gospel of Christ." And it is so now; you cannot take up a missionary journal, but you find men but a year or two ago heathen, and given up to all wickedness, now receiving the Gospel with a simplicity, and carrying out its precepts with a faith and fervour which puts to shame the coldness and apathy of hereditary believers.

30. "And behold, there are last which shall be first," &c. These words are said by the Lord on at least three different occasions (here and in Matth. xix. 30, and xx. 16). The "last" seems to represent those who have only just received the word of God, and from them little might be expected. The "first" means those who have been educated in its principles, and from them God looks for much. Thus Theophylact, "We, as it seems, are "the first" who have received from our very cradles the rudiments of Christian teaching, and perhaps shall be last in respect of the heathen who have believed at the end of life." And Bede, "Many also, at first burning with zeal, afterwards grow cold; many, at first cold, on a sudden become warm; many despised in this world will be glorified in the world

360 HEROD WILL KILL THEE. [ST. LUKE.

31 ¶ The same day there came certain of the Pharisees, saying unto him, Get thee out, and depart hence: for Herod will kill thee.

32 And he said unto them, Go ye, and tell that fox, Behold, I cast out devils, and I do cures to day and to morrow, and the third *day* [u] I shall be perfected.

u Heb. ii. 10.

---

31. "The same day." So later Uncials, most Cursives, old Latin, Vulg., Sah., Cop., Syriac (Schaaf), Arm., Æth.; but ℵ, A., B., D., L., and about fifteen Cursives, read, "the same hour."
32. "I shall be perfected." "I am perfected" (Revisers).

to come: others renowned among men will, in the end, be condemned." (Catena Aurea.)

31. "The same day there came certain of the Pharisees . . . . kill thee." Was this enmity of Herod a fabrication on the part of the Pharisees, desiring, for their own ends to scare the Lord from Galilee, or was there any real ground for their caution? We must take as our key to the significance of the advice, the fact that Herod, so far from seeking the life of our Lord, earnestly desired to see Him, in order that he might see some miracle done by Him (Luke xxiii. 8). The rumour, then, was a mere invention on the part of those who desired our Lord's removal from a part of Judæa where He was, humanly speaking, safe, and where He was daily increasing in the affections of the people, to another district where He would be more in the power of his enemies, the chief priests and the rulers, or Sanhedrim.

32. "And he said unto them, Go ye, and tell that fox," &c. This enigmatical answer of our Lord has presented considerable difficulty. At first it seems as if the particular Pharisees who had bidden Him beware of the malice of Herod, were his emissaries; but if Herod sought to kill the Lord why should he give Him warning to remove out of his territories? This has occasioned some to interpret "that fox" or rather "this fox," of the craftiness of those present, as if He said, "I know perfectly well your deceit, but I am totally unmoved by it: whether your pretended sender or you yourselves, desire my absence, I shall go on as I have done. I cast out devils, and I do cures to-day and to-morrow (meaning by to-day and to-morrow a short but indefinite time), and the third day (after I have finished the work allotted to Me by My Father), I shall be, or I am perfected, that is, by My sacrificial Death."

CHAP. XIII.]   O JERUSALEM, JERUSALEM.   361

33 Nevertheless I must walk to day, and to morrow, and the *day* following : for it cannot be that a prophet perish out of Jerusalem.

34 ˣ O Jerusalem, Jerusalem, which killest the prophets, and stonest them that are sent unto

ˣ Matt. xxiii. 37.

---

33. "Nevertheless I must walk to-day, and to-morrow, and the day following . . . Jerusalem." This "nevertheless" may allude to His death. He should walk as He had done, *i.e.*, He should exercise an active ministry of teaching and healing to the very week, or almost to the day of His death. Williams paraphrases the two verses, "In executing this My last Mission, there is no power of preventing me during this period, for this is not the place of my departure. 'For it cannot be that a prophet perish out of Jerusalem.' I have a journey to perform to Jerusalem, and there will be an end ; out of Jerusalem there is no fear; that is the place of all wickedness, and the consummation of crime, the law with all its types requires that the great sacrifice should be in Jerusalem."

34. "O Jerusalem, Jerusalem, which killest the prophets, and stonest them," &c. This apostrophe to Jerusalem is almost word for word the same as that in St. Matth. xxiii. 37, and yet the latter was delivered in Jerusalem, this in Galilee. It is exceedingly difficult to believe that it was uttered twice, and yet if only poured forth once, the occasion in St. Matthew seems by far the most appropriate. But still, the words which the Lord had just been saying, respecting no prophet perishing out of Jerusalem, seem a most fitting and natural introduction to the words as contained in St. Luke. Godet even prefers the idea that it was said in Galilee. " Were not the Pharisees whom Jesus had before Him, the representatives of that capital. Compare v. 17. There were Pharisees and doctors of the law sitting by, which were come out of every town of Galilee and Judæa and *Jerusalem*. . . . Such an apostrophe to Jerusalem regarded from a distance has something about it more touching than if He had been already within its walls."

"Which killest the prophets, and stonest them that are sent unto thee." What a mystery of sin and evil. Jerusalem—the vision of peace—the city of the great King, in whose midst was the palace not for man, but for the Lord God ; the place where God had set His Name, where He dwelt between the cherubims, this Jerusalem

thee; how often would I have gathered thy children together, as a hen *doth gather* her brood under *her* wings, and ye would not!

---

killed the prophets and stoned them which were sent unto her from the very God Who dwelt in her, and this has she done for so many centuries that the Lord said, "It cannot be that a prophet perish out of Jerusalem." But such a city must have been long ago given up by God. Not so, for here we have the Son of God saying :—

"How often would I have gathered thy children together, as a hen doth gather," &c. As I said in my notes on St. Matthew, this must not be taken as referring merely to former visits to Jerusalem, such as those recorded in St. John, but to all the dealings of the Pre-existent Word with them from the time of Moses to the time of the Lord's personal coming.

Keble has a wonderful sermon on this text, the mere name of which is full of instructive warning of the deepest character, for it is entitled, "The Disappointments of our Lord." "Christ is God; He has the mind, the will, the power, the love, the omniscience of God. 'He that hath seen Him, hath seen the Father.' Now as Christ exhibits to us all other features of God's character, so this among them, that He respects our freedom. He sets bounds to the power of His loving mercy in that He allows Himself to be rejected by those whom He takes pains to save. When He says 'How often would I have gathered thy children together as a hen gathers her brood under her wings,' it is as if he should have said, 'Do you know how anxious I am, how much I care for your souls. Look at those whom I have created to be mothers, how wholly their minds are wrapped up, as it were, in their offspring. Look at so common a thing as a hen with her young brood: she minds nothing but how to feed and how to defend them; though naturally timid, she is bold as a lion when she sees a hawk coming; she longs to gather them under her wings, and to feel that they are safe.' Such is Christ's care for Jerusalem, but Jerusalem cares neither for herself nor for Christ. 'I would have gathered you, but ye would not. I came down from heaven and was made one of you, that ye might be partakers of Me: but as far as doing good to you is concerned, My coming has been in vain.'"

35. "Behold, your house is left unto you desolate." If the word

CHAP. XIII.] DESOLATE. 363

35 Behold, ʸ your house is left unto you desolate: and verily I say unto you, Ye shall not see me, until *the time* come when ye shall say, ᶻ Blessed *is* he that cometh in the name of the Lord.

ʸ Lev. xxvi. 31, 32. Ps. lxix. 25. Is. i. 7. Dan. ix. 27. Mic. iii. 12.

ᶻ Ps. cxviii. 26. Matt. xxi. 9. Mark xi. 10. ch. xix. 38. John xii. 13.

---

35. "Desolate;" omitted by ℵ, A., B., K., L., R., S., V., Γ, Δ, Π, 80 Cursives, some old Latin (e, ff², g², i), Vulg. (Cod. Amiat), Sah., Copt., Arm.; but retained by D., E., G., H., M., U., X., Δ, 33, and many other Cursives, old Latin (a, b, c, f, g¹, l, q), Syriac (Cureton and Peshito), some Copt., Æth.

"desolate" is to be retained, then the utter desolation shortly to overtake the city and temple, and indeed the whole Jewish state of things was principally in the Lord's eye. If the word is to be rejected, the sense is yet very good and significant. "Your home, your state of things is left unto you. Deserted by God you are as a church and nation left to yourselves, to the desolation of your own pride, and wilful ignorance and selfishness." We have a wonderful comment on the whole passage in the eighty-first psalm: "I am the Lord thy God who brought thee out of the land of Egypt: open thy mouth wide and I will fill it. But my people would not hearken to my voice; and Israel would have none of me. So I gave them up unto their own hearts' lusts, and they walked in their own counsels. O, that my people had hearkened unto me, and Israel had walked in my ways! . . . I should soon have subdued thine enemies . . . with honey out of the stony rock should I have satisfied thee."

"Verily, I say unto you, Ye shall not see me, until the time come when ye shall say," &c. Most probably the meaning is, "Ye shall not see me effectually, so as to be benefited by the sight": in the sense of the word "seeing" in John xiv. 19, "The world seeth me no more, but ye see me." All Jerusalem saw Him, and shouted, "Blessed is He that cometh in the name of the Lord." But this was to no purpose; it did not hinder them from crying, "Crucify Him." Hereafter when the heart of the nation is turned to the Lord, and they look for Him, and bless the signs of His appearing, then He shall be seen again, and be seen for ever.

CHAPTER XIV.

AND it came to pass, as he went into the house of one of the chief Pharisees to eat bread on the sabbath day, that they watched him.

2 And, behold, there was a certain man before him which had the dropsy.

3 And Jesus answering spake unto the lawyers and Phari-sees, saying, ^a Is it lawful to heal on the sabbath day?

^a Matt. xii. 10.

---

3. "Is it lawful to heal on the Sabbath day?" So A., all later Uncials, almost all Cursives, some old Latin (a, c, ff², i, l), Vulg., some Sah., Syriac (Schaaf), Arm.; but ℵ, B., D., L., 1, 13, 69, 124, and some old Latin (b, e, f, q), some Sah., Copt., Cur. Syriac, add, " or not," " Is it lawful to heal or not?"

1. "And it came to pass, as he went into the house of one of the chief Pharisees ... watched him." This miracle is so very similar in its circumstances to several others, especially that in the previous chapter (xiii. 11, 17), that few remarks need be made upon it. It appears that the Jews constantly gave feasts on the sabbath, though one cannot suppose that such entertainments were allowed to contravene the law of Exod. xxxv. 3, "Ye shall kindle no fire throughout your habitations on the sabbath day."

2. "And, behold, there was a certain man before him which had the dropsy." Was this man invited, or placed by them before the Lord with an evil purpose? Very probably; though very likely unknown to the sufferer. "They watched him," whether He would observe the sufferer and heal him, for apparently the man did not put himself forward, or ask to be healed. It is noticeable that this is the only case in which the Lord heals the disease of dropsy.

3. "And Jesus answering spake unto the lawyers and Pharisees, saying, Is it lawful," &c. What did the Lord answer, because apparently, no one had spoken? No doubt He answered their secret thoughts. They were asking in themselves, will He heal this man on this day, as He has healed many others. "Is it law-

4 And they held their peace. And he took *him*, and healed him, and let him go;

5 And answered them, saying, ᵇ Which of you shall have an ass or an ox fallen into a pit, and will not straightway pull him out on the sabbath day? <small>ᵇ Ex. xxiii. 5. Deut. xxii. 4. ch. xiii. 15.</small>

6 And they could not answer him again to these things.

7 ¶ And he put forth a parable to those which were bidden, when he marked how they chose out the chief rooms; saying unto them,

8 When thou art bidden of any *man* to a wedding, sit not down in the highest room; lest a more honourable man than thou be bidden of him;

<small>5. "An ass." So ℵ, K., L., X., Π, 1, 33, old Latin (a, b, c, i, l), Vulg., Copt., Arm., Æth.; but A., B., E., G., H., M., S., U., V., Γ, Δ, Λ, about one hundred and thirty Cursives, some old Latin, Sah., Cur. Syriac, read, "a son." D. reads a "sheep."</small>

ful to heal?" because, no doubt, it would entail upon the Lord no labour: indeed, nothing like the labour and trouble of laying the feast.

4. "And they held their peace. And he took him, and healed him, and let him go." He did this no doubt by His word, and by His touch when He took or laid hold of the man.

5, 6. "And answered them, saying, ... could not answer him again to these things." It would be gross inhumanity to let an ox or an ass continue in a state of suffering when you are at hand, and able to help him; and it is much more contrary to all brotherly feeling to allow a fellow creature to remain in a state of distress, when, by a simple word, he can be restored to the enjoyment of life.

7. "And he put forth a parable to those which were bidden, ... saying unto them," &c. This parable seems to have been spoken at a different feast to that at which He had just performed the miracle. The miracle requires a state of comparative quiet in which they could watch the Lord. But here all would be bustle and anxiety on the part of those present to secure the best places.

8. "When thou art bidden of any man to a wedding, sit not down in the highest room." The "room" signifies, and should rather be rendered "first couch," or reclining place. All took

9 And he that bade thee and him come and say to thee, Give this man place; and thou begin with shame to take the lowest room.

^c Prov. xxv. 6, 7.

10 ^c But when thou art bidden, go and sit down in the lowest room; that when he that bade thee cometh, he may say unto thee, Friend, go up higher: then shalt thou have worship in the presence of them that sit at meat with thee.

---

10. "Of them that sit at meat with thee." So D., Γ, Δ, Λ, Π, later Uncials, most Cursives, old Latin, Vulg., Goth., Arm.; but ℵ, A., B., L., X., about twelve Cursives, Sah., Copt., Syriac, Æth., read, "all them."

place in one room, or apartment, in which the shame of him who was made to give place, and the honour conferred on him who had a better place assigned to him, could be observed by the whole body of the guests.

9. "And he that bade thee and him come and say to thee, . . . lowest room." Here it is implied that the host, coming in last, brings with him the more honourable guests who had probably been lodging with him, and for whom places near to himself had been reserved, into one of which the person supposed to be addressed may have intruded.

"To take the lowest room." Because all the others were filled up, and he was not sufficiently honourable or respectable to have room made for him, which would have required some one's degradation to a lower place.

10. "But when thou art bidden, go and sit down . . . worship in the presence of them that sit at meat with thee." Does the Lord here inculcate a feigned humility? By no means; He simply enjoins that a man should mortify his individual pride and self-seeking, an act of self-discipline which is in itself always wholesome and beneficial. If the man deserved the lowest or a lower place, then all was right; he took that to which alone he was fairly entitled. If he took a place below what he was entitled to, then he left it to the master of the feast, the only fountain of honour, to redress matters. Anyhow he set an example of "minding not high things," but "in lowliness of mind esteeming others better than himself." It is to be remembered that in one of any real worth the outward act would react on the inward spirit. The pride of

CHAP. XIV.] THE HUMBLE EXALTED. 367

11 ᵈ For whosoever exalteth himself shall be abased; and he that humbleth himself shall be exalted.

ᵈ Job xxii. 29.
Ps. xviii. 27.
Prov. xxix. 23.
Matt. xxiii. 12.
ch. xviii. 14.
James iv. 6.
1 Pet. v. 5.

spirit is fostered by outward self-assertion, and mortified by outward self-abasement.

11. "For whosoever exalteth himself shall be abased; and he that humbleth," &c. With respect to the spiritual meaning of the parable we have a remarkable key to it in the passage referred to in the marginal references (Prov. xxv. 6, 7), "Put not forth thyself in the presence of the king, and stand not in the place of great men. Far better is it that it be said unto thee, Come up hither; than thou shouldst be put lower in the presence of the prince whom thine eyes have seen." The Lord must have had this place in His eye; He must have meant Himself by the prince, for it was He Who, as the wisdom of God, inspired this passage. All pride, all self-assertion, all seeking of great things takes place in the presence of a King, the supreme Fountain of honour, the Lord of both worlds, the present and the future. It is very necessary for us to remember this, for the shame and confusion of face which in this parable is represented as the lot of mortified pride does not always follow it in this world. Self-assertion, self-assumption, forwardness, and boasting do not always entail a disgraceful fall upon the man who displays them. The meek do not as yet "inherit the earth;" though, if we can trust the words of Christ, they assuredly will. David asks, how is it that ungodly men "speak so disdainfully, and make such proud boastings." Men who are ambitious and self-seeking at times attain to the height of their ambition, provided, of course, that they have other qualities, such as prudence, cleverness, and perseverance. But a day is coming when the words of Christ, with which the parable concludes, will be verified in the case of every man. He Himself is the King before Whom all pride displays itself, and before Whom it will be abased. And there is the greater reason that He should do so, for when He had the highest place in the universe next to the Eternal Father, He abased Himself, and took the lowest place, even the place of the Cross and of death, in order that He might exalt those who have "followed the example of His humility."

The Judge at that day will remember and humble every act of

12 ¶ Then said he also to him that bade him, When thou makest a dinner or a supper, call not thy friends, nor thy brethren, neither thy kinsmen, nor *thy* rich neighbours; lest they also bid thee again, and a recompense be made thee.

---

pride, just as He will remember and reward every act of humility. Does this seem too much? Not for One Who numbers the hairs of our heads, and without Whose permission no sparrow falls, and Who has engaged to bring every idle word into judgment, and make manifest the secrets of all hearts. Should it not, then, be a matter of prayer that God may humble us here rather than hereafter? It may be very bitter to have our pride mortified now, but it will be a thousand fold more bitter to have it mortified before men and angels, above all in the presence of the Prince Whom our eyes have seen.

12. "Then said he also to him that bade him, When thou makest a dinner or a supper," &c. It may be that there had been something very pretentious about the banquet; so that a number of guests of consideration were there, and these would naturally stand upon ceremony and precedence.

When the Lord says, "When thou makest a dinner or a supper, call not thy friends," &c. His words are to be understood somewhat on the principle that His other words, "If any man will come after me and hate not his father and mother," &c., are to be received. He really means that hospitality is first to be exercised towards those who need it, because of their narrow means, and to whom kindness of this sort is more pleasant, because they receive such little notice from the world. These are to be *first* recipients of our hospitality, and *after* them our friends, relatives, and neighbours, who may be supposed to be able to ask us again. This, of course, is directly contrary to the practice of the world. Now I do not think that we obey this injunction of the Lord by following its spirit (as the saying is) rather than its letter. It has been said that "The essence of the beatitude, as distinct from its form, remains for all who give freely, to those who can give them no recompense in return, who have nothing to offer but their thanks and prayers," and that "relief, given privately, thoughtfully, discriminately, may be better both for the giver, as less ostentatious, and for the receiver, as tending to the formation of a higher character than the

13 But when thou makest a feast, call ᵉthe poor, the maimed, the lame, the blind: ᵉ Neh. viii. 10, 12.

14 And thou shalt be blessed; for they cannot recompense thee: for thou shalt be recompensed at the resurrection of the just.

---

open feast of the Eastern form of benevolence." But it is to be noticed that the Lord is not speaking of relief, *i.e.*, of almsgiving, but of hospitality. It is one thing to send relief in a basket to some poor person from your house, and quite another yourself to proffer to the same person food upon your own table of which you and he jointly partake. By relief or alms you almost, of necessity, constitute yourself his superior; by hospitality you assume that he is far more on the same level with yourself. Partaking of food in common has, by the absolutely universal consent of mankind, been esteemed a very different thing to the mere gift of food. If it be said that such hospitality, as the Lord here recommends, is contrary to the usages of even Christian society amongst us, we answer, "of course it is;" but, notwithstanding this, it is quite possible that the Christianity of our Christian society, of which we have so high an opinion, may be very imperfect indeed, and require reformation, if not regeneration, and that "the open feast of the Eastern form of benevolence" may be worthy of more imitation amongst ourselves. Look at the extravagant cost of some entertainments: viands set before the guests simply because they are costly and out of season; and consider that the difference between a fair and creditable entertainment and this extravagance would enable the giver to act ten times more frequently on the principle which the Lord inculcates, and for which he would be rewarded; consider this, and the folly of such waste, not to say its wickedness, is manifest.

As in the case of the parable of the good Samaritan and many others, as, for instance, in that of the very last one He had given utterance to, respecting taking the lowest room, so here the Lord Himself has first set the example before He inculcates the precept. "I appoint unto you," He says, "a kingdom, as My Father hath appointed unto Me, that ye may eat and drink at My table in My kingdom." He goes even further than this, where He says respecting those servants whom He shall find watching, that at His own table He will wait on them. (Luke xii. 37.)

15 ¶ And when one of them that sat at meat with him heard these things, he said unto him, ᶠ Blessed is he that shall eat bread in the kingdom of God.

16 ᵍ Then said he unto him, A certain man made a great supper, and bade many:

17 And ʰ sent his servant at supper time to say to them that were bidden, Come; for all things are now ready.

ᶠ Rev. xix. 9.

ᵍ Matt. xxii. 2.

ʰ Prov. ix. 2, 5.

15, 16, 17. "And when one of them that sat at meat with him heard these things," &c. The man who made this exclamation seems to have been moved by the words of the promise, that those who extend their hospitality to such as cannot recompense them in this world shall be abundantly rewarded on the Day of the Resurrection. He seems to have uttered the words in a self-satisfied spirit—he recalled, perhaps, some works of charity or almsgiving which he had done, and he felt sure that such as he could not miss receiving the final recompense.

Our Lord's parable was uttered to convince him, and such self-satisfied Jews as were like him, that before he could eat bread in the kingdom of God he must accept an invitation which numbers like himself, indeed, the vast bulk of his countrymen, might and would reject. The kingdom of God in which he must eat bread, was not wholly in the future, though its final consummation might be long delayed. It was a present reality, at least it was a closely impending reality. In a very short time, perhaps in two or three months, certainly within that year, he and his fellow-countrymen would be invited to enter, and take their places at the feast, *i.e.*, they would be invited to enter into the Church of Christ. They would be invited to accept Him as the Christ, to be washed in the Blood of His all-atoning Sacrifice, and through this to receive a gift of the Holy Ghost, such as men had never received before. They would be invited to be baptized unto His mystical Body, and to eat His Flesh and drink His Blood, so that He should dwell in them and they in Him. Through the reception of the Catholic faith they would be invited to entertain the highest conceivable views of the Godhead, and through instruction in the Life of Christ to have before them as their example the highest pattern of holiness, and through Christian worship, especially the Eucharistic oblation, they would join in that of which all their previous worship had been but the shadow.

18 And they all with one *consent* began to make excuse. The first said unto him, I have bought a piece of ground, and I must needs go and see it: I pray thee have me excused.

19 And another said, I have bought five yoke of oxen, and I go to prove them: I pray thee have me excused.

If not then, yet very shortly they would hear the words, " Come, for all things are now ready : " the Gospel is preached, the Church is set up, the Sacraments are administered. Surely one and all would crowd to eat such bread in the kingdom of God. No, the Saviour warns His hearers that it would not be so—all with one consent would begin to make excuse.

18, 19, 20. " And they all with one consent," &c. The first said, " I have bought a piece of ground, and I must needs go and see it . . . . therefore I cannot come." Now a very little thought will show to us that all these are mere empty excuses, one and all meaning that they declined to come to such a feast. If one had said, " my father is on the point of death and I must run to soothe his last moments," or another had said, " my dearest friend is haled up before the judge, and I must lose no time in witnessing to his innocence," there might have been some show of reason in the refusal: but the land which the one had bought would not disappear, he could just as well fulfil his engagement and see it the next day. And so the second would have lost nothing by postponing the "proving" of his oxen, for a day or two, and the third, if he could not have brought his wife with him might have left her at home for a few hours, as he certainly would have done if the feast had been to his mind. It seems to me a mistake, though we have such high authority as Augustine for it, to say that these three excuses represent the " all that is in the world " of St. John. The lust of the flesh, " I have married a wife." The lust of the eyes, " I have bought five pairs of oxen." The ambition of life, " I have bought a farm." This seems beside the mark, for the one was not called upon to part with his farm, or the other with his oxen, and assuredly the third was not required to put away his wife. No. The point of the parable is that they were all on the face of them empty excuses, and when we consider that according to Jewish custom this was the second invitation following upon one which they had accepted (or the announcement that all was ready would

20 And another said, I have married a wife, and therefore I cannot come.

21 So that servant came, and shewed his lord these things. Then the master of the house being angry said to his servant, Go out quickly into the streets and lanes of the city, and

---

not have been sent), it is clear that they were mere shifts to break a disagreeable engagement.

Now this exactly answers to the case of the Jews. By their religion, by their Scriptures, by their national hopes, by their own individual confession of expectancy, they were bound to accept the Messiah Whom God would send. It was not as if they were invited for the first time, and so had no choice. The man who exclaimed, " Blessed is he that shall eat bread in the kingdom of God," by this very exclamation showed that he entertained strong hopes of the coming, perhaps the speedy coming, of the Messiah, to usher in a state of blessedness, which would commence with a feast. The excuses then, as I said, were empty subterfuges to escape that which they were bound to accept. They may have even been falsehoods. Any how if these had not been forthcoming they would have found or invented others.

And is it not so with nominal Christians? Do they not for the present cast about for any excuse whereby they may postpone the acceptance of the claims of Christ? There is only this difference: the Jews were invited to enter as for the first time into the place of the feast: nominal Christians are presumed to have already entered into but are in no sense enjoying, the unspeakable blessings with which they are surrounded; they have to wake up even as from the dead (1 Cor. xv. 34, Ephes. v. 13, 14), and claim their part in the feast, or they may be ignominiously cast out, as we learn from the sister parable in St. Matthew. (The wedding garment, Matth. xxii. 1-14.)

21. " So that servant came, and shewed his lord these things. Then the master of the house," &c. Quesnel interprets this servant as being the Son of God, " God sent His own Son clothed in the form of a servant, to invite and conduct us to the heavenly supper; all things are ready because He has done all things necessary to our salvation—is Himself the banquet, and is gone to prepare the place for us." But even His patience may be exhausted. After

bring in hither the poor, and the maimed, and the halt, and the blind.

22 And the servant said, Lord, it is done as thou hast commanded, and yet there is room.

23 And the lord said unto the servant, Go out into the

---

years of intercession He may turn and "show the Father" the way in which all offers of grace have been perseveringly rejected. This is what He did in the case of His own countrymen. At last he became the minister of Divine Vengeance, for we know that the destruction of Jerusalem was His coming in vengeance.

But here, inasmuch as the day of salvation is not closed when the first bidden guests refuse, He is sent into the streets and lanes of the city to bring in the poor, the maimed, the halt, and the blind. Now inasmuch as these streets and lanes are the streets and lanes of the city within its walls or enclosure, we must understand these poor and maimed of the more ignorant and despised of the Jews, those whom the rulers and Pharisees and Scribes looked down upon as the people, the common herd, who, knowing not the law, were cursed (John vii. 49); and to whom our Lord alludes when He speaks of the publicans and the harlots entering into the kingdom of heaven before the Scribes and Pharisees. (Matth. xxi. 31.)

The Epistle of St. James, which seems to embody or represent the teaching and preaching to the Circumcision, is especially addressed to such poor and despised Jews, as for instance: ii. 5. "Hearken my beloved children, hath not God chosen the poor of this world?" "Do not rich men oppress you, and draw you before the judgment seats?" and again especially, v. 1, "Go to now, ye rich men, weep and howl for your miseries which shall come upon you," &c.

To such the invitation of the Gospel was addressed, and they accepted it, but not so as to fill up the places of the great banquet.

22-23. "And the servant said, Lord, it is done as thou hast commanded, and yet, &c. . . . . may be filled." This, no doubt, represents the call of the Gentiles, who were accounted by the Jews to be homeless vagabonds, and in truth their religion compared with that of the chosen people was as the miserable shelter of a hedge compared to that of a house in a walled city.

374 COMPEL THEM TO COME IN. [St. Luke.

highways and hedges, and compel *them* to come in, that my house may be filled.

ⁱ Matt. xxi. 43. & xxii. 8. Acts xiii. 46.   24 For I say unto you, ⁱ That none of those men which were bidden shall taste of my supper.

"Compel them to come in," *i.e.*, by holding out to them the threatenings of the law, and the promises of the Gospel. "Compel them," not of course by persecution, but by earnest pleading, by importunity, by taking no denial.

24. "For I say unto you, That none of those men which were bidden," &c. It is to be noticed that the Saviour here interposes, and Himself claims to be the giver of the Feast, or at least so One with Him that the feast is His Feast.

He here teaches us that God will not for ever call men. There will be an end of His offers, and those who have persistently neglected them shall be finally shut out.

Let us now gather up some of the permanent lessons of the parable, and before doing so translate it into the language of modern life. We shall find it very startling. A man, evidently a very rich and great man, makes a great entertainment, invites his very respectable neighbours, such as those who dwell in the suburbs and squares, and on their refusal calls the indigent poor, those who dwell in the streets and lanes, and when these are not enough, then fills it with the refuse of the common lodging houses. This is no exaggeration. It is literally what is described in the parable. When put thus, it is, as I said, very startling, and was evidently intended to be so in order the more deeply to impress upon us some hard lessons.

The first may be this, that mere respectability without godliness is no passport to eternal happiness. A man may be thoroughly respectable, well to do, unexceptionable in outward conduct and demeanour, a good and useful member of this world's society, a business man, a family man, and yet be all his life refusing the calls of God. Thorough respectability as regards this world, and deep-rooted ungodliness, may be united in the same man.

A second lesson is this, that those who from their place in Christian society, and their knowledge and their education, one would suppose to be marked out by God to be the pillars and ornaments of His Church, are perpetually falling short of God's high calling. God looks to find fruit on them and finds none, whilst abundant fruit is unexpectedly found on those from whom we hope nothing.

25 ¶ And there went great multitudes with him: and he turned and said unto them,

---

A third and very consoling lesson is this, that heaven will at last be full. It is said in prophecy of Jesus its King, that "He shall see of the travail of His soul and shall be satisfied," and we say it with all reverence, it will take much to satisfy His soul.

The Apostle saw "an innumerable multitude which no man could number, standing round about the throne." God's home will be filled, but by whom? Let the prophet answer. "I was found of them that sought me not, I was made manifest to them that asked not after me;"—by such the places in His house will be filled: but the prophet proceeds, "All the day long have I stretched forth my hands unto a disobedient and gainsaying people."

Wonderful mystery that of God's election, that God has a multitude of souls innumerable to us, but which He knows! And it ought to be a consoling thing to think that God's purposes of mercy will not be thwarted. His house will be filled, but by whom? By those who accept and receive, and realize, and enjoy the promises, the truths, the Eucharists of the Gospel.

It remains to say that this parable is not the same as that of Matth. xxii. 1-14. The first part resembles that in St. Matthew, but with important differences. The principal figure in that of St. Matthew is a king, who acts like a king, inasmuch as he sends forth his armies and destroys the murderers of his servants and burns up their city. The "certain man" of St. Luke's parable acts throughout like a private person whose only punishment to those who despise the invitation is exclusion from his feast. The occasions also which gave rise to each respectively are as different as possible. In the one case the parable is suggested by the exclamation of one of the guests at a feast; the other follows close upon another parable, that of the wicked husbandman, setting forth God's dealings with the chosen people under the similitude of one who required fruit of them and they refused it.

25. "And there went great multitudes with him: and he turned and said," &c. We now come to a passage of no ordinary difficulty: at least we must judge so from the great difference amongst commentators in the interpretation of it. Archbishop Trench has a chapter upon it in his "Studies of the Gospels;" and, though I cannot say that in all respects I agree with him in his exposition,

26 ᵏ If any *man* come to me, ˡ and hate not his father, and mother, and wife, and children, and brethren, and sisters, ᵐ yea, and his own life also, he cannot be my disciple.

27 And ⁿ whosoever doth not bear his cross, and come after me, cannot be my disciple.

ᵏ Deut. xiii. 6. & xxxiii. 9.
Matt. x. 37.
ˡ Rom. ix. 13.
ᵐ Rev. xii. 11.
ⁿ Matt. xvi. 24. Mark viii. 34. ch. ix. 23.
2 Tim. iii. 12.

---

yet if any one would at all properly face the difficulties of these ensuing verses (25-32) and see their intimate connection, and form anything like a clear and sensible idea of the lessons which the Lord teaches us in them, he must procure a sight of this book and read very carefully the chapter entitled the " Unfinished Tower and the deprecated War."

The key to the whole is to be found in the very first words setting forth how there went great multitudes with the Lord, and He turned and instead of welcoming them discouraged them. He bid them count the cost of following Him as His disciples.

Now it is most needful, first of all, to make up our minds as to what this following of our Lord on the part of the multitude really meant. It was evidently not a following in the sense of accepting His teaching and obeying His precepts of holy living. It is impossible to suppose that our Lord would bid them calculate what would be involved in believing what He said, or obeying what He commanded, so that if, on consideration, they found that it would demand more than they had strength for, they must forthwith cease from listening to Him, and from attempting to practise what He taught them. On the contrary, the Lord had distinctly likened the believing on Him with the view of obeying Him, to a man building —building, not a tower, but a house—and the process of building, the laying of stone upon stone, was the hearing of His sayings and the doing of them. Again, though He does not in any of His parables liken the following of Him in faith and obedience to a warfare, yet He intimates precisely the same thing when He speaks of " the kingdom of heaven suffering violence, and the violent taking it by force." It is impossible then that He could have meant to tell them that before they set out on the path of faith and obedience they must calculate the chances of failure, so that if they discovered that they were too poor to build and too weak to fight, they must fall back into the ranks of the world.

COUNTETH THE COST.

28 For °which of you, intending to build a tower, sitteth not down first, and counteth the cost, whether he have *sufficient* to finish *it?*

° Prov. xxiv. 27.

For what then were they following our Lord? Evidently with the view of attaching themselves, so far, that is, as such a considerable multitude could, to His person, much as the Apostles had done, but without a particle of their religion or their devotion. They no doubt believed that the Lord was the Messiah, and that He would shortly manifest Himself as such. This they learnt from the parable of the great Supper which the Lord had just given utterance to. They wished to be present at this manifestation, and to reap any temporal benefits, and a few of them, perhaps, hoped for some higher blessings, which might accrue to those who had ranged themselves on His side. The more I think of it, the more it seems to me impossible that these great multitudes went with Him with any distinct spiritual purpose, such as the blotting out or subjugation of their sins, or their acceptance in Him, or their attainment of such a heaven—such a state of holiness and spiritual happiness after death, as He set forth.

The conduct of these great multitudes, and their reception on the part of our Lord, seems to me the exact counterpart of the offer of the scribe and the Lord's reception of it in Matth. viii. 19. "A certain scribe came and said unto him, Master, I will follow thee whithersoever thou goest," and the Lord's answer was, "Foxes have holes, and the birds of the air have nests, but the Son of man hath not where to lay his head." This means, "If you follow me as my apostles or disciples are doing, you must surrender everything, you must even consent to give up that which the poorest of them—which even animals and birds have—a home.

This, then, is what the Lord said to this ignorant mixed multitude. "You desire to go with Me, not merely in the sense of hearing and keeping My sayings, but as these My apostles and evangelists are doing. If after such sort you desire to cast in your lot with Me, you must be as they are. They have given up home, parents, brothers, sisters, relatives, friends—they, like Me, have no certain dwelling-place, they are prepared to surrender their lives if I call upon them so to do. They are all prepared, in following Me, to take up the cross, and you must cast in your lot with them, for I

29 Lest haply, after he hath laid the foundation, and is not able to finish *it*, all that behold *it* begin to mock him.

30 Saying, This man began to build, and was not able to finish.

---

cannot now, at this fast approaching crisis, be encumbered with a mixed following, attached partly to Me and partly to the world. You see that you must count the cost, or you may ignominiously fail and fall away. These My Apostles have counted the cost. I have set before them what is meant by 'drinking of my cup,' and ' being baptized with my baptism.' And they have deliberately said ' We are able.' And you must count the cost too. They have proposed to themselves to do what may be likened to building no mean tower and engaging in no petty warfare, and you must look well to your resources, if you propose to do the same."

Such, I cannot but think, must be the meaning of the Lord's appeal, or rather caution, to the multitude. It is absurd to suppose that the Lord would counsel men to deliberate, to balance chances of failure, to count the probable cost of self-denial that they might have to undergo if they began a life of ordinary Christian faith and obedience. Can He mean that when the providence of God brings them in front of the strait gate and the narrow way, they may deliberate about entering and turn aside with impunity? Impossible. But what He undoubtedly means is that they must deliberate, if they would follow Him in the Apostolic Life. One man, and he one of the twelve, did not so deliberate or count the cost, and his failure was terrific. Another man, Demas, did not count the cost of following the Lord's life, as set forth in the life of the Apostle Paul, and his failure was disgraceful. His name has been a byword in the Church for those who love the world before Christ.

A few questions more must be answered before we have done with this difficult but most interesting passage.

1. Is anything in the common Christian life or warfare meant by the tower, and the more powerful king? Taking into consideration the analogy of many other places of Scripture, in which the Christian life is compared to the building of a house upon the rock, or the building upon a foundation laid by the Christian preacher (1 Corinth. iii. 10); there seems to be at first sight no difficulty about what this tower is, but the crux is that the Lord evidently

31 Or what king, going to make war against another king, sitteth not down first, and consulteth whether he be able with

---

31. "Going to make war against;" or rather, "as he goeth to encounter" (Revisers).

sets forth the building of the tower as something not necessary in the case of every one who desires to follow Him, because the Lord's words seem to have no meaning except on the assumption that the man who meditates the building of the tower, may, after consideration, decline the work. Whereas it is not in the power of anyone who has so much as once heard the Gospel to decline the building up of himself upon his most holy faith, except at the peril of his soul. The first hearing of the Gospel puts a man under the responsibility of receiving it or not. If he receives it he is bound to build his spiritual home upon it, *i.e.*, upon the rock, and the only alternative is rejecting it and so refusing to save his soul.

So that if the tower means anything, it means the erection of something far more costly, and difficult, and dangerous than the building up of the house of each man's Christian life, and the only things which seems to me to correspond to this, is the self-denial, the poverty, the ceaseless labour, and the dangers of the Apostolic life. (1 Corinth. iv. 9-14; 2 Corinth. vi. 4-10; xi. 23-30.)

But what can the more powerful king, who can put into the field 20,000 men against the other's 10,000 signify? Strange to say, it has been held to signify both God and Satan. The latter seems absurd, for is it to be supposed that the Lord would ever put it within the range of possibility that a man should make terms with Satan, much less send an embassage to the Evil One and desire conditions of peace?

And it seems exceedingly difficult to explain the more powerful king as being God, for though it is quite true that a man at enmity with God ought seriously to consider the boundless resources of vengeance of Him Whom he so madly opposes, yet the gist of the whole passage is against such an interpretation; for the Lord is considering not what a man must do, but what he can apparently innocently decline doing. Now the weaker king meditates war, whereas the impenitent sinner merely desires to be let alone by God. Add to this, that it is extremely improbable that our Lord should compare the Almighty to a king who has only just double the strength of his opponent, seeing that a commander of genius

ten thousand to meet him that cometh against him with twenty thousand?

---

and skill in handling his troops, and who can choose his ground, may easily defeat another who can bring twice the number of men into the field.

I do not think that we can give with any certainty a definite meaning to either the tower or the more powerful king. The one thing which, it seems to me, the Lord desired to bring before those who were desirous of following Him in the Apostolic Life, was the possibility of leading such a life, and yet the absolute need of deliberation, and men looking well into themselves, as to whether they were at all even in the way of being fitted for it. For, with all deference to the opinion of many good and pious men, I do not think that the Lord here intends to teach that either the tower-builder or the weaker king must look to his own resources, and that if he finds that he has not sufficient (which of course he assuredly will find out, if he is in the least degree honest in dealing with himself), he must invoke the resources of Divine Grace, for the man is not bound either to begin the tower or undertake the war.

The true state of the case may be put thus. A man thinks he is called upon to follow the Lord, literally sharing with Him the life He was then leading. Before he does this, he must set before himself the sort of life which he proposes to himself, a life of extreme self-denial and very patient endurance indeed. Now it will not be sufficient for such an one to say, " God's grace is all-sufficient. I will cast myself upon it." No; God works by means, and, of course, by fitting means. The man in question must, so far as he is able, see to himself as to whether he is at all likely to be one of such fitting means ; he must count the cost, by seeing narrowly to his past life, whether it has been a life of self-indulgence, or self-restraint—whether he has had his entire self under control. If he has not, he has no right to count upon the grace of God to enable him to lead a life of extraordinary endurance in close companionship with Christ. God may choose to call such a man, but the Lord is here speaking, not of what God sets forth before the man, but of what the man sets forth before himself. If God clearly and distinctly sets a particular form of life before a man, such an one has no alternative. He is not to hesitate a moment. Thus, in

32 Or else, while the other is yet a great way off, he sendeth an ambassage, and desireth conditions of peace.

33 So likewise, whosoever he be of you that forsaketh not all that he hath, he cannot be my disciple.

---

this very Gospel, we are told that the Lord said to one, "Follow me;" and when the man rejoined, "Lord, suffer me first to go and bury my father," he was cut short with the words, "Let the dead bury their dead, but go thou and preach the kingdom of God " (ix. 60).

If it be rejoined to all this, that we are giving a somewhat narrow and temporary explanation, by referring these two illustrations to the Apostolic life and ministry, we reply, " By no means." For the Apostolic ministry is, throughout the New Testament, the type and example of all other. We have throughout the Acts and Epistles no account of the life and work of the ordinary Christian minister of modern times. The bishops, or presbyters, and deacons, over whom Timothy and Titus had the oversight, may have been such, but, as I said, we have no account of either their life or work, whereas the pages of the New Testament contain very fully the account of the Apostolic ministry. Now if this be the rock whence we are hewn, it may be well for us to look to it far more than we do. In the providence of God, we may at any time be forced to adopt this as our standard: so that those who are entering upon the Christian ministry, or are purposing to adopt some higher form of it, such as the missionary life, must "count the cost;" must see as to their own resources of self-command and strong will, and resistance to temptation, as well as to the promises of Divine assistance. Romanist commentators, such as Cornelius a Lapide, interpret these two illustrations as referring to entering upon a life of Christian perfection, such as the monastic; but the Lord's words, in verse 26, go far beyond this. It is true that such an one gives up his property, and engages to live under strict rule, but he has a home and a settled maintenance, both of which the Apostles and first followers of the Lord surrendered at the outset.

33. " So likewise, whosoever he be of you that forsaketh not all that," &c. These words are evidently the sequel of the preceding ones. They set forth in the plainest way the extent to which the "counting of the cost" must go. It must go to the extent of

34 ¶ ᵖ Salt *is* good: but if the salt have lost his savour, wherewith shall it be seasoned?

ᵖ Matt. v. 13.
Mark ix. 50.

---

giving up all that a man hath, and living a life of daily dependence on God's particular providence. Because, however, the injunction seems so universal, and the taking of our Lord at His word so exceedingly rare, expositors have cast about for some interpretation which they think will include a larger number in the net of discipleship, and they think they have found this in the discarding of a man's own righteousness, and the desire to be found before God clothed only in the righteousness of Christ. Thus one of great and deserved eminence writes: "But this self which needs to be renounced is oftentimes a very subtle one; the self of him who purposes to serve God, but to serve Him in his own strength, and not in God's, and thus to have wherein to glory; who may have renounced much, but has not renounced a vain confidence in his own powers, and that these will enable him to carry to a successful end a service thus undertaken." Now the answer to this is, that the Apostolic life was not a surrender of one's own righteousness, but a surrender of friends, home, reputation, property and life. The same Apostle who said, "I desire to be found in Him not having mine own righteousness, which is of the law, but that which is through the faith of Christ" (Phil. iii. 9), said also of himself and his fellows, "Even unto this present hour we both hunger and thirst, and are naked, and are buffeted, and have no certain dwelling-place" (1 Cor. iv. 11). It is to this aspect of the life of His first followers to which the Lord evidently alludes, and, I believe, to no other.

34. "Salt is good: but if the salt shall have lost his savour, wherewith shall it be seasoned?" &c. The connection between this and the preceding verses seems sufficiently clear. The Apostles, and those who followed them as they followed Christ, were to act in the moral world as salt does in the natural. They were to preserve from corruption those with whom they came in contact who would receive their teaching. But this could only be if they retained the savour of Divine Grace. They might lose this savour—indeed of the very foremost of them one would lose it. And who were more likely to lose it than those who had intruded into the Apostolic ministry without counting the cost, without very deep

35 It is neither fit for the land, nor yet for the dunghill; *but* men cast it out. He that hath ears to ear, let him hear.

---

and earnest self-examination as to their motives, and their sincerity, and the self-control and self-denial which, by God's grace, they had hitherto been able to exercise? Such would become like that salt so familiar to those who have traversed salt deserts. "Maundrel, near Gebal, found some salt perfect to the eye, but completely insipid from long exposure to air, rain, and sun." Schoettgen speaks of a fragrant bituminous salt from Lake Asphaltites strewn largely over the sacrifices, to overpower the smell, and facilitate combustion, which, when it lost its aromatic virtue, was sprinkled over part of the temple pavement to prevent the priests slipping. (Notes on the Four Gospels, by F. M.)

No doubt this illustration of the salt losing its savour, and becoming worthless, is first of all intended for the Apostles, and those who followed the Lord as they did; for in the parallel place (Matth. v. 13), it is to the Apostles that Christ speaks when He says: "Ye are the salt of the earth;" but these last verses are of more general application than the preceding—all Christians are, by their example, even more than by the teaching of some among them, to be the salt of the earth; but if they lose their religion, their case seems more hopeless than those who have never repented or been converted.

"Wherewith will ye season it? What new motives to repentance or holiness can ye bring to bear on them, seeing they have already received them, and now are unmoved by them? Their terrible case is described by the Apostle. "It had been better for them not to have known the way of righteousness than, after they have known it, to turn from the holy commandment delivered unto them." (2 Peter ii. 21).

CHAP. XV.

THEN ᵃ drew near unto him all the Publicans and sinners for to hear him.

2 And the Pharisees and Scribes murmured, saying, This man receiveth sinners, ᵇ and eateth with them.

ᵃ Matt. ix. 10.
ᵇ Acts xi. 3.
Gal. ii. 12.

1. "Then drew near unto him all the Publicans and sinners for to hear him." They were not repelled by His holiness, as at first thoughts we might have imagined, but rather attracted by it, for God had begun a work of grace within them, and they came to Him as being both Divinely compassionate and Divinely holy. He was compassionate, and so they felt that He would receive them; and yet He was holy so that though He loved their souls He yet hated their sin, and so would put forth His almighty power to rid them of it.

"All the Publicans." I have noticed elsewhere that there can be little doubt but that God was having mercy upon the Publicans as a class, and so it is said that "*all* the Publicans drew near." Their calling was full of temptation, and yet not absolutely unlawful. It might be followed honestly and respectably, whereas the Jews, no doubt from national feeling, treated it as absolutely unlawful, so God, by raising up amongst them such men as Matthew and Zacchæus, showed that He did not brand it as an essentially sinful calling.

"And sinners." No doubt the open, wilful sinners, such as the woman of chap. vii. 37.

2. "And the Pharisees and Scribes murmured, saying, This man receiveth sinners," &c. Not only received them, that is absolved them, encouraged them, instructed them, and in all respects acted toward them as a loving pastor; but even eat with them as a token that on their repentance He had communion with them. As Thirsch well says, "He gave the impression which one of us would do, who allowed himself to be seen in company with convicts recently released from prison."

They "murmured," as supposing that such a reception would confirm sinners in their sins. They did this because their whole

IF HE LOSE ONE OF THEM.

3 ¶ And he spake this parable unto them, saying,

4 ^c What man of you, having an hundred sheep, if he lose one of them, doth not leave the ninety

^c Matt. xviii. 12.

---

cast of mind was unsympathizing. They only understood the severe, harsh, unloving mode of treatment; whereas even their own law, their own national history, such accounts as the reception and restoration of their great hero David, on his repentance, ought to have taught them better.

And now the all merciful Lord, not merely with the view of correcting false notions of God's mercy, but with the view of enshrining God's loving and joyful reception of penitents for ever in the mind of His Church, uttered three parables, which have been fitly called parables of grace, each one advancing beyond the other in its enunciation of the loving joy of Himself and His Father in the contemplation of the return of sinners.

In the first He likens this loving joy to that of a man who having lost one out of a hundred sheep finds it again and brings it home. In the second, to a poor woman who had missed one out of ten pieces of silver, and after very much trouble and turning the house upside down, recovers it: and in the third, to a father who had but two sons, and, to all appearance, one of them became a reprobate, and yet through God's mercy he returns to gladden the heart of his father.

4. "What man of you, having an hundred sheep, if he lose one of them, doth not," &c. The first thing to be noticed is that the Lord appeals to their own feelings, "What man of you," so that the Lord teaches us that our better human feelings are the reflection of what is in the Divine mind. God has not so deserted us that we cannot, upon the whole, "of ourselves judge what is right." Then it is to be noticed that the man owns a comparatively small flock, not so small in number as the pieces of silver in the purse of the woman, not so small as the family of two sons only, but still a flock so small that if but one sheep were lost it would be an object to him to recover it.

And it was an object, for it is said that on discovering the loss he forthwith left the ninety and nine, and went after the lost one.

He left the ninety and nine. Does this sound as if he was

and nine in the wilderness, and go after that which is lost, until he find it?

5 And when he hath found *it*, he layeth *it* on his shoulders, rejoicing.

---

careless about them, and left them in comparative insecurity, or in an unprotected state? Common sense teaches us that this is impossible; for if the loss of a single sheep was the cause of such anxiety and gave him so much trouble, he would surely take care not to run the risk of losing fifty more. He left them, no doubt, under the care of his servants, and probably in a fold: but still, why is it said particularly that, he left the ninety and nine and went after the straying one? I answer, simply to emphasize the fact that he himself went after it: he did not stay with the ninety and nine and send another man after the lost one—he took upon himself the more difficult and troublesome task, and went in person after the lost sheep, and by this we are taught the value which he put upon every single sheep of the flock.

"And go after that which is lost until he find it." From this we should gather that he eventually finds and brings home every sheep after which he goes: and in Divine things, in the spiritual application of the parable, it seems difficult to suppose that it can be otherwise. It seems impossible that the toil and labour of the good Shepherd after any lost sheep should be thrown away, and yet in an expression in the corresponding parable in St. Matthew we seem to have the freedom of the will asserted when it is written, "if so be that he find it," instead of the absolute "when he hath found it."

It may be wrong to insist much upon this, but it would be equally wrong to leave it unnoticed.

5. "And when he hath found it, he layeth it on his shoulders, rejoicing." Gregory of Nyssa remarks on this: "When the shepherd hath found the sheep he did not punish it, he did not get it back to the flock by driving it, but by placing it upon his shoulder and carrying it gently, he united it to his flock."

6. "And when he cometh home, he calleth together his friends and neighbours, saying," &c. Both sorrow and joy ask for sympathy. As it adds bitterness to our sorrow to grieve alone, so it adds sensibly to our joy when others share it with us.

7. "I say unto you that likewise joy shall be in heaven over one

6 And when he cometh home, he calleth together *his*

---

sinner," &c. This is the point of the parable. This is its one great lesson. The Pharisees and Scribes had murmured because He received sinners. The Lord shows them that their murmuring betrays a character the very opposite to that of the angels in heaven —the very opposite to that of God Himself.

Such is the parable of the lost sheep. It was at first addressed to Jews, and was intended to reprove those who had a zeal of God, and yet utterly mistook His character and purposes. He is the only fountain of holiness, and His hatred of sin is shown, not in His repelling sinners, and bidding them remain as they are, and await His punishment; but in His desire that they should come to Him to be freed from sin and become again His true children.

But the application to Christians is so much closer, and so much more in accordance with the whole parable and every circumstance of it, that we must address ourselves to bringing out its present bearing on the members of the mystical Body.

Now, in the first place, the foundation of the whole parable, that, in fact, which is its first necessity as a parable, is, that the sheep which was lost belonged to the owner of the flock—was, no doubt, marked with his mark and strayed out of his fold. The straying sheep could not have belonged to another person, it could not have belonged to his enemy, much less could it have been a wild sheep which required altogether reclaiming from its natural state. This is the starting point, as it were. The sheep is first of all in a flock belonging to an owner who had a flock of one hundred. And so whenever the Christian goes astray he leaves a home—a home of grace—a fold in which he is safe if he continues in it. What is this home? Practically it is the grace of our Baptism. If by Baptism we are brought into a state of grace, one of the least things that can be said of this state is, that whilst we continue in it we are in the fold of Christ, owned by Him as one of His sheep, and marked with His mark. The Spirit in the Scriptures says very much more of the grace of Baptism than this, for He says that in it we are buried and raised again with Christ, that in it in some sense we are "saved," that in it we are all baptized by one Spirit into one Body; but what I have said will suffice so far as this, that we must account ourselves as having been brought into the flock of Christ and numbered amongst His sheep.

friends and neighbours, saying unto them, Rejoice with me;
for I have found my sheep ^d which was lost.

^d 1 Pet. ii. 10, 25.

What is the straying of the sheep? It is not leaving the outward fold of the Church, but it is running counter to the grace which we received when we were first born into that flock or family. We may be outwardly in the flock, and yet the searching eye of the Good Shepherd may discern that in spirit and in life we are very far indeed from it. He who reads the heart can discern little or nothing of the stamp of grace upon the soul. The straying of the sheep of the flock of Christ is the continuance in sin, wilful or open, and the neglect or contempt of the means of grace. The eye of Christ alone can measure spiritual distances, so that in the sight of our brethren we may be in the fold, or very near it, and in His eye we may be very far off indeed. Of course those who are living in drunkenness, and sensuality, and uncleanness, and fornication, are lost sheep, but men are lost also through sins of the spirit. The proud, unhumbled, implacable, unforgiving, are in very deed lost, wandering sheep, if Christ be the humble, forgiving Saviour that the Scriptures represent Him to be. A man may be a lost sheep through idleness and sloth in the matter of his Salvation.

And now what is the going after the lost sheep on the part of the Good Shepherd, seeing that He never locally moves out of His place, nor they out of theirs? What can it be but the workings of conscience, its misgivings, its stings, its wounds? What can it be but visions of future wrath? What can it be but the memories of the innocence of the past, contrasted with the cheerlessness of the present and the loomings of the future? Or it may be the Lord finds them by loss of friends, loss of health, loss of means, loss of prospects, loss of children or of wife, ingratitude where they looked for some return of lovingkindness, disappointments where they were so sure—all these may be the pursuing footsteps of the Good Shepherd to find His lost sheep.

But is this, or something like this, the conduct of the Shepherd with every lost sheep, seeing there are such multitudes? Assuredly we are bound to believe that it is, for the secret action of Christ with regard to each soul is hidden from us, sometimes hidden from the soul itself, and will never be known till the last day. At that day, when the secrets of all hearts shall be disclosed, it will

7 I say unto you, that likewise joy shall be in heaven over

---

be found that Christ has in some way or other pursued with His love every soul.

But what is there now in the Christian dispensation which answers to the calling together of the man's friends and neighbours that they should rejoice with him, because of the recovery of the lost one?

The Lord Himself seems to explain it. He makes known to the angels, and no doubt to the spirits of just men made perfect, His success in the recovery of every lost member of His Body, and they rejoice with Him. The Lord uses the expression, "Joy shall be in heaven." But where in heaven? First of all, evidently in the breast of the Great Shepherd. His heart can contain the whole multitude, and His mind can discriminate each one, and His Intercession is not for all in a mass but for each one, and He rejoices separately, as it were, over the return of each one, and He makes this joy known to all the redeemed and glorified family, that they may rejoice with Him. The reader will remember the words, "Enter thou into the joy of thy Lord." The greatest joy which created beings can feel, is that which they share with God. If God be the Greatest and Highest of beings, His joy must be the greatest and highest joy, and His Son tells us here that His joy is in the triumph of Goodness and the discomfiture of evil, when He tells us that it is over the repentance of the sinner.

"More than over ninety and nine just persons which need no repentance." It is surprising how many commentators give a sinister meaning to the ninety and nine—that they are self-righteous and suppose that they have no need of repentance, that they represent the Scribes and Pharisees who were murmuring against the Lord because He received sinners. Even Archbishop Trench writes: "The one view of the parables which seems to afford a solution of the difficulties appears to be this, that we understand these 'righteous' as really such, but also that their righteousness is a legal one, is of the old dispensation, so that the least in the kingdom of heaven is greater than they."

But I cannot think that such is the meaning—indeed, it seems to me to make the whole parable unreal. For what is the joy of the parable? It is the joy after labour, after sorrow, after anxiety. It is the joy of recovery, of restoration; but to understand aright its

one sinner that repenteth, ᵉ more than over ninety and nine
just persons, which need no repentance.

ᵉ ch. v. 32.

relation to other joy, we have only to consider what the owner of the one hundred sheep would have said if this had been put to him : " You have felt intense joy at the recovery of this lost sheep, much more than you feel at the contemplation of the safety of your ninety and nine ; had you not better throw down the fences of your fold, and dismiss your servants, so that the remainder may go astray in order that you may have the same joy over again at finding them and bringing them back ? " We may imagine what the man would have said if such folly had been seriously proposed to him ; and what will God say to those teachers who virtually assert that there is no such thing as growing up in the grace of His covenant, that there was no such thing under the Old Covenant as growing up from the root of circumcision, imperfect though it was, and that there is now no such thing as growing up in the fold of grace from the Baptismal root—that no one can be properly accounted a true Christian who has not broken his baptismal vows, made naught of baptismal grace, and plunged into wilful sin ?

It is to be remembered that the true type of the Jew was not the Scribe or Pharisee. It was rather men of the stamp of John the Baptist, Zacharias and Elizabeth, Simeon, Anna, and St. Joseph, and if it be lawful to name her with others, the Blessed Virgin. It was rather the first called Apostles, and Barnabas, and Timothy, and Saul, who even in his unconverted state lived in all good conscience before God; and if we go back to the Old Dispensation, Daniel, and the three holy children, David in his youth, Joseph and Joshua, and others. Now these men would all confess sin ; their very holiness being the infusion of God's Spirit, would make them bewail shortcomings, but they needed not repentance such as David did after his fall, as Solomon after his declension, as Manasseh did after provoking God with the provocations which required the national retribution of the seventy years' captivity.

If then the ninety and nine be sincere followers of God, whether Jews before Pentecost or Christians after, how does God regard them? Surely it seems absurd to ask the question, but seeing that commentator after commentator seems to think that because the joy over the finding of the lost sheep is emphasized, therefore there is no joy worth speaking of over the ninety and nine, let us out

8 ¶ Either what woman having ten ‖ pieces of silver, if she lose one piece, doth not light a candle, and sweep the house, and seek diligently till she find *it?*

9 And when she hath found *it*, she calleth *her* friends and *her* neighbours together, saying, Rejoice with me; for I have found the piece which I had lost.

‖ *Drachma*, here translated *a piece of silver*, is the eighth part of an ounce, which cometh to seven pence halfpenny, and is equal to the Roman penny, Matt. xviii. 28.

---

of a thousand places just name one, "The Lord's delight is in them that fear him, and put their trust in his mercy;" and another, "He will fulfil the desire of them that fear him;" and again, "The eyes of the Lord are over the righteous, and his ears are open unto their prayers;" and if we ask how this joy is reflected in the breasts of the true servants of God, let us think how one servant says, "Now we live if ye stand fast in the Lord" (1 Thess. iii. 8); (could he have expressed himself more strongly?) And another says as heartily, "I have no greater joy than to hear that my children walk in truth" (3 John 4).

8, 9. "Either what woman having ten pieces of silver, if she lose," &c. . . . "I have found the piece which I had lost." This parable seems intended to teach precisely the same lesson as the one we have just expounded. Several differences have been noticed in their respective lessons, which, on closer examination, seem to me to be made out with difficulty. One, for instance, is this. The owner of the lost sheep goes in search of it from a feeling of pity and humanity, the idea of self-interest being ignored. Whereas the woman searches for her lost coin solely from a feeling of self-interest, and because the piece of money is a dead thing, humanity or pity cannot be thought of in connection with it; the lost money is simply valuable or necessary, and so she searches diligently, and calls her friends and neighbours to rejoice with her on its recovery. But surely to give the man credit for such feelings of humanity is an anachronism. It is to transfer back to well-nigh two thousand years ago, the feelings (exceedingly good and right, but exceedingly modern) of the present century, the century of humane and animal protection societies. The man set out to recover his lost property with just the same intention as the woman began to sweep the house to recover hers. The one great point to which all else is

10 Likewise, I say unto you, there is joy in the presence of the angels of God over one sinner that repenteth.

11 ¶ And he said, A certain man had two sons:

---

subordinate is, that in the one case the sheep was his, and so in his flock before it strayed, and in the other case the drachma was hers, and in her purse or girdle before it rolled away.

If there be a difference in the teaching of the parables, it appears to me to be somewhat of this sort. When the owner sets out to find his sheep, it may, for anything he knows, be irrecoverable; it may have perished by falling down some precipice (St. Matthew says, " he goeth into the mountains "), or it may have been devoured by wild beasts. He has a large tract of country to traverse, and if he finds it, a long way to bring it home on his shoulders : whereas, in the other case, the drachma, though lost, is evidently somewhere in the house, and if due diligence is used it is almost certain to be found. This last parable then *seems* to indicate a far less wide departure, and so a more hopeful search, but I am not at all sure about such an application.

Again the woman has been supposed to be the Church, the lighting of the candle the ministry of the word, which is a light unto our feet, and a lantern unto our paths. The drachma, stamped with the image of a king, the soul or spirit of man stamped with the image of God. The trouble taken by the woman in sweeping the house and peering into the corners, the diligence of the Church in preaching the word and exercising discipline, so that not one who bears the image of God may be useless and unavailable for purposes of good. All these may be true interpretations, but they must not be allowed for a moment to interfere with *the* lesson, which is that the man in the one case and the woman in the other, lost their own—their property, and missed it at once, and were annoyed at the loss, and at once took steps to recover it, and at the recovery expressed more joy than at the quiet possession of that which had not been in danger of being lost.

11, 12. " And he said, A certain man had two sons . . . divided unto them his living." This most wonderful parable follows upon and emphasizes the teaching of the two preceding ones. In all three the Lord tells us in different ways that God cares for the souls of those who have left Him, and gone astray, and rejoices at their

12 And the younger of them said to *his* father, Father, give me the portion of goods that falleth *to me*. And he divided unto them ᶠ *his* living.   ᶠ Mark xii. 44.

---

12. "The portion of goods which falleth to me." "The portion of *thy* [or the] substance which falleth to me."

recovery more than at the safety of those whom He has not lost. The exhibition of grace in the parable of the prodigal son is far beyond that of the other two, for whereas in the first an unreasoning creature strays, not knowing or reflecting upon what it does, and in the second a senseless thing is lost, in the third a human being in the full use of his faculties, determinedly chooses evil and refuses good, and yet, notwithstanding his wilfulness, his selfishness, his extravagance and debauchery, is, on his repentance, received back, not only freely and joyfully, but without a word of reproach.

This individual application must be firmly held to as *the* teaching of the parable. It springs out of the same root as the teaching of the other two, viz., that the Lord received certain gross sinners on their coming to Him to be delivered from the burden of sin, and that certain others, Scribes and Pharisees, were scandalized at such freeness of grace and welcome. If we take the chief lesson of the parable to be its reference to certain large classes into which mankind is divided, such as Jews and Gentiles, it seems to weaken the impression of the deep personal feeling and exuberance of love of the old father, both to him who had wrung his heart by unkindness and to him who was irreconcilable. The teaching of the parable is that there is joy in the heart of the Eternal Father over a penitent returning sinner, no matter how he has sinned, and that the same Eternal Father bears with, and by condescending kindness would overcome evil-mindeness of another sort altogether—that which exhibits itself in uncharitableness, moroseness, churlishness, envy, and ill-temper.

12. "And the younger of them said to his father, Father, give me the portion of goods . . . divided unto them his living."

"The portion of goods that falleth to me," *i.e.*, we suppose, "the share which would be mine if you were to die now."

"He divided unto them his living." This seems to imply that he assigned to each of them their interest in the property or estate. In the original it is "the living." Alford writes upon this, "The

THE YOUNGER SON.

13 And not many days after the younger son gathered

first-born had two-thirds of the property. (See Deut. xxi. 17.) The father, as implied in the parable, reserves to himself during his life power over the portion of the first-born. (See verse 31.) The parable sets before us, very strikingly, the permission of free will to man." Certainly not, we answer, unless the elder had the same power of disposing of his share as the younger had. It is not at all impossible that the father divided between them the estate: certainly the words taken literally seem to imply it. If it be objected that this would be contrary to common prudence, we are to remember that the wisdom of the old man in the matter does not come into consideration at all, but only his overflowing goodness.

13. "And not many days after the younger son gathered all together . . . riotous living." No doubt this was his intention when he asked to have his share given to him. He hated the restraints of his father's house, and he desired to get as far from it as he could, so he took his journey into a far country, where there would be nothing to remind him of the home which he had left, and from whence, as we trust, he hoped that no tidings of his profligacy would reach his father's ears. His case, as described by the Lord, is a very bad one, and was intended to be taken as such, in order to subserve the purpose of the parable. It is difficult to say which is the worst, his selfishness, his love of sinful pleasure or his undutifulness and want of all filial feeling. There is a picture of Vernet's which brings out with extraordinary power his character of selfish unconcern for the feelings of his father. It represents the courtyard of an Eastern house in which he is taking leave. The mother is leaning, in the depths of distress, against the side of the door, the father is bending towards him with a countenance full of yearning affection and grief, as if his heart would break; a leading domestic, perhaps "the steward of the house," clenches his hands as unable to restrain his feelings of indignation, astonishment, and shame at his cool indifference as he turns away from his father's embrace to a groom who is holding a high-mettled and richly-caparisoned steed, so that he may mount it at once and take his departure. Altogether it is a dreadful picture; but it may have been, and no doubt was, far below the reality of a multitude of such scenes, vividly present to the all-comprehending mind of the Divine Speaker.

Chap. XV.]   HE BEGAN TO BE IN WANT.   395

all together, and took his journey into a far country, and there wasted his substance with riotous living.

14 And when he had spent all, there arose a mighty famine in that land; and he began to be in want.

15 And he went and joined himself to a citizen of that country ; and he sent him into his fields to feed swine.

" Wasted his substance with riotous living."

" Riotous living," living riotously ; but the word signifies far more than noise and clamour at feasts, and rather describes excess of profligacy. Some commentators have, in excuse, expressed their doubts as to whether it need comprehend fornication and such vices ; but is it at all in accordance with common sense to suppose that a rich young libertine, one who had abandoned himself to all sorts of debauchery, should have kept " his body in chastity " ?

14. " And when he had spent all, there arose a mighty famine in that land," &c. This famine is brought in to explain the extremity of his want, for the scarcity and dearness of the common necessaries of life would press most hardly upon such as he, who had squandered all his money, who had pampered desires such as only money could minister to, and who knew not how to obtain any decent means of employment.

I do not think it is well to give any intellectual meaning to this famine and consequent want, so as to make it less vulgar, as Godet, who explains it as " the absolute void of a heart which has sacrificed everything for pleasure, and which has nothing left but suffering." Why not suppose that if it had not been for the pressure occasioned by this famine he might have lived on his friends, and his return not taken place ? The famine would be felt by all, and a stranger like himself would be the last to be cared for or relieved. Much better what Alford suggests, that the famine is providential. It is the Shepherd seeking His sheep which was lost.

15. " And he went and joined himself to a citizen of that country : and he sent him," &c. This is the extremity of indignity. The last and bitterest drop of his bitter cup, that he, a Jew, of course, should be reduced to herd the swine of the heathen man of the far country.

16. " And he would fain have filled his belly with the husks," &c., . . . " gave unto him." These husks are supposed to be, not the pods of our ordinary leguminous plants, such as peas, or beans,

16 And he would fain have filled his belly with the husks
that the swine did eat: and no man gave unto him.

---

or lentils, but the pods of the carob tree. "In shape they resemble
a bean-pod, though larger, and curved more into the form of a
sickle, thence called keration, or little horn." (Trench.) They are
sometimes eaten by the very poor, but oftener used for the foddering of cattle. When it is said, he would fain have filled his belly
with these husks, it seems to imply that he was not allowed by the
owner even to do this; or it may be understood with what follows,
that he desired to eat these because no man gave him anything, *i.e.*,
anything fitter for human food.

"No man gave unto him." Not one of the false friends, or the
harlots on whom he had squandered his money would give him the
smallest trifle to save him from starving.

This is the end of the first stage of his history. At its beginning,
when he left his father's house with the purpose of being far away
from its restraints, so that he should live a life of undisturbed sensual gratification, he had fallen morally as low as he could; for the
gratification of sensual lusts is not lower than determined selfishness and filial ingratitude, and through God's mercy he has been
steeped in misery and degradation, a poor, ragged, starved swineherd; so that his final outward or worldly condition was the exact
counterpart of his first spiritual state: as at first he was without the
commonest feelings of virtue, so he is now without the commonest
necessaries of life: as at first he fed his filthy lusts, so now he has
to feed swine.

Now in reviewing this part of the parable, it seems to me that a
great mistake is made by giving an intellectual colouring to it.
There is a great temptation to do this, if we take the real design of
the parable to represent the departure of the Gentiles from their
first knowledge of God. In this case the famine is supposed to represent the wants of the soul or spirit, to which the philosophies
and mythologies, and traditions of heathenism were as unsatisfying husks. The citizen of the country has been explained as the
representative of the wisdom and knowledge—the maxims of
worldly prudence, or principles of ethics, without religion—which
for a time sustain the soul, and "still the hungry edge of appetite,"
and keep it from sinking utterly, while yet they leave it in its
wretchedness.

CHAP. XV.] WHEN HE CAME TO HIMSELF.

17 And when he came to himself, he said, How many hired

Now all such intellectual colouring detracts very seriously from the application of the parable to common life, and, still worse, seems to weaken its principal point, which is, the readiness of God to receive individual returning sinners—for, I need not say, every sinner must come back personally to God. Of course amongst the Gentiles in their best state there was a woeful famine of the knowledge of God; but the famine, if one would do justice to the parable, must be taken as literally as possible, as representing the sharp worldly disappointments and distresses which in so many cases are the means by which sinners are brought to their senses. The incidents of the parable are vulgar in the sense of common or familiar, because they represent what is constantly occurring in daily life. It is true that few men have in their youth a fortune given them to squander in vice or extravagance, but most men leave the home of religion or grace through some gross sin or other—drunkenness, fornication, evil company, gambling, betting, or some sort of dishonesty. In vast numbers of cases, where they are reclaimed, it is through the sharp discipline of want, disappointment, sickness, pain, or distress, according to the words of the Psalm, "Before I was afflicted I went astray, but now have I kept thy word." Or at least these things contribute, through the good providence of God, to their restoration. Some may wander through Agnosticism, Rationalism, or various forms of Scepticism, but these must be comparatively few, and the teaching of the Lord is not for the few but for the many.

17. "And when he came to himself, he said, How many hired servants," &c. He came to himself, or, in other words, when he came to his senses. In spiritual matters, the coming to one's self is the coming to God; for it is coming to understand our true interests as immortal beings, our true place in God's creation, or rather family, as His sons, and our true nobility; and yet how all this has added to our sin, in that we have forsaken God! In the case of the prodigal himself, we must be careful, if we would not make the parable unreal, not to credit him with all the thoughts and feelings of Evangelical Christianity, as if he lived in Gospel, not in Jewish times. The thing that awoke him, as it were, was the remembrance of the overflowing plenty of his forsaken home compared with his present want.

servants of my father's have bread enough and to spare, and I perish with hunger!

18 I will arise and go to my father, and will say

"I perish with hunger." So A., P., Q., X., T., Δ, Λ, Π, later Uncials, most Cursives, &c.; but ℵ, B., D., L., some Cursives, old Latin, Vulg., Copt., Syriac, &c., read, "perish here."

"How many hired servants of my father's have," &c. Again, we must be careful how we project the spiritual, or Christian, interpretation into the story itself, and so confuse the parable, and rob it of some of its most salient points. One commentator, for instance makes these "hired servants" to "represent those heathen proselytes who had a place, although a very inferior one (the outer court) in the temple, and who might thus from afar take part in the worship." Another sees in them "those who, with no very lofty views about living to the glory of God, with no very lively affections towards Him, do yet find their satisfaction in the discharge of their daily duties; who, though they do His work more in the spirit of servants than of sons, rather looking to their hire than out of the free impulses of love, are not without their reward."

But, we must ask, what did the prodigal himself mean by these hired servants? Evidently the lowest, meanest, and least cared for people in his father's employment. In ancient times the hired servant was far worse off than the slave, for the slave was always sure of his food, his clothing, his lodging, his attendance when sick; whereas the hired servant had simply his day's wages, and when these were paid, he went off to his hovel, and there was an end of all care for him. He had his liberty, it is true, but that was too often liberty to starve; so that when the prodigal envied the lot of the hired servants, he envied the lot of the lowest of those who had anything to do with his father.

18. "I will arise and go to my father, and will say unto him, Father, I have," &c. There must have been some struggle within to enable him to determine upon this. There was the shame on the one side, the shame of meeting his father and the household, and the elder brother, but it was overborne by the remembrance of his father's kindness in time past. He could not believe that he had changed.

"My father." He feels that he is his father, and that there is no hope for him on earth except in the name of "father."

CHAP. XV.] FATHER, I HAVE SINNED. 399

unto him, Father, I have sinned against heaven, and before thee,

19 And am no more worthy to be called thy son: make me as one of thy hired servants.

20 And he arose, and came to his father. But ^g when he was yet a great way off, his father saw him, ^g Acts ii. 39. Eph. ii. 13, 17.

"Father, I have sinned against heaven, and before thee." "Against heaven," *i.e.*, against the God of heaven. "Before thee." Notice that we are yet in the parable, and so we must not *at present* identify the father of the parable with God, the Eternal Father of the Eternal Son. The father is the natural father of the prodigal, and he resolves to return to him confessing the twofold guilt of his sin against heaven and before him. Godet considers this "before thee" to mean when in the presence, and under the roof of his father he gathered all together, and when his father beheld him with grief, "he defied his last look, and obstinately turned his back upon him." It may be, however, that he knew that his reckless career had become known to his father.

19. "And am no more worthy to be called thy son." Here we have the truth so constantly recurring in Scripture, that it is one thing to be in relationship to a person, God or man, and another to live according to that relationship—one thing to be a son, another to live as a son should live. Thus St. Paul, "Now are ye light in the Lord, walk as children of light" (Ephes. v. 8).

"Make me as one of thy hired servants." Again he thinks of the lowest and poorest in his father's employment and desires to take his place amongst them.

20. "And he arose, and came to his father." Apparently he made no delay. The sharp discipline of want and shame had had its desired effect.

"But when he was yet a great way off, his father saw him." His father was on the look-out for him. He knew, no doubt, that there was but one way by which he could return. It seems impossible to suppose that he had been totally without any information respecting his son, and so hearing of his extremity, he might expect him back. If, however, the Lord would have us suppose that he had no knowledge of it, what a picture have we of a father's yearning for the lost, that he should go out daily, perhaps many times a

and had compassion, and ran, and fell on his neck, and kissed him.

21 And the son said unto him, Father, I have sinned against heaven, ʰ and in thy sight, and am no more worthy to be called thy son.

ʰ Ps. li. 4.

---

21. "And am no more worthy." "And" omitted by אּ, A., B., D., K., L., Π, 1, 6, 131, and a few others, old Latin, Vulg., Sah., Copt.; but E., G., H., M., P., Q., R., other Uncials, most Cursives, Syriac, &c., retain "and."

21. אּ, B., D., U., X., add to end, "make me as one of thy hired servants." A., L., P., Q., R., other Uncials, almost all Cursives, old Latin, Vulg., &c., omit it.

day, and strain his eyes in the direction of the "far country," hoping against hope that his son might have some sense of his sin—some memory of the goodness of his home vouchsafed to him by God! He knew that he had long earnestly prayed for this, and it may be that he had faith in the promises of God that He would answer his prayers.

"His father saw him." His heart at once told him that the indistinct figure in the dim distance was his son. He forgot in a moment all the unkind, unfilial treatment which he had received. His bowels yearned over him, and

"He ran, and fell on his neck, and kissed him." This apparently before the son had time to say a word. His return was the best proof of his repentance, but there was also the deep sorrow and anguish of his face, his soiled and tattered garments, his erect form bowed down with shame. By all this the father saw at a glance that his son was "alive again."

21. "And the son said unto him, Father, I have sinned against heaven," &c. The unlooked for kindness of his reception does not stay for a moment the penitent's confession. The acknowledgment of sin seems perfect.

"I have sinned against heaven," *i.e.*, against God and His law and holy will, and before thee. His absence from a good and righteous home, and the company of a loving father was, he knew, ever before his father. His abject poverty and wan looks were the proof, before the eyes of all, of his vicious extravagance.

"And am no more worthy to be called thy son." Here was the acknowledgment of his father's goodness and righteousness. How could such a profligate be the son of such a father? and yet he is

CHAP. XV.] BRING FORTH THE BEST ROBE. 401

22 But the father said to his servants, Bring forth the best robe and put *it* on him; and put a ring on his hand, and shoes on *his* feet:

---

22. "Bring forth quickly" (ταχὺ). So ℵ, B., L., X. (D. τάχεως), old Latin, Vulg., Goth., Copt., Arm., Æth.; but A., later Uncials, all Cursives, Sah., Syriac, omit and read as in Rec. Text.

his father. This is admirably put by Quesnel, "The particular marks of God's favour and goodness towards a true penitent never cause him to lay aside the resolution of humbling himself ever after at His footstool. He is faithful to his purpose, and it is even an effect of the goodness of God that he is so. How unworthy soever he may acknowledge himself to be called a child of God, yet he cannot forbear calling Him Father: it is a contest between confidence and humility; the former restores what the latter takes away."

22. "But the father said to his servants, Bring forth the best robe .... shoes on his feet." If we are to bear in mind the intention of the parable which is to teach us how God rejoices over the penitent, we must postpone all consideration of the spiritual or mystical meaning of the robe, or ring, or shoes, and consider for the present only what they would signify if the parable was the relation of an occurrence which actually took place about that time. In such a case the robe would not be the robe which the prodigal used to wear before he left home (if it was a costly or gorgeous one, why when he gathered all together should he have left it behind?), but the best festive robe in the house. The father, being a man of wealth and consideration, would have festive robes with which he would clothe any guest whom he wished to honour (see particularly notes on Matth. xxii. 11); so that the young man was welcomed back, not merely with the tenderest affection, but in the highest festive way as the most honoured guest; the giving of a ring was a sign of the highest honour which princes could bestow. (Genesis xli. 42, Esther iii. 10, viii. 2.) The putting on of shoes or sandals on his feet, was not because he was weary and footsore, but because the being shoeless was a mark of mourning (2 Sam. xv. 30, Ezekiel xxiv. 17); and so all signs of mourning must be removed; besides, we are told that slaves could not wear shoes or sandals, so that this investiture was a token that he was not for a moment to be considered as a slave, notwithstanding his poverty.

D D

23 And bring hither the fatted calf, and kill *it;* and let us eat, and be merry :

---

23. "And bring hither the fatted calf, and kill it," &c. In those old times, when each great man killed the meat for his feasts, and at any time might be called to entertain persons of distinction, some beasts were always ready fattened (Gen. xviii. 7); so that the penitent is, in all respects, treated as a distinguished guest who had suddenly arrived, and towards whom suitable and generous hospitality was to be exercised.

24. "For this my son was dead, and is alive again," &c. . . . "began to be merry." We are not at first to give these words their high spiritual meaning, though I confess that it is hard not to do so. Still any good and virtuous man who had similarly lost one of his family, would almost naturally say the same. "My son was dead to all better feelings, all self-respect, all sense of what is looked for from a member of my family, and all these good and right feelings are revived in him, so that he is to me as one alive from the dead. He was lost to myself, to his family, to society, and religion, and is found.

Such is the parable. I have studiously kept quite in the background all spiritual, all evangelical, all mystical meanings, because all such seem to me, if brought forward *at the first*, to detract from the power of the teaching, which is to set forth the heavenly joy in the bosom of God, and of the angels of God, at the restoration of the penitent, by means of a most graphic picture of high and pure earthly joy at the return of a reprobate to his earthly father's house. The circumstances of the parable are intensely human, or, to use the word most fashionable with expositors, intensely anthropomorphic, and were intended by the Lord to be so, so that of ourselves—ourselves, of course, in our best state—we might judge what is right.

And the lesson is beyond measure astonishing. The Eternal Son, Who is in the bosom of the Father, and Who knows every beat of that Father's heart, sets forth here what He alone knows, the mind of God towards the penitent. In the two former parables this mind is set forth in somewhat general language, " Rejoice with me, for I have found my sheep," " Rejoice with me, for I have found the piece which I had lost ; " but here is the liveliest picture of the joy itself, the seeing afar off, the compassion, the embrace, the kiss, as

CHAP. XV.] DEAD AND ALIVE AGAIN. 403

24 [i] For this my son was dead, and is alive again; he was lost, and is found. And they began to be merry.

[i] ver. 32. Eph. ii. 1. & v. 14. Rev. iii. 1.

---

prelude to the festive robe, the ring, the sandals, the best provision, the feast itself, the mirth of the feast.

Such is the human or earthly picture by which the Lord would have us judge of the mind and heart of His Father towards penitent sinners. And now, having kept the picture on its human side clear, so that it may bring out in stronger relief the one great purpose of the parable, we can the better consider its evangelical application, because it was evidently intended, not for a mere handful of Jews, but for us, for the Church of Christ, the Church Catholic in all ages and in all countries.

In the spiritual application, the loving and forbearing Father is God. By some German commentators it has, to serve their rationalistic purposes, been made a difficulty that the Son of God, and His Mediation are not alluded to in a parable which seems to require some reference to them; but the whole Godhead—Father, Son, and Spirit—is the Head of the house; the prodigal sins equally against the love of the Father, the covenant of the Son, and the sealing of the Spirit.

It will be now at the outset necessary to settle distinctly in our minds as to what the home is from which the prodigal, or the erring Christian, departs; for this lies at the root of the parable itself, and of any spiritual application of it. It has been taken by Catholic commentators to be the state of baptismal grace or membership in the mystical body of Christ, in which, assuming that infant baptism is according to the will of God, and that He will accompany it with grace suitable to the needs of the child, the son has been brought up from his earliest years. Only two hypotheses seem possible. This to which we have alluded, that the prodigal was brought up in a state of grace answering to that mentioned in the catechism, "I heartily thank our heavenly Father, that he hath called me to this state of salvation through Jesus Christ our Saviour; and I pray unto God to give me his grace, that I may continue in the same." Or that the youth entered into a state of grace by an act of conscious conversion later in life, which would necessitate that he should be the son of another father, brought up in an altogether different home, and that much later in life, perhaps two or three years before his departure, he deliberately chose for himself another father, and then, for the first time, became an inmate of the good and holy home which he left when he became the prodigal. It is absolutely necessary, I say, that we should settle this matter, for the fact that the prodigal left the house of a father, in which he was living in peace and plenty at the time of his departure, is not one of the accessories of the parable, but its dominant feature. It is the root, the foundation of the whole matter. I do not see how in either this dispensation, or indeed in the Jewish, the parable could be applied to individual souls without it. The doctrine of baptismal grace, as set forth in Scripture and the formularies of the Church,[1] supplies the idea of the home; and, as far as I can see, nothing else can. And a home of love and grace in which a child can be brought up must be assumed, or the whole parable seems meaningless.

Such is the home; and now for the circumstances of the departure. The younger son first asked that his portion of goods might be given to him, so that he might do what he liked with it, and the father at once gave it to him. This is interpreted on the part of the Eternal Father as the gift of free-will, and on the part of the prodigal as representing that inherent selfishness which is at the root of all wilful sin, or that love of independence which even caused the fall of our first parents; but I ask, is it not essential to the construction of the sort of parable or story which the Lord intended to produce? He desired to represent a man well brought up wasting his patrimony in vice and extravagance, and also his kind reception by his father after he had incurred severe discipline. And this necessitates that he must have means wherewith to be sinful and profligate; and so his father must give him his share at the outset. The conduct of the father, if it represents the conduct of God, seems to me to set forth the terrible truth, that when men depart from God, He does not take away His gifts from them, but permits them to misuse them, so that they may see that all temporal gifts are curses when enjoyed apart from Him.

The taking a journey into the far country, and there wasting his substance must be what it is described as being, plunging into a

---

[1] Or what, of course, exactly answers to it under the old covenant, the reception of the Jewish child by circumcision into the elder family of God.

course of open and deliberate sin, accompanied by drunkenness and fornication, as well as waste and extravagance. The latter part of the parable forbids us to interpret it as any form of ill-temper, or moroseness, or even self-righteousness which, if persisted in, will destroy religion. It must be open and deliberate sin, and be it remembered that open profligacy has the additional aggravation that it involves others in sin. The evil companions, male and female, of the prodigal must have been, some of them, at least, hardened, not only by his example, but by the means of sinful indulgence which the squandering of his great wealth afforded them. Some of them may have owed their first experience in evil to him.

Add to this that the greater part of those to whom we preach repentance seem mostly to fall away from God by gross sin of some sort, especially the poor.[1]

The "far country" has been interpreted as alienation from God. To Christians it may also mean deliberate withdrawing from the reception of those means of grace which remind the soul of God and eternal things.

The "mighty famine" must not be taken to be a "famine of the word of God," or of spiritual satisfaction, because this sort of want was most pressing when he was in the height of his carnal pleasures. Then his soul was dying of spiritual starvation when he least realized such needs. The famine is rather, as I have said, the afflictions and distresses both of body and soul by which God so often brings wilful sinners to their senses.

The "feeding swine" seems to depict the lowest state of abasement that could well enter into the Jewish mind. The consistency of the outward framework of the parable seems to require that it should not be understood as the gratification of very debasing lusts, because he had not the means of so doing, and had not wherewithal to assuage his hunger.

The "coming to himself" and his soliloquy about the hired servants seems to betoken the awaking of the soul to its true needs, perhaps the remembrance of bygone pleasures of religion, perhaps the consciousness that those only who are in the home of God's grace enjoy true happiness.

---

[1] The late Archbishop Sumner in his "Apostolical Preaching considered," notices this as showing the wisdom of the Apostles in preaching against gross rather than refined forms of sin.

"I will arise, and go to my Father." Here is the first thing, to arise out of the mire and degradation of sin, and go even to God.

"To my Father." Here is the sense of the Fatherhood of God, which gives its life to Evangelical repentance: without it all is cold formalism, or forsaking of sins on mere prudential motives, or despair.

"Father, I have sinned against heaven, and before thee." "He shows his repentance to have been divinely wrought, a work of the Holy Spirit, in that he acknowledges his sin at its root as transgression of the Divine Law—as wrought against God. Thus did David say, 'against Thee, Thee only have I sinned,' while yet his offences had been against the second table. For we may injure ourselves by our evil, we may wrong our neighbour, but strictly speaking we can *sin* only against God; and the recognition of our evil as first and chiefly an offence against Him, is of the essence of all true repentance, and distinguishes it broadly from remorse, and all other kinds of sorrow which may follow upon evil deeds." (Trench).

"And am no more worthy to be called thy son." See observations on pp. 399 and 400.

"When he was yet a great way off, his father saw him," &c. This is far truer of the spiritual reality than of the parabolic picture; for it is the heavenly Father, Who when he is almost totally alienated, brings the sinner to his senses by corrective discipline, brings him to himself, shows him how his sin is against heaven, gives him the mind to resolve, and secretly upholds him in putting his resolution into effect; and when he is come back, and is nearing home, gives him such a foretaste of heavenly joys as dispels his fears and encourages him, and fills him with hope and makes him resolve that come what will, he will never again wring the heart of so forbearing a Father. Quesnel aptly remarks, "A pastor to whom a penitent comes as a father, ought to have the heart and deportment of one, and imitate Him Whose place he holds."

As to the robe, the ring, the shoes, the fatted calf, we have seen how they denote high festival: and I think it is well to keep them as such, and not endeavour to minutely particularize everything. Thus the robe has been explained as the "Righteousness of Christ thrown over the sinner," but the great gift of the New Covenant is not an outward, but an inward thing. Jewish righteousness is

MUSICK AND DANCING.

25 Now his elder son was in the field: and as he came and drew nigh to the house, he heard musick and dancing.

---

comparatively external, whilst Christian righteousness, that of the new and better covenant is "I will put my law in their hearts" (Hebrews x. 11). Again, the ring has been explained as the sign of betrothal, "I will betroth thee unto me in faithfulness," and the shoes somewhat lamely have been associated with Ephes. vi. 15.

The killing of the fatted calf has been said to be the Death of Christ; but as Trench well remarks, "That sacrifice is not a consequence of the sinner's return, as the killing of the fatted calf is the consequence of the prodigal's, but the ground which renders such a return possible."

With respect to the Eucharistic feeding, which the feast on the fatted calf is, by so many spiritual divines, said to symbolize, I cannot help saying that I hesitate so to apply it. The figures which compose this delightful parable are exceedingly engaging, loving, instructive, necessary, but they are elementary. They appear to me to be in a sphere below those set forth in John vi. The Eucharistic feeding, that in it we may partake of the full nature of the God-Man, has to do with the conveyance of Life, spiritual and eternal Life, and the Resurrection of the Body, whilst the fatted calf has to do with the festivity of a welcome home. The ideas associated with the welcome home are very beautiful, but still ordinary religious ideas, God meeting the penitent, encouraging him, diffusing joy into his heart; whereas the ideas associated with the Eucharistic Oblation, and the feeding on the Body and Blood of the Adorable Victim, are transcendental.

The second part of the parable teaches us the same lesson as the first part, viz: the exceeding goodness and forbearance of the father, in dealing with and endeavouring to win over to a better mind, one whose conduct seems morose and churlish to the last degree. It begins with

25. "Now his elder son was in the field: . . . music and dancing."[1] Now his elder son was in the field, *i.e.*, he was about his

---

[1] "Musick and dancing." As I desire to keep my remarks on this parable free from all considerations which may distract the reader's attention from its great lesson, I think it better to throw the following into a footnote.

On the "dancing" Dean Alford remarks:—" This is one of those by-glances into the lesser occupations and recreations of human life, by which the Lord so often stamps hi

26 And he called one of the servants, and asked what these things meant.

father's business, and considering that the framework of the parable has to do solely with home duty, or the neglect of it, nothing better could be said of him. It is quite evident that the Lord means by this notice to contrast his conduct with that of his brother's, and also to shew us, perhaps by way of some exculpation, that having been absent about the farm work when the younger son returned, he had not seen the deep marks of contrition exhibited in his whole demeanour nor heard his penitent confession. In fact we shall see he had not heard one word of his brother's change of heart till he heard it from his father in the very last words of the parable.

Let the reader remember that I do not say this to vindicate him,

---

tacit approval on the joys and unbendings of men. Would these festal employments have been here mentioned by Him on so solemn and blessed an occasion, if they really were amongst those works of the devil which He came into the world to destroy?" Upon this another commentator, Bishop Ryle, remarks :—" I can see no force in arguments of this kind. There is not the slightest proof that the dancing referred to in this place was at all like the dancing of modern times. There is no proof that it was at night, or that it was a dance of men and women mingled together." But is not this commentator aware that the most abominable of all dancing is that where the sexes—especially the females—dance apart? The thing which purifies dancing in these Western countries is the intermingling of the sexes, just as the same mixture goes very far (humanly speaking) to purify society. The vilest state of society is that where men and women are kept apart.

With respect to dancing itself, it is a natural way of expressing joy, and so is common, in some shape or other, to the whole human family. It is abundantly recognized in scripture as a natural and innocent mode of recreation. Thus Jeremiah xxxi. 13, " Then," *i. e.* in Messianic times, " the virgins shall rejoice in the dance, both young men and old together: for I will turn their mourning into joy, and will comfort them, and make them rejoice from their sorrow." Also Jer. xxxi. 4. " Thou shalt be built . . . . and shalt again go forth in the dances of them that make merry." It was also, like music, capable of a religious use. Psalm cxlix. 3, cl. 4; Exod. xv. 20; II. Samuel, vi. 14; which it could not be if it was essentially ungodly. Of course like every other amusement, or, indeed, occupation, it requires strict Christian watchfulness, lest it occupy the mind ; and wherever it takes place in houses of public resort it requires to be put under the strictest regulation as to hours, company, &c. I cannot help concluding this note without expressing my conviction—that in past years untold harm has been done to tender consciences by religious guides of a certain school making that to be a sin which is no sin. The young have been taught that an amusement is essentially unclean, which God has not pronounced to be unclean. Not being "fully persuaded in their own minds," they have engaged in it, as the Apostle says, " with offence," and from this they have received permanent injury to their souls rather than from any evil connected with the amusement itself; but we trust that this, being the fault of others, will not be imputed to them.

CHAP. XV.]   HE WAS ANGRY.   409

27 And he said unto him, Thy brother is come; and thy father hath killed the fatted calf, because he hath received him safe and sound.

28 And he was angry, and would not go in: therefore came his father out, and intreated him.

---

28. "Therefore came his father out." So almost all later Uncials, almost all Cursives, Vulg., Syriac; but ℵ, A., B., D., L., R., X., 1, 33, 131, 157, old Latin, Goth., Copt., Arm., read, "and his father."

---

but rather to vindicate the father, whose words of affection and regard to him are utterly out of keeping with the character of mere superficial show of heartless obedience, with which the majority of commentators credit him.

26. "And he called one of the servants and asked what these things meant. . . . safe and sound." This enquiry without going in himself is also alleged against him by Archbishop Trench as indicating the ungenial character of the man, and still more offensively by Godet. " Every free and joyous impulse is abhorrent to the spirit of Pharisaism. Rather than go straight into the house, the elder son begins by gathering information from a servant: he does not feel himself at home in the house." But it seems to me that the Lord introduces this minor incident with a double purpose. First, as part of the necessary machinery, so to speak, of the parable. It was necessary in order to bring out into the strongest relief the exceeding kindness and forbearance of the old man, that he should himself come out and himself personally entreat his son to come in; all which would have been lost if the son had gone in at once. And, besides this, it is probably intended by the Lord to be in some measure exculpatory, for the servant, as I before remarked, said nothing whatsoever of the younger brother's repentance, merely that the father had received him safe and sound, and the sinful irreconcilability of the elder brother scarcely began, till he, having heard the imperfect statement of the servant, refused to come in, which, with the father's conduct consequent upon it, is thus described.

28. "And he was angry, and would not come: therefore came his father," &c. It is to be remembered that he had not heard the circumstances which were in his brother's favour. This, *i.e.*, his deep sorrow and humiliation, he heard for the first time when his father came out and described his brother as one risen from the dead.

29 And he answering said to *his* father, Lo, these many years do I serve thee, neither transgressed I at any time thy commandment: and yet thou never gavest me a kid, that I might make merry with my friends:

He ought of course to have anticipated his father's kindness, or, as Godet says, to have considered himself more at home, but, if he had, we should have missed the latter part of the parable.

29. "And he answering said to his father, Lo, these many years do I serve thee, neither at any time," &c. Let the reader remember that these words in the actual parable itself, as distinguished from its spiritual import, may not have been said in the vain-glorious spirit which they seem to us to proceed from. Looking at them simply and merely as what passed between a human father and his son, many a son may have been able to say this to his father, just as I have heard more than one father say of his son, "That dear lad has never given me one moment's uneasiness." If St. Paul in the view of the approval of his Divine Father could say, "Men and brethren, I have lived in all good conscience before God until this day" (Acts, xxiii. 1), and could describe his former Judaical state in the words "touching the righteousness which is of the law blameless," surely this young man, looking back at his past years of industrious farm work, office work, home work, might say what he did.

Of course, considered theologically in the light of the new views of things brought us by the fulness of New Testament teaching, respecting works and grace, he could not for a moment say anything like this to his heavenly Father. Taking the fulness of gospel truth into account, and considering the father of the parable not as a human, but as the Eternal Father, he must be held to have sinned and come short of the glory of God, and must be justified freely by God's grace, just as his own father, rather just as Abraham, Isaac, and Jacob, and the prophets must have been justified. But looking at the parable on its human side, it was quite possible that he could, without falsehood, have said this to the father whose estate he had managed, and whose household had been probably very much under his control.[1]

---

[1] I cannot gather less than this from verse 31.

SON, THOU ART EVER WITH ME.

30 But as soon as this thy son was come, which hath devoured thy living with harlots, thou hast killed for him the fatted calf.

31 And he said unto him, Son, thou art ever with me, and all that I have is thine.

"And yet thou never gavest me a kid, that I might," &c.

Though in all probability there was not a sumptuous entertainment given by his father for years past in which he had not played the part next to the head of the household.

30. "But as soon as this thy son was come, which hath devoured thy living," &c. Nothing can be worse than the spirit of this remonstrance. He repudiates the name and relationship of brother. This *thy* son—not *my* brother, but *thy* son: thereby tacitly reproaching his father for having such a son. I cannot help remarking that he would not have expressed himself in such language if his brother and he had been on loving terms before the departure of the former. Up to that time it is not probable that they had had much in common. The elder one a business man devoted to husbandry and the management of the estate: the younger not so.

But this exceeding moroseness and ill-temper did not for one moment alienate the heart of his father from him. Quite the contrary—the father not only bears with it, but tries to bring him round in words of such extraordinary approval and affection that one cannot but be astonished at the father's wonderful forbearance in that he should at that time, in the face of the insulting speech which he has just received, have given utterance to them.

31, 32. "And he said unto him, Son, thou art ever with me, and all that I have is thine. It was meet that we should make merry, and be glad," &c. Here the father pronounces upon the state of the two sons—of the first, notwithstanding the sinful outbreak of uncharitableness and ill-temper, he says, "Son, thou art ever with me, and all that I have is thine." Of the other he says, "This thy brother was dead, and is alive again; and was lost, and is found."

Now both these expressions must be understood according to the same principle of interpretation. They must both be understood, first of all, in a worldly or lower sense, that is, within the limits of

32 It was meet that we should make merry, and be glad:
k ver. 24. *k* for this thy brother was dead, and is alive again;
and was lost, and is found.

the parable, taking it to be a story of what might have occurred at any time in the history of a wealthy family; and then they must be understood according to the spiritual interpretation of the parable as an earthly story setting forth some heavenly and spiritual reality.

In the first case "thou art ever with me" means thou art ever in my house—about my person—consulted by me on all points connected with my estate and my household; and " all that I have is thine" means thou hast the present enjoyment and the future disposal of all that belongs to me.

In the second case " this thy brother was dead " means that " to me he was as one dead, his affections were seemingly alienated from me, and his conduct was a disgrace to my name, but now " he is alive again," his affection to me is revived; his conduct promises to be virtuous, and his life will be a source of happiness to me: he was lost to all sense of decency, lost to all better feeling, to all usefulness, and now all this is reversed, it is as if it had not been, he is found."

But the parable sets forth spiritual realities. We must believe, as I said, that the Lord spake it for the edification of his Church to the end of time. If ever there was a Gospel parable framed with reference to Gospel times, it is this. No other parable more naturally lends itself to the exhibition of Gospel realities.

Now, as evangelically understood, what must be the significance of "this my son (or thy brother) was dead and is alive again?" It can have but one, which is set forth in the words of the apostle: "Awake, thou that sleepest, and arise from the dead, and Christ shall give thee light." The being dead must be "dead in trespasses and sins," the being alive again must be "yielding ourselves unto God as those that are alive from the dead," or in the words of another apostle, "we being dead to sin live unto righteousness." For this resurrection to newness of life we pray every time we stand by the grave of a departed brother. "We meekly beseech thee, O Father, to raise us from the death of sin unto the life of righteousness." And the same with the expressions "lost" and "found." The being lost can have but one spiritual meaning, the loss of the soul through sin. Similarly the being "found" can only have but one meaning, the salvation of the soul through Christ: the soul being brought to itself, converted, forgiven, and established by Him Who came "to seek and to save that which is lost." But if the words respecting the second son have this spiritual application, and this only, what must we say of the words said to the first son? Are we to understand the words said to the younger spiritually, and those to the elder carnally? Impossible. This is not dealing honestly with the word of God. If the words to the younger are intended by the Lord to apply spiritually to the members of His Church, so must the words to the elder; and they too can have but one meaning. "Thou art ever with me" can only mean "Thou abidest in Me, in My love, in My grace—notwithstanding thine infirmities, thy sinful infirmities, thy outbursts of passion, or even uncharitableness, thou art ever with Me. Thou hast not fallen away, thou hast not sinned unto death. And 'all that I have is thine' cannot but mean "thou art yet an inheritor of the kingdom of heaven, all things are thine if thou yet belongest unto Me."

If the words said of the younger son respecting his restoration to life are to be understood spiritually, so must the words to the elder son respecting his abiding in life, or at least in the favour of God. And there is a heartiness about both sets of expressions, an affectionateness, a plainness, which seems to assure us that the Father meant what He said in each case.

But there is undoubtedly a difficulty, which to some minds, I believe, is insuperable, in acknowledging the reality of the father's words to the elder son, and it is this, that it is taken for granted that he is intended to represent the Scribes and Pharisees, who at the beginning of the chapter are set forth as murmuring against the Lord, because He received sinners and eat with them; but I believe that this identification of the elder son with the Pharisees is a great mistake, and cannot be held consistently with our Lord's conduct to the Pharisees, or his words respecting them. His words to them are always words of very strong and withering denunciations. "Woe unto you Scribes and Pharisees, hypocrites, for ye pay tithe of mint and anise and cummin, and have omitted the weightier matters of the law, judgment, mercy, and faith." Think of some of the things of which He accuses them in Matth. xxiii. "Ye shut up the kingdom of heaven against men;" "Ye devour widow's houses;" "Ye make the proselyte twofold more the child of hell than before;" "Ye make clean the outside of the cup and platter, but within they are full of extortion and excess;" "Ye are like whited sepulchres, full of all uncleanness." I appeal to the reader, is it possible that the Lord should denounce the Pharisees as a body in this way, and then, as in this parable, address a typical or representative Pharisee with such words as " Son, thou art ever with me, and all that I have is thine?" Common sense seems to forbid it. No. We must take the elder son to be the representative not of the Pharisee, but of the Jew—the religious Jew. And if it be asked, Is it possible to suppose that any religious Jew would grumble, and manifest ill-feeling at the ready reception of a penitent, we answer, we have a case exactly to the point in one of the most remarkable characters in the Old Testament—in no other than the prophet Jonah. His outburst of extreme ill-temper at God's ready reception of the Ninevites, and God's patient forbearance with him, seem the exact counterpart of the conduct exhibited by the elder son and God's patient forbearance towards *him*. [Jonah iv.]

Be it remembered that the ill humour of the elder brother was not directed against *any* reception of the returning penitent, but against the joy and festivity which accompanied the particular reception. If it had been put to him he would probably have said, "by all means let him be received, but let him be made to feel the disgrace that he has brought upon us, let him be put under discipline, let him be treated as one of the hired servants," forgetting, or it may be, being willingly ignorant that his brother had been made to undergo very severe discipline indeed, in the starvation of his body through the famine, and in the distress and anguish of his mind through his repentance. He required not discipline, but reassurance, and this he could hardly have without some very manifest tokens of the restored love of his father. In the most penitential of Psalms we are taught to pray, " Make me hear of joy and gladness, that the bones which thou hast broken may rejoice," and " restore unto me the joy of thy salvation."

With respect to the saying of the elder son, " Lo, these many years do I serve thee, neither transgressed I at any time thy commandment," I say that those who impute this to him as sinful Pharisaical self-righteousness must be extraordinarily ignorant of the language of the Old Testament, especially of the book of Psalms. I have counted about twenty similar and parallel expressions in the 119th Psalm alone (verses 31, 51, 55, 56, 59, 60, 70, 101, 111, 112, 121,

129, 161-178.[1] See also Psalm xviii. 19-26, and Neh. xiii. 14, 22, 31).

The words and conduct of the elder brother thus represent, not Pharisaism, but religious Judaism, which, one might almost say, of necessity lacked that deep view of sin, or of the sinfulness of all human nature which can only, as far as we can see, be brought about by the full exhibition of the Life and Death of the Son of God. Under such a system—an imperfect and (compared to the Christian) a superficial system—individual goodness as contrasted with the shortcomings of others was naturally a matter of glory, and because of the same imperfection in the system, returning sinners would be more harshly dealt with. The deeper the view of sin the more will love be applied in dealing with it, because the depth of love can only reach the depth of sin in the soul.

One word more. I have said that this parable is in its very nature adapted to the times of the Gospel, but can the conduct and spirit of the elder son be reproduced now? One would imagine that the influence of this parable itself, apart from any other teaching of Christ, would have made such a thing impossible, but it has not. In the early ages sects flourished for centuries whose separation from the Catholic Church was on the sole ground of its supposed too easy reception of penitents. The whole spirit of the elder brother seems reproduced in the later life and many of the sayings of Tertullian. And if we could read hearts, we should perhaps find that many devout Christians need the teaching of the parable,[2] though undoubtedly much of the popular preaching of the day ignores the prodigal's deep and hearty repentance, and would account him to be received back with no signs of contrition at all.

---

[1] 31. "I have stuck unto thy testimonies."

51. "The proud have had me greatly in derision, yet have I not declined from thy law."

55. "I have remembered thy name, O Lord, in the night, and have kept thy law."

56. "This I had, because I kept thy precepts," &c. &c.

[2] Thomas Scott, the Evangelical Commentator, has a remarkable note opposing the views of Dr. Adam Clarke, another Evangelical Commentator, which is much to the point. Adam Clarke had written: "They would never say that He (Jesus) was a friend to

Such is the parable. I have, with much regret, taken a view of it different to that of many Christian commentators, but my reasons are these:

I believe that of all parables it is the most Evangelical, and this, I think, mainly arises from its lending itself so readily, indeed from its requiring an individualizing application; but to this two things are necessary.

1. That the groundwork of the parable—the human story of what might have occurred in any wealthy family of the time, must be first of all set forth naturally, because the taking of it naturally and literally sets forth, more than anything else can do, the exuberance of forgiving love in the old father—the head of the family. The love of the eternal Father in receiving sinners, is imaged by the love of an earthly father, and the Lord has drawn the picture of an earthly father's love which brings home to us with exceeding emphasis the heavenly Father's love.

2. That all introduction of the reception of classes of men, such as Jews and Gentiles, before Christ, or in the time of Christ, or after it, seriously interferes with the individual application of the parable.

---

prostitutes, because it does not appear that such persons ever came to Christ, or that He in the way of His ministry ever came to them " (Dr. A. Clarke, note on Luke viii.). " Dr. Clarke, however," Scott rejoins, "allows that the prodigal son was among harlots. I trust that he did not, in his zealous defence of Mary Magdalene from the unjust charge brought against her, recollect at the moment the conclusion which might readily be deduced from this statement. Are the harlots ($\pi o \rho v a \iota$) so immensely more criminal and hopeless than their male associates and often seducers ($\pi o \rho v o \iota$), that while one of the latter was selected by our Lord Himself, for the encouraging pattern of our gracious God's ready mercy to the penitent, however vile their previous character; the former are to be considered merely as the objects of His frown and studied disregard?" I remember well that some years ago a leading Evangelical newspaper denounced very strongly the zeal with which the members of the Catholic School threw themselves into the good work of reclaiming fallen women. Surely the teaching and spirit of this parable was needed here.

3. That the parable being the most Evangelical of all, was mainly intended for the use of the Catholic Church, *i.e.*, for gospel times; and so such expressions as "This my son was dead, and is alive again," and "Son, thou art ever with me," must be interpreted according to Christian, rather than to Jewish ideas, or else we detract from our power of applying the parable to the case of any fallen Christian.

Add to this that the Jews did not reject Christ because of His reception of the Gentiles, but because He was a totally different Messiah to what they expected: "We preach Christ crucified, to the Jews a stumblingblock." The Pharisees who were afterwards converted to the faith gave much trouble, not because they opposed the conversion of the Gentiles, but because they desired that they might be circumcised that they might 'glory in their flesh.' (Gal. vi.)

My view of the scope of the parable is mainly that taken in a note at the end of Archbishop Trench's exposition, which reproduces the view of Cajetan. It is this: "Cajetan's view of the displeasure of the elder brother is interesting, and in its main features, original. He speaks first of the sweetness which the penient often finds at his first return unto God, 'the music and dancing;' for him all the glories of the Gospel have the freshness of novelty, an overpowering gladness, which they cannot possess for one to whom they have been familiar from the beginning. The joy of the latter has been infinitely greater than this one burst of gladness, but spread over larger spaces of time: so that, seeing the exultation of the newly converted, he may be tempted to ask, with a transient feeling of discontent, why to him also is not given this burst of exulting joy? why for him the fatted calf has been never slain? The answer is, because he has been ever with his father, because his father's possessions are, and always have been, his. His joy, therefore, is soberer and more solid—not the suddenly swelling mountain torrent, but the deep but smooth, silent river; and what is given to the other is given to him just because he was a beginner."

I see also that my view of the elder brother's state is in the main that of Wesley, who ends his remarks on the parable with, "Let no elder brother murmur at this indulgence, but rather welcome the prodigal back into the family. And let those who have been thus received, wander no more, but emulate the strictest piety of those who for many years have served their heavenly Father, and not transgressed His commandments."

CHAP. XVI.

AND he said also unto his disciples, There was a certain rich man, which had a steward; and the same was accused unto him that he had wasted his goods.

1. "And he said also unto his disciples, There was a certain rich man . . . . wasted his goods." I cannot altogether agree with the great majority of expositors in considering this parable as one of very great difficulty. The difficulty appears to me to vanish if we hold very fast and firm to the fact that it teaches but one lesson, and that, apart from this one lesson, it has no typical or mystical meaning. The lesson which is the key to the whole of it, is contained in verses 8 and 9. "The children of this world are, in their generation, wiser than the children of light, and I say unto you, Make to yourselves friends of the mammon of unrighteousness," &c. The Lord simply inculcates spiritual prudence or foresight, and in this respect I think only teaches the children of light to take example from the children of this world in their exercise of worldly prudence or foresight. Many things in the parable, I fully grant, seem to suggest a spiritual sense, but this sense cannot possibly be applied to all the circumstances of the parable without obscuring its one great lesson. Take, for instance, that which at first sight seems so obvious, that the rich man signifies God, that the steward is the soul to whom God has committed goods which do not belong to the soul, but to Him; that the soul, being sinful, has wasted its Master's goods instead of making the best of them to His glory, that God will call each and every soul to account for what He has committed to its keeping, that the time of this calling to account is either death or the judgment; that the soul called thus to account exclaims "What shall I do?" thus the lesson of the parable is the need of preparation for the inevitable issue of this calling to account, but here the spiritual interpretation begins to fail; for when God calls us to account for the deeds done in the body, it is too late to make preparation for a future world. 'The harvest is past, the summer is ended.' 'The master has risen up and shut to the door.' And, as we proceed, the interpretation I have alluded

GIVE AN ACCOUNT.

2 And he called him, and said unto him, How is it that I hear this of thee? give an account of thy stewardship; for thou mayest be no longer steward.

---

to fails still more signally, for even supposing that God says to the soul while there is yet time to make preparation, "How is it that I hear this of thee?" yet His demand can only be to wake the soul to repentance, but the steward in the parable, instead of repenting, adds sin to sin, and by further acts of dishonesty prepares a future home for himself by evil deeds, which in the spiritual and eternal reality he can only make provision for by good deeds.

The more seemingly obvious spiritual meaning thus failing, a variety of others have been suggested, some of them to be commended for their extraordinary ingenuity, but for nothing else. Archbishop Trench gives an interpretation from Vitringa, which may be taken as a sample, in which the rich man is God, the steward the ecclesiastical rulers of the people, the accusers of these rulers, the prophets, as Ezekiel xxxiv. 2 ("Woe be to the shepherds of Israel that do feed themselves,") Malachi ii. 8 ("Ye are departed out of the way; ye have caused many to stumble at the law," &c.), the accusation is "that they wasted the Lord's goods, they used the teaching and other powers committed to them for purposes of self-exaltation. They feel the justice of this, and see that there is nothing but condemnation from God before them." Therefore they now seek to make themselves friends among the Lord's debtors, and to retain their hold upon them though forsaken by God. And the device by which they seek to retain the people is by lowering the standard of righteousness, by substituting an outside instead of a heart righteousness. They invent convenient glosses for evading the strictness of God's law. They suffer men to put away their wives for any trifling cause. This gives a distinct meaning to the lowering of the bills, "write fifty," "write fourscore." I have abridged the above from Trench. The answer is that it is much too clever, much too ingenious, and above all, much too original. The lesson of the parable is obscured by it. The lesson is a very important one for every Christian soul, and must be very plainly set forth in the parable itself, instead of very circuitously, and very obscurely as in the explanation of this Vitringa.

We now proceed to examine the parable.

"There was a certain rich man which had a steward," as we

3 Then the steward said within himself, What shall I do? for my lord taketh away from me the stewardship: I cannot dig; to beg I am ashamed.

4 I am resolved what to do, that, when I am put out of the stewardship, they may receive me into their houses.

---

should call him, an agent. It is probable that he did more than receive rents, for the most feasible explanation of what follows is that he received the produce of the estate in kind, and sold it to merchants and dealers.

"And the same was accused unto him that he had wasted (or was wasting) his goods." We must adhere to the meaning of the word "wasting;" it is the same as that applied to describe the extravagance of the prodigal son. He wasted his lord's money over himself in extravagant living. This accounts for the fact that when put out of his office he had nothing to fall back upon, but was penniless. He had not robbed his master and put his ill-gotten gains in a place of safety, but had lived in extravagance beyond the income or share of the profits which he was allowed.

2. "And he called him and said unto him, How is it that I hear?" &c. The lord had not only heard the accusation, but was convinced that it was true, so he calls upon him to give account—not with a view to his acquittal, about that the lord had made up his mind—but that his accounts might be handed over to his successor: besides, it is in the preparation of the account that the fraud took place.

3. "Then the steward said within himself, What shall I do?" &c. It is clear that he had nothing to urge in excuse, or even in mitigation. He had no hope of any further consideration from his lord.

"I cannot dig;" perhaps, "I am not strong enough to dig."

"To beg I am ashamed." And yet he was not ashamed to commit a fraud.

4. "I am resolved what to do, that, when I am put out," &c. As if he had turned the matter over in his mind and a sudden, and, as he deemed, a happy thought struck him: and he lost not a moment in carrying it out, for indeed no time was to be lost.

5. "So he called every one of his lord's debtors unto him, and said unto the first," &c. Notice how the abruptness of the narra-

5 So he called every one of his lord's debtors *unto* him, and said unto the first, How much owest thou unto my lord?

6 And he said, An hundred ‖ measures of oil. And he said unto him, Take thy bill, and sit down quickly, and write fifty.

7 Then said he to another, And how much owest thou? And he said, An hundred ‖ measures of wheat. And he said unto him, Take thy bill, and write fourscore.

‖ The word *Batus* in the original containeth nine gallons three quarts: See Ezek. xlv. 10, 11, 14.
‖ The word here interpreted *a measure* in the original containeth about fourteen bushels and a pottle.

---

tive indicates the rapidity with which the nefarious business is carried out. No account is given of the thought and resolution immediately following upon it. We learn what it was from the way in which it was carried into execution.

"And he said, An hundred measures of oil . . . write fifty . . . write fourscore." From the steward asking the question and using the expression *thy* bill, it has been supposed that, contrary to our custom, the debtors made out each his own account, which, when he brought in, was examined and certified by the steward as correct. Very probably it was so: but one thing is quite certain, that the steward's voucher for the correctness of the bill was, in law, binding on the lord, who could not alter it, but must accept it as a true account of the debt.

But why is it said that he remitted one man fifty per cent. and the other twenty only? Very ingenious spiritual reasons have been given for this: but was it not a part of the steward's shrewdness or cunning? It seems to me (but of course no two persons will regard this in the same light), that if he had made an uniform deduction from each bill the fraud would have been more easily detected. Again, as to the difference in the amount of what was remitted, it might be alleged, that the circumstances of each debtor or farmer required to be taken into account: and so the lord, who seems to have been a man who left his concerns pretty much in the hands of others, would take the longer time in finding out the exact nature and extent of the fraud.

Such was the fraud, a very clever one, perhaps one which, except for some accident, would not have been discovered for a long time.

8 And the lord commended the unjust steward, because he

He had been able, at the last moment, to make each of these debtors a present of a considerable sum of money, and he counted on their gratitude and perhaps on their fears that he might make his home at one or other of their houses for some time to come.

8. "And the lord commended the unjust steward, because he had done wisely." Done wisely, or rather prudently, in that at the very last moment he had provided himself a home with money which he had for a very short time, perhaps only for a day or two, under his control. He had to give up his account, part of that account must be the amount of money owing to the lord or rich man. It was not in his power to apply to his own use any deduction he might make in each case, because when found out he could have been compelled to repay it, and the debtor, being in no way under an obligation to him, would have been first to accuse him, but his voucher or signature was good against his master, so that the lord could not sue the debtor for more than was on the bill.

Altogether it was a very clever fraud, and so the lord praised him for his prudence and forethought. And the Lord Jesus Himself now comes in, and adds the moral. "For the children of this world are in their generation wiser than the children of light." What is the significance of this 'for' [ὅτι] ? Some, and amongst them Alford, seem to think that it refers to the lord, or rich man, as a child of this world, in a measure sympathizing with and so praising the unjust steward for his clever fraud; but we have no right to assume this of the rich man, for the little we are told of him seems to show that he was by no means watchful in the management of his concerns.

Is not the explanation of it rather in the *wisely* (φρονίμως), and *wiser* (φρονιμώτεροι), as if He said, 'though the wisdom of this world, in all its branches, is foolishness with God, yet there is a certain wisdom in which the children of this world excel, and this is the wisdom of self-interest ; and so his lord praised the steward in this sense, and he could well do so because the children of this world present so very many examples of this lower earthly wisdom.'

"Are in their generation wiser than the children of light." It has been thought that the word "wisely" is not a good rendering, because in the most part of Scripture the word "wise" is applied

had done wisely: for the children of this world are in their generation wiser than ᵃ the children of light.   ᵃ John xii. 36.
Eph. v. 8.
1 Thess. v. 5.

to the wisdom from above—the highest wisdom, and it has been suggested that it would be better to render it by "prudent"—"prudently," but this latter word by no means sufficiently recognizes the extraordinary cleverness of the transaction, in which ingenuity was united with rapidity of execution. The word "shrewd," however, would be better rendering of the Greek. Perhaps the word which exactly expresses the idea is our word, "sharp," which would combine the forethought of the man, the ingenuity of his conception, and the quickness with which he carried it out.

"In their generation." The very literal rendering is "towards their generation," which would seem to mean towards the men of their generation, and the idea is supposed to be that the steward, and the debtors benefited by him were all of one race, children of the ungodly world; and the Lord's declaration is that the men of this world make their intercourse with one another more profitable, obtain more by it, manage it better for their interests, such as those are, than do the children of light *their* intercourse with one another. "For what opportunities," He would imply, "are missed by these last by those among them to whom a share of the earthly mammon is entrusted; what opportunities of laying up treasure in heaven, of making to themselves friends for the time to come by showing love to the poor saints, or generally of doing offices of kindness to the household of faith, to those of the same generation as themselves,—whom notwithstanding this affinity they yet make not to the extent they might receivers of benefits to be returned hereafter a hundredfold into their own bosoms." (Trench.) This is exceedingly good, but is not the application much too narrow? for surely a man makes himself friends of the mammon of unrighteousness, when he supports missions to the heathen abroad, or to those who are utterly alienated from the Church and virtually heathen at home. I acknowledge, of course, that there is a peculiar blessing upon those who do good to Christians, as Christians, or the Apostle would not have said, "While we have time let us do good unto all men, and *specially* to them who are of the household of faith." I cannot, however, help thinking that if possible the paraphrase of Alford, which gives a wider application, is to be preferred. "The sons of this world are far more shrewd for (towards the pur-

9 And I say unto you, ᵇMake to yourselves friends of the || mammon of unrighteousness; that, when ye fail, they may receive you into everlasting habitations.

ᵇ Dan. iv. 27. Matt. vi. 19. & xix. 21. ch. xi. 41. 1 Tim. vi. 17, 18, 19.
| Or, *riches.*

---

9. "When ye fail." So later Uncials, nearly all Cursives, some old Latin (b, e, f, ff², q), Vulg.; but ℵ, A., B., D., L., R., Π, old Latin (a, c, l), Cop., Syr., Arm., Æth., read, "they fail."

---

poses of) their own generation, for the purposes of their self-interest, than the sons of light." If we take the term "generation" to signify the time in which each generation lives, and along with it the interests, opportunities, &c., of that time, then, the word may mean, "in matters pertaining to this world," which is, I think, the true idea. Be it remembered, however, that the Lord speaks generally, for many a child of this world throws away his earthly prospects, just as some children of light have in their pursuit of the true and eternal riches, far exceeded the wise of this world in their pursuit of this world's good things.

9. "And I say unto you, Make to yourselves friends of the mammon," &c. We must first consider the broad, general meaning of this saying of the Lord, and then the particular terms in which it is expressed.

The Lord introduces His lesson with, "I say unto you." In this He seems to contrast Himself with the lord of the unjust steward. "He, the lord, commended the unjust steward because he made such good use, for his own purposes, of money over which he had control for so very short a time. And I, your Lord and Judge, commend the same prudence and forthought to you, My disciples and hearers. As he made himself friends by the money over which he had control, so I say unto you make to yourselves friends by means of that which it is now in your power to use to your eternal advantage."

The Lord's saying is virtually the same as His saying in Matthew vi. 19. 20. "Lay not up for yourselves treasures upon earth," "lay up for yourselves treasures in heaven;" the same as, "Sell that thou hast and give to the poor, and thou shalt have treasure in heaven." The same as that in Luke, "Sell that ye have and give alms, provide yourselves ... a treasure in the heaven that faileth not." The same as that in 1 Tim. vi. 19, "Charge

10 ᶜ He that is faithful in that which is least is faithful also in much: and he that is unjust in the least is unjust also in much.

ᶜ Matt. xxv. 21. ch. xix. 17.

---

them that are rich in this world that they do good, laying up in store for themselves a good foundation ... that they may attain eternal life." In fine it is one of those many places which give a place to almsgiving of the first importance, which make it a means of calling down from God especial grace, and which seem to make it almost, if it may be lawful to say so, "propitiatory"—not of course expiatory, but propitiatory in the sense of making God propitious to us according to the Lord's words, "Blessed are the merciful, for they shall obtain mercy."

But why does the Lord express himself in such terms as "Make to yourselves friends of the mammon of unrighteousness?" We answer, to carry on the analogy of the parable. The Lord had given utterance to a very graphic parable, in all probability founded upon an actual occurrence in which a man by unjust use of what was not his own made himself friends, who would receive him into their temporal habitations; and the Lord would have us in a way very acceptable to God, make by means of the same money which, though we have the disposal of it, is not strictly our own, friends who will receive us into eternal habitations. The expressions are clearly highly figurative or poetical. The friends who will receive us to the everlasting habitations, are either the good deeds personified, of which we have abundant instances in Scripture, as when, for instance, the hire of labourers is said to cry against oppressors of the poor (James v. 4), or when Abel's blood is said to cry to God against Cain, or it may be the friends whom we have won by our almsgiving, who will pray for us in this world, or if they die before us will welcome us into Paradise. I very much prefer the former meaning.

The Lord calls this world's riches unrighteous mammon, either because it is so often amassed, or at least increased by crooked means, or hard dealing, or because it so often produces covetousness, or worldliness, in those who possess it.

10. "He that is faithful in that which is least is faithful also in much: and he," &c. The Lord here seems to pass from the unfaithfulness of the steward in dealing with that which was his

11 If therefore ye have not been faithful in the unrighteous || mammon, who will commit to your trust the true *riches*?

|| Or, *riches*.

master's to the detriment of his master, to the general subject of faithfulness to our trusts and its opposite. He lays down that faithfulness is a principle, and, as such, will be seen in the performance of the smallest duties as much as in the greatest. "There is nothing small which God has either commanded, or expressed His pleasure respecting it, that we should do it. His greatness makes all about Him to be great. Nothing is little by which God may be pleased or may be offended. A thought is a little thing, and yet it may be a great provocation of the Divine Majesty; for every sin has the whole principle and virus of sin. So every duty, even the least duty, involves the whole principle of obedience, and little duties make the will dutiful, that is, supple and prompt to obey. The daily round of duty is full of probation and of discipline: it trains the will, heart, and conscience. To be holy we need not be prophets or apostles. The commonest life may be full of perfection. The duties of home are a discipline for the ministries of heaven. It is specially the common unnoticed duties of life which are the safest and most searching tests. They have no ostentation or excitement, but are done from inward force and a fruitful principle of duty." (Manning, "Sermons," vol. iv. Sermon ii.)

11. "If therefore ye have not been faithful in the unrighteous mammon, who will," &c. The unrighteous mammon means the goods of this world, the use or disposal of which God has made a part of our probation. If we are faithful in the use of these, we show our fitness to have what the Lord here calls the "true" entrusted to us. Our translators have supplied the word "riches" to complete the sense: but the word which the parallelism strictly demands is "mammon"—"the true mammon": but as such a rendering is absolutely inadmissable, perhaps the best word would be "goods," or "good things," which is more comprehensive than riches. There is a very deep and important truth in this place, for how is it that the faithful use of this world's mammon or goods is the condition without which we cannot be entrusted with the true good? Evidently because the true good, whatever it be, has to be employed throughout eternity in the service of God. There will be no selfishness amongst the blessed in the eternal world. All

12 And if ye have not been faithful in that which is another man's, who shall give you that which is your own?

---

12. "That which is your own." So ℵ, A., D., all other Uncials, Cursives, &c., &c.; but B., L., read, "our own," thereby destroying the sense. This surprising blunder of the officious scribe of B., who had not the least idea of the true meaning of the passage, is virtually adopted by Westcott and Hort, without even a note to vindicate their adhesion to a manifest blunder of two MSS. against the testimony of all the rest of Christendom.

their powers, faculties, possessions, will be ever laid at the feet of God. They will be ever used, not for themselves, but for Him. If, then, men have here in this life considered that which God has committed to them as absolutely their own to be used selfishly, and with little or no thought of God's ownership in it, how can the mere passage through death or the grave so change them that in eternity they will employ all that may be given them unselfishly, and to the sole glory of God? The rewards of the future world are never represented in Scripture as an eternity of mere rest, or of mere singing of praise, or even of mere rapture. Taking into full account such places as Luke xix. 17, 19, and the obedience of those hosts of angels to whom we shall be made like, and the analogy of all God's dealings with intelligent creatures, it will be an eternity of employment, in the faithful execution of higher and still higher trusts committed to us. And to fit us for this it is evident that we must not only receive grace, but also education, and the Lord here assures us that a great part of our education for these higher trusts will be our fulfilment of the lower trust—the unrighteous mammon.

12. "And if ye have not been faithful in that which is another man's, who shall," &c. At first sight the reason for this is not apparent. If anything can be called our own why should we not have it? and supposing that any person commits some thing of value to us, is it not possible that we might be very careless about looking to his interests and very careful about our own in any matter which we really think belongs to us? So it would be if what is here called "our own" were our own absolutely now in this life, and we were not accountable to anyone for its due use; but what our Lord means is this: "Our own" is only that which is eternally our own, which is inalienable. Now the things of this life are not our own, because we must part with them at death: but they are God-ordained means in the due use of which we may be

GOD AND MAMMON. [St. Luke.

13 ¶ ᵈ No servant can serve two masters: for either he
ᵈ Matt. vi. 24. will hate the one, and love the other; or else he
will hold to the one, and despise the other. Ye cannot serve
God and mammon.

---

prepared to serve God in another world with that which in a far higher sense can be called " our own " because inalienable. The true good, ἀληθινὸν, cannot be given to any one ; only to those who are prepared to use it for ever to the glory of God. The enlarged gifts, faculties, and powers of the undying nature if given to those alienated from God would simply make them devils.[1]

13. " No servant can serve two masters : for either he will hate the one, and love the other," &c. The connection between this and what goes before is extremely difficult to ascertain. One commentator supposes that the connecting link is the fact that the unjust steward attempted to serve both his lord and the mammon by which he at last made himself friends, but it appears to me that he never even attempted to serve his lord—only himself; at first by extravagance, then by fraud. The better connection is that we are put in trust of the unrighteous mammon, and must not allow it to become our master. If we employ it in the service of God, we are its master. If we employ it to feed our selfishness, or our covetousness, we become its slave. And the Lord seems to desire to impress upon us that there is no alternative. We must every one of us rule on God's part the unrighteous mammon, or be ruled by it. (See notes on Matth. vi. 24.) Mammon, of course, means

---

[1] There is a wonderful illustration of the truth of this at the conclusion of one of the most remarkable poems in our language, Southey's " Curse of Kehama." A wicked king by the performance of sacrifices, acts of worship, and austerities obtains possession of the whole universe ; heaven, earth and hell are at his feet. He has subdued to himself all living existences except the Triad. (Brakma, Vishnu, Siva.) Immortality alone is wanting. In the last scene he stands side by side with a chaste virgin, and the cup of Eternal Life is handed to both. The maiden drinks it, and it infuses into her immortality capable of unbounded happiness. He drinks it and he becomes a molten statue, the fire within him ever burning and never exhausted.

14 And the Pharisees also, ᵉ who were covetous, heard all these things: and they derided him.   ᵉ Matt. xxiii. 14.

15 And he said unto them, Ye are they which ᶠ justify yourselves before men; but ᵍ God knoweth your hearts: for ʰ that which is highly esteemed among men is abomination in the sight of God.   ᶠ ch. x. 29.   ᵍ Ps. vii. 9.   ʰ 1 Sam. xvi. 7.

16 ⁱ The law and the prophets *were* until John: since that time the kingdom of God is preached, and every man presseth into it.   ⁱ Matt. iv. 17. & xi. 12, 13. ch. vii. 29.

---

every good thing of this world. Not only money, but money's worth, as the saying is. A man must serve either God or the world. He cannot serve neither and he cannot serve both.

14. "And the Pharisees also, who were covetous, heard all these things: and they derided him." There seems to be here the point of a new departure. The Lord's words which follow, *i.e.*, from the fifteenth to the eighteenth verses inclusive, seem to be the fragments of a much longer discourse which appears to have been upon the errors or sins of the Pharisees. The fifteenth verse denounces their show of mere outside formal righteousness. The sixteenth opposes their worst error—the idea that the Old Testament dispensation was final, and that their exposition of it had put the top stone to its fabric. So far from this being the case the old state of things really came to an end in John and his preaching. Then the kingdom of God was proclaimed, and the publicans and harlots were pressing into it before them; but lest they should think that the passing away of the law in its ancient form implied its destruction, He assured them that it would pass away by being fulfilled in every tittle— nothing of it should fail. It would be like the passing of the bud into the flower, or that of the flower into the fruit. The ancient law would be regenerated, or transfigured, as it were, and become the everlasting Gospel—the narrow polity of the earthly Israel would pass into the Catholic or Universal Church—the partial atonement by sacrifices would be absorbed into the one universal Atonement of the One Oblation—the ten commandments written on tables of stone would become spiritual as well as literal, so that they should be written on the tables of the heart—the outward circumcision of

17 ᵏ And it is easier for heaven and earth to pass, than one tittle of the law to fail.

18 ˡ Whosoever putteth away his wife, and marrieth another, committeth adultery: and who-

ᵏ Ps. cii. 26, 27. Is. xl. 8. & li. 6. Matt. v. 18. 1 Pet. i. 25.
ˡ Matt. v. 32. & xix. 9. Mark x. 11. 1 Cor. vii. 10, 11.

the flesh would give way to a Baptism conveying the grace of Christ's Resurrection to enable men to " walk in newness of life "— the feeding on the Paschal Lamb would give place to a Sacrament in which men eat the Flesh of the Son of Man and drink His Blood, so that they may have His very Life in them—the various Sacrifices setting forth the Death of Him Who was to come would all merge in the one Eucharistic Oblation which set forth, which pleaded, which re-presented, the all-reconciling Death.

18. " Whosoever putteth away his wife, and marrieth another, committeth adultery," &c. The extraordinary abruptness with which the saying is introduced, standing, as it seems to do, wholly out of connection with what precedes respecting the impossibility of any part of the law failing, and with the parable of the rich man and Lazarus which succeeds, can only be explained on the assumption I have alluded to, that verses 13-19 are only fragments of a longer discourse respecting the sins and errors of the Pharisees. The Pharisees were, as a body, covetous, and proud, or self-justifying. They held that the law in its outward form was for ever binding, and that it was not to be superseded by any future " kingdom of God," and they justified divorce for very trivial grounds. Respecting this last the Lord now reproves them. If we had all the discourse we should most probably find that He repeated the arguments used by Him in Matth. xix. 4, 9, respecting the older law being that of the indissolubleness of marriage, and the permission of Divorce introduced because of the " hardness of men's hearts."

I have treated this subject so fully in my notes on Matth. xix. that I must refer the reader to what I said there, merely drawing attention to the fact that in this place (Luke xvi. 18) there is no mention of the relaxation of the *principle*, even in the case of adultery. I cannot but draw from this the conclusion that adherence to the original principle founded on the creation of one male and one female is the safest for the sake of society. It seems clear

CHAP. XVI.] MARRIAGE OF THE DIVORCED.

soever marrieth her that is put away from *her* husband committeth adultery.

---

that to allow the guilty parties to marry is contrary to the words of the Lord and an encouragement to sin.[1]

We now come to the Parable (or, it may be, narrative,) of the Rich Man and Lazarus. There is much difference of opinion as to whether it be a parable, or an account of what actually took place, first in this world, then in the world of spirits—for all that takes place in either world is "naked and open" before the eyes of Him Who uttered what follows. But whether it be an account of what actually took place or not, is immaterial. It is a parable to us, just as the Good Samaritan, the Unjust Steward, and the account of the Prodigal Son are parables, in the lesson taught by each, and yet every particular in each one of them may have been historical.

---

[1] Since writing the above I have had my attention directed by a friend (the Rev. J. B. Sweet) to a review by a Presbyterian minister of America, the Rev. S. Dike, of the fearful state of things respecting Divorce in the United States, particularly in some of the New England States. In Connecticut, in the year 1878, there was one divorce to between ten and eleven marriages. In 1880 one to a little under fourteen marriages. In Massachusetts, in 1860, there was one divorce to fifty-one marriages, but so rapidly has the practice increased that in 1878 there was one to twenty-one marriages. But this is by no means all. We have to deduct Roman Catholic marriages, because that Church does not allow divorce, and it appears to keep such a hold upon those belonging to it that they abstain from it; but if the number of Romanist marriages be taken into account and deducted, then in 1878 the proportion of divorces to marriages was, in Connecticut, one in between eight and nine, and in Rhode Island about the same. The author, the Rev. S. Dike, Presbyterian, makes the following statement. "The current (in favour of divorce) was set wrong in part by the early Puritan dread of everything like Ecclesiasticism. Marriage at the first was made a civil contract only, and a religious ceremony forbidden or discouraged." ("Marriage Laws in the United States, and their Results." Published by Vacher & Sons.)

What gave rise to this parable? Has it any connection with any word which the Lord had been uttering? Some think that it was addressed as a warning to the Pharisees, "who were covetous," and had "derided" the Lord. Others that it follows up the teaching of the Unjust Steward, inasmuch as we have the lot of one in the unseen world who, through his selfishness, had failed to "make to himself friends of the mammon of unrighteousness," and so had no one to welcome him into "the everlasting habitations." Others think that by the fate of the rich man the Lord foreshadows that of Herod, but the difficulty of supposing that it applies to the Pharisees is that as a rule they seem to have been austere rather than luxurious in their mode of living. Our Lord describes them in another parable as "fasting twice in the week," and Josephus speaks of them as self-denying and plain in their living. One expositor describes the rich man as a Pharisee who lived as a Sadducee—another (Trench) as an unbeliever, and if so, he could hardly have been a Pharisee; a third as a self-justifier, because the Lord had just said, "ye are they which justify yourselves before men," and endeavours to show that his words to Abraham are, when narrowly examined, so much self-exculpation.

Now it seems that the principal means for ascertaining the scope of the parable, and most certainly realizing the width of its practical application, is the fact that nothing whatsoever is said of the vice, or sin, of the rich man which brought him to such fearful punishment, just as nothing whatsoever is said of the virtue, or faith, or even patience of Lazarus which caused him to be so rewarded. Before the death of each nothing is said respecting the one, except what describes his prosperity, just as nothing is said of the other except what brings out the depth of his misery. And this reticence is wonderfully emphasized by the utter want of reference, in the words of Abraham, to the moral character of either the one or the other. Abraham says not, "Son, remember that thou in thy lifetime wast selfish, and hard hearted," but simply "thou receivedst thy good things," just as he says not, "Lazarus was poor in spirit, and patient, and believing," but "Lazarus received evil things." That the rich man by his want of true faith or charity, by his "doing" or his "leaving undone," deserved his punishment, we naturally infer with the utmost certainty, from what we believe of the perfect justice of God; but nothing is said of the guilt of the rich man, or of the faith of Lazarus. And this reticence is so marked, indeed,

19 ¶ There was a certain rich man, which was clothed in purple and fine linen, and fared sumptuously every day:

---

compared with the general tenor of our Lord's teaching, so extraordinary, that it seems to me to be the key of the parable. The teaching of the parable may be summed up in one word—Contrast. The contrast which may be, and in cases of which God only knows the number, actually IS, between the state of any man before and after his death. The depth of misery—of what the world esteems misery—and the height of happiness. The height of happiness—of what the world esteems happiness—and the depth of misery. So that the parable is the most graphic illustration conceivable of what is implied in the Lord's question, "What shall it profit a man if he gain the whole world and lose his own soul?"

And this interpretation, far more than any other, makes all parts of the parable cohere. The extremity of the misery of the unseen world is that it must be suffered without alleviation and without sympathy—of course, availing sympathy. One who has such a place in Paradise as Abraham cannot alleviate or send any one to alleviate, the misery of one whom he acknowledges as his son (child); and even the latter part of the parable, where the rich man prays that one should be sent from the world of spirits who, by his witness to its realities, may bring his brethren to repentance, is a most fitting conclusion to the whole, for its intention is to teach how this absolute reversal of our state from happiness to misery may be avoided by listening to the word, and by believing and accepting the Revelation of God; to the Jew this was Moses and the Prophets, to the Christian it is Christ and the Apostles. Let the soul that desires that its present happiness be not quenched in misery, let the soul which desires that its present wretchedness and poverty be so sanctified by grace that it may make it fit for a place in the Paradise of God, listen to this: for this Revelation of God in His Word is sufficient, and no other message from the eternal world apart from it can be of any avail.

19. "There was a certain rich man who was clothed in purple and fine linen." Such was his wealth and love of display that he clothed himself as if he were a king. The fine linen (byssus) was from the looms of Egypt. In Revelations xviii. 12, it has a foremost place amongst the most costly merchandize. "Gold,

20 And there was a certain beggar named Lazarus, which was laid at his gate, full of sores,

21 And desiring to be fed with the crumbs which fell from the rich man's table: moreover the dogs came and licked his sores.

---

21. "With the crumbs which fell." So A. (D.), P., X., Γ, Δ, Λ, Π, later Uncials, almost all Cursives, old Latin, a, f, g¹, Vulg., Goth., Syriac; but ℵ, B., L., old Latin (b, c, e, i, l, m, q), Sah., read, "with what fell."

silver, precious stones, pearls, fine linen (byssus), purple and silk." Edersheim tells us that "The white garments of the high priest on the day of atonement were made of it. To pass over exaggerated accounts of its costliness, the high priest's dress of Pelusian linen for the morning service of the day of atonement was said to have cost about £36, that of Indian linen for the evening of the same day, about £24. As regards purple, which was obtained from the coasts of Tyre, wool of violet purple was sold at that time by the pound, at the rate of about £3 the Roman pound."

"Faring sumptuously," translated literally, "enjoying himself splendidly."

20. "And there was a certain beggar named Lazarus." The name Lazarus is the same as that of Eleazer, signifying "God is my help," the Lord apparently signifying by this that he had no help but in God.

"Which was laid at his gate, full of sores." "Laid at his gate," so that the rich man saw the wretched object every time he went in or out of his mansion; and the poor man heard the sound of joyous revelry, and perhaps saw the abundance under which the tables groaned, so that his utmost desire was to partake of the broken fragments.

"Full of sores." St. Luke here uses a medical term, "ulcerated all over." These ulcers, however, could not well have been the effect of leprosy, as some suppose, or he would have been confined to a particular quarter of the city.

"Moreover the dogs came and licked his sores." Commentators are divided as to whether this is noticed as an alleviation of, or an addition to his pains. I think the former, but the fact that these unclean creatures, the scavengers of the streets of an Eastern city, should be able to pollute him with their tongues, sensibly increases the degradation of his state.

THE BEGGAR DIED.

22 And it came to pass, that the beggar died, and was carried by the angels into Abraham's bosom: the rich man also died, and was buried;

23 And in hell he lift up his eyes, being in torments, and

---

22. "And it came to pass that the beggar died, and was carried by the angels, &c. . . . was buried." No mention is made of his funeral. It seems as if he died as he lived, utterly forgotten, his body cast out of sight into some hole, whereas since the Lord expressly mentions the burial of the rich man, we must infer that his funeral was costly and magnificent as was his life. And now begins the contrast, the absolute reversal of the two conditions of each respectively.

Though perhaps there was no one friend or relative to soothe the last moments of Lazarus, and see to his decent interment, angels were watching the moment of his departure, that they might bear him through the gates of Paradise to the bosom of Abraham.

Whereas respecting the passage of the soul of the rich man into the unseen, the Lord says nothing; his soul, weighed down by luxury, by selfishness, by unforgiven sin, sunk down to the place of punishment which God had assigned to it, and the Lord says:

23. "In hell he lift up his eyes, being in torments, and seeth," &c. As this is one of the very, very few places in which God is pleased to lift up a little corner, as it were, of the veil which hides from us the unseen spiritual world, almost every syllable of the fearful account should be reverently and carefully examined.

The place, then, in which the rich man lifts up his eyes is not Gehenna but Hades, not the place of everlasting torment, but the place in which the souls of those who die before the Lord's coming exist in blissful or in doleful expectation of the end at that coming. This is noticed by all commentators who desire to set forth honestly what is in Scripture. Thus Alford, "Hades (Sheöl) is the abode of all disembodied spirits, till the Resurrection, not the place of torment, much less *hell* as commonly understood in the English Version. Lazarus was also in Hades, but separate from Dives, one on the blissful, the other on the baleful side . . . the Lord Himself went into the same Hades, of which Paradise is a part." So also Wordsworth, Plumptre, Godet, Stier, &c. Cornelius à Lapide writes, "in inferno, id est in Purgatorio," quoting Faber Stapulensis, but goes on to say that in this case it is equivalent to hell, *i.e.* Gehenna.

seeth Abraham afar off, and Lazarus in his bosom.

"Being in torments." The whole of the account would lead us to believe that these torments were not merely spiritual torments, such as anguish of mind, or despair, but bodily.

If it be asked how can a disembodied spirit feel bodily pain, or what is equivalent to it, and must be described in the same language, we answer by asking the question, "What is it within us which feels pain?"—evidently not the mere wounded fleshly muscle, but the animal life, the soul in fact ($\psi v \chi \acute{\eta}$), to which the nerves which permeate all parts of the body, carry to and fro the sensations which the soul feels, for if the nerve which forms its link of communication with the stricken or burnt limb be severed or withered, the self or soul feels no pain. Just then as the soul can think independently of the brain, though the brain is in some way, unknown to us, its instrument in the act of thinking, so the soul may feel that which can only be described in the terms which indicate bodily pleasure or pain, though it is apart from the body.

"And seeth Abraham afar off, and Lazarus in his bosom." Was this a special revelation, or are the inhabitants of the regions on each side of the impassable gulf able to see one another, and not only to see but to converse. We have reason to believe that in the unseen world there is not the same sense of distance as there is in this. I have heard of one of very great piety and intellect, having a vision of things after death, and the most prominent fact of that vision to him was that, in that state of existence, space seemed annihilated, and he and others were at once able to hold communication with those who, judged by our ideas of space, would be at an almost infinite distance. In the last chapter of Isaiah, it seems that the righteous, or at least the worshippers of God, were able to go forth and look upon the carcasses of impenitent sinners, "whose worm shall not die, neither shall their fire be quenched, and they shall be an abhorring to all flesh" (lxvi. 22-24).

Another question presents itself. Was the holiness of Lazarus such that he should have a permanent place in the bosom of the greatest saint of the Old Covenant? This seems as if it required that the place should not be taken strictly literally, and it is to be remarked that the bosom of Abraham was a Jewish phrase for the highest, or a very high state of bliss, and it was the intention of the Lord, in order to emphasize the teaching of the parables, to bring

24 And he cried and said, Father Abraham, have mercy on me, and send Lazarus, that he may dip the tip of his finger in water, and ᵐ cool my tongue; for I ⁿ am tormented in this flame.

ᵐ Zech. xiv. 12.
ⁿ Is. lxvi. 24. Mark ix. 44, &c.

---

on the scene the highest human inhabitant of the unseen world as unable to alleviate the sinner's punishment.

24. "And he cried and said, Father Abraham, have mercy on me," &c. Most extraordinary misapprehensions, as at least they seem to me, have been entertained by commentators upon this passage. The rich man is supposed to have carried into the other world his unbelief in things unseen, and his realization only of things seen, and so he is supposed to pray to Abraham rather than to God, but how do we know that in his misery he had not invoked God? The rich man's words to Abraham are not a prayer at all, taking prayer to be calling upon a Divine Being, or one whom we suppose to be one. They are words which we should address to any one whatsoever whom we supposed could hear and help us, as for instance, if we were in danger from fire or drowning. Abraham was within the reach of his voice, and he begged him, not to deliver him out of his misery—that he knew only God could do; but to afford him a very slight alleviation; and one which, taking into account their respective conditions, did not seem to demand any very great exercise of power.

"Father Abraham." It has been said that his invocation of Abraham as his father was an outcome of the Jewish superstition that none of the circumcised seed of Abraham could perish, but if he knew that the being on whom his eyes rested was Abraham, the most likely and natural thing for him to do was to call upon him as his father, which, of course, Abraham was.

"Send Lazarus, that he may dip the tip of his finger in water, and cool my tongue," &c. He is supposed, by some, from these words to have had the same feelings of fancied superiority towards Lazarus in Paradise as he had upon earth, and so he desired Abraham to *send* Lazarus, as if he were a servant, but it stands to reason that if he saw one in Abraham's bosom whom he recognized, he should ask the great Patriarch to send him, rather than come himself.

But why did he put his request for a little alleviation in such a

25 But Abraham said, Son, °remember that thou in thy lifetime receivedst thy good things, and likewise

° Job xxi. 13. ch. vi. 24.

form? Evidently as a contrast to what had taken place upon earth. Lazarus had desired to be fed with the crumbs. He desired that he should bring him but a drop of water, just as Lazarus had desired to be fed with the crumbs from his table. As I said, the main teaching of the parable is contrast: and here is the most salient point of such contrast.

With respect to the question whether, in his earthly prosperity, he had denied Lazarus the crumbs, I think this petition seems to indicate that he had not. Why is it said that Lazarus *desired* to be fed with the crumbs? Evidently because the fragments of such abundance as covered the rich man's table would have been an ample meal for him. If the crumbs did not find their way to Lazarus, it was probably owing to the selfishness or dishonesty of the menials, and the rich man's sin most probably was that he was utterly careless as to whether any of his exceeding abundance relieved the hunger of Lazarus or not. It seems to me that the two, the crumbs and the drop of water, form part of the fearful contrast, and the rich man would scarcely have asked that Lazarus should have been sent to him with the one, if he had wholly denied him the other. With respect to the apparent slightness of the alleviation, it has been supposed that he thought that one drop of the water of Paradise would very sensibly and permanently relieve his torment.

25. "But Abraham said, Son, remember that thou in thy lifetime receivedst," &c. This answer of Abraham, rightly understood, seems to furnish the key to the leading teaching of the parable, which is, *contrast*—the comparison between the state of the reprobate man, no matter what the sin or sins may have been for which he is rejected by God, and the accepted man, no matter what the particular good disposition which Divine grace has wrought in him for which God rewards him.

For Abraham says nothing about the vice or sin of the rich man. He makes not the slightest mention of unbelief or infidelity, or luxury, or selfishness, or pride, or extravagance, or other grosser sins which usually accompany "fulness of bread" (see particularly Ezek. xvi. 48, 49); just as he makes no mention of the faith or love, or patience, or devoutness of Lazarus. Between the state of any sinner that is lost, and any sinner that is saved, there is the same

Lazarus evil things: but now he is comforted, and thou art tormented.

26 And beside all this, between us and you there is a great gulf fixed: so that they which would pass from hence

---

25. "He is comforted." אׁ, A., B., D., all Uncials, one hundred Cursives, Syriac, Copt., Sah., Arm., Æth., read, "He *is here* comforted." Old Latin and Vulg. doubtful; a few Cursives as in Text. Recept.

---

fearful difference. And so, in order that the lesson from this contrast may be as wide as possible, no particular sin on the one side, and no particular grace on the other is mentioned. But, of course, common sense teaches us that the rich man must have made the worst use of his riches; he failed to lay up treasure in heaven—he failed to make himself friends of "the Mammon of unrighteousness," and so had no one to receive him "into everlasting habitations." The Lord, no doubt, means to teach us that his wealth was the principal cause of his soul's ruin. It, and the world's flattery which accompanied it, had no doubt blinded his eyes to the realities of the future world. ["How can ye believe," &c., John v. 44.] He was an example of the truth of the Lord's words, "Woe unto you rich, for ye have received your consolation." (Luke vi. 24.)

Commentators notice, and with reason, that Abraham says, "Thou receivedst thy good things," as if all that the rich man really regarded as *good* was his wealth, and the luxury and magnificence which accrued to him from it. Of course this is true. If he had realized the higher good he would not have been where he was, but I doubt whether Abraham intended this, or the Lord intended that such an emphasis should be laid on Abraham's words.

Some Rationalists, in order to disparage the authority of St. Luke as a teacher of the truth of God, endeavour to make us believe, that in this Parable we have the Ebionite tendencies of this evangelist— the rich man being condemned for the mere possession of riches; but the fact that the request is answered and refused by one who, in all probability, whilst on earth was far richer than Dives, but made a good use of his wealth, is sufficient disproof of the idea.

26. "And beside all this, between us and you there is a great gulf fixed," &c. But cannot those who are in the unseen world, and have put off their gross heavy bodies, pass over any gulf? To this we answer that we have not the least knowledge of the conditions

to you cannot; neither can they pass to us, that *would come* from thence.

27 Then he said, I pray thee therefore, father, that thou wouldest send him to my father's house:

---

under which the spirits in Hades exist; what are their powers, how they exercise them, and their limitations. One thing, however, is certain, that the whole structure of the parable requires that the gulf or chasm should have a real objective existence. It cannot be explained as solely the difference between their two moral states— between established holiness and entire unmitigated wickedness. What we must gather from its description is the absolute separation between the two conditions, or rather places; so that the wicked cannot escape into Paradise, or the righteous descend to bring them alleviation. (One did descend there, but when this was spoken He had not done so.) Beyond this we can say absolutely nothing.

We are not to gather from this the absolute fixedness of the rich man's state. Stier well says, "Not as if the power of God were unable to fill up even this chasm, but it is not in the power of the θέλοντες [they which would] to pass from the one side to the other." We shall have to advert to this again at the conclusion of our remarks, and must pass on to the second part of the dialogue.

27-31. "Then he said, I pray thee, therefore, father, that thou wouldest send him, &c. . . . though one rose from the dead." The parable so far as its great lesson is concerned finishes with the twenty-sixth verse, in which Abraham asserts the impossibility of granting the rich man's request. The second request, its denial, or rather Abraham's assertion of its needlessness, and counter assertion of the all-sufficiency of the Revelation already given to save the rich man's brethren from falling into his condition, is, as it were, by the way; but the merciful Lord Who would have no man lost, appends it, in order to show His hearers how the punishment of the rich man is to be avoided. It would seem that if sinners had more light, more direct warning, more certain knowledge of the fearful mysteries of the unseen state, they would repent. A messenger from Paradise, Whom they had known when He was living here on earth, and who had also been witness of the punishment of their impenitent brother, would certainly arouse their slumbering consciences, and bring them to repentance, but it would

CHAP. XVI.]   I HAVE FIVE BRETHREN.   441

28 For I have five brethren; that he may testify unto them, lest they also come into this place of torment.

---

not be so. The appearance of a messenger from Paradise or Hades, the Lord, Who knows all things, knew would startle and terrify for a time, but would do no more; whereas the witness of God's revelation in the Scriptures, even of the Old Testament only, would, if received and obeyed, prepare them for much more than avoiding future misery. It has been noticed that Abraham's answer goes far beyond the rich man's prayer in this respect; that the rich man says, "If one went unto them from the dead," whereas Abraham rejoins, "neither will they be persuaded though one rose from the dead." Not one only, but two rose from the dead; first Lazarus, one bearing the same name as that given by the Lord to the poor beggar, and they were not persuaded, for they took counsel how they might put Lazarus to death; then the Lord Himself rose, and they bribed the soldiers, and spread abroad the report that He was stolen away whilst the guard slept.

One question yet remains. Is the parable intended to teach us that the rich man's state was unalterably fixed for all eternity? I will now set before the reader what has been said by good and learned men on this matter; and I earnestly pray that I may be withheld from either overstating or understating anything whatsoever bearing on the inference, whatever it be, which the Lord intends us to gather from His account.

Those who contend that we are to infer the eternal condemnation of the sinner, appeal, of course, to the words of Abraham, " Between us and you there is a great gulf fixed, so that they which would pass from hence to you, cannot, neither can they pass to us who would come from thence." Cornelius à Lapide, who believes that the rich man was undergoing eternal condemnation, uses this argument to show that though at the outset he is said to be in Hades, yet this mention of the "great gulf fixed," shows that we are to understand that the Lord asserts the sufferings of Gehenna.[1]

---

[1] "In inferno. Id est in purgatorio, ait Jacobus Faber Stapulensis (censet ergo ipse Epulonem salvatum esse, post purgationem gulæ in igne Purgatorii): verum hoc est paradoxum, unde alii passim infernum damnatorum hîc accipiunt, asseruntque divitem hunc esse damna-

29 Abraham saith unto him, ᵖ They have Moses and the prophets; let them hear them.

Marginal refs: p Is. viii. 20. & xxxiv. 16. John v. 39, 45. Acts xv. 21. & xvii. 11.

But it is not improbable that he is swayed by his Romish views of Purgatory, according to which substantial relief can be granted to those suffering in it, through the prayers and Eucharistic oblations of their friends, and so, of course, by the intervention of such a saint as Abraham. Alford also holds the same view of the eternity of the punishment, and actually uses it to disparage the seeming affection displayed by Dives. "This expression [is fixed for ever] precludes all idea that the following verse indicates the beginning of a better mind in the rich man." And on verse 27 he writes, "This is the believing and trembling of James ii. 19. His eyes are now opened to the truth, and no wonder that his natural sympathies are awakened for his brethren. That a lost spirit should feel and express such sympathies is not to be wondered at; the misery of such will be very much heightened by the awakened and active state of those higher faculties and feelings, which selfishness and the body kept down here." So Dean Alford; but this is amazing! The higher faculties and feelings more fully developed in hell in a soul absolutely lost, because of the absence of selfishness!! Could he have seriously thought of what he was putting on paper when he wrote this?

Such is the argument, and apparently the only one, which can be drawn from the contents of this parable respecting the eternal fixedness of the torments of the rich man.

The arguments of those who, with fear and trembling desire, in submission to God, to take a more merciful view of his case are as follows.

First of all he is represented as being in Hades, which is not a final state, though the condition of many souls in it must be final.

Secondly, the moral state of the rich man as indicated by his words. The general description of the state of the lost is that they

---

tum, idque satis colligitur ex versu vigesimo tertio et vigesimo quarto, et maxime versu 26 ubi dicitur chaos magnum inter Abraham et Epulonem firmatum esse," &c.

30 And he said, Nay, father Abraham: but if one went unto them from the dead, they will repent.

---

never open their lips except for blasphemy—this blasphemy being the outcome of the eternal hate which reigns within them which they share with Satan and his angels. But, on the contrary, the words of the rich man are exceedingly submissive. Making no excuse, urging no self-vindication, he asks for a very small alleviation. He asks for no deliverance, and therefore cannot be said to pray to Abraham as if he were in the place of God.

And when his request is refused, instead of replying in anger and cursing, he prays for others—for his brethren. Whatever be his motive in this, it is very contrary to the disposition of many amongst us, who when they have ruined their own souls feel a diabolical pleasure in compassing the ruin of others.

It is quite true that he uses a bad argument. He overrates the influence of a supernatural appearance and underrates the power of the Scriptures, but one of the most distinguished preachers of righteousness of modern times was known to say that if he could only prove the reality of the fact of the appearance of a ghost or spirit he would be able to silence all infidelity.

From his words, then, naturally interpreted, we must gather that his soul was not lost in the sense of being utterly bad and deprived of all remains of goodness, as the soul of a devil is supposed to be.

The words of Abraham also to the rich man are not such as we can well suppose to be addressed to an utterly "cursed" spirit in everlasting fire prepared for the devil and his angels.

First of all he addresses him as "son" (child, $τέκνον$), using a somewhat more endearing word than Son.

Then he bids him "remember." Stier remarks upon this, "Remember my son, saith Abraham, think upon it, and thou wilt discern that thy present torment is just, and therefore the best thing that God can and will send thee: thus may thy pondering find the right way out of this present unto another future. For the 'but now' ($νῦν δέ$) does not constitute an irrevocable and final end, if there is yet left to him a 'remember' ($μνήσθητι$). If a father graciously says to his son under chastisement, 'reflect, my son!' there glimmers through all the punishment the distant design of

31 And he said unto him, If they hear not Moses and

love, and in the very words there is an exhortation to a right return to self, and to an earnest repenting." [1]

Godet, whose remarks on this parable are far too short, writes on verse 25, "The words 'comforted' and 'tormented' are not the equivalents of *saved* and *damned*, absolutely taken. Nothing could be final among the members of the ancient covenant till they had been brought into contact with Jesus Christ. 'The Gospel,' says St. Peter (1 Epistle iv. 6) 'was preached to them that are dead,' that they might be capable of being judged. The knowledge of Jesus Christ is the condition on which the pronouncing of the final sentence is based. The hour of this judgment has not yet struck for the rich man."

With respect to the second request of the rich man Godet writes : " Some commentators, unable to allow any good feeling in one damned, have attributed this prayer of the rich man to a selfish aim. According to them he dreaded the time when his own sufferings would be aggravated by seeing those of his brethren. But would not even this fear still suppose in him a remnant of love ? And why represent him as destitute of all human feeling ? He is not yet, we have seen, damned in the absolute sense of the word."

In writing, or selecting from the writings of others, the foregoing remarks, I desire it to be very distinctly understood that I refer to nothing except the single case of the man mentioned in the narrative, if it be a true history. How far he may represent a class it is impossible to speculate upon. There may have been others stand-

---

[1] It is right, however, to state that Stier at the conclusion considers his ultimate repentance and restoration to be very doubtful, because he thinks he discerns in the rich man's request to have Lazarus sent to his brethren a flavour of self-justification. And so literally and truly this good man Stier is in doubt of him, because his words may be understood as somewhat contrary to the Lutheran formula of Justification. I could give instance upon instance of this extraordinary enslavement of mind in these commentators in that they expect clear views of justification by faith long before it was revealed as a distinct and defined doctrine.

the prophets, ^q neither will they be persuaded, though one rose from the dead.

^q John xii. 10, 11.

ing by his side in the same place of torment to whose case they do not apply, inasmuch as their rebellious and blasphemous words would show that they were in very deed utterly lost: but the Saviour has given the account of a man whose words are not words of rebellion and blasphemy, but humble words of deprecation and submission, and regard for others.

With respect to the opinions of commentators I cannot help thinking that their doctrinal views respecting the state after death prevent many from taking all that is said of this rich man into full account. Romanists are afraid that if this man's state be Purgatorial, it militates against their view of the alleviation of the pains of Purgatory by the intercession, or intervention, of saints or other means: Protestants take the darkest view because if the man's state be capable of change they suppose that it proves the existence of Purgatory.

CHAP. XVII.

THEN said he unto the disciples, ^a It is impossible but that offences will come: but woe *unto him*, through whom they come!

^a Matt. xviii. 6, 7. Mark ix. 42. 1 Cor. xi. 19.

1. "Then said he unto the disciples, It is impossible but that offences will come," &c. Scarcely any two commentators are agreed as to the connection between these verses 1-10 with what goes before, or with one another. But do we not go too far in endeavouring to make out the origin, in the course of events, or in the Lord's Mind, of everything which He says. Many of His most precious words are perfectly independent of time and circumstances because they are general truths, capable of the widest application. To make them spring out of certain local or temporary incidents does not add to the universality of their application, but rather weakens it.

"It is impossible, but that offences will come." Wherever there

446   IF HE REPENT, FORGIVE.   [St. Luke.

2 It were better for him that a millstone were hanged about his neck, and he cast into the sea, than that he should offend one of these little ones.

^b Matt. xviii. 15, 21.
^c Lev. xix. 17.
Prov. xvii. 10.
James v. 19.

3 ¶ Take heed to yourselves: ^b If thy brother trespass against thee, ^c rebuke him ; and if he repent, forgive him.

---

3. "Thy brother trespass against thee." So D., X., Γ, Δ, Λ, Π, all later Uncials, almost all Cursives, some old Latin (c, e, q), and some editions of Versions; but ℵ, A., B., L., 1, 42, 131, 209, 254, 346, some old Latin (a, b, f, ff², g¹, i, l, m), Vulg. (Cod. Amiat.), Goth., Copt., Syriac, omit "against thee."

---

is sin in a Christian, or indeed in any human being, there will be offences. Numbers of those who see sin in a fellow Christian will either be encouraged to do the like, or speak against the holy religion possessed by him as too weak to preserve him from evil, and so it may be safely neglected. What numbers among the poor profess to see no good in Holy Communion, because of the inconsistent lives of some communicants. Let men take good heed lest by their impure conversation they infuse impurity, or by their sceptical remarks they shake the faith of their brethren, for assuredly the Judge of all will some day or other make good His threat. " It were better for him that a millstone were hanged about his neck and he cast," &c. The millstone cast round the neck will cause the body to sink to the lowest depth, and will render its burial impossible ; " but far more terrible to be cast into hell with the weight of another's ruin on one's conscience." If any have thus brought religion into contempt, or seduced innocence, there must be reparation of the wrong done. Public, if the scandal has been known by all—personal if it has been a private wrong, as the seduction of innocence, or the undermining of faith, or partnership in fraud, or the teaching of any evil habit.

3. " Take heed to yourselves: If thy brother trespass [against thee], rebuke him," &c. The reader will see from the critical note above that the words " against thee " are very doubtful. More doubtful than the same words in Matth. xviii. 15. It seems, however, imperative upon us to understand them, because the words in the next clause, " if he repent forgive him," can only apply to trespasses of one man against another, not to trespasses against God. Godet well remarks, " Holiness and love meet together in this pre-

CHAP. XVII.] LORD, INCREASE OUR FAITH. 447

4 And if he trespass against thee seven times in a day, and seven times in a day turn again to thee, saying, I repent; thou shalt forgive him.

5 And the apostles said unto the Lord, Increase our faith.

6 [d] And the Lord said, If ye had faith as a grain of mustard seed, ye might say unto this sycamine tree, Be thou plucked up by the root, and be thou planted in the sea; and it should obey you.

[d] Matt. xvii. 20. & xxi. 21. Mark ix. 23. & xi. 23.

---

4. "Seven times in a day." "In a day" omitted by א, B., D., L., a few Cursives, most old Latin, Copt., Arm.; but retained by A, Γ, Δ, Λ, Π, later Uncials, most Cursives, Vulg., Syr., Æth., &c.

6. "If ye had faith." So D., F., G., H., many Cursives, and Vulg.; but א, A., B., F., K., L., S., U., other later Uncials, above forty Cursives, read, "If ye have faith."

cept; holiness begins with rebuking; then when the rebuke has once been taken, love pardons. The pardon to be granted to our brethren has no other limit than their repenting, and the confession by which it is expressed."

5. "And the apostles said unto the Lord, Increase our faith." The need of more faith seems to have been impressed upon them by this command of unlimited forgiveness of one another. A man who would thus forgive another, must have a very vivid realization indeed of unseen and eternal things. And faith is the "evidence of things not seen." He must be very full of the sense of his constantly recurring need of forgiveness—of what God has done through the Incarnation and Redemption of Christ to bring forgiveness near to himself and to his brethren, of the necessity of constant conformity to the mind and will of his forgiving Father, if He would fulfil this precept of forgiveness.

6. "And the Lord said, If ye had [or have] faith as a grain of mustard seed," &c. I have enlarged so fully on the teaching of these words in my comments on the parallel passages, Matth. xvii. 20, and xxi. 21, and Mark ix. 23, and xi. 23, that I must refer the reader to my notes on those places.

I would, however, remark on a matter I before omitted to notice. The Lord does not, in any of these words, deny that the Apostles had any faith, especially if we consider that His words really were not "if ye *had* faith," but "if ye *have* faith." They had certainly faith in Himself as having come out from God, and for this He specially thanks the Father (John xvi. 27, xvii. 8, 25). But

7 But which of you, having a servant plowing or feeding cattle, will say unto him by and by, when he is come from the field, Go and sit down to meat?

8 And will not rather say unto him, Make ready wherewith I may sup, and gird thyself, ᵉand serve me, till I have eaten and drunken; and afterward thou shalt eat and drink?

ᵉ ch. xii. 37.

---

their faith looked at from His point of view as that of One Who from moment to moment lived consciously in the Father, referred all to Him, did all in and through Him, was exceedingly small—smaller than that which was proverbially the smallest of seeds; but yet the smallest conceivable seed has a living principle within it, and so may grow to be the greatest of trees, and thus it was with the Apostles' faith. The Lord answered this their prayer. He added to their faith. And this smallest seed of faith which they had, though then scarcely perceptible, grew shortly to be the greatest power of life in a dead world.

7, 8. "But which of you, having a servant plowing or feeding cattle . . . . drink." This short parable teaches us one lesson, how we are ourselves to look upon all services which we render to God. It does not contemplate for a moment the way in which God is pleased to look upon our services or to reward them. It simply regards us as creatures of God's hands; to Him we belong, body and soul, for He has made both; and having made us, He has kept us in being from moment to moment. He cannot need anything of us, for "He giveth to all life, and breath, and all things:" so that it is impossible to suppose that we can be profitable to Him in the sense in which we can be profitable to our fellows, who, more or less, depend upon us. Nor is this relation between our services and God's all-sufficiency in the least degree altered by Divine grace. St. Paul asks Christians, his converts, who were inclined to boast against one another, "Who maketh thee to differ from another, and what hast thou that thou didst not receive? now if thou didst receive it, why dost thou glory, as if thou hadst not received it?" (1 Corinth. iv. 7.)

So that the case against any idea of merit on our part is as strong as can possibly be stated. The master who possesses the servant possesses him as a slave, to whom he owes nothing, neither thanks

DOTH HE THANK THAT SERVANT? 449

9 Doth he thank that servant because he did the things that were commanded him? I trow not.

---

9. "I trow not." Omitted by ℵ, B., L., X., 1, 2, 8, 118, 131, 157, 209, old Latin (a, e), Copt., Arm., Æth.; but retained by A., D., all other Uncials, most Cursives, most old Latin, Vulg., Goth., Syriac.

nor wages. For his own profit he keeps him in food and clothing under his roof, but because he belongs to him, he never thinks of thanking him; but after all, as members of the same human family, the slave is on a sort of equality with his master. He did not receive his being from his master, nor his strength of body, or intelligence of soul, whereby he can serve him, whereas everything that we can name as belonging to us we owe to God only. In no sense then can God owe us anything, and this we must both feel and acknowledge. Even though through the ignorance and blindness of our Old Adam, we may not realize our utter unprofitableness, we are yet to confess it, for the Lord says, "When ye have done all these things which are commanded you, *say*, We are unprofitable servants: We have done that which is our duty to do." If we do not feel this unprofitableness, if we have not this estimate of our best services, it is a sign that we do not realize the greatness and all-sufficiency of Almighty God, and we have need to put up the prayer of the Apostles, "Lord, increase our faith." Stier, quoting Gerlach, says, "The lack of faith has its ground pre-eminently in self-righteousness, in the reliance upon our own merit."

Let us now see as to the way in which the Lord brings out this truth. He brings forward a very strong case. A man has a servant, apparently his only servant, who has been at work all day in the fields, or in the sheep walk. When he comes home, instead of allowing him to rest and refresh himself, he sets him upon housework. "Make ready wherewith I may sup, and gird thyself and serve me." This seems hard, and that is what the Lord intended it to seem. He draws the picture of a man who, without being a cruel master, evidently intends to get the fullest amount of work possible out of his slave. He does this, and does not think that he is in the least degree obliged to him, and this because he belongs to him. If he had thanked the slave he would have confessed his obligation to him. He does not thank him, because he conceives that he is in no way indebted to him, even for what we may deem extra work. Now the Lord in effect says, "When you think of

10 So likewise ye, when ye shall have done all those things which are commanded you, say, We are ᶠ unprofitable servants: we have done that which was our duty to do.

f Job xxii. 3.
& xxxv. 7. Ps.
xvi. 2. Matt.
xxv. 30. Rom.
iii. 12. & xi. 35.
1 Cor. ix. 16,
17. Philem. 11.

your work which God distinctly demands of you, no matter how long and toilsome it seems, no matter how it accumulates upon you, even when you think you need rest; look upon it all as simply your duty. God, in strictness, owes you not even thanks for it: much less can He, Who is all-sufficient, be profited by it. So, just as the man in My parable treats his servant as if he were unprofitable to him, giving him no thanks even, so do you treat yourselves; so do you estimate your services to One to Whom you owe all things, even the body and soul in which you serve Him.

Such is the parable, but it is to be remembered that it is the one sole place in our Lord's discourses in which He would have us measure our services by God's all-sufficiency only. In innumerable other places He would have us regard God as delighting in, as praising, as rewarding, our feeblest endeavours. He very emphatically promises that the gift of a mere cup of cold water shall not lose its reward. He promises to reward openly secret prayer, almsgiving, and fasting. He actually identifies Himself with His needy fellow-creatures: " Come ye blessed, receive the kingdom, for I was an hungered, and ye gave me meat." This is a great mystery, rather a sacred paradox, that the God Who is in one way so all-sufficient that He is infinitely above the reach of our services, in another way, and that the way of the Incarnation, has abased Himself so that He can be our debtor, and so account Himself as relieved by us when we relieve the poor members of His Body.

Must not our Lord also in the expressions He made use of in giving us this parable, have had regard to other words of His recorded in this very Gospel, in extreme contrast with those now before us. Here He represents God under the figure of an exacting master, bidding the servant, after his day's work, gird himself and serve him, whereas in Luke xii. 37, He says, " Blessed are those servants whom the Lord when he cometh shall find watching: verily I say unto you, that he shall gird himself and make them to sit down to meat, and will come forth and serve them." Just as in the former we have the Lord for a purpose regarded simply and solely as all-

CHAP. XVII.] TEN MEN THAT WERE LEPERS. 451

11 ¶ And it came to pass, ᵍ as he went to Jerusalem, that he passed through the midst of Samaria and Galilee.   ᵍ Luke ix. 51, 52. John iv. 4.

12 And as he entered into a certain village, there met him ten men that were lepers, ʰ which stood afar off :   ʰ Lev. xiii. 46.

---

sufficient, and nothing else—so in the latter, we have the same Divine Being regarded simply and solely as all-condescending, all-loving, all-rewarding.

These two views of God, as at once all-sufficient and all-loving, must be held together, or we may fall into grievous error. The heathen feigned that the gods dwelt at ease, regardless of the sins and the sufferings of mortals; and Eliphaz, the friend of Job, seems to have been on the brink of the same error, when he says : " Can a man be profitable to God as he that is wise may be profitable unto himself? Is it any pleasure to the Almighty that thou art righteous, or is it gain to him that thou makest thy way perfect?" Our perfection is no gain to God; but that it is pleasing in His sight every word of Scripture assures us.

11. "And it came to pass, as he went to Jerusalem, that he passed through," &c. It is, of couse, impossible to suppose that if our Lord was going southward to Jerusalem, He would pass first through Samaria, and then turn back again into Galilee. So most commentators explain this verse as teaching that He went eastward along the confines of the two provinces, skirting both till He came to Jordan, and crossed over it into Peræa, near Scythopolis, where there was a bridge, and so entered Peræa, and then left Peræa by Jericho on His last journey towards Jerusalem (Luke xviii. 31, 35; xix. 1). The Galilean Jews who went up to the feasts usually went round by Peræa to avoid the dangers of passing through Samaria, the Samaritans, as related in Josephus, having massacred about this time a number of Jews on their way to the Temple. The fact of one Samaritan, a member of the less numerous people, consorting with nine Jews, seems to indicate that the miracle probably took place in a border district.

12. "And as he entered into a certain village . . . stood afar off . . . have mercy upon us." "Stood afar off." This was in order to obey the law that they were to keep at the distance of one hundred paces from all whom they met: so being obliged to keep at

452   JESUS, MASTER.   [St. Luke.

13 And they lifted up *their* voices, and said, Jesus, Master, have mercy on us.

14 And when he saw *them*, he said unto them, ¹ Go shew yourselves unto the priests. And it came to pass, that, as they went, they were cleansed.

¹ Lev. xiii. 2. & xiv. 2. Matt. viii. 4. ch. v. 14.

---

such a distance they had to cry very loudly to make themselves heard.

This cry was undoubtedly the cry of faith. They would not have so cried unless they had heard that the Lord had healed many who were similarly afflicted, and they believed that He was both able and willing to heal them.

14. "And when he saw them, he said unto them, Go shew yourselves unto the priests," &c. In this the Lord acted as He had done when He healed the man mentioned in Matth. viii. 4, and Luke v. 14. He sent the lepers to the priests because, no matter how perfect their healing seemed to be, they could not be restored to religious worship in the synagogues or temple except by the verdict of the priests. The priests' function was not to cleanse or heal, but to pronounce them clean.

The question has been gravely asked and discussed, whether, seeing one of them was a Samaritan, the Lord sent him to the Samaritan priest; but is it likely that the Lord would thus formally recognize a religion of whose votaries He had said, "Ye worship ye know not what" (John iv.)? The healing which the man experienced at the hands of a Jew was better than ten thousand arguments to convince him that the religion which Jesus by His constant attendance at the feasts so devoutly observed was the true one: so that the Lord no doubt took for granted that he would give up his idle superstition.

"And it came to pass, that, as they went, they were cleansed." It is to be remarked that there is implied in this a further and a far greater act of faith on the part of all the ten. The Lord had not bid them come to Him, and touched each, one by one, and dispelled the leprosy by His touch; on the contrary, when they obeyed His command, and set out, they were unhealed. It was only after they had commenced their journey that the signs of leprosy began rapidly to disappear. They might have said, with Naaman, "Let Him come and lay His hands upon us. Why should we go to the

15 And one of them, when he saw that he was healed, turned back, and with a loud voice glorified God.

16 And fell down on *his* face at his feet, giving him thanks: and he was a Samaritan.

Temple till we are actually cleansed?" They did not thus object, but at once set out, in the belief that before they reached the priests they would be such as the ministers of the Temple might receive and dismiss as clean.

So far, then, as the healing of their bodies was concerned, nothing was wanting in their faith.

But though the ten were healed, but one felt gratitude to the Healer.

15-16. "And one of them, when he saw that he was healed ... he was a Samaritan." It is necessary to notice the saving element in this man's gratitude. We can imagine them saying to the Samaritan, as he turned back, "We are as grateful to God as you are, but we will return our thanks in the temple of God. There are certain acts of worship, certain sacrifices ordained in the law by God Himself. In the due performance of these we will thank God in His own appointed way. He Who healed us is a great Prophet, but it is the power of God alone which has cleansed us." Now the Samaritan was not content with this. His faith worked by love, taking the form of thankfulness. He at once left the nine to their journey, and, without delay, threw himself at the feet of the Lord. He felt that his was not a common healing—not a healing in the way of nature, by the disease exhausting itself in time. It was a supernatural healing, through the intervention of a particular Servant of God; and this Servant [or, perhaps, he had heard that Jesus claimed to be more than a servant, even the Son of God], must be thanked and glorified. If God had healed him in the ordinary course, the sacrifices prescribed for such healing would have sufficed. But God had healed him in an extraordinary way— by His Son, by One Who was far greater than any prophet; and so, if God was to be glorified, it must be in connection with this extraordinary channel of blessing, this Mediator. With this agrees what follows.

17, 18. "And Jesus answering said, Were there not ten cleansed? but where are the nine? ... There are not found that returned," &c.

17 And Jesus answering said, Were there not ten cleansed? but where *are* the nine?

18 There are not found that returned to give glory to God, save this stranger.

19 ᵏ And he said unto him, Arise, go thy way: thy faith hath made thee whole.

20 ¶ And when he was demanded of the Phari-

ᵏ Matt. ix. 22. Mark v. 34. & x. 52. ch. vii. 50. & viii. 48. & xviii. 42.

Here the Lord distinctly claims that His action in the matter as the special representative of God, even His Son, must be recognized. In falling down "at His (Jesus') feet, giving Him thanks," this Samaritan, and he alone, gave glory to God. Here we have not obscurely set forth the truth so often insisted on by the Lord in His discourses as given by St. John, that the Father that dwelt in Him did the works, and that men must honour Him as they honour the Father; and that these nine ungrateful Jews, in neglecting to honour the Son, "honoured not the Father which had sent him."

"Save this stranger"—rather, save this alien. The Samaritans were not Jews, but Gentiles. By the fact that he who set the example of gratitude was an alien and a misbeliever, we are taught that God constantly raises up men from systems outside the pale of His Church, to set examples of faith and devotion to those who, though "of Israel," are not, by their unbelief, the true Israel.

19. "And he said unto him, Arise, go thy way: thy faith hath," &c. But were not the nine made whole by faith? They had faith to ask the Lord to heal them. They had faith to act as if He intended to heal them. And yet their faith was not "saving," for it saved them not from the sin of ingratitude. The Lord, by the words "thy faith hath saved thee," must allude to a far higher salvation, of which the salvation from leprosy was but the type. For the faith of this Samaritan, so far as was possible before the Resurrection and Ascension, joined him to the Son of God. The same grace which had made him grateful to Christ would make him believe in the Lord, and accept His salvation from sin and an evil world. Perhaps he was one of those who by their testimony to the power of Christ prepared their countrymen to receive the message of the Gospel at the lips of the Evangelist (Acts viii.).

20, 21. "And when he was demanded of the Pharisees, when the kingdom of God . . . within you." The key to the explanation of

CHAP. XVII.] LO HERE! OR, LO THERE! 455

sees, when the kingdom of God should come, he answered them and said, The kingdom of God cometh not ‖ with observation:

‖ Or, *with outward shew.*

21 ¹ Neither shall they say, Lo here! or, lo there! for, behold, ᵐ the kingdom of God is ‖ within you.

1 ver. 23.
ᵐ Rom. xiv. 17.
‖ Or, *among you,* John i. 26.

21. "Lo there." This "lo" omitted, ℵ, B., L., and some old Latin; but A., D., all later Uncials and Cursives, old Latin (a, b, c, f, g), Vulg., &c., retain it.

this passage is the character and expectations of the questioners. They expected a carnal kingdom, a great prince at the head of the nation, leading it to victory in the sight of the world; but it was not to be so. The kingdom of God was not to come with observation, *i.e.*, in such a way that men would say "lo here! or, lo there!" On the contrary, it would come about, one might say, stealthily. Men, before they were aware of it, would be caught in the net, and overcome; or, on the contrary, the signs of its being at work in their midst would be so contrary to all carnal expectation that they would reject it. We may take what happened to the Lord Himself as an illustration. If the kingdom of God had come when He entered into Jerusalem in a sort of triumph, as was prophesied of Him, and had then visibly displayed Divine power in the subjugation of His opposers—then it would have come "with observation." But it came with its greatest, its most triumphant power, when He was crucified: for then it came in its atoning and reconciling power. It came with still greater power at His Resurrection; but no one saw Him rise. It came with renewed power at His Ascension; but only a favoured few saw Him ascend.

But they make a great mistake who suppose that the kingdom of God was always to be unobserved or unobservable. The Lord, so far as its outward aspect was concerned, had compared it to the grain of mustard seed which was, at first, the least of all seeds, but in a short time grew to be the greatest among herbs. It was destined to become the most powerful of human institutions; but when the Pharisees asked this question, it was in its beginning. And when it became in a degree an outward organization, as at Pentecost, it was not one that flaunted itself before the eyes of the world. Men could oppose it, and scorn it, and deny it to be "of God." Years after, when it was spreading in the seats of Greek

22 And he said unto the disciples, ⁿThe days will come, when ye shall desire to see one of the days of the Son of man, and yet shall not see *it*.

ⁿ See Matt. ix. 15. John xvii. 12.

---

culture and learning, it could be said of it, "not many wise men after the flesh, not many mighty, not many noble are called" (1 Cor. i. 26).

All this bears upon the vexed question, What is the meaning of " within you " ? " Within you " usually means "in your hearts," but it sometimes has the meaning of " among you." It is difficult to believe that the Lord, in addressing the Pharisees, would say that " the kingdom of God was within them ; " for it assuredly was not in them in the sense of their spiritually apprehending it; and it was amongst them in the persons of the Lord and his first followers, but not so that they should discern it.

The reader will remember that St. Paul writes, "the kingdom of God is not meat and drink, but righteousness and peace and joy in the Holy Ghost;" but surely such a description of an internal state of holiness applies least of all to these Pharisees. If by ἐντὸς the Lord alludes to any merely internal spiritual aspect of His kingdom, He can only mean the power of discerning it is "within you." " You can only discern it by the soul's eye, the eye of faith;" but such an interpretation seems very unlikely.

22. "And he said unto the disciples, The days will come, when ye shall desire to see," &c. These words are said expressly to the disciples, so that they cannot allude, as some have supposed, to an earnest longing for one of the days of the Messiah's power in the fearful time when the Jewish polity was fast coming to a close. They no doubt express what would be in the minds of the Apostles or early disciples who had seen the Lord, and the acts of His power and goodness, and who would be then assailed by persecution and opposition from without, and dismayed by the decline of love, and multiplying of heresies within. Would that we could see again but one of the days in which He fed the multitudes, and stilled the tempest, and enlightened us with His teaching, and made all His adversaries ashamed !

They should not see it: not even one of such days. And this would make them more fervently long for *the* day of His coming: as the last of them did who prayed, " Even so come Lord Jesus."

23 ° And they shall say to you, See here; or, see there: go not after *them*, nor follow *them*.

° Matt. xxiv. 23. Mark xiii. 21. ch. xxi. 8.

24 ᴾ For as the lightning, that lighteneth out of the one *part* under heaven, shineth unto the other *part* under heaven; so shall also the Son of man be in his day.

ᴾ Matt. xxiv. 27.

25 ᵠ But first must he suffer many things, and be rejected of this generation.

ᵠ Mark viii. 31. & ix. 31. & x. 33. ch. ix. 22.

26 ʳ And as it was in the days of Noe, so shall it be also in the days of the Son of man.

ʳ Gen. vii. Matt. xxiv. 37.

---

24. "In his day." So ℵ, A., L., later Uncials, nearly all Cursives and Versions; but B., D., 220, old Latin (a, b, e, i), omit "in his day."

23, 24. "And when they shall say to you, See here; or, see there: . . . Son of man be in his day." This is one of those many places which assure us that the Second Coming of the Son of Man will not be a mere providential coming, as at the destruction of Jerusalem, when not He Himself in person, but the armies of the Romans executed His purposes of vengeance. Nor will it be a spiritual coming, as in the more rapid and successful propagation of the Gospel; but it will be a sudden and personal appearance to all men at once, so that no one need point out to his neighbour where the Lord is. As one says, "Men do not run here or there to see a flash of lightning: it shines simultaneously on all points of the horizon." So the Lord will appear at the same moment to the view of all living. The judgment will not be as now in the secret place of each man's conscience, but in the sight of all mankind.

25. "But first must he suffer many things, and be rejected of this generation." "This generation" means, in the first place, the generation in which the Lord then lived, but, by implication, the men of the world from the day of Pentecost to the Second Advent.

The world, as the world, as a whole has rejected Christ. Whilst in His Mediatorial kingdom He has controlled and ordered all things, He has yet reigned in the hearts of but a few. Very few have rendered to him the obedience of faith. Even where His Name has been professed, and His true doctrine vindicated, the strictness and holiness of His teaching has been set at naught.

26, 27. "And as it was in the days of Noe . . . destroyed them

27 They did eat, they drank, they married wives, they were given in marriage, until the day that Noe entered into the ark, and the flood came, and destroyed them all.

^s Gen. xix. 28 ^s Likewise also as it was in the days of Lot ; they did eat, they drank, they bought, they sold, they planted, they builded ;

^t Gen. xix. 16, 24. 29 But ^t the same day that Lot went out of

all." The flood came upon men suddenly, unexpectedly, universally [that is, to the then inhabited parts of the earth : there was no need that it should overwhelm tracts, perhaps whole continents, on which no foot of living man had then trod], so that there was no escape. And yet they had had above a hundred years of warning. They had a preacher of righteousness, an upholder of the truth of God, and a prophet of the coming destruction in Noah; but his testimony was utterly disregarded, and no doubt the sign patent to all that he believed his own testimony in the long continued building of the ark before their eyes, was scoffed at. And so at last destruction came upon them as in a moment, and there was no escape.

It is worthy of notice how the fact that "they married wives," "they were given in marriage," seems to signify something contrary to the will of God in the marriages then contracted ; and so we read that "the sons of God saw the daughters of men that they were fair ; and they took them wives of all which they chose." (Gen. vi. 2.) That these marriages were impious or ungodly there seems to be no doubt, and the Lord alludes to them as exhibiting the carnal security of the time.

28, 29. "Likewise also as it was in the days of Lot; they did eat, they drank . . . destroyed them all." The account of the destruction of Sodom is so very fragmentary that nothing is said in the narrative in Genesis of any warning which they had been vouchsafed ; but the notice of this catastrophe in the Second Epistle of St. Peter, where it is said that "that righteous man, dwelling among them, in seeing and hearing, vexed his righteous soul from day to day with their unlawful deeds," seems to imply that Lot witnessed to them of righteousness, temperance, and judgment to come.

Both these cases are cited because of the suddenness, completeness, and inevitableness of the judgment in each case.

CHAP. XVII.] IT RAINED FIRE AND BRIMSTONE. 459

Sodom it rained fire and brimstone from heaven, and destroyed *them* all.

30 Even thus shall it be in the day when the Son of man is revealed. ᵘ ᵘ 2 Thess. i. 7.

31 In that day, he ˣ which shall be upon the housetop, and his stuff in the house, let him not come down to take it away: and he that is in the field, let him likewise not return back. ˣ Matt. xxiv. 17. Mark xiii. 15.

"It rained fire and brimstone from heaven, and destroyed them all." Here the Lord vouches for the truth of the manner of the destruction of the Sodomites—a matter called in question by sceptical writers, and by those semi-believers who think that, though we in our sphere can bring to bear various natural forces for the destruction of our enemies, God in His sphere cannot—in a word, that He is less powerful in His sphere than we are in ours.

In each of these cases—that of the Flood and of the destruction of Sodom—the course of the world, its businesses, its pleasures, was going on just as usual, when the all-reaching destruction came on without a moment's warning of its being close at hand. And so it will be at the last day.

30. "Even thus shall it be in the day when the Son of man is revealed." It is much to be noticed that the Lord does not allude to the extreme wickedness of the Antediluvians or the Sodomites, but to the things which showed their carnal security, their sporting upon the brink of destruction.

31, 32. "In that day, he which shall be upon the housetop . . . Remember Lot's wife." All these verses seem to refer to the Second Coming of the Lord in glory, and not to the destruction of Jerusalem. And yet these two verses appear to refer to a catastrophe from which it may not be impossible to escape, if when it bursts upon us we are perfectly unencumbered. Godet writes: "Jesus describes that disposition of mind which, in this last crisis, shall be the condition of salvation. The Lord passes with His heavenly retinue; He attracts all the inhabitants of the earth who are willing and ready to join Him; but it transpires in the twinkling of an eye. Whosoever is not already loosed from earthly things, so as to haste away without hesitation, taking flight towards Him, freely and joyously, remains behind. Thus precisely had Lot's wife perished

460   REMEMBER LOT'S WIFE.   [ST. LUKE.

y Gen. xix. 26.
z Matt. x. 39. & xvi. 25.
Mark viii. 35.
ch. ix. 24.
John xii. 25.

32 ʸ Remember Lot's wife.

33 ᶻ Whosoever shall seek to save his life shall lose it ; and whosoever shall lose his life shall preserve it.

---

33. "Seek to save." So ℵ, A., R., later Uncials, almost all Cursives, old Latin (a, e, f, ff², l), Vulg.; but B., L., old Latin (b, c, i, q), read, "Seek to gain" or "possess" his life.

with the goods from which she could not part. Agreeably to His usual method Jesus characterizes the dispositions of mind by a series of external acts, in which it is concretely realized." But the objection to this is that *the* great day is not represented as a procession of a bridegroom (as in Matth. xxv. 1-13), but as a Judge coming in the clouds of heaven, and calling all before Him to receive their award. I think it is most probable that it refers to some absolute surrender of earthly things which will be required of the true elect before the Lord's actual appearance, which will be clear to those and those only whose hearts are right with God (Daniel xii. 10, " None of the wicked shall understand, but the wise shall understand ").

32. "Remember Lot's wife." Lot's wife was destroyed because, at the very last moment, when the wicked city was just about to be consumed—even, perhaps, whent he work of destruction had begun, she looked back with longing eyes at a place in which she had lived in comfort and peace, regardless of the extreme wickedness of its inhabitants. And the Lord teaches us here that the world, notwithstanding its ungodliness, is yet so fascinating that it will retain some hold upon the spirits of Christ's people, even when the signs of His coming to condemn it are all around. Lot's wife was destroyed when all belonging to her were fleeing for their lives from the coming wrath. And so this example of Lot's wife is cited by the Lord as a warning at all times against looking back—looking back on the world—looking back with pleasure at the commission of past sins. Thus Quesnel: " A man is sometimes so great an enemy to his own good that he regrets the loss of wicked company, and of those opportunities of ruining himself from which he has been delivered through the Divine mercy. This is a piece of ingratitude which the Lord cannot bear, and which He punishes very severely. We must readily give up our friends and relations, our wealth and temporal advantage, and count them but loss for Christ, when they

CHAP. XVII.] IN THAT NIGHT. 461

34 ^a I tell you, in that night there shall be two *men* in one bed; the one shall be taken, and the other shall be left.

^a Matt. xxiv. 40, 41. 1 Thess. iv. 17.

35 Two *women* shall be grinding together; the one shall be taken, and the other left.

36 ‖ Two *men* shall be in the field; the one shall be taken, and the other left.

‖ This 36th verse is wanting in most of the Greek copies.

---

36. "Two men shall be in the field," This verse omitted by אּ, A., B., L., Q., R., all other later Uncials, many Cursives; but retained by D., U., most old Latin, Vulg.

become obstacles to our salvation. We love them with a criminal fondness, when at His command we leave them with grief and anxiety."

33. "Whosoever shall seek to save his life shall lose it; and whosoever . . . . preserve it." This saying of our Lord was uttered by Him not once or twice, but apparently many times. It contains a truth which should ever abide with us: We require it every day of our lives, for almost every day we are called upon in some shape or other to choose between that self-indulgence which pleases our earthly perishing life, and that self-denial which nourishes our eternal life. I have commented on it somewhat fully in my notes on Matth. x. 39, on Mark viii. 35, on ix. 24 of this Gospel, and on John xii. 25; and can only now remark that as it is here introduced amongst sayings which refer entirely to the Second Advent, there will be particular need of it when that Advent is close at hand. All Scripture teaches that the last trial of the Church will be the greatest. May God prepare us for it.

34-36. "I tell you, in that night there shall be two men in one bed . . . . the other left." The Lord would very strongly emphasize what He is now about to say, for He begins it with "I tell you."

"In that night." This has been used to support the view that our Lord will come in the night, literally, as a thief in the night; but as one remarks, it will be night to one half the world and day to the other; another says that "that night," is descriptive of the world's condition, when the lightening of the day of Christ shall burst upon it; in other words, shrouded in the darkness of sin and unbelief. In the three illustrations which follow, one, the two

37 And they answered and said unto him, ᵇ Where, Lord?
And he said unto them, Wheresoever the body *is*,
thither will the eagles be gathered together.

ᵇ Job xxxix. 30. Matt. xxiv. 28.

in one bed, is appropriate to the night, but the grinding, and the working, or walking in the field, is more consonant with the day time. But the fact is, it will be neither day nor night. If the presence of the sun makes the day, he will not be seen. So far as the good are concerned, it will be the dawn of eternal day, to the wicked it will be the closing in of eternal night.

"Two men in one bed; the one shall be taken, and the other left." No doubt the word "taken" is to be understood in a good sense. "The one shall be taken up to the Lord" (1 Thess. iv. 17). The other left to perish. The one shall be received to Himself (John xiv. 3). The other disowned by Him.

It has been noticed that there are three gradations of close intimacy: occupying the same couch, working at the same domestic work, walking together in the field.

Many have a secret feeling that because they are the friends or relatives of true Christians, and consort with them, and listen to them with something of approval, they will be right at last: but this is a miserable deception, God will then bring to judgment the secrets of man. The state of the heart will make the difference.

37. "And they answered and said unto him, Where, Lord? And he said unto them," &c. To those who did not thoroughly realize the universality of the separation at the judgment, this was a very natural question. Our Lord's answer seems to assure them that wherever there are human beings of different characters to be separated, there will be the ministers of separation. The saying, "Wheresoever the body is," &c., was probably a proverbial one, grounded upon the almost immediate appearance of the vultures wherever there is a dead body. Some accounts of the power of vultures in discerning a carcase immediately after it has been slain seem miraculous. No one will be able to escape the all-observing, all-sifting, all-separating judgment.

CHAP. XVIII.

AND he spake a parable unto them *to this end*, that men ought ^a always to pray, and not to faint;

^a ch. xi. 5. & xxi. 36. Rom. xii. 12. Eph. vi. 18. Col. iv. 2. 1 Thess. v. 17.

1. "That (men) ought." So D., E., G., H., Λ, many Cursives; but ℵ, A., B., K., L., &c., nearly sixty Cursives, Copt., Arm., read, "that they ought" (adding αὐτούς).

1. "And he spake a parable unto them to this end, that men ought always," &c. These words of the Saviour seem to fix the application of the parable as perfectly general. They teach us that men ought always to pray, that is, we ought to pray at all times—not merely at stated times, as at morning, and noonday, and evening—but at all times; particularly when God puts within us the thought of our adversary, who has, through the fall, got access to our soul, or of our besetting sin by which we constantly fall, and by which our whole spiritual progress is hindered. The application, I say, the Saviour seems to desire to make perfectly general, so that every soul should account itself the widow, and look upon every sin or spiritual evil as its adversary, and regard God as being the very opposite of this unjust judge; as ever more ready to hear than we to pray, as being, in very deed, on our side against the world and sin, Who when He is weary, is weary not with our constancy and perseverance in prayer, but with our forgetfulness of His presence and cessation from prayer.

I think we should keep this before us as the design of the parable, and that we should be somewhat cautious in considering the widow to be the Church, and the avenging speedily as the sudden cessation of the tribulation of the last days by the coming of the Lord. This is its secondary application, and can only be effectually realized through its primary one, because the Church is a Body made up altogether of individual souls or persons, so that when the Church as a person, *i.e.*, a widow, cries to God it can only mean, as far as I can see, a spirit of prayer diffused through the hearts of the particular members of the Church, and exercised by them individually.

2 Saying, There was †in a city a judge, which feared not
God, neither regarded man:

† Gr. *in a certain city*.

3 And there was a widow in that city; and she came unto him, saying, Avenge me of mine adversary.

4 And he would not for a while: but afterward he said within himself, Though I fear not God, nor regard man;

---

3. "And she came;" rather, "and she kept coming," "came oft," Revisers.

We now come to the parable.

2. "Saying, There was in a city a judge, which feared not God, neither regarded man." Isaac Williams illustrates it "As fearing not God, having no mercy: as regarding not man, having no wish to appear better:" as we should say, dead to all better motives, divine or human.

3. "And there was a widow in that city," &c. In those Eastern countries, for above 1,500 years, widows seem to have had no protector but God. Amongst us especial favour is granted to them by society. Every effort is usually made to alleviate their sorrows. Unbounded indignation pursues those who wrong them, whereas through long ages, reaching to our Lord's time, they seem to have been a special object of prey to their unscrupulous relations or neighbours. Thus God calls Himself "a father of the fatherless, and the defender of the cause of the widow." When Isaiah calls the people to do "works meet for repentance," they are "to judge the fatherless and plead for the widow" (Isaiah i. 17).

"And she came unto him, saying, Avenge me of mine adversary." The idea is not so much "avenge me" as "do me justice" against mine adversary. Some powerful and wicked neighbour had taken away her land, her house, her cattle, and she called aloud to the judge to "right" her. "Avenge" conveys a wrong impression. It was not so much vengeance or the punishment of her oppressor that she wanted, as the restoration of her rights; though I grant that if the widow is taken to be the Church, her martyrs are represented, in Rev. vi. 10, as calling for vengeance.

4. "And he would not for a while: but afterward he said within himself, Though I fear not God," &c. "Though I fear not God." He is represented by the Lord as not only wicked, but conscious of his wickedness, and glorying in it, and boasting to himself that no consideration can move him except that of his own ease.

5 ^b Yet because this widow troubleth me, I will avenge her, lest by her continual coming she weary me. ^b ch. xi. 8.

6 And the Lord said, Hear what the unjust judge saith.

7 And ^c shall not God avenge his own elect, ^c Rev. vi. 10.

---

5. "She weary me," "she wear me out," Revisers; and in margin, "bruise me," but see below.

5. "Yet because this widow troubleth me, . . . she weary me." The word translated "weary" seems to have properly a far more startling meaning. It is "lest by her continual coming she smite me on the face." As if he was afraid that the widow would assault him; the same word in 1 Cor. ix. 27 (where alone it occurs except in this passage) signifying "buffeting and, as it were, mortifying the body by various self-denials." Perhaps "plague me" would preserve the strong meaning, and yet be without the seeming vulgarity. But it is to be remembered that the Lord is drawing the picture of a man regardless of self-respect and decency.

6. "And the Lord said, Hear what the unjust judge saith." Notice how the Lord directs attention not so much to the importunity of the widow, as to her success in causing this bad, selfish man to listen to her.

7. "And shall not God avenge his own elect, which cry day and night," &c. No doubt but that by the elect is meant the Church, but the Lord, by using a plural noun, and not the collective word Church in the singular, would desire us to take to ourselves, each one for himself, this most gracious promise. We have a right to the promise only as members of the Church, but we exercise that continual prayer which entitles each one of us to his share in the promise individually.

"His own elect." Who are the elect? What is the mark by which we may know ourselves to be of the number? Evidently earnest and continual prayer (His own elect which cry day and night unto him).

"Avenge His own elect." This avenging, of course, will have its consummation at the Second Coming, when the Church, as such, will be avenged of the world, and the prince of the world : but it would be a poor promise for those who have fought, or are fighting their fight *now*, to be told that their avenging will be that of another generation at the last day. They feel the power and tyranny

which cry day and night unto him, though he bear long with them?

8 I tell you ^d that he will avenge them speedily. ^d Heb. x. 37. 2 Pet. iii. 8, 9.

---

7. " Though he bears long with them " " and he is long-suffering over them," Revisers. (μακροθυμῶν in T., Δ, Λ, R., later Uncials, almost all Cursives, Syriac (Schaaf), μακροθύμῖι in א, A, B., D., L., Θ, X., 1, 157, 209), but see below.

of their adversary *now* : *now* at this present he oppresses them—now sin finds an entrance into their mortal bodies—now they cry, " O wretched man that I am, who shall deliver me from the body of this death?" Their earnest desire, their cry is that God should bruise Satan under their feet shortly. The warfare is within, the oppression is within, and the avenging, the deliverance, must be within if they are to have part in the final deliverance. So *now* they cry for cleansing—for the casting out of the evil spirit—the spirit of anger, envy, concupiscence, foul thoughts, wordly ambition.

Some have made it a difficulty that the Lord is here compared to a judge of iniquity, but He is not compared to such a judge, He is *contrasted* with him. If the unjust judge is made by the perseverance of the widow to yield and do justice, much more will the just and holy God Who has commanded us always to pray and not to faint, and Who is on our side in the warfare we are maintaining with the evil within and without us—much more will such a God take the part of His Own.

" Though he bear long with them." This may mean, " Though, like the judge, He bear long with their cry, deferring his answer," or, it has sometimes been interpreted, " though He bear long with their remaining sinfulness : " or, " though He bear long with those which oppress them."

8. " I tell you that he will avenge them speedily." Williams well remarks : " It is the same contradiction which always pervades this subject, for the Lord is always described as appearing to be long in coming to avenge His elect; and yet, in fact, coming ' speedily.' This very word occurs in another place in the same way: 'The Lord is not slack concerning his promise as some men count slackness; but is longsuffering to us-ward' (μακροθυμῶν), (2 Peter iii. 9). For that which seems long with men is very short with God, and with them that are with God, and who come to the mind of God."

A PHARISEE. A PUBLICAN.

Nevertheless when the Son of man cometh, shall he find faith on the earth?

9 And he spake this parable unto certain ᵉ which trusted in themselves ‖ that they were righteous, and despised others:

ᵉ ch. x. 29. & xvi. 15.
‖ Or, *as being righteous.*

10 Two men went up into the temple to pray; the one a Pharisee, and the other a Publican.

"Nevertheless when the Son of man cometh, shall he find [the] faith on the earth?" This has been understood as if, before the Second Coming prayer will have become less fervent through lack of faith: but such a meaning seems scarcely to do justice to the passage. In it the Lord asks a question, and seems to express a doubt as to the answer He should receive. "When the Son of man cometh shall he find, think you, the faith (not faith, but *the* faith) on the earth?" I cannot but think that this faith is the faith once delivered to the saints, the faith of the Gospel, and the creeds—*the* faith in Christ, the Eternal Son of God Incarnate, Crucified, Risen, Ascended, and Returning. This faith will be in the pages of Scripture, and in the creeds of the Church. It may not, perhaps, be denied, but it will not be *held*. And yet without the realization of these great eternal verities there can be no faith, in the New Testament sense of the word.

Already this faith grows weaker and weaker. It has been said that faith is "turned inward," and a miserable "turning" it is: for what is there *within* the sinner to raise him up to God and unite him to the Supreme? It is the exhibition of the love of God in His Son which breeds faith in the soul. It is the same exhibition which sustains it, and the same which perfects it.

9. "And he spake this parable unto certain which trusted in themselves," &c. This declaration on the Lord's part fixes the meaning and purpose of the parable. Its application is perfectly general, and any application to classes, such as Jews and Gentiles, however seemingly appropriate, must be put quite in the background.

10. "Two men went up into the temple to pray; the one a Pharisee, and the other a Publican. Why are two men out of these two classes chosen? Evidently because the Pharisees were the most popular religionists of the day, and the Publicans the most

468 GOD, I THANK THEE. [ST. LUKE.

^f Ps. cxxxv. 2.
^g Is. i. 15. &
lviii. 2. Rev.
iii. 17.

11 The Pharisee ^f stood and prayed thus with himself, ^g God, I thank thee, that I am not as

despised of all Jews. According to the popular view, a Pharisee could not be unjustified, and nothing that he could do would justify Publican so long as he continued in his hated calling.

"Went up," naturally because the temple was on an elevation. Went up to pray. They went up, that is, for private prayer. The temple being the one place of sacrificial worship, was naturally the place of prayer. Whilst the sacrifices of the law and the burnings of incense were going on, men would desire that their particular prayers and thanksgivings should unite with the smoke of the offerings, and be thus borne up to heaven. It is a great scandal that our churches are not open for prayer at all times. It is to be hoped that the time is not far distant when this will be first possible and then universal. Any poor Jew could escape from the noise and worry of his crowded home, and use this most splendid of all places, raised to the honour of God, as his oratory. Why should not every poor English Christian have the same privilege?

11. "The Pharisee stood and prayed thus with himself, God, I thank thee, that I am not as," &c. Why does the Lord draw attention to the standing of the Pharisee, seeing that standing was the common posture of the Jews in prayer? Evidently because he stood erect, without even an inclination of the head or the body, as if he had no sin to be ashamed of, no wrath to deprecate, no spiritual want to be supplied.

"Prayed thus with himself." "With himself" does not depend upon "standing," as if it were standing aside by himself, but upon "prayed." He prayed thus with himself, as we say, to himself, in his mind, though his words may have been heard by those near.

"God, I thank thee that I am not as other men are, extortioners, unjust, adulterers," &c. It seems to me a great mistake to endeavour to bring in this man guilty of the sins which he here thanks God that he does not commit, as Stier, for instance, seems to do. "If we could suppose God to answer him by setting before him the true catalogue, with the question appended in each case, Art thou not such thyself, at least in My sight? then might a revealing light have penetrated to his soul, and he might have recognized in in himself the extortioner, and even the adulterer (according to John viii. 9), and especially in the spiritual meaning." This seems

other men *are*, extortioners, unjust, adulterers, or even as this Publican.

12 I fast twice in the week, I give tithes of all that I possess.

---

to me to undo the lesson of the parable, which is the evil of the man's self-righteousness and self-complacency, *per se*. Giving him the fullest credit for keeping the letter of the law, that he was neither extortionate, unjust, or adulterous; the wrong thing was that he prided himself upon his outward observance of these precepts, that he was proud, self-righteous, and self-complacent. To such an extent was he this, that he did not utter even a prayer. His prayer was, in fact, no prayer at all. It was a soliloquy rather, in which, whilst formally addressing God, he really ran over to himself his virtues, his abstainings, his superiority to all others, or, at least, to the general run of men, his self-denials, his offerings.

"Even as this publican." As he looked round upon this man, he must have observed the signs of contrition and humility in his whole demeanour. And yet he took no account of them. He knew he was a Publican, and so, though knowing nothing of his real state before God, he credited him with the Publican's vices, no doubt particularly extortion and injustice. All this showed his guilty state of heart, because it proved his shameful ignorance of the spirit of his own scriptures, embodied in such striking passages as "Thus saith the high and lofty One that inhabiteth eternity . . . . I dwell in the high and holy place, with him also that is of a contrite and humble spirit, to revive the spirit of the humble, and to revive the heart of the contrite ones."

"I fast twice in the week." Does the Lord here speak in disparagement of fasting, seeing that He Himself had fasted forty days and forty nights; seeing that He had said to His followers, "When ye fast, be not as the hypocrites." "Thou when thou fastest, appear not unto men to fast, but unto thy Father which is in secret, and thy Father, which seeth in secret, shall reward thee openly.' What, then, does the Lord blame? Not the fasting, but the complacent dwelling upon it; the displaying it before God; the mentioning of it as if it was an end in itself, and not the means to an end; for it is to be remarked that he does not even plead his fasting that God may give him something; he has no sense of any want, for there is no prayer whatsoever, as I noticed before, throughout his soliloquy.

13 And the Publican, standing afar off, would not lift up so much as *his* eyes unto heaven, but smote upon his breast, saying, God be merciful to me a sinner.

"I give tithes of all that I possess." Does the Lord here discourage carefulness and exactness in our transactions with God, so that we should give to Him His full tenth? No; because the Lord Himself, in speaking of the tithing of such small matters as pot-herbs, mint, rue, and anise, says, "These (the tithes of such things) ought ye to have done, and not to leave the others (justice, mercy, and faith) undone."

What, then, does He blame? The complacent dwelling upon it, the secret regarding of God as his debtor, because he gave Him what others neglected to give.

Such was the Pharisee's prayer. To us it seems incredible that one taught in the scriptures of God should so address Him; and yet prayers conceived in this spirit seem to have been common. Edersheim gives two or three. One is, "I thank Thee, O Lord, my God, that Thou hast put my part with those who sit in the academy, and not with those who sit at the corners (money changers and traders). For I rise early, and they rise early: I rise early to the words of the law, and they to vain things. I labour, and they labour: I labour and receive a reward, they labour and receive no reward. I run, and they run: I run to the life of the world to come, and they to the pit of destruction."

13. "And the Publican, standing afar off, would not lift up so much as his eyes," &c. "Standing afar off" seems to signify that, whilst the Pharisee pressed as near to the most sacred part of the temple as he was allowed to do, the Publican stood far behind him, scarcely venturing to pass through the entrance, feeling that one so unholy must not tread on holy ground.

"Would not lift up so much as his eyes unto heaven." Showing, in the curved posture of his body, and his downcast look, the deepest feeling of personal guilt.

"But smote upon his breast," thereby not taking credit for repentance, but taking shame for sin.

"God be merciful to me a sinner." We are to remember that this cry for mercy was the utterance of the agony of his inmost spirit. There was no prescribed ritual which put into his mouth

14 I tell you, this man went down to his house justified

14. "Justified rather than the other." "Above" or "beside the other" read by ℵ, B., L., 11, 94, 209, Sah., Copt., old Latin (b, c, e, f, ff², i, l, q); but A., all later Uncials, &c., as in Rec. Text.

such words as, "Thou, O Lord, have mercy upon us, miserable offenders." It was, as we said, private prayer, though in a public place; as the Pharisee's prayer was extempore, the overflowing of his own heart, so was the Publican's, though the words he chose are to be found in many Psalms.

14. "I tell you, this man went down to his house justified," &c. That is, he went down to his house, having had his prayer for mercy heard and accepted by God; whilst the other, having prayed for nothing, received nothing, because he had simply displayed himself before God, and so came under a curse rather than a blessing, as it is written, "Everyone proud in heart is abomination to the Lord."

A question now presents itself upon the words, "justified rather than the other" (or as the neutral text MSS. read, "above the other") which is forced upon us by the treatment which this passage receives at the hands of some good and able divines. Thus one writes that the Pharisee was unjustified, not so much because of his pride, but because it is said that the Publican was "justified rather than he was," and as there can be "no degrees in justification," the Pharisee must be altogether unjustified; and so it is assumed that the one went to his house with "a sweet sense of assurance," which he may have had, but of which nothing is said, and the other was secretly "without peace," being in reality ill at ease, which we should have seen if we could have only read his heart.

But is it possible thus to apply to the Publican's case the Pauline, or rather Christian sense of justification? I think it is absurd to do so, and that it seriously interferes with the reality and naturalness, so to speak, of the parable. For what is the Pauline doctrine of justification? It is justification of life (Rom. v. 18); that life being not the natural, but the supernatural life, resulting from the communication to us of the Lord's Risen Life. It is, consequently, the result of the Lord's Resurrection, and of nothing else, and is made over or supposed, by St. Paul at least, to be made over to each man on his believing the resurrection of the Lord (Rom. iv. 23-25, x. 9),

472   JUSTIFIED.   [St. Luke.

^h Job xxii. 29. *rather* than the other: ^h for every one that exalteth
Matt. xxiii. 12.
ch. xiv. 11.
Jam. iv. 6. 1
Pet. v. 5, 6.

and is sealed to him on his submitting to receive a rite in which he is mystically raised again with Christ (Rom. vi. 3, 4). This is the only view of Christian justification given after Pentecost, by the only Christian writer who systematically entertains the subject.

To connect the Publican's justification and the Pharisee's want of justification with this is not only a misleading anachronism, but an introduction of an element of unreality. The Publican was justified, *i.e.*, accepted and blessed because of his self-abasement, and the Pharisee, the popular religious professor of the day, was unjustified and unblessed, because of his self-conceit and self-assertion, according to the Divine words, "Though the Lord be high, yet hath he respect unto the lowly; as for the proud, he beholdeth them afar off."

One word more. When the Publican thus confessed himself a sinner, and asked mercy, we are not to suppose that he confessed mere sinfulness, common to all men alike, but that in all probability he had committed the sins to which the Publicans as a class were liable, fraud, extortion, injustice, false accusation. The whole virtue of the parable is in this, that he had led an actually evil life, and from this he was delivered, and not only from certain spiritual sins to which there is no particular shame attached.

So that the words with which the Lord concludes are absolutely true. "Every one that exalteth himself," no matter how free from blame his outward conduct, no matter how high his profession is, no matter to what pretentious sect he belongs,—"Every one that exalteth himself shall be abased, and he that humbleth himself" —no matter how evil his former life—" shall be exalted." He shall be high in the favour of Him whose loving-kindness is better than the Life itself.

And now for the application of this to Christian times.

We must remember that such things as self-esteem and self-complacency depend very much on the system in which men are brought up, and to which they continue to belong. Under a legal system, a man will pride himself upon legal, *i.e.*, outward righteousness; under a spiritual system, a man will esteem himself on account of his spiritual discernment—his clear views of the doctrines of grace and their relations one to another, particularly of the

himself shall be abased; and he that humbleth himself shall be exalted.

---

relative positions of justification and santification—of imputed and imparted righteousness, and such things. In my own youth I was thrown much amongst such persons, and though I remember many among them of the deepest, because the humblest piety, walking to all appearance as closely with God as any can do on this side of eternity, yet I have in my recollection not a few whose whole souls seemed to be permeated with the self-complacent, self-asserting, self-conscious spirit of this Pharisee. Their self-gratulation was that they were enlightened, that they had clear views, and the worst sign in their eyes of the condition of a fellow-creature was, that he had not such. The view of illuminating grace which they entertained was, I need not say, very different from that of the Apostle, where he writes, "He that hateth his brother is in darkness, and walketh in darkness, and knoweth not whither he goeth, because that darkness hath blinded his eyes" (1 John ii. 11). How many pride themselves upon their conversion, not remembering that our Lord in speaking of conversion says not merely, "except ye be converted," but, "except ye be converted and *become as little children*, ye shall in no case enter into the kingdom of heaven." [1]

We Christians then have to take heed lest we resemble the Pharisee. In such a spiritual dispensation as that in which we are, our outward confession may have not one word like his, and yet our whole heart and mind may be pervaded by his spirit of self-esteem. The worst part of his address were the words, "Even as this publican." The moment we find ourselves comparing our-

---

[1] Such persons are very much decreasing in the Church of England. They have taken refuge principally among the so-called "Brethren." Their uncharitableness in the matter of "judging" would now seem incredible. I remember, as if it were yesterday, being in a company of religious persons of this school, very shortly after the death of the late Dr. Arnold. An article in a religious newspaper of the day was discussed, in which it was asserted that Arnold had only just light enough to save him. Upon which one of the leaders in the company (I assure the reader far above the average) expressed, by no means flippantly, but in all seriousness, the opinion that he had nothing like light enough to save him.

474   THEY BROUGHT TO HIM INFANTS.   [St. Luke.

15 [1] And they brought unto him also infants, that he would
touch them: but when *his* disciples saw *it*, they
rebuked them.

[1] Matt. xix. 13.
Mark x. 13.

---

selves with others to our own advantage, then we have reason to
fear the spirit of Pharisaism.[1]

Lastly we see, from the example of the Publican, what God requires of sinners. He requires of them that they should seek Him, and throw themselves simply and entirely upon His mercy. In coming to God, then, let us extenuate nothing. Let us not say that such or such a temptation, under which we fell, was too strong for us, because He, no doubt, remembers what we forget, that there was a way of escape provided, if we would have seen it, and not turned away our eyes from it. Do not let us plead our circumstances, because God, perhaps, may be able to show that others under more adverse circumstances have endured where we have failed. It is the safest to come to God cloaking nothing, extenuating nothing, mentioning nothing but His promises of mercy in Jesus Christ.

15. "And they brought unto him also infants that he would touch them," &c. What blessing did the parents of these children expect from the Lord? It could not have been healing, for they were not sick, and it could not have been any high spiritual grace. Origen says that they thought that 'no ill-chance, or evil spirit could harm those infants on whom Jesus laid His hand, and by His touch infused virtue into them. Augustine, however, goes deeper. "To whom are they brought to be touched, but to the Saviour?

---

[1] An almost ludicrous yet very instructive illustration of the form in which this spirit not unfrequently displays itself, I heard but a day or two ago. A well-known and much esteemed minister of the Church entered a place where a prayer meeting was being held. He was asked to stay, as in a minute or two he would be privileged to listen to the experiences of some convert well known in the locality. He did stop, and did hear a long confession, but not of the man's own sins, but of *those of his father*. Scarcely a word was said of his own wrong doings; it was full from beginning to end of the drunkenness, the neglect of prayer, and other signs of his own father's irreligion.

16 But Jesus called them *unto him*, and said, Suffer little children to come unto me, and forbid them not: for [k] of such is the kingdom of God.

17 [l] Verily I say unto you, Whosoever shall not receive the kingdom of God as a little child shall in no wise enter therein.

[k] 1 Cor. xiv. 20. 1 Pet. ii. 2.
[l] Mark x. 15.

And as being the Saviour they are presented to Him to be saved, Who came to save that which was lost. But with regard to these innocents, when were they lost? The Apostle says, 'By one man sin entered into the world.' Let then the little children come as the sick to a Physician, the lost to their Redeemer." I have very fully examined the import of this beautiful incident in my notes on St. Mark's Gospel (x. 17). I need hardly remind the reader that the Church, in her Baptismal Office for Infants, uses it to stir up our faith in the gracious presence and working of our Saviour at every baptism. We are not to "doubt, but earnestly believe that he will likewise favourably receive this present infant; that he will embrace him with the arms of his mercy," &c. The strict logical deduction from the transaction (taking our Saviour's Divine power and Godhead into account) is that He will confer spiritual blessings upon those who, at the time, cannot pray to Him, or consciously apprehend the gift He bestows.

"Suffer little children to come unto me." Here we see that the Lord accounts that children who are brought to Him come unto Him. He takes their tender age into account, and dispenses for the time with their conscious coming.

"Of such is the kingdom of God." The kingdom of God is composed of children, and of such as are, in respect of their humble and teachable disposition, like unto children.

17. "Verily I say unto you, Whosoever shall not receive the kingdom of God," &c. We cannot but infer from this, that after Baptism our continuance in the kingdom of God depends upon our preserving the humble, teachable, child-like spirit. If we are received into the Church of Christ as infants, and afterwards become worldly, proud, questioning, sceptical, we fall away from the grace of our adoption, and have to re-enter the kingdom not only by being converted, but by being converted so as to become as little children.

18 ᵐ And a certain ruler asked him, saying, Good Master, what shall I do to inherit eternal life?

ᵐ Matt. xix. 16. Mark x. 17.

18. "And a certain ruler asked him, saying, Good Master, what shall I do," &c. We now come to our third exposition of this remarkable incident, for we have it fully reported in each of the three synoptics. I have examined it very fully in my notes on St. Mark—particularly with reference to two things: first, to our Lord demanding of the young ruler why he called Him good; secondly, with respect to our Lord directing the young ruler to follow Him in the way of perfection, not as an ordinary Christian, but as an Apostle, or quasi-Apostle, (such as Matthias and Joseph, surnamed Barsabas) parting with all that he had at the outset. Respecting these matters I must refer the reader to the notes on St. Mark. There are, however, one or two points in this most instructive incident which will require further handling.

I would make one observation at the outset, that the internal, or spiritual, character of the man, *i.e.*, his state before God, must be judged from the fact that our Lord, not before, but after he had given the answer, "All these have I kept from my youth up," "looked upon him and loved him." Now it is the prerogative of our Lord, as partaking fully of the Divine Nature, to read the heart. He could not have said this if the man had been a hypocrite, or proud, or insincere in his first question, or a boaster, or self-righteous after the example of the self-righteousness of the Pharisee of the last parable.

" And a certain ruler asked him, saying, Good Master, what shall I do," &c. St. Luke alone tells us that he was a ruler—most probably a ruler in a synagogue. We should gather from this that he had, at least, a reputation for being learned in the Scriptures, as well as that he was highly esteemed for his moral life.

"What shall I do to inherit eternal life?" There was nothing blameable in this question, *i.e.*, in asking what he should "do." The way of faith in a crucified and risen Saviour was not revealed, at least it was not apprehended even by the Apostles (Luke xviii. 34), and if they, as yet, could not apprehend it, much less this ruler. It is to be observed that the Lord does not blame him for putting this question, but rather for using unreal words.

19. "And Jesus said unto him, Why callest thou me good?" &c. See my note on St. Mark. He had, according to St. Matthew,

CHAP. XVIII.] ALL THESE HAVE I KEPT. 477

19 And Jesus said unto him, Why callest thou me good? none *is* good, save one, *that is*, God.

20 Thou knowest the commandments, ⁿ Do not commit adultery, Do not kill, Do not steal. Do not bear false witness, ᵒ Honour thy father and thy mother.

ⁿ Ex. xx. 12. 16. Deut. v. 16-20. Rom. xiii. 9.
ᵒ Eph. vi. 2. Col. iii. 20.

21 And he said, All these have I kept from my youth up.

---

19. "Save one, *that is* God" (ὁ Θεός). So A., D., and apparently all other authorities except ℵ and B. (first hand), which, omitting article, read, "save one God."

asked "what good thing shall I do?" and the Lord would rectify his ideas respecting goodness, by not allowing him to call even Himself good unless he realized something of the meaning of the words he used.

20. "Thou knowest the commandments, Do not commit adultery, do not kill," &c. All these commandments are good, according to the words of the Spirit by St. Paul, "The commandment is holy, and just, and good." (Rom. vii. 12). And as these commandments are good, so the doing of them, even in the letter, is good. It is good, for instance, to keep the first of these things which the Lord here mentions, for otherwise human society becomes a filthy sty, as it is becoming in places where a lawless Gospel is preached.

21. "And he said, All these have I kept from my youth up." We are to judge of these words by two things. First by the way in which the Lord receives them. He utters not one word of reproach to the man because of the seeming self-righteousness he evinced. On the contrary, it is said by St. Mark that then "Jesus beholding him, loved him." Now it was impossible for the Lord to have thus spoken if the man had been animated by anything of the spirit of the Pharisee in the last parable, for the look of Jesus penetrates into the innermost depths of the soul. Could the all-knowing Saviour, after searching him through and through, and then loving him, have thought of him as a modern Evangelical expositor does who writes, "An answer more full of darkness and self-ignorance it is impossible to conceive! He who made it could have known nothing rightly either about himself, or God, or God's law." Surely if the Lord entertained the same view of his state of heart as Bishop Ryle here does, He would have plainly told him that he had never kept one of God's commandments. Then, in the

22 Now when Jesus heard these things, he said unto him,

next place, we must estimate them by the standard of the dispensation in which they were uttered. They are not one whit more self-righteous than the words of Hezekiah, " Remember now, O Lord, I beseech thee, how I have walked before thee in truth, and with a perfect heart, and have done that which is good in thy sight" (Isaiah xxxviii. 3), or than those of David in a hundred places in the Book of Psalms; take, for example, Psalm xxvi., beginning, "Be thou my judge, O Lord, for I have walked innocently: my trust hath been also in the Lord, therefore shall I not fall." Or Psalm xviii. 20-26, " The Lord shall reward me after my righteous dealing, according to the cleanness of my hands shall he recompense me." We are to remember that the essential difference between the dispensations is that the one was of the letter, the other of the Spirit. (2 Corinth. iii. 6, 7). Men now take a far deeper view of sin, and a far wider view of God's law, because of the Incarnation and its consequences. " The Spirit was not then given because that Jesus was not then glorified." The Spirit is now given to conform men to the example, and to infuse into them the mind of the Eternal Son: so that now they know no standard but His Life, no righteousness by the side of His Righteousness; but before the Resurrection and Pentecost it was not so, and could not have been so. Men then, such as David, Hezekiah, and this ruler, expressed themselves not vain-gloriously, but naturally, according to their standard. Their standard was a legal one, and, in a great measure, an external one. The young ruler could have kept perfectly the letter of the commandments which Christ mentioned. That he should have kept them in the spirit, or taken a spiritual view of their full requirements depends upon this, whether God in his case chose to anticipate the principal feature of the New Dispensation as distinguished from the Old, which is this, " I will put my law in their minds and write it in their hearts." (Heb. viii. 8-10, x. 16.)

22. " Now when Jesus heard these things he said unto him, Yet lackest thou," &c. St. Matthew alone makes the ruler ask, " What lack I yet ? " St. Mark and St. Luke both make the Lord first allude to the one thing lacking.

It is commonly supposed that this man was exceedingly covetous. One writes, " It was a case of desperate and idolatrous love of money, and so there was but one remedy, ' Sell all and distribute.' "

CHAP. XVIII.] YET LACKEST THOU ONE THING. 479

Yet lackest thou one thing: P sell all that thou hast, and distribute unto the poor, and and thou shalt have treasure in heaven: and come, follow me.

p Matt. vi. 19, 20. & xix. 21. 1 Tim. vi. 19.

23 And when he heard this, he was very sorrowful: for he was very rich.

Well I can only say that in this our England there are numberless cases of such covetousness, and yet no preachers and no commentators that I ever heard of have preached so severe a remedy. The Lord not only bid him sell all, but "follow" Him, *i.e.*, in the way of the Apostolic life, as the twelve were doing, and to this he was not equal. The Lord, be it remembered, did not bid him sell all in order that he might have eternal life hereafter—respecting that He had said, "If thou wilt enter into life, keep the commandments" —but in order that He might live the Apostolic life and obtain the Apostolic crown.

I am thankful to see that this view which I have advocated in my notes on the two first synoptics is in the main that taken by so Evangelical a commentator as Godet. "This look of love was also a scrutinizing look by which Jesus discerned the good and bad qualities of the heart, and which dictated to Him the following saying. He determined to call this man into the number of His permanent disciples. The real substance of his answer, indeed, is not the order to distribute his goods, but the call to follow Him. The giving away of his money is only the condition of entering upon that new career which is open to him (see at ix. 61, and xii. 33). In the proposal which He makes to him Jesus observes the character which best corresponds to the desire expressed by the young man. He asked of Him some work to do; and Jesus points out one, and that decisive, which perfectly corresponds to his object, inasmuch as it assures him of salvation."

23, 24. "And when he heard this, he was very sorrowful .... And when Jesus saw that he was very sorrowful, ... How hardly," &c. This shows that this young man was not exceptionally covetous or fond of riches, but that he was one of a class, and that he did not rise above his class. He was an example of a danger shared in by very many. For instance, the Lord, in describing the persons which refused the Gospel invitation, makes the first to be one who had bought a piece of land, and the second one who had bought five yoke of oxen. The Lord seems to lay down that all worldly

24 And when Jesus saw that he was very sorrowful, he said, ⁹ How hardly shall they that have riches enter into the kingdom of God!

q Prov. xi. 28.
Matt. xix. 23.
Mark x. 23.

25 For it is easier for a camel to go through a needle's eye, than for a rich man to enter into the kingdom of God.

26 And they that heard *it* said, Who then can be saved.

27 And he said, ʳ The things which are impossible with men are possible with God.

r Jer. xxxii. 17. Zech. viii. 6. Matt. xix. 26. ch. i. 37.

---

24. "When Jesus saw that he was very sorrowful." So A., I., P., R., X., Γ, Δ, Λ, Π, all later Uncials, almost all Cursives, most old Latin, Vulg., Syriacs; but א, B., L., 1, 131, 157, 209, Copt., read, "And Jesus seeing him, said."

24. "Shall they that have riches enter." So א, A., D., all other later Uncials, most Cursives, old Latin (f, l), Syriac, &c.; but B., L., read, "do enter."

---

possessions have a tendency to make men worldly. One man may cling to a small estate more detrimentally to his soul than another may cling to a larger. Riches, too, are a matter of degree. Every shilling of the incomes of many rich men is anticipated, and must be expended upon others as soon as received. Whilst many working men, who would class themselves as poor, are able to expend in some districts of this country as much as two pounds a week in low sensual pleasures, and do so.

25, 27. "For it is easier for a camel to go through a needle's eye, than for a rich man . . . . possible with God." Here the Lord lays down the impossibility, humanly speaking, of a rich man entering into the kingdom of God; and He somewhat qualifies what He was saying from His own divine standpoint, "The things which are impossible with men are possible with God."

Now what is our duty as ministers of God, living in the midst of an exceedingly wealthy community, as regards these sayings? Evidently not to make the one neutralize the other, but to assert manfully and courageously the danger of wealth, and all other worldly advantages, and that men can only deprive them of their poison by giving liberally; far, far more liberally than the standard even of the Church recognizes as liberality, and that all mental powers, accomplishments, &c., are to be laid at the feet of the Lord and consecrated to His service. The preaching and inculcation of almsgiving bears no proportion in modern books on religion, or sermons, to what it does in the New Testament.

CHAP. XVIII.] LO, WE HAVE LEFT ALL. 481

28 ªThen Peter said, Lo, we have left all, and followed thee.   ª Matt. xix. 27.

28. "Lo, we have left all." So ℵ, A., P., R., X., Γ, Δ, Λ, Π, all later Uncials, most Cursives, Vulg., Goth.; but B., D., L., some Cursives, 1, 13, 49, 118, 131, 209, 346, Copt., Syr. (Schaaf), most old Latin, read, "left our own."

And yet it was not so in the first ages. Almost every sermon or lecture of Chrysostom on St. Matthew or the Epistles ends with some inculcation of almsgiving or generosity, sometimes couched in the most trenchant language possible.

The Apostles, though they themselves had given up all, were astonished at this saying. Perhaps some part of their astonishment arose from the marked difference between the two dispensations in this very matter. Of the man under the Old Covenant that feareth the Lord, it is said, " Riches and plenteousness shall be in his house," but for the New Dispensation, the Lord said, " Blessed are ye poor," " woe unto you rich." Outward blessings are now not the sign of the Divine favour as they were under the old state of things—rather the contrary; so that it seems beside the mark to cite the cases of Abraham, David, Hezekiah, Jehoshaphat, Josiah, Job, and Daniel, as rich men who were saved; for in and after Christ's time matters were utterly reversed. The Lord, the first Apostles, St. Paul, and his companions, were very poor; all the first teachers of the Christian religion were very poor.

Let nothing that we say upon this very serious matter undo the force of the Lord's words, " How hardly," for if the truth was unflinchingly declared, many a rich man now at ease in his possessions might be aroused, and led to lay hold of that grace, the first effect of which will be to make him part with his wealth, and succour his needy fellow creatures, and lay up treasures in heaven, escape the terrible lot of Dives, do good, be rich in good works, ready to distribute, and so lay up in store for himself a good foundation against the time to come, that he may lay hold on eternal life (1 Tim. vi. 18, 19).

28—30. " Then Peter said, Lo, we have left all .... world to come life everlasting." For the explanation of the great truth contained in this passage, I must refer the reader to my notes on Mark x. 29, 30. Suffice it now to notice one or two things.

1st. The Lord does not reply to Peter's question so far as regards himself and those on whose behalf he spake, but gives an answer of the widest application. " Verily, I say unto you, *there is no man*

I I

29 And he said unto them, Verily I say unto you, ᵗThere
is no man that hath left house, or parents, or
brethren, or wife, or children, for the kingdom of
God's sake,

30 ᵘ Who shall not receive manifold more in
this present time, and in the world to come life
everlasting.

t Deut. xxxiii. 9.

u Job xlii. 10.

---

that hath left house," &c.; so that there is no man, no matter in what age of the Church he lives, who has followed the example of the apostles, but will receive as far as possible the rewards of the apostles; I say as far as possible, for the promise accorded in Matth. xix. 38, respecting the twelve thrones, is of course limited to the twelve.

With respect to the words "in the present time," which are evidently opposed to the words "in the world to come" of the next clause, they teach us that we must be careful to explain the "manifold more," as given in this world. Homes, parents, brethren, wives, children, are things to be desired, because they call forth the highest and purest affections, the exercise of which sheds abroad in the heart the highest and sweetest human joy and satisfaction. Now a man's conversion to the faith of Christ, though it at times, perhaps almost always, estranged him from a heathen home and family, gave him another home, and a far wider family, attached to him in far firmer and closer and, withal, more holy bonds, and these were brethren and sisters, fathers and mothers in Christ. The exercise of purified love and affection, and, we may add, reverence towards these, would diffuse through his heart a far holier and deeper joy than he had ever experienced in his former unholy heathen state. Take, for instance, the last chapter of the Epistle to the Romans; look at the number of Christians to whom the apostle sent salutation. In no one case were these salutations a mere heartless form. In every case they were accompanied by the overflow of Christian love, by memories of how they had laboured and suffered together in the same holy cause; in most cases, perhaps, they were the greetings of a father to his children in the faith. What a sea of satisfaction and holy joy does all this disclose! And so it was, though, of course, in different degrees, and under various forms, with every Christian who had given up any worldly advantage for Christ's sake.

31 ¶ ˣ Then he took *unto him* the twelve, and said unto them, Behold, we go up to Jerusalem, and all things ʸ that are written by the prophets concerning the Son of man shall be accomplished.

32 For ᶻ he shall be delivered unto the Gentiles, and shall be mocked, and spitefully entreated, and spitted on:

33 And they shall scourge *him*, and put him to death: and the third day he shall rise again.

34 ᵃ And they understood none of these things: and this saying was hid from them, neither knew they the things which were spoken.

x Matt. xvi. 21. & xvii. 22. & xx. 17. Mark x. 32.
y Ps. xxii. Is. liii.
z Matt. xxvii. 2. ch. xxiii. 1. John xviii. 28. Acts iii. 13.

a Mark ix. 32. ch. ii. 50. & ix. 45. John x. 6. & xii. 16.

---

31. "Then he took unto him the twelve, and said unto them, Behold, we go up . . . . Neither knew they the things which were spoken." "Then took he unto him;" *i.e.*, according to St. Matthew, "he took them apart by the way." "He shall be delivered unto the Gentiles." Mark the words. He must first be delivered to the Gentiles by His own people before they could touch Him. (See my note on John xix. 11.)

34. "And they understood none of these things," &c. And yet nothing could be plainer or more circumstantial than the Lord's prophecy. It was not deep doctrine respecting His union with the Father, but the plainest possible intimation of His sufferings. He shall be mocked, spitefully entreated, spitted on, scourged, put to death.

Why was it that they understood not such things, that they were hidden from them, that they knew them not? Some think that it was because their whole soul rejected the thought of what was impending. They would not entertain it, but when we read the words "it was hid from them," we cannot but think that there was something supernatural in this "hiding" or "concealing." It was as if God for His own all-wise purposes had cast a veil over these plain things, and if the thirty-fourth verse principally refers to the prophecy respecting His Resurrection on the third day, their inability to understand this may have been, in a sense, judicial. They were bound to receive all the Lord's words as the utterances of the Incarnate Truth, and as they had not received the intimations of

35 ¶ ᵇ And it came to pass, that as he was come nigh unto Jericho, a certain blind man sat by the way side begging:

ᵇ Matt. xx. 29. Mark x. 46.

36 And hearing the multitude pass by, he asked what it meant.

37 And they told him, that Jesus of Nazareth passeth by.

38 And he cried, saying, Jesus, *thou* Son of David, have mercy on me.

39 And they which went before rebuked him, that he should hold his peace: but he cried so much the more, *Thou* Son of David, have mercy on me.

40 And Jesus stood, and commanded him to be brought unto him : and when he was come near, he asked him,

---

His sufferings because they gave way to their natural dislike to the thought of such things, so when He announced the termination of these sufferings in His rising again, they were, by a judicial act of God, unable to apprehend it. Through God's all-ruling providence this slowness on their part to believe in the Resurrection is, for these latter days, one of the greatest proofs of its reality. They did not expect it, and so they did not figure it to themselves, or imagine it, and so could not have imposed upon themselves an appearance which never had any external or objective reality.

35. "And it came to pass, that as he was come nigh unto Jericho, a certain blind man," &c. I have commented so fully upon this incident in my notes on St. Mark's Gospel, that I can do little more than refer the reader to that volume. St. Mark gives by far the most circumstantial account; St. Luke's narrative differs from his mainly in this, that he considers the miracle to have taken place as the Lord came nigh to Jericho; whereas St. Mark says, "As he went out of Jericho." It has been supposed that the principal blind man, that is Bartimæus, first accosted the Lord as He entered Jericho, and not having, for some reason or other, attracted His notice he sat by the wayside, and called to Him along with another, who had joined his company, as He departed. I see that Godet quotes an author or reviewer who mentions that Josephus and Eusebius distinguish between the Old and the New Jericho, and

41 Saying, What wilt thou that I shall do unto thee? And he said, Lord, that I may receive my sight.

42 And Jesus said unto him, Receive thy sight: ^c thy faith hath saved thee.

^c ch. xvii. 19.

43 And immediately he received his sight, and followed him, ^d glorifying God: and all the people, when they saw *it*, gave praise unto God.

^d ch. v. 26. Acts iv. 21. & xi. 18.

---

that the two blind men might have been found, the one as they went out of one city, the other at the entrance of the other."

Be this as it may, the lessons to be derived from the parable are the same.

First, that the Lord is ever passing by. He is ever coming near to us, and though we see Him not, giving proofs of His nearness to encourage us to call upon Him for spiritual sight.

Secondly, that the more we are forbidden, whether by false friends or by seemingly discouraging circumstances, to call upon Him, the more we should call. True faith is that which overcomes all discouragements.

Thirdly, that if we do thus perseveringly call, He will stand; He will cause us to be brought to Him; He will give us what we cry for: especially will He give us spiritual sight, "the eyes of our understandings being enlightened, we shall know the hope of His calling."

Fourthly, that it will be Christ, Who gives us the light of truth and salvation, and yet it will be our faith—our faith in Him as a living person, as the Son of David, and, therefore the Inheritor of all the promises, and the Wielder of all the power ascribed to that Son of David. It is remarkable that amidst all the glorious titles of Christ such as God, as Word, as Only Begotten, as Saviour and Redeemer, the Church has not forgotten this one of "Son of David." "O Son of David," we call in our Litany, "O Son of David, have mercy upon us."

And lastly, when we have received this spiritual sight, if it be true spiritual sight, we shall follow Him, glorifying God. We shall follow Him in the path of faith and love and obedience, and those around us, when they see our holy and consistent walk, will "give praise unto God."

CHAP. XIX.

AND *Jesus* entered and passed through Jericho.
2 And, behold, *there was* a man named Zacchæus, which was the chief among the publicans, and he was rich.

3 And he sought to see Jesus who he was; and could not for the press, because he was little of stature.

1, 2. "And Jesus entered and passed through Jericho. And behold, there was a man named Zacchæus," &c. The account of Zacchæus we owe to St. Luke alone. The name is a Jewish or Hebrew name, and is the Grecized form of Zaccai (Ezra ii. 9).

"Which was the chief among the publicans." It was only natural that Jericho, from its position close to the fords of Jordan (Josh. ii. 7), and as the frontier city on entering the Holy Land from Peræa—situated, too, as it was, in the richest plain of Palestine, from which the costly balsams passed from Gilead on their way westward, should be the seat of a revenue collector of superior rank.

3, 4. "And he sought to see Jesus who he was . . . he was to pass that way." Why did he seek to see the Lord? It must have been from some strong interest he took in Him, and this could not well be other than a spiritual one. He is another instance of that which we have several times noticed in the course of this commentary, that from many hints in the Gospels, it seems that a work of grace was going on amongst the publicans as a class. (See Luke iii. 12; v. 29; vii. 29; xv. 1; xviii. 10. These should be taken together.) He was very probably one of those who had strong feelings towards religion, and deep yearnings after what is good and right, but, as yet, had not been able to separate himself from the peculiar sins of his dangerous calling. The good Shepherd discerned him, and secretly but irresistibly led him to seek Him, though at first in the way of curiosity, perhaps, as much as from any deeper longings. The means he took to see the Lord were very remarkable, very unwonted for a man in his position, a rich man, chief of a wealthy class. Regardless of ridicule, and of any compromise of his dignity, he ran and climbed into a roadside tree, as if he were a boy, in

ZACCHÆUS, MAKE HASTE.

4 And he ran before, and climbed up into a sycomore tree to see him: for he was to pass that *way*.

5 And when Jesus came to the place, he looked up, and saw him, and said unto him, Zacchæus, make haste, and come down; for to day I must abide at thy house.

6 And he made haste, and came down, and received him joyfully.

---

order to get a sight of the Lord as He passed. As Trench remarks, "He has not, or if he has he overcomes, that false pride, through which so many precious opportunities, and oftentimes in the highest things of all, are lost." It is noticed by commentators that the tree into which he climbed has wide-spreading lateral branches which made it easy for a man to climb and stand in it.

5. "And when Jesus came to the place, he looked up," &c. He brought Zaccai out of his concealment, perhaps to his momentary discomfiture, as He did the woman with the issue of blood. He had far more grace in store for him than the mere sight of His Person.

"Zacchæus, make haste and come down, for to-day I must abide at thy house." Words of extraordinary grace, for while the Lord *accepted* many invitations (Luke vii. 36, xi. 37, xiv. 1), yet we do not read that He honoured any but this publican by thus offering Himself to his hospitality. As Augustine says, "He who thought it a great blessing to behold Jesus passing by, hath, of a sudden, merited to receive Him into his house." The reader will remember the words of the Lord to the Church of Laodicea. "If any man hear my voice, and open the door, I will come in to him and sup with him, and he with Me." (Rev. iii. 24.)

6. "And he made haste, and came down, and and received him joyfully." This seems to imply that Zacchæus sought to see the Lord out of far more than a feeling of mere curiosity. He must have heard much about the Lord's miracles, His teaching, above all, His receiving publicans, thus to welcome Him. He must, I think, have been looking for Him, as One in some way sent from God, to separate men from their past evil lives.

7. "And when they saw it, they all murmured, saying, That he was gone to be," &c. So they murmured when, at the house of Matthew, He eat with Publicans and sinners; so they murmured

7 And when they saw *it*, they all murmured, saying,[a] That he was gone to be guest with a man that is a sinner.

8 And Zacchæus stood, and said unto the Lord; Behold, Lord, the half of my goods I give to the poor; and if I have taken any thing from any man by [b] false accusation, [c] I restore *him* fourfold.

[a] Matt. ix. 11.
ch. v. 30.

[b] ch. iii. 14.
[c] Ex. xxii. 1.
1 Sam. xii. 3.
2 Sam. xii. 6.

---

when He allowed the penitent woman to anoint His feet. They all murmured—the crowd murmured—because He shared the hospitality of a hated tax-gatherer and extortioner. The Pharisees, probably—the leaders of the then religious world—that He was gone to be the guest of one excommunicated.

8. "And Zacchæus stood, and said unto the Lord; Behold, Lord, the half of my goods," &c. This is as if he rose from his seat where he was sitting surrounded by many other guests as well as the Lord and His disciples, and made a solemn profession or confession. Some have supposed that he stood up to profess the benevolence of his private life and conduct in opposition to those who had said that the Lord had gone in to eat with a sinner. And they explain his last words, "If I have taken any thing from any man by false accusation, I restore him fourfold," by such a supposition as, "In a profession like his, it was easy to commit involuntary injustice. Besides Zacchæus had under his authority many employés, for whom he could not answer."—Godet. But it seems rather to be a profession of repentance, and the consequent determination to lead a new life—a life exactly contrary to his old one. For inasmuch as his former life was devoted to the accumulation of money, now, at one stroke, he gives up half his property; whereas before he had given way to the practices frequent in his profession, of extortion and underhand dealing, now he openly repudiates all such unlawful ways of gain.

It is very probable that the single Greek word (ἐσυκοφάντησα), rendered in English by the whole sentence, "if I have taken (any thing) by false accusation," had a wider meaning than is implied in its derivation, and includes many species of fraud besides that directly connected with false witness.

"I restore him fourfold." The thief had to restore fourfold (Exod. xxii. 1). So that, by such a restoration, Zacchæus publicly

SALVATION COME TO THIS HOUSE.

9 And Jesus said unto him, This day is salvation come

confessed that his frauds were breakings of the eighth commandment.

"The half of my goods I give to the poor . . . . I restore fourfold." These are indeed worthy fruits of repentance. There seems to be nothing like them in this our day. When a man in the worldly position of Zacchæus is converted, or becomes religious, it is reckoned an adequate sign of it if, out of perhaps an income far above one thousand a year, he gives a few guineas to a few societies, helps a little more liberally the parish schools and the parish benefit clubs, and so on. On the other hand, Cornelius à Lapide, and others anxious to show that from that time he embraced a life of voluntary poverty, tell us that he only retained the other half in order that out of it he might pay the "fourfold" to those whom he had defrauded; but this is absurd on the face of it: for we have no reason to believe, from the narrative, that he threw up his position as chief of the publicans. The Lord did not bid him follow Him, as He did the young ruler, in the way of apostolic poverty; and it is not to be imagined that he continued fraudulent practices in order that he might make amends to the sufferers with the other half of his income. In all probability, with the Lord's express sanction, he continued in his occupation, in order that he might set an example to others of his class, showing them that a calling which does not involve the commission of sin is a lawful one, and may be pursued innocently and honestly; and in order that he might restrain those, over whom he acted as chief, from extortion and other crimes.

9. "And Jesus said unto him, This day is salvation come to this house," &c. To many houses had the Lord come, and even He had not brought salvation to the inmates, because they received Him as a mere guest, and not as the Messiah or special representative of God to save them from sin; but to this man the coming of the Lord, and His holy converse, had been the turning point in his soul's life. He had probably made many resolutions before, and had had much conflict with the evil within him; but now, encouraged by the presence, and assisted by the secret power of Christ, he vigorously snapped asunder the chains of the world, and became a new man, denying his covetousness, confessing and making amends for his fraud and extortion, entering upon a life of benevolence and regard

to this house, forsomuch as ^d he also is ^e a son of Abraham.

10 ^f For the Son of man is come to seek and to save that which was lost.

11 And as they heard these things, he added and spake a parable, because he was nigh to Jerusalem, and because ^g they thought that the kingdom of God should immediately appear.

^d Rom. iv. 11, 12, 16. Gal. iii. 7.
^e ch. xiii. 16.
^f Matt. xviii. 11. See Matt. x. 6. & xv. 24.
^g Acts i. 6.

---

for others, and acknowledging the claims of Him whose presence had wrought so marvellous a change.

Thus had salvation come to his house, because the Lord had come in saving power to him.

"Forsomuch as he also is a son of Abraham." The import of this seems to be that, notwithstanding the detestation under which his class was held by his fellow-countrymen, the covenant of God with him as a son of Abraham held good that, on his repentance, he should be restored to all the privileges of the Israel of God. Those who hold that he was a Gentile by birth, suppose that by these words the Lord claimed him as a son of Abraham by faith, as one of the spiritual seed of Abraham, but I do not think this is possible.

"For the Son of man is come to seek and to save that which was lost." We learn from this, that though Zacchæus seemed to seek the Lord to see Him, yet the Lord was secretly seeking Zacchæus, both assisting and fostering the better thoughts which were taking possession of his soul, and also exciting his innocent curiosity so as to bring about His sojourn in his house, which was, of course, the occasion of much closer intercourse than Zacchæus would otherwise have enjoyed.

11. "And as they heard these things, he added and spake a parable .... immediately appear." They knew that He was going up to Jerusalem for no ordinary purpose,—not merely to teach or work miracles, but to bring about a crisis. What He had expressly told them respecting this crisis, as involving His own sufferings and shameful death before He entered into His glory, they put from them, and would not entertain the idea; but they knew that He was going up to establish the Messianic kingdom. This kingdom they, in their carnal views, understood to be one of "ob-

12 ʰ He said therefore, A certain nobleman went into a far country to receive for himself a kingdom, and to return.

13 And he called his ten servants, and delivered them ten ‖ pounds, and said unto them, Occupy till I come.

14 ⁱ But his citizens hated him, and sent a message after him, saying, We will not have this *man* to reign over us.

ʰ Matt. xxv. 14. Mark xiii. 34.

‖ *Mina*, here translated a pound, is twelve ounces and a half: which according to five shillings the ounce is three pounds two shillings and sixpence.

ⁱ John i. 11.

---

13. "Occupy till I come." So Γ, Δ, Λ, most later Uncials, almost all Cursives; but ℵ, A., B., D., K., L., R., Π., and about twenty Cursives, read, "during the time that I come," *i.e.*, "whilst I am away."

servation," of outward show and pomp; and He now puts forth a parable which teaches them that there must be a long period of probation, during which His servants would be on their trial, during His prolonged absence, and must win their places of rule in His kingdom by the use they made of the gifts which He committed to them.

This parable bears in some of its features a resemblance to that of the Talents in Matth. xxv.; but in its great lesson is essentially different. I have dwelt at some length upon the difference in my notes on St. Matthew's Gospel, but it may be well now shortly to re-state it.

The two parables, taken together, represent the sum of human accountability. All human beings whatsoever are accountable to God for the use which they make of His gifts; but these gifts may be divided into two classes, those which God gives to all alike, and those which He gives to each diversely in different proportions. To the heathen, even, He gives to all alike the gifts of life and breath, and the use of speech and sight and hearing, and such things; but he gives such gifts as health and riches, and strength of body and intelligence to each one in different proportions, so that no two men are exactly alike in their possession of these gifts. Now the Parable of the Talents has to do with each man's use or neglect of this latter set of gifts, or Talents as we have come to call them. In it the man travelling into the far country commits to each one of his servants his property in very different shares or proportions: to

15 And it came to pass, that when he was returned, having received the kingdom, then he commanded these

one five talents, to another two, according to their several ability; and as each man has different abilities, each has a different share. When the time of recompense comes, no difference seems to be made between him who has made his five talents into ten, and him who has made his two into four. They have each done their best, according to their ability, and are both welcomed into the joy of their Lord; but in this parable of the Pounds or Minas it is altogether different. The nobleman, on his leaving to receive for himself a kingdom, gives one and the same sum to each one of ten servants. One trades so well with his mina, that he increases it, or rather it increases under his hands into ten, another into five: and these are made rulers over ten and five cities respectively. The treatment of the man who makes no profit by his pound, but hides it in a napkin, is similar to that of the man who buried his talent in the earth. It is taken from him, and given to him that hath ten.

Now, first of all, this parable of the Minas, or Pounds, is much more closely connected with the manifestation of the kingdom, or Church, of Christ than that of the Talents. It was uttered because some thought that the kingdom of God should "immediately appear,"—*i.e.*, be manifested in power and glory. The great man of the parable is not a householder, but a nobleman, one well born (εὐγενὴς), who goes into a far country to be invested by the emperor, or greater sovereign, with the kingly rule of a province. At his departure he calls to him his ten servants (ten, of course, standing for any large number), and commits to them one mina each, which he left in their hands to trade with. Then there comes a sort of episode. His fellow-citizens hate him, and send after him an embassage to the emperor, or greater sovereign, with the words, "We do not desire this man to rule over us."[1] The length of the

---

[1] This part of the parable seems to have been founded on an historical fact. Archilaus, on the death of his father, Herod the Great, went to Rome to receive from Augustus the same royal dignity, and the Jews sent at the same time a deputation to the Emperor, begging him to deliver them from this evil house, and to convert this

servants to be called unto him, to whom he had given the †money, that he might know how much every man had gained by trading.

† Gr. *silver*, and so ver. 23.

---

time during which he is absent is the real answer to those who thought that the Messianic reign would at once be manifested. There must first be a probation of his servants, during which time his enemies remain unpunished, and this may be a considerable time, but he does return, and rewards his servants in exact proportion to what they have gained. The reward is in accordance with what we should expect that an Eastern king would give to faithful servants. They reign with and under him. One is made ruler over ten, the other over five cities; and after the idle servant is deprived of his power, the parable concludes with condign punishment executed before the king himself on the rebels.

Now taking into account the close connection of the parable with the kingdom, or church, of Christ, its points of contrast with the Parable of the Talents, particularly in regard of the equality of the sum committed to each of the ten, and their reward strictly according to the faithfulness and industry of each, there can be no doubt whatsoever what these minas, or pounds, denote. They must denote something which is the same to all, so that no one at the first can have more than another, and yet this something is of such a sort that it can be very differently employed, or increased by each one, not so much according to his ability, as according to his faithfulness or industry. Now there is one thing common to all Christians, which all receive alike, which is exactly the same to one as to another, and that is the Church taken in connection with its means of grace. Baptism is the same to all, for it is a grafting into One Body, so that the person baptized is made a member of Christ, no more and no less. The Scripture, or the Word of God, whether written or preached, is the same to all; its great leading truths, the being and attributes of God—the Incarnation, Life, Death,

---

country into a Roman province. At this very Jericho, where the Lord was speaking, Archelaus had built for himself a magnificent palace. He received from the Emperor only a part of his father's dominions, with the inferior title of Ethnarch, and on his return put to death those who had opposed his pretensions.

16 Then came the first, saying, Lord, thy pound hath gained ten pounds.

17 And he said unto him, Well, thou good servant: because thou hast been [k] faithful in a very little, have thou authority over ten cities.

[k] Matt. xxv. 21. ch. xvi. 10.

18 And the second came, saying, Lord, thy pound hath gained five pounds.

19 And he said likewise to him, Be thou also over five cities.

---

and Resurrection of the Son of God, are the same to each and all. The gift of the Spirit, at least the initial gift, is common to all, for the Apostle very emphatically says, "The manifestation of the Spirit is given to every man to profit withal" (1 Corinth. xii. 7) The Eucharist is the same to all. It is the Body and Blood of Christ, but one may so receive it that he "dwells in Christ and Christ in him," and another so profanes it that he "eats and drinks his own condemnation, not discerning the Lord's Body." And so with the promises of God that He will hear all our prayers, so with the example of Christ and His saints—all these things are the same to each. The early Christians had no means of grace which we have not. The Eucharist was the same Body and Blood of Christ to St. Paul as to the weakest believer. The profiting by it was according to the faith and prayer exercised in each case.

Such are these minas, or pounds. I do not see that any other meaning can be given to them. So that the difference between Christian and Christian—between nominal Christian and real believer, and between one real believer and another—is simply the use, the cultivation, the employment of, the perseverance in—the means of grace—the common means of grace which all Christians have, or are able to have, alike.

One objection, however, may be made. It may be said that the means of grace are withheld or mutilated, or given in very different proportions to different Christians. Amongst a vast body of Christians half the Sacrament of the Eucharist is withheld from the great body of the faithful, inasmuch as they are communicated only in one kind. Amongst us of the Church of England, about seventy or eighty years ago, there were multitudes of churches in which the

HERE IS THY POUND.

20 And another came, saying, Lord, behold, *here is* thy pound, which I have kept laid up in a napkin :

21 [1] For I feared thee, because thou art an austere man : thou takest up that thou layedst not down, and reapest that thou didst not sow.

22 And he saith unto him, [m] Out of thine own mouth will I judge thee, *thou* wicked servant. [n] Thou knewest that I was an austere man, taking up that I laid not down, and reaping that I did not sow :

[1] Matt. xxv. 24.
[m] 2 Sam. i. 16. Job xv. 6. Matt. xii. 37.
[n] Matt. xxv. 26.

Eucharist was only celebrated twice or three times a year. Again, with respect to other means of grace, many through defect of education could not read the Scriptures. Again, the preached word was very differently dispensed in different parishes. Now taking all this into the fullest account, there are yet abundant indications that God can, and does, make up for such seemingly serious losses in a marvellous way. Many devout Romanists seem to profit by their mutilated Sacrament more than many of us do by our full rite. God's good Spirit sometimes savingly impresses a few scattered and disjointed truths on the minds of poor Christians, so that they are far nearer to the mind of God than those whose knowledge is infinitely more varied and systematic and, we must say, intelligent. The guilt of withholding or depraving God's Word, and mutilating His Sacraments is with the teachers or administrators of Christian systems; and God by His marvellous grace not seldom makes up to private Christians what, through no fault of theirs, they have been deprived of.

A second matter for consideration is the method of rewarding the faithful servants. They are rewarded exactly in proportion to the way in which they have increased the sum of one mina committed to each. One is made to rule over ten cities, another over five.

Now, without at all pressing this literally, as that the reward of the future state will always be government or rule over others, perhaps in other worlds than this, such a theory of reward is perfectly incompatible with the popular idea of "heaven." I am not, I am sure, caricaturing the usual view of heaven, when I say that most Christians look upon it as a vast hall, into which those saved are admitted on their death; and we are constantly told that if we arrive at the

23 Wherefore then gavest not thou my money into the bank, that at my coming I might have required mine own with usury?

24 And he said unto them that stood by, Take from him the pound, and give *it* to him that hath ten pounds.

25 (And they said unto him, Lord, he hath ten pounds.)

26 For I say unto you, °That unto every one which hath shall be given; and from him that hath not, even that he hath shall be taken away from him.

° Matt. xiii. 12. & xxv. 29. Mark iv. 25. ch. viii. 18.

---

entrance, and can show our order of admission, we shall not be asked a word respecting the road by which we have come to the gate. Once admitted within the four walls, there will be no room for anything approaching to the gradations of reward set forth in this parable, for the only possible difference which the popular idea admits of is that one may have a seat nearer the place of honour—another nearer the door. The employment of the place is but one, no other which can properly be called employment has ever been suggested, one endless hallelujah, one never-ending song of praise. Now let the reader remember that I am writing nothing in the smallest degree contrary to what God's saints have ever held, respecting the wondrous rapture and glory of the beatific vision. But the same adorable Lord Jesus, the Ruler of all worlds seen and unseen, the Bestower of all grace here and all glory hereafter—this same Lord and Judge has not only said, " Blessed are the pure in heart, for they shall see God," but He has also said that He will say to those whom He accepts, " Come, ye blessed, inherit the kingdom—not merely enter into the hall, or even the palace, but inherit the kingdom," and He says, in strict accordance with this, to one, " Be thou ruler over ten," to another, " Be thou ruler over five cities." The idea of the reward which the Lord sets before us here is strictly just; His servant sets forth the same idea in more general terms when He says, " Every man shall receive his own reward according to his own labour" (1 Cor. iii.), and it is also natural, and points to the highest development of our natural faculties ; for the guidance, the direction, the protection, the administration of justice which is implied in " rule," and " kingship," taxes the best and highest faculties of the creature to the uttermost.

27 But those mine enemies, which would not that I should reign over them, bring hither, and slay *them* before me.

28 ¶ And when he had thus spoken, [p] he went before, ascending up to Jerusalem. p Mark x. 32.

29 [q] And it came to pass, when he was come nigh to Bethphage and Bethany, at the mount called *the mount* of Olives, he sent two of his disciples, q Matt. xxi. 1. Mark xi. 1.

---

27. "But those mine enemies, which would not that I should . . . slay them before me." One word more respecting that which seems at first sight apart from the great lesson of the parable, the embassy and subsequent treatment of the rebels.

"We will not have this man to reign over us." "Those mine enemies . . . bring hither and slay them before me." It seems impossible to avoid the conclusion that the Lord here of set purpose makes a difference between the slothful, and therefore evil servant, and the open enemies. The one has his mina taken from him, and, we suppose, like the man who had buried his talent, is cast into the darkness without, though this is not said; the others are treated as enemies, and slain. Those who send the embassy to the greater sovereign represent, in the first instance, the Jews, but the Jews themselves in this case must be taken to represent those who, when the reign of Christ is established, wilfully refuse obedience. It seems to stand to reason that if men knowingly and wilfully refuse the rule of Christ, they should be punished with greater severity than one who makes no use or increase of his gifts. This place is valuable as giving the lie to the notion that the Lord can inflict but one punishment, and that of the extremest severity.

The excuse of the slothful servant, the Lord's reproof of him, and his punishment are so similar in the account of the unfaithful servant in the Parable of the Talents, that I must refer my reader to my remarks on Matth. xxv. 24-30.

29. "And it came to pass, when he was come nigh to Bethphage and Bethany." We learn from St. John's Gospel that Jesus did not go up to Jerusalem without halting by the way. He stayed the night at Bethany, at the house of the sisters. At Bethany he was entertained by Simon the leper, and was by Mary anointed for His burial. On the next day (Palm Sunday) He made His

498 THE LORD HATH NEED OF HIM. [St. Luke.

30 Saying, Go ye into the village over against *you*; in the which at your entering ye shall find a colt tied, whereon yet never man sat: loose him, and bring *him hither*.

31 And if any man ask you, Why do you loose *him*? thus shall ye say unto him, Because the Lord hath need of him.

32 And they that were sent went their way, and found even as he had said unto them.

33 And as they were loosing the colt, the owners thereof said unto them, Why loose ye the colt?

34 And they said, The Lord hath need of him.

r 2 Kings ix. 13. Matt. xxi. 7. Mark xi. 7. John xii. 14.

35 And they brought him to Jesus: r and they cast their garments upon the colt, and they set Jesus thereon.

---

public entry into Jerusalem. All the three Synoptics give accounts of this, but if we had not the fourth Gospel, it would be impossible to understand how it was that He was met and followed by such a multitude. St. John tells us that the people met Him because they heard that He had "done this miracle," *i.e.*, that He had called Lazarus out of his grave.

30. "Saying, Go ye into the village over against you . . . bring him hither." We have remarked upon the extraordinary contrast between this incident and all others in the life of the Lord. On all other occasions the Lord refused all demonstrations of popularity—He forbade men even to mention His miracles. He conveyed Himself away when a multitude gathered together (John v. 13). When they would have taken Him by force, to make Him a king, He departed into a mountain Himself alone (John vi. 15). Now, on the contrary, He deliberately prepared to receive the all but worship which He alone knew would be rendered to Him; He laid Himself out for it, He encouraged it, and what is more, in very extraordinary words, as we shall see, He vindicated His right to it. First of all, He sent two disciples, most probably Peter and John, with the direction that they should find in a certain place two creatures, an ass and its colt, on which He intended to ride into Jerusalem, these creatures being those mentioned in the prophet Zachariah as those on which the Messiah-King should ride in triumph into the Holy City. St. Luke and St. Mark and St. John, however, only men-

BLESSED BE THE KING.

36 ˢAnd as he went, they spread their clothes in the way.   ˢ Matt. xxi. 8.

37 And when he was come nigh, even now at the descent of the mount of Olives, the whole multitude of the disciples began to rejoice and praise God with a loud voice for all the mighty works that they had seen:

38 Saying, ᵗBlessed *be* the King that cometh in the name of the Lord: ᵘ peace in heaven, and glory in the highest.   ᵗ Ps. cxviii. 26. ch. xiii. 35. ᵘ ch. ii. 14. Eph. ii. 14.

39 And some of the Pharisees from among the multitude said unto him, Master, rebuke thy disciples.

---

38. "Blessed be the King that cometh." So A., L., R., Γ, Δ, most later Uncials, most Cursives, Vulg., Goth., Copt., Syriac (Cureton and Schaaf); D. reads, "he that cometh;" א*, "the King in the name of the Lord;" but the Text. Recept. has no doubt the true reading.

tion the young ass or colt. Anticipating some difficulty on the part of the owners, He foretold that this would immediately vanish when they heard the royal demand, "The Lord hath need of him." Then when they had brought him to the Lord, He permitted them to do to Him what from the Old Testament we learn was done to those who claimed kingly power. They put their garments on the colt, and then they spread their garments in the way, that He might ride over them; they strewed the road with palm branches, and shouted before Him words which welcomed Him as King, "Blessed be the king that cometh in the name of the Lord," and no ordinary king, but one whose reign would be felt in heaven itself, "Peace in heaven and glory in the highest." Surely He was bound to restrain all this, for it was not merely enthusiasm, it was worship. The hosannas, the blessings, seemed to be given to Himself as well as to God. So thought the Pharisees, and accordingly they remonstrated, as well they might, if He were not a Divine King. "Master," they say, "rebuke thy disciples. These shouts of hosanna, these invocations of blessing trench on the honour due to God only."

The answer of the Lord is very wonderful, and, understood in the light of the rest of Scripture, is one of the strongest possible claims to divine worship on the part of the Lord.

500   THE STONES WOULD CRY OUT.   [St. Luke.

40 And he answered and said unto them, I tell you that,
if these should hold their peace, ˣthe stones would
immediately cry out.

41 ¶ And when he was come near, he beheld the city, and
ʸwept over it.

ˣ Hab. ii. 11.
ʸ John xi. 35.

---

40. "And he answered and said unto them, I tell you that, if these should hold their peace, the stones would immediately cry out." This has been designated as an hyperbole, but it is one that is very common in Scripture—the Prophets and the Psalms are full of such expressions; for do they not abound in words of praise and adoration which make all inanimate nature feel the presence of God? His presence is assumed to give life and tongue to mountains, to hills, to trees, to fields, to woods, to seas and their waves. "The mountains skipped like rams." "The hills melted like wax at the presence of the Lord." "Let the heavens rejoice, and let the earth be glad, let the sea roar and the fulness thereof." "Let the field be joyful, and all that is in it, then shall the trees of the wood rejoice." Now, of course, all this is poetry, but then it is poetry which is only given to God, only composed and poured forth to the honour of the Supreme. And when the Lord here says that if the disciples withheld their hosannas, the very stones would cry out, He claimed, not with indifference or hesitation, but with a very strong "I tell you" the same worship on the part of inanimate nature which, in a wondrous figure, if indeed it be a figure, is accorded to God only.

Such was the adoration which the lowly Son of Man received and claimed as His due on the way to the Holy City. And yet this way of kingly triumph was the way of the Cross. As I have shown in my notes on St. Mark, it was this triumphant entry, and this alone, which gave the chief priests their only possible opportunity of accusing Him to Pilate as claiming kingship in any sense.

> "Ride on! ride on in majesty,
> In lowly pomp ride on to die;
> Bow Thy meek head to mortal pain,
> Then take, O God, Thy power and reign."

41. "And when he was come near, he beheld the city, and wept over it." The exact spot where this most affecting scene must have occurred, can be pointed out. It is thus described by Dean Stanley:

IF THOU HADST KNOWN.

42 Saying, If thou hadst known, even thou, at least in this thy day, the things *which belong* unto thy peace! but now they are hid from thine eyes.

---

42. "At least" omitted by some MSS. and authorities, as also is "thy" in "This thy day." A. reads, "If thou hadst known, even thou, at least in this day." Vulgate agrees with authorized, and so does Tischendorf.

"The road descends a slight declivity, and the glimpse of the city is again withdrawn behind the intervening ridge of Olivet. A few moments, and the path mounts again, it climbs a rugged ascent, it reaches a ledge of smooth rock, and in an instant the whole city bursts into view. As now the dome of the mosque El-Aksa rises like a ghost from the earth before the traveller stands on the ledge, so then must have risen the Temple tower; as now the vast enclosure of the Mussulman Sanctuary, so then must have spread the Temple courts; as now the grey town with its broken hills, so then the magnificent city with its background—long since vanished away—of garden and suburbs on the western plateau behind. Immediately below was the valley of the Kedron, here seen in its greatest depth, as it joins the valley of Hinnom, and thus giving full effect to the great peculiarity of Jerusalem, seen only on the eastern side, its situation as of a city rising out of a deep abyss. It is hardly possible to doubt that this rise and turn of the road, this rocky ledge, was the exact point where the multitude paused again, and He, when He beheld the city, wept over it. Nowhere else on the Mount of Olives is there a view like this—still less is there any point where, as here, the city and temple would suddenly burst into view, producing the sudden and affecting impression described in the Gospel narrative."

42. "Saying, If thou hadst known, even thou, at least in this thy day, the things which belong," &c. "If thou hadst known." This is a phrase common in both Testaments for, "O, that thou hadst known."

"Even thou." "Thou daughter of Zion, which art so deeply fallen."

"At least in this thy day." Thy day of grace, the day in which God has come to thee as He had never come before. In past days He came to thee by prophets, by judges, by righteous kings; now, at last, He has come to thee in this thy day personally, in the power of His Godhead; for He has sent, last of all, His Son.

43 For the day shall come upon thee, that thine enemies shall cast a trench about thee, and compass thee round, and keep thee in on every side,

---

"The things which belong unto thy peace." The things taught by Me which would have reconciled thee to God, so that thou shouldest be as thy name denotes—The Vision of Peace—so that from this time thou shouldest be a joy and praise in the earth.

"But now they are hid from thine eyes." Now as a city, a church, a people, thy doom is sealed. Thou canst not now believe and be turned; but a remnant in the midst of thee shall go forth, and be the root of a more glorious Zion, a more heavenly city, a more faithful spouse of God.

43. "For the days shall come upon thee that thine enemies shall cast a trench," &c. Thy day of doom shall be delayed for a little space till these are gathered out of thee, and then the end shall come.

"Thine enemies shall cast a trench." "Trench," literally, "stockade with mound." Josephus, who has a most graphic description of its erection, describes it as a wall—meaning, of course, not a stone wall, but a safe enclosure. "Titus gave his opinion, which was that, if they aimed at quickness, joined with security, they must build a wall round about the whole city, which was, he thought, the only way to prevent the Jews from coming out any way, and then they would entirely despair of saving the city, and so would surrender it up to him . . . Titus gave orders that the army should be distributed to their several shares of this work, and indeed there now came upon the soldiers a certain Divine fury, so that they did not only part the whole wall that was to be built among them, nor did only one legion strive with another, but the lesser divisions of the army did the same. Now the length of this wall was forty furlongs, only one abated . . . and the whole was completed in three days: so that what would naturally have required some months was done in so short an interval as is incredible." So rapidly and completely was the Lord's prophecy fulfilled.

"And shall lay thee even with the ground, and thy children within thee . . . time of thy visitation." Josephus' account is the best comment upon this. "Now as soon as the army had no more

CHAP. XIX.] NOT ONE STONE UPON ANOTHER. 503

44 And ^a shall lay thee even with the ground, and thy children within thee; and ^b they shall not leave in thee one stone upon another; ^c because thou knewest not the time of thy visitation.

^a 1 Kings ix. 7, 8. Mic. iii, 12.
^b Matt. xxiv. 2. Mark xiii. 2. ch. xxi. 6.
^c Dan. ix. 24. ch. i. 68, 78. 1 Pet. ii. 12.

---

people to slay, or to plunder, because there remained none to be the objects of their fury, Cæsar gave orders that they should now demolish the whole city and temple. . . . This wall (*i.e.*, part of the west wall) was spared, in order to afford a camp for such as were to lie in garrison : as were the towers also spared, in order to demonstrate to posterity what kind of city it was, and how well fortified, which the Roman valour had subdued : but for all the rest of the wall, it was so thoroughly laid even with the ground by those that dug it up to the foundation, that there was nothing left to make those who came thither believe it had ever been inhabited."

Such was the fate of the city of God, and the Lord wept over it as loving it; but was He not the Lord of the spirits of all flesh ? Could He not have in one moment turned every heart in Jerusalem to Himself? He could, if we regard Him as simply power; but He was more than mere power, He was the just Judge—the righteous Ruler of intelligent spirits who have freedom of will, and He must respect this freedom of will with which He has endowed His creatures. So He must not act upon them by mere irresistible force, but must sway them, if possible, by motives, and draw them to Him by exhibitions of love and truth and goodness, so that they should willingly yield their hearts to Him. This He had assayed to do often and often. " How often would I have gathered thy children together, as a hen gathereth her chickens under her wing," but they would not be gathered. And now there was an end; the decree had gone forth, and though a remnant was to be gathered the nation must be cast away—the city destroyed. And if God be a just Ruler and Judge, so it must be now with us, with nations, with churches, with souls.

With nations, for these are the "times of the Gentiles"—as long as Jerusalem is trodden down, and trodden down it is now under the Turk ; the times of the Gentiles—the day of visitation for each Gentile nation is going on. If we have national life, that life should surely be national Christian life. National recognition of God,

HE WENT INTO THE TEMPLE. [ST. LUKE.

d Matt. xxi. 12. Mark xi. 11, 15. John ii. 14, 15.

45 ᵈ And he went into the temple, and began

national worship, national teaching of God's truth, or at least no hindrance to its teaching, putting away of national sins, such as traffic in slaves, which has been repudiated, and traffic in opium, which is not repudiated.

With churches. The Lord Himself tells us how He visited the seven churches of Asia, and the Lord is now of a certainty visiting us of the Church of England. May our prayer now be,— "Let Thy continual pity cleanse and defend Thy Church, and because it cannot continue in safety without Thy succour, preserve it evermore by Thy help and goodness."

And souls. "Our Redeemer does not cease to weep through His elect whenever He perceives any to have departed from a good life to follow evil ways. Who, if they had known their own damnation hanging over them would, together with the elect, shed tears over themselves. But the corrupt soul here has its day, rejoicing in the passing time; to whom things present are its peace, seeing that it takes delight in that which is temporal. It shuns the foresight of the future, which may disturb its present mirth : and hence it follows: "*But now are they hid from Thine eyes.*" (Gregory in "Cat. Aurea.")

As it was with Jerusalem so it is with the soul. There is the time of each soul's visitation. There is the time when Jesus comes, stands at the door, and knocks. This time may be very early, when the thought first occurs to the child that it must live for ever. Or it may be at confirmation, or first communion. It may be when the full-grown man has to choose between the world and Christ. It may be at the hearing of a sermon, or when a word has been dropped by a religious friend, or when there has been some sudden and startling danger imminent, or when some bitter grief has well-nigh overwhelmed the soul.

But can these things be the visitation of the Son of God ? Certainly. Nothing can happen to us except by His will, and if that which has happened has been in the way of awakening or illuminating the soul, it has not only happened according to His will, but by His special direction, and is a token that He is searching for the lost sheep that He may bring it home.

45. "And he went into the temple . . . ye have made it a den of

HE CAST OUT THEM THAT SOLD.

to cast out them that sold therein, and them that bought.

---

45. "Them that sold therein, and them that bought." "Therein" omitted by ℵ, B., C., L., 1, 69, 209, and ten other Cursives, old Latin (e, l, s), Cop., Arm.; retained by A., D., R., later Uncials, most Cursives, most old Latin, Vulg., Syriac.

"Them that bought," omitted by ℵ, B., L., 1, 209, Copt.; retained by A., C., D., R., all other Uncials, most Cursives, old Latin, Vulg., Goth., Syriac, &c.

thieves." Here we have Christ, who had in fulfilment of prophecy entered Jerusalem as its king, now asserting His Divine and Kingly authority in the temple of God. The chief priests had let out the area of the court of the Gentiles to cattle-dealers, money-changers, and others, and, no doubt, received much revenue from this profanation, and now the Lord thrusts aside their authority in what they thought to be their own house, to be used for their vile, covetous gain, and asserts His Kingship and Headship over His Father's house; and by an act of supernatural power, drove out these wretches apparently by a mere act of will, not even with the "whip of small cords" which at His first cleansing (John ii.) He had used for this purpose. Origen, and Jerome after him, consider this one of the most wonderful acts of Divine power exercised by our Lord. I have considered in my notes on St. Mark how this action teaches us reverence for all holy places and things,—not only for our churches, but for our bodies as along with our souls and spirits dedicated to God; and in my notes on St. Matthew how this action shows the attitude of our Lord towards the whole Sacrificial system, of which the temple was the centre, how till in His providence He actually abolished and superseded it, He treated it as in very deed the service of the Most High, and so everything connected with it as most holy. Suffice it now to say that in this action the Fathers seem to see the dislike of the Lord for all that approaches to traffic in religion; thus Origen: "Now I consider that the Church is the temple built of living stones, and that there are therein certain persons who live not as in the Church, but as they that war after the flesh, who through their wickedness make the house of prayer, built of living stones, a den of thieves. For who that hath perceived the sins that prevail in some Churches by those who consider the godliness of others to be their own gain: and when they ought to live entirely according to the Gospel alone, instead of doing so, collect wealth and great possessions—who seeing this will not say that the mystical holiness of Churches has become a den of thieves." (So also Ambrose and Augustine, quoted in J. Williams.)

A DEN OF THIEVES. [St. Luke.

46 Saying unto them, ^e It is written, My house is the house of prayer: but ^f ye have made it a den of thieves.

47 And he taught daily in the temple. But ^g the Chief Priests and the Scribes and the chief of the people sought to destroy him.

48 And could not find what they might do: for all the people ‖ were very attentive to hear him.

^e Is. lvi. 7.
^f Jer. vii. 11.

^g Mark xi. 18. John vii. 19. & viii. 37.

‖ Or, *hanged on him*, Acts, xvi. 14.

---

46. "Is the house of prayer." So A., C., D., other Uncials, most Cursives, and old Latin; but אc, B., L., R., a few Cursives, &c., read, "shall be."

Quesnel has a valuable application. "Every one of the faithful is the temple of God; and, therefore, ought to have the same zeal for the purity of his own heart, which Christ had for the sanctity of His visible temple. Avarice, self-interest, fondness for temporal things, and other lusts of this life, which fill the heart, are the buyers and sellers which must be cast out of this house of God, consecrated by Baptism for the offering up of prayer and adoration."

47, 48. "And he taught daily in the temple .... attentive to hear him." We are taught by these verses two things; first, how the Lord, to the very last, taught not only in the streets but in the temple itself—and none dare touch Him, because of the attention of the people; and, secondly, how the treachery of Judas was a necessary step before He could be taken and crucified; for He could only be betrayed "in the absence of the multitude" by one who knew where He resorted for secret prayer.

CHAP. XX.

AND ^a it came to pass, *that* on one of those days, as he taught the people in the temple, and preached the gospel, the chief priests and the scribes came upon *him* with the elders,

2 And spake unto him, saying, Tell us, ^b by what authority doest thou these things? or who is he that gave thee this authority?

^a Matt. xxi. 23.

^b Acts iv. 7. & vii. 27.

---

1. "The chief priests." So ℵ, B., C., D., L., M., Q., R., many Cursives, &c.; but A., F., G., H., K., S., other later Uncials, and about one hundred Cursives, read "the priests."

1. "And it came to pass, *that* on one of those days . . . . with the elders." That is, on the Tuesday, or the Wednesday in Holy Week. Edersheim gives reasons for supposing it to have been on the Tuesday. It must have been as soon as possible after the cleansing of the Temple.

The chief priests, whose authority in their own domain had been interfered with by the casting of the buyers and sellers out of the sacred precincts, were no doubt the principal instigators of this inquiry, and they brought with them scribes, men learned in the law, that if He appealed to Scripture for His authority they might oppose Him—the elders, no doubt, belonged to the Sanhedrim.

2. "And spake unto him, saying, Tell us, by what authority doest thou these," &c. No doubt this means, By what authority dost thou claim to interfere in the regulation of the Temple—but we are also to remember, that, for a man amongst the Jews to teach with authority required a commission. "There was no principle more firmly established by universal consent than that authoritative teaching required previous authorization. Indeed this logically followed from the principle of Rabbinism. All teaching must be authoritative, since it was traditional—approved by authority, and handed down from teacher to disciple. The highest honour of a scholar was that he was like a well-plastered cistern, from which not a drop had leaked of what had been poured

3 And he answered and said unto them, I will also ask you one thing; and answer me:
4 The baptism of John, was it from heaven, or of men?

into it. The ultimate appeal in cases of discussion was always to some great authority, whether an individual teacher, or a decree by the Sanhedrim." So Edersheim, who proceeds to describe how the disciples sat before the Sanhedrim in three rows, how the Sanhedrim was recruited from the first row—how there was a form of ordination, probably by laying on of hands, and so on. All this seems to show how deeply inrooted in the Jewish mind was the question of authorization.

This was not wrong in itself, for the heads of this system had a right to demand, indeed it was their duty to demand, that all teachers should be well instructed in that which they had to teach; but they ought to have seen well to two things; first, that the authorized teaching was according to the Scriptures, and did not make void the plain commandments of God; and secondly, that God reserved to Himself the right of raising up special messengers, not to found rival systems, or organizations, but to recall the minds of men to the essential holiness of their own system. In what had just occurred Jesus had actually vindicated the holiness of the temple and the sacrificial worship of which it was the centre against its own administrators—who were Sadducees, and consequently had no real belief in the Divine authority of anything.

3-8. " And he answered and said unto them . . . by what authority I do these things." " The Baptism of John, was it from heaven," &c. Our Lord here designates John's whole dispensation, his doctrine, profession, preaching, and the like by this one word, his Baptism. As Maldonatus well observes, "as the circumcision of Moses implied a keeping of the whole law, so the Baptism of John implied all his teaching." This Baptismal dispensation of John had no meaning except as pointing to Christ. It is described by the Apostle Paul as simply and merely a preparation. " John verily baptized with the baptism of repentance, saying unto the people, that they should believe on him which should come after him, that is, on Christ Jesus." [Acts xix. 4.]

When, then, the Lord asked this question, He really asked, " Was John's witness to Me and preparation for Me from God or from men?"

5 And they reasoned with themselves, saying, If we shall say, From heaven; he will say, Why then believed ye him not?

6 But and if we say, Of men; all the people will stone us: ^c for they be persuaded that John was a prophet.

^c Matt. xiv. 5. & xxi. 26. ch. vii. 29.

7 And they answered, that they could not tell whence *it was*.

And so, if they said from heaven, as was the universal opinion, then the absolutely necessary inference was that his testimony to Jesus was from heaven, and if they had believed this they would have accepted the Lord Jesus as the Christ. But they—these chief priests, scribes, and elders—had treated it as if it were "of men," because they had not accepted St. John's one doctrine—his one testimony—the one purport of his mission. And yet they dare not confess it to be "of men." The people were convinced, not by John's miracles, for he did no miracles, but by the holiness of his teaching, by his self-denying life, by his faithful reproof of sin in all men, in kings and courtiers, in Pharisees, publicans, soldiers, common people, all alike, that he was from above; he could not have been sent from man, he must have been sent from God.

This dilemma presented itself, as Jesus foresaw, to their minds. They must either condemn themselves, as professing to believe that a certain prophet came from God, and yet treating him as mistaken in his own message, or they must reject his mission, and seriously endanger their whole religious influence with the people and indeed their lives, and so they say, "We cannot tell." "We do not know," *i.e.*, "We refuse to entertain the question, being assured that if we did, it would go against us." This was not an absolute lie, as some have treated it, but a form of self-deception common to all human beings. Certain good reasons are presented to men's minds for accepting a clearly revealed truth of God, or altering a hurtful plan of life, and as soon as they perceive the goal to which these reasons tend they at once draw back, they refuse to go on the direct road, because of its disagreeable termination, and stand still, or turn aside.

Now it is not to be supposed that they—*i.e.*, those of them who had any remains of a conscience, entirely rejected the claim of John. They would have said, no doubt, that he was a prophet, that he was

8 And Jesus said unto them, Neither tell I you by what authority I do these things.

9 Then began he to speak to the people this parable; ^d A certain man planted a vineyard, and let it forth to husbandmen, and went into a far country for a long time.

^d Matt. xxi. 33.
Mark xii. 1.

---

raised up by God to do much good, to be "useful" to publicans and soldiers and common people, and that it would have been better for Herod if he had attended to him, and so on. But John was not sent to reprove Herod, or to reform publicans, but to point to a certain man and say, " Behold the Lamb of God," and to say, " He that cometh after me is greater than I—He shall gather His wheat—He shall burn the chaff—He shall baptize with the Holy Ghost." In fact, they rejected that in John's mission which was especially Divine, Messianic, and Supernatural.

And are not numbers of men, semi-agnostics, and Rationalists, acting in the same way towards Christ. They allow that he was the teacher of a higher morality, a purer worship, a deeper sense of truth, justice, and mercy, but they reject that for which He came, to reconcile men to God, to endue them with supernatural grace, to raise their bodies from the grave, and their souls from the death of sin by His Spirit. To these things their answer is, "We cannot tell." And so these chief priests and scribes, with every means of forming a correct judgment both of John's mission and that of the Lord, refused to do so. And the Lord retorted on them, "Neither tell I you by what authority I do these things." It would have been waste of words answering such double-minded men. There was enough to assure them of the authority of Christ—the prophets could have told them—John the Baptist told them—the signs of the times assured them—the teaching of Christ, all on the side of goodness and holiness—the miracles of Christ which, according to one of themselves, no man could do except God were with Him—all were witnesses to His authority.

9. " Then began he to speak to the people this parable ; A certain man planted," &c. This parable of the "Wicked Husbandmen" serves a double purpose.

The Jews had asked, " By what authority doest Thou these things, or who is he that gave Thee this authority ? " He did

CHAP. XX.] THE HUSBANDMEN BEAT HIM. 511

10 And at the season he sent a servant to the husbandmen, that they should give him of the fruit of the vineyard: but the husbandmen beat him, and sent *him* away empty.

11 And again he sent another servant: and they beat him also, and entreated *him* shamefully, and sent *him* away empty.

12 And again he sent a third: and they wounded him also, and cast *him* out.

---

then these things as the "beloved Son of God," and the Father had expressly sent Him as the last special Messenger to the Jewish Church and people to demand of them those fruits for the sake of which God had planted them.

Then in the next place it exhibits to us the extreme long-suffering of God. For 1500 years He had not only borne with the sin of the Jewish priests and prophets, but He had for the time condoned their persecution of His first prophets so far as to send others, and when they were rejected, to send His only and well-beloved Son.

In my notes on the two first synoptics I have very fully considered the circumstances of the parabolic history, so far as it relates to the Jewish people: but the long-suffering of God as detailed in the parable, and His perseverance in sending messenger after messenger to receive the fruit due to Him, naturally suggest two other applications—His dealing with Churches and His dealing with particular souls.

The dealings of our Lord with the Seven Churches of Asia by the mouth of His last surviving Apostle, are examples of His conduct to churches. He begins with acknowledging, so far as He can do so, what is good in them, their works, their faith, their patience, and then He has a "few things" to say, as to their shortcomings, and He ends with promising a reward to those among them who endure and are faithful, but threatens the Church itself with the loss of His Grace if, as a Church, it is unfaithful. In all this He addresses, not the Church itself, but the chief minister or angel, and of course through him, the other ministers. And it will be found at the last that He has done so with all churches. He has certainly done so with the Church of England. During the last century, the time of her deepest declension, He sent such an one as Wesley, who did his best to minister faithfully to the Church as

13 Then said the lord of the vineyard, What shall I do?
I will send my beloved son : it may be they will reverence
him when they see him.

14 But when the husbandmen saw him, they reasoned
among themselves, saying, This is the heir : come, let us kill
him, that the inheritance may be our's.

15 So they cast him out of the vineyard, and killed *him*.
What therefore shall the lord of the vineyard do unto them?

---

13. "When they see him." Omitted by אּ, B., C., D., L., Q., 1, 33, 131, 157, 209, some old Latin (a, c, ff², i, l, q), Copt., Syriac (Cur.), Arm. ; but retained by A., R., Γ, Δ, Λ, Π, later Uncials, most Cursives, Vulg., Goth., Syriac (Schaaf).

14. "Come." Omitted by A., B., K., M., Q., 1, 209, most old Latin, Vulg., Goth., Arm. ; retained by אּ, C., D., L., R., Γ, Δ, Λ, later Uncials, most Cursives, &c.

---

such, never allowing the ministrations of his own body to take place when her doors were open, requiring all his preachers and people to attend the celebrations of the Eucharist in Church, and I believe that, notwithstanding all provocations, he was in no way answerable for what took place after his decease. Then after his time a body of earnest and faithful men in the Church were sent to proclaim the necessity of preaching the power of the atonement and the cleansing and sanctifying work of the Spirit, and the need of personal coming to Christ, and lastly God raised up a band of men, the leaders of them of very great saintliness of life, to proclaim the reality of the visible Church and the peculiar grace of its Sacraments, that Christ has one mystical Body, and that He cares for the unity of this body, as well as calls for its energy in proclaiming the Gospel. In these ways has He demanded fruit from our branch of the Church. May God grant that we may render to Him something of what He looks for.

Then, in the second place, the vineyard is each soul. He is its Maker and so its Proprietor, and we have to cultivate it, each one of us for himself. By the gift of the Spirit and the Scriptures, and the ministry and the Sacraments He has done all that can be done to enable it to bear fruit : and this fruit which we have to give back to Him is His service, and His worship. These things may be compared to the hedge, the tower, the winepress, which in the other synoptics complete the idea of the vineyard. And in order to receive from us that fruit, the rendering of which is infinitely more profitable to us than to Him, He constantly sends messengers to the

16 He shall come and destroy these husbandmen, and shall give the vineyard to others. And when they heard *it*, they said, God forbid.

17 And he beheld them, and said, What is this then that is written, ᵉ The stone which the builders rejected, the same is become the head of the corner?   ᵉ Ps. cxviii. 22. Matt. xxi. 42.

18 Whosoever shall fall upon that stone shall be broken; but ᶠ on whomsoever it shall fall, it will grind him to powder.   ᶠ Dan. ii. 34, 35. Matt. xxi. 44.

soul. The watchfulness of parents, the instruction of Christian teachers, the exhortations of ministers, the reproofs and rebukes of godly friends; above all, at times He comes Himself; certainly it will be found that once, at least, He has come close to each soul. He has stood and knocked at its door. If it has opened the door, it has received Him to its salvation. If it has closed the door, it has, so far as it can, cast Him out, and crucified Him afresh. It has said within itself, "The inheritance shall be ours. We will be our own. In our thoughts, in our wills, in our bodies, in our society, in our possessions, we will be our own masters." And the end of Jerusalem is a true forecast of the end of that soul.

16. "He shall come and destroy those husbandmen .... grind him to powder." They perceived that the parable was aimed at themselves, and in them at the body of the Jewish people who, under their influence, were rejecting the Lord.

Bede notices two interpretations, "He who is a sinner, yet believes on Christ, falls indeed upon the stone and is shaken, for he is preserved by penitence unto salvation. But upon whomsoever it shall fall, that is, upon whom the Stone itself has come down because he denied it, it shall grind him to powder, so that not even a broken piece of a vessel shall be left, in which may be drunk a little water. Or he means by those who fall upon Him, such as only despise Him, and therefore do not yet utterly perish, but are shaken violently so that they cannot walk upright. But upon whom it falls, upon them shall He come in judgment with everlasting punishment, therefore shall it grind them to powder, that they may be as the dust which the wind scatters from the face of the earth." (Bede in "Caténa Aurea.")

20. "And they watched him . . . authority of the governor."

THEY SENT FORTH SPIES. [St. Luke.

19 ¶ And the Chief Priests and the Scribes the same hour sought to lay hands on him; and they feared the people: for they perceived that he had spoken this parable against them.

^g Matt. xxii. 15.
20 ^g And they watched *him*, and sent forth spies, which should feign themselves just men, that they might take hold of his words, that so they might deliver him unto the power and authority of the governor.

^h Matt. xxii. 16. Mark xii. 14.
21 And they asked him, saying, ^h Master, we know that thou sayest and teachest rightly, neither acceptest thou the person *of any*, but
‖ Or, *of a truth*. teachest the way of God ‖ truly:

---

21. "But teacheth the way of God truly." "But of a truth teacheth the way of God." Revisers.

From this place we should gather that these spies were emissaries of the chief priests and scribes only. From SS. Matthew and Mark we learn that they were sent forth by the Pharisees, and were their disciples, so that the chief Pharisees kept in the background for fear of being committed to the views of the Herodians who joined with them. Taking all three Evangelists together, it seems that all the enemies of Jesus—the Sadducean High Priests, the Scribes, the Pharisees, and the adherents of Herod—were united in putting this question following. St. Luke alone expressly mentions that the intent was that they might "deliver him unto the power and authority of the governor." From this we gather that they expected from Him an answer adverse to the claims of Cæsar, and in their ignorance they supposed that if He claimed to be the Messiah He must desire to get rid of foreign ascendancy in his own kingdom.

"Should feign themselves just men," *i.e.*, men who asked the question honestly and not captiously, with a view to ensnaring Him.

21. "And they asked him, saying . . . teachest the way of God truly." Of course the reader will mark how they condemned themselves by this impudent flattery. If He said and judged rightly and taught the way of God truly, why did they not believe His teaching?

CHAP. XX.]   WHY TEMPT YE ME?   515

22 Is it lawful for us to give tribute unto Cæsar, or no?

23 But he perceived their craftiness, and said unto them, Why tempt ye me?

24 Shew me a ‖ penny. Whose image and superscription hath it? They answered and said, Cæsar's.   ‖ See Matt. xviii. 28.

---

23. "Why tempt ye me?" So A., C., D., F., P., Γ, Δ, Π, later Uncials, most Cursives, most old Latin, Vulg., Goth., Syriacs; but omitted by ℵ, B., L., 1, 116, 118, 131, 157, 209, old Latin (e), Copt., Arm.

24. ℵ, C., L., some Cursives (1, 13, 33, 69, &c.), old Latin (c), Copt., &c., add, "and they shewed it to him, and he said;" but A., B., D., all other Uncials, most Cursives, most old Latin, Vulg., Goth., Syriac (Cureton and Schaaf), &c., omit these words.

22. "Is it lawful to give tribute to Cæsar or not?" It seemed to them a dilemma from which, to Him at least, there was no escape. If He said "It is lawful," His popularity with the multitude, who hated the Roman yoke, would be gone: for here was a Messiah, they would say, who belied the very first idea they entertained of the expected One, that He should make them free, and deliver them from all foreign ascendancy.

If, on the contrary, He said, "It is not lawful," they would accuse Him to the governor with some apparent ground of truth for their accusation.

23-25. "But he perceived their craftiness . . . and unto God the things that are God's." The image and superscription on the coin would show them to whom all obedience in civil matters was due. "And observe that He says not give, but return [ἀπόδοτε, *reddite*]. For it is a debt. Thy prince protects thee from enemies, renders thy life tranquil. Surely, then, thou art bound to pay him tribute. Nay, this very piece of money which thou bringest thou hast from him. Return, then, to the king the king's money. God also has given thee understanding and reason; make, then, a return of these to Him." (Theophylact.)

Many expositors have commented on this place in such a way as to imply that if men would only observe these two precepts of rendering their dues to God, and to the civil powers, they would avoid all difficulty, for there would be no collision between the two. But this betrays great ignorance. For what was it that occasioned the greater part of the martyrdoms and persecutions of the first three centuries, but this, that the civil power required Christians to

25 And he said unto them, Render therefore unto Cæsar the things which be Cæsar's, and unto God the things which be God's.

26 And they could not take hold of his words before the people: and they marvelled at his answer, and held their peace.

27 ¶ ¹Then came to *him* certain of the Sadducees, ᵏ which deny that there is any resurrection; and they asked him,

¹ Matt. xxii. 23. Mark xii. 18.
ᵏ Acts xxiii. 6, 8.

---

burn incense to false gods, and especially to the genius of the Emperor. It may be that under the influence of a false and spurious liberalism the civil power in this country may endeavour so to "widen the basis" (as the cant expression is) of the Church of England that it should include those who deny the Divinity of Jesus Christ, or even His special mission as the Son of God. Such a change would deprive the Church of the first and foremost reason for her existence, and would have, under God, to be resisted to the death. May God avert such a danger, and may we each in our spheres strive to render it impossible by indoctrinating all those under our influence with the full truth of God.

25. "And he said unto them, Render therefore unto Cæsar the things which are Cæsar's." Tribute, custom, honour, obedience in things temporal, loyalty, generous support.

"And unto God the things which are God's." The belief, fear, and love of the whole heart, the worship of the body and of the spirit, the submission of the intellect, the careful observance of all matters, great and small, respecting which God has made His will known.

26. "And they could not take hold of his words before the people." This question had been asked in the temple, no doubt, before a crowd of bystanders. It was put out of the deepest malice, but God so overruled it that we owe to it one of the great household words of our religion, "Render the things of Cæsar to Cæsar, and the things of God to God."

27. "Then came to him certain of the Sadducees, which deny that there is any resurrection." The Sadducees hitherto seem to have taken no notice of the Lord, but to have treated His teaching with

CHAP. XX.]   MOSES WROTE UNTO US.   517

28 Saying, Master, ¹Moses wrote unto us, If any man's brother die, having a wife, and he die without children, that his brother should take his wife, and raise up seed unto his brother.   ¹ Deut. xxv. 5.

29 There were therefore seven brethren: and the first took a wife, and died without children.

30 And the second took her to wife, and he died childless.

31 And the third took her; and in like manner the seven also: and they left no children, and died.

---

28. "And he die without children." So A., Γ, Δ, Λ, Π, later Uncials, most Cursives, old Latin (e, f, i), Goth.; but ℵ, B., L., P., some Cursives, 1, 16, 33, 118, 131, 157, 209, 254, old Latin (a, ff², g¹, l, q), Vulg., Copt., Arm., Æth., Syr. (Cur. and Schaaf), read, "he be without children."

30. ℵ, B., D., L., 157, omit all this verse except the first words, "and the second;" but A., all later Uncials, almost all Cursives, old Latin, Vulg., as in Rec. Text.

31. "The seven died also, and they left no children." Perhaps, "the seven also left no children, and died."

---

contempt. On one occasion only before this do they seem to have opposed him, when they united with the Pharisees in seeking from Him a sign from heaven (Matth. xvi. 1).

He had put to silence both the High Priest's emissaries and the Pharisees' disciples who had united with the Herodians; and now they would prove Him by themselves, and hoped, of course, by His discomfiture to show the hollowness of the popular belief in the existence of the unseen universe, particularly in the existence of souls after death; and, of course, if they could throw doubt upon the separate existence of the soul, much more upon the union of that soul to its own glorified and spiritualized body. They imagine an absurd and, humanly speaking, impossible case, of a woman who by the Levirate law had seven husbands, who all died before her, and they demanded, "in the resurrection, whose wife should she be?" Having, as might be expected, only the lowest and grossest view of the condition of man after death, the Lord first answers them by exposing their shortsighted and miserable materialism. They had no elevating hopes of the future dignity and glory of their own race. They could only imagine a future in which men should be under the same low conditions, and subject to the same gross and carnal desires as now.

The Lord answers them by setting before them a far more glorious

32 Last of all the woman died also.

33 Therefore in the resurrection whose wife of them is she? for seven had her to wife.

34 And Jesus answering said unto them, The children of this world marry, and are given in marriage:

35 But they which shall be accounted worthy to obtain that world, and the resurrection from the dead, neither marry, nor are given in marriage:

---

34. "The children of this world." Properly "sons."

future, more consonant with the power of God, and with the true dignity of a race whose nature He Himself had assumed.

The children of this world or *aiön*, or of the present state of things, marry and are given in marriage. They marry, and are given in marriage, because otherwise the race would become extinct by reason of death, but it shall not be so in the better—the eternal and more spiritual state of things to which the righteous look forward.

35. "But they which shall be accounted worthy to obtain that world, and the resurrection from the dead, neither marry nor are given in marriage." Mark the words: "They which shall be accounted worthy to obtain that world, or future state, or *aiön* of glory." Not all who die will pass into the better state (Luke xii. 47), though God will continue all in a state of existence. Some will pass into a state of punishment proportioned to their wrong doings. Some may have so thrown away all their better hopes, and so cut themselves off from God and goodness that they must share the lot of evil spirits. But some will be accounted worthy. Who are these? Are they all who will escape punishment? Probably the Lord here alludes to the first Resurrection, what St. Paul calls the Exanastasis, when he writes, "If by any means I might attain to the Resurrection from among the dead" (Phil. iii. 11); and St. John alludes apparently to the same when he writes in the Apocalypse: "But the rest of the dead lived not again till the thousand years were finished." "Blessed and holy is he that hath part in the first Resurrection: on such the second death shall have no power" (Rev. xx. 6). And the words of the Lord in this Gospel (τῆς ἀναστάσεως τῆς ἐκ νεκρῶν, Vulg. *resurrectione ex mortuis*) seem to point

CHAP. XX.] EQUAL UNTO THE ANGELS. 519

36 Neither can they die any more: for ^m they are equal unto the angels; and are the children of God, ⁿ being the children of the resurrection.

37 Now that the dead are raised, ° even Moses

^m 1 Cor. xv. 42, 49, 52.
1 John iii. 2.
ⁿ Rom. viii. 23.
° Ex. iii. 6.

---

36. "The children of God, being the children of the resurrection." Rather, "sons of God, sons of the resurrection."

this way. And the Lord in the next chapter seems to indicate a select few when He says, "Watch ye therefore, and pray always, that ye may be accounted worthy . . . to stand before the Son of man."

36. "Neither can they die any more: for they are equal unto the angels"—*i.e.*, equal in the condition of their frames as being above the reach of death. The angels seem not to be pure thought, or will, or intellect, but to have frames of so ethereal a nature that they are above the reach of decay; and the glorified bodies of the saints, being raised in the likeness of Christ's Body, will be equally above corruption and death. Thus, of the future body, St. Paul says, "It is sown in corruption, it is raised in incorruption; it is sown in dishonour, it is raised in glory; it is sown in weakness, it is raised in power; it is sown a natural body, it is raised a spiritual body."

"And are the children of God, being the children of the resurrection." There are four senses, one rising above another, in which men are the children of God. They are children of God by nature (Mal. ii. 10); they are children of God by adoption in Baptism by being grafted into the body of His Son (1 Corinth. xii. 13); they are children of God by being conformed by His Spirit to His likeness (Matth. v. 9, 44, 45; Rom. viii. 14); and they are the children of God in the highest sense, when they have overcome (Rev. xxi. 7), and are "worthy to obtain that world and the Resurrection from the dead."

37. "Now that the dead are raised, even Moses shewed at the bush," &c. "Even Moses"; why does the Lord say "*even* Moses"? Evidently because the declarations of a future state and a resurrection are much clearer in the later books of the Old Testament than in the earlier. Thus the most absolute declaration of a Resurrection is in Daniel xii., a book written towards the conclusion of the captivity, the dates of the book of Job, and some of the Psalms

shewed at the bush, when he calleth the Lord the God of Abraham, and the God of Isaac, and the God of Jacob.

38 For he is not a God of the dead, but of the living: for ᵖ all live unto him.

ᵖ Rom. vi. 10, 11.

---

which contain intimation of the Resurrection being posterior to the writing of the Pentateuch.

"Shewed," rather "indicated." "The choice of the word μηνύω, 'to give to understand,' shows that Jesus distinguishes perfectly between an express declaration which does not exist, and an indication such as that which He proceeds to cite." (Godet).

"At the bush," *i.e.*, in the section of Exodus which describes the appearance of the Burning Bush. It was God Himself who spake out of the bush the words, "I am the God of Abraham, and the God of Isaac, and the God of Jacob." No doubt the exact words which the Lord used are those in St. Matthew and St. Mark.

38. "When he calleth the Lord the God of Abraham, and the God of Isaac, and the God of Jacob. For he is not a God of the dead, but of the living," &c. On the views of the Sadducees who held no future state of existence, this place means that God is the God of three dead corpses—rather, inasmuch as those corpses had long been wholly decayed, the God of a little dust. I have shown, in my comment on St. Matthew, that God is not a proper name, but a title of the Supreme Being which implies an abiding relation to any one of whom He calls Himself the God ; and the root of the word "God" in the Semitic languages more particularly implies a being exercising power over, or on behalf of, those of whom He is the God—power to protect them, guide them, sustain them, reward them, and so on. So that it would be as incongruous for God to call Himself the God of Abraham, if Abraham had no distinct existence after death, as it would be for Him to call Himself the ruler or guide of Abraham, if Abraham existed nowhere in the unseen world.

"For all live unto him." The best comment on these words is that of St. Paul: "Whether we live, we live unto the Lord; or whether we die, we die unto the Lord : whether we live therefore, or die, we are the Lord's. For to this end Christ died and lived again, that He might be Lord of both the dead and the living." When the soul passes from the body it merely passes from one de-

39 ¶ Then certain of the scribes answering said, Master, thou hast well said.

40 And after that they durst not ask him any *question at all.*

41 And he said unto them, q How say they that Christ is David's son?

q Matt. xxii. 42. Mark xii. 35.

---

partment of God's realm to another, it is as much in His love and under His care as before death, and is probably employed by Him according to its capacities, and trained by Him for a still higher and more perfect state when it shall be raised up in the body.

The question, however, presents itself, Do these words of God imply the Resurrection of Abraham's body? They do, because the Scriptures do not teach men to look forward to a state in which they will be disembodied ghosts, such as is described in Homer, but to a state in which they will be what they are now, body and soul: the soul a purified and holy soul, the body a spiritual body corresponding to the purity of the soul. Man in his present state is not a bodiless being, and when God calls Himself the God of Abraham He means that He is the God of a holy soul awaiting its complete state in a natural and perfected body to which God in due time will reunite it.

39, 40. "Then certain of the scribes answering said . . . . durst not ask him any question at all." The Scribes, holding the Resurrection, were delighted with the answer by which He had silenced the Sadducees. They now perceived that it was dangerous to question Him because He could invariably turn their questions on themselves.

It was now, however, His turn to question them, and His question was exceedingly remarkable, as its aim was simply to bring out and assert His Divine Dignity and Power, if He was the Messiah, or Christ, which He claimed to be. It is thus very shortly stated by our Evangelist.

41, 44. "And he said unto them, How say they that Christ is David's son? . . . . how is he then his son?" The Lord constantly spoke and acted as claiming to be the Christ, Who should come into the world. On three remarkable occasions He allowed His followers to confess Him to be the Christ. Twice when He received from Peter the confession, "Thou art the Christ, the son of

42 And David himself saith in the book of Psalms, ʳ The LORD said unto my Lord, Sit thou on my right hand,

ʳ Ps. cx. 1.
Acts ii. 34.

43 Till I make thine enemies thy footstool.

44 David therefore calleth him Lord, how is he then his son ?

45 ¶ ˢ Then in the audience of all the people he said unto his disciples,

ˢ Matt. xxiii. 1.
Mark xii. 38.

---

the living God" (Matth. xvi. 16, John vi. 69). Again when He received from Martha the same confession (John xi. 27). He asserted it to the woman of Samaria (John iv. 26); to the messengers of John the Baptist (Matth. xi. 4-7). He made it a condition of salvation when He said, " If ye believe not that I am he, ye shall die in your sins" (John viii. 24). And now He puts to them a question respecting who this Christ was which admitted of but one answer—that He was such an One that He could be at once the Lord, and the Son of David : David, speaking of one of his descendants who should be born a thousand years after his own decease, calls Him "my Lord." How could He be the Lord of the greatest King of Israel? Only on the same principle that after the decease of Abraham, God could be his God. If when David wrote the one hundred and tenth Psalm, He could call One his Lord, that One must then have been in existence, and we know that He was in existence for He was the Word Who was with God, and was God, Who when He came upon earth said, "Before Abraham was I am," *i.e.*, above one thousand years before David lived " I am." Well, then, has Godet written : " The three Synoptics have preserved, with slight differences, this remarkable saying which, with Luke x. 21, 22, and some other passages, forms the bond of union between the teaching of Jesus in these Gospels, and all that is affirmed of His Person in that of St. John. If it is true that Jesus applied to Himself the title of David's Lord, with which this king addressed the Messiah in Ps. cx., the consciousness of Divinity is implied in this title as certainly as in any declaration whatever of the fourth Gospel."

45, 47. " Then in the audience of all the people . . . . the same shall receive greater damnation." These three verses represent the denunciation uttered by Him against the Scribes and Pharisees in Matth. xxiii. The substance of that withering exposure is given us

46 ᵗBeware of the scribes, which desire to walk in long robes, and ᵘlove greetings in the markets, and the highest seats in the synagogues, and the chief rooms at feasts;   ᵗ Matt. xxiii. 5.
ᵘ ch. xi. 43.

47 ˣWhich devour widows' houses, and for a shew make long prayers: the same shall receive greater damnation.   ˣ Matt. xxiii. 14.

---

by St. Luke xi. 37-53, and our Evangelist here contents himself with gathering up in very few words the character and doings of the Scribes and Pharisees of which He bids the disciples beware, such as their pride and vanity, " they desire to walk in long robes, and love greetings in the markets, and the highest seats in the synagogues, and the chief rooms at feasts; " then their greed and extortion—" They devour widows' houses," which probably means, they lay themselves out for getting hold of the property of unprotected persons, such as widows, and under the pretence of managing it for them, rob them; and their hypocrisy—" for a shew they make long prayers."

" The same shall receive greater damnation," or greater condemnation, which, of course, implies heavier punishment. It is one of those places which show that there are degrees in punishment as well as in reward, and the heaviest punishment will be awarded to those who under the pretence of greater religion rob the credulous and unsuspecting.

CHAP. XXI.

AND he looked up, ᵃand saw the rich men casting their gifts into the treasury.   ᵃ Mark xii. 41.

1-4. " And he looked up, and saw the rich men . . . all the living that she had." This beautiful incident of the widow and her two mites, and the Lord's commendation of her is one of the very few places common to St. Mark and St. Luke, only St. Mark, as we should have expected, gives it more circumstantially: St. Luke as

2 And he saw also a certain poor widow casting in thither two ‖ mites.

‖ See Mark xii. 42.

3 And he said, Of a truth I say unto you, ᵇ that this poor widow hath cast in more than they all:

ᵇ 2 Cor. viii. 12.

4 For all these have of their abundance cast in unto the offerings of God: but she of her penury hath cast in all the living that she had.

---

4. "Offerings of God." So A., D., G., Γ, Δ, Λ, Π, later Uncials, nearly all Cursives, old Latin, Vulg., Syriac (Sch.); but ℵ, B., L., X., 1, 118, 131, 209, Copt., and Cur. Syriac, omit " of God."

if he received it from the same source as St. Mark received his accounts, but in a slightly abridged form.

It may be instructive to draw attention to the differences.

St. Mark speaks of the Lord "sitting over against the treasury," *i.e.*, the row of trumpet-shaped vessels at the entrance between the court of the women and the inner court, so that it was accessible to the women; and that He watched the people offering their gifts, and the rich, many of them casting in much; and that the poor widow cast in two mites, which he explains to his Roman readers as making a farthing. St. Luke only mentions that the Lord saw the rich giving, and then the widow casting in her two mites.

St. Mark then mentions that the Lord called His disciples, and told them of the widow's gift; for she must have given it and gone her way before they could come up. St. Luke more shortly says that the Lord remarked it, as if speaking to the bystanders, and they both conclude with the same lesson, not however in exactly the same words.

The one great lesson from this account is that God estimates the value of what men give for His poor, or His Church, by one standard only—by the self-denial they exercise in parting with their money or their goods.

When it is said that this mite was all this woman's living, it must, of course, mean all her living for that day. She threw herself upon the providence of God to supply her with her evening meal or night's lodging.

From what she gave, which the Lord brought to light and commended, the expression " I give my mite " has passed into a

5 ¶ ᶜAnd as some spake of the temple, how it was adorned with goodly stones and gifts, he said,   ᶜ Matt. xxiv. 1. Mark xiii. 1.

6 *As for* these things which ye behold, the days will come, in the which ᵈ there shall not be ᵈ ch. xix. 44. left one stone upon another, that shall not be thrown down.

---

proverb, which in the mouths of many who use it is ridiculous, if not profane. What ought to be the mite of one in a good business which yields him several hundreds a year clear profit? What ought to be the mite of a professional man in good practice, after all reasonable family claims are provided for? A man with an income of at least two or three hundred a year once said to me, when I called upon him for assistance in keeping up a national school, "I will think about it, sir, and I will give you my mite." He did think, and his mite was two shillings. Contrast this with the following. Two aged paupers, having only the usual parish pay, became communicants. They determined that they would not neglect the offertory; but how was this to be done, as they were on starvation allowance? Well, during the week before the celebration they did without light, sat up for two or three hours in the dark, and then went to bed, and gave the few pence which they saved in oil or rushlights to be laid on the altar of God.

5-7. "And as some spake of the temple, how it was adorned ... thrown down." We now enter for the third time on the exposition of the prophecy of the Lord respecting the destruction of the city and temple, and His Own Second Coming. It will be well particularly to notice the differences between the Lord's words, as reported in St. Luke and in the two first Synoptics. We shall see that some of the things peculiar to St. Luke clear up some of the principal difficulties in the other two reports. The discourse, as given in our Evangelist, is as full, or nearly as full as those in the other Synoptics, up to the point of the taking of Jerusalem; after that it hurries on to the consummation, and concludes with the parable of the fig-tree, and two or three verses only of warning to those who shall be alive when the Lord actually appears.

"As some spake of the temple, how it was adorned with goodly stones and gifts." St. Mark tells us that it was one of His disciples which drew attention to the stones, evidently to their vast size; and that such was the character of the remark, appears from this, that

7 And they asked him, saying, Master, but when shall these things be? and what sign *will there be* when these things shall come to pass?

8 And he said, ᵉTake heed that ye be not deceived: for many shall come in my name, saying, I am *Christ;* ∥ and the time draweth near: go ye not therefore after them.

ᵉ Matt. xxiv. 4. Mark xiii. 5. Eph. v. 6. 2 Thess. ii. 3.
∥ Or, *and, The time,* Matt. iii. 2. & iv. 17.

---

8. "Go ye not therefore." So A., Γ, Δ, Λ, Π, later Uncials, almost all Cursives, f, q, Vulg.; but ℵ, B., D., L., X., 157, 346, old Latin (a, c, e, ff², i, l, s), Copt., Cur. Syriac, Arm., and Æth. omit "therefore."

according to St. Luke the Lord does not allude to the goodliness of the stones and gifts, but to the displacement of the stones. This looks rather to their size than their preciousness, and is almost verbatim the same in all three Evangelists.

7. "And they asked him, saying, Master, but when . . . . come to pass?" St. Luke omits all mention of this question being asked as the Lord sat on the Mount of Olives, and by Peter, James, John, and Andrew. He also omits the very important part of it given by St. Matthew, "What shall be the sign of thy coming, and of the end of the world?" The question, as reported by both Luke and Mark has principally, if not wholly, to do with the destruction of the temple.

In the answer of the Lord there are four divisions.

First, the apparent signs which may be deceptive as to the nearness of the catastrophe. (8-20.)

Second, the real and unmistakable sign that the catastrophe is close at hand, which will assure the believing Jews that if they desire to escape not a moment is to be lost. (20-22.)

Third, the catastrophe itself and the clear declaration that its effects shall be prolonged, which prolongation covers the period of "the times of the Gentiles." (24.)

Fourth, the signs of the Second Coming to Judgment, and the appearance of the Son of Man. (25-28.)

After this comes the parable of the fig-tree, which, from the way in which it is introduced by St. Luke, seems to be uttered after a pause, or some break in the discourse.

8. "And he said, Take heed that ye be not deceived: for many shall come in my name," &c. We do not read of any false Christs

9 But when ye shall hear of wars and commotions, be not terrified: for these things must first come to pass; but the end *is* not by and by.

10 ᶠThen said he unto them, Nation shall rise ᶠ Matt. xxiv. 7. against nation, and kingdom against kingdom:

---

9. "By and by." Rather, "immediately." Revisers.

who claimed to set the Lord aside and substitute themselves in His place, and yet such a man as Simon Magus could deceive those who were on the very threshold of Christianity, so that they accepted him as "the great power of God" (Acts viii. 10). And we know that at a very early period indeed, *i.e.*, before the writing of the second of the Epistles (2 Thess.) St. Paul found it needful to warn his converts that " they be not shaken in mind, or be troubled, neither by spirit, nor by word, nor by letter as from us [as if men forged letters in his name] as that the day of Christ is at hand. And that no man should deceive them by any means, as that the day was absolutely close at the doors " (2 Thess. ii. 2, 3).

"Go ye not after them." It seems impossible to suppose that the Apostles themselves needed such warnings; they must rather have been intended for the early converts as represented by, or contained in, the Apostles.

9. "But when ye shall hear of wars and commotions." The whole extent of the Roman Empire was agitated, and in the brief space of eighteen months four Emperors—Nero, Galba, Otho, and Vitellius—died by violence. With respect to the regions nearer to Judæa, Josephus in his "Antiquities," (book xx., ch. iii. sec. 4, and chap. iv. sec. 2) relates wars between the Parthian king, Artabanus, and Izates, of Adiabene, and, probably, if one had the history of those regions more in full, we should learn of many more.

10. " Then said He unto them." How is it that these words are, as it were, interjected, as there is nothing answering to them in the two first Synoptics ? Godet throws out the hint that this passage (verses 10-19) might have been inscribed here by Luke as a fragment borrowed from a separate document differing from the source whence he took the rest of the discourse. They should be accounted for, and yet most expositors take no notice of them.

10. "Nation shall rise against nation, and kingdom against kingdom." I have noticed that these international conflicts seem

11. And great earthquakes shall be in divers places, and famines, and pestilences; and fearful sights and great signs shall there be from heaven.

---

to look rather to these latter times, when Europe and the adjacent parts of Asia and Africa are divided into so many independent sovereignties, than to a time when there was but one great empire, which, as it were, kept the peace amongst the smaller nationalities. Nevertheless there seems to have been at this time fearful conflicts between the Jews and those nations amongst which they were dispersed. "In Cesarea twenty thousand Jews were slain in an old contention with the Syrians, fifty thousand in Alexandria, and two fierce factions raging in every city." (See Josephus, "Wars of the Jews," bk. ii., ch. xviii., sec. 1.) "Every city was divided into two armies, encamped one against another, and the preservation of the one party was in the destruction of the other; so that the day time was spent in shedding of blood, and the night in fear;" and (bk. iv. ch. iii., sec. 2), "There were besides disorders and civil wars in every city, and all those that were at quiet from the Romans turned their hands one against another."

11. "And great earthquakes shall be in divers places." An earthquake destroyed Laodicea, Hierapolis, &c., in 67 or 68 A.D.

"Famines." There was the famine prophesied of by Agabus in Acts xi. 28, which came to pass in the days of Claudius Cæsar. Josephus also mentions a famine in Jerusalem, in which the people were relieved by the bounty of Helena, the mother of Izates of Adiabene (Ant. xx., ch. ii., sec. 5).

Pestilences, the usual consequences of famines, "and fearful sights and great signs shall there be from heaven."

By the signs from heaven, Godet says, we are to understand meteors, auroras, eclipses, &c., phenomena to which the vulgar readily attach a prophetic significance. Josephus gives a remarkable illustration. Speaking of the band of Idumæans, who had been excluded from the city, he writes: "They lay all night before the wall, though in a very bad encampment: for there broke out a prodigious storm in the night, with the utmost violence, with very strong winds, with the largest showers of rain, with continued lightnings, terrible thundering, and amazing concussions and bellowings of the earth, which was in an earthquake." And he adds:

12 ᵍ But before all these, they shall lay their hands on you, and persecute *you*, delivering *you* up to the synagogues, and ʰ into prisons, ⁱ being brought before kings and rulers ᵏ for my name's sake.

13 And ˡ it shall turn to you for a testimony.

14 ᵐ Settle *it* therefore in your hearts, not to meditate before what ye shall answer:

g Mark xiii. 9. Rev. ii. 10.
h Acts iv. 3. & v. 18. & xii. 4. & xvi. 24.
i Acts xxv. 23.
k 1 Pet. ii. 13.
l Phil. i. 28. 2 Thess. i. 5.
m Matt. x. 19. Mark xiii. 11. ch. xii. 11.

"These things were a manifest indication that some destruction was coming upon men, when the system of the world was put into this disorder; and anyone would guess that these wonders foreshowed some great calamities which were coming." The Lord here, it will be noticed, strives to correct such very inferences as Josephus drew from the war of the elements.

12. "But before all these, they shall lay their hands on you, and persecute you." Almost immediately after Pentecost persecutions commenced; the Apostles were brought before the rulers as early as the time of Acts iv. Paul was brought before a king (Agrippa), and, perhaps, before Nero. Persecutions are narrated as having occurred at Jerusalem (Acts viii. 1, xii. 4), at Antioch (xiii. 50), at Lystra (xiv. 19), at Ephesus (Acts xix.), and in every city where the Gospel was preached (Acts xx. 23).

13. "And it shall turn to you for a testimony." The words parallel to this in St. Mark are "for a testimony against them "— that is, against those kings and rulers who would condemn them. Their behaviour when on their trial, and the words which Christ put into their mouths, would not be without effect. It would be a testimony to their truthfulness, and to the falsehood of their accusers and unjust judges.

14. "Settle it therefore in your hearts, not to meditate before," &c. The parallel words in St. Mark are, "Whatsoever shall be given you in that hour, that speak ye: for it is not ye that speak, but the Holy Ghost."

The reader will remember how that, when St. Paul spake of righteousness, temperance, and judgment to come, Felix, the unjust governor, trembled. This promise, however, of course, is limited to cases of emergency, as when they are brought before magistrates, and have orators and advocates such as Tertullus hired against

YE SHALL BE BETRAYED.

15 For I will give you a mouth and wisdom, ⁿ which all your adversaries shall not be able to gainsay nor resist.

16 ° And ye shall be betrayed both by parents, and brethren, and kinsfolks, and friends; and ^p *some* of you shall they cause to be put to death.

17 And ^q ye shall be hated of all *men* for my name's sake.

a Acts vi. 10.
o Mic. vii. 6.
Mark xiii. 12.
p Acts vii. 59.
& xii. 2.
q Matt. x. 22.

---

16. "Both by parents." Rather, "even by parents." Rev.

them. It is not for a moment to be taken as implying that they may safely neglect such things as preparation for public teaching or preaching. For the application to those who are called upon on a sudden to answer the arguments of infidels, I must refer to my notes on St. Mark xiii. 11.

With respect to the words, "a mouth and wisdom," Theophylact remarks: "Many men have often wisdom in their mind, but being easily provoked to their great disturbance, mar the whole when their time of speaking comes."

This was fulfilled particularly in the case of St. Stephen: "They were not able to resist the wisdom and the spirit by which he spake" (Acts vi. 10).

16. "Ye shall be betrayed both by parents, and brethren, and kinsfolks, and friends," &c. I gave some instances of this in my notes on St. Mark. Williams well writes: "When deep principles are actively set afloat, especially if on great matters, an agreement on those principles is the strongest bond of union among those who hold them in earnest as true and important; the same therefore is the strongest cause of division among such as differ on these points.... For this reason nothing is so exciting as the stirring of religious principles; the whole mass of society is moved and shaken in the centre when these are stirred; besides which there is an intrinsic hatred of goodness in the human heart which ever heightens religious discord"—*i.e.*, the discord between those who hold a religion essentially impure and false as heathenism, and those who hold a purifying and elevating faith.

If any of my readers desire to see the intense antagonism which the introduction of Christian principles must have occasioned in a

18 ʳ But there shall not an hair of your head perish.
19 In your patience possess ye your souls.   ʳ Matt. x. 30.

heathen family, let them read some remarks of Tertullian in his "Second Book to his Wife," secs. 3, 4, 5.

18. "But there shall not a hair of your head perish." How is this to be reconciled with the previous words: "Some of you shall they cause to be put to death"? It has been supposed that the words are to be taken spiritually. Thus one expositor writes: "They form a proverbial saying. They teach us that whatever sufferings a disciple of Christ may go through, his best things can never be injured." But surely the Lord would never express a man's "best spiritual things" or interests by such a term as the "hairs of his head." And, besides, all the rest of these predictions are to be taken literally, why should this one among them be taken spiritually? Godet's view seems still more unsatisfactory: "There shall, indeed, be some individual believers who shall perish in the persecution; but the Christian community of Palestine, as a whole, shall escape the extermination which will overtake the Jewish people." It seems that there can be but one reconciliation, which is to me, at least, most obvious. Some, as the Lord expressly says, will endure martyrdom for His sake; but they will, as the saying is, be immortal till their work is done. Not a hair of their head shall perish, except by the Divine permission. We cannot but refer back to the Lord's own saying to these same men, "The hairs of your head are all numbered." This does not imply that death cannot overtake them, but that every event which can occur to them is absolutely ordered by God, so that they suffer nothing, except by the express permission of God.

19. "In your patience possess ye your souls." The parallel expression to this in St. Matthew and St. Mark is, "He that shall endure to the end, the same shall be saved." The word "possess" should rather be translated "win" or "acquire," so the Revised Version, "In your patience ye shall win your souls." "Their condition is to be one of patience, that is to say, peaceful waiting for the Divine Signal, without being drawn aside either by the appeals of a false patriotism, or by persecution, or false signs, and Anti-Christian seductions." The words seem to teach the same as the words of the Lord by the prophet Isaiah, "In quietness and confidence shall be your strength."

20 [a] And when ye shall see Jerusalem compassed with armies, then know that the desolation thereof is nigh.

[a] Matt. xxiv. 15. Mark xiii. 14.

---

20. "And when ye shall see Jerusalem compassed with armies, then know," &c. Hitherto the Lord had been warning them against being disturbed and "shaken in mind," by things which are always occurring—wars, commotions, insurrections, earthquakes, signs in heaven, &c.; these things may take place at all times in the history of the world, and people magnify their intensity by their nearness to themselves, or by their supposed political or religious influence.[1] Now the Lord gives the true and unmistakable sign, Jerusalem compassed about with armies. In my notes on the Gospel of St. Mark (xiii. 14), I directed the reader's attention to the fact that St. Luke makes no mention of that sign which the Lord evidently would have them regard as the sure and unmistakable one, the "abomination of desolation" spoken of by Daniel the prophet as "standing in the Holy Place" (Matthew), "standing where it ought not" (Mark). It is also to be noticed that the compassing of the city by the Roman armies is immediately followed, in St. Luke, by the same express direction verbatim, "Let them which are in Judæa flee to the mountains," as is the sight of "the abomination of desolation" in the Holy Place, in St. Matthew's and St. Mark's report. There can be little doubt, therefore, but that the "abomination of desolation" is either the presence of the Roman armies, whose very standards were the objects of idolatrous worship, round the city on ground which, being the suburbs of the Holy City, was itself considered holy, or that it refers to something in the siege, or rather immediately before it, which has not come down to us.

---

[1] A clever and intellectual man, sober-minded in everything but the interpretation of prophecy, gravely assured me that he considered the invasion of France by the Prussians in 1870 to be the fulfilment of the prediction of the "great hail" of Rev. xvi. 21. Perhaps the reader will remember the excitement caused by the republication of Fleming's book about the time that Louis Philippe was dethroned, and within a year succeeded by Louis Napoleon. The Crimea at the time of the Crimean War, and Constantinople at the time of the Russian invasion of Turkey, were both oracularly pronounced by two excellent clergymen of our Church to be the scenes of the battle of Armageddon. Such interpretations, in which oneself, and one's own country, and one's own religious views are the centre, are not merely ridiculous, but extremely mischievous. They tend to disparage the study of prophecy, and probably will be one of the means by which many Christians will not be able to read the true signs of the time of the Advent.

CHAP. XXI.] FLEE TO THE MOUNTAINS. 533

21 Then let them which are in Judæa flee to the moun-

I speak with some hesitation where I differ from such able expositors as Wordsworth and Alford, but I doubt much whether the "abomination of desolation" means the possession of the Temple by the Sicarii, or Assassins ; such would not be a sign to those in Judæa, for the possession of the temple by the Sicarii took place some time before the siege, whereas the sign in question, whatever it was, was to be the signal of flight so hasty that they were not even to go back to the house to take anything out of their house. Besides, as I have shown, the Hebrew word which is translated "abomination" always alludes to an idol, or idolatrous worship, whereas the Assassins, though guilty of every species of violence and bloodshed, could not be accused of this.

It is needful, however, to consider how the beleaguering of the city by the Roman armies could be a sign to the Christians to "depart out," seeing that the besieging army hemmed them in so that there was no escape ? It is to be remembered that the city of Jerusalem was twice threatened—once, some time before the arrival of Titus, by Cestius Gallus, who having drawn up his army before the city, when by a single stroke he might have taken it, and prevented the subsequent carnage and desolation, suddenly, and for no apparent reason, withdrew his army, so that all who had fears respecting the issue of the impending struggle fled to Pella. This retreat is thus described : " The people, upon this, took courage, and when the wicked part of the city gave ground, thither did they come in order to set open the gates, and to admit Cestius as their benefactor, who, had he but continued the siege a little longer, had certainly taken the city ; but it was, I suppose, owing to the aversion God had already at the city, and the sanctuary, that he was hindered from putting an end to the war that very day. It thus happened that Cestius was not conscious either how the besieged despaired of success, nor how courageous the people [*i.e.* the better minded Jews] were for him ; and so he recalled his soldiers from the place, and by despairing of any expectation of taking it, without having received any disgrace, he retired from the city, without any reason in the world." (" Wars of the Jews," II. ch. xix. 6, 7.)

It may have been at this time that that which is related by Eusebius took place, that "the whole body of the Church of Jerusalem having been commanded by a Divine Revelation given to

tains: and let them which are in the midst of it depart out; and let not them that are in the countries enter thereinto.

22 For these be the days of vengeance, that ᵗall things which are written may be fulfilled.

ᵗ Dan. ix. 26, 27. Zech. xi. 1.
ᵘ Matt. xxiv. 19.

23 ᵘ But woe unto them that are with child, and to them that give suck, in those days! for

---

23. "But woe unto them." "Woe" omitted by B., D., L., and old Latin (a, c, e, ff², i, 1, q); but retained by ℵ, A., C., all later Uncials, all Cursives, f, Vulg., Copt., Syriac, &c.

---

men of approved piety there before the war, removed from the city, and dwelt at a certain town beyond the Jordan, called Pella."

21. "Then let them which are in Judæa flee to the mountains," *i.e.*, to the very rugged and mountainous country beyond Jordan, perhaps the ancient Gilead.

"Let not them that are in the countries [*i.e.*, the country districts] enter thereinto."

22. "For these be the days of vengeance, that all things which are written may be fulfilled." All things that are written in Deut. xxviii. 49-58, especially the most terrible and horrible of all, " The tender and delicate woman among you which would not adventure to set the sole of her foot upon the ground for delicateness and tenderness, her eye shall be evil towards the husband of her bosom, and toward her son, and toward her daughter . . . and towards her children which she shall bear: for she shall eat them for want of all things in the siege and straitness wherewith thine enemies shall distress thee in thy gates." An instance of this—one amongst many—is given by Josephus. ("Wars of the Jews," VI. ch. iii. 4.) It is too horrible and sickening to give here.

Let the reader also remember the words of the Lord, "Upon you shall come all the righteous blood shed upon the earth . . . verily I say unto you, all these things shall come upon this generation" (Matth. xxiii. 35, 36).

23. " Woe unto them that are with child, and to them that give suck . . . wrath upon this people." That is, God's blessing of fruitfulness is turned into a curse. There was no safety for any inhabitant of the doomed land but in immediate flight, but how could

CHAP. XXI.] THE TIMES OF THE GENTILES. 535

there shall be great distress in the land, and wrath upon this people.

24 And they shall fall by the edge of the sword, and shall be led away captive into all nations: and Jerusalem shall be trodden down of the Gentiles, ˣ until the times of the Gentiles be fulfilled.

ˣ Dan. ix. 27. & xii. 7. Rom. xi. 25.

---

such flee so quickly as to save themselves? The reader will remember the Lord's words in the Gospel, "Daughters of Jerusalem, weep not for me, but weep for yourselves and for your children," &c.

24. "And they shall fall by the edge of the sword, and shall be led away captive into all nations." Eleven hundred thousand perished by famine or the sword; above ninety thousand were sold as slaves. Great numbers were sent among the provinces to be the prey of wild beasts in the amphitheatres.

"And Jerusalem shall be trodden down of the Gentiles until the times of the Gentiles be fulfilled." The latter part of this 24th verse is peculiar to St. Luke, and goes very far in clearing up the principal difficulty of the discourse as contained in the three first Gospels. For in the reports of the discourse in St. Matthew and St. Mark there is mention of a tribulation which from its position in the prophecy must be the destruction of Jerusalem (Matth. xxiv. 15-26; Mark xiii. 14-23). This is called in St. Matthew, "The tribulation of those days," and immediately after the tribulation shall the sun be darkened, and the other signs of the immediate return of the Lord to judgment shall be manifest. We should gather, then, from the first two Synoptics, that the tribulation was the siege and fall of the devoted city, and the subsequent horrors, and that the Second Coming of the Lord would be immediately after; but by St. Luke's version it is clear that the tribulation may be an indefinite period, probably long—it may be very long, for "Jerusalem shall be trodden down of the Gentiles until the times of the Gentiles be fulfilled." Jerusalem is now trodden down, and has been since the time of its final overthrow. The Christian Jerusalem of the Fathers—the Jerusalem of the succeeding ages—the Jerusalem of the present time is not Jerusalem. As regards its inhabitants at all these periods they were none of them, or at least a mere fragment of them, Jews. The Jerusalem of old continues trodden

25 ¶ ʸ And there shall be signs in the sun, and in the moon, and in the stars; and upon the

ʸ Matt. xxiv. 29. Mark xiii. 24. 2 Pet. iii. 10, 12.

down; indeed, is non-existent; the present city in no respect represents it. City after city has grown up on the ruins of its foundations, but none of them have taken its place.

And all this will be "till the times of the Gentiles be fulfilled." The present desolation, moral and religious, of the ancient people of God is set forth in the words of the prophet. "The children of Israel shall abide many days without a king," *i.e.*, of the line of David; "and without a prince," *i.e.*, a leader or judge to unite them; "and without a sacrifice," that is, without the God-ordained Levitical Ritual; "and without an image," *i.e.*, without the worship of any false god or idol; "and without an ephod," *i.e.*, without oracular guidance from the true God (1 Sam. xxiii. 9, 10): "and without teraphim," *i.e.*, idolatrous and unlawful means of divination. "Afterwards," *i.e.*, after the time of the Gentiles, "shall the children of Israel return, and seek the Lord their God, and David their king, and shall fear the Lord and his goodness in the latter days" (Hosea iii. 4, 5). The above is the substance of Dr. Pusey's note on this prophecy in his "Minor Prophets." It concludes with the words, "There will be a more full fulfilment, of which St. Paul speaks, when the eyes of all Israel shall be opened to the deceivableness of the last Antichrist, and Enoch and Elias, the two witnesses, shall have come to prepare our Lord's Second Coming, and shall have been slain (Rev. xi. 3), and by God's converting grace all Israel shall be saved."

"The Jews are dispersed into all nations, to proclaim and show to all the world what a people or a soul is without Christ, what it is to have let slip the time and opportunity of repentance, and what it is to have heard, without bringing forth any fruit, the Saviour and His Gospel. That which has happened to this people, happens to everyone who is finally impenitent; but after a manner which is much more dreadful." (Quesnel.)

25. "And there shall be signs in the sun, and in the moon .... upon the earth distress of nations .... the sea and the waves roaring." That these signs in the sun and in the moon, &c., will not be the waning of spiritual or religious light, or the dethronement of great sovereigns, or desolating revolutions, is evident from this, that such things will occur in addition to the heavenly signs, for,

earth distress of nations, with perplexity; the sea and the waves roaring;

25. "With perplexity, the sea and the waves roaring." So D., Γ., Δ, Λ, Π, most later Uncials, most Cursives, old Latin, Vulg.; but א, A., B., C., L., M., R., X., a few Cursives, Copt., Syriac, Arm., read, "with perplexity at the roaring of the sea," &c.

according to St. Luke the Lord adds the words, "upon the earth distress of nations, with perplexity." With respect to the signs in the sun, we know so very little of what is the cause of its light that to assert that there can be no changes in the photosphere, as it is called, which may seriously affect our share of that light is the extreme of infidel dogmatism.

On two great occasions in the religious history of the chosen people, God made the phenomena of the natural world to witness to the awful nature of what was taking place in the moral world: when He revealed His law on Mount Sinai, and when He revealed the reconciliation of justice and mercy on Calvary: and the second coming of the Incarnate Word will be the greatest open manifestation of God, both in His Person and in His moral attributes, which the universe has ever seen. The shaking of the whole frame of nature and the suspension of its highest laws are very small matters compared to the Revelation of the Unseen and Eternal God which will then take place.

To one who believes that the Divine, the moral, and the spiritual is infinitely greater than the natural, Godet's remark on the process by which God may bring about this seems reasonable and according to common sense when he writes: "In the midst of this carnal security, alarming symptoms will all at once proclaim one of those universal revolutions through which our earth has more than once passed. Like a ship, creaking in every timber at the moment of its going to pieces, the globe which we inhabit (ἡ οἰκουμένη) and our whole solar system shall undergo unusual commotions. The moving forces (δυνάμεις), regular in their action till then, shall be, as it were, set free from their laws by an unknown power; and at the end of this violent but short distress, the world shall see Him appear Whose coming shall be like the lightning which shines from one end of heaven to the other."

"The sea and the waves roaring." Some MSS. connect this with the preceding word "perplexity." Perplexity (of nations) at the roaring of the sea and the waves. But inasmuch as but a small part

26 Men's hearts failing them for fear, and for looking after those things which are coming on the earth: *for the powers of heaven shall be shaken.

27 And then shall they see the Son of man ᵃ coming in a cloud with power and great glory.

*Matt. xxiv. 29.

ᵃ Matt. xxiv. 30. Rev. i. 7. & xiv. 14.

---

of the inhabitants of the earth dwell on the sea coast, this seems unlikely. If we take the sea and the waves to be the political agitation of the people, then we have a figurative expression used amongst literal ones, apparently for no purpose; still many take it to mean universal fear at the frequency of revolts and tumults. We are to remember, however, that any disarrangement of the influences of the heavenly bodies would be felt throughout all nature, especially the sea and the air.

26. "Men's hearts failing them for fear, and for looking after those things," &c. Is it not, however, said that the wicked will be in a state of carnal security? Yes, but the two statements are perfectly reconcilable: for in the first place their security will be suddenly and rudely broken up, and they will be filled with forebodings which will make their hearts fail for fear: and yet they will not know which way to turn. As the fears and distresses of the Jews in the siege of Jerusalem did not make them turn to their true Refuge, so men will then be unable to turn to Him Who is so close at hand; for, when the sight of Him bursts upon them, they will call upon the mountains and rocks to cover them and hide them from His Wrath.

27. "And then shall they see the Son of man coming in a cloud with power and great glory." The Son of Man coming openly, visibly, gloriously—not spiritually, as when He comes to each soul at its conversion to Himself—not providentially, as He came in vengeance at the destruction of Jerusalem: but as the lightning which lighteth from the east and shineth even to the west, so that every eye shall see Him, so that they who have pierced Him shall look on Him Whom they have pierced, and they who look for Him shall say, "Lo, this is our God! we have waited for Him and He will save us."

"In a cloud"; thus the Lord claims to be that Son of Man, Whom the Prophet Daniel saw in vision: "One like unto the Son of man came with the clouds of heaven" (vii. 13).

Chap. XXI.] LIFT UP YOUR HEADS. 539

28 And when these things begin to come to pass, then look up, and lift up your heads; for ᵇyour redemption draweth nigh. ᵇ Rom. viii. 19, 23.

29 ᶜ And he spake to them a parable; Behold the fig tree, and all the trees; ᶜ Matt. xxiv. 32. Mark xiii. 28.

30 When they now shoot forth, ye see and know of your own selves that summer is now nigh at hand.

31 So likewise ye, when ye see these things come to pass, know ye that the kingdom of God is nigh at hand.

"With power and great glory." As He Himself expresses it, "in His own glory, and in His Father's, and of the Holy Angels." (Luke ix. 26.)

"In power and majesty will men see Him Whom in lowly stations they refused to hear, that so much the more acutely they may feel His power as they are now the less willing to bow the necks of their hearts to His sufferings." (Gregory.)

28. "And when these things begin to come to pass, then look up . . . . your redemption draweth nigh." What does the Lord mean by "these things?" Does He mean that which occupies the principal part of His discourse, *i.e.*, the signs of the impending vengeance on the Jewish nation, or does He mean that which He had last warned them about, that is, His Second Coming? He may mean either, but indeed He probably means both. In the first case, when they heard of the armies of the Romans entering the bounds of the Holy Land, then their redemption, in the sense of their deliverance from the fast approaching calamities, was at hand : and in the second case, when men see the unusual signs in the heavens, and the widespread distress and perplexity, and the elemental war, and the shaking of the powers of heaven, then their last and final redemption, " to wit, the redemption of their bodies " from corruption and sin, draws nigh. Here redemption is put for the final, the crowning effect of the redeeming Death. As the Apostle writes, "not only they, but ourselves also, who have the first-fruits of the Spirit, even we ourselves groan within ourselves, waiting for the adoption, *to wit*, the redemption of our body" (Rom. viii. 23).

29-31. "And he spake to them a parable; Behold the fig tree, and all the trees . . . . the kingdom of God is nigh at hand." To the mass of mankind who cannot read or compute time, the near

32 Verily I say unto you, This generation shall not pass away, till all be fulfilled.

---

approach of summer is known, not by the almanack, but by the shooting forth of the fig tree (as being the most conspicuous), and all the trees; and so to believing souls the swift coming of the kingdom of God is known by the signs of the times. God will make the near approach of His Son, in providence to judge Jerusalem, or in person to judge the world, as certain to those who have eyes to see, and ears to hear, as He makes the approach of the summer certain to the labouring man by the bursting forth of all nature into life.

32. "Verily I say unto you, This generation shall not pass away, till all be fulfilled." The key to this place is, as I have shown in my notes on Matth. xxiv. 32-34, the words which were really the occasion of the whole discourse, which are to be found at the conclusion of the denunciation of the Scribes and Pharisees in Matthew, chap. xxiii., "Verily, I say unto you, all these things," that is, the blood of all the prophets from Abel to Zacharias, shall come upon this generation." This is followed by "Your house is left unto you desolate, and ye shall not see me till ye shall say, Blessed is he that cometh in the name of the Lord." These remarks of the Lord suggested the question of the Apostles, "When shall these things be?" and upon this follows the whole discourse. Now the discourse which the Lord utters is occupied with two things: the first, the signs of the impending vengeance, which was of special interest to that generation; the second, the signs of the approaching advent, which was of the utmost concern to a more remote one, which would be in existence after the "times of the Gentiles were fulfilled." The Lord, then, in the words, "This generation shall not pass away," &c., must refer to the first of these, which mainly occupies the first part of the discourse, and which, be it remembered, is an exposition of the all-important words—all-important, that is, to the men then living, "All these things shall come upon this generation." To make any difficulty about this in deference to an absurd literalism, and to understand the Lord to mean by "generation," the whole future existence of the Jewish people or of the Christian Church, is to insist that the words of the Lord "Jerusalem shall be trodden under foot of the Gentiles, till the times of the Gentiles be fulfilled,"

MY WORDS SHALL NOT PASS AWAY.

33 ^d Heaven and earth shall pass away: but my words shall not pass away.

^d Matt. xxiv. 35.

34 ¶ And ^e take heed to yourselves, lest at any time your hearts be overcharged with surfeiting,

^e Rom. xiii. 13.
1 Thess. v. 6.
1 Pet. iv. 7.

---

signify perhaps half-a-dozen years, whilst on the very face of it they signify a considerable period of time.

33. "Heaven and earth shall pass away: but my words shall not pass away." God in the Scriptures constantly foretells the passing away of the present earth and heaven to give place to a world far more worthy of being the habitation of the children of the Resurrection. Thus Isaiah lxv. 17, "Behold, I create new heaven and a new earth: and the former shall not be remembered, nor come into mind." And, again, 2 Peter iii. 13, "We, according to his promise, look for new heavens and a new earth, wherein dwelleth righteousness." So that the present outward frame of nature, stable as it seems, has no real promise of continuance, whereas whatsoever is in the mind of God, and is made known to us by His Son, cannot fail of being fulfilled in its time. We have reasons for believing in the immutability of Christ's words which the first disciples had not. Nothing could, humanly speaking, be more unlikely, than that such a temple as that before them would be levelled with the ground, its huge stones of glittering marble broken to atoms, and its very site ploughed over, and rendered indistinguishable, and yet within forty short years all this took place just as the Lord foretold; and when this happened, a vengeance was executed on the former people of God, which could only be likened to the blood of all former martyrs and prophets of God being required of that particular generation. And since then "their house has been left desolate"; all the powers of earth could not reverse the Lord's words; a heathen emperor tried to build up its ruins, and ignominiously failed. All mediæval Christendom united to effect a sort of Christian restoration, but to no purpose. We may settle it in our minds, then, that if the words of Christ respecting the destruction of such a temple, and the scattering of such a nation pass not away, no words of His will pass away—all will be fulfilled in their season.

34, 35. "And take heed to yourselves, lest at any time your hearts be overcharged . . . . the whole earth." It is sad to reflect that the disciples of Christ need to be warned not only against spiri-

and drunkenness, and cares of this life, and *so* that day
come upon you unawares.

<small>f 1 Thess. v. 2.
2 Pet. iii. 10.
Rev. iii. 3. &
xvi. 15.</small> 35 For ^f as a snare shall it come on all them that dwell on the face of the whole earth.

<small>34, 35. "That day come upon you unawares. For as a snare." So A., C., later Uncials, almost all Cursives; but ℵ, B., D., L., old Latin (a, b, c, e, ff, i), Copt., read, "Come upon you unawares as a snare : for it shall come," &c.</small>

tual sins, but against fleshly ones ; not only against cares of this life, which may be innocent, but against surfeiting and drunkenness. But must not all poor Christians be exposed to cares respecting their living, and must not this interfere with their watching and taking heed ? Yes, unless they obey the Apostolic precept, "Casting all your care upon him, for He careth for you."

"So that day come upon you unawares. For as a snare shall it come," &c. Here we have our Evangelist giving us words of the Lord which answer to those recorded by his brother Evangelists respecting the duty of watching and waiting for the coming of the Son of Man; not watching to be draughted out of this world by death, but watching for the Lord Himself coming again to this world to reward His faithful ones, and take vengeance on His enemies.

"To them that look for Him shall He appear the second time without sin unto salvation." We are not only to believe, but to watch; not only to love, but to watch; not only to obey, but to watch. Besides all other Christian dispositions there is to be this of watching, for it alone recognizes the very distinct enunciations of the Lord respecting the secrecy and suddenness of his Second Coming. The crown which the Lord will give at the last will not be to Apostles only, but "to all them that love his appearing." See particularly my notes on St. Matthew xxiv. pp. 364-366, and on St. Mark xiii. pp. 324-326. And what is this watching ? It is not going out and gazing up into heaven. It is not imagining that every national distress or natural catastrophe is the immediate forerunner of the end. It is not dogmatically asserting that such an occurrence is the fulfilment of such an Apocalyptic vision; but it is the living in the constant belief that the present state of things may, at any moment, disappear and give way to another, and this by the coming of the Lord Himself. It is best described by the Apostle in the words,

CHAP. XXI.]   WATCH YE THEREFORE.   543

36 ⁵ Watch ye therefore, and ʰ pray always, that ye may be accounted worthy to escape all these things that shall come to pass, and ⁱ to stand before the Son of man.

⁵ Matt. xxiv. 42. & xxv. 13.
Mark xiii. 33.
ʰ ch. xviii. 1.
ⁱ Ps. i. 5.
Eph. vi. 13.

---

36. "Ye may be accounted worthy." So A., C., D., R., Γ, Δ, Λ, Π, all later Uncials, most Cursives, old Latin, Vulg., Syriacs, Arm.; but ℵ. B., L., X., 1, 33, 36, 57, 131, 157, 209, Copt., read, "that ye may have strength."

"This I say, brethren, the time is short; it remaineth, that both they that have wives be as though they had none; and they that weep, as though they wept not; and they that rejoice, as though they rejoiced not; and they that buy, as though they possessed not; and they that use this world as not abusing it: for the fashion of this world passeth away" (1 Cor. vii. 29, 30).

36. "Watch ye therefore, and pray always . . . . stand before the Son of man." This is a very fearful verse. I know none that brings out with such alarming power and distinctness the difficulty of final acceptance, and the danger of coming short. "Watch ye, therefore (be wakeful) at all seasons, praying that ye may be accounted worthy to escape all those things that shall come to pass, and to stand before the Son of man. For what end such unremitting watchfulness and such constant prayer? Is it that we may have the highest posts of honour, and sit on His right hand and on His left in His kingdom? No! but that we may be safe. He Who died for us, Love Infinite! bids us watch, praying at all seasons, that so we may . . . . stand before the Son of Man." (Pusey.) The Holy Spirit, by the mouth of the Apostle Paul, gives us a similar earnest, piercing call. "Take unto you the whole armour of God, that ye may be able to withstand in the evil day, and having done all to stand." With such words uttered by the Lord Himself, and His servants, how can men have the face to teach others that salvation is the matter of a moment—that the moment a man is converted and believes, he is safe for ever—that a man is to be rewarded with the fruits of victory before he has struck a blow? It seems an astonishing delusion, preached and believed in in spite of the plainest words of Christ, and yet it is the most popular delusion of the day.

I am not speaking against sudden conversions. Conversions with the most of men ought to be sudden, not a moment is to be lost in

37 [k] And in the day time he was teaching in the temple: and [l] at night he went out, and abode in the mount that is called *the mount* of Olives.

[k] John viii. 1, 2.
[l] ch. xxii. 39.

38 And all the people came early in the morning to him in the temple, for to hear him.

---

turning from the wrong way to the right, from sin to holiness, from the world to God, from self to Christ. But in the face of Scripture and of all human experience, to say of those who have scarcely begun to fight the fight, and to run the race, what an Apostle such as St. Paul disclaimed respecting himself, does seem a folly which, we should think, no sane Christian, who cares for the words of Christ, would be guilty of. "O God, whose blessed Son was manifested that He might destroy the works of the devil, and make us the sons of God and heirs of eternal life, grant us, we beseech thee, that, having this Hope, we may purify ourselves, even as He is pure, that when He shall appear again with power and great glory, we may be made like unto Him in His eternal and glorious kingdom."

37, 38. "And in the day time he was teaching in the temple . . . . to hear him." Why does the Evangelist tell us this? Not only to teach us of our Lord's assiduity to the very last, and that to the very last He kept up the deep interest of the people in what He taught; but also to assure us that till the very hour decreed in the councils of the Trinity He was safe, and could not be taken. Before He could be taken He must be betrayed by one of the twelve, the Passover must be eaten, the Eucharist instituted, the Agony endured.

CHAP. XXII.

NOW ᵃ the feast of unleavened bread drew nigh, which is called the Passover.
2 And ᵇ the Chief Priests and Scribes sought how they might kill him; for they feared the people.

ᵃ Matt. xxvi. 2. Mark xiv. 1.
ᵇ Ps. ii. 2. John xi. 47. Acts iv. 27.

1. "Now the feast of unleavened bread drew nigh, which is called the Passover." I have noticed in my remarks on the other Gospels how very closely the Lord's death is connected with the Passover. This is still more conspicuous in the Gospel of St. Luke, inasmuch as he omits all mention of the supper in Bethany, and of the anointing which took place at it, which is inserted in the narratives of St. Matthew and St. Mark out of its proper chronological order.

"The feast of unleavened bread," not merely the single feast on the Paschal Lamb, but the whole eight days in which it was unlawful to eat anything leavened.

"Which is called the Passover." This explanation is given for the sake of the Gentile readers of the Gospel.

2. "And the Chief Priests and Scribes sought how they might kill him, for they feared the people." Emphasis is here to be laid on the word *sought*. It was a matter of difficulty, because the last notice of Him in the last chapter is, "All the people came early in the morning to him in the temple to hear him." The temple was, as it were, their own domain, but because of the crowds which flocked to hear Him He could not be taken there. So that if they were to apprehend Him at all, it must be "in the absence of the multitude:" in some place to which He retired for rest and devotion.

3. "Then entered Satan into Judas surnamed Iscariot, being of the number of the twelve." The account of Judas in St. Luke occupies a midway position between the accounts of the two first Synoptics and that of St. John. In SS. Matthew and Mark nothing whatsoever is said of him, *i.e.*, to his disparagement, till he perpetrates his crime. In St. John, on the contrary, we have the steps

N N

JUDAS SURNAMED ISCARIOT. [St. Luke.

3 ¶ c Then entered Satan into Judas surnamed Iscariot, being of the number of the twelve.

c Matt. xxvi. 14. Mark xiv. 10. John xiii. 2, 27.

which led to it, by which he hardened his own heart through repeated small acts of theft from the bag which contained the small sums which were given to Jesus and the Apostolic band for their maintenance. He committed these acts of dishonesty all the time that he was in close companionship with the Lord, seeing all His miracles, hearing all His discourses, especially those upon the danger of covetousness; and being, no doubt, perfectly conscious that Christ knew well all about his secret peculations—so that at last he ripened himself to commit the greatest crime that any human being has ever been guilty of. It is a fearful thing to think that an Apostle should fall by the commission of sins for which we should send a little servant-maid to a reformatory, but it was so. And it should teach us that any one of us may fall, not by high spiritual, but also by low carnal sins. It is surprising to see how many godly commentators of this day try to excuse this man, and to divest his sin, if possible, of its vulgarity and commonplace character. One would make his "deflection" from the Lord to be wholly on political grounds. In order that he might be a patriot he became a traitor. Another supposes that he betrayed his Lord in order to force Him to proclaim Himself to be the Messiah. A third, whilst allowing and deprecating his crime, "wraps it up" in as soft words as he well can. "This disciple, on joining the service of Jesus, had not taken care to deny his own life, as Jesus so often urged His own to do. Jesus, instead of becoming the end to his heart, had remained the means. And now, when he saw things terminating in a result entirely opposed to that with which he had ambitiously flattered himself, he wished at least to try to benefit by the false position into which he had put himself with his nation, and to use his advantages as a disciple in order to regain the favour of the rulers with whom he had broken." But is it at all likely that the rulers knew anything whatsoever about him till he offered to betray Jesus? Must we not assume that he originally belonged to the same order of society as the rest? If anything can be urged in mitigation of his crime on solid Scripture grounds, let it be so; but the lesson of Scripture is that one fell from the companionship of the Son of God, and from an apostolic throne, by miserable, vulgar, contemptible acts of sin.

CHAP. XXII.] HOW HE MIGHT BETRAY HIM. 547

4 And he went his way, and communed with the Chief Priests and captains, how he might betray him unto them.

5 And they were glad, and ᵈ covenanted to give him money.   ᵈ Zech. xi. 12.

6 And he promised, and sought opportunity to betray him unto them ‖ in the absence of the multitude.   ‖ Or, *without tumult*.

7 ¶ ᵉ Then came the day of unleavened bread, when the Passover must be killed.   ᵉ Matt. xxvi. 17. Mark xiv. 12.

---

7. "Must be killed;" rather, "must be sacrificed."

The lesson for each and every Christian is that, if he had the gifts and graces of an Apostle, this must not exempt him from taking heed to the precept, "Let him that thinketh he standeth take heed lest he fall."

4, 5. "And he went his way, and communed with the Chief Priests and captains . . . . money." St. Matthew only mentions the sum—thirty pieces of silver. St. Mark and St. Luke agree in noticing the alacrity with which the chief priests accepted the offer.

6. "And he promised, and sought opportunity," &c. For this diabolical purpose he again rejoined the holy company, being on the watch the whole time for some word to fall from His Master respecting His movements. He was present at the Passover, received the first Eucharist, and allowed the Lord to wash his feet. ["Ye are clean, but not all."]

7. "Then came the day of unleavened bread, when the Passover must be killed." As the Jews began their reckoning with the evening, at six o'clock, this, in our way of reckoning, would mean, "then came the Thursday evening, the commencement of the day which with us would begin at twelve o'clock that night, which day is our Good Friday." I must refer the reader to my notes on St. Matthew xxvi. 1, p. 400, and St. Mark xiv. 12, p. 335, for the discussion of the question, On what day did our Lord eat His Passover? I have shown that in all human probability (for there must always be some uncertainty on a question which has been debated ever since the second century of our era) He eat it twenty-four hours before the usual time. I may mention in passing that I

8 And he sent Peter and John, saying, Go and prepare us the Passover, that we may eat.

9 And they said unto him, Where wilt thou that we prepare?

10 And he said unto them, Behold, when ye are entered into the city, there shall a man meet you, bearing a pitcher of water; follow him into the house where he entereth in.

---

am glad to see that such an unprejudiced and thoughtful commentator as Godet is of this opinion.

8. "And he sent Peter and John, saying, Go and prepare us the Passover," &c. According to SS. Matthew and Mark the disciples had asked Him " Where wilt thou that we go and prepare the Passover?" According to our evangelist, the Lord takes the initiative. I believe that St. Luke's account is the strictly accurate one. The Lord, desiring to eat it beforehand, first mentioned the matter. It may be, however, that the disciples, knowing the difficulty of procuring a suitable apartment when such multitudes had flocked to the city for the same purpose, had mentioned it as desiring to be sure of some apartment.

9. "And they said unto him, Where wilt thou that we prepare?" This is precisely the same question as in the two first Synoptics, and may either have been an answer to the Lord's direction, or spontaneous on their part, feeling that if they were to have a room no time must be lost.

10. "And he said unto them, Behold, when ye are entered into the city .... he entereth in." Why does He indicate in so comparatively indirect a way how they are to find the house and not name the house? Evidently because He desired that Judas might not know the spot, because, if so, the emissaries of the chief priests might come upon Him whilst He was celebrating the Passover.

"Where he entereth in." He was a servant, and not the master of the house who is now mentioned as the "good man."[1]

---

[1] "The sign indicated—a man drawing water from a fountain—is not so accidental as it appears. On the evening of the 13th, before the stars appeared in the heavens, every father, according to Jewish custom, had to repair to the fountain to draw pure water with which to knead the unleavened bread." So Godet, but he does not give any authority for this from any Jewish or other writer, and it is not mentioned by any other commentator that I am aware of. Indeed, it might have confused those who were sent, seeing that many bearing pitchers might on that day be going on the same errand.

CHAP. XXII.] WHERE IS THE GUESTCHAMBER. 549

11 And ye shall say unto the goodman of the house, The Master saith unto thee, Where is the guestchamber, where I shall eat the Passover with my disciples?

12 And he shall shew you a large upper room furnished: there make ready.

13 And they went, and found as he had said unto them: and they made ready the Passover.

---

11. "And ye shall say unto the goodman . . . . he shall shew you a large upper room furnished," &c. According to Edersheim, we miss much of the significance of this incident by not sufficiently distinguishing between the two rooms. It is generally supposed that the Lord directed them to ask for the same room—the best, or festal apartment—which was given to Him, but it appears that in asking for the katalyma, rendered "Guest chamber," He asked for a lower rank of apartment on the ground floor opening into the court, whereas the goodman, as He foretold, shewed the disciples a large upper room (anögeon]. "The disciples were not bidden to ask for the chief or upper chamber, but for what we have rendered, for want of better, by 'hostelry,' or 'hall'—κατάλυμα—the place in the house where, as in an open khán, the beasts of burden were unloaded, shoes and staff, or daily garment and burdens put down —if an apartment, at least a common one, certainly not the best. Except in this place, the word only occurs as the designation of the 'inn,' or hostelry (κατάλυμα), in Bethlehem, where the Virgin Mother brought forth her first-born Son, and laid Him in a manger. He Who was born in a 'hostelry' (katalyma) was content to ask for his last meal in a katalyma." (Edersheim, vol. ii. p. 483).

13. "And they went, and found as he had said unto them: and they made ready the Passover." "They made ready the Passover." That is, all things that were then held to be needful for fulfilling the institution. No doubt they went with a lamb which they had purchased to the temple, and had its blood thrown at the bottom of the altar by the officiating priests; they procured the unleavened cakes, the wine, the bitter herbs, and perhaps the sweet sauce (Haroseth); but it is to be remembered that most of the details which are given in the Talmud and other Jewish authorities cannot

14 ʳAnd when the hour was come, he sat down, and the twelve apostles with him.

15 And he said unto them, ‖ With desire I

ʳ Matt. xxvi. 20. Mark xiv. 17.
‖ Or, *I have heartily desired.*

14. "Twelve" omitted by ℵ, B., D., 157, old Latin (a, b, c, e, ff², i, l), Sah., Syr. Cur., but retained by A., C., P., R., Γ, Δ, Λ, Π, all later Uncials, almost all Cursives, old Latin (f, q), Vulg., Copt., Syriacs (Schaaf, &c.), Arm., Æth.

be traced to our Lord's time, but first appear in written documents composed many centuries afterwards.

14. "And when the hour was come, he sat down, and the twelve apostles with him." "He sat down." This does not mean that He and the twelve observed a sitting posture during the whole succeeding solemnity. On the contrary, there came prayers, and thanksgivings interspersed with prayers, in which they would naturally assume an attitude of devotion.

"And the twelve apostles with him." St. Matthew has "with the twelve," St. Mark, "he cometh with the twelve." This is one of those places to which I have before directed attention, in which the Lord, for His own most wise purposes, draws a line of distinction between the twelve and all His other followers. Some of us may, in our secret hearts, object to this, as implying a small and narrow basis for the Church, instead of a broad and wide one, and some have even hazarded the assertion (which is not only without a shadow of proof, but is directly contrary to every word of the Spirit), that there were others present to receive the commission to celebrate the Eucharist. That there were only twelve is evident from the after declaration, that those present, except the traitor, were to sit on thrones, judging the twelve tribes of Israel. (See my note in St. Matthew on The Resurrection, p. 470.)

15. "And he said unto them, With desire I have desired to eat this Passover," &c. To estimate the force of these words, which, properly rendered, would read, "I have most earnestly, most heartily, desired to eat this Passover with you," we must remember that everything which the Lord did and said was laid down for Him by His Father. He could not die at any time; it must be when His hour was fully come. He could not die at any feast; it must be at the Passover. He could not die at any Passover; it must be at *that* Passover, because not till then had He "finished the work which God gave Him to do." And the particular Passover which

have desired to eat this Passover with you before I suffer:

He was then about to celebrate was a necessary precedent of His own immolation, because in it He, as I have shown, parted with all power over His own life. No one could take His life from Him till He surrendered it; and inasmuch as He died, not as a mere martyr, but as the One All-atoning Sacrifice, He must surrender up His life, not in a common, but in a priestly way. As I wrote in my note on St. Matthew, "In this taking and breaking of bread He formally surrendered that life which He had so emphatically declared that 'no one could take from Him.' It was the moment in time when He formally, federally, and sacerdotally ratified that purpose which He had conceived and resolved on through eternity, of giving Himself for His people. As a priest He must offer the Victim, that is, Himself. He could not slay Himself, but in the breaking of bread He offered Himself to be slain."

And besides this, He had it in His mind " to institute and ordain Holy Mysteries," " a perpetual memory of that His precious Death." Now this Mystery could not have been ordained by Him at any time. It must be most closely and intimately connected with two things—the Passover and His own Death. In its origin it was a part of the Paschal solemnity, to which part He gave a new life and meaning, that " Christ our Passover is sacrificed for us ; " and in its origin it must be also just before His Death, on its very eve, as close to that Death as the other circumstances of His Passion would permit, or it would lose all its significance.

So, taking all this into account, we can see why He said, " With desire I have desired to eat this Passover with you before I suffer."

But the words sound to us as if, humanly speaking, there might have been an hindrance: and so there might. For instance, if, instead of indicating the place where He desired to eat the feast somewhat obscurely, by telling them to follow the man with the pitcher of water, He had distinctly named the name of the host, Judas would have gone at once about his evil work, and the Lord's last Passover might have been interrupted. And very likely He, Who knew all contingencies, might have foreseen others ; but now all was, as it were, safe. And there is a sound of satisfaction about the words, " With desire I have desired to eat this Passover," as if nothing now could hinder it.

552   DIVIDE IT AMONG YOURSELVES.   [St. Luke.

16 For I say unto you, I will not any more eat thereof,
^g ch. xiv. 15.   ^g until it be fulfilled in the kingdom of God.
Acts x. 41.
Rev. xix. 9.   17. And he took the cup, and gave thanks, and
said, Take this, and divide *it* among yourselves:

---

16. "Any more" omitted by ℵ, A., B., C., H., Z., four Cursives, old Latin (a), Sah., Copt.; retained by D., P., R., X., Γ., Δ, Λ, Π, later Uncials, almost all Cursives, most old Latin, Vulg., Syriacs, Arm., Æth.

17. "The cup." So A., D., K., M., U., Π, about twenty-five Cursives. "A cup" with ℵ, B., C., E., G., H., L., S., V., most Cursives.

16. " For I say unto you, I will not any more eat thereof, until it be fulfilled," &c. The best exposition I have seen of this is that of Bede : " I will no more celebrate the Mosaic Passover until, being spiritually understood, it is fulfilled in the Church. For the Church is the kingdom of God."

But does the Lord mean by this "until" that when the kingdom of God shall have come and the Passover fulfilled in it, He will eat a Passover, or that into which the Passover shall have been transformed ? One divine writes: " Our Saviour's words obviously imply that He will never partake of the Paschal supper any more."

But when we know that our Lord did actually eat and drink with His disciples (Luke xxiv. 42, 43 ; Acts x. 41) after His Resurrection, it would be well if we did not express ourselves so dogmatically. The Lord says (verse 80), " That ye may eat and drink at my table in my kingdom." Could it be called His table if He never partook with His guests of what was on it ? Godet writes: " Jesus means to speak of a new banquet which shall take place after the consummation of all things. The Holy Supper is the bond of union between the Israelitish and typical Passover, which was reaching its goal, and the heavenly and Divine feast, which was yet in the distant future. Does not the *spiritual* salvation, of which the supper is the memorial, form in reality the transition from the *external* deliverance of Israel to that salvation at once spiritual and external which awaits the glorified Church ? "

17. "And he took the cup, and gave thanks, and said, Take this, and divide it," &c. Was this the same cup as that of verse 20 ? Impossible ; though some difficulties might be avoided by identifying them. There were four cups, at least, solemnly blessed and used at the Passover solemnity, and this was most likely the second. This has been called " the cup of the Old Testament" or

CHAP. XXII.] THE FRUIT OF THE VINE. 553

18. For ʰI say unto you, I will not drink of the fruit of the vine, until the kingdom of God shall come.   ʰ Matt. xxvi. 29. Mark xiv. 25.

18. "I will not drink." So A., C., X., Γ, Δ, Λ, three later Uncials, most Cursives, most old Latin, Vulg., Syriac (Schaaf); but ℵ, B., K., L., M., Π, fifteen Cursives, e, Sah., Copt., &c., read, "I will not drink henceforth." So also D., G., in somewhat different order.

"Covenant," being strictly a part of the ancient Passover, which was then for ever passing away. The next cup (that of verse 20) being part of the new rite—the Eucharistic sacrament—into which a somewhat later part of the solemnity, of breaking bread and blessing and handing round a cup, was turned by the Lord.

Did the Lord then partake of this cup? If verses 17 and 18 are strictly parallel to verses 15 and 16, He did. Just as He partook of the passover, which "with desire he had desired to eat;" so of this cup, which He would have His own to consider as the last part of the waning solemnity. On this Alford writes:—"Some suppose that it is here implied that our Lord did not drink the cup Himself. But, surely, this cannot be so. The two members of the speech are strictly parallel: and if He desired to *eat* the Passover with them, He would also *drink of the cup*, which formed a usual part of the ceremony. This seems to me to be implied in δεξάμενος; λαβών is the word used by all evangelists *afterwards*, when He did *not* partake of the bread and wine. This most important addition in our narrative amounts, I believe, to a solemn declaration of the *fulfilment* of the Passover rite in both its usual divisions—the eating of the flesh of the Lamb, and drinking the cup of thanksgiving. Henceforward, He Who fulfilled the law for man will no more eat and drink of it. I remark this, in order further to observe that this division of the cup is not only not identical with, but has no reference to, the subsequent one in verse 20. That was the institution of a new rite; this the abrogation of an old one now fulfilled, or about to be so, in the Person of the true Lamb of God."

With respect to the fact that the words after "this cup" are the same, or nearly the same, as those after the cup of the New Testament in Matth. xxvi. 29, and Mark xiv. 25, it is quite possible that the Lord said these words, or words very much resembling one another, twice. So Alford. Williams, however, lays stress on the difference. "It may be further observed that although our Lord uses a similar expression afterwards in appointing the Eucharist,

[Matt. xxvi. 26. Mark xiv. 22.] 19 ¶ ¹And he took bread, and gave thanks,

yet He does not speak here (*i.e.* in St. Luke) as He does there, of their drinking the *new* wine, or of His drinking the *new* wine with them."¹

These words respecting the drinking of the fruit of the vine, or drinking it new with them, are so exceedingly mysterious that I marvel exceedingly that their seeming repetition (and yet with a marked difference) has induced some Christian critics to make them a handle for throwing doubt on the genuineness of the reading of these verses as they are in our Received Text, which, as the reader will observe, if he turns to the critical notes, have an immense preponderance of authority in their favour.

19-20. "And he took bread, and gave thanks, and brake it, and gave unto them, saying, This is my body which is given for you: this do in remembrance of me." "Likewise also the cup after supper," &c.

We now come to the words of Institution as they are to be found in St. Luke's Gospel. And first of all we are bound to investigate the source from which St. Luke, unless the words were made known to him by a special revelation, must of necessity have derived them.

For they contain certain additions to the traditional account (assuming that traditional account to be that which we find in St. Matthew and St. Mark), which St. Luke must have received from some source of the highest authority.

Now this source was undoubtedly the Apostle St. Paul, with whom not only was St. Luke associated as a companion, but his Gospel in very early Fathers was identified with that of St. Paul. (See Preface to this vol.)

For in the first place the words of Institution in St. Luke are the same as those in 1 Corinth, xi. 24-25, particularly in the words in which St. Paul's account differs from the received tradition in

---

¹ The words in St. Luke after the giving the previous cup are: "I say unto you, I will not drink of the fruit of the vine until the kingdom of God shall come." Those in St. Matthew are, "I say unto you, I will not drink henceforth of this fruit of the vine until that day when I drink it new with you in my Father's kingdom," or, as in St. Mark, "in the kingdom of God."

and brake *it*, and gave unto them, saying, This is my body

"this is the new covenant in my blood," and "do this in remembrance of me."

And, in the second place, there is another somewhat latent, but most remarkable coincidence between the two narratives.

St. Luke distinguishes the Institution of the Eucharist from the preceding Paschal solemnity more sharply than either St. Matthew or St. Mark; for the Passover Festival in St. Luke clearly ends with the distribution of the first cup, and then the Institution of the Eucharist comes in somewhat abruptly. Now this exactly corresponds with the fact that in St. Paul's account there are no Passover associations whatsoever. The Institution with him takes place not so much on the night of the Passover, as on the night of the betrayal. And yet St. Paul is the one Apostle who identifies the Lord as the true Paschal Sacrifice when he writes in the same Epistle, "Christ our Passover is sacrificed for us, therefore let us keep the feast" (1 Cor. v. 7). So that in St. Luke we have the clearest connection between the Jewish and Christian Passover, and yet the clearest distinction.

But from whom was the account in St. Paul's Epistle derived? He himself tells us. He prefaces his account of the Institution with the words, "I have received of the Lord that which I also delivered unto you" (1 Cor. xi. 23). So that here is one of the very chiefest facts of historical Christianity respecting which the Apostle of the Gentiles received the account from the Lord Himself.

The reader will perceive that this account is the most direct of all. There is but one link between the Evangelist and the Divine Institutor, and that is the Apostle Paul. To this account, then, let us in all reverence and humility address ourselves.

19. "And he took bread, and gave thanks, and brake it, and gave to them, saying, This is my body," &c. These are the words which enshrine the mystery, a mystery which can in no way be explained so as to be understood or comprehended by the mere intellect. They are addressed to faith, and can only be received by faith, just as the corresponding mystery of the Nature and Person of the great Institutor Himself can only be received by faith. For the two mysteries are parallel, just as the Lord is in one Person God and Man, the Godhead not quenching the manhood, and the manhood not lowering or detracting from the Godhead, so this

which is given for you: ᵏthis do in remembrance of me.

---

19. Properly, "is being given." He was then sacerdotally and formally surrendering it. The words from "this do in remembrance," &c., to end of next verse, are in all Greek MSS., except D., *i.e.* they are contained in א, A., B., C., E., F., G., H., K., L., M., S., U., X., V., Γ, Δ, Λ, Π, all Cursives and Versions except old Latin and Cur. Syriac. They are distinctly alluded to by Justin Martyr. If doubt is thrown upon them because of their omission in one or two most untrustworthy MSS., what passage of Scripture is safe?

Mystery or Sacrament has, as the Church says, two parts. An outward part, which is bread and wine, which the Lord hath commanded to be received, and an inward Part or Thing signified, which is "The Body and Blood of Christ, which are verily and indeed taken and received by the faithful in the Lord's Supper." The link of connection between these two parts, so that they should be both in their integrity in the One Sacrament, the secret of their identification, so that the Lord, with the full view of the future of His Church before Him, should say of the bread which He held and brake, "this is my body," and of the contents of the Cup which He commanded them to drink, "this is my blood," or the New Covenant in My blood—this link of connection between the Bread and the Body, this manner of identification by which He gives us the bread as His Body, is one of the secret things of God, and is absolutely unknown to us, and as long as we continue human beings, imperfect both in faith, love, knowledge, and intellect, must be unknown to us; but though the secret of the mystery is unknown, the purpose for which the Lord has ordained the Sacrament which enshrines it is clearly revealed. It is that in the due and faithful use of this Sacrament, we should realize the promise which He gave to us in the most wonderful and mysterious discourse which He ever uttered; in which discourse He assures us that if we eat His Flesh and drink His Blood, we shall have eternal life, and He will raise us up at the last day; and that he that eateth His Flesh and drinketh His Blood dwelleth in Christ, and Christ in Him.

That the Eucharist is the means by which we can appropriate to ourselves this promise, is clear from this, that unless we receive His Flesh and Blood in it, there is no other means ordained by which we can know that we receive such things at all. The promise that in the reception of His Flesh and Blood, we shall receive the

20 Likewise also the cup after supper, saying, ¹This cup

1 Cor. x. 16.

extraordinary benefits set forth in the discourse in John vi. is not an ordinary promise—there is no other at all like it—no other even remotely like it—for it is that we shall receive the highest benefits which His Incarnation has brought within our reach, not through partaking of His Spirit alone, but through partaking of His Flesh —His Flesh and Blood; and this really means that we shall receive these highest things through partaking of the lower part of His human nature rather than of the higher part of the same; for the lower part is flesh and blood, and the higher is spirit and intellect.

Again, unless the Eucharist be the means of the fulfilment of the promise in John vi. we have the extraordinary and unaccountable fact that Christ instituted His Sacrament in such terms as "This is my body," "This is my blood," and had previously given the disciples no preparation by which they might receive such things worthily, and with faith, and holy desire. Surely they, just as much as we, required some previous knowledge, some definite instruction, or a very Holy Thing seems offered to those who through want of due teaching cannot appreciate it.

"And he took bread." This taking, being expressly mentioned in each one of the four accounts, there must have been something peculiarly solemn in His manner of doing it; so that it at once arrested their attention.

"And gave thanks." In St. Matthew and St. Mark He is said to have blessed it. And no doubt the "giving thanks" and the "blessing" were united. What the words which He used were has not been recorded; but if the Church has been guided by the Holy Spirit in any one particular of her mode of celebrating this most holy rite, it has been in the fact that she has adopted in all her branches a form very much the same as that of our Consecration Prayer, in which we recount, in a prayer before God, the words of the Lord in instituting the Eucharist, and pray that we may partake of the benefits attached to the devout reception of so inexpressibly Great and Holy a Thing as the Sacrament of His Body and Blood.

"And brake it." In every one of the accounts this "breaking" is expressly mentioned. By it, of course, He betokened that His Body should, within a very short time, be bruised, and broken, and

is the new testament in my blood, which is shed for you.

---

tortured, and slain upon the cross. But it far more than merely betokened this; for in its fracture He solemnly and sacerdotally surrendered His Body to be bruised and slain the next day. He must thus surrender Himself, for no one could take His Life from Him. He must lay it down of Himself; and now by this His act and deed He gave His Body to be immolated on the cross. This was His most priestly act. He acted as a Priest after the Order of Melchizedec, who brought forth bread and wine; only with this difference, that the act of Melchizedec was the type, and the Act of the Lord was the Antitype—the act of Melchizedec, as far as we know, ended with Abraham, the act of our Lord ended with His own Death, and our eternal Life through that Death.

It has been remarked by Archdeacon Freeman that this fraction, or breaking, has a higher position in our Liturgy than in any other; for in our Liturgy alone does it occur in the consecration, as it evidently did when our Lord first blessed or gave thanks, whereas in most others it occurs more towards the conclusion, long after consecration.

"And gave unto them, saying, This is my body which is given for you." It is to be remarked that St. Luke omits the words, "Take eat," but the use of bread is to be eaten, and so we must understand when we read his account that the Lord said this; just as when we read St. Matthew's account we must understand that the Lord said, "Do this in remembrance of me," though we owe the record of these latter words to St. Paul and St. Luke.

"This is my Body." Does the Lord here institute a merely figurative rite? Impossible, for the kingdom of God is not a kingdom of figures, but of realities. The Mosaic institutions were shadows. If God hath provided some better thing for us, this better thing must be a system of realities. And this is the difference between the signs of the Law and those of the Gospel. The ceremony and offerings of the Law are bare signs, having no inward and spiritual grace. The Sacraments of the Gospel are outward and visible signs of inward and spiritual grace.

But is not the bread which the Lord brake a sign or figure? Assuredly, but a sign or figure of what? Of something present, or something absent? We believe that it is the sign, not of what is absent, but of what is present. We believe that the outward part is the sign of the presence of the inward Part. There is no need of any outward sign to assure us of the existence of the Body of Christ in heaven, but there is need of an outward sign to assure us that we can receive that Body now, whilst we live on earth.

Again, the bread and wine cannot be a sign of what is already within us, or what is usually within us, through some other means. How can the outward reception of anything assure us of what is already within us. If there be any use in eating it is to bring that which is without us, and which God designs for our nourishment, within us, so that we should be strengthened and refreshed by it.

Again, the partaking of the consecrated Elements cannot be a sign to assure us of some spiritual truths, such as that we must each individually believe in Christ, and "assimilate" our part in Him. The act of eating is not a sermon about the need of taking nourishment, but an act of taking as nourishment into ourselves what such a sermon as John vi. says we must receive into ourselves, if we would be truly united to Christ.

In this way we might go through all the subterfuges by which men endeavour to get rid of the fact that the Sacrament is ordained to make us partakers of the Body and Blood of Christ. One and all they come to this, that it would have been better if Christ had avoided the use of the terms. But we who believe Him to be the Word and the Wisdom of God, believe Him to know all the needs of our nature. We believe that He knows that one of these needs is that we must partake of the elements of His lower nature, so that through this we should receive the opposite of that which we receive through the nature—the flesh and blood of Adam. We wish to receive His words without so spiritualizing them as to weaken their meaning. We are afraid of any explanation, such as Transubstantiation, which turns the mystery into a miracle. We believe that we have in the service which God's providence has provided for us in the Prayer Book the most ample recognition of the fact that in the Eucharist we must expect to receive, and that we do receive, nothing less than the Body and Blood of Christ, and for the purposes which in His discourses in the synagogue He declared to be of the utmost necessity, and we rest here, and are content.

"This do in remembrance of me." These words are peculiar to St. Luke and St. Paul. I mean the record of them: because the Lord certainly said them when He instituted the Eucharist, though for some reason or other they were not in the original tradition which is contained in the two first Gospels.

On their right understanding the whole theory of Eucharistic worship depends. Let us first consider what those who first received would, in all human probability, understand by the word remembrance, or anamnesis; and then what they would understand by the word "do."

The words, literally rendered, are, "Do this for my commemoration," or "for my memorial." They mean something very much more than, "When you do this remember me;" they mean something very much more than, "Do this to remind yourselves of me," or "in order that you may not forget me." They mean, do this in order to make before God and the Church a solemn commemoration or memorial of My Death. They mean, do this to show before God the Sacrifice of My Death, and in your Church assemblies, as the united body of Christ, to plead it on earth, and join yourselves with My pleading of it in heaven. The word Anamnesis, except in connection with the Eucharist in this place, and in 1 Cor. xi., is used but once in the New Testament, and that is in Hebrews x. 3: "In these sacrifices there is a remembrance (anamnesis) again made of sins once every year." Now the Apostolic writer here alludes to a sacrificial act of the Jewish high priest on the great day of Atonement, which was the great sacrificial function of the Jewish year, and was to be so exclusively before God that no man was to be in the tabernacle when he performed it (Levit. xvi. 17). In two other places in the Septuagint is the word anamnesis used with respect to sacrifices, and in each of these it is expressly mentioned that the anamnesis is before God (Levit. xxiv. 7), "the incense may be on the bread for a memorial, even an offering made by fire unto the Lord," and Numb. x. 10. So that when the Lord bid them "Do this for His Anamnesis," He used a word which indicated a very solemn sacrificial memorial, and not a private act of reminding themselves, or one another.

Now this is very much intensified by the word which the Lord, whether in Hebrew or in Greek, used for "do." The word ποιειν in the Septuagint, as well as the word עשה in the Hebrew Bible, when used with reference to religious worship, signifies "sacrifice this," or "offer this." Thus Ps. lxvi. 15, "I will offer (ἀνοίσω) to thee burnt sacrifices of fatlings, with the incense of rams; I will offer (ποιήσω) bullocks and goats." Then, with respect to daily

Sacrifice, ποιεῖν is a regular liturgical word. Thus, Levit. ix. 7, "And Moses said to Aaron, Draw nigh to the altar, and offer (do, ποιήσον) thy sin-offering ... and offer (do, ποιήσον) the gifts of the people." Again (Exod. x. 25), "Thou shalt give us whole burnt-offerings and sacrifices, which we will sacrifice (do, ποιήσομεν) unto the Lord our God." I give some other instances in a note.[1]

But it may be asked, why should He say, "Offer this for my anamnesis," seeing that in outward form it differed altogether from the sacrifices of the Jews? To which we answer, that He ordained a Passover—a new Passover, in which the Paschal Lamb was Himself, and, through the consecrated elements of this Sacrament, Himself, as the Passover Lamb, was to be partaken of by all His Church at all times and in every place. The same word was used with respect to the celebration of the Passover as for other sacrifices, viz., the word ποιεῖν, which the Lord here used. Thus (Numbers ix. 2), "Let the children of Israel also keep (do, ποιείτωσαν) the Passover," &c. "On the fourteenth day of the first month at even, thou shalt keep it (do, ποιήσεις) in its season," &c. Thus the oldest Greek father of whom we have any considerable remains, Justin Martyr, who must have been born within seventy years after the death of Christ, writes: "The offering of the flour commanded to be offered (προσφέρεσθαι) for persons cleansed from leprosy, was a type of the offering of the bread of the Eucharist which our Lord Jesus Christ gave command to offer (do, ποιεῖν) for a memorial (ἀνάμνησιν) of the sufferings which He underwent for those whose souls are cleansed from all iniquity" ("Dialogue with Trypho," chap. 41).

Thus Irenæus, who wrote A.D. 180: "He took that created thing, bread, and gave thanks, and said, 'This is my body;' and the cup likewise, which is part of that creation to which we belong, He confessed to be His Blood, and taught the oblation of the New Covenant, which the Church, receiving from the Apostles, offers to God throughout all the world."

In an appendix to my work, "The One Offering," I have given

---

[1] "Now this is that which thou shalt do (ποιήσεις) upon the altar, two lambs of the first year day by day continually. One lamb thou shalt do (i.e., offer) in the morning, and the second lamb thou shalt do (offer) in the evening." (Lev. ix. 7.) Again, "And the priest of his sons that is anointed in his stead shall offer it" (do it). (Lev. vi. 22.) "And ye shall do (i.e., offer) that day when ye wave the sheaf, an he lamb without blemish." "And they shall sacrifice (do) one kid of the goats for a sin offering. Again, in Ezekiel xlvi. 12, 13-15, almost at the end of the prophetical dispensation, there is the same use of *poiein*, or "do," for "offering a sacrifice."

extracts of similar significance from Clement of Rome, Tertullian, Hippolytus, Origen, Cyprian, Cyril of Jerusalem, Ambrose, Jerome, Augustine, and Chrysostom; and amongst English divines from Bishop Ridley, Bishop Andrews, Bishop Hall, Mede, and Bishop Jeremy Taylor.

Bishop Ridley, for example, says, "As though our Unbloody Sacrifice of the Church were any other than the sacrifice of praise and thanksgiving, than a commemoration, a showing forth, and a sacramental representation of that One only Bloody Sacrifice, offered up once for all."

I will give one extract from Mede, the anti-papal expositor of the Apocalypse, which, better than any other that I know, sets forth the theory of the sacrificial Eucharistic Oblation. "Instead, therefore, of the slaying of beasts and burning of incense, whereby they called upon the name of God in the Old Testament, the Fathers, I say, believed our Saviour ordained this Sacrament of bread and wine as a rite whereby to give thanks, and make supplication to His Father in His Name. The mystery of which rite they took to be this: that as Christ, by presenting His Death and Satisfaction to His Father, continually intercedes for us in heaven (Rev. v. 6), so the Church on earth semblably approaches the Throne of Grace by representing Christ to His Father in these Holy Mysteries of His Death and Passion."

But no English divine has set forth this truth of Eucharistic sacrificial worship better than Wesley in some of his sacramental hymns. I will give two verses.

Hymn CXVII.

"Thou Lamb that sufferest on the tree,
And in this dreadful mystery
  Still offerest up Thyself to God,
We cast us on Thy Sacrifice,
Wrapt in the sacred smoke arise,
  And covered with the atoning Blood."

And again—

CXXIII.

"By faith we see thy sufferings past
  In this mysterious rite brought back,
And on Thy grand Oblation cast,
  Its saving benefit partake."

But what do we of the Church actually do? We do all that the Lord did. We take the bread, we use all the words that we know were said by Him, we break, and we receive and give. We, in fact, as the oldest Liturgy expresses it, "fulfil His Institution." And we do all this not in a sermon to the people, but in an act of worship offered to God the Father.

20. "Likewise also the cup after supper, saying, This cup is the new testament in my blood." This is virtually the same as the words recorded in the two first synoptics, "This is my blood of the new testament." Only we gather from it the exceeding importance of the chalice. It contains the Lord's Blood, but this Blood for the highest of purposes, our continuance in the New Covenant. The contents of the cup as mere wine, or as mere mixed wine, are ignored by the Lord. It is the Blood of the New Covenant answering to the blood of the paschal lamb. The Passover was a covenant ordinance. It was intended to assure each Israelite who partook thereof that he continued in the covenant that God made with Israel. The Lord also may allude to the ratification of the covenant in Exod. xxiv. 8: "Behold the blood of the covenant which the Lord hath made with you."

But should this Blood be drunk, seeing that it was unlawful under the old covenant to drink blood? Yes. "In the figure (Exod. xxiv. 8), the blood of the victim was sprinkled externally on the people, or at the Passover on the door posts of the door, where they were assembled. But in the fulfilment, the Blood of the Redeemer was to penetrate the inmost recesses of our being, and hence was given to the Apostles to drink."

The change from the words, "My blood of the new covenant," into "The new covenant in my blood" in no way detracts from the mystery of the sacramental presence of the Blood. For the covenant either of the Old or New Testament was not in wine, but in Blood. What is particularly emphasized by the Blood is forgiveness. So that the Holy Sacrament is not only to the believer a channel of strength and union in the Body of Christ, but to the penitent an assurance of forgiveness. If he is in a contrite state of heart, and receives in any effectual way the Blood of Christ, he receives it for the forgiveness of his sins.

21. "But, behold, the hand of him that betrayeth me is with me on the table." This is the only sorrowful allusion which St. Luke records that the Lord Himself made to the treachery of Judas. It seems certain that it is intended to teach us that Judas had been present at the Institution and received what the rest did, but received it to his damnation; as Stier writes: "This hand, which

21 ¶ ᵐ But, behold, the hand of him that betrayeth me *is*
with me on the table.

22 ⁿ And truly the Son of man goeth, ° as it
was determined: but woe unto that man by whom
he is betrayed!

23 ᵖ And they began to enquire among themselves, which of them it was that should do this thing.

24 ¶ ᑫ And there was also a strife among them,
which of them should be accounted the greatest.

ᵐ Ps. xli. 9.
Matt. xxvi. 21,
23. Mark xiv.
18. John xiii.
ⁿ Matt. xxvi.
24.
° Acts ii. 23.
& iv. 28.
ᵖ Matt. xxvi.
22. John xiii.
22, 25.

ᑫ Mark ix. 34.
ch. ix. 46.

---

yesterday received the reward of treachery, and to-day dippeth with me in the dish, receiveth the Bread and the Cup of Mystery."

22. "And truly the Son of man goeth, as it was determined: but woe unto that man," &c. God, Who knows the end of everything from the beginning, foresaw how the crimes of the Jews, and of Judas, and of the chief priests and Pilate, would meet at this dread time, and culminate in the crucifixion of the Lord, and He not only allowed these things to take their course, but solemnly determined and decreed that this exceeding wickedness should end in atonement and salvation; but not the less did He determine to punish the authors of all this wickedness, for the good which He brought out of the evil in no way diminished its turpitude.

23. "And they began to enquire among themselves, which of them it was that should," &c. This enquiry is evidently that which is described in Matth. xxvi. 21, 25, where they said one after another, "Is it I?" The matter is narrated in St. Luke somewhat out of its place.

24. "And there was also a strife among them, which of them should be accounted the greatest." It is scarcely possible to suppose that this strife took place after they had received such a lesson upon humility as the washing of their feet had taught them, though Greswell places it after this abasement of the Lord. A similar exhibition of desire of self-advancement is recorded in Mark ix. 34, which the Lord had reproved by taking the little child and setting him in the midst as a pattern to which they were to conform themselves. The words with which St. Luke introduces this account are just those of one who was desirous of including in his narrative whatever occurred about the time: "There was *also* a strife," &c.

CHAP. XXII.] THE KINGS OF THE GENTILES. 565

25 ʳAnd he said unto them, The kings of the Gentiles exercise lordship over them; and they that exercise authority upon them are called benefactors. ʳ Matt. xx. 25. Mark x. 42.

26 ˢBut ye *shall* not *be* so: ᵗbut he that is greatest among you, let him be as the younger; and he that is chief, as he that doth serve. ˢ Matt. xx. 26. 1 Pet. v. 3. ᵗ ch. ix. 48.

27 ᵘFor whether *is* greater, he that sitteth at meat, or he that serveth? *is* not he that sitteth at meat? but ˣI am among you as he that serveth. ᵘ ch. xii. 37. ˣ Matt. xx. 28. John xiii. 13, 14, Phil. ii. 7.

---

25. "And he said unto them, The kings of the Gentiles exercise lordship," &c. I have commented so fully upon this in my notes on Mark x. 42-44 that I must refer the reader to that place: suffice it to say that here, as well as there, the spirit of all church rule is described as to what it is not, and as to what it is. It is not to be the rule of the earthly king, much less of such Gentile sovereigns as were then lording it over the world; even though such persons may call themselves, or insist upon being called, "benefactors." Their rule, at the best, was a rule of mere power—mere will—mere command—whereas the Christian rule was to be that of a servant who, if he be called upon by the providence of God, or by the voice of the Church, to exercise authority or discipline, must do it in the spirit, not of a master, but of a servant—knowing that all over whom he exercises rule are his equals in Christ, perhaps many among them his superiors in piety, in good works, in grace, and humility.

26. "He that is greatest [or greater] among you let him," &c. The Lord here recognizes that some must be greater—some must be chief. And in every well ordered community it must be so. There must be either the lead of those who are appointed, or there must be the lead of heads of parties, who rise into their positions by powers of debate, and the arts by which men obtain and keep together majorities. The former has been the practice of the Catholic Church—the latter of bodies extraneous to her.

Each of these systems—indeed, any system worked by human beings—must present temptations to ambition and self-seeking; and there is but one remedy, the mind of Christ worked in us by His Spirit, and that mind we have in what follows.

27. "For whether is greater, he that sitteth at meat, or he that serveth . . . . I am among you as he that serveth." The life of

28 Ye are they which have continued with me in ʸmy temptations.

ʸ Heb. iv. 15.

---

28. "Ye are they." "But ye are they" (Revisers); (ὑμεῖς δέ); *vos autem estis* (Vulg.).

the Son of God was one of uninterrupted service: serving God so that He could say, "My meat and drink is to do the will of him that sent me;" serving man, always teaching, always healing, journeying, having no settled home, no servant—always, as one may say, at the beck and call of everyone who needed His help—living on the bounty of others—carefully abstaining from all mere human precedence, power, or judgeship, ["man, who made me a ruler and a judge over you?"]—serving His Own, His chosen—always on the watch for opportunities of instructing them, always bearing with them, always acting towards them as a shepherd, always watching them as a nurse would watch a wayward child—and now at this time actually about to demean Himself to do a menial office for them, for I cannot but think that the feet washing takes place at this time.

One writes: "These expressions, 'He that sitteth at meat,' 'He that serveth,' leave no doubt that the fact of the feet washing was the occasion of this saying." But may not this saying have equally been the occasion of the feet washing? He said the words, "I am among you as he that serveth," and to enforce this He began literally to act as a servant.

28, 29. "Ye are they which have continued with me in my temptations. And I appoint," &c. The connecting thought seems to be something of this kind. "I have spoken to you as if your highest glory is to be servants, as I myself came not to be served, but to serve; but you are not to understand this, as if you will be ultimately without any reward of glory and honour. On the contrary in My kingdom ye shall have glory next to Mine."

"Ye are they which have continued with me in my temptations." "Ye have continued steadfast to Me, notwithstanding my rejection by the rulers of your nation and the heads of your religion." It required no small grace to accept the Messiah under the lowly guise in which He first appeared, and to adhere to Him though He constantly and systematically destroyed every Messianic hope which the worldlings of his people so dearly cherished. He had refused all worldly praise and honour. He had even gone so far as to say

CHAP. XXII.]   I APPOINT UNTO YOU A KINGDOM.   567

29 And ᶻI appoint unto you a kingdom, as my Father hath appointed unto me;

30 That ᵃye may eat and drink at my table in my kingdom, ᵇand sit on thrones judging the twelve tribes of Israel.

ᶻ Matt. xxiv. 47. ch. xii. 32.
ᵃ 2 Cor. i. 7.
2 Tim. ii. 12.
ᵃ Matt. viii. 11.
ch. xiv. 15.
Rev. xix. 9.
ᵇ Ps. xlix. 14.
Matt. xix. 28.
1 Cor. vi. 2.
Rev. iii. 21.

that no true believer in Himself could desire it when He asked, "How can ye believe, who receive honour one from another, and seek not the honour which cometh from God only?"

"And I appoint unto you a kingdom, as my Father," &c. As He would be invested with visible glory and majesty, such as the universe had never seen, so they should share His glory.

30. "That ye may eat and drink at my table in my kingdom, ... twelve tribes of Israel." What is the meaning of this promise, which is the same as that in Matth. xix. 28? Do the thrones mean actual thrones? What is implied in the "judging?" Are the twelve tribes the literal, or the spiritual Israel? Now in the first place we must remember that if the Lord meant to reassure His Apostles that they should not be without a visible and tangible reward, the words that He used betoken the highest glory which in their then state of mind they could conceive. If He had given them simply spiritual promises, they would not have understood them in the least. They would have been no promises to them. But that they should eat and drink at the table of the Messiah Himself, and that they should each one rule as a judge over a tribe, and be the Patriarchs of the glorified Israel—this was beyond their fondest imagination. I have no doubt whatever that now in the unseen world, as well as in the kingdom of glory to be revealed at the Second Advent, the Apostles, as such, have a place, and power, and authority, which none (except St. Paul) will share with them. How far this is connected with the spirits of the justified Israel, the sealed out of the twelve literal tribes, is hidden from us. Under what form or circumstances the restoration of God's ancient people, the ten tribes now lost, will take place, so that they should be visibly ruled by these twelve first followers of the Lord, is not revealed; but the promise seems so definite as to the Apostles on the one side, and the tribes on the other, that our safest and humblest course is take it literally. We must remember that He Who made

31 ¶ And the Lord said, Simon, Simon, behold, ^c Satan hath desired *to have* you, that he may ^d sift *you* as wheat:

^c 1 Pet. v. 8.
^d Amos ix. 9.

32 But ^eI have prayed for thee, that thy faith

^e John xvii. 9, 11, 15.

31. "And the Lord said." So ℵ, A., D., G., X., Γ, Δ, Λ, Π, all later Uncials, almost all Cursives, old Latin, Vulg.; but B., L., T., Sah., Copt., omit the words.

this promise has all time at His disposal and all power at His command—that the first notice of His first Advent is that "God shall give to him the throne of his father David," and that on His Cross was the title, "The King of the Jews." We believe that the promise will be fulfilled, and also more than fulfilled; but how, when, where, we know not.

31. "And the Lord said, Simon, Simon, behold, Satan hath desired to have you, that," &c. It is supposed that on this evening our Lord warned St. Peter no less than three times. The first instance being that recorded in John xiii. 36-38. When Peter said, "Why cannot I follow thee now? I will lay down my life for thy sake." The second that mentioned here by St. Luke, which, according to our Evangelist, took place in the same chamber as that in which He had instituted the Eucharist. The third in Matth. xxvi. 34, when they were on their way to the Mount of Olives. No warnings could have been more direct: "Verily I say unto thee," "Verily, verily, I say unto thee," "I tell thee, Peter." No warnings could have been more circumstantial: "The cock shall not crow," "The cock shall not crow this day," "This night before the cock crow." And yet he heeded it not, he remembered it not, he believed it not. Marvellous that men can believe in Christ, and yet not believe very express words of His, and yet it is so!

"Satan hath desired to have you," *i.e.*, the twelve, "that he may sift you as wheat." "Satan asks the right of putting the twelve to the proof; and he takes upon himself over against God, as formerly in relation to Job, to prove that, at bottom, the best of the disciples is but a Judas."

"But I have prayed for thee." Why is it that St. Peter is prayed for in particular? "I have prayed for thee, that thy faith fail not." It seems as if Satan was not allowed to sift the rest, at least as he sifted Simon. They all fled, but they kept out of the way of temptation, which Peter did not. Peter then, as their repre-

CHAP. XXII.] STRENGTHEN THY BRETHREN. 569

fail not : ^f and when thou art converted, strengthen thy
brethren.

f Ps. li. 13.
John xxi. 15, 16, 17.

33 And he said unto him, Lord, I am ready to
go with thee, both into prison, and to death.

---

32. "And when thou art converted." "And do thou, when once thou hast turned again, stablish thy brethren " (Revisers).

sentative, was sifted as wheat, and it was because the prayer of the Lord prevailed so that, in the depth of His own distress, He might turn and give Peter the saving look, that Peter's faith failed not. It was like the hand of the Lord stretched out once before on the sea just in time. It looked him into repentance, and that repentance was both the revival, and the sign of the faith which yet survived in him.

"When thou art converted"—*i.e.*, when thy miserable cowardice, and thy disregard of My clearest warnings, and thy want of sympathy with Me in the hour of My distress, are turned into deep and bitter repentance, with tears and shame, then "strengthen thy brethren."

This "strengthen thy brethren" seems to refer to his brother Apostles, between the time of the Lord's Death and His Resurrection. It was he that had confessed the good confession, that Jesus was the Christ, the Son of the living God. If that faith failed not, he might with some words of consolation unknown to us be able to revive or keep alive the failing faith of the Eleven—that all was not lost, and that God might yet work out His purposes through the power of Christ in heaven ; for though he did not realize the Resurrection he certainly believed that the Lord's glorified Spirit might wield the power of God, and establish His kingdom.

33, 34. "And he said unto him, Lord, I am ready to go with thee, both into prison, and to death . . . thrice deny that thou knowest me." The stronger man believes himself to be, the weaker he is, for his promising himself a great deal from his own strength is a sign that God has already left him to himself. This Apostle thought that the love he had for his Master would be proof against every temptation, and it was the love of his own life which prevailed and caused him to fall.

"The cock shall not crow this day"—the day, of course, begin-

34 ⁵ And he said, I tell thee, Peter, the cock shall not
crow this day, before that thou shalt thrice deny
that thou knowest me.

⁵ Matt. xxvi. 34. Mark xiv. 30. John xiii. 38.

35 ʰ And he said unto them, When I sent you
without purse, and scrip, and shoes, lacked ye any
thing? And they said, Nothing.

ʰ Matt. x. 9. ch. ix. 3. & x. 4.

36 Then said he unto them, But now, he that hath a
purse, let him take *it*, and likewise *his* scrip: and he that
hath no sword, let him sell his garment, and buy one.

---

ning at six o'clock that evening. Thus St. Mark adds the words,
"this day, even in this night."

35, 36. "And he said unto them, When I sent you without purse
... Nothing ... sell his garment, and buy one." These words
are peculiar to St. Luke, and they are very difficult, for they seem
to intimate that the Apostles are not to rely upon the power of
Christ for the supply of their temporal wants as they had done in
time past; and that besides this they must rely on ordinary human
means, as the sword, for their defence. They are even to sell their
garments to buy one; and yet they are not to use the sword when
bought. "Put up thy sword into his sheath, for all they that take
the sword shall perish by the sword."

Some, as Theophylact, or those referred to by him, seem to think
that at least what the Lord says about swords is ironical. "But
some say that our Lord said, 'It is enough,' ironically, as if He
said, 'Since there are two swords, they will amply suffice against
so large a multitude as is about to attack us.'"

Mr. Blunt explains the words about the purse and scrip, as if
they had only a temporary application to the time between the
Lord's Death and His Ascension. He was about to be taken from
them, and they were for a time to be left to themselves. It was
this necessity of providing for themselves which led Simon Peter to
the resolution, "I go a fishing," and to others of the Apostles saying, "We also go with thee." He takes, however, no notice of our
Lord's words about the sword. I cannot help taking it to be a
prophecy that, on His departure, they would enter upon a different
outward life. Hitherto, for instance, in their journeyings they had
taken no provision whatsoever, either in money or food; now they

37 For I say unto you, that this that is written must yet be accomplished in me, ¹And he was reckoned among the transgressors: for the things concerning me have an end.

¹ Is. liii. 12.
Mark xv. 28.

38 And they said, Lord, behold, here *are* two swords. And he said unto them, It is enough.

---

were to equip themselves for their journeys. They were to be supported, not by the bounty of those with whom they lodged, but with what was supplied them by the Church: for it would be best that at first, at least, they should take nothing from the Gentiles amongst whom they preached. If need be, they were even to work with their hands (Acts xviii. 3). Still, at the same time, as before, they were to amass no property, and to live lives of faith.

With respect to the mention of the sword, it has been taken as if His words meant that they were to resort to all means of self defence short of the sword, which the Lord certainly forbad; but this is exceedingly unsatisfactory. It seems not intended to be taken literally at all, but to be an intimation of coming persecutions, which would destroy some of them, if not all—from which persecutions they had hitherto been shielded by the Lord's power.

37. "For I say unto you, that this that is written . . . have an end." This betokened the fearful rapidity with which the final stroke would come upon Himself and them. He was now to be reckoned among the transgressors. He was to be treated by the chief priests as if He were a blasphemer; by Pilate, whilst the same Pilate asserted His faultlessness, as if He were a rebel; and He was to be literally crucified between two transgressors who deserved punishment.

It is to be remarked that the Lord here claims the great Messianic prophesy of Isaiah liii., as referring to Himself. If He was the One Who was to be reckoned with the transgressors, then He was equally the One Who was to "bear the sins of many," and in Whose hand "the pleasure of the Lord should prosper."

38. "And they said, Lord, behold, here are two swords." It is an interesting question, had they at once acted literally on the Lord's advice, and gone out and purchased these swords, or were they already in their possession? It seems strange that the latter should have been the case; but very probably, being much struck with

39 ¶ ᵏ And he came out, and ˡ went, as he was wont, to the mount of Olives; and his disciples also followed him.

40 ᵐ And when he was at the place, he said

ᵏ Matt. xxvi. 36. Mark xiv. 32. John xviii. 1.
ˡ ch. xxi. 37.
ᵐ Matt. vi. 13. & xxvi. 41. Mark xiv. 38. ver. 46.

---

the prophesies of the Lord, respecting His speedy apprehension and betrayal, they had secretly purchased these two weapons. It must have been brought about by the providence of God, for it was with one of these that St. Peter nearly killed the servant of the high priest, and so enabled the Lord to demonstrate to His enemies that His kingdom was not of this world, and also to show those who were come to capture Him His supernatural and Divine power and goodness, so that they might have no excuse.

"It is enough." These words have been taken to mean, "I have said enough. Let us now go hence" (John xiv. 31, "Arise, let us go hence"); or they may be said somewhat ironically, "Two swords are, indeed, sufficient for any use which you can make of such weapons."

39. "And he came out, and went, as he was wont, to the mount of Olives," &c. "As he was wont." There is here evidently a reference to what is written in xxi. 37, "In the day time he was teaching in the temple, and at night he went out and abode in the Mount that is called the Mount of Olives."

40. "And when he was at the place, he said unto them, Pray that ye enter not into temptation." The place, evidently Gethsemane, is alluded to by our Evangelist as a place well known.

We now come to the account of the Agony. St. Luke is here very compendious. He says nothing about the three disciples, whom the Lord "took with Him" (Matth. xxvi. 37). Whereas St. Matthew states that the Lord prayed three times, he only mentions one prayer. Whereas St. Matthew mentions three awakenings of the disciples, St. Luke only has one. And yet St. Luke gives some most precious additions to what we get from the other Synoptics. It is to him that we owe the name by which this awful passage in the Lord's life is known, for St. Luke alone names it as "agony," "Being in an agony." He alone mentions the strengthening by the angel, and the sweat of blood.

I have commented so fully upon the cause, so far as we may

unto them, Pray that ye enter not into temptation.

---

reverently surmise it, of this mysterious and fearful feature in the Lord's Passion in my notes on St. Matthew and St. Mark, that I can only now briefly summarise what I have there written.

First then, our Lord had perfectly in His foreknowledge, not only the physical and mental sorrows which were shortly to come upon Him, but the extraordinary wickedness of the human agents of the evil one in bringing this about. He had perfectly in His mind the treachery of Judas, all that led to it, and all its fearful consequences in the loss of his soul, and what is implied in the words, "Good were it for that man if he had never been born!" He had perfectly in His foreknowledge the extraordinary wickedness and disregard of justice of the chief priests, who were in His eyes the chief ministers of a religion which, in His pre-existent state, He Himself had ordained, and which was then the only religion on the face of the earth in which God could be purely and holily worshipped. He had perfectly before him the prostitution of justice and kingly power in the person of Pilate. 'He had perfectly before Him the cruelty and blasphemy of all the subordinate agents. His holy soul realized, as our polluted souls cannot, the iniquity of it all—and above all, how it was called out and intensified by His own power and holiness, according to His own words, "If I had not come and spoken to them, they had not had sin. If I had not done among them the works which none other man did, they had not had sin; but now have they both seen and hated both me and my Father" (John xv. 22, 24).

And may there not have been present vividly before Him the ruin and scattering of His own nation and people, which would be the punishment of their sin in rejecting and crucifying Him? These I have considered in my notes on St. Matthew.

Then, in my commentary on St. Mark, I have noticed how our Lord alone of all men knew the real nature of death, as the opposite to that Life which was inherent in Himself as One to Whom the Father had granted to have Life in Himself. There is something exceedingly mysterious about death, putting out of the question any pains and agonies. It is in human beings the penalty of sin. It is reckoned in the Law of God, which must give us a true account of matters, not only as a painful, but as an unclean thing.

All these, which must have been fully in the Lord's conscious-

574   REMOVE THIS CUP FROM ME.   [ST. LUKE.

41 [n] And he was withdrawn from them about a stone's cast, and kneeled down, and prayed,

42 Saying, Father, if thou be † willing, remove this cup from me: nevertheless [o] not my will, but thine, be done.

[n] Matt. xxvi. 39. Mark xiv. 35.
† Gr. *willing to remove.*
[o] John v. 30. & vi. 38.

---

ness, were, we are sure, no small part of the extreme bitterness of His cup, in addition to what is implied in such assertions of the Spirit as "God made him, who knew no sin, to be sin for us." "The Lord hath laid on him the iniquity of us all." "He himself bare our sins in his own body on the tree."

"Pray that ye enter not into temptation." This has been understood by some to mean "pray that ye enter into temptation so as not to yield to it." But may it not, looking to the extreme frailty of human nature, rather mean "Pray that ye be not tempted?" It is, I think, our duty to desire not to be tempted, to shun all nearness of evil, such as is implied in temptation.

41. And he was withdrawn from them about a stone's cast, and kneeled down, and prayed." "He was withdrawn." The word withdrawn is much stronger in the Greek (ἀπεσπάσθη) and also in the Latin version (avulsus est), and perhaps implies some involuntary impulse of extreme grief, as in our Lord's temptations after His Baptism, of which St. Mark says, "The Spirit driveth Him into the wilderness." It is as if He was dragged away by anguish.

"And kneeled down and prayed." He kneeled down at first, but afterwards, according to St. Matthew, "He fell on His face and prayed, and Mark, "He fell on the ground and prayed." "Thus He Who bore our sicknesses and interceded for us, bent His knee in prayer, by reason of the man which He had assumed, giving as an example, that we ought not to exalt ourselves at the time of prayer, but in all things be conformed to humility." (Greg. Nyss. in Cat. Aurea.)

42. "Saying, Father, if thou be willing . . . . not my will, but thine, be done." If the Lord has a perfect human nature, He must have a perfect will, which, of necessity, shrinks from those things, such as pain, suffering, and death, which tend to the dissolution of that nature; for, for this purpose as well as others, God has endowed human nature with an intelligent, reasonable will. Here then that will shows itself, but then it no sooner shows itself, but it

CHAP. XXII.] AN ANGEL STRENGTHENING HIM.

43 And there appeared ᵖ an angel unto him from heaven, strengthening him.

ᵖ Matt. iv. 11.

---

43. "This and the next verse are contained in the vast majority of MSS. and versions, in ℵ, cD, F., G., H., K., L., M., Q., U., X., Λ, and most Cursives. They are also contained, but marked with asterisks, in E., S., V., Δ, and five Cursives (24, 36, 161, 166, 274). In Γ and four or five Cursives they are obelized. They are contained in all Syriac versions, and in old Latin (a, b, c, e, ff², g¹ ², i, l, q), and the Vulgate. They are distinctly alluded to by Justin Martyr and Irenæus. They are omitted in A., B., R., T, 124, in the Memphitic, and in some Thebaic and Armenian Codices, and in f of the old Latin. Epiphanius says that they were in his time omitted by the Orthodox as derogatory to our Lord's Divine dignity. The preponderance of authorities in their favour is immense.

submits to the higher Will of the Father, which the Eternal Son came into the world to fulfil. If the Lord had been without a human will which shrinks from suffering and death, there would have been no virtue in His sufferings. If the Lord had had a will which asserted itself against the will of God, then He would have been like the rest of our fallen race, and could not have redeemed us; but He had a Will which shrunk from death, and yet in the very act of shrinking submitted to the Highest—the Divine Will. And this it was which gave His sufferings and Death their redeeming virtue. This, I need not say, is written also for our sakes, to show us that there is no sin in having a natural human will which may shrink from what God sees to be in store for it, if we, at the same time, say with all our hearts, "Thy will be done."

43. And there appeared an angel unto him from heaven, strengthening him." This wonderful place has a twofold significance. It teaches us our Lord's true humanity, and it teaches us the numberless ways in which God may make use of the angels to execute His purposes.

1. Our Lord's true humanity. The angels are ministering spirits sent forth to minister to those who shall be heirs of salvation. Our Lord then, by becoming man, was made a little lower than the angels, and so humbled Himself to receive good offices at their hands. Thus, after His long fast at the time of His temptation, angels came and ministered unto him. And now, in the extremity of His agony, God strengthens Him for the coming conflict, not directly from Himself, but mediately through the intervention of an angel.

2. We are taught, secondly, that there can be no limits to the employment of these ministering spirits in executing the purposes

44 ᑫ And being in an agony he prayed more earnestly:
and his sweat was as it were great drops of
blood falling down to the ground.

ᑫ John xii. 27.
Heb. v. 7.

---

of God. Nothing can be conceived more intimate than the union betwixt God and His Son. If then God strengthened His Son by an angel, what does He not do at the hands of angels? What natural law may be exempt from their working and control? What special providence which may not be altogether brought about by them? What movement of men's minds may they not shape and direct? Indeed, the Book of the Revelations teaches that the whole course of the world is, under God and Christ, administered by them. For nothing can come up to this, that God strengthened the human nature of His own Son by an angel.

But how did the angel strengthen the Lord? In what way, or under what form, did he infuse strength into Him? I cannot think that the angel infused spiritual strength into the Lord by presenting to His mind arguments and reasons for trust in God. I know that this is held by many Catholic commentators, as Cornelius à Lapide and I. Williams, but it seems to me incredible. For did not the bloody sweat which took place at the time of the appearance of the angel, or immediately after it, betoken an action of the soul or spirit on the body, which must have been followed by such a prostration as would seem to be the precursor of its dissolution? The Lord's redeeming work upon which He was now entering, required physical strength as well as spiritual; and this physical strength the angel was sent by God to infuse, in some way unknown to us. This seems to me the more reverent way of regarding this awfully mysterious matter.

44. "And being in an agony he prayed more earnestly: and his sweat was as it were," &c. Extreme agony, through fear or mental conflict, has brought about this sweat of blood in others, besides our Saviour. Thus Maldonatus speaks of having heard from those who had seen or known him, of a man at Paris in robust health, who, when he heard that he was condemned to death, sweat blood. And Thuanus (quoted in Notes by F. M.), narrates of the governor of Monte Maro, treacherously decoyed by Maggi and the bastard of Saluces, and menaced with death for refusing to betray his trust, that it was noticed that he was so shaken in mind with vehement

45 And when he rose up from prayer, and was come to his disciples, he found them sleeping for sorrow,

46 And said unto them, Why sleep ye? rise and ʳpray, lest ye enter into temptation. ʳ ver. 40.

---

fear of so unworthy a death, that he poured forth a bloody sweat from his whole body. (Thuanus, ix. 1.[1])

This bloody sweat was the outward visible sign of a conflict in the Saviour's soul, intense beyond conception, and so the Church mentions it before the Lord in the deprecations in her Litany: "By thine Agony and bloody Sweat—Good Lord, deliver us."

This account of the appearance of the angel and the Bloody Sweat was, strange to say, distasteful to some calling themselves orthodox, and so they had the audacity to remove it from certain MSS. of the fourth century, though it is quoted by two of the very earliest Fathers, Justin Martyr and Irenæus, in the second century.

St. Ambrose commences a passage of wonderful power and sweetness with a reference to this unworthy fear of the orthodox: "Many are shocked at this place, who turn the sorrows of the Saviour to an argument of inherent weakness from the beginning, rather than taken upon Him for the time. But I am so far from considering it a thing to be excused, that I never more admire His mercy and majesty: for He would have conferred less upon me had He not taken upon Him my feelings. For He took upon Him my sorrow, that upon me He might bestow His joy. With confidence, therefore, I name His sadness, because I preach His cross. He must needs then have undergone affliction that He might conquer. For they have no praise of fortitude whose wounds have produced stupor rather than pain. He instructs us, therefore, how we should conquer death, and what is far greater, the anguish of coming death." (Ambrose in Cat. Aurea.)

45, 46. "And when he rose up from prayer .... enter into temptation." Sleeping for sorrow. St. Luke is the only one of the Evangelists who gives this reason, indeed excuse, for the sleep of the apostles; *i.e.*, of course, of the three. It was not in the tradition,

---

[1] The passage from Aristotle quoted by Alford is not at all to the point, as it describes the effect of disease. And the same also may be said of the fatal illness of Charles IX. of France.

JUDAS, ONE OF THE TWELVE. [St. Luke.

47 ¶ And while he yet spake, ^a behold a multitude, and he that was called Judas, one of the twelve, went before them, and drew near unto Jesus to kiss him.

^a Matt. xxvi. 47. Mark xiv. 43. John xviii. 3.

48 But Jesus said unto him, Judas, betrayest thou the Son of man with a kiss?

49 When they which were about him saw what would follow, they said unto him, Lord, shall we smite with the sword?

50 ¶ And ^t one of them smote the servant of the high priest, and cut off his right ear.

^t Matt. xxvi. 51. Mark xiv. 47. John xviii. 10.

51 And Jesus answered and said, Suffer ye thus far. And he touched his ear, and healed him.

---

and St. Mark, who wrote what St. Peter preached, could hardly have given it. It may have come to St. Luke from the Highest Source.

47, 48. "And while he yet spake .... betrayest thou the Son of man with a kiss?" No doubt Judas came forward far in the front, and being one of the twelve, would be supposed to be a friend, and would not strike those about the Lord with fear, and so there would be neither resistance nor flight till the multitude had had the person of the Lord clearly indicated to them.

"Judas, betrayest thou"? And the Lord gives him his proper name, which was rather like one lamenting and recalling him, than one provoked to anger. (Chrysostom.)

He says, Betrayest thou with a kiss? that is, dost thou inflict a wound with the pledge of love? with the instruments of peace dost thou impose death? (Ambrose.)

49-51. "When they which were about him .... touched his ear, and healed him." St. Luke alone records that they asked the question, shall we smite? From this we cannot but gather that he got the account from one present. It is true he gives neither the name of Peter, or of the servant, or any of the sayings of the Lord (Matth. xxvi. 52, 54, John xviii. 11), to which the incident gave rise, and yet St. Luke alone gives the miracle which followed.

"Suffer ye thus far." More than one meaning has been given to these words. They have been supposed to have been spoken as

CHAP. XXII.] THE POWER OF DARKNESS. 579

52 ^u Then Jesus said unto the chief priests, and captains of the temple, and the elders, which were come to him, Be ye come out, as against a thief, with swords and staves? u Matt. xxvi. 55. Mark xiv. 48.

53 When I was daily with you in the temple, ye stretched forth no hands against me: ^x but this is your hour, and the power of darkness. x John xii. 27.

---

a preliminary to the healing. Our Lord had just been seized and was being held fast, and so could not touch the wounded man, as He was wont to do when He performed miracles on the bodies of men—and so He asked that His hand might be allowed to be set free for a moment, in order that He might touch the ear, and so show that the healing proceeded from Him Whom they were treating with such indignity. Or they may have been spoken to the disciples with a view to restrain them from further violence. Thus Godet: "*Stop there;* strike no such second blow; this one is quite enough." This act of violence compromised the Lord's cause. If it had gone further He could hardly have said to Pilate, "If my kingdom were of this world, then would my servants fight." So it was needful not only that He should compel his ardent follower to sheathe the sword, but also that He should restore the servant's ear; thereby showing that the act of violence was done in direct opposition to His will. It is also suggested that they were addressed to the servants and officers, that they should not visit His followers with punishment for this one act, as its ill effects would be instantly remedied.

52, 53. "Then said Jesus unto the chief priests, ... your hour, and the power of darkness." St. Luke alone mentions the presence of "chief priests"—of course not Annas, or Caiaphas, but some of the heads of the courses. Their presence shows how thoroughly they were alarmed at the growing influence of the Lord, so much so that more than one of them accompanied the band of men and officers to see that there was no slackness in doing their work.

"Against a thief." The Lord felt deeply the degradation of the proceedings taken against Him. His miracles, His teaching, His innocence of life, His influence, were all ignored, He was treated as a common criminal, "He was numbered with the transgressors."

"This is your hour, and the power of darkness." What a fearful

580 PETER SAT DOWN AMONG THEM. [St. Luke.

54 ¶ ʸ Then took they him, and led *him*, and brought him into the high priest's house. ᶻ And Peter followed afar off.

55 ᵃ And when they had kindled a fire in the midst of the hall, and were set down together, Peter sat down among them.

56 But a certain maid beheld him as he sat by the fire, and earnestly looked upon him, and said, This man was also with him.

y Matt. xxvi. 57.
z Matt. xxvi. 58. John xviii. 15.
a Matt. xxvi. 69. Mark xiv. 66. John xviii. 17, 18.

---

55. "Hall." "Court" (Revisers).
"Among them," or, "in the midst." So B., L., T., but all other authorities, ℵ, A., all other Uncials as in Rec. Text.

thing that it could be said of any human beings that they were so in league with Satan as that their hour was his. This is peculiar to St. Luke, who says nothing of the flight of the Apostles.

54-60. "Then took they him, and led him . . . Peter followed afar off . . . the cock crew." Rather, "they seized him, and led him away." It may be well to remind the reader of the events of this fearful night in their order. First of all (John xviii. 13), they led Him to the house of Annas, and this was done, as I have said in my notes on St. John, to give a show of legality to the proceedings: for Annas must have been the real high priest. At the house of Annas nothing took place except to send Him bound to Caiaphas. At the palace of Caiaphas was the first examination, evidence was taken, and the Lord was condemned; but His actual legal condemnation took place in the morning, as soon as it was day, at a fuller and more formal meeting. At the house of Caiaphas the denials by Peter occurred.

St. Luke gives us nothing whatsoever of the trial in the night before Caiaphas, but mentions the insults which the Lord received. His account is wholly taken up with the denials of Peter.

The first denial was to a maid of the high priest (Matth. xxvi. 69, 70, Mark xiv. 67, 68, Luke xxii. 56, 57). From St. John we learn that she was the porteress (John xviii. 17).

In the account of the second denial there is apparently a discrepancy between St. Luke and the two first Synoptics, for whereas in St. Matthew and St. Mark it is a female servant, in St. Luke it is a man (ἕτερος).

57 And he denied him, saying, Woman, I know him not.

58 ᵇAnd after a little while another saw him, and said, Thou art also of them. And Peter said, Man, I am not.

ᵇ Matt. xxvi. 71. Mark xiv. 69. John xviii. 25.

59 ᶜAnd about the space of one hour after another confidently affirmed, saying, Of a truth this *fellow* also was with him: for he is a Galilæan.

ᶜ Matt. xxvi. 73. Mark xiv. 70. John xviii. 26.

60 And Peter said, Man, I know not what thou sayest. And immediately, while he yet spake, the cock crew.

---

57. "And he denied him." So A., D., E., G., H., U, V, Δ, Λ, most Cursives, old Latin (d), Vulg., Syriac. "Him" omitted by ℵ, B., K., L., M., S., T., XII., above forty Cursives, old Latin (a, b, c, f, l), Sah., Copt., Syriac (Cureton and Schaaf), Arm., Æth.

In the account of the third there is no real discrepancy. St. Matthew and St. Mark make the denial to be made to them that stood by; St. Luke to another, a male (ἄλλος). And with St. Luke St. John agrees, and describes the servant as a kinsman of him whose ear Peter cut off. If several were standing by, it is most probable that one would take the lead in accusing Peter.

Respecting the discrepancies between the accounts, and the impossibility of completely reconciling them, I have commented in my notes on St. Matthew's history, and shown that we cannot have four independent accounts of a transaction of such a sort as this was without discrepancies. If there were no discrepancies, the Evangelists must have compared notes, and the account would consequently be deprived of very much of its value, for it would be then one carefully prepared narrative, instead of four natural ones.

"The difficulties of reconciling the various narratives of the denials have been indefinitely increased by adhering to the absurd and unnatural supposition, that in a crowd of menials only one spoke at a time; that they spoke only to Peter, or must all be assumed to speak only to him; that each denial on the part of Peter consisted of but one sentence. Whereas we have only to imagine a scene in which a single person is beset and worried by perhaps a dozen others, to be convinced how true the account is to nature, and how impossible it would be for any two bystanders, if afterwards examined, to give an exactly coherent account of all that was said and done." (From notes on St. Mark.)

61 And the Lord turned, and looked upon Peter. ᵈ And Peter remembered the word of the Lord, how he had said unto him, ᵉ Before the cock crow, thou shalt deny me thrice.

62 And Peter went out, and wept bitterly.

63 ¶ ᶠ And the men that held Jesus mocked him, and smote *him*.

ᵈ Matt. xxvi. 75. Mark xiv. 72.
ᵉ Matt. xxvi. 34, 75. John xiii. 38.
ᶠ Matt. xxvi. 67, 68. Mark xiv. 65.

---

61. "Before the cock crow." So A., D., Γ, Δ, Λ, six later Uncials, almost all Cursives, old Latin (a, e, e, f, i, q), Vulg., Cur. Syriac, and Schaaf, Arm.; but ℵ, B., K., L., M., T., XII., twenty-five Cursives, Copt., &c., read, "to-day"—"before the cock crow to-day."

There are three points in St. Luke's narrative which seem to make it almost certain that he received the account from an eye-witness. First, that the maid or porteress earnestly looked (ἀτενίσασα) upon him, as if she scanned his features by an imperfect light, as that of a fire would be. Secondly, that another "confidently affirmed." Why confidently? except there was something in the tone of his voice which penetrated very deep. Thirdly, that the Lord turned and looked upon the fallen Apostle, and by His look recalled him to repentance, to faith, to love.

I have commented so largely on the fall of St. Peter elsewhere that I cannot here say more than that it was the fruit of self-confidence and remissness in prayer. If he had been less over-weening, he would have taken more seriously the warnings of the Lord, and like Him prayed more earnestly that such a disgraceful fall might have been averted.

61, 62. "And the Lord turned, and looked upon Peter," &c. "Blessed are the tears which wash away guilt! *They* at length mourn upon whom Jesus looks. Peter denied the first time, and wept not, because the Lord looked not on him. He denied a second time, and wept not, for as yet the Lord had not looked on him. He denied also a third time, Jesus looked on him, and he wept most bitterly. Lord Jesus, look on us, that we may know how to weep for our sin, and wash out the guilt!" (St. Ambrose.)

63-66. "And the men that held Jesus mocked him .... spake they against him." One would have thought that the fact that he had done many miracles, and all these miracles of mercy—alleviating suffering, restoring sight, even raising the dead—all which these

CHAP. XXII.] WHO IS IT THAT SMOTE THEE ? 583

64 And when they had blindfolded him, they struck him on the face, and asked him, saying, Prophesy, who is it that smote thee?

65 And many other things blasphemously spake they against him.

66 ¶ [g] And as soon as it was day, [h] the elders of the people and the chief priests and the scribes came together, and led him into their council, saying,

67 [i] Art thou the Christ? tell us. And he said unto them, If I tell you, ye will not believe:

[g] Matt. xxvii. 1.
[h] Acts iv. 26. See Acts xxii. 5.
[i] Matt. xxvi. 63. Mark xiv. 61.

---

64. "Struck him on the face, and." So A., X., Γ, Δ, Λ, six later Uncials, most Cursives, Vulg., but omitted by B., K., L., M., T., Π, Copt., Sah., Cur. Syriac.

67. "Art thou the Christ? tell us." "If thou art the Christ tell us" (Revisers).

---

minions of the chief priests must have known, would have saved the Lord from such insults as these.

Upon the blindfolding, Quesnel remarks: "These soldiers abuse the Son of God without knowing Him; and Christians affront the God Whom they know as audaciously as if He were blindfolded, and could only guess at those who insult Him." And, again: "Thou sanctifiest these things by enduring them in Thy Divine Person; Thou makest of them a sacrifice to Thy Father, a pattern of patience and humility to me, and a fountain of grace to Thy whole Church."

66. "And as soon as it was day, the elders of the people and the chief priests," &c. This was a more formal meeting of the Sanhedrin: that which had taken place in the house of Caiaphas being a preliminary one to collect evidence, and confront the prisoner with the witnesses. It appears that it was a rule among the Jews that no sentence could be passed in the night. The Evangelists Matthew and Mark mention this meeting in the early morning, but give no account of its proceedings whatsoever. St. John makes no mention of it, but seems to imply that they led Jesus from the palace of Caiaphas to the hall of judgment, i.e., the Prætorium. It is quite possible, however, that on this occasion the more formal morning council assembled also in the house of Caiaphas. St. Luke, who has given no account of the judicial proceedings in the night before

68 And if I also ask *you*, ye will not answer me, nor let me go.

^k Matt. xxvi. 64. Mark xiv. 62. Heb. i. 3. & viii. 1.
69 ^k Hereafter shall the Son of man sit on the right hand of the power of God.

70 Then said they all, Art thou then the Son of God? And he said unto them, ^l Ye say that I am.

^l Matt. xxvi. 64. Mark xiv. 62.

68. "Me, nor let me go." So A., D., all later Uncials, almost all Cursives, old Latin, Vulg., Syriacs, but omitted by ℵ, B., L., T., 22, 131, 157, 209, Copt.
69. "Hereafter." "But from henceforth" (Revisers).

Caiaphas, seems to transfer these proceedings to the second assembly, for the narrative in our Evangelist of their questioning Him as to whether He was the Christ, and the Lord's answer, "Hereafter shall the Son of man sit on the right hand of God," and His avowing Himself to be the Son of God, seems to be a shortened account of the substance of what is recorded in St. Matthew and St. Mark.

No doubt the notes of what was of most importance in the midnight proceedings would be read before the more important assembly, or verbally given to them, and St. Luke might speak of these as if they were the actual proceedings; or again, after they had read the notes they might ask whether He allowed the substantial allegation against Him in such words as "If thou be the Christ tell us," and He would repeat His claim in the words "Hereafter shall the Son of man sit on the right hand of the power of God." This would either awaken them to the infinite greatness of Him Whom they were judging, or harden and condemn them.

70. "Then said they all, Art thou then the Son of God?" &c. But, in the words He had just said, He had claimed to be the Son of Man—in fact, the Son of Man of Daniel vii. How then could they ask Him whether He was the Son of God? Because they knew full well that His claim to be, in an unique sense, the Son of Man, carried with it a far higher claim. He claimed to be the Son of Man, not having his origin from the race, but as having come into the race from above. They knew well how He had habitually called Himself "the Son," and with Himself, as the Son, He had habitually associated "the Father," even God. Besides, the night before, the solemn adjuration of the High Priest was in the words, "I adjure thee by the living God that thou tell us whether thou

71 ᵐ And they said, What need we any further witness? for we ourselves have heard of his own mouth. ᵐ Matt. xxvi. 65. Mark xiv. 63.

be the Christ, the Son of God." And He had answered " Thou hast said. Nevertheless, I say unto you, Hereafter shall ye see the Son of man sitting on the right hand of power." So that on His lips when speaking of Himself, " Son of Man," and " Son of God " were convertible terms. He was Son of Man in a sense, and with claims and pretensions which would not be possible unless He were the very Son of God.

"Ye say that I am." This is a Jewish form of affirmation. "I am what ye say." Your question expects from Me the answer, "I am," and you are right. St. Mark, it is to be remembered, writing for Gentiles at Rome, makes the answer to be, "I am."

71. "And they said, What need we . . . . own mouth." This proves beyond the shadow of a doubt that they took the word " Son of God " in a sense which, in their view of Christ, implied blasphemy worthy of the severest punishment. They proceeded, through the hands of Pilate, to inflict upon Him a most cruel death. This He suffered them to do, though by one word, such as "I am a mere man, as thou art," He might have rescued Himself and saved them from the guilt of crucifying Him ; but He withheld this word, and was crucified because He made Himself the Son of God. He left it to God to vindicate the truth of His Sonship, which that God did by raising Him from the dead, and, further than this, God visited the people which, through their rulers and representatives, thus condemned Him, with the most terrific punishment, because they continued in the denial of His Sonship. And even more than this, God superseded a religion whose ministers maintained the strict solitary unity of the Divine Being, by a religion which maintained an Unity in Trinity. Such was the verdict of these men, and such the verdict of God upon them.

"Thou sittest at the right hand of God, in the glory of the Father. We believe that thou shalt come to be our Judge. We therefore pray thee help thy servants whom thou hast redeemed with thy precious blood."

CHAP. XXIII.

AND ᵃ the whole multitude of them arose, and led him unto Pilate.

2 And they began to accuse him, saying, We found this *fellow* ᵇ perverting the nation, and ᶜ forbidding to give tribute to Cæsar, saying ᵈ that he himself is Christ a King.

3 ᵉ And Pilate asked him, saying, Art thou the King of the Jews? And he answered him and said, Thou sayest *it*.

ᵃ Matt. xxvii. 2. Mark xv. 1. John xviii. 28.
ᵇ Acts xvii. 7.
ᶜ See Matt. xvii. 27. & xxii. 21. Mark xii. 17.
ᵈ John xix. 12.
ᵉ Matt. xxvii. 11. 1 Tim. vi. 13.

2. "The nation." So A., E., G., S., U., V., X., Γ, Δ, Λ, most Cursives; but א, B., D., H., K., L., M., R., T., sixty Cursives, old Latin, Vulg., Sah., Copt., Syriacs, Æth., read, "our nation."

1. "And the whole multitude of them arose, and led him unto Pilate." "The whole multitude." This seems to imply that there were many spectators and attendants in the morning sitting of the Sanhedrin. Their extraordinary earnestness in bringing about His condemnation is shown in their not sending a few of their body, but rising *en masse* and accompanying Him to the Prætorium.

2. "They began to accuse him, saying, We found this fellow perverting the nation," &c. The reckless wickedness and injustice of their proceedings is shown from the very first. At their two assemblies not a word had been said respecting His forbidding to give tribute: it was all connected with His making Himself the Son of God. Pilate, of course, would not have listened to them for a moment if they had come with such a charge, which would have been to him simply unintelligible; so they impudently and unscrupulously shifted their ground and accused of sedition the man who a day or two before had said, "Render unto Cæsar the things which are Cæsar's."

"Saying that he himself is Christ a King." In their own assemblies they accused him of pretending to be Christ the Son of God: to Pilate, of pretending to be Christ a King.

3, 4. "And Pilate asked him, saying, Art thou the King of the

CHAP. XXIII.] I FIND NO FAULT IN THIS MAN. 587

4 Then said Pilate to the chief priests and *to* the people, ^f^ I find no fault in this man. ^f^ 1 Pet. ii. 22.

5 And they were the more fierce, saying, He stirreth up the people, teaching throughout all Jewry, beginning from Galilee to this place.

6 When Pilate heard of Galilee, he asked whether the man were a Galilæan.

7 And as soon as he knew that he belonged unto ^g^ Herod's jurisdiction, he sent him to Herod, who himself ^g^ ch. iii. 1. also was at Jerusalem at that time.

---

6. "When Pilate heard of Galilee." So A., D., R., X., Γ, Δ, Λ, Π, later Uncials, all Cursives, old Latin, Vulg., Sah., Syriacs; but "of Galilee" omitted by ℵ, B., L., T., Copt.

Jews? . . . no fault in this man." If we only possessed this Gospel, or if we were without that of St. John, we should have here a great difficulty; for if any man had claimed to be king of so rebellious and excitable a people as the Jews, Pilate was bound to make some sort of inquiry; for this Man against whom such pretensions were alleged had lately made a sort of triumphal entry into Jerusalem, the excited crowds shouting before him, "Blessed be the king that cometh in the name of the Lord;" but instead of investigating the matter, Pilate dismisses it with the words, "I find no fault in this man." He had investigated, and he had been assured that Christ's Kingdom was not of this world, and that the mark of His subjects was witnessing to the truth. And so he answered the Lord's accusers with "I find no fault in him"—in this man. (John xviii. 33-38.)

5, 6, 7. "And they were the more fierce, saying, He stirreth up the people . . . at that time." Pilate, who heartily desired to have nothing to do with the matter, eagerly caught at the word Galilee, and finding that the Lord's usual abode was there, he sent Him to Herod, the tetrarch of Galilee, who was up at Jerusalem for the feast. He had had also a quarrel with Herod, and it is not at all improbable but that he wished to make this up, and endeavoured to do so by this acknowledgment of Herod's jurisdiction over these Galilæans who were sojourning in Jerusalem to attend the feast.

8. "And when Herod saw Jesus, he was exceeding glad . . . . done by Him." This was Herod Antipas, the adulterer, and the

8 ¶ And when Herod saw Jesus, he was exceeding glad:
for ʰ he was desirous to see him of a long *season*,
because ⁱ he had heard many things of him; and
he hoped to have seen some miracle done by him.

9 Then he questioned with him in many words; but he
answered him nothing.

ʰ ch. ix. 9.
ⁱ Matt. xiv. 1.
Mark vi. 14.

---

8. "He had heard many things." So A., R., X., Γ, Δ, Λ, later Uncials, most Cursives, old Latin, Vulg., Syriacs; but ℵ, B., D., K., L., M., T., Π, 1, 131, 157, 209, and ten other Cursives, Sah., Copt., Syr. (Cureton), omit "many things."

murderer of St. John the Baptist. Our Lord's judgment on his character is to be found in His words, "Go ye and tell that fox." Being the tetrarch of Galilee he must have constantly heard of the miracles of our Lord. The wife of a member of his household, Joanna the wife of Chuza, Herod's steward, was one of our Lord's followers, who ministered to Him of their substance. It is from St. Luke ix. 8, that we hear that a long time before this he desired to see our Lord out of curiosity. He desired to see some miracles in the same spirit as he would desire to see any other curious and unaccountable matter, but with not the smallest intention of acknowledging the claims which the Lord founded on His miracles. "One would apprehend he was in that most fearful state into which persons sometimes fall, when they have had their feelings once excited on the subject of religion, but still kept their vices; and also still continue to entertain an interest and curiosity in matters of religion, having lost godly fear." However, at last he had his wretched desire gratified; he was face to face with the Lord, but only to his greater condemnation. Instead of seeing a Divine miracle, he sees One apparently powerless and deserted, Whom it is in his power to insult and mock; and being angry and disappointed that, though a king, no notice is taken of him, he turns round upon the Lord and becomes His persecutor.

9. "Then he questioned with him in many words; but he answered him nothing." This may have been out of just indignation, inasmuch as Herod was the murderer of the Lord's forerunner, or it may have been out of mercy; for men have to give account of all messages from God, which any word from our Lord would have been, and assuredly Herod in his then state of mind could profit by nothing which the Lord said.

A GORGEOUS ROBE.

10 And the chief priests and scribes stood and vehemently accused him.

11 ᵏ And Herod with his men of war set him at nought, and mocked *him*, and arrayed him in a gorgeous robe, and sent him again to Pilate. ᵏ Isai. liii. 3.

12 ¶ And the same day ˡ Pilate and Herod were made friends together: for before they were at enmity between themselves. ˡ Acts iv. 27.

13 ¶ ᵐ And Pilate, when he had called together the chief priests and the rulers and the people, ᵐ Matt. xxvii. 23. Mark xv. 14. John xviii. 38. & xix. 4.

---

11. "Gorgeous." Rather, "white."

10-11. And the chief priests and scribes stood and vehemently accused him ... sent him again to Pilate." Notice the eagerness of the chief priests, in following him about. They seemed to have felt that their whole future influence in the so-called Theocracy depended on the Lord's condemnation.

"Arrayed him in a gorgeous robe:" not a purple, but a white robe. St. Ambrose draws a mystical meaning from it. "It is not without reason that He is arrayed by Herod in a white robe, as being a sign of His immaculate Passion."

12. "And the same day Pilate and Herod were made friends together ... enmity between themselves." What the occasion of this enmity was we are not told. Some have supposed that it arose from Pilate's cruelty in the slaughter of the Galilæans, mentioned in xiii. 1, and was on a matter of jurisdiction, and that Pilate by acknowledging Herod's jurisdiction over the Lord in some sort made amends.

I cannot but think that many good men make a serious mistake in citing this case of the reconciliation of Pilate and Herod as an illustration of the way in which wicked men of different parties will unite against Christ. Pilate had send Christ to Herod for the very purpose of avoiding passing sentence upon Him; and, no doubt, was, in his heart, sore displeased at His being sent back again. Herod had mocked Him because he was disappointed at not seeing a miracle, but he appears to have paid no attention to the vehement accusations of the chief priests against the Lord.

13-16. "And Pilate, when he had called together . . . . worthy of

14 Said unto them, ⁿ Ye have brought this man unto me,
as one that perverteth the people: and, behold, ᵒ I,
having examined *him* before you, have found no
fault in this man touching those things whereof ye accuse him:

15 No, nor yet Herod: for I sent you to him; and, lo,
nothing worthy of death is done unto him.

16 ᵖ I will therefore chastise him, and release him.

17 ᑫ (For of necessity he must release one unto them at the feast.)

18 And ʳ they cried out all at once, saying,
Away with this *man*, and release unto us Barabbas:

ⁿ ver. 1, 2.
ᵒ ver. 4.
ᵖ Matt. xxvii. 26. John xix. 1.
ᑫ Matt. xxvii. 15. Mark xv. 6. John xviii. 39.
ʳ Acts iii. 14.

---

15. "For I sent you to him." So A., D., (H.), X., Γ, Δ, Λ, later Uncials, most Cursives, most old Latin, Vulg., and Syriacs; but ℵ, B., K., L., M., T., Π, 157, and twenty other Cursives, f, Sah., Copt., read, "For he sent him back to us."

17. ("For of necessity . . . feast.") This whole verse omitted by A., B., K., L., T., Π, old Latin (a), Sah., Copt.; retained by ℵ, (D.), X., Γ, Δ, Λ, later Uncials, all Cursives, old Latin (b, c, e, f, ff², g ¹², l, q), Vulg., some Copt., Syriacs.

---

death is done unto him." The account of the proceedings narrated in these four verses is peculiar to St. Luke. Pilate very solemnly avouches for the Lord's innocence and appeals to the conduct of Herod as having virtually acquitted Him, but he now ventures on another step. He remembers that the time is come when according to the custom of the feast he must release to them one prisoner. He suggests that it should be the Lord, but in order to gratify their malice he offers to chastise Him first and then release Him. If He had committed no crime, but was entirely innocent, why should He suffer the cruel punishment of a Roman scourging, under the pain of which many sunk?

16 and 17. "I will therefore chastise him, and release him. (For of necessity he must release one unto them at the feast.)" The words of Pilate were probably those of St. John and St. Luke combined, "But ye have a custom that I should release unto you one at the passover (John xviii. 39), I will therefore chastise him and release him."

18. "And they cried out all at once, saying, Away with this man, and release," &c. But the people, instigated by the chief priests (Mark xv. 11), had already made up their minds upon the

CRUCIFY HIM, CRUCIFY HIM.

19 (Who for a certain sedition made in the city, and for murder, was cast into prison.)

20 Pilate therefore, willing to release Jesus, spake again to them.

21 But they cried, saying, Crucify *him*, crucify him.

22 And he said unto them the third time, Why, what evil hath he done? I have found no cause of death in him: I will therefore chastise him, and let *him* go.

23 And they were instant with loud voices, requiring that

---

prisoner whom they would have released. They apparently took no notice of Pilate's hint about the Lord, but crying aloud began to desire him "to do as he had ever done unto them." Then Pilate, in bitter mockery at both priests and people of a despised race, asked whether the prisoner to be released should not be "the King of the Jews," and then burst forth the cry from every lip, "Away with this man and release unto us Barabbas."

19. "Who for a certain sedition made in the city," &c. There can be little doubt, as I said in my notes on St. Matthew, that this sedition was not a political outbreak, but a raid for plunder, or St. Peter would not have reproached the Jews with "desiring a murderer to be granted unto them."

It is most probable that just before this he had received the message from his wife, which made him doubly anxious for the Lord's release, and so we read,

20-23. "Pilate therefore, willing to release Jesus . . . . . Crucify him, crucify him. And he said unto them the third time . . . . . requiring that he might be crucified." St. Luke alone mentions distinctly the three successive appeals of Pilate. The reader will remember the words of St. Peter in the Acts, "how the people denied him in the presence of Pilate, when he was determined to let him go."

The events immediately following this we find in John xix. 1-15, and Mark xv. 19. How the Lord was scourged, crowned with thorns, saluted with "Hail, King of the Jews," smitten with the reed and with the soldiers' hands, spit upon, worshipped in mockery, brought forth again wearing the crown of thorns and the purple robe, with the words "Behold the man." Again rejected with "Crucify him, crucify him." Then another awakening of

he might be crucified. And the voices of them and of the chief priests prevailed.

24 And ᵃ Pilate || gave sentence that it should be as they required.

25 And he released unto them him that for sedition and murder was cast into prison, whom they desired; but he delivered Jesus to their will.

ᵃ Matt. xxvii. 26. Mark xv. 15. John xix. 16.
|| Or, *assented*, Exod. xxiii. 2.

23. "And of the chief priests." So A., D., P., X., Δ, Λ, Π, later Uncials, all Cursives, old Latin (c, f), Syriacs, but omitted by א, B., L., a, b, e, ff², g¹², l, Sah., Copt.

Pilate's fear when he heard that Jesus claimed to be the Son of God. Then a return to the judgment hall, another questioning by Pilate, "Whence art thou?" Then fresh efforts of Pilate to release Him. Then still further cries of "Crucify him." Then the abjuration of the theocracy by the chief priests, "We have no king but Cæsar," and then Pilate's hand-washing, and then the final sentence in the words of St. Luke.

23-26. "And the voices of them and of the chief priests prevailed . . . . . he delivered Jesus to their will." What a sublime condemnation of human nature there is in these touching verses! The voices of them—of the rabble, the scum of Jerusalem—and of the chief priests, the successors of Aaron, Eleazer, Zadok, Joshua, the chief ministers of the only God-ordained religion then existing, prevailed—prevailed against innocence, and in favour of brutal guilt. And Pilate—who as a judge was by his office the minister of God for good—gave sentence that it should be as they required— gave sentence, not according to his conscience, not according to his perfect knowledge of the Lord's innocence, but according to his fears, his cowardice, his self-love,—as they required. They required not only blood, but blood shed in the most cruel way in which it could well be shed.

"And he released unto them him that for sedition and murder was cast into prison." A hardened villain guilty of the worst crimes against human society, and one who for plunder, no doubt, had destroyed life. But he delivered Jesus—One Who had in numberless instances prolonged life, alleviated the sufferings of life, restored the dead to life, above all, planted in innumerable breasts the hope of eternal life—"he delivered Jesus to their will."

"He delivered Jesus to their will." Mark this word "deli-

CHAP. XXIII.] ONE SIMON, A CYRENIAN. 593

26 ᵗ And as they led him away, they laid hold upon one Simon, a Cyrenian, coming out of the country, and on him they laid the cross, that he might bear *it* after Jesus.

ᵗ Matt. xxvii. 32. Mark xv. 21. See John xix. 17.

27 ¶ And there followed him a great company of people, and of women, which also bewailed and lamented him.

28 But Jesus turning unto them said, Daughters of Jeru-

---

livered," for in it the cruelty and wickedness of man, and the goodness and mercy of God meet.

As He had prophesied, He was delivered to the Gentiles, but it was by the determinate counsel and foreknowledge of God. (Acts ii. 23.) He was delivered to His enemies, but He was delivered "for our offences." Pilate seemed to deliver Him, but in a far higher sense God "delivered Him up for us all." He was delivered to the power of darkness, but it was that He might deliver us from the same power of darkness, and translate us into His kingdom. (Coloss. i. 13.)

26. "And as they led him away, they laid hold . . . . . bear it after Jesus." Simon is the type of all true followers of the Lord, for what he bears actually they bear spiritually. According to the words of the Lord, "He that will come after me, let him deny himself, and take up his cross and follow me;" and of His servant, "Let us go forth therefore unto him without the camp, bearing his reproach" (Heb. xiii. 13).

27. "And there followed him a great company of people and of women," &c. Apparently the multitude were mainly those who were indifferent or hostile: it was the women who are noticed as bewailing and lamenting. It is very remarkable that women seem always to have more readily than men received the teaching of the Lord and taken part with Him. A woman, a virgin, bore Him— a woman anointed His feet, a woman anointed Him for the burial, women followed Him, and "ministered to him of their substances:" women were attending beside the cross, women were first at the sepulchre. He seems to have removed the curse from the sex, so that they now are more ready to receive His truth than men.

28. "But Jesus turning unto them said, Daughters of Jerusalem, weep not for me," &c. St. Luke alone gives the account of His weeping over Jerusalem. And now instead of thinking of the sea

Q Q

594   WEEP FOR YOURSELVES.   [ST. LUKE.

salem, weep not for me, but weep for yourselves, and for your children.

u Matt. xxiv. 19. ch. xxi. 23.
29 ᵘ For, behold, the days are coming, in the which they shall say, Blessed *are* the barren, and the wombs that never bare, and the paps which never gave suck.

x Is. ii. 19.
Hos. x. 8.
Rev. vi. 16.
& ix. 6.
30 ˣ Then shall they begin to say to the mountains, Fall on us; and to the hills, Cover us.

---

of anguish which was about to engulph Him, He thinks rather of His countrymen and countrywomen, and their helpless little ones, and the doomed city.

"Weep not for me." Does He reject their sympathy? No. But He tells them that they and theirs have much more need of tears than He has, for though His sufferings will be unspeakably bitter, they will be short. On that very evening they will be all over, and on the day after the morrow He will come forth from the tomb incorruptible and impassible, but not so with the people and the city which reject Him.

29. "For behold the days are coming in the which," &c. To those among them who will survive and to their children the blessings of motherhood and of offspring will be turned into a curse. They shall see them perishing of hunger, slain barbarously, murdered, carried captive to be the bondmen and bondwomen of depraved and cruel Gentile masters. They shall even hear of those, perhaps their neighbours, in whom would be fulfilled the words of their great prophet, that their eyes should be evil towards their children that they should bare, and that they should eat them in the siege and straitness wherewith their enemies should distress them (Deut. xxviii. 56, 57.)

30. " Then shall they begin to say to the mountains, Fall on us; and to the hills, Cover us." We are told by Josephus that those who escaped the destruction of Jerusalem hid themselves in the dens and in the rocks of the mountains, but the words used by the Saviour forcibly remind us of the prophecy in the Book of Revelations, when, not the Jews, but all the impenitent, " Kings, great men, rich men, chief captains, every bondman, every freeman, will hide themselves in the dens and caves of the mountains, and call upon the mountains and rocks to fall upon them and hide them

CHAP. XXIII.] WHAT SHALL BE DONE IN THE DRY? 595

31 ʸFor if they do these things in a green tree, what shall be done in the dry?

32 ᶻAnd there were also two other, malefactors, led with him to be put to death.

33 And ᵃwhen they were come to the place,

y Prov. xi. 31.
Jer. xxv. 29.
Ezek. xx. 47.
& xxi. 3, 4.
1 Pet. iv. 17.
z Is. liii. 12.
Matt. xxvii. 38.
a Matt. xxvii. 33. Mark xv. 22. John xix. 17, 18.

from the wrath of the Lamb." So that in this short prophecy we have the same feature as in the longer prophecy of the Lord—the Lord passing from the destruction of Jerusalem and its people to the day of final vengeance on all the impenitent, of which the overthrow of the devoted city was but a type and forecast.

"Weep not for me, but weep for yourselves." "The admonition we cannot but consider as intended for us all; that when we feel our human sympathies and compassions moved towards Him at the recital of His sufferings, we are to think that He turns to us, and tells us to think of ourselves, and of our own sins, that occasioned those sufferings; that when we venture to approach and gaze on Him, by these contemplations we forget not ourselves also."

31. "For if they do these things in a green tree, what shall be done in the dry?" This seems to have been a proverbial expression among the Jews. If the fire seizes and consumes green wood which has life and sap in it, and is yet capable of bearing fruit, how much more speedily and effectually will it consume dry, sapless, dead wood. And so, if God allowed for our sakes One Who had done no wrong, but had always served Him, to suffer such things, what will He bring upon those who have no life of God in them, and are dead in trespasses and sins, because they finally reject the offer of Life in the Crucified?

32. "And there were also two other, malefactors, led with him," &c. St. Luke alone mentions that these malefactors were led with Him—that is, for the whole, or part of the way. From the other evangelists we should suppose that they were brought singly to the place of execution. If it be as is reported by St. Luke, it adds emphasis to the prophecy, "He was numbered with the transgressors."

33. "And when they were come to the place which is called Calvary . . . crucified him." It is impossible in this age to realize

which is called ‖ Calvary, there they crucified him, and the malefactors, one on the right hand, and the other on the left.

‖ Or, *The place of a skull.*

these words, since crucifixion is a thing of the past, for Constantine abolished it. It was no longer meet that vile criminals should suffer the form of the Redeeming Death.

We cannot even in imagination realize its pain, and we are still less able to realize the shame of a Death by which the Son of God got the victory over moral evil, by which He abolished Death, by which He reconciled God and sinners, by which He won the highest place in the universe, and a throne in the hearts of all the people of God.

We cannot add to what we have written in our notes on St. Matthew and St. Mark, respecting the pain and ignominy of this form of death; but we must say something more upon the purpose for which God suffered His Son to undergo such a death at the hands of His creatures.

It fulfilled the purpose for which the Word became Flesh. The flesh which He took was capable of exquisite pain and death; and the Eternal Word took this flesh in order that, suffering and dying in it, He might atone for our sins, and through the Resurrection of this crucified Body endue us with His Life. Thus the Psalmist, as interpreted by the Apostolic writer: " Sacrifice and burnt offering thou wouldest not, but a body hast thou prepared me. In burnt offerings and sacrifices for sin thou hast had no pleasure. Then said I, Lo, I come (in the volume of the book it is written of me) to do thy will, O God. By the which will [of the Eternal Father] we are sanctified through the offering of the Body of Christ once for all " (Heb. x. 5, 8, 10).

Again, similar words: " Forasmuch, then, as the children are partakers of flesh and blood, he also himself likewise took part of the same; that, through death, he might destroy him that had the power of death, that is, the devil; and deliver them who, through fear of death, were all their lifetime subject to bondage " (Heb. ii. 14).

Such is the purpose of the Death on the Cross.

It exhibits the character of God as nothing else can, for it exhibits God sacrificing Himself. The Deity, as long as He dwelt in His own unapproachable Light, could not sacrifice Himself. He took upon Him a nature capable of the uttermost self-sacrifice, in order

CHAP. XXIII.]   FATHER, FORGIVE THEM.   **597**

34 ¶ Then said Jesus, Father, ᵇforgive them;   ᵇ Matt. v. 44.
Acts vii. 60.
1 Cor. iv. 12.

34. The uncritical reader will be surprised and shocked to know that the first word upon the Cross—the Divinest, the most Evangelical word in the New Testament—is marked with doubt by some modern critics because it is not in two Uncial MSS. (B. and D.). It is to be found in ℵ, A., C., F., G., H., K., L. (which so often sides with B.), M., Q., S., U., V., Γ, Δ, Λ, Π, all Cursives except two (38, 435), most old Latin (c, e, f, ff², l), Vulg., all Syriac, all Memphitic except two, Arm., Æth. Judged by the Divine character of the utterance, and the weight of the evidence of all parts of Christendom in its favour, its omission from any manuscript must be that manuscript's utter condemnation.

that He might exercise the uttermost self-sacrifice. "Herein is love, not that we loved God, but that he loved us, and gave his Son to be the propitiation for our sins."

It exhibits the value of the soul. "Come (says this crucified God by the voice of His Blood), come and see by the expense of what I suffer, how great the value of thy soul is. Thou esteemest thyself, but not sufficiently. Contemplate attentively thyself in Me: thou wilt see what thou art, and what is thy value. Thou must prize thyself by My merits, for I am thy price; and that salvation which thou givest up on so many occasions is nothing but what I am Myself, since I deliver myself up for the securing of it. In this manner He speaks to sinners . . . . . The mystery of the Cross is, therefore, a mystery of the Divine Wisdom. For, as St. Chrysostom argues, a mystery that gives me such high ideas of God, that inspires me with an infinite horror of sin, that makes me value my salvation preferable to all past, present, future, and even possible things, in whatever point of view I behold it, should appear in my eyes a mystery of wisdom. . . . . For this reason the Apostle of the Gentiles, possessed with a belief of this mystery, made open profession of knowing nothing except Jesus Christ, and Him crucified. For in this crucified Jesus he found whatever he wanted to know —that is, the eminent knowledge of God, and the salutary knowledge of himself. 'I judged not to know anything among you, save Jesus Christ, and him crucified.'" (Bourdaloue, "Sermon on the Passion of our Saviour.")

34. "Then said Jesus, Father forgive them; for they know not what they do." These are the first of the seven words upon the Cross. The Lord was in Himself the Priest and the Victim in one Person. At the moment that He surrendered Himself to die as the Victim, He acted as the all-prevailing Priest : for as it was foretold of Him, "He made intercession for the transgressors." (Isaiah liii.)

for ^c they know not what they do. And ^d they parted his raiment, and cast lots.

^c Acts iii. 17.
^d Matt. xxvii. 35. Mark xv. 24. John xix. 23.

And now also He set us an example that we should love and pray for our enemies. He had before said to us, "Love your enemies; pray for them which despitefully use you and persecute you;" and now in His own person He carries this out.

But who are they for whom He prays? Not, surely, the soldiers only. They were only obeying orders; though they might have shown by their rough and pitiless demeanour that the horrible work was not distasteful to them.

But did the intercession embrace Pilate—the Jews and their rulers? Certainly; for St. Peter said expressly, "And now, brethren, I wot that through ignorance ye did it, *as did also your rulers*" (Acts iii. 17). And St. Paul: "The hidden wisdom, which *none of the princes of this world knew*, for, had they known it, they would not have crucified the Lord of Glory" (1 Cor. ii.).

But do these words embrace all sinners? Especially do they include baptized sinners? Are we not told that by wilful sin we crucify the Son of God afresh? Does the Lord here pray for those who do this? I cannot tell. I will endeavour to answer the question; but I will answer it, as far as one dare answer it, in the words of one who has had far, far more experience than most pastors in dealing with individual souls. Keble writes: "We have put forth our hands, and have helped to crucify Him; and that although we knew, or ought to know what we are doing, what reason have we to hope that we, too, may be of the number of those for whom He prayed, 'Father, forgive them; for they know not what they do'?"

"Truly, we could have no hope, were it not for that infinite overflowing mercy of His which, if we do but now truly and perseveringly repent, will, we know, make allowance for all our weaknesses and errors and ignorances. We dare not make allowance for them ourselves—we know not how far they were our own fault; but if we truly and unfeignedly give ourselves up, soul and body, to do and suffer His Will, He will allow for them. He will forgive us the grievous and shameful things for which we cannot forgive ourselves. Even of the best instructed among Christians it may be truly said that he knows not what he does, when he breaks his baptismal vow. Who can measure the pain, the shame, the dis-

CHAP. XXIII.]   LET HIM SAVE HIMSELF.   599

35 And ^e the people stood beholding. And the ^f rulers also with them derided *him*, saying, He saved others; let him save himself, if he be Christ, the chosen of God.

e Ps. xxii. 17. Zech. xii. 10.
f Matt. xxvii. 39. Mark xv. 29.

36 And the soldiers also mocked him, coming to him, and offering him vinegar,

37 And saying, If thou be the king of the Jews, save thyself.

---

35. "And the rulers also." "Also" omitted by א, D., and five Cursives, but retained by A., B., C., L., all other Uncials and Cursives, &c.

"With them" omitted by א, B., C., D., L., Q., X., 33, 47, 69, 157, 346, old Latin (b, c, e, ff², l), Copt., Syriac (Schaaf), but retained by A., Γ, Δ, Λ, Π, all later Uncials, most Cursives, f, Vulg., and Cur. Syriac.

"Christ, the chosen of God," or, " If this is the Christ of God, His chosen" (Revisers).

order which a single bad action in a Christian person may cause in the world and kingdom of the Almighty, each part of which is so wonderfully linked and entwined with every other part?" (From sermons on "Words on the Cross" in Holy Week.)

"And they parted his raiment, and cast lots." In all cases of crucifixion the raiment seems to have been the perquisite of the soldiers who kept guard. It is probable that they cast lots twice, once for their choice of the garments which were parted into four divisions, and a second time for the seamless vesture.

35. "And the people stood beholding. And the rulers also with them," &c. Some expositors, holding the words, "with them," to be no part of the text, consider that the people were apathetic, and gazed as they would have done at any other execution, and that the rulers only derided Him; but this is contrary to the testimony of St. Matthew and Mark, "And they that passed by reviled him," &c. These bad men must have known His miracles of Salvation. How He had in numberless instances saved men from disease, from blindness, from lameness, from the power of evil spirits. Above all, they knew perfectly how He had but a short time before saved a man from the dominion of death. But He heeded not these mockeries. In all probability He interceded in Spirit for those who cast them in His teeth.

36, 37. "And the soldiers also mocked him, . . . king of the Jews, save thyself." The soldiers, as I have said, could have had no malevolent feelings against Him on account of His teaching, or

600   THIS IS THE KING OF THE JEWS.   [St. Luke.

38 ᵍ And a superscription also was written over him in letters of Greek, and Latin, and Hebrew, THIS IS THE KING OF THE JEWS.

39 ¶ ʰ And one of the malefactors which were

ᵍ Matt. xxvii. 37. Mark xv. 26. John xix. 19.
ʰ Matt. xxvii. 44. Mark xv. 32.

38. "In letters of Greek, and Latin, and Hebrew." So ℵ, A., C³., D., all later Uncials, all Cursives, most old Latin, Vulg., Syriac (Schaaf), Arm., Æth.; omitted by B., C., L., a, Sah., Copt., Syriac (Cureton).

Messianic claims. They simply regarded Him as a Jew, a fanatical or perhaps disaffected Jew: and these reproaches were aimed at the despised Jewish race, of which they assumed Him to be the pretended king. With respect to their offering Him vinegar it has been said, "The soldiers pretend to treat Jesus as a king, to whom the festive cup is presented."

38. "And a superscription also was written over him in letters of Greek, ... This is the king of the Jews." This inscription was written by Pilate himself. Of course it was written in mockery and scorn, but not so much of Jesus Himself as of His crucifiers. They, feeling the insult, desired that the title should be altered into a mere assertion of His pretensions. They would have it worded, "He said—This Man said—I am the King of the Jews." But Pilate refused to alter it: being in this, as I firmly believe, upheld by a higher power: for Jesus was, both by descent and through God's election, the King of the Jews: for the angel had said unto Mary before His conception, "The Lord God shall give unto him the throne of his father David."

But was He not far more than the King of the Jews? was He not to be the King of all men, the King of Kings? Yes, but this King of a world-wide dominion, foretold in so many prophecies, was first to be the King of Zion, "Yet have I set my king upon my holy hill of Zion."

Respecting the trilingual form of the inscription, Theophylact aptly remarks: "It is said in Greek, Latin, and Hebrew, by which it was signified that the most powerful of the nations (as the Romans), the wisest (as the Greeks), those who most worshipped God (as the Jewish nation), must be made subject to the dominion of Christ.

39. "And one of the malefactors which were hanged railed on him, saying, If thou be," &c. This most remarkable and instructive

SAVE THYSELF AND US.

hanged railed on him, saying, If thou be Christ, save thyself and us.

39. "If thou be Christ." So A., all later Uncials, and all Cursives, old Latin (c, f, q), Vulg., Syriacs; but ℵ, B., C., L., some old Latin (a, b, ff²), Sah., Copt., Cureton Syriac, Arm., Æth., read, "Art thou not the Christ?"

incident is found only in St. Luke. St. Luke alone, who here relates the conversion of one of them, calls them "malefactors" (workers of evil, κακοῦργοι). St. Matthew and St. Mark call them robbers. St. John in no way indicates their crimes, or even that they were criminals, but simply speaks of them as "two other." Archbishop Trench, whose chapter upon them in his "Studies of the Gospels" is as exhaustive as any study of such a Scripture incident can well be, supposes that they were not even common robbers in the sense of men who got their living by plunder and violence, but belonged to a band of those Jews who resisted by violence the Roman yoke, and, being outlawed, betook themselves to plunder as a means of subsistence. These were the zealots who at the time of the siege of Jerusalem had developed into the Sicarii, whose possession of the temple brought such unutterable misery upon Jerusalem. He even supposes that they may have been of the same company, or band, as Barabbas, and that as Pilate was forced to release Barabbas, he revenged himself by sending his two principal adherents to be crucified with the King of the Jews: so that Pilate made these men partakers of our Lord's crucifixion, rather in scorn of the Jews than in hatred or contempt of Jesus. In this way the vulgarity of their lives of crime is diminished, and some explanation attempted to be given of the fact that one who was punished for crimes of violence should exhibit such nobleness of character. But the Scriptures are totally silent about this. In St. Luke's eyes they are simply "evil workers;" and Barabbas is supposed to be a mere murderer. He was cast into prison for sedition and murder, and St. Luke represents St. Peter as saying, "Ye desired a murderer to be granted unto you." Since, then, nothing extenuating is said of them, it is safer to suppose that they were criminals of a bad type, though one might have possessed much better dispositions than the other, and so the Lord's Almighty Grace is the more magnified in the plucking of one of them as a brand from the burning.

"Railed. . . . . If thou be Christ, save thyself and us." The rail-

40 But the other answering rebuked him, saying, Dost not thou fear God, seeing thou art in the same condemnation ?

41 And we indeed justly; for we receive the due reward of our deeds: but this man hath done nothing amiss.

---

ing here is in the scornful expression of unbelief. Canst thou be the Christ if thou sufferest thy subjects to treat thee so?

" And us." He believed that the Lord could save neither them nor Himself.

40. "But the other answering rebuked him, saying, ... same condemnation." SS. Matthew and Mark seem to tell us that both the robbers joined in the insults offered to the Lord. They may have both done so at the first, and the one who repented may have been brought to a better mind by seeing the patience and forbearance, and submission of the Lord. Or it may be that the impenitent one was from the first more bitter and violent, and seemed to answer for the other, who may have for some time held his peace, and so was accounted by the bystanders to be of the same mind towards the Lord. I much incline to this latter, for if he had joined in the other's insults, he could hardly so soon have reproached his fellow with the want of the fear of God.

" Dost not thou fear God ? " This is a question which implies that his fellow had no fear of God, and this notwithstanding the agony of pain he was then suffering. " It is nothing so strange, he would say, that secure sinners, whom justice has not yet overtaken, for whom God's judgments are, as yet, far out of sight, should dare thus to open their mouths against the Holy One of God; but thou, upon thy cross, with such teaching as that might give thee, with such evidence as that affords that God is not mocked, that men eat at last of the fruit of their doing, dost thou venture upon the same ? " (Trench.)

" The same condemnation," sharing the same awful suffering might have softened his heart, and inspired him with some pity for a patient fellow sufferer.

41. " And we indeed justly; for we receive the due reward of our deeds." No expression of conviction of sin can be more practical than this: he was suffering the most horribly cruel punishment; and remembering his past life of violence and bloodshed he accepts it in the words, " We, indeed, justly, for we receive the due reward of our deeds."

CHAP. XXIII.]   LORD, REMEMBER ME.   **603**

42 And he said unto Jesus, Lord, remember me when thou comest into thy kingdom.

43 And Jesus said unto him, Verily I say unto thee, To day shalt thou be with me in paradise.

---

42. "And he said unto Jesus, Lord, remember me." So A., א{c}, C². , all later Uncials, all Cursives, old Latin, Vulg., Syriacs (Cureton and Schaaf), Æth.; but א, B., C., L., Sah., Copt., read, "He said, Jesus remember me."

"But this man hath done nothing amiss." These words have been interpreted as if he here asserts the theological truth of the absolute sinlessness of the Lord, but such cannot be. He could not have known the Lord personally, much less intimately; and he could not have had a special revelation about so deep a thing: but no doubt he had heard of the Lord's life—how He went about doing good, healing the bodies of men, and teaching their souls the best truths of God, and so he rightly judged that such an one had done nothing worthy of the slightest punishment, much less of one of such extreme cruelty.

42. "And he said unto Jesus, Lord, remember me when thou comest," &c. All seem agreed that no prayer of faith of which we have any record equals this.

"To believe that He whose only token of royalty was the crown of thorns that still clung to His bleeding brows, was a King, and had a kingdom; that He on whose eyes the mists of death were already hanging, was indeed the Prince of life, wielding in those pierced hands, nailed so helplessly to the cross, the keys of death and hell . . . . . that it would profit something, in that mysterious world whither they were both hastening, to be remembered by this crucified Man—that was a faith indeed . . . . . Everything seemed to give the lie to Christ's pretensions. Disciples and Apostles themselves had fallen away and fled . . . . . and then in the midst of this universal unbelief, one, all whose anterior life might seem to have unfitted him for this heroic act of faith, does homage, not indeed in outward act, for his limbs are nailed to the tree, but in heart and word, to Jesus as the King of Israel, as the Lord of the spirits of all flesh." (Trench.)

43. "And Jesus said unto him, Verily I say unto thee, To day shalt thou be," &c. This is the second word on the Cross, and it also is the word of the Great High Priest. As the first word was one of Intercession, so this of Absolution—full, free, immediate. I

604 DARKNESS. [ST. LUKE.

44 [1] And it was about the sixth hour, and there was a darkness over all the || earth until the ninth hour.

[1] Matt. xxvii. 45. Mark xv. 33.

|| Or, *land*.

44. "And it was about." So ℵ, A., C., D., Q., R., X., Γ, Δ, Λ, Π, all later Uncials, all Cursives, old Latin, Vulg., Syriacs, Sah., Arm.; but B.. C*., L., Copt., read, "And it was now about."

dare not comment upon it. I rather reproduce the words of a sermon preached within a stone's throw of the place where this Divine and most gracious utterance proceeded from the Lord. "What power, O robber, enlightened thee? Who taught thee to worship that despised Man, thy companion on the Cross? O Eternal Light, which givest light to them that are in darkness. . . . . . Thy deeds are not such as should make thee be of good cheer; but that the King is here, dispensing benefits. The request reached unto a distant time; but the grace is very speedy. 'Verily, I say unto thee, *this day* shalt thou be with Me in Paradise;' because *to day* thou hast heard My voice, and hast not hardened thine heart. Verily, speedily I passed sentence upon Adam, very speedily I pardon thee. To him it was said, 'In the day wherein thou eatest thou shalt surely die;' but thou to-day hast obeyed the faith, to-day is thy salvation. Adam by the tree fell; thou by the tree are brought into Paradise. I say not unto thee this day shalt thou depart, but, this day shalt thou be with Me.

"O mighty and ineffable grace! 'Where sin abounded, there grace did much more abound.' They who had borne the burden and heat of the day had not yet entered; and he of the eleventh hour entered. Let none murmur against the good man of the house, for he says, 'Friend, I do thee no wrong; is it not lawful for me to do what I will with mine own?' The robber has a wish to work righteousness, but death prevents him. I wait not exclusively for work, I have accepted faith. I am come who feed My sheep among the lilies. I am come to feed My sheep in the gardens. I have *found a sheep*, a *lost* one, but I lay it on My shoulders, for he believes, since he himself has said, 'I have gone astray like a lost sheep. We receive the due reward of our deeds. Lord remember me when Thou comest in Thy kingdom.'" (Cyril of Jerusalem.)

44-45. "And it was about the sixth hour, and there was a darkness . . . . . rent in the midst." This could not have been an

CHAP. XXIII.] THE RENDING OF THE VEIL. 605

45 And the sun was darkened, and ᵏ the veil of the temple
was rent in the midst.   ᵏ Matt. xxvii.
51. Mark xv.
38.

45. "And the sun was darkened." So A., D., Q., R., X., Γ, Δ, Λ, Π, all later Uncials, most Cursives, old Latin (a, b, c, e, f, ff², l, q), Vulg., Syriac (Cur. and Schaaf); but ℵ, B., C*., L., some evangelisteria, and Sah., read, "The sun being eclipsed" (or, the sun's light failing) (τοῦ ἡλίου ἐκλίποντος).

eclipse, for such a phenomenon can only happen when there is a new moon, and it was then full moon. Besides, the obscuration of a total eclipse can only last a few seconds. Very many so-called natural causes, some within the range of our atmosphere, others beyond it,¹ as in the sun's photosphere, might have occasioned it, that is, if we are forced on such an occasion to seek for a natural cause. If it was owing to a natural cause, as the intervening of a very dense cloud, still the occurrence at that particular juncture was brought about by an act of God's special power, and was designed to reveal to all in Jerusalem—very probably to all in Palestine—that the Death of the Crucified was no common death; the very frame of nature itself seemed to mourn for it.

These phenomena in the outer world—the darkness, the rending of the veil, the opened graves, could not have been without their effect. They must have been remembered long after Pentecost, and no doubt contributed somewhat to the readiness with which so vast a number of the dwellers in Jerusalem then received the Gospel.

"And the veil of the temple was rent in the midst." This is narrated by our Evangelist a little before its proper place. I have commented very fully upon it in my notes on the two first synoptics. The Epistle to the Hebrews teaches us its significance—that the way into the holiest of all, into the very presence chamber of God, is made manifest by the Death of Christ. There is now no obstacle between us and God. The existence of the veil in the

---

¹ Godet in a note mentions a remarkable instance of the obscuration of the sun at midday, the cause of which seems to have been beyond the limits of our atmosphere. "M. Liais, a well-known naturalist, relates that on the 11th of April, 1860, in the province of Pernambuco, while the sky was perfectly clear, the sun became dark about midday to such a degree that for some seconds it was possible to look at it. The solar disc appeared surrounded with a ring having the colours of the rainbow, and quite near it there was seen a bright star which must have been Venus. The phenomenon lasted for some minutes. M. Liais attributes it to cosmical nebulæ floating in space beyond our atmosphere. A similar phenomenon must have occurred in the years 1106, 1208, 1547, and 1706." ("Revue Germanique," 1860.)

46 ¶ And when Jesus had cried with a loud voice, he said, [1]Father, into thy hands I commend my spirit: [m]and having said thus, he gave up the ghost.

[1] Ps. xxxi. 5. 1 Pet. ii. 3.
[m] Matt. xxvii. 50. Mark xv. 37. John xix. 30.

temple betokened that there was not as yet perfect reconciliation. Now there is, but solely through the Death of Christ. If God had opened the eyes of any godly Jew to understand its significance, it would have been to him the most perfect outward sign or parable of completed reconciliation conceivable.

46. "And when Jesus had cried with a loud voice, he said, Father, into thy hands," &c. All three Synoptics record that the moment before His Death He cried *with a loud voice*, thereby showing that "His natural force was not abated." He died not through weakness, but by an act of His own will. At the moment of His saying the seventh and last word, He breathed out His Spirit to God.

"Father, into thy hands I commend my spirit." These words show that the cloud, the horror of darkness, which for a brief season had made him feel as if forsaken by God, had rolled away. He died in the full consciousness of His Father's presence and love.

"Father, into thy hands I commend my spirit." These were human words, issuing from the depths of His lower and assumed nature. They are for us—for all the dying. Because He said them we are emboldened to say them. But not only in the hour of death, but in the hour of temptation—in the conflict of our natural with our spiritual man, we must say them too. *They* only can hope to say these words with acceptance at the hour of death who have all their lives lived in the spirit of them. In lives full of changes and chances like ours, we who know not what a day or an hour may bring forth, have reason to say them constantly. Immense numbers of Christians never retire to rest without commending themselves to God's keeping in these words.[1]

The fact that the Lord thought good to say such a prayer teaches us the awfulness of death—even the death of the most righteous. Death, though its sting is removed, is not to be thought lightly of.

---

[1] Because the office of Compline—the last of the seven "hours"—contains the first verses of Psalm xxxi., in which verses they occur.

47 ⁿ Now when the centurion saw what was done, he glorified God, saying, Certainly this was a righteous man.

<small>n Matt. xxvii. 54. Mark xv. 39.</small>

48 And all the people that came together to that sight, beholding the things which were done, smote their breasts, and returned.

49 ° And all his acquaintance, and the women that followed him from Galilee, stood afar off, beholding these things.

<small>o Ps. xxxviii. 11. Matt. xxvii. 55. Mark xv. 40. See John xix. 25.</small>

It is a fearful mystery. The Church does well in teaching us to say, "In the hour of death, Good Lord, deliver us," and in putting into our lips such words as, "O holy and merciful Saviour, suffer us not at our last hour, for any pains of death, to fall from thee."

47. "Now when the centurion saw what was done, he glorified God, saying," &c. According to SS. Matthew and Mark he confessed Him to be the Son of God. No doubt he said both the things attributed to him: "This was a righteous man," "This was the Son of God." We are to remember that the term "righteous One" was especially applied to Christ by the men of His day and country. He was treated as the worst of sinners, and yet was the righteous, the just One (Acts iii. 14; vii. 52; and perhaps James v. 6).

48. "And all the people that came together to that sight . . . . smote," &c. It is probable that the blaspheming part of the multitude had been scared away by the signs and portents, and that those who remained were, most of them, somewhat better disposed, and now smote their breasts, as if they felt that some terrible wickedness had been committed, and that it would be visited upon their city and nation; and so thy did what the publican in the parable did. They smote on their breasts in token of contrition, and in deprecation of the wrath they had too good reason to fear.

49. "And all his acquaintance, and the women that followed him," &c. At some time during the latter part of the crucifixion certain of the women (according to St. John, the Lord's mother, her sister Mary of Cleophas, and Mary Magdalene) stood by the cross. His mother was led away by St. John, and the others, perhaps, accompanied her, and afterwards were not permitted to come near to the cross.

50 ¶ ᵖ And, behold, *there was* a man named Joseph, a counseller; *and he was* a good man, and a just: 51 (The same had not consented to the counsel and deed of them;) *he was* of Arimathæa, a city of the Jews: ᑫ who also himself waited for the kingdom of God.

ᵖ Matt. xxvii. 57. Mark xv. 42. John xix. 38.

ᑫ Mark xv. 43. ch. ii. 25, 38.

52 This *man* went unto Pilate, and begged the body of Jesus.

53 ʳ And he took it down, and wrapped it in linen, and laid it in a sepulchre that was hewn in stone, wherein never man before was laid.

ʳ Matt. xxvii. 59. Mark xv. 46.

---

51. "Who also himself." So A., E., F., G., H., S., V., Δ, Λ, most Cursives (1, 33, 131, 209); but ℵ, B,, C., D., L., 69, old Latin (a, b, e, l), Sah., Copt., omit "also himself."
53. "Wrapped it." So A., L., P., X., Γ, Δ, Λ, Π, all later Uncials, most Cursives; but ℵ, B., C., D., most old Latin, Vulg., &c., read "Him."

50-56. "And, behold, there was a man named Joseph . . . . according to the commandment." The account of the Lord's burial by Joseph of Arimathea is virtually the same in the first three Gospels. St. Luke says somewhat more respecting his moral character—that he was a good man and a just, and that he had not consented to the counsel and deed of them; from which it would seem that he had attended the meetings of the Sanhedrim, and had opposed the wicked ruling of the majority.

"And he took it down, and wrapped it in linen . . . before was laid." The Burial of the Lord is a part of the Gospel. Thus St. Paul: "I declare unto you the Gospel which I preached unto you . . . . that Christ died for our sins, according to the Scriptures; and *that he was buried*, and that he rose again the third day" (1 Cor. xv.). His Burial was an assurance that His Resurrection was a reality: for His Body was taken down by friends in the presence of foes, who knew that He was dead, and deposited by them, not in a common tomb, but in a cave, hollowed out of a hill side, with a great stone rolled to block up the entrance, which was guarded by the soldiers of Pilate.

His burial, also, was the last humiliation offered to Him, for though Joseph and Nicodemus and the women who assisted performed it as a work of piety and love, yet in it He was not the less

54 And that day was ⁸the preparation, and the sabbath drew on.   ˢ Matt. xxvii. 62.

55 And the women also, ᵗwhich came with him   ᵗ ch. viii. 2. from Galilee, followed after, and ᵘ beheld the   ᵘ Mark xv. 47. sepulchre, and how his body was laid.

56 And they returned, and ˣ prepared spices and   ˣ Mark xvi. 1. ointments; and rested the sabbath day ʸ according   ʸ Ex. xx. 10. to the commandment.

---

associated with us, whose bodies must be committed to the ground, earth to earth, ashes to ashes, dust to dust; He was the incorruptible, and yet was buried, and they prepared to embalm Him as if He had been corruptible. In birth from a womb, and in burial in a tomb, He was one with His sinful brethren.

And the burial of the Lord is in a remarkably mysterious way connected with our Baptism. The font represents the grave of the Lord, in which, as having died with Him, we are mystically and sacramentally buried, and from which we rise again, endued with new life from Him, as He rose from His grave endued with new life. Thus St. Paul: "Buried with him in Baptism, wherein also ye were raised with him through faith in the working of God which raised him from the dead" (Coloss. ii. 12, Revised Version). And, again, "We were buried with him, therefore, through Baptism into death, that like as Christ was raised from the dead through the glory of the Father, so we also might walk in newness of life" (Rom. vi. 1-4, Revised Version).

54. "And that day was the preparation." It was the Friday evening, before six o'clock, when the Sabbath commenced. And in that year that Sabbath, being at once the Passover festival and the Sabbath, was a very great day indeed.

"Beheld the sepulchre, and how his body was laid." It is remarkable that each of the Synoptics mentions how the women observed the place of the body. St. Matthew mentions particularly that "they were sitting over against the sepulchre;" St. Mark, that "they beheld where he was laid;" St. Luke, "how his body was laid."

56. "(They) rested the sabbath day according to the commandment." So strictly did they observe this Sabbath, for it was the last. Henceforth the Lord's day was to take its place.

CHAP. XXIV.

NOW [a] upon the first *day* of the week, very early in the morning, they came unto the sepulchre, [b] bringing

[a] Matt. xxviii. 1. Mark xvi. 1. John xx. 1.
[b] ch. xxiii. 56.

1. " Now upon the first day, . . . very early in the morning," &c. The discrepancies between St. Luke and the other Evangelists in their accounts of the occurrences of the morning of Easter Sunday seem insuperable. I shall endeavour to show that there is a plain principle by which the narratives can be reconciled, and this is, steadily to keep in view the purpose which each Evangelist had in giving us his particular history of the events of the Resurrection morning.

St. Matthew, beyond all doubt, writes for his countrymen, or rather selects that part of the body of tradition which they, as Jews, most required. On this account he brings forward the angel of the Lord, the special messenger of the God of their fathers, as descending, rolling away the stone, striking the keepers with deathly fear, and encouraging the devoted women. After this, having given one appearance of the Lord to the women, with a message to the disciples, he passes on to refute the falsehood spread far and wide among the Jews that the Lord had been stolen away whilst the guard slept; and he concludes with the appearance of the Lord in Galilee, which was not only the most important because of the Apostolic commission, but was the one which the Lord had specially promised.

St. Mark, writing most probably for Roman Christians, relates the account of the appearance of the angel to the women, but breaks off in his narrative before the appearance of the Lord to the women which we have in St. Matthew; so that his account cannot be critically compared with that of St. Luke, though he evidently records in a very abbreviated form the appearance on the way to Emmaus.

St. John mentions the visits to the sepulchre of no women except Mary Magdalene, to whom the Lord first appeared, and through whom He sent a message to His disciples respecting the Ascension,

the spices which they had prepared, and certain *others* with them.

1. "And certain others with them." So A., D., X., Γ, Δ, Λ, Π, all later Uncials, almost all Cursives, f, q, Sah., Syriacs, Arm.; but omitted by א, B., C., L., 33, 124, a, b, c, e, ff², g¹, l, Vulg., Copt.

and not respecting the meeting in Galilee. St. John's narrative respecting the Magdalene seems intended as a preparation for his account of the meeting with the two. The mysterious words, "Touch me not, for I am not yet ascended to my Father; but go to my brethren, and say unto them, I ascend unto my Father and your Father," &c., seems to prepare us better for the unutterable mystery of the words, "As my Father sent me, so send I you," "Receive ye the Holy Ghost."

And now let us come to St. Luke. What is his purpose? Evidently to arrive, as soon as possible, at what he conceived to be his special communication—the appearance of the Lord to the two disciples on the way to Emmaus. But this account must have some introduction, because it reports a conversation with two persons, who had set off for a journey into the country before any account of any appearance of the Lord had reached the body of disciples whom they left in Jerusalem. These two were evidently present with those disciples to whom the women brought the account of the vision of angels, but, like the rest, they seemed to them as telling "idle tales, and they believed them not"; and having heard that Peter had gone to the sepulchre without having had any further revelation, they set out on their way. This, of course, must have occurred before the return of Mary Magdalene from the sepulchre with the account of the appearance of the Lord to her, and His message respecting His Ascension. (I shall explain the occurrence of Mary Magdalene's name in the 10th verse when I come to it.)

We will now examine the first ten verses.

"Now upon the first day of the week, very early in the morning, they came," &c. Who came? If we look back two verses—to xxvii. 55—they were the women who followed Him from Galilee, and among these were Joanna, the wife of Chuza, and Susannah, and many others.

But as I noticed in my comment on St. Mark, there were, most probably, two companies of women, one that of Mary Magdalene,

2 ᶜAnd they found the stone rolled away from the sepulchre.

ᶜ Matt. xxviii. 2. Mark xvi. 4.

3 ᵈAnd they entered in, and found not the body of the Lord Jesus.

ᵈ ver. xxiii. Mark xvi. 5.

4 And it came to pass, as they were much perplexed thereabout, ᵉbehold, two men stood by them in shining garments:

ᵉ John xx. 12. Acts i. 10.

---

3. " The body of the Lord Jesus." So ℵ, A., B., C., L., all other Uncials, except D., all Cursives, old Latin, c, q, Vulg., Copt., Syriacs, Arm., Æth.; but D. and some old Latin, a, b, e, ff², l, omit " of the Lord Jesus."

---

and Mary the mother of James and Salome (Mark xvi.), and the other that of Joanna and the women from Galilee. The former were parted from Mary Magdalene, who preceded them a little, first saw the sepulchre open, the stone having been rolled away, and taking for granted that the Lord's body had been stolen away by His enemies, left her companions, and ran to tell Peter and John. Those who remained saw the angel, received the message to the disciples that the Lord would see them in Galilee, and later on were favoured with the sight of the Lord Himself. The second company (assuming there to have been a second) came somewhat later, saw two angels, and were addressed by them in words totally different from those which the one angel had addressed to the first company, and then went to the disciples and told them of the angelic vision. This was before Cleopas and his friend departed for Emmaus, so that they set out having only heard the account from the Galilean women of the appearance of the angels. If they had had any word of the Lord Himself having been seen, they probably would not have left Jerusalem. But it is next to certain that the company or college of the Apostles were not assembled together till towards the evening: so that the accounts of the Lord's appearance to the Magdalen, or to the other women, may have been made known to some groups of disciples and not to others.

2, 3. " And they found the stone rolled away .... body of the Lord Jesus." St. Matthew alone gives the action of the angel in this; but each of the four accounts notices the rolling away of the stone. St. Luke alone distinctly mentions that they found not the Lord's body.

4. " And it came to pass, as they were much perplexed there-

CHAP. XXIV.] HE IS NOT HERE, BUT IS RISEN. 613

5 And as they were afraid, and bowed down *their* faces to the earth, they said unto them, Why seek ye ‖ the living among the dead?

‖ Or, *him that liveth.*

6 He is not here, but is risen: *f* remember how he spake unto you when he was yet in Galilee,

7 Saying, The Son of man must be delivered into the hands of sinful men, and be crucified, and the third day rise again.

f Matt. xvi. 21. & xvii. 23. Mark viii. 31. & ix. 22.

---

6. "He is not here, but is risen." These words found in all other MSS. versions, &c., except D., a, b, e, ff², l.

about," &c. This seems to show that they were a different party to that of Mary Magdalene, for the women, as recorded in both SS. Matthew and Mark, saw the angel as soon as they entered the sepulchre, and had not time to be perplexed, as these were.

5. "And as they were afraid, ... Why seek ye the living among the dead?" There is somewhat of reproach in this question. In bringing the spices to preserve His Body from corruption, they were manifesting their love and grateful remembrance, and not their faith; for they came to preserve a Body from corruption, which, if they had known the Scriptures (Ps. xvi), or believed His own words, they would have known to be incapable of corruption. The Lord demands our love to Himself; but He first of all demands our faith. The very love which He asks for is to have its root in faith. Unless we believe in Him as He is revealed, our love is not worthy of Him, for it does not love Him as being God Incarnate and Man incorruptible.

6, 7. "He is not here, but is risen: remember how he spake .... third day rise again." The words said in Galilee, as reported in St. Luke, were, "The Son of man must suffer many things, and be rejected of the elders and chief priests and scribes, and be slain, and be raised the third day;" but these seem, from the context, to have been said only in the hearing of the Apostles; so that it is most probable that the saying of the Lord quoted by the angel was said, perhaps more than once, to the outer body of believers, or indeed to the people. Its value is this, that it shows that the people enjoyed just the same intimation of the Resurrection that the Apostles did, and were as unbelieving.

8 And ^g they remembered his words,

9 ^h And returned from the sepulchre, and told all these things unto the eleven, and to all the rest.

10 It was Mary Magdalene, and ⁱ Joanna, and Mary *the mother* of James, and other *women that were* with them, which told these things unto the apostles.

<small>g John ii. 22.
h Matt. xxviii. 8. Mark xvi. 10.
i ch. viii. 3.</small>

---

9. "From the sepulchre." These words found in all other MSS. and versions, &c., Cop., a, b, c, e, ff², l, Arm.

8. "And they remembered his words." The reader will call to mind the words in St. John's Gospel respecting the temple of Christ's Body, "When therefore he was risen from the dead his disciples remembered that he had said this" (John ii. 22).

9. "And returned from the sepulchre, and told all these things unto the eleven," &c. We are not to suppose from this that the eleven were all in one room when these tidings were brought; most probably the communication was not made at once, but it took some time to inform all; and so, later in the day, Mary Magdalene, who had remained at the sepulchre after Peter and John had left, saw the Lord, and bore His message to the disciples.

"And to all the rest," *i.e.*, to such disciples as Cleopas and his companion, and Barnabas and Matthias.

10. "It was Mary Magdalene, and Joanna, and Mary the mother of James . . . unto the apostles." How are we to reconcile the fact that Mary Magdalene, who had seen the Lord and carried from Him a message to the eleven, is here numbered amongst those who had only seen the angel or angels? Very clearly in this way. This verse 10, with the names of the women, is thrown in, as it were, by the way, to show how all the women who visited the sepulchre bore their testimony to the angelic vision, and were disbelieved. We are to remember that, according to St. Mark, Mary Magdalene's account of the Lord having appeared to her was at first disbelieved. We shall see further that this also is introductory to the account which follows. I. Williams says: "St. Luke is speaking (v. 10) of all the women, who severally brought the accounts to the apostles, and none of which they believed: and he here introduces the mention of these women, evidently in no immediate connection with what went before, but as a summary of all the intelligence conveyed

CHAP. XXIV.]   IDLE TALES.   615

11 ᵏ And their words seemed to them as idle tales, and they believed them not.

<small>ᵏ Mark xvi. 11. ver. xxv.</small>

12 ˡ Then arose Peter, and ran unto the sepulchre; and stooping down, he beheld the linen clothes laid by themselves, and departed, wondering in himself at that which was come to pass.

<small>ˡ John xx. 3, 6.</small>

13 ¶ ᵐ And, behold, two of them went that same day to a village called Emmaus, which was from Jerusalem *about* threescore furlongs.

<small>ᵐ Mark xvi. 12.</small>

---

12. This whole verse omitted by D., a, b, e, l; but retained by all other MSS. and versions, &c.

13. "Three score furlongs." א, I., K., N., Π, 158, 223, 237, 420, old Latin, g, read, "one hundred and sixty;" but A., B., D., L., and all others, read, "sixty."

by the various women at various times during this eventful morning."

11. "And their words seemed to them as idle tales, and they believed them not." Very likely the fact that these appearances were related at the first only by women had something to do with their rejection of them, for in immediate sequence comes the visit of the foremost man of the Apostles to the sepulchre.

12. "Then arose Peter, and ran unto the sepulchre . . . . come to pass." This is evidently the visit recorded in John xx., where, however, Peter is accompanied by John. Peter's name is no doubt mentioned because he first went into the sepulchre, and observed the order of all within, but the absence of the Body; though it is to be noticed that the same words are applied to the action of him who went in, as to that of John before he went in—"stooping down and saw the linen clothes lying." In verse 24 the presence of another besides Peter is recognized, " certain of them (τινες τῶν σὺν ἡμῖν) which were with us."

13. "And, behold, two of them went that same day to a village called Emmaus," &c. A place apparently mentioned by Josephus, which Titus assigned, after the siege of Jerusalem, to 800 veterans of his army, and thence was called Kolonieh, situated exactly sixty furlongs (a little more than seven miles) from Jerusalem. Who the two were it is impossible to conjecture. The name of one, Cleopas, is given, and the other, because his name is not given, has

14 And they talked together of all these things which had happened.

15 And it came to pass, that, while they communed *together* and reasoned, [n] Jesus himself drew near, and went with them.

16 But [o] their eyes were holden that they should not know him.

[n] Matt. xviii. 20. ver. xxxvi.
[o] John xx. 14. & xxi. 4.

---

been supposed by many to have been St. Luke himself, just as the unnamed young man who fled naked from the scene of the Lord's apprehension is said to have been St. Mark. No other reason can be given, and from no other hint in his writings can we gather that St. Luke was in the company of the disciples during the Lord's lifetime.

14, 15. "And they talked .... Jesus himself drew near, and went with them." Theophylact remarks, "The disciples above mentioned talked to one another of the things which had happened, not as believing them, but as bewildered at events so extraordinary."

"Jesus himself drew near, and went with them."

It seemed as if a stranger, of whose nearness they were unaware because of the earnestness of their conversation, suddenly overtook them, and began to walk by their side.

16. "But their eyes were holden that they should not know him." St. Mark describes this as the appearing in another form; and, indeed, if they saw him so closely as to discern his features it must have been so. He must have presented a different appearance to what they had been accustomed to, or they would have instantly recognized Him.

"Having now obtained a spiritual body, distance of place is no obstacle to His being present to whom He wished, nor did He any further govern His Body by natural laws, but spiritually and supernaturally. Hence, as Mark says, He appeared to them in a different form, in which they were not permitted to know Him; for it follows, 'And their eyes were holden that they should not know him;' in order, truly, that they might reveal their doubtful conceptions, and uncovering their wounds may receive a cure, and that they might know that although the same Body which suffered rose again, yet it was no longer such as to be visible to all, but only to

17 And he said unto them, What manner of communications *are* these that ye have one to another, as ye walk, and are sad?

18 And the one of them, p whose name was   p John xix. 25. Cleopas, answering said unto him, Art thou only a stranger in Jerusalem, and hast not known the things which are come to pass there in these days?

---

17. "As ye walk, and are sad." There is some authority, א, A. (?), B. (L.), for the alteration, "and they stood, looking sad;" but most MSS. and versions are in favour of the reading in the Rec. Text.

18. "Art thou only a stranger in Jerusalem, and hast not known." Revisers translate this in their text, "Dost thou alone sojourn in Jerusalem?" and in margin, "Dost thou sojourn alone in Jerusalem, and knowest thou not," &c.?

those by whom He willed it to be seen." (Theophylact, in Cat. Aurea.)

17. "And he said unto them, What manner of communications are these that ye have one to another," &c. The words which the Lord uses imply rather debate and discussion—what are these words which ye throw one against another? It would seem from what follows that they were arguing whether the cruel and shameful death of the Lord was a complete and final disproof of all His Messianic claims or not.

"And are sad?" Rather "downcast," not merely a passing sadness, but as if their hopes were blighted, and they could not lift up their heads again.

18. "And the one of them, whose name was Cleopas, answering said unto him," &c. Cleopas: not the same as Clopas, which was Aramaic (Cholphai), but a Greek word, short for Cleopatros. Dean Plumptre suggests that his name indicates Hellenistic and probably Alexandrian antecedents. This may in part, perhaps, account for his imparting to St. Luke what had not found its way into the current oral teaching of the Hebrew Church at Jerusalem as embodied in the narratives of St. Matthew and St. Mark.

"Art thou only a stranger in Jerusalem, and hast not known," &c. This has been more probably rendered, "Dost thou sojourn alone in Jerusalem, and knowest thou not?" &c. A mere stranger in Jerusalem, especially if he were one from Galilee or Peræa, would know all about what had occurred within the last eventful week. The man who had heard nothing of the events which had touched

19 And he said unto them, What things? And they said unto him, Concerning Jesus of Nazareth, ᑫ which was a prophet ʳ mighty in deed and word before God and all the people:

20 ˢ And how the chief priests and our rulers delivered him to be condemned to death, and have crucified him.

21 But we trusted ᵗ that it had been he which should have redeemed Israel: and beside all this, to day is the third day since these things were done.

q Matt. xxi. 11. ch. vii. 16. John iii. 2. & iv. 19. & vi. 14. Acts ii. 22.
r Acts vii. 22.
s ch. xxiii. 1. Acts xiii. 27, 28.
t ch. i. 68. & ii. 38. Acts i. 6.

---

every heart with either pity or fear, must have dwelt alone, by himself, having no communication with any one.

19-22. "And he said unto them, What things? .... these things were done." The Lord asks "What things?" in order to draw out from them what their mind was respecting Himself after His rejection and crucifixion. Their answer is exceedingly valuable, for it teaches what their belief had been concerning Him. They believed that He had been a prophet—perhaps the greatest of the prophets, "mighty in deed and word before God and all the people." But could He have really been this if the chief priests— the chief ministers, not of an ordinary natural state of things, but of a Theocracy—had condemned Him and crucified Him—that is, put Him to no ordinary death, but to a death inflicted only on those who were held to be accursed of God. (Gal. iii. 13.)

21. "But we trusted that it had been he which should have redeemed Israel." We believed Him to have been the long expected Messiah: but now our hopes are shattered, for God would not have suffered His Holy One to die such a death.

"Redeemed Israel." Did they mean by this a spiritual redemption or a carnal one, such as is indicated in Acts i. 6: "Lord, wilt thou at this time restore again the Kingdom to Israel?" They cannot have had any idea of a spiritual redemption through the Blood of the Crucified One ; much less a redemption from the power of the grave.

Such was their belief, or rather such had been their belief—that He was a very great prophet—perhaps a Redeemer. This shows what must have been at its best the state of mind respecting the Lord in

22 Yea, and ᵘ certain women also of our company made us astonished, which were early at the sepulchre; 23 And when they found not his body, they came, saying, that they had also seen a vision of angels, which said that he was alive.

u Matt. xxviii. 8. Mark xvi. 10. ver. ix. 10. John xx. 18.

24 And ˣ certain of them which were with us went to the sepulchre, and found *it* even so as the women had said: but him they saw not.

x ver. 12.

---

the outer and very numerous circle of the ordinary disciples—those not of the twelve. There is nothing in their confession of faith answering to the words of St. Peter, "Thou art the Christ, the Son of the living God." And yet these two must have been devoted followers of the Lord.

"And besides all this, to day is the third day," &c. What is the ground of this allusion to the third day? It may be a lingering reminiscence of the promise of the Resurrection. This is the third day, it is already on the wane, and nothing is yet manifested to drive away our despair: and yet they had not given up all hope, there was yet an uncertain glimmer.

22, 23. "Yea, and certain women also of our company made us astonished . . . . he was alive." The reader will notice how the first verses of this chapter are, as we said, written as an introduction to this. The women had astonished the disciples by their report that the sepulchre was empty. His Body was gone, how they knew not, only it was not there. They said that angels had told them that he was alive, but weak women led away by affection and imagination, might be deceived in all this. Why should angels give the first intimation to Galilean women?

24. "And certain of them which were with us went . . . him they saw not." Notice how two apostles are simply described as "certain of them which were with us." The two, Cleopas and his friend, were speaking to an apparent stranger, and they never thought of indicating the position among themselves of the two who went to ascertain the truth of the women's story, only the fact that they went, and found that the women had brought a correct report respecting the Body not being there; but nothing further. "Him they saw not." Perhaps in this there may be an allusion to some

SLOW OF HEART TO BELIEVE.

25 Then he said unto them, O fools, and slow of heart to believe all that the prophets have spoken:

26 ʸ Ought not Christ to have suffered these things, and to enter into his glory?

ʸ ver. xlvi.
Acts xvii. 3.
1 Pet. i. 11.

---

rumour which reached their ears just before their departure, that He had appeared to Mary Magdalene. Anyhow, the absence of any appearance to those who went to the sepulchre to ascertain the truth of matters was in their minds a proof against the reality of the angelic appearance to the women.

25, 26, 27. "Then he said unto them, O fools, and slow of heart ... the things concerning himself." Notice, in the eyes of the Lord a fool is one who is "slow of heart to believe." And is it not according to common sense? If men profess to accept a certain book or series of books as containing a revelation from God, what greater folly than only partially to believe it, or accept its statements respecting what suits our earthly hopes and wishes, and reject all in it which would raise up our aspirations to the higher things above this world! Considering what sort of creatures we are, is not a revelation from God more likely to correct and rebuke our worldly, carnal, low ideas than to fall in with them?

26, 27. "Ought not Christ to have suffered such things ... ? And beginning at Moses," &c. The Jews always believed that the books of Moses were the greatest of all, and written with the highest degree of inspiration. The Lord, then, would naturally begin with them, for they contain the seed of all. It was a rooted principle in the Jewish mind, that the various facts related in the books of Moses had a far wider and deeper significance than what was on the surface,—that they hinted at, betokened, shadowed forth, or as we should now say, typified, great moral and spiritual realities. To tell these Jews, as most probably the Lord did, that the bruising of the heel of the seed of the woman, implied some deeply mysterious truth, and that Abraham receiving his son back again on the third day, as from the dead, betokened something equally mysterious respecting the same truth, and that Moses lifting up a serpent of brass upon a pole, that those who looked to it should live, pertained also to the same mystery, and that this truth or mystery was to be connected with, or embodied in, the prophet that the

CHAP. XXIV.] BEGINNING AT MOSES. 621

27 ᶻ And beginning at ᵃ Moses and ᵇ all the prophets, he expounded unto them in all the scriptures the things concerning himself.

ᶻ ver. xlv.
ᵃ Gen. iii. 15. & xxii. 18. & xxvi. 4. & xlix. 10. Num. xxi. 9. Deu. xviii. 15.
ᵇ Ps. xvi. 9, 10. & xxii. & cxxxii. 11. Is. vii. 14. & ix. 6. & xl. 10, 11. & l. 6. & liii. Jer. xxiii. 5. & xxxiii. 14, 15. Ezek. xxxiv. 23. & xxxvii. 25. Dan. ix. 24. Mic. vii. 20. Mal. iii. 1. & iv. 2. See on John i. 45.

Lord God would raise up from among His brethren like to Moses,—all this was in accordance with the religious mind which had been formed in the godly Jews by the study of the Old Testament.¹ It all sprung from the great principle that the word of such a Being as God would contain much more than at first sight it seemed to contain.

As it is said that He "began at Moses," we may reasonably, indeed, with almost certainty, surmise that He began with such considerations as would naturally lead to those revelations of suffering, very closely followed by glory, which we have in the two greatest Messianic prophecies, Ps. xxii. and Isaiah liii.

In the first of these, Ps. xxii., we have extreme suffering (having certain marks and outward features which meet only in crucifixion), closely followed, apparently in the same person, by a state of glory, in which the sufferer bows the hearts of all men to God and to Himself. In the second, the sufferings of a certain human being have atoning and expiatory terms applied to them which are nowhere else applied to any man, and are supposed to terminate in an universal priestship and kingly rule, for we read, "The pleasure of the Lord shall prosper in his hand:" "He bears the sin of many, and makes intercession for the transgressors." So that, instead of the sufferings of Jesus being a stumbling-block, they ought to enforce all His claims. Ought not the Redeemer of Israel to be a Son of man, to have His hands and feet pierced, to be brought into the dust of death, to have His garments parted, to have lots cast for His vesture? If these things had not happened unto Him, how could all the ends of the world remember themselves and be turned to the Lord through Him, how could the pleasure of the Lord prosper in His hand, how could He divide the great for his portion, and the strong for his spoil? Ought they not, if they be-

---

¹ See Galatians iv. 21. St. Paul would not have argued in this way with Judaizers unless they acknowledged its soundness.

28 And they drew nigh unto the village, whither they went: and ^c he made as though he would have gone further.

29 But ^d they constrained him, saying, Abide with us: for it is toward evening, and the day is far spent. And he went in to tarry with them.

30 And it came to pass, as he sat at meat with them, ^e he took bread, and blessed *it*, and brake, and gave to them.

c See Gen. xxxii. 26. & xlii. 7. Mark vi. 48.
d Gen. xix. 3. Acts xvi. 15.
e Matt. xiv. 19.

---

lieved Moses and the Prophets, to have expected that Christ would suffer such things before He entered into His glory?

28. " And they drew nigh unto the village, whither they went . . . went in to tarry with them." By this He tried them whether they were so sufficiently absorbed in what He had said, as to desire to hear more. He actually would have gone further unless they had detained Him, but by their constraining Him to abide with them, they showed their desire to hear from Him more of the precious truth which He had been communicating to them. I. Williams notices many instances of similar conduct on His part, as for instance, to the blind man by the roadside, to the Canaanite woman; so when they were in the storm at sea, He seemed as if He would have passed by them. " So now He manifests not Himself to them, but is passing by, till constrained to come in and abide; showing them that although Christ was risen indeed, yet He would not be as Christ risen unto them, unless they put forth their hands unto Him, and earnestly sought for Him."

" Thus also now is He to us each day of our lives : He passes by, in opportunities of good that occur, and if neglected, pass, never to return; but if we constrain them, they become means of manifesting Christ to us, *i.e.*, of fulfilling His commandments, which enlighten the eyes to discern His presence."

30, 31. " And it came to pass as he sat at meat with them . . . vanished out of their sight." We should naturally suppose that this act of taking bread and blessing it, and breaking it and giving it, was Eucharistic. For these are the very words in which St. Matthew and St. Mark describe the Institution. Jesus took ($\lambda\alpha\beta\grave{\omega}\nu$) bread, and blessed it ($\epsilon\dot{\nu}\lambda\acute{o}\gamma\eta\sigma\epsilon$, in Matthew the participle $\epsilon\dot{\nu}\lambda o\gamma\acute{\eta}\sigma\alpha\varsigma$), and brake it ($\kappa\lambda\acute{\alpha}\sigma\alpha\varsigma$, in Matthew $\emph{ἔ}\kappa\lambda\alpha\sigma\epsilon$), and gave ($\emph{ἐ}\pi\epsilon\delta\acute{\iota}\delta ov$, in Matthew $\emph{ἐ}\delta\acute{\iota}\delta ov$). Again, in describing to the assembled disciples what took

CHAP. XXIV.]   THEY KNEW HIM.   623

31 And their eyes were opened, and they knew him; and he ‖ vanished out of their sight.

32 And they said one to another, Did not our

‖ Or, *ceased to be seen of them.*
See chap. iv. 30. John viii. 59.

place here, Cleopas and his friend do it in the words, "How he was known unto them in the breaking of bread " (v. 35), the very words which St. Luke uses to describe the Eucharist in Acts ii. 42, "They continued steadfastly . . . . in the breaking of bread " (τῇ κλάσει τοῦ ἄρτου).[1] The Lord was manifested to them not whilst He brake, but whilst they received. "He gave to them, and their eyes were opened." Receiving Him into themselves, they *naturally*, one is almost tempted to say, discerned Him. All that had previously occurred led up to this, that they should discern Him personally in this Eucharistic act. Their previous instruction in the witness of all Scripture to the sufferings and glory of the Messiah was not sufficient, even though the words made their hearts burn within them; their actual recognition of Him was reserved to the moment of their reception of His Body. Quesnel remarks: "The Eucharist by faith becomes to us the bread of life, and of saving knowledge. One communion sometimes opens the eyes more, with respect to matters of faith, than all the discourses and instructions of men."

32. "And they said one to another, Did not our heart burn within us," &c. ? They had read these Scriptures respecting the Messiah from their youth, and their hearts had never thus burned

---

[1] The only reason which can be brought against an Eucharistic Significance is that wine or the cup is not mentioned; but surély there was not likely to be bread on the table and not wine, meat and not drink. Wine in that country and time was not a luxury, but an ordinary drink, as in all the South of Europe now. When it is said that it makes for the giving of the Sacrament in one kind only, we answer that the description of the Eucharist in Acts ii. 42, equally omits all mention of the cup. And in fact what need was there to wait for the cup, since He vanished as soon as they had received Him in the bread? The word "break" (κλάω), in connection with bread (ἄρτος), is never used in the New Testament of ordinary breaking of bread at an ordinary meal. It is used sixteen or seventeen times in the New Testament; nine times in direct connection with the Eucharist, Matt. xxvi. 26, Mark xiv. 22, Luke xxii. 19, Acts ii.42 and 46, xx. 7 and 11, 1 Cor. x. 16, xi. 24 ; five times in connection with that miraculous feeding of the multitudes which foreshadows the Eucharistic feast, and directly led to the Eucharistic discourse in John vi.; once in the account of St. Paul's shipwreck, where, with very peculiar solemnity, as if he was performing a religious act, " he took bread, and gave thanks to God in presence of them all, and when he had broken it he began to eat." The meat of the remainder of the persons on the ship being described by a different word (τροφῆς). The remaining place is this one, Luke xxiv. 30.

heart burn within us, while he talked with us by the way, and while he opened to us the scriptures?

---

within them. It was not the mere letter of Scripture, though that is the foundation of all, but it was the letter of Scripture expounded and brought home by One of surpassing holiness and love. It was the voice of God and the power of the Spirit which kindled the fire. And is it not the same now? Does not one man preach and read, and there is coldness and listlessness, and men say, "How stale is all this! we know it all as well as he"? And does not another man preach, or teach, or read perhaps the same words, and the soul catches fire, and truths well known become engraven, and truths forgotten rise to mind, and prayer ascends, and life is quickened?

And now let us shortly review this beautiful episode.

It seems, next to that in St. John xx., the most important of all our Lord's appearances. The revelation of the Risen Lord in John xx. seems given for the ministry in the Apostles, this one seems for ordinary disciples, for devout Christian wayfarers, one might say for lay-people. And though not perhaps anterior to the appearance to St. Peter, it is anterior to that to the college or body of Apostles.

This account of the walk to Emmaus shows us the state of belief among the body of the disciples. They accounted the Lord a very great prophet, perhaps the greatest of the prophets. They revered His memory to the uttermost. Their love seemed unwavering, but their faith in Him as the Christ the Redeemer seems to have sunk to nothing, or next to nothing. We may take this state of mind as representing that of those who were not Apostles. So that after the Lord's Death none, absolutely none, in the Church looked for His Resurrection. Then, in the next place, the account in St. Luke is intermediate between the traditional account as represented in St. Matthew, and that in St. John, on the matter of the mysterious nature of the Lord's Body. In this account He appears and disappears at His Will, but the spiritual nature of His Body is not emphasized as it is by the mention of the closed doors in the fourth Gospel, through which He must have passed as a spirit would. Then, in the next place, this account shows us that our Lord's appearances or disappearances are not regulated by any so-called law. The supposed law is that they who are in accord with Him spiri-

CHAP. XXIV.]   THE LORD IS RISEN INDEED.   625

33 And they rose up the same hour, and returned to Jerusalem, and found the eleven gathered together, and them that were with them.

34 Saying, The Lord is risen indeed, and ᶠ hath appeared to Simon. ᶠ 1 Cor. xv. 5.

---

tually will apparently, quite independently of His Will, see Him in His spiritual body, if He be near them: but if there be any such law He ought to have been seen by them when their hearts burned within them. But their recognition of Him was deferred till the very moment when He communicated them in His Body. In fact, it entirely and wholly depended upon His Will.

And, in the last place, the whole narrative leads up to their discernment of Him in their reception of the Eucharist—not in their apprehension of Him in the written Word, even though expounded and applied by Himself. His Blessed Will, then, is that over and above the liveliest apprehension of Himself, as set forth in the pages of Scripture, there is to be a Sacramental Apprehension of His Presence.

There are very many other lessons drawn out by holy and spiritual men—as, for instance, that He may be very near to us and we not know it—that He comes near to us in our way, as we walk through life, and, though invisible, teaches us, consoles us, reproves us, particularly when we speak with one another about Him—that we must constrain Him and He will not leave us—that we must look for special tokens of His love in His Sacrament. All these are very good, but they must not be allowed to interfere for a moment with the revelation in the narrative, which is, the manifestation to ordinary believers of the Risen Body of the Lord.

33. "And they rose up the same hour, and returned to Jerusalem," &c. No time must be lost to declare what they had seen. The unbelief which they had left in those from whom they parted that morning must be at once dispelled.

"And found the eleven gathered together, and them that were with them." These that were with them must have been, as we shall see, those who were in the same state of mind with reference to the Lord's Resurrection as Cleopas and his friend.

34. "Saying, The Lord is risen indeed, and hath appeared to Simon." Their unbelief was now turned to faith, but there was no *triumph* of faith in this, as some say. They believed when they had

S S

35 And they told what things *were done* in the way, and how he was known of them in breaking of bread.

---

seen. It is remarkable that this appearance to Simon is not mentioned except by St. Paul in 1 Cor. xv.

Respecting this appearance to Simon Peter nothing whatsoever has come down to us. It is probable that the Lord enjoined secrecy upon him for some time respecting any revelation He made to him. If it be lawful to hazard a conjecture, the Lord may have made known to him something of what occurred between His dying and His rising again. St. Peter alone relates the activity of the Lord in the unseen state. [1 Pet. iii. 19.]

85. " And they told what things were done in the way, and how he was known of them," &c. Their account was, by some at least, apparently received with incredulity ; for St. Mark evidently alludes to the appearance to Cleopas and his friend in the words, " After that he appeared in another form unto two of them as they walked and went into the country," but he proceeds to say, " And they went and told it to the residue ; neither believed they them." How is it that apparently, according to St. Mark's account, they received with suspicion, to say the least, the account of the two disciples, whilst in St. Luke they met these very men with the words, "The Lord is risen indeed, and hath appeared unto Simon " ? It may be that amongst the body of the disciples there were different degrees of assent. It may be that, even in one large room, there were groups, and one of them threw doubts on the appearance on the way to Emmaus. Or may there not have been a readiness to accept the testimony of Simon Peter because he was the undoubted leader, and a tendency to reject the account of appearances to persons not so prominent in the little society ? " Why should He appear to these and not to us ? Why should He appear to women—to Mary Magdalen—to those two who would not wait to see the end, but were actually leaving Jerusalem ? "

But, in fact, need we go further for an explanation than the inconsistency of human nature ? I have consulted a large number of commentators and expositors in the writing of this commentary on the four Gospels, and have come across an abundance of what is good, of what springs from the sincerest Christian faith, the brightest Christian hope, and the warmest Christian love : but (and I write this, feeling that someone may say the same of myself) I

HANDLE ME AND SEE.

36 ¶ ᵍAnd as they thus spake, Jesus himself stood in the midst of them, and saith unto them, Peace *be* unto you.

37 But they were terrified and affrighted, and supposed that they had seen ʰ a spirit.

38 And he said unto them, Why are ye troubled? and why do thoughts arise in your hearts?

39 Behold my hands and my feet, that it is I myself: ⁱ handle me, and see; for a spirit hath not flesh and bones, as ye see me have.

g Mark xvi. 14. John xx. 19. 1 Cor. xv. 5.
h Mark vi. 49.
i John xx. 20, 27.

---

36. "Jesus himself." So A., E., G., K., M., S., and other later Uncials, and almost all Cursives, &c.; but "Jesus" omitted by ℵ, B., D., L., 61, 255, a, b, c, Sah., Cur. Syriac.

The latter part in all MSS., &c., except D. and some old Latin, a, b, c, ff², l.

---

have come across the most surprising inconsistencies in accepting some accounts in the Gospels, and ignoring, if not rejecting, others. One man will accept a miracle as undoubtedly historical and reject another close to it in the narrative as unhistorical. One man will accept in its fulness a plain saying of the Lord, and the same man will with all his might endeavour to get rid of another equally plain. One man cries up pure morality, high motives, constant regard to truth, &c., and yet writes as if he believed that the four Evangelists had no regard for the historical truth of their narratives, and were base enough to manipulate that most sacred deposit with which they had to do, not only for advancing their "party," but out of sheer hatred to persons, as, for instance, to Simon Peter, or to Judas Iscariot.

So that, if some of the followers of Christ believed heartily and some with hesitation—if one man believed in the appearance to an Apostle, and hesitated as to the appearance to a woman, it was only human nature.

36-43. "And as they thus spake .... as ye see me have .... did eat before them." This is apparently the same meeting of the Lord with His disciples as that described in John xx. 19-23; but the reports of the two Evangelists are so exceedingly dissimilar, that they read like the account of two wholly different meetings with different persons.

Let us reverently draw attention to these differences, for we do

40 And when he had thus spoken, he shewed them *his* hands and *his* feet.

k Gen. xlv. 26.
l John xxi. 5.

41 And while they yet believed not ᵏ for joy, and wondered, he said unto them, ˡ Have ye here any meat?

42 And they gave him a piece of a broiled fish, and of an honeycomb.

m Acts x. 41.

43 ᵐ And he took *it*, and did eat before them.

---

40. This verse omitted by D.; but retained by ℵ, A., B., L., all later Uncials, Cursives, &c.

42. " And of an honeycomb." So E., H., K., M., N., S., U., V., X., Γ, Δ, Λ, a, b, ff², l, q, Vulg., Copt.; but omitted by ℵ, A., B., D., L., Π, e.

not deal honestly with the Word of God unless we do, and there may be a meaning in the fact that two such different reports are given.

First, then, St. John alone mentions that the doors were shut. This shows that he was perfectly alive to subordinate circumstances, and alluded to them if he thought they were necessary.

The salutation of the Lord is the same in both, " Peace be unto you." But the effect upon those assembled in each case was exceedingly different. St. Luke tells us that they were "terrified and affrighted, and supposed that they had seen a Spirit." St. John says, " Then were the disciples glad when they saw the Lord." Of course it be may said that before they were assured that it was the Lord by the sight of the marks of the spear and nails they were affrighted, and that not till then was their fear dispelled; but this is very unsatisfactory, for St. John is by no means backward in setting forth what was in the minds of the Apostles, even when it is to their discredit ; as, for instance, that St. Peter, in contrast with St. John, believed not even when he saw the sepulchre empty—that they knew not the Scripture that He must rise from the dead—and the unbelief of Thomas.

The impression from St. John's account is, that they saw Him at the first with joy. But there is absolutely nothing answering in St. John's account to what we find in the next three verses of St. Luke: " And he said unto them, Why are ye troubled? and why do thoughts arise in your hearts? Behold my hands and my feet, handle me, and see; for a spirit hath not flesh and bones, as ye see me have. And when he had thus spoken, he shewed them his hands and his feet." Now it is impossible to suppose that all this occurred to

CHAP. XXIV.] ALL MUST BE FULFILLED. 629

44 And he said unto them, ⁿ These *are* the words which I spake unto you, while I was yet with you, that all things must be fulfilled, which were written in the law of Moses, and *in* the prophets, and *in* the psalms, concerning me.

ⁿ Matt. xvi. 21. & xvii. 22. & xx. 18. Mark viii. 31. ch. ix. 22. & xviii. 31. ver. 6.

---

dispel the unbelief of the ten between the Lord's salutation and their seeing Him with gladness, as told us by St. John. So difficult is it that many commentators (and among them apparently Godet) suppose that St. Mark and St. Luke mix up the two accounts of the appearance to the ten on Easter day and to the eleven on the next Sunday, and so they apply to the rest, *i.e.*, the ten, words which were addressed only to Thomas, viz., "Behold my hands and my feet, handle me and see," &c.

Then, from the forty-first verse, we gather that their unbelief was even then not wholly dispelled; and, in order to destroy it entirely, he asked, "Have ye here any meat?" and they gave Him the broiled fish and the honey-comb, and then He ate before them. Now in St. John even in the account of the meeting on the eighth day after, when Thomas was present, we have not a word of such circumstances, nor are they possible, for the only one remaining who required his unbelief to be dispelled, was Thomas, and his confession, "My Lord and my God," followed instantly on his feeling the wounds in the hands and side.

But we now come to the final and most important difference of all.

44-47. "And he said unto them, These are the words which I spake unto you . . . . rise from the dead the third day: And that repentance and remission of sins . . . . Jerusalem." The reader will notice that St. John gives not one word of this. According to the fourth Evangelist, the Lord gives to the ten, and to the ten only, a very remarkable commission, couched in the most startling language in Scripture (except, perhaps, that in John vi.); words which must, by their very nature, have been remembered by anyone who heard them, and these words were accompanied by an outward and visible act of a kind such as He had never performed before. He breathed on them, and saith unto them, "Receive ye the Holy Ghost. Whosesoever sins ye remit, they are remitted unto them; and whosesoever sins ye retain, they are retained."

Not one word of this, the most important commission ever given to human beings, appears in St. Luke. On the contrary, from his

45 Then ° opened he their understanding, that they might understand the scriptures,

° Acts xvi. 14.

46 And said unto them, ᵖ Thus it is written, and thus it behoved Christ to suffer, and to rise from the dead the third day:

ᵖ ver. 26.
Ps. xxii. 1s.
l. 6. & liii. 2,
&c. Acts
xvii. 3.

---

46. "And thus it behoved." So A., C²., N., X., Γ, Δ, Λ, Π, later Uncials, almost all Cursives, f, q, Vulg., Syriacs; but omitted by ℵ, B., C¹, D., L., a, b, c, e, ff², l, Copt., Æth.

narrative we should gather that no commission of any sort was then given. According to St. Luke the only words spoken were a reference to other words which are not given, and which seem to refer to what was spoken to the two disciples on the way to Emmaus: "These are the words which I spake unto you, while I was yet with you, that all things must be fulfilled, which were written in the law of Moses, and in the prophets, and in the Psalms concerning me."

Such are the two inspired accounts of the same meeting, but with scarcely a feature in common. The account in St. John is that of an eye-witness, one of the innermost circle of believers—one on whose mind such tremendous words, accompanied with so extraordinary an act, must have been for ever impressed. St. Luke certainly was not present, and yet his account is so circumstantial, so graphic, that if he be a truthful Evangelist, it must have come from one present. How are we to account for all this?

I believe in one way, and in only one. It was a large room. There was a large assembly of the followers of the Lord, and there were amongst them two or three distinct groups. One of these groups stood somewhat by itself, and was formed of the Apostles alone. The Lord appeared amongst these. They recognized Him with joy, and words passed between them, very brief, which were unheard by the others. The "others," or many of them, were terrified and affrighted, as at an apparition. But He went amongst them, and reassured them, bid them feel His flesh and bones, and finally ate something in their presence. These, the greater part, would not know, or very indistinctly hear what He said to the ten: the full account of this was reserved to the writing of the last Gospel.

If any one objects to this explanation, let him do so. But let him

CHAP. XXIV.]   YE ARE WITNESSES.   631

47 And that repentance and ⁹ remission of sins should be preached in his name ʳ among all nations, beginning at Jerusalem.

48 And ˢ ye are witnesses of these things.

49 ¶ ᵗ And, behold, I send the promise of my Father upon you: but tarry ye in the city of Jerusalem, until ye be endued with power from on high.

q Dan. ix. 24. Acts xiii. 38, 46. 1 John ii. 12.
r Gen. xii. 3. Ps. xxii. 27. Is. xlix. 6, 22. Jer. xxxi. 34. Hos. ii. 23. Mic. iv. 2. Mal. i. 11.
s John xv. 27. Acts i. 8, 22. & ii. 32. & iii. 15.
t Is. xliv. 3. Joel ii. 28.

49. "Of Jerusalem." So A., C², X., Γ, Δ, Λ, Π, all later Uncials, all Cursives, f, q, Syriac, Arm., and Æth.; but omitted by ℵ, B., C¹, D., L., a, b, c, e, ff², g², l, q, Vulg., Copt.

John xiv. 16, 26. & xv. 26. & xvi. 7. Acts i. 4. & ii. 1, &c.

---

remember what he is bound to account for. He is bound to account for the fact that two inspired writers give a history of what occurred at the same time and place without one feature in common. The impression made by the Lord's appearance, His conduct, and His words to dispel their fear, and, above all, His final words are totally different in each narrative.

That the eleven (or ten) were somewhat apart from the rest, so as to receive a commission by themselves, was no new thing. On the contrary, it is in accordance with all Christ's dealings with them. They were chosen apart from the rest; they received separate instruction as the twelve; they received promises as a body of twelve, and no more; they only were present at the institution of the Eucharist. Their segregation continues in the history of the founding of the Church. One is very solemnly added to fill up the mystic number. "Peter stood up with the eleven," and "of the rest durst no man join himself unto them." (Acts i. 26, ii. 14, v. 13.)

From St. Luke we gather that there were more persons besides the ten, but not one word of any commission addressed to them: only that, in accordance with prophecy, repentance and remission of sins should be preached in His name among all nations. This, if it implies a commission merely to preach, is very indirect, whereas the commission in St. John to remit or retain sins is the most direct conceivable.

Much has been made of the presence of others besides the Apostles as noted by St. Luke. These "others," of whom we know nothing

50 ¶ And he led them out ᵘ as far as to Bethany, and he lifted up his hands, and blessed them. 51 ˣ And it came to pass, while he blessed them, he was parted from them, and carried up into heaven.

ᵘ Acts i. 12.
ˣ 2 Kings ii. 11. Mark xvi. 19. John xx. 17. Acts i. 9. Eph. iv. 8.

51. "And carried up into heaven." So A., B., C., L., X., Γ, Δ, Λ, Π, later Uncials, all Cursives, c, f, q, Vulg., Syriacs; but omitted by ℵ, D., a, b, e, ff².

except that they were so terrified that the feeling of the Lord's flesh and bones, and the sight of His hands and feet were not sufficient to dispel their doubts, are (the reader will scarcely credit it) supposed to represent the whole Church as apart from the Apostles, and so to receive a commission to remit and retain co-ordinately with the Apostles: so that the Lord here desires to nullify that peculiar position in which He had endeavoured to place the twelve between Himself and the rest of His followers, and which they appear to have reassumed after Pentecost.

But this is contrary to all which we can gather from the narrative. For if "the others" had heard any such commission, which, if addressed to them, the Lord would have taken care that they should have heard, they would have remembered it, and St. Luke, who is very circumstantial in his account, would have recorded it from the report of some one of them: and so his silence is the plainest proof that no such commission was addressed to those outside the twelve.

44-49. "And he said unto them . . . on high." We have now to notice another remarkable matter in St. Luke's narrative, which is, that if we understand the words of the Lord recorded in the forty-fourth verse as said now, then seeing that from the forty-fourth to the fiftieth verses there is one continuous narrative, he seems to place the Ascension immediately after this meeting: but this is impossible. We must then suppose that between the account of His eating before them, and the words narrated in verses 44 or 46 and 47 there is to be inserted the narratives of all the meetings related by St. Matthew, St. Mark, and St. John, during the great forty days.

"Then opened he their understanding," &c. This is in all probability as stupendous a miracle as any in the Lord's history. That men should in a moment receive a power of mental comprehension which they had not before, and that this power should enable them to see the true import and meaning of a book which

CHAP. XXIV.] THEY WORSHIPPED HIM. 633

52 ʸ And they worshipped him, and returned to Jerusalem with great joy:

53 And were continually ᶻ in the temple, praising and blessing God. Amen.

ʸ Matt. xxviii. 9, 17.
ᶻ Acts ii. 46. & v. 42.

---

52. "And they worshipped him." Omitted by D. and old Latin, a, b, e, ff², l; but retained by all other MSS., Uncials and Cursives, c, f, q, Vulg.
53. "Praising and blessing God." D. and some old Latin omit "blessing." Some, א, B., C., L., omit "praising." "Praising and blessing" in A., later Uncials, and all Cursives, some old Latin, Vulg., &c.

had hitherto been closed to them, seems greater than any acts of healing, or feeding of multitudes, or stilling of tempests. It implies Divine power over our spiritual and intellectual nature such as God only can exercise. And yet it is the commonest of all miracles, and the one which survives amongst us. The opening of the mind and heart to the things of God is constantly now going on. To many—we may say to all—who submit their wills and understandings to God, the Scriptures are unlocked, a new light is shed upon every part of them, especially upon the works and words of the Lord. This power of a risen Christ we claim every time we put up to God one of the most familiar of all our prayers, that " by patience and comfort of His holy Word we may embrace and ever hold fast the blessed hope of everlasting life " in Jesus Christ.

49. "And, behold, I send the promise of my Father upon you: but tarry ye in ... Jerusalem," &c. This certainly was said but a little before the Ascension. It must have been said after they had seen Him in Galilee. It is the substance of what is recorded in Acts i. 4-8.

"The promise of my Father." The only distinct promises of the sending of the Holy Spirit are in St. John's Gospel, so that this place both requires and recognizes the teaching of the last discourses of that Gospel, John xiii. to xvii.

50, 51. We must reserve all remarks on the Ascension to our notes on the Acts of the Apostles, which contain the fullest report. The speciality of the Gospel account is that the Lord was parted from them in the act of blessing them.

52. "And they worshipped him, and returned to Jerusalem with great joy." This worship of One Who was by the act of His Ascension exalted into the sphere of Deity was an act of Divine Worship.

53. "And were continually in the temple, praising and blessing

God." So we read, Acts ii. 46, iii. 1, &c. There was no sharp line drawn between the worship of the Old and the New Covenant. Till the temple was destroyed the Christian Jews were its constant attendants. The twilight of Judaism gradually gave place to the bright and clear morn of the Gospel.

THE END.

www.ingramcontent.com/pod-product-compliance
Lightning Source LLC
Chambersburg PA
CBHW052039290426
44111CB00011B/1561